Human Resource Management

2nd Edition

Debashish Sengupta

Published by:

An Imprint of dreamtech PRESS

© **Copyright 2015 by the Author**

The book may not be duplicated in any way without the express written consent of the publisher, except in the form of brief excerpts or quotations for the purpose of the review. The information contained herein is for the personal use of the reader and may not be incorporated in any commercial programmes other books, databases, or any kind of software with written consent of the publisher. Making copies of this book or any portion thereof for any purpose other than your own is a violation of copyright laws.

Limits of Liability/ Disclaimer of Warranty

The author and publishers have used their best efforts in preparing this book. The author makes no representation or warranties with respect to the accuracy or completeness of the content of this book, and specifically disclaims any implied warranties of merchantability or fitness for any particular purpose. There are no warranties which extend beyond the description contained in this paragraph. No warranty may be created or extended by sales representatives or written sales materials. The accuracy and completeness of the information provided herein and the opinion stated herein are not guaranteed and warranted to provide any particular results, and the advice and strategies contained herein may not be suitable for every individual. Neither Biztantra (An Imprint of Dreamtech Press) nor the author shall be liable for any loss of profit or any commercial damages, including but not limited to special, incidental, consequential, or other damages.

Trademarks

All brand names and product names used in this book are trademarks, registered trademarks, or trade names of their respective holders. Dreamtech Press is not associated with any product or vendor mentioned in this book.

ISBN: 978-93-5119-779-9

Edition: 2015

Printed at: *Radha Offset, Delhi*

To my dear parents

Ranjit & Shyamali

Foreword

Human resource function has not quite been truly reinvented per se in the last few years. An increasing realization that people are key differentiators when it comes to ensuring the success of any firm and are at the same time inimitable, have converged the human resource management spotlight. That decidedly makes quantifiable and qualitative difference in the performance of an organization.

Human Resource function is confronted with several challenges. A multigenerational workforce is a major one that has been compounded by the fact that there is an influx of large number of generation Y or millennial generation employees into the workforce. India is on the way to become the youngest nation in the world. Hence, at least three generations are at work together - the baby boomers—almost on their way out, the Generation X—at senior and mid-management levels and the generation Y—at entry to mid-level. The new generation Y workforce is challenging many pre-set existing organizational designs, cultures, work systems and workplace behaviours. Consequently, there has been rise in friction between the older and newer generation, leading to formation of certain myths about millennials. This multi-generational workforce on one hand is a challenge to deal with, but on the other hand promises to be a great opportunity for organizations for leveraging on innovation and sustainability. How this diverse workforce is managed ultimately will make the difference. The balance could swing both ways.

However generational diversity is not the only challenge that managers and leaders face in terms of managing workforce. With a significant number of women entering the workforce, gender-diversity, gender-sensitivity and gender-inclusivity are important issues that need to be addressed, with much greater focus and attention. The trend of temporary workers is also growing and managing a mix of permanent and temporary workers at the same time poses to be a challenge for the companies. The global nature of the workforce also means greater cultural diversity, need for cross-cultural management and training people on cultural sensitivity in conducting business.

With an army of young graduates available every year for recruitment, hiring has not been that easy as it may seem to be. India especially is confronted with a unique demographic challenge. Employability skills amongst new graduates continue to be a challenge. To convert this demographic advantage into a demographic dividend this skill-gap must be bridged. Hiring managers and recruitment heads have been overwhelmed in terms of figuring out how this can be achieved. Government has set an ambitious target of imparting skills to over 30 crore people, one out of every four Indians, by 2020 to help them secure jobs as part of the new national skills development policy. But the question that human resource managers have to ask themselves is what they are going to do as a more proactive measure from their end.

Talent retention continues to be a challenge and most companies seem to be grappling with keeping their key talent engaged. With market being upbeat and lots of jobs being available, there will be an increase in the overall attrition percentage. The attrition level across sectors is likely to go up to 20 per cent in 2015. This may further compound the war for talent.

Technology is impacting workplaces and workers in a big way. Trends like crowdsourcing in hiring, social media recruitment, BYOD, virtual workspaces, remote working etc., are relatively new challenges that HR managers have to come to terms with.

With growing need for HR to play a part in the business and not just be a part of business, the need to bring in more purpose in the way performance of people are managed and the way they are rewarded and developed are seeing major transformations. It is no surprise that people management is cited to be by far the most substantial challenge facing companies over the next five to ten years, according to a recent survey of 636 C-level and senior executives by The Economist Intelligence Unit, sponsored by the SHRM Foundation.

We need all the knowledge and insights that we can get in order to deal with these challenges and create a competitive advantage through people and systems. Systematic practice-oriented theoretical frameworks, like the one this book so eloquently and thoughtfully presents, shall benefit business scholars, researchers and business managers in gathering right knowledge and acumen on managing people. Dr. Debashish has made this book a unique text in many ways. Firstly, it's a strong blend of theory and practical insights in the form of elaborate set of case studies. Secondly, the book addresses several contemporary aspects of human resource management. Thirdly, the book never loses sight of the big picture of the business and also discusses the strategic nature of managing people. And finally, the book has included several unconventional discussions, rich set of reading exhibits and examples that make the book rich, insightful and comprehensive.

I strongly recommend this book to everyone interested in building a strong, contemporary, incisive knowhow on human resource management.

Madhukar Angur,
B. Tech. (NIT); PGDM (IIM-A); Ph. D. (Texas),
Founder Chancellor, Alliance University, Bangalore

April 2015

Preface

Preface to Second Edition

As the field of human resource management is continuously evolving, new additions are both important and necessary to keep the text contemporary and relevant. The first edition was received well by the readers and certain valuable suggestions made by few researchers and academicians were also incorporated in the second edition.

The second editions contain 3 new chapters and 6 new case studies. The first chapter 'Overview of human resource management' has been added to make readers familiar with the concept and evolution of human resource management. The last two chapters namely – 'Strategic management of human resource in organizations' and 'International human resource management' are also new additions. They have been added to articulate with more assertiveness the fast evolving strategic and global role of human resource function. The second edition also has 6 new case studies that further add ammunition to existing rich inventory of cases in the book. Attempt always has been to make the book more practice-oriented and consequently help the readers develop not only knowledge, but the requisite skills required to manage workforce effectively.

There is age old adage that says – 'Change is the only constant'. Hopefully the changes and additions made in the second edition would make the book more meaningful and useful to the readers and result in greater learning.

Preface to First Edition

One of the first questions that I asked myself before writing this book and perhaps you as a reader would be asking as well is why another book on HRM? Well, believe me that it was tougher for me to convince myself before I finally decided to ink the text.

On November 26, 2008, when terrorists struck the TajMahal Palace in Mumbai, as they did simultaneously at various other locations in the city, something extraordinary happened amidst a severe hostage crisis that lasted two nights and three days. Apparently none of the hotel employees fled the scene and put the safety of the guests before their own. Waiters, room cleaners, busboys who knew the various exit routes from the hotel, guided the guests to safety, kitchen employees formed a human shield to protect the guests, evacuated telephone operators, came back to the hotel to help the guests; these are only handful stories of extraordinary courage displayed by the ordinary employees of the hotel, many losing their lives in the process. The general manager of the hotel, Kang, who lost his whole family in the attack, was reportedly the last man to leave the hotel much after the seize was over.

What prompted these ordinary men and women to risk their lives and respond in such a unique manner to a sudden crisis? No organization rules were binding upon them in such a scenario nor would anyone have blamed them if they had chosen to save their lives. After all it was an extreme situation! Yet they chose to stay and take care of their guests. When Rohit Deshpande published this as a case in HBR he underlined deep seated HR philosophy of the company behind such a response which even the mangers of the company found difficult to explain. No one should be surprised that Taj Hotels feature very highly in Gallup's engagement rankings, globally. This incident however showed the unimaginable benefits and importance of good people management. The potential returns shall continue to surprise both the scholar and the practitioner. My belief that I should attempt to present this subject in the way I have seen it for the last dozen years was strengthened.

Besides this, Human resource management as a discipline and practice shall never stop evolving. The kind of changes that HRM has seen in the past decade especially in countries like India is huge and continues to transform. For instance, Pangea3, a legal process outsourcing firm (LPO), introduced sometime back an innovative performance appraisal system known as one year 'anniversary appraisal cycle'. An employee who has completed one year comes-up for appraisal without having to wait for the organization's annual evaluation to end. The appraisal system has also been uniquely designed by the company under which they account for not only the quantitative client contact metrics but also qualitative aspects and the throughput (volume errors). Every quarter an employee is engaged with an engagement form that provides visibility to the individual regarding his/her performance position. The employee of the year gets to fly-out with his spouse/fiancée for a paid-up vacation on a foreign locale.

The HR transformation in India is at its various stages of evolution and requires students and practitioners to be equipped with contemporary skills and knowledge to manage today's employees so as to convert them into strategic partners of the company. This book is an attempt towards presenting similar colours and contours of the ever changing and challenging human resource management.

About the Book

It was on September 15, 2008 that Lehman Brothers filed for bankruptcy. A more than 100 year old firm, with a huge reputation in the market, collapsed and with $639 billion in assets and $619 billion in debt, Lehman's bankruptcy filing was the largest in history, as its assets far surpassed those of previous bankrupt giants such as WorldCom and Enron. Lehman was the fourth-largest U.S. investment bank at the time of its collapse, with 25,000 employees worldwide. What led to the collapse of this giant? Lehman was perhaps one of the biggest victims of the US subprime crisis. However its failure is mainly attributed to gross miscalculations done in terms of acquisitions and policy overlook that caused this colossal collapse. Lehman was let down by its own people and their deeds. The decision to massage the bottom-line without looking at sustainable growth cost the firm dearly. Lehman had the reputation to attract and pockets to afford the best talents from all over the world. Yet it failed! All the knowledge, skill and experience could not be of any use! The question is why? Was it greed? Was it shortsightedness? Or was it a mad-rush to push profits? May be all of these...

The Lehman episode however shows that despite the fact that a firm might have the best of the best talent in its fold, the crème-de-la-crème working for it but if it fails to manage them effectively then it could still have a 'titanic' affect. Titanic that boasted of its size, strength and skill, ignored all the warning signs and hit a giant iceberg at full speed to meet its doom and created one of the worst shipping disasters in the world, that continues to intrigue one and all even after 100 years of its sinking. Similarly Lehman Brothers despite having a hundred year old legacy, enviable talent and reputation hit the subprime bubble at a speed that spelt its doom.

Treating human as a resource and managing them in a way that the firm's strategic objectives can be actualized to ensure both profitability in the present and sustainability in the future, is a challenge that confronts every firm today. Lehman example also shows that the cost of poor people management is unforgiving.

This book also assumes that people management is everyone's job and not just the job of the HR department. The Line specialists are the prime-drivers of the HR management and the CEO-the Chief Engagement officer. The HR department and the Chief Human Resource officer of the firm are the owners and facilitators of the process, as well as the strategic partners to core business. And hence, when it comes to people management, everyone assumes responsibility. In words of SAS CEO Jim Goodnight - *"I guess 95% of my assets drive-out of the front gate every evening and it's my job to bring them back."* No wonder SAS lead people management practices which has translated with greater business success. Engaged, talented employees are vital to a knowledge-based company like SAS. In 2010, SAS was named No. 1 on the 'Best

Companies to Work for' lists in Belgium, Norway, Sweden and the US. It is not coincidental that 2010 was a year of milestones for SAS – as an innovator, employer and corporate citizen. The year also marked its 35th consecutive year of growth and profitability, with record global revenue of US$2.43 billion, an increase of 5.2 percent over 2009.

This book is an attempt towards building a case for not only the management of people but good people management that is having both speed and direction. Each chapter has been carefully constructed to address both theory and practice. The idea is to develop a book that not only equips readers with knowledge but also imparts practical skills needed to manage the human resource.

The book has 23 chapters and 30 case studies. Each chapter covers a relevant topic in human resource management. Chapters are followed by review questions to help learners reflect on their learning. Additional reading exhibits have been included that are based on articles written on issues concerning human resource management by certain eminent researchers and practitioners, to provide additional insights into managing people in a way to gain competitive advantage.

Chapter 1 – The first chapter introduces the readers to concept and evolution of human resource management. It highlights how modern HRM is different from traditional HRM and the importance of human resource management. The chapter introduces various HR systems and processes and prepares the readers what to expect in the rest of the chapters.

Chapter 2 – This chapter explains why employees are the best brand ambassadors that any company can have and how this can be a win-win situation, both for the firm and for the employees. It also suggests a 10 E model for developing employees as brand ambassadors. The chapter concludes with successful examples of Maruti, Samsung, and Whirpool in their quest to create brand ambassadors out of employees.

Chapter 3 – HR cannot operate as a silo. The HR imperatives cannot appear out of thin air. The chapter 2 discusses how the external environmental variables (political, economic, social, cultural, technological, legal and environmental factors) shape the business imperatives; and how the business imperatives of a firm in turn shape the HR imperatives of a firm. The chapter ends by deriving seven new age HR roles that a people manager needs to do so as to be efficient and effective.

Chapter 4 – Human Resource Planning programs have primarily three implications on any organization - Cost implications, Talent implications and Organizational Readiness. The chapter 3 focuses on the aspects of human resource planning and explains techniques like Markov Analysis in detail to make it more practical and useful.

Chapter 5 – Job analysis is often fundamental to the success of many HR processes, yet it is often an ignored process in itself in many firms. This chapter tries to bring back the focus on good job analysis and how it can be linked to other HR sub-functions. Exhibits of Job Analysis tools used in the real world (Arizona State University) make the chapter more enriching. Sample exhibits of actual Job Analysis are also given at the end of this chapter.

Chapter 6 – Recruitment is the first step in hiring and can be crucial in the success of a firm's acquisition plan. The Chapter 5 not only throws light on recruitment process and factors affecting recruitment but engages in some very practical discussions like the seven types of candidates that a firm must avoid or the positioning strategy that can be used to design recruitment advertisements strategically etc. At the end of the chapter there is an excellent reading exhibit on recruitment process outsourcing from the Human capital institute.

Chapter 7 – The selection process has been documented and mapped, with each step explained with clarity. The Graphology test exhibit from Business Balls U.K. is a unique tool used in making selection decisions. Selection Interviews and the need to train interviewers on the dos and don'ts during a selection interview and how interviewers can avoid sub-conscious bias have been highlighted. The cost of a wrong hire is roughly 25 times of the cost of a normal hire. Hence the topic of reference check or background verification has been given due weightage in the chapter.

Chapter 8 – How does a firm know conclusively that its selection systems have reliability and validity? Is there a way to statistically ascertain the reliability of a selection system? The chapter 8 discussions are mathematical and practical. The chapter talks about methods like Cronbach Alpha, Spearman Brown prophecy formula, Point-biserial correlation etc.

Chapter 9 – The chapter on performance management system is designed primarily for training the line managers. The managerial intervention in the PMS process has been highlighted, mapped and discussed in detail. The role of a manager in performance planning, review, appraisal and feedback has been explained from a practitioner's perspective.

Chapter 10 – When you appraise an employee, how do you know whether the same is in line with company's strategic objectives? When an employee achieves a performance goal, how do you know whether it is contributing to the achievement of the organization's goals? When you set development targets for the employee, do you know for sure that those skill sets are the ones required for the job? The chapter Competency-based PMS is thoroughly practical and from a manager's standpoint. The whole process of Competency Mapping has been discussed in detail. Concluding exhibits of actual competency maps, using the process explained in the chapter lend credibility to the discussions.

Chapter 11 – Developing a resource should be the ultimate objective of any performance management system. This chapter is foundation to designing adequate & effective training systems. Understanding the learning styles of the trainees is an important step towards learning. The chapter discusses various learning styles, theories of learning & their implications for trainers and ultimately about transfer of learning. How much of whatever is learnt in the training rooms gets translated into actual job place performance, is an issue that evry trainer and training organization faces, in terms of ensuring the effectiveness of training. Transfer of training deals with such issues.

Chapter 12 – This chapter is an exhaustive discussion on the various nitty-gritties of training. The journey from Training Need Identification (TNI) to ROI on training has been captured as objectively as possible. The highlight of the chapter is discussion on training evaluation, especially on ROI on training. The practical issues in ROI computation have been captured from the perspectives of practicing training heads. The chapter closes with exhibits of actual training needs assessment of professionals.

Chapter 13 – The issue of compensation can never be under-estimated. Right compensation strategies and not only good compensation are important towards achieving engagement targets. The various components of compensation and the sub-components within them, pricing the jobs, compensable factors etc., have been discussed in detail. The hay group Spectrum published with requisite permission of the Hay Group and the reading exhibit on Internal wage Structure have added richness to the discussions.

Chapter 14 – What do the organizations pay their employees for? Do they pay them for the time that they spend in the organization? Do they pay them for their inputs? Do they pay them for their skills? Or do they pay them for their performance? These are some of the questions that have been raised at the beginning of this chapter that focuses on performance-based compensation. The logic behind performance-based compensation and the various types of performance-based pays have been discussed.

Chapter 15 – A safe and secure working place is one of the very basic requirements that every employee aspires for. The chapter goes beyond the normal course of workplace safety discussions and also focuses on a very important aspect of workplace violence, and ways to deal with this growing menace.

Chapter 16 – Industrial relations has come back with a bang in reckoning with the recent spate of industrial strikes hitting not only India, but in many other parts of the world. The chapter addresses the issues of approaches to IR, trade unions, various laws related to IR in a detailed yet objective manner.

Chapter 17 – The idea of dedicating a chapter on Women and the much needed HR response to the same does not stem from the perception that women are in anyway lesser employees but from the fact that despite the all-round brilliance of women it is still very much a man's world and the odds are loaded in all possible ways against women. This is true even for the most developed countries of the world like US. The chapter addresses some of the key concerns that exist when it comes to the state of the women employees in the organization and ways to address the same.

Chapter 18 – The chapter 18 deals with three important and futuristic topics in HR i.e. automation, audit and accounting of HR and HR systems. The issues have been dealt keeping in mind the present as well future potential of such practices.

Chapter 19 – One of the most contemporary chapters in the book that deals with the various application that social media offers to the organizations in terms of better management of its human resources. From social media recruitment to back-channel referencing to aspects of networking & communication, all have been dealt with proper examples.

Chapter 20 – One of the key concerns that every firm faces today is managing talents. Talent has become key to a firm's potential to translate its strategies into action. The chapter deals with the complexities associated with talent management and suggests relevant talent management strategies. The chapter also proposes a talent pipeline that an organization can build.

Chapter 21 – Employee engagement happens at two levels – at rational level and at emotional level. Engagement is key to successful management of human resources. Many a times organization look at retention and productivity of employees as an objective in itself. However that is a huge error. Actually engagement should be the objective. Once that is achieved, then productivity, contribution and retention of employees automatically become an outcome. The chapter introduces readers to the basics of employee engagement. The chapter also consists of some case excerpts from my previous book *'Employee Engagement'* (Biztantra, 2011).

Chapter 22 – This chapter discusses the strategic nature of managing human resources and how the same can add value to the business. HRM effectiveness is connected to business effectiveness and HR needs to understand the business and business strategy to accordingly develop HR strategy that meets business needs and employee needs, both. Various approaches to strategic human resource management have been discussed in this chapter.

Chapter 23 – Global nature of business has necessitated managing people across national boundaries. Parent-country, hoist-country, third-country national being employed in various subsidiaries of the companies at various locations of the world has meant expatriates. Consequently, expatriation and repatriation issues have also come into existence. The complexities of managing human resources across boundaries are even more and this chapter introduces readers to the international management of human resources.

Case Studies

The book has **30 case studies**. The cases have been derived from the actual incidents and problems that have occurred in various companies. The cases cover a wide-range of areas in human resource management and are designed to help the readers to appreciate the practical problems that managers encounter when it comes to managing people. The Cases have been written to enable learners to analyze, reflect and discuss real life human resource management situations.

The cases in the book cover a wide-range of HR problems in various organizations including HR lag in companies, Work-life imbalance, workforce planning, hiring mistakes, issues in managing employee performance, skilling challenge faced by companies, designing right compensation packages, industrial conflicts and employee relations, problems in gender inclusivity, sexual harassment, automation, impact of social media on HR and leadership issues in managing people.

The case studies in the book help readers learn about the practice of human resource management and accomplish the following learning objectives -

1. Enhance one's understanding of what managers should and should not do in managing and building a healthy workforce.
2. Providing in-depth exposure to real-life HR issues and problems and learn from experience.
3. Developing one's skills in assessing a company's HR strengths and shortcomings and in conducting strategic analysis in a variety of competitive situations.
4. Gain valuable practice in identifying key HR issues that need to be addressed, evaluating best possible alternatives, and formulating practical plans of action.
5. Augment one's sense of judgment and developing solutions, instead of being served ready-made answers to problems.
6. Learning-by-doing is encouraged using case method of teaching and learning.

About the Author

Dr. Debashish Sengupta is the author of a Crossword bestseller book – *'Employee Engagement'* (Biztantra -Wiley India, 2011). The book has been cited by *KPMG* in one of its report. He has also authored four other books *'Business Drama: How Shakespearean insights help leaders manage volatile contexts'* (Zorba Publishers, 2014), *'Human Resource Management'* (Biztantra-Wiley India, 2012) *'You Can Beat Your Stress'* (Excel, 2007) and *'FMI'* (Excel, 2010). He has been a book editor and reviewer for the prestigious *Emerald Group Publishing, London (U.K.)*

He writes a blog on people engagement - http://www.peopleengagement.blogspot.in. The blog deals on contemporary issues concerning engaging the modern day employee on an emotional as well as rational plane, with an objective of nurturing a productive & happy workforce. He was recently invited to write an invitational blogpost for a blog on employee happiness, by Institute for Employee Wellbeing, Bellevue University, Nebraska, U.S. Dr. Sengupta is among the exclusive 26 authors invited from all over the world, and the only Indian on this list.

Debashish is an avid researcher and besides the books authored by him, he has contributed several research papers in International Journals, in refereed and peer-reviewed national journals, columns in popular business media, book chapters and articles in business magazines.

He occasionally writes columns for reputed business dailies like The Hindu 'Business Line' and for leading business magazines like 'Outlook Business'. His interviews have appeared in dailies like Telegraph, Pioneer and The Hindu.

Debashish is also a much sought speaker at various business forums. He became the first non-CEO to be invited by CII – HRD Forum, Karnataka State (India) to give a talk on Employee Engagement, in the year 2011. His invited talk on Engaging gen Y for the entire HR fraternity of TCS Bangalore was contributory in design of a Gen Y policy of the company', it should be written 'His series of invited talks titled 'Engaging Gen Y', based on his research, have contributed to the design of policy on Gen Y workers in a number of companies.' He is a resource person in several MDPs, corporate training programs. His training programs have been attended by people of the rank of CEO, Regional Directors, Chief General Managers, GM-HR, DGM-HRs COO, Senior Bank Officers, Senior Indian Army Officers up to the rank of Commandant, Chartered Accountants, and Directors. His training videos on stress management techniques are on You Tube. He has also been a resource person for visiting Consulting & Executive MBA students of various global business schools.

Debashish holds a degree of Ph.D. in Management and specializes in Employee Engagement and Strategic Human Resource Management. He is also certified in Leadership Development by the Japan Management Association Management Centre (JMAM) and in Social Psychology from Wesleyan University, USA.

Presently, Debashish is involved in teaching business post-graduate and doctoral students at Alliance School of Business, Alliance University. He lives with his wife Vandana and son Arnab at Bangalore (India).

Acknowledgements

I would like to express my deepest sense of thanks and gratitude to all those who supported me in this project for their excellent suggestions and advice. My special thanks to the editorial team of Biztantra especially to **Mr. Yoginder Singh** and his team for their painstaking work and for their patience, time and devotion. I thank **Mr. Rahul Gupta** managing director of Biztantra.

I express my deep sense of gratitude to **Dr. Madhukar Angur,** Hon'ble Chancellor of Alliance University for his extra-ordinary support throughout this project. He has been very kind in writing foreword for the book.

I would like to thank all those who permitted reproduction of copyrighted material in this book. This book has been enriched by their brilliant pieces -

- **Mr. Alan Chapman** (ac@alanchapman.com), Businessballs, United Kingdom
- **Mr. Bernard O'Meara** (b.omeara@ballarat.edu.au), University of Ballart, Australia
- **Ms. Carol Hurst** (Carol.Hurst@asu.edu), Arizona State University, USA
- **Ms. Caroline Liguori** (cliguori@ccl-cca.ca), Canadian Council on Learning / Conseil canadien sur l'apprentissage c/o University of Ottawa, Ottawa, Ontario, Canada
- **Mr. David R. Shetterly** (dshetterly@troy.edu), Troy University, AtlantaRegion, USA
- **Mr. Ganesh Chella** (ganesh@totusconsulting.com), Totus Consulting, India
- **Mr. Gregorio Billikopf** (gebillikopf@ucdavis.edu), University of California, USA
- **Mr. Jeffrey M. Miller, Shidoshi,** (jmmiller@warrior-concepts-online.com), Warrior Concepts International, Sunbury, USA
- **Mr. Kerry Jothen** (kerryjothen@shaw.ca), Human Capital Strategies, Canada
- **Ms. Laura Presland** (Laura.Presland@haygroup.com), Hay Group, USA
- **Mr. Robert Masternak** (robert@masternak.com), Masternak & Associates, Ohio, USA
- **Mr. Ross Jones,** Human Capital Institute
- **Mr. Rosalio Pagano,** Human Capital Institute
- **Mr. Sriram Ramanujam** (sriram_ramanujam@infosys.com), Infosys, India

I would also like to thank all those who read chapters and cases of my book and wrote authoritative testimonials for my book. They include **Mr. Buddhadeb Das Gupta,** COO- Nous Infosystems, **Dr. Anil Kumar Mulpur,** V.P. & Clinical Director, Narayana Hrudayalaya, **Dr. J. Sadakkadulla,** Principal, Reserve Bank Staff College, Chennai & **Mr. K.G.Umesh**, Head - Human Resources, The Himalaya Drug Company. I thank them for their valuable time and precious words for my book.

I dedicate this book to my parents and would like to put on record my thanks to my brother **Subhashish** for his support.

The last two people whom I wish to thank are my wife **Vandana** and my nine year old son **Arnab**. This book would not have been possible without them.

Dr. Debashish Sengupta
Bangalore (India)

Brief Contents

Foreword	v
Preface	vii
About the Book	ix
About the Author	xv
Acknowledgements	xvii

PART I: TEXT — 1

CHAPTER 1: Overview of Human Resource Management	3
CHAPTER 2: The New Brand Ambassadors	17
CHAPTER 3: The New Age HRM	27
CHAPTER 4: Human Resource Planning	65
CHAPTER 5: Job Analysis	89
CHAPTER 6: Recruitment	123
CHAPTER 7: Selection	165
CHAPTER 8: Reliability & Validity in Selection	191
CHAPTER 9: Performance Management Systems	207
CHAPTER 10: Competency Based Performance Management	229
CHAPTER 11: Learning Process & Trainers	253
CHAPTER 12: Employee Training & Development	263
CHAPTER 13: Compensation & Benefits	295

CHAPTER 14: Performance-based Compensation — 339

CHAPTER 15: Workplace Health & Safety — 369

CHAPTER 16: Industrial Relations — 391

CHAPTER 17: Women Workforce & HR — 413

CHAPTER 18: Human Resource Automation, Audit & Accounting — 429

CHAPTER 19: Social Media Applications in Managing Human Resource — 453

CHAPTER 20: Talent Management — 461

CHAPTER 21: Employee Engagement — 477

CHAPTER 22: Strategic Management of Human Resource in Organizations — 493

CHAPTER 23: International Human Resource Management — 507

PART II: BUSINESS CASES — 525

1. Chink in the Giant — 527
2. No Time to Holiday — 530
3. Why Indian Firms go Wrong when Hiring US Sales Teams? — 533
4. Selection Blues — 536
5. Faulty Appraisals — 538
6. Appraisals at Hexagon Foods — 540
7. The Skills Gap in Canada — 542
8. The Best Archer — 550
9. Bharti Airtel Trains for Customer Service — 552
10. Training for Safer Roads — 553
11. Compensation Woes of Engineering Faculty — 556
12. ESOPs in GMT Bank — 558

13.	Sexual Harassment at Simon Logistics	560
14.	Strike at Spark Automatives & Precision Engineering	562
15.	Strike at Maruti Suzuki India	564
16.	Air India Strikes	570
17.	Women Participation in Workforce	572
18.	Automating to Match Scale	576
19.	Employee-voices on Social Media	578
20.	On-boarding at Taj Hotels	582
21.	YUM Increasing Footprint through Effective Talent Management	585
22.	Indian Problem, Singaporean Solution – Will it Work?	587
23.	S(kill) Sales: Gaps in Sales Training	589
24.	Strike at MRF Tyre Plant	592
25.	The New Generation Army	594

PART III: COMPREHENSIVE CASES — 597

1.	HRP for 2010 Winter Olympic Games	599
2.	A Metropolitan University	627
3.	Job Characteristics of Officers & Agents	647
4.	Debacle of Dream Films Productions Limited (DFPL)	675
5.	Skill-gap & Talent Shortage in India	681

INDEX	689

Detailed Contents

Foreword	*v*
Preface	*vii*
About the Book	*ix*
About the Author	*xv*
Acknowledgements	*xvii*

PART I: TEXT — 1

CHAPTER 1: Overview of Human Resource Management — 3

Business Byte	4
What is Human Resource Managment?	4
Organizational Design & Policies	5
HR Systems & Processes	5
Evolution of Human Resource Management	8
Traditional versus Modern Human Resource Management	10
Importance of Human Resource Managment	11
Job Satisfaction versus Employee Engagement	14
Essay Questions	15
Application Questions	15
Bibliography	16

CHAPTER 2: The New Brand Ambassadors — 17

Introduction	18
How to Develop Brand Ambassadors?	20
Success Stories	24
The Maruti Salesman	24
Spreading Magic @Whirlpool	24
Singing what Samsung	25

Essay Questions	25
Application Questions	25
Bibiolography	25

CHAPTER 3: The New Age HRM — 27

Introduction	28
Political Factors	29
Business Imperatives Driven by Changed Political Climate	31
HR Imperatives Driven by Political Context	32
1. Managing Cultural Change	32
2. Talent Management	32
3. Structural Change in Organization	33
4. Training and Development	33
5. Employee Engagement	33
6. Increase in Use of Temporary Employment Practices	33
7. Focus on Key Players	34
8. Increasing use of Technology and Business Intelligence	34
Economic Factors	34
Business Imperatives Driven by Changed Economic Climate	36
HR Imperatives Driven by Economic Environment	38
Social Factors	39
Business Imperatives Driven by Changed Social Context	42
HR Imperatives Driven by Social Context	42
Cultural Factors	44
Business Imperatives Driven by Changed Cultural Environment	45
HR Imperatives Driven by Cultural Context	47
Legal/Regulatory Factors	48
Business Imperatives Driven by Changed Legal/Regulatory Climate	49
1. Ease of Trade	49
2. Restructuring	50
3. Security	50
4. Parity	51
HR Imperatives Driven by Legal Environment	51
Technological Factors	53
HR Imperatives Driven by Technological Context	55
New Age HRM Roles	59
Essay Questions	62
Application Questions	62
Bibliography	62

CHAPTER 4: Human Resource Planning — 65

Introduction	66
Human Resource Function	66

Human Resource Planning	67
Key Elements of HR Planning	68
Implications of HR Planning on Organisation	68
Factors Affecting Human Resource Planning	69
The Macro Environmental Factors	69
The Micro (Industry Specific) Factors	70
The Company Specific Factors	75
Demand Forecasting	76
A. Qualitative Methods	81
B. Quantitative Methods	81
Supply Forecasting	82
Markov Analysis	82
Sample Exercises on Markov Analysis	85
Essay Questions	86
Application Questions	86
Bibliography	86

Chapter 5: Job Analysis — 89

Introduction	90
What is a Job?	90
What is Job Analysis?	90
Primary Actors in Job Analysis	91
Use of Job Analysis Data	91
Process Steps in Job Analysis	92
Data Collection Methods	93
Job Analysis Interview Format	93
Position Analysis Questionnaire	95
Overview and Instructions	95
General Information	96
Organizational Relationships	96
Essential Functions (Duties/Responsibilities)	97
Additional Job Information	98
Decision Making/Problem Solving	98
Working Environment	99
Minimum Qualifications	100
Primary Purpose (Position Objective)	100
Supervisor's Section	101
Instructions for Completing PAQ	102
Topics to Cover	102

Logistics	104
Factors to be Considered in Collection of Job Analysis Data	105
Sample Exhibits of Actual Job Analysis using PAQ	105
Exhibit 1: JA of a Senior Manager in India's Premier Commercial Vehicle Manufacturers Training Provided by the Organization	109
Exhibit 2: JA of a Manager-Software Development of a Leading Internet Solutions & Networking Company	109
Exhibit 3: JA of a Project Manager in a Global Management Consulting, Technology Consulting and Technology Outsourcing Company	114
Additional Job Information	116
Decision Making/Problem Solving	116
Working Environment	118
Minimum Qualifications	118
Primary Purpose	118
Training for Senior/Middle Level Management	119
Development Activities	120
Essay Questions	120
Application Questions	120
Bibliography	120

Chapter 6: Recruitment — 123

Introduction	124
Recruitment	124
Species of Candidates to be Avoided	124
Recruitment Objectives	126
Various Factors Affecting Recruitment	127
External Factors	127
Internal Factors	129
Sources of Recruitment	129
A. Internal Sources	129
B. External Sources	129
Recruitment Process	131
Recruitment Advertisements – More than a 'Vacancy' Announcement	132
e-Recruitment Advertisements	135
Advantages of e-Recruitment Advertisements	136
Reduced Costs	136
Reduced Time to Hire	136
Increase Efficiency of the Process	136
Creative Design	136

Greater Access	136
Flexible and Scalable	136
SWOT Analysis of e-recruitment Advertisements	137
Strengths	137
Weaknesses	137
Opportunities	137
Threats	138
Social Media Recruitment	139
About Human Capital Institute	139
RPO in Today's Economic Environment	140
Talent Acquisition and RPO - The Current State	141
Defining RPO	142
Why Use RPO?	143
What Recruiting Practices Drive RPO Today?	144
Linking Strategic Priorities and Recruiting Practices	148
Strategy & Analysis	148
RPO - Challenges and Opportunities	149
Conclusion	154
Summary	156
Survey	157
Findings	157
An Opportunity for Competitive Advantage	158
Appendix 1: Methodology and Demographics Methodology	158
Appendix 2: Factor Analysis of Critical Talent Acquisition Practices	161
Essay Questions	163
Application Questions	163
Bibliography	163

CHAPTER 7: Selection — 165

Introduction	166
Selection Process	166
Selection Tests	168
Exhibit 1: Sample English Ability Test	171
Exhibit 2: Sample Aptitude Test	172
Exhibit 3: Businessballs Handwriting Quick Self-test	173
Graphology Explanation	173
The Basic Features of Handwriting	174
Graphology - The Basic Analysis	175
The Three Cases - Divisions of Personality	176

Some Other Simple Indicators	177
Cold Calling	178
Sorting the Curriculum-Vitae (CV)	178
Selection Interview	179
Dos	179
Don'ts	180
How to Avoid Sub-conscious Bias?	181
Reference Checking / Background Verification	181
Why Verify?	181
Exhibit 4: Cost of the Wrong Hire	182
What to Verify?	183
What not to Verify?	183
Exhibit 5: Backchannel Referencing	184
Exhibit 6: National Skills Registry (NSR)	184
Where to Verify?	184
How to Verify?	185
Essay Questions	186
Application Questions	187
Bibliography	188

CHAPTER 8: Reliability & Validity in Selection   191

Introduction	192
Kinds of Errors in Selection	192
Selection Errors	193
Omission Errors	193
Other Errors	193
Reliability	193
Types of Reliability	194
Limitation of Test-retest Reliability	194
a) By Altering the Length of the Test	196
b) By Altering the Quality of Question in a Test	197
Interpreting Point Biserial Correlation Coefficient (rpbi) Values	200
Validity	201
Kinds of Validity	201
Relationship Between Reliability & Validity	203
Interpreting Validity Coefficients	203
Essay Questions	204
Application Questions	204
Bibliography	205

Chapter 9: Performance Management Systems 207

Introduction	208
Scope of Performance Management	209
Setting Objectives	211
Key Result Areas (KRAs)	211
Core Responsibilities (CRs)	211
Individual Contribution Areas (ICAs)	211
Use of Balanced Score Card (BSC) in Setting KRAs	212
Anomaly of Assessment	212
Four Parameters & Cascading Principle	213
Objective Setting & Cascading Principle	213
Managerial Role in Setting Objectives	216
Don'ts	217
Dos	217
Mid-term Review	217
Annual Appraisal	218
Traditional Appraisal Methods	218
Doubts on Accuracy of Performance Appraisals	220
Contemporary Appraisal Methods	221
Management by Objectives (MBO)	221
360º Performance Appraisal Method	222
Merits	222
Demerits	222
Steps in Annual Appraisal Process	223
The Appraisal Interview	224
Feedback	224
Manager's Role in Feedback	225
Conclusion	225
Essay Questions	226
Application Questions	226
Bibliography	227

Chapter 10: Competency Based Performance Management 229

Competency	230
Competency and Organizational Strategy	231
Competency and other HR Processes	232
Recruitment	232

Performance Management System	232
Individual Development	232
Succession Planning	232
Leadership Development	232
Competency Dictionary	232
Competency Buckets	233
Exhibit 1: Competency Bucket for Head of the Department of Watch Assembly	233
Exhibit 2: Competency Bucket for Head of the Department of Watch Assembly - Quality	234
Exhibit 3: Competency Bucket for Team Member of Watch Assembly	235
Exhibit 4: Competency Bucket for Team Member of Watch Assembly - Quality	235
Exhibit 5: Competency Bucket for Team Member of Watch Assembly - Coordination with other Units	226
Preparing Competency Buckets	237
1. Sensitization	237
2. Identification of Functional and Role Competencies	237
Accountability	238
Competency Gap	238
Types of Competencies	239
1. Functional Competencies	239
2. Behavioural Competencies	239
Competency Mapping Process	239
Exhibit 6: Competency Mapping of Mr. Thomas Varghese, Senior Consultant (IT)	241
Functional Competencies	242
Behavioural Competencies	242
Functional Competencies	243
Behavioural Competencies	244
Exhibit 7: Competency Mapping of Mr. Arnold Hopkins, Director Consultant in a Strategic Consulting Group	246
Functional Competencies	246
Behavioural Competencies	246
Essay Questions	250
Application Questions	250
Bibliography	251

CHAPTER 11: Learning Process & Trainers — 253

Introduction	254
Learning	254
The Process of Learning	254
Learning Styles	255

Learning Theories	257
a. Social Learning Theory	257
b. Adult Learning Theory	259
Implications of Adult Learning Theory for Trainers	259
The Learning Curve	260
Implications for Trainers	260
Transfer of Learning	261
Essay Questions	261
Application Questions	261
Bibliography	262

CHAPTER 12: Employee Training & Development — 263

Introduction	264
Training	264
Training versus Education	264
Training versus Development	265
Relationship between Learning, Training, Education & Development	265
Competency & Competency Gap	265
Reading Exhibit 1	266
Reading Exhibit 2	266
The Training Process Model	266
Training Need Analysis	267
a. Organizational Training Need Analysis	268
b. Operational Training Need Analysis	268
c. Individual Training Need Analysis	268
Approaches to Training Need Assessment (TNA)	268
Reading Exhibit 3	269
Reading Exhibit 4	269
Reading Exhibit 5: Proactive TNA by IBM	269
Training Plan	270
Training Methods	271
Commonly Used Training Methods	271
Simulation	271
Role Play	271
Case Studies	271
Reading Exhibit 6: Triage Training (Virtual Training)	272
Outbound Training	272
Reading Exhibit 7: Outbound Training @ Cognizant	272

Computer Based Training (CBT)	272
Outbound Training	272
Reading Exhibit 8: Team Building through Drumming	273
Choosing the Right Training Method – The 3-C Model	273
Training Evaluation	275
Why Evaluate?	275
What to Evaluate?	275
When to Evaluate?	275
How to Evaluate?	277
Return on Investment in Training	278
Categories of Return of Investment (ROI)	278
Practical Issues in ROI Computation	279
1. Does Performance Result in increase of Organizational Revenues/Billing?	279
2. Are Improvements Always Quantitative?	279
3. Can Effects of Training be Isolated?	280
Reading Exhibit 9: A Training Need Analysis Sample	280
Company Profile	280
Group of Companies	281
Training Need Analysis & Results	285
A. Organizational Analysis of Training Needs	285
B. Operational Training Need Analysis	285
C. Person Analysis	286
Reading Exhibit 10: Training Employees at Titan	286
Process of Training Need Analysis at Titan	288
Senior Leadership Development based on PPM's	289
Capability Gaps for a Given Role	289
Performance Management System/KRA's	289
Talent Group Requirements	291
Corporate Initiatives	291
External Benchmarking/Developments	291
Essay Questions	292
Application Questions	293
Bibliography	293

CHAPTER 13: Compensation & Benefits — 295

Introduction	296
What is Compensation?	296
Factors Governing Compensation	297
Objectives of a Compensation System	297

1. Equity	297
2. Efficiency	298
Components of a Compensation Package	298
Base Pay Structure (Fixed component)	298
Basic Component	298
HRA (House Rent Allowance)	299
DA (Dearness Allowance)	299
Leave Travel Allowance	299
Mobile Expenses	299
Medical Allowance/Reimbursements, etc.	299
Variable Pay Programs	299
Variable Pay Plans for Sales	299
Variable Pay Plans for Non-sales	300
Bonus	300
Commissions	300
Mixed Plans	301
Incentives	301
Sign on Bonuses	301
Profit Sharing Payments	301
Stock Options	301
Benefits	302
Types of Benefits	303
Paid Time off (also referred to as PTO)	303
Insurance Programs	303
Fringe Benefits	303
Social Security	304
Provident Fund	305
Gratuity	305
Reading Exhibit 1: HSBC (USA)	306
Rewards & Recognition	307
Pricing the Jobs	308
Job Evaluation	309
Reading Exhibit 2: Hay Group Spectrum - Job Evaluation for a New Generation	309
Compensable Factors	310
CF - Category I: Skill	311
CF - Category II: Responsibility	311
CF - Category III: Effort	312
CF - Category IV: Working Conditions	312
Non-quantitative Techniques of Job Evaluation	313
Ranking Method	313

Job Classification Method	313
Quantitative Methods of Job Evaluation	314
Point Method	314
Factor Comparison Method	316
Market Pricing/Benchmarking	317
Reading Exhibit 3: Internal Wage Structure	319
Pay Fairness (Pay Equity)	319
What is Behind Pay Differences?	321
Job Evaluations and Market Consideration	323
Job Evaluation	323
Market Considerations	325
Reconciling Market & Job Evaluations	326
Elements of A Wage Structure	326
Maintaining A Pay Structure	328
Seniority-based Raises	329
Merit-based Raises	329
Promotion Pay	331
Out-of-line or Color Rates	332
Cost of Living Adjustments (COLAs)	333
Flat vs. Percentage COLAs	333
Wage Compression & Minimum Wage	334
Summary	334
Essay Questions	335
Application Questions	335
Bibliography	336

CHAPTER 14: Performance-based Compensation   339

Introduction	340
Performance-based Pay/ Variable Pay	341
Types of Performance-based Pays	341
Merit Pays/Increments	342
Individual Incentives	342
Gain-sharing & Profit-sharing	343
Employee Stock Options (ESOPs)	344
Performance Bonus	346
The Payment of Bonus Act, 1965	347
Reading Exhibit 1	349
Reading Exhibit 2	349
Performance Milestones	349

Reading Exhibit 3	350
Gainsharing or Profit-sharing: The Right Tool for the Right Organization	350
Story	351
The Moral of the Story	352
Profit-sharing	353
History	353
Gainsharing	356
History	356
Line-of-sight & Measurement	359
Family of Measures	360
Essay Questions	366
Application Questions	366
Bibliography	367

CHAPTER 15: Workplace Health & Safety — 369

Introduction	370
Accidents/Industrial Disasters	370
Some of the Worst Industrial Accidents & Disasters	371
The Ten Worst Worldwide Mining Disasters	373
Four Levels of Safety Interventions	375
Legal Angle	376
The Factories Act, 1948	376
Some Other Acts	378
The Mines Act, 1952	378
The Dock Workers Act, 1986	378
Workmen's Compensation Act, 1923	379
OSHA, 1970	379
Workplace Violence	380
Growing Menace	380
Reading Exhibit: Top of Form	383
Essay Questions	388
Application Questions	388
Bibliography	388

CHAPTER 16: Industrial Relations — 391

Introduction	392
Theoretical Approaches to Industrial Relations	393
Systems Model Approach	393
Roles of Industrial Relations	394

Trade Unions	395
Labour Acts	395
List of Various Central Labour Acts	396
The Trade Unions Act, 1926	400
The Minimum Wages Act, 1948	400
Payment of Wages Act, 1936	401
Workmen's Compensation Act, 1923	402
Equal Remuneration Act [Act 25 of 1976 Amended by Act 49 of 1987]	403
Employee State Insurance Act, 1948	404
Payment of Gratuity Act	404
Employees' Provident Funds & Misc. Provisions Act, 1952	405
The Industrial Employment (Standing Orders) Act, 1946	405
The Payment of Bonus Act	405
The Shops and Establishments Act	406
The Maternity Benefit Act, 1961	406
The Industrial Disputes Act, 1947	407
The Factories Act, 1948	408
Apprentices Act, 1961	408
Future of Industrial Relations in India	408
Essay Questions	409
Application Questions	410
Bibliography	410

CHAPTER 17: Women Workforce & HR — 413

Introduction	414
Unequal Worlds	416
Work-life Imbalance	416
Sexual Harassment & Physical Insecurity	417
Pay Discrimination & Glass Ceiling	418
Work Stress	418
Women Resource	419
Exhibit 1: IBM India	420
Exhibit 2: Ernst & Young	421
Exhibit 3: American Express, India	422
Exhibit 4: Hindustan Unilever Limited (HUL)	422
Exhibit 5: Taj Group of Hotels	423
Exhibit 6: PepsiCo	424
Exhibit 7: Marriott International, Inc.	424
Exhibit 8: Deloitte	425

Exhibit 9: Accenture	425
Essay Questions	426
Application Questions	426
Bibliography	427

CHAPTER 18: Human Resource Automation, Audit & Accounting — 429

Automation	430
Payroll Automation	430
Performance Management Automation Systems	431
Recruitment Automation Systems	431
Employee Self-service Systems	431
Benefits & Pitfalls of Automation	432
Audit	432
Rationale of Audit	433
Approaches to Audit	435
Legal Approach to HR Audit	435
Benchmarking Approach	435
Strategic Approach to HR Audit	435
Reading Exhibit 1: Sample HR Audit	436
Employee Communications & Documents	436
Recruitment, Employment and Selection	436
New Hire Orientation	436
Compensation & Wage Administration	436
Benefits	436
Employee Training & Development	437
Performance & Behavior Feedback Processes	437
Termination	437
Human Resource Responsibilities	437
Accounting	437
Methods of Calculating HRA	438
Cost Approach	438
Economic Value Approach	439
HRA at Infosys	440
Education Index	441
Is HRA Useful?	441
Arguments against Human Resource Accounting	442
Future of Human Resource Accounting	442

Reading Exhibit 2: Thoughtful HRIT Strategy and Preparation: Indispensable
Precursor to HCM Solution Adoption 442
Future of Human Resource Accounting 442
HRIT Strategy: Points to Ponder 443
    In-house versus Outsource 445
    Aspects of Preparation 448
    Preparation of People 448
    Conclusion 449
    Permission 449
Essay Questions 450
Application Questions 450
Bibliography 451

CHAPTER 19: Social Media Applications in Managing Human Resource — 453

Introduction 454
Social Media Recruitment 454
Reference Checks 456
Networking & Communication 457
Essay Questions 458
Application Questions 459
Bibliography 460

CHAPTER 20: Talent Management — 461

Is Talent Management an 'Oxymoron' 462
Who is a Talent? 463
Who Owns & Drives Talent Management? 465
Talent Management – Priorities or Prescription 468
Talent Management in a Bust Economy 469
Talent Management: The New HRM Approach 473
    Talent Wheels 473
Essay Questions 475
Application Questions 475
Bibliography 476

CHAPTER 21: Employee Engagement — 477

Three Entities of Engagement 478
Is Employee Engagement More than Job Involvement? 478

Why Engagement?	478
Introducing Employee Engagement	478
Engagement Models	479
Levels of Engagement	479
(i) 'The Engaged'	479
(ii) Almost Engaged	480
(iii) Honeymooners and Hamsters	480
(iv) Crash & Burn	480
(v) The Disengaged	481
Building Blocks of Engagement	481
Trust	482
Treat your Employees Well	482
Deliver Promises	482
Envision	483
Career Growth	483
Design Jobs	483
Place of Work	483
Collaborate	484
Exhibit 1: Engagement through Idea Sharing and Team Participation @ Titan	484
Empower	484
Communicate	485
Work-life Balance & Engagement	485
Exhibit 2: People Philosophy at Taj Hotels	485
Exhibit 3: Multi-channel Communication @ TCS	485
Work-life Balance Myths	486
Impact of Work-life Imbalance	486
Towards Greater Work-life Balance	487
Measuring Employee Engagement	488
Commonly used Methods	488
Gallup Q. 12	488
USAID 26- item Measurement Tool	488
DDI's E3	489
Engagement Trends in India	489
Challenges Ahead	489
Essay Questions	490
Application Questions	490
Bibliography	491

Chapter 22: Strategic Management of Human Resource in Organizatons — 493

Business Byte	494
HRM Effectiveness and Business Success	495
Strategy & Strategic Management	496
Types of Strategies	498
Corporate Strategies	498
Competitive Strategies	499
Functional Strategies	499
Strategic Management Process	500
Strategic Human Resource Management	500
Approaches to Strategic Human Resource Management	501
HR Strategies	502
Essay Questions	503
Application Questions	503
Bibliography	504

Chapter 23: International Human Resource Management — 507

Introduction	508
Strategic View of International Human Resource Management	509
Human Resource Strategies & Roles in a Multinational Company	512
Internationalization Strategies	512
International HR Strategies	512
International Human Resource Management Roles	513
International HRM Activities	514
International Staffing	515
Cultural Challenge	515
Reading Exhibit 1: 'Nitaqat'	517
What is NITAQAT?	517
It's Political, Too	517
Effect on India	517
Reading Exhibit 2: 'Glocal Hiring'	518
Reading Exhibit 3: Map of National Cultures (Hofstede, Practical Applications of Hofstede's Cultural Dimensions, 2013)	519
International Labour Relations	519

International Compensation	519
Health and Safety of Expatriates	522
Essay Questions	522
Application Questions	523
Bibliography	523

PART II: BUSINESS CASES — 525

1.	Chink in the Giant!	527
2.	No Time to Holiday	530
3.	Why Indian Firms go Wrong when Hiring US Sales Teams?	533
4.	Selection Blues	536
5.	Faulty Appraisals	538
6.	Appraisals at Hexagon Foods	540
7.	The Skills Gap in Canada	542
8.	The Best Archer	550
9.	Bharti Airtel Trains for Customer Service	552
10.	Training for Safer Roads	553
11.	Compensation Woes of Engineering Faculty	556
12.	ESOPs in GMT Bank	558
13.	Sexual Harassment at Simon Logistics	560
14.	Strike at Spark Automatives & Precision Engineering	562
15.	Strike at Maruti Suzuki India	564
16.	Air India Strikes	570
17.	Women Participation in Workforce	572
18.	Automating to Match Scale	576
19.	Employee-voices on Social Media	578
20.	On-boarding at Taj Hotels	582
21.	YUM Increasing Footprint through Effective Talent Management	585

22. Indian Problem, Singaporean Solution – Will it Work? ... 587
23. S(kill) Sales: Gaps in Sales Training ... 589
24. Strike at MRF Tyre Plant ... 592
25. The New Generation Army ... 594

PART III: COMPREHENSIVE CASES — 597

1. HRP for 2010 Winter Olympic Games ... 599
2. A Metropolitan University ... 627
3. Job Characteristics of Officers & Agents: Results of a National Job Analysis ... 647
4. Debacle of Dream Films Productions Limited (DFPL) ... 675
5. Skill-gap & Talent Shortage in India ... 681

INDEX — 689

Part I

TEXT

Chapter 1

Overview of Human Resource Management

Outline

- Business Byte
- What is Human Resource Management?
- Organizational Design & Policies
- HR Systems & Processes
- Evolution of Human Resource Management
- Traditional versus Modern Human Resource Management
- Importance of Human Resource Management
- Job Satisfaction versus Employee Engagement
- Essay Questions
- Application Question
- Bibliography

Key Terms

- HR System
- Control System
- Evolution of HR
- Traditional HRM
- Modern HRM
- Job Satisfaction

Business Byte

Tata Group, one of India's premier business conglomerate stands-out from the rest of the business houses in the country in terms of its strong commitment towards people and their welfare. At a time when other companies are struggling with their contract workers and have been accused of being inhumane and discriminatory towards them, facing huge backlash as a result, Tata Steel does something unique. Tata Steel employs large number of contract workers and generally gets the supply of contract workers from recognized suppliers. The suppliers generally have a large 'pool' from which they pick-up the ones to be deployed at Tata Steel facility on a regular basis. Tata Steel maintains computerized records of all the contract labours who work even once in their facility. Hence, although, the ones that are deployed in the factory may vary, however whenever they report for work their records help in their placement and allocation of work. For instance, the contract workers who have fear of height or spinal issues may not be deployed on high-rise structures inside the facility. The company also takes care of the contract workers and has never had a problem with them. Such harmony has meant a win-win proposition for all.

Tata Steel maintains computerized records of all the contract labours who work even once in their facility.

What is Human Resource Management?

Various terms have defined a person employed in an organization and earning his livelihood. They have been called labour, workers, employees and finally human resource. They are still used interchangeably and many times to classify various kinds of people who work for an organization. Blue-collared of working population are often called as labour or workers while the white-collared ones are generally called employees. More terms have evolved over time like Talent, Human Capital etc.

HRM is the process of managing human talent to achieve an organization's obejectives.

While a functional definition or classification of the working population of a company has existed, the leadership belief and concept of their employees has led to them being called/considered human resource. The fact that they have been called a resource shows that the organization has recognized them as an asset and believes that they can grow and can be groomed; and most importantly they are valuable. Human Resource is not only the only animate asset of an organization but also one of the few assets that has the potential of appreciating over time.

Human resource management involves managing the employees in a way that they can be productively engaged to the organization and that elicits voluntary initiatives and organizational citizenship behaviour.

Organizational Design & Policies

Every organization is designed consciously by the founding leaders and the design is sustained by the subsequent leadership of the company. The organizational design comprises of three basic elements: organizational structure, organizational culture and control systems. The organizational structure refers to how people are organized in the company and how they report/communicate with each other. Hierarchical structures have been contrasted with flat structures, where the former is more top-down characterized by power centralization and bureaucratic reporting structures, while flat structures on the other hand are more open, democratic and characterized by open channels of communication and lack of rigid lines of reporting. Organizational culture is a sum total of belief, philosophy, rituals, artifacts, norms, symbols etc., in the organization. Again, open cultures have been contrasted with closed cultures. Open cultures are more accommodating and built on greater transparency and trust; while closed cultures believe in secrecy and skepticism. Control systems in an organization refer many times to the kind of reward systems that have been put in place. Command and control, hire & fire are contrasted with systems that are based on individual & mutual accountability and greater levels of self-discipline. The design pretty much determines how an organization turns out to be and how most people behave in the organization. For instance, rigid hierarchical structures, closed culture and command & control system will have a different impact on individual & group decision-making in the organization compared to flat structured, open cultured and accountable systems. In short, the organizational design shapes the policies that dictate the broad ideology of people management in any organization.

> The organizational structure refers to how people are organized in the company and how they report/communicate with each other.

> Organizational culture is a sum total of belief, philosophy, rituals, artifacts, norms, symbols etc., in the organization.

> The organizational design shapes the policies that dictate the broad ideology of people management in any organization.

HR Systems & Processes

The HR system and processes refer to the functional part of human resource management. Various systems, sub-systems and processes are engineered and executed to manage the various human resource functions in an organization.

> Hiring or recruitment is the process of acquisition of employees by an organization.

Hiring System: The hiring system consists of HRP, recruitment and selection sub-systems. HRP or human resource planning refer to forecasting demand and supply of human resource and designing strategies to deal with shortage and surplus of employees in an organization. The recruitment function refers to activating the process of acquisition of employees by an organization, attracting candidates and creating a large pool of potential candidates from which the right hires can be chosen. The selection function involves selecting the right hires from this pool by employing various selection tools.

Performance Management System (PMS): The performance management systems has been employed to enable an organized, structured, scientific and fair method of managing and measuring the performance of an employee. The core objective of PMS is development of the employee and consequently of the organization.

Training & Development System: The training and development system is designed to build capabilities of the employees through assessment of their competencies (knowledge, skills and attitudes) and mapping the same with those required for the job, analyzing competency gaps and developing development programs to plug those gaps.

> Compensation is a payment made in cash to the employee in return of the contribution that he/she makes in the organization.

Compensation & Benefits System: Compensation system in an organization takes care of the payroll and benefits administration in an organization. Designing pay packages, pricing jobs, fringe benefits, social security benefits, income tax aspects etc., fall under the ambit of compensation system. Equity principle governs the entire compensation system and strategies.

Workplace Health & Safety: Workplace health and safety deals with making work and workplace secure against any hazard at workplace. Safety awareness, safety standards and safety training form an integral part of the system. Workplace safety also covers the issue of workplace violence, focusing on creating awareness, reporting mechanisms of any such incident, action against the perpetrators and preventive mechanisms.

> Industrial relation is the relationship between the employer and employee in an organization.

Industrial Relations: Industrial relations deal with relations between employer and employee. Labour unions, collective bargaining, labour laws, industrial disputes, conflicts and negotiations, industrial harmony form an integral part of the discussions.

HR Automation: The marriage of technology with HR has given rise to the study and practice of HR automation. Essentially, it involves automating various HR processes to bring-in greater levels of efficiency and speed.

HR Accounting: Employees being considered an asset for a company, its valuation in monetary terms is studied under HR accounting. Its primary use for the company is estimating the value of its HR and evaluating the appreciation or depreciation in value over the years at an aggregate level.

> HR Accounting is used in a company estimating the value of its HR and evaluating the appreciation or depreciation in value over the years.

HR Audit: HR Audit is a system of measuring existing HR processes against benchmarks and improving them on a continuous basis. Quality remains at the core of audit systems.

HR Analytics: Human resources analytics is the application of advanced data mining and business analytics techniques to human resources (HR) data, with an objective of improving employee performance and therefore getting a better return on investment. HR analytics correlates business data and people data and establishes a cause-and-effect relationship between what HR does and business outcomes.

> HR analytics correlates business data and people data.

Talent Management: Talent management means adding a premium on few human resource in the organization. Their positions or they themselves may be considered critical for the organization. Managing them requires different configuration then other employees in the organization, considering that talent is in high-demand, scarce and costly. Talent Management deals with management of such resources in the firm.

> Talent management is an HR process designed to attract, develop, motivate and retain productive engaged employees.

Social Media Applications in HR: Social Media has revolutionized the world. For the first time 'many-to-many' communication became possible and in turn exponentially accelerated the speed and spread of communication. Human Resource function has not been untouched by the same and many of its functions have been leveraged by the new media.

Employee Engagement: Employee Engagement is cognitively and affectively engaging people within the organization so as to make them productive and elicit voluntary participation and innovative behaviour from them.

HR Strategy: HR strategy links HR with business. It defines and describes how anything and everything that HR does directly or indirectly impacts business. The idea is to develop the HR business partner role and ensure that HR has a positive impact on business and helps both the organization and individuals to achieve their goals.

> Employee Engagement is a workplace approach designed to ensure that employees are committed to the organisation's goals and values.

Evolution of Human Resource Management

The earliest form of recruitments dealt with hiring of soldiers in the armies. The industrial revolution in England in the 18th century set the ball rolling for the manner and scale at which people working for an enterprise needed to be managed. Rapid changes in the production technologies coupled with changes in legislations about the way workers were to be paid etc., made people management a discipline that needed to be studied and addressed by any firm. There was also a growing realization that happy and satisfied workers were more productive.

However it was not until the beginning of the 20th century that major changes happened in the way people were hired and employed by any firm. The social order, political systems had started to change and awareness levels as well as expectation were altering. Some major events like Triangle Waist company accident altered the dynamics altogether. The fire at Triangle Waist Company in 1911 is widely considered a pivotal moment in the US history. It led to the transformation of the labor code of New York State and to the adoption of fire safety measures that served as a model for the entire US. The fire that killed close to 150 workers, mostly women shook the US and the entire world. The New York Factory Investigative Commission was instrumental in writing thirty-six of the new labor related bills that the state legislature eventually adopted. The work done by the local governmental agencies and unions was also significant which adopted fire safety measures and monitored conditions in factories. Thus the labour unions were born and so was the concept and practice of Personnel Management. It was dealing with issues, introducing the new law requirements. It had the responsibility for the implementation of different social and work place safety programs. Productivity and safety of workers became a key concern. The Trade Unions became a force to reckon with and protection of the rights of the workers their main motive. Skill development of workers also received attention during this period because of the focus on productivity.

Towards the latter half of the 20th century the onset of economic reforms world-wide and the emergence of LPG (Liberalization, Privatization, Globalization) policies changed the landscape of people management drastically and the concept of talent was born. The employees started to be considered as resource and assets. The real practice of human resource management thus began. Transformation and not Transactional HR was the need of the hour and the personnel departments of companies were fast changing to HR departments. By the end of the 20th century and the onset of

The industrial revolution led to growth of labour unions, because some factory workers were made to work long hours and paid less wages. To deal with workers unrest industrial relations department emerged.

The industrial relations (i.e., relations between employee or employer) department also called personnel management department had to be capable of politics and diplomacy. Lateron the same personnel department used to be called HR department.

the 21st century technology made many otherwise seemingly impossible things possible. Job satisfaction principle had lost its sheen primarily and Employee Engagement was the new buzz word. It was no more enough to satisfy people to make them productive; rather it was significant to engage them productively & creatively to the organization.

Talent Management, Managing people across boundaries, HR Analytics, HRIS, Employability Skills & Capacity-building are important HR issues that companies grapple with, day-in and day-out. The role of leadership, especially that of the CEO in managing people and devolution of HR responsibilities to the line managers has become a necessity. HR is fast emerging as a business partner, than being a mere back-office mute spectator. New age start-ups are much more people-focused and agile, forcing bigger corporations to take note without risking becoming 'titanic' themselves. Human Resource Management has never been more exciting than before.

> HR is fast emerging as a business partner, than being a mere back-office mute spectator.

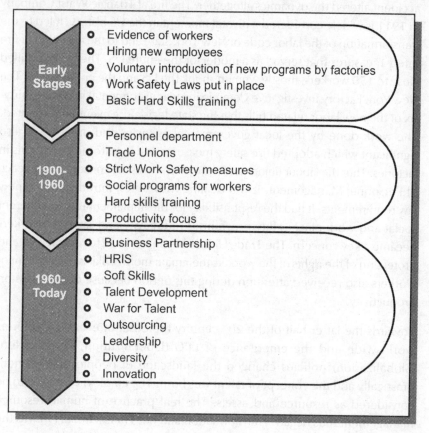

Figure 1.1: Evolution of HR

Traditional versus Modern Human Resource Management

Traditional HRM is hierarchical in nature and policies & rules are enacted in a centralized manner. Employees are expected to follow the same.

The traditional management of employees has been adhoc and mostly reactive in nature. It responds to an organizational problem related with man or manpower whenever and wherever it occurs and attempts to find at least a quick short-term solution to the same. It is primarily concerned with day to day management of workforce and addressing the concerns related to the same. Traditional HRM is hierarchical in nature and policies & rules are enacted in a centralized manner. Employees are expected to follow the same. Compliance is expected and appreciated. HR spends most of its time in managing process and problems and hardly any time in terms of strategy formulation or execution. HR is also thought to be exclusively the responsibility of the HR department and generally assigned a back-office status, concerned with processing payrolls, keeping a record of leaves, absenteeism and attendance. Perceptually employees view HR department as a tool in the hands of the management to execute their plans through them. It is typically carrot and stick management. Monitoring, interference-based supervision and keeping a tight leash on the employees is believed to be important. The employee relations are based on a pluralist approach and HRM is more transaction-based. Cost-minimization approach is the mantra of such organizations and mandate for their HR departments. Seniority-based promotions and increments are common. Training is seen and managed as a cost-center and hence limited in its application, mostly to rectify erroneous employees.

Perceptually employees view HR department as a tool in the hands of the management to execute their plans through them.

The modern HR management is about performance management, internal equity, succession planning, talent development, and providing competitive benefits.

Modern HR management first of all recognizes employees as vital and most significant assets of the company. The belief is centered around the fact that although it is possible to replicate almost all other assets and aspects of successful company by a rival concern, if managed well, it may be an uphill task for the latter to copy the kind of engaged workforce that it boasts of. Hence modern HR is proactive by its very nature and uses sophisticated tools and techniques to forecast the HR needs – both in terms of numbers and skills, hires them using the best recruitment methods, sources & platforms, invests in skill development, develops compensation strategies that are not narrowly focused on paying people for the jobs they do but for larger good of the individual & the organization, manages their performance and charters unique career paths for its talent, providing them both opportunity to ideate and a conducive environment to make those ideas a business proposition. HR policies are evolved using employee participation and are based on superordinate goals. Difference of opinion is not seen as a non-compliance issue; rather it is seen as an opportunity to explore something new for the organization. HRM is no more the exclusive responsibility of the HR department or managers; line managers and the senior leadership assume HR responsibilities as well. People management is everyone's job in the organization. HR departments become the chief architect of the HR policies, processes and plans, the CEO/top leadership become the drive, the line managers become active contributors & in-charge of execution of HR strategies and employees become both the recipients well as participants in the process. Business success, customer delight and good governance become the core parameters of success of HR strategies that is mutually shared. Cost-optimization and not minimization is the focus and the cost-benefit analysis of all HR plans is done to ensure maximum ROI (return on investment). Modern HR management aspires to be more transformational, than transactional in its disposition and outcome.

> HRM is no more the exclusive responsibility of the HR department or managers; line managers and the senior leadership assume HR responsibilities as well. People management is everyone's job in the organization.

Importance of Human Resource Management

In 2014 HDFC Bank – a private sector bank in India, announced a change in HR policy that allowed the bank to rehire its old employees. The bank planned to rehire about 3000 former employees who had good performance track record and were presently doing well in their current organization. While the practice of creating alumni relations, alumni chapters and alumni reunions have been a common practice among universities, the corporate sector has rarely focused on alumni network of its ex-employees. A concept that was pioneered by McKinsey, employee-alumni relations have not been too popular in India. Not surprising - considering India has not particularly done well in employee engagement.

> The importance of HR department is that it makes optimum, utilization of available human resources to meet organizational goals.

Global consultants like PwC, KPMG have employee-alumni network portals to enable its ex-employees to reconnect should they want to at any point of time. They actively consider re-hiring ex-employees or considering referrals from their ex-employees. Post-recession, some Indian companies started showing similar intent and Infosys, Wipro considered re-hiring employees laid-off during recession.

> Re-hiring ex-employees can be beneficial because they have been tried and tested and once back they bring fresh ideas.

The rationale of re-hiring ex-employees comes from the fact that they are not only accustomed to the corporate culture but they have been tried and tested hands, with proven record of previous performance. Besides since they left, they have had other experiences. Hence once back they bring fresh ideas and perspectives on the table that could help the company get a competitive edge.

HDFC Bank is the latest to join this growing tribe. The bank, which had 68,165 employees at the end of March, aims to re-hire as many as 3,000 former employees over the next 12-18 months. As the bank plans to grow with stability old hands may be good back home.

Very contrastingly though ICICI Bank– another prominent private sector bank in India had announced a change in policy that barred the bank from re-hiring ex-employees. Earlier the bank had a fixed period moratorium on hiring employees who have left the company and only after the moratorium period was over could they be reconsidered for employment in the bank. However in 2013 they put a blanket shutdown on any possibility of re-hiring of ex-employees not only in the bank but in all ICICI group companies. ICICI Group being one of the industry leaders has been a fertile hunting ground for recruiters in the financial services industry in the recent past. Top talents like Shikha Sharma (now CEO of Axis Bank), Kalpana Morparia (now with JP Morgan) and V Vaidyanathan (now with Capital First) have been poached from ICICI Bank. The new HR policy is possibly designed to act as a potential deterrent for employees who might want to jump ships to the newer players.

> The new HR policy is possibly designed to act as a potential deterrent for employees who might want to jump ships to the newer players.

However HR experts say this is a contrarian strategy at a time when several companies are actively engaging with alumni, some even looking at them as unannointed brand ambassadors and potential customers. Most companies are keeping intact the 'revolving door' policy when it comes to recruiting talent.

> Most companies are keeping intact the 'revolving door' policy when it comes to recruiting talent.

HDFC Bank and ICICI Bank both seem to have adopted complete bipolar strategies when it came to considering ex-employees for re-hiring. Which one do you agree with? It's worth talking a pause for a minute and thinking about the issue. You can even consider a discussion with your group and debate on agreements and disagreements.

Interestingly though the banks differ in their policy regarding re-hiring ex-employees, the concern seems to be common. In light of serious talent crunch in the financial sector, both banks seem to be taking measures to keep talent in the fold. While one is flattening barriers to allow for their talent to do the 'home run', the other seems to be building barriers to keep its talent pool intact.

With talent being the common concern of both these leading players in the banking sector in India, the importance of human resource management could not be highlighted or outlined more appropriately.

Poor State of Engagement

Peter Drucker had once said "So much of what we call management consists in making it difficult for people to work." Often organizations manage their most precious asset, their people, in the most clumsy and dysfunctional way. No wonder only 13% of employees worldwide are engaged at work, according to Gallup's new 142-country study on the State of the Global Workplace.

Often organizations manage their most precious asset, their people, in the most clumsy and dysfunctional way.

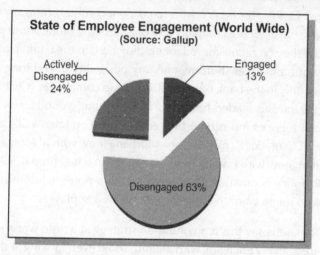

Figure 1.2: Employee Engagement (World Wide)

The bulk of employees worldwide are 'not engaged' or even worse the rest are 'actively disengaged'. While the 'not engaged' employees lack motivation and are less likely to invest discretionary efforts towards achieving organizational goals or outcomes, the 'actively disengaged' ones are not only unhappy and unproductive but also likely to spread negativity among other co-workers. This could be potentially damaging for the company.

The 'not engaged' employees lack motivation and are not only unhappy and unproductive but also likely to spread negativity among other co-workers.

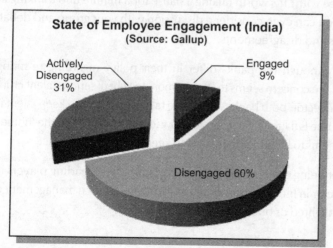

Figure 1.3: Employee Engagement in India

The 'disengaged' category, where the maximum population resides currently, represents both opportunity and threat. The opportunity is to convert them to 'engaged' set and since they have not drifted too far away it may not be too difficult to bring them back in the fold. However the threat comes from the 'actively disengaged' ones - remember they may spread negativity. They are potential disruptive and their efforts may result in more getting pulled from 'disengaged' to 'actively disengaged'. The question remains who succeeds - the companies or the actively disengaged segment?

With the new generation entering the workforce in large numbers and with clear indications of their growing conflicts with the older generation, these figures could become even worse. Most companies around the world have struggled to manage their human resource in a manner so as to elicit motivation and discretionary efforts from employees towards achieving organizational goals or outcomes.

Disengagement remains a common problem and Engagement remains a common challenge around the world. People spend their maximum time at their workplaces. It is very natural for them to look for cognitive and emotional reasons to stay glued to places where they spend most of their time. Only companies need to take the wake-up call and realize that engagement is a business solution and an engaged workforce represents a business opportunity in helping them create greater value in their firms for their customers and meeting the companies and shareholders objectives.

Job Satisfaction versus Employee Engagement

As discussed before, the concept and practice of job satisfaction has gradually lost its sheen and engagement principles have gained ground. Such changes have been centered around the growing importance and relevance of human resource management. Job satisfaction and engagement take completely opposite routes to happiness of employees. Job satisfaction school of thought believes that employee must be made happy. And the assumption has been that if an organization can do so then these happy employees would be more productive. So, organizations simplify work, reduce work hours, dole out benefits etc., to make their employees happy, in anticipation that this will make them work harder. However this theory has largely not worked, for if it had then all our PSU establishments would have been in Fortune 500. On the other hand, the Engagement school of thought believes that the organization should do everything possible to maximize chances and opportunities for an employee to contribute. So if an organization provides benefits then it does not do so to make employees happy rather it does so to take away the worries from the mind of the employees and hence leave a large part of his/her mindshare for thinking about work. At workplace the entire leadership, all resources, facilities and systems work towards making sure that the employee finds more avenues and interest to contribute. When an employee finds such a space, he/she can effectively contribute; it also maximizes his/her achievements and consequently the recognition & the rewards. Higher pay-offs and a sense of achievement & fulfillment lead to happiness.

In short, while job satisfaction approach treats happiness as an input, engagement treats happiness as an output! Evidence from practice and research shows that the latter approach has worked much more than the former.

The next two chapters focus on how employees can become most effective brand ambassadors for any company and the new age HRM – contextually responsive and consequently the new age HRM roles.

Essay Questions

1. What is human resource management? How does organization design and policies shape the philosophy of managing human resource?
2. What are various HR systems and processes? Write brief note on each of them.
3. Write a short note on the evolution of human resource management.
4. Contrast traditional and modern human resource management.
5. Outline the importance of human resource management.
6. Why is poor engagement of employees a concern for organizations? Contrast the concepts of job satisfaction and employee engagement. Which is a more relevant concept in terms of modern practice?

Application Question

1. Using internet find a reputed Indian company whose organisation design and policies have resulted in job satisfaction. Compare the same with those of another such company.

Bibliography

Brief History of Human Resources and HR Management, Creative HRM.com

Chakraborty, S. (2014, December 9). *HDFC Bank to welcome back its former employees.* Retrieved from Business Standard: http://www.business-standard.com/article/finance/welcome-back-hdfc-bank-tells-its-former-employees-114120800135_1.html

Chakraborty, Somasroy; Subramanian, Sundaresha. (2013, March 29). *ICICI Bank Shuts Door on Ex-employees.* Retrieved from Business Standard: http://www.business-standard.com/article/finance/icici-bank-shuts-door-on-ex-employees-113032900127_1.html

Cornell. (2011). *Legacy of the Triangle Fire.* Retrieved from Cornell Edu: http://www.ilr.cornell.edu/trianglefire/legacy/index.html

Crabtree, S. (2012). *Worldwide, 13% of Employees are Engaged at Work.* Retrieved from Gallup: http://www.gallup.com/poll/165269/worldwide-employees-engaged-work.aspx

Economist. (2013, September 28). *Winning the Generation Game.* Retrieved from The Economist: http://www.economist.com/news/business/21586831-businesses-are-worrying-about-how-manage-different-age-groups-widely-different

PBS. (n.d.). *American Experience.* Retrieved from Triangle Fire: http://www.pbs.org/wgbh/americanexperience/features/introduction/triangle-intro/

Sen, V. (2010, December 13). *Infosys, Wipro, TCS want to hire fired ex-employees.* Retrieved from Tech Eye: http://news.techeye.net/business/infosys-wipro-tcs-want-to-hire-fired-ex-employees

Sindhu Hariharan. (2014, December 13). *Out of sight, but still part of the mind.* Retrieved from The Times of India: http://timesofindia.indiatimes.com/business/india-business/Out-of-sight-but-still-part-of-the-mind/articleshow/45500839.cms

Vorhauser-Smith, S. (2012, February 7). *How to Stop Employee Turnover in India.* Retrieved from Forbes: http://www.forbes.com/sites/sylviavorhausersmith/2012/07/02/how-to-stop-employee-turnover-in-india/

Chapter 2

The New Brand Ambassadors

Outline

Introduction

How to Develop Brand Ambassadors?

Success Stories

The Maruti Salesman

Spreading Magic @Whirlpool

Singing what Samsung

Essay Questions

Application Questions

Bibliography

Key Terms

Brand Ambassador

Corporate Brand

Effective Communication

Effective Processes

Employee Pride

The 10 E Model

Introduction

Consumer brands rely on brand ambassadors. **Cadbury's** had Amitabh, **Toyota** had Aamir Khan, **BSNL** had Preity Zinta, **Taj Mahal** tea has Saif Ali Khan, **Sunfeast** had Shah Rukh Khan, **Aviva** like so many others had Sachin Tendulkar as a brand Ambassador. What actually is a brand then? Is it just a logotype, colour, trademark or a symbol? Perhaps, not! Brand is an experience to relate with. It's a whole set of abstract nuances with which a customer associates himself or herself. The common thread in all this is that the communication is external, driven by mass media communication. However the fact may be that these brand ambassadors may have very little to do with the company or its values. They are used because marketers believe there is a strong fit between the brand ambassador's personality and what consumer aspires for. Whilst one recognizes the need for brand ambassadors for some brands, it is perhaps important to recognize what every corporate brand needs. Every corporate brand needs champions. And these champions are within the company. They are its employees. They impact, mould and convey the brand values to various target consumers.

Consider for instance the experiences of a young corporate manager named Sebastian –

Sebastian was thinking about a place for dinner. Anniversary was always special and special days called for some special treats. He wanted to take his wife to some nice and new place. Just then an advertisement in the local newspaper caught his attention. The ad showed some celebrity endorsing a brand new restaurant that had come-up in the town. That's the place I was wanting', he thought. In the evening all dressed-up, he alongwith his wife and 6 year old daughter went to that restaurant. Upon reaching there he found that parking was a huge problem. Somehow with lot of difficult maneuverings he could successfully park the car. As he and his family were entering the restaurant another rude shock was awaiting them. The guard at the gate did not notice Sebastian's small daughter following him and left the swinging door soon after Sebastian entered. Had it not been the agility of Sebastian, his young daughter would have been seriously injured. After giving the guard a piece of mind the 'family' moved-on. But then hardly anything went right for them. From too oily and tasteless food, to 'deaf' waiters, unapologetic manager and round-about everything went tipsy-turvy. The only thing which seemed to work in their restaurant was the billing-machine. So after paying a 'good' sum for a 'poor' evening Sebastian and his family left the place, swearing never to visit the place again, not even in

> Brand ambassadors may have very little to do with the company or its values, but they are used because marketers believe there is a strong fit between the brand ambassador's personality and what consumer aspires for.

the wildest of dreams. On reflecting Sebastian found that advertisement, that celebrity's promise so very unfulfilled and so very away from the reality. 'Is this what you call brand ambassadors' – he thought...

In any organization (especially service organizations) the biggest brand ambassadors are the employees. Every employee in a company should understand, believe and know that servicing customers (directly or indirectly) through constant value-additions and building a positive perception is the most important factor for gaining or retaining an old customer and not anything else.

The customer has already picked-up the company when they compared prices, quality or other aspects. Even if they are still evaluating the above factor, an average employee can make a world of difference to his/her final decision. The employee can help create a positive or a negative perception about the product or service. What's more important to understand is that irrespective of what decision the customer takes at that moment, the perception will last much longer, affecting even the future decisions. And then the powerful word-of-mouth' will play its own role.

'Recently during our visit to Ooty - Southern hill station in India, we experienced something similar. We had booked a hotel through an agent. After a long and tiring travel, we checked-in the hotel, at around 9:45 p.m. While checking-in we asked at the reception whether the dinner was available (since it was raining outside and we were feeling terribly hungry so it was an obvious question). The front-desk executive at the reception assured us with a smile that the food was available. Around twenty minutes later after checking-in the hotel and after settling down a bit, at around 10:05 p.m. I called the room service and ordered for the dinner. To my utter surprise, I was rudely from the other end that after 10 p.m. no orders were being taken. I was aghast...was this the way to treat customers? If they were having this rule they should have told us at the reception itself. We would have adjusted accordingly. It was only after jostling a bit with the hotel manager that our order was taken and the food was served.

If we ever go back to Ooty, given a choice, I will never like to stay in the same hotel, irrespective of it having nice interiors and location.

'Bringing a well-designed customer experience to life requires aligning every point of customer contact with the brand promise, from the storefronts to the call-centers, to the website, from the first service to the ongoing service interaction. The most important factor in creating a successful customer experience is a company's workforce.'

> Every employee in a company should understand, believe and know that servicing customers (directly or indirectly) through constant value-additions and building a positive perception is the most important factor for gaining or retaining customers.

It is the human factor which many-a-time makes greatest impact on how a customer feels about a company.

Lufthansa is known for personally thanking the high-flier customers even when they are traveling in the economy-class. It hardly costs the airline anything but brings in a nice image and of course customer back again.

Contrastingly, another international Airways not so long ago acquired the dubious reputation of being the worst baggage handlers in the industry. In 2007, they lost the baggage of the Indian Cricket team which was returning after winning the Future Cup in South Africa. That was a high-profile case but frequent travellers say the problem is common with the airline.

As the airlines grapple with the problem, the passengers run from pillar to post for no fault of their own, except perhaps choosing to fly with the airlines.

How to Develop Brand Ambassadors?

Most of us tend to believe that brand is the CEO's baby or perhaps of the brand managers'! The reality however is that brand belongs to each and every employee. It has not only to be communicated but also to be internalized.

Let us look at the '10 E' model to understand how to develop brand ambassadors out of our employees:

The '10E' Model

Educate

The first step towards educating the employees on brand consciousness is to find out whether an employee understands the brand philosophy, the way the company perceives it or not and then plugging-in the gaps. Then starts the process of explaining the brand concept and how people are expected to represent the same.

1. Educate: It's important to understand how the various interactions with the brand happen both internally as well as externally. In other words the first step to educate the employees on brand consciousness is to find out whether an employee understands the brand philosophy the way the company perceives it or not. If any gaps are seen at this stage, they are plugged-in. Then starts the process of explaining the brand-concept and how people are expected to represent the same. It may be through dress-code, informal talks, social gatherings, official parties, stationeries etc. But the reinforcement of the brand consciousness and an ability on part of the employees to align with brand values are critical to developing brand ambassadors.

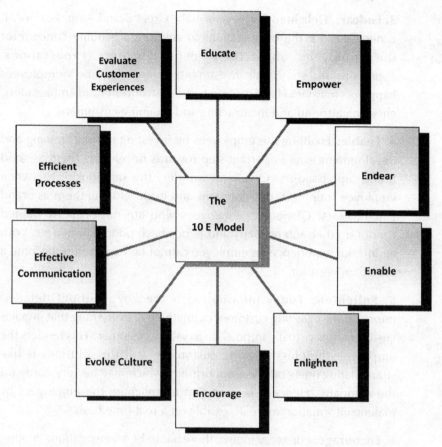

Figure 2.1:
The 10 E Model (How to Develop Brand Ambassadors?)

2. Empower: There is this famous story of a 'Virgin Atlantic' flight attendant. While organizing a wedding, she got a feel of the hassles associated with it. She felt a one-stop shop would just be the perfect idea of doing away with these hassles. She went to the 'Virgin Atlantic' boss Branson and rest is history. 'Virgin Brides', a chain of stores that would cater everything a bride needs, was born.

How many times would the same thing happen in our organizations? How many times would we be encouraged to share our idea with the CEO of the company and how many times would he/she listen and respond if the idea is great?

It's important to give employees reasonable autonomy and a feeling of virtual ownership of their jobs. This not only makes them more enthusiastic about their job but also about the brand.

Empower

Giving employees reasonable autonomy and a virtual ownership of their jobs.

Endear

Cultivating genuine concern for employees and investing in their happiness.

Enable

Poorly trained employees have poor experiences themselves, that they pass-on to the customer.

Enlighten

Providing information to employees on real-time basis to help to help them serve customers better.

Encourage

Aligning goals of individuals to organizational goals and motivating them to do better.

Evolve Culture

Evolving value-based culture, sharing success stories goes a long way in developing real brand ambassadors.

3. Endear: 'Delighted Employees make Great Brand Ambassadors'. It is necessary for the organizations to cultivate a genuine concern for the employees; about their needs, concerns, expectations, apprehensions etc. Small investments in ensuring one's employees happiness may yield large gains in terms of stronger brand ambassadors, checking attrition and in attracting and retaining customers.

4. Enable: Enabling the employees by investing in their training and development is an important step towards developing them as good brand ambassadors. One may wonder, the relationship between employee training & development and in developing them as brand ambassadors! Obviously, employees who are not properly trained cannot do their job properly and hence have poor experiences. With an inferior experience an employee cannot be expected to become a brand ambassador.

5. Enlighten: Today information is the key. Without detailed information regarding customer or anything & everything that impacts customer, it is virtually impossible to satisfy customer. This renders the employees helpless. Making customers wait for solutions is like strangulating one's business opportunity which may be very costly for the company. Hence it is important to enlighten the employees by making information more accessible on a real-time basis.

6. Encourage: For every motive there has to be an inspiration; in other words there must be enough motivation. New employees may look for salary or for nice treatment from their seniors, senior employees may look for prestige & status; women may look for fairness; needs may be different but goals of every individual have to be aligned with the organizational goals. Keeping employees motivated presents an opportunity in itself.

7. Evolve Culture: Couple of years back a marketing executive, of a private insurance company, in his over-zealous bid to out-do his competitor came-up with a shocking nomenclature to his campaign named after one of the most wanted outlaw of the world. The marketing executive was arrested & the company faced a lot of flak. Evolving a value-based success culture is key to developing real brand ambassadors of any organization. Success stories must be shared and not simply pinned – on the display boards for general consumption. Employees have to live & breathe the brand.

8. Effective Communication: Effective communication applies equally to between company & employees, to between employees & customers. Effective communication has at least four components.

   a. Sender must be able to communicate what he/she intends.
   b. Receiver must understand the message.
   c. There must be no misunderstanding.
   d. The recipient must engage in intended action by the sender.

Any misunderstanding or communication-gap between company & employees & between employees & customers could be like air bubble in the veins. It ultimately leads to relationship – hemorrhage. The communication between employees and customers can only be streamlined when communication between company & employees is effective. Few companies have gone a step further in corporate communication. Employees now form a part of the corporate presentations mostly used for hiring fresh/new recruits.

Effective Communication

Misunderstandings between company & employees, and subsequently between employees & customers could lead to relationship hemorrhage.

Example: I-GATE Global Solutions has moved over the earlier drab corporate presentations featuring mostly company history, industry environment & job roles. Brand ambassadors are the latest addition to the presentations, which help them to focus in 'marked differentiators'.

Similarly at Aricent (previously Flextronics Software system) employees are not only a part of the corporate film shown during presentation, but they also travel with the hiring team to campus. The idea is absolutely clear – no one better then the true brand ambassadors (employees) help to lend credibility & differentiation to the company.

9. Effective Processes: Dependence on age-old systems, reluctance to switch to more efficient ones, inefficient & unresponsive back-office, computers or other equipments which run slower than snail, bureaucratic step-up approach etc could leave an average employee hassled & harassed. On the other hand efficient & responsive systems & processes could induce employee morale & in-turn can drive his will to contribute more.

Effective Processes

Efficient & responsive systems and processes would induce employee morale, driving him/her to contribute more.

10. Evaluate Customer Experiences: It takes years to win-over a customer, it takes a moment to drive them away. Just as a company produces goods & services, it also 'manufactures' the kind of experiences its customers might encounter. Hence as it is important to evaluate the quality of products & services, it is also important to evaluate what kind of experiences the customer is having while buying that product or while using those services. Positive as well as negative

Evaluate Customer Experiences

Evaluating Customer Experiences & communicating them early to employees helps arrest any decline in service or offerings.

experiences must be communicated to the employees. Early detection of negative customer experiences helps employees to rectify the error & return the customer.

Success Stories

The Maruti Salesman

Amidst the din and clutter of the busy shop floor in the Maruti car factory, Gurgaon, Mukesh Kumar supervises men who put together the 'people's car'. Wearing overalls and a yellow helmet, he has been diligently doing this for the past 13 years.

But these days, he's impatient for his eight hour shift to end. The reason: After a hard day's work, Kumar dons another cap – that of a salesman. For the past two months, he has also been selling cars he helps make. It's a whole new experience and he's loving it. So far, he has sold 138 cars – 800s, Altos, WagonRs and Omnis – to friends, relatives, villagers, et al. 'My aim is to sell 150 cars by August end' – says Kumar. For the record, he's just a matriculate with an ITI diploma and has no background in sales.

(**Source:** *Confessions of the new salesman, Sujata Dutta Sachdev, The Times of India, August 26, 2007, pg.8)*

Kumar is not alone. Hundreds of Maruti employees are using their free time to sell cars to boost bottom lines. The company believes every employee is a brand manager and a sales man, came out with this idea and launched "Lalkar". In the year 2000-01 when the company faced loss for the first time, Jagdish Khattar came out with his 'Lalkar'. Everyone was encouraged to sell at least one car per month. This resulted in healthy competition cutting across levels & designations. The company claims to have sold 5000 cars in a short time. The net result has been very encouraging, while most car makers have reported decline in sales, Maruti has seen its domestic sales went up by 18.3% compared to the same time last year. This besides the enthusiasm & motivation it has caused to employees has been priceless.

Spreading Magic @Whirlpool

Like Maruti, Whirlpool also recognizes employees as its best ambassadors. The enthusiasm in the company says it all. Before the management could come up with an idea of encouraging employee to sell the company's products, employees on their own inundated the management for such an opportunity. The result was a campaign called 'Spread the Magic'. Employees on their own ensure that 'Whirlpool' is a talking point in most of the parties. Under this campaign till now thousands of company's products have been sold. In April 2005, Whirlpool India launched its unique Brand Ambassador Program. The program was launched in two phases:

Phase 1: Teasers were mailed across the organization. This was done to evoke curiosity and create an awareness among employees.

Phase 2: An interactive teleconference followed to sell the proposition to the employees.

Singing what Samsung

Samsung also believes that employees are the best brand ambassadors. But unlike Whirlpool & Maruti it does not think that there needs to any incentive to motivate employees don the role of a salesman. The company believes that if the employees are passionate about Samsung then they will rope-in new customers on their own. And that's what most members of Samsung are doing. Even the new recruits are checked on their incidence of using Samsung products, just to see how much conviction they have in the company and its products.

The program that was launched to leverage employee pride and passion in the brand and the company, increase customer base and build customer loyalty, became a runaway success.

Essay Questions

1. Discuss in detail the '10-E' model of developing employees as brand ambassadors.

2. Do you think customer satisfaction and delight is linked to how much employees of a company take over the brand ambassador role? Exemplify.

Application Questions

1. Browse the net and read through any 'best employer survey'. Find out how some companies are developing their employees as brand ambassadors?

2. Interview three people working in the same organization, one belonging to the Top management, the other to Middle management, and third belonging to the Entry level. Ask them how they feel about their organization and to what degree they feel they are brand ambassadors for their company. Compare the findings.

Bibliography

Alkadry, Mohamad G., and Leslie E. Tower. 2006. Unequal Pay: The Role of Gender. and Family-Friendly Benefits Practices in Local Governments: Results from a National Survey. *Public Personnel* and Retention of Entry-Level, Hourly Employees? Brief no. 2, Families and Work Institute.

Armstrong, M. 2000. *Performance Management: Key Strategies and Practical Guidelines*. 2nd Edition. London: Kogan Page Ltd.

Bascal, R. 2000. *Performance Management*. New York: McGraw-Hill.

Beagrie, S. 2003. 'How to Influence Employee Behaviour through Internal Marketing', *Personnel Today*, August: 35.

Bendapudi, N. & Bendapudi, V. 2005. 'Creating the Living Brand', *Harvard Business Review*. 82(5):124-128.

Bond, James T., and Ellen Galinsky. 2006. How Can Employers Increase the Productivity?

Bryman, A. 1989. *Research methods and Organization Studies*. London: Routledge.

Casper, Wendy, and Christopher M. Harris. 2008. Work–life Benefits and Organization.

Czaplewski, A.J., Ferguson, J.M. & Milliman, J.F. 2001. 'Southwest Airlines: How Internal Marketing Pilots Success', *Marketing Management*, 10(3): 14-18.

Das, S. 2003. 'Vacant or Engaged?' *Employee Benefits*, March: 24-28.

Drummond, G. & Ensor, J. 1999. *Strategic Marketing: Planning and Control*. Oxford: Butterworth-Heinemann,.

Fram, E.H. & McCarthy, M.S. 2003. 'From employee to brand champion', *Marketing Management*, 12(1): 24-30.

Greatplacetowork. 2004. [online] URL: http://www.greatplacetowork.com. Accessed 6 March 2004.

Ind, N. 2004. *Living the Brand*. 2nd Edition. Great Britain: Kogan Page.

Jacobs Rick, 'Turn Employees into Brand Ambassadors', ABA Bank Marketing, April 2003: 23-26

James, D. 2000. 'Don't Forget Staff in Marketing Plan', *Marketing News*, 34(6):10-12.

Keller, K.L. 2003. *Strategic Brand Management – Building, Measuring, and Managing Brand Equity*. 2nd Edition.

Naff, Katherine C. 2001. *To Look Like America: Dismantling Barriers for Women and Minorities in Government*. Boulder, CO: Westview Press.

Newman, Meredith, and Kay Mathews. 1999. Federal Family-Friendly Workplace Policies: Barriers to Effective Implementation. *Review of Public Personnel Administration* 19(3): 34–48.

Newman, Meredith. 1994. Gender and Lowi's Thesis: Implications for Career Advancement.

Pfau, Bruce N., and Ira T. Kay. 2002. *The Human Capital Edge: 21 People Management Practices Your Company Must Implement (or Avoid) to Maximize Shareholder Value*. New York: McGraw-Hill.

Roberts, Gary E. 2000. An Inventory of Family-Friendly Benefit Practices in Small New Jersey Local Governments. *Review of Public Personnel Administration* 20(2): 50–62.

Roberts, Gary E., Jerry A. Gianakis, Cloff ord McCue, and XiaoHu Wang. 2004. Traditional

Sutherland, M. & Jordaan, W. 2004. 'Factors affecting the retention of knowledge workers', *SA Journal of Human Resources Management*, 2(2): 55-64.

Upper Saddle River, New Jersey: Prentice Hall. Kotler, P. 2003. *Marketing management*. 11th Edition.

Welbourne, T. 2003. 'Employee engagement, doing it vs. Measuring it', *Journal of People Dynamics*, November & December: 30-31.

Yin, R.K. 1984. *Case Study Research – Design and methods*. Applied Social Research Methods Series Vol. 5. California: Sage Publications.

Chapter 3

The New Age HRM

Outline

Introduction
Political Factors
Economic Factors
Social Factors
Cultural Factors
Legal/Regulatory Factors
Technological Factors
New Age HRM Roles
Essay Questions
Application Questions
Bibliography

Key Terms

- Business Imperative
- Change Management
- Economic Factors
- Engagement Architect
- HR Imperatives
- Managing Diversity
- Political Factors
- Social Behaviour
- Social Networking
- Social Relations
- Talent Catalyst
- Technological Factors

Introduction

The nature and scope of human resource management has undergone a serious transformation in the past couple of decades. What used to be once a purely 'hire and fire' function mostly executed by administrative people has changed into treating employees as assets or resources and managing them in a way so as to create competitive advantage for the firm and win-win proposition for both. The purely back-office personnel function has changed into a strategic board room game. HRM from being a game-bench has changed into the new game-changer.

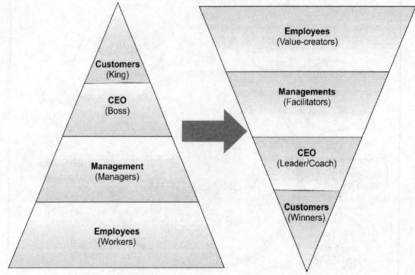

Figure 3.1: Customer to Employees: New Age, New Roles

The conventional wisdom has been turned upside down (figure 3.1). Employees have changed from workers to value-creators. As a result the role of manager and the CEO have also undergone a transformation. In the earlier concept of customer being the king, although the customer had been given the ultimate tag, however that did not ensure that the 'king' would end-up on the winning side always. The new wisdom however ensured that the customer (minus the decorative tag) always end-up as the winner in the process, something every business-firm would badly want today in the era of competition to seal better customer loyalty and retention. Through this chapter we shall try to explore why this change has happened in the very fabric of managing people, what drove that change and what are the new roles that HR has to don in the changed context.

Human Resources cannot operate in a silo and if it does it hardly has any relevance except being a blocker in the entire process of change. HR transformation is driven by the business imperatives that any firm faces, which in turn are driven by the macro-environmental variables (refer to figure 3.2).

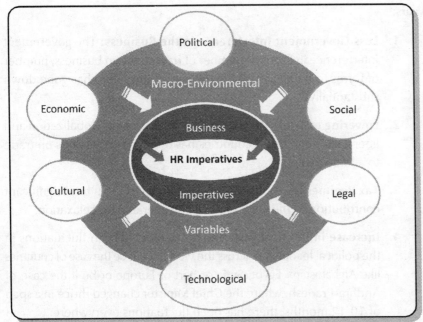

Figure 3.2: New Age HRM Model (Relationship between HR Imperatives, Business Imperatives & Macro-environment)

The macro-environmental variables like Political factor, Economic factor, Social Factor, Cultural Factor, Legal factor and Technological factor influence the business imperatives of any firm. This shapes the business strategy of the firm which consequently shapes the HR imperatives or the HR strategy. To understand the new age HRM it is important to understand the dynamics of the New Age HRM Model.

Political Factors

Political factors determine how and to what degree a government intervenes in the economy. Political factors include areas such as -

- Tax policy
- Labour law
- Environmental law

- Regional blocks
- Trade restrictions & Tariffs
- Political stability

The following changes have been observed in the political context over the years:

1. **Less Government Interference in the Business:** The government interference in terms of number of days to set up business, number of forms to be filled and the regulations therefore has gone down substantially.

2. **Lowering of Trade Restrictions:** Introduction of globalization and liberalization in many countries has removed restrictions on trade to a large extent.

3. **Tax Regimes Becoming more Liberal:** Sectors that have significant contribution to the GDP enjoy a considerable tax relaxation.

4. **Increase in Political Instability:** There have been fluctuations in the political leadership across the world. Say it be the case of countries like Afghanistam, Egypt, Syria or part of Europe or be it the case of Andhra-Pradesh, where the Chief Minister changed thrice in a span of 10-12 months, there has been fluctuations everywhere.

5. **Power-shift, Emergence of Regional Blocks:** If we take a close look at the global scenario it's no more the case where a single economy drives all others. Many regional blocks have started emerging with great potential to influence each other.

6. **Emerging Markets (India, China) Altering Political Equations:** The political factor along with some other factors has its effect on the demography of the country and thus different countries specialize in different products or services.

Example: If we consider the Asian countries, we find that whereas India has specialized in services, China has specialized in manufacturing.

7. **People-power (Democratization):** Politics has become more people driven after the introduction of democratic way of leading in many countries.

8. **Rise of Environmental Driven Policies:** Considering the limited availability of resources and increased amount of pollution, political

parties have come up with policies to have a check on the same. The concepts like carbon credits have come came into the picture.

Business Imperatives Driven by Changed Political Climate

Based on the above changes in the political context the following imperatives have become a part of the business.

1. A business should understand the political undercurrents and not just read policy changes.

The example of Tata Nano - Singur case excellently describes the impact of the undercurrents on business.

2. It is necessary for a business to ensure that the political neutrality and policy (concrete steps) are aligned, so that the business runs smoothly.

3. Businesses are shifting towards free trade and there's an uprising of disguised competition.

Example: China & ASEAN (Association of Southeast Asian Nations) countries have free trade between them. The removal of the trade barriers lowers the costs of trade transactions, and increases ASEAN-China trade. It also enhances economic efficiency, boosting real income in both ASEAN and China as resources flow to sectors where they can be more efficiently and productively utilised.

4. Have a 'stakeholder's approach' rather than only 'shareholder's approach'.

Having a stakeholder's approach would ensure everyone's engagement in the business and help the organization identify various dimensions of the business and thus the path towards achieving its goals.

5. Retaining the flexibility of a small organization (mobility and entrepreneurial mindset).

6. Understanding popular political moods and mood swings.

It is important for a company to be proactive in analysing the political situations surrounding the business environment. Thus several organizations have a Business Intelligence department that helps them keep a track on such situations.

7. A business should focus on both fundamental & incremental innovation to retain flexibility.

8. Business and stakeholders (key) loyalty overrides all other loyalties.

The uprising of the people power overrides all other loyalties of a business. A business is now governed more by the people rather than the political bodies having an upper hand.

9. Business sectors enjoying liberal governmental regulation are growing at a fast pace.

> **Example:** Textile Industry (the textile manufacturer's strike on March 7, 2011), government's tight regulation on alcoholic beverages.

10. Businesses now have a customer centric approach. They design or develop product based on the needs of the customers.

HR Imperatives Driven by Political Context

The HR imperatives as a result of the changed political climate and the business imperatives necessitated by the same are as follows:

1. Managing Cultural Change

Since now organizations have a diverse workforce it's necessary for businesses to manage the cultural change happening.

Recruitment: Also now that businesses are spread across the globe it is necessary that care be taken while recruiting a diverse workforce and accepts the culture with an open mind.

2. Talent Management

Due to the dynamic nature of workforce it is necessary that organizations have an appropriate talent management strategy to acquire, develop, retain and replenish the workforce.

Personal Development: Now that there is a shift from collectivism to individualism it is necessary organizations focus on an individual's career development, develop future leaders etc.

Cross-cultural Training: It is necessary to provide training to individuals on the various cultures they are going to work when businesses are going global.

> **Example:** It is required to train an employee on the cultural aspects of China if suppose the firm was to establish their business in China. This will ensure the sustainability of the business.

3. Structural Change in Organization

With reduced political barriers it is an imperative that businesses have:

- A flat hierarchy
- The power distance be reduced
- Empowerment of employees
- Communication barriers be reduced

Communication should be Instant (decisions be made quickly and also feedback be provided instantaneously) and transparent.

4. Training and Development

With changing business context it is necessary that employees be trained to sustain in the market with the changing technology. Also they are provided cross functional training, so that they can be employed with the changing business needs.

5. Employee Engagement

For the success of a business it is necessary that the workforce be highly engaged and therefore it is the need of every business to keep its employees engaged.

Employee engagement is necessary to make the employees aware of various business activities, manages employee turnover and boost business growth.

6. Increase in Use of Temporary Employment Practices

Businesses are moving towards a temporary workforce due to various reasons. They are easy to hire, flexible to any work timings, though they have high pay rates and they are low cost to the company in the long run.

> **Example:** Many companies have temporary workforce or rather 'Free-lancers' even for top positions. The temp does the work on a particular project and once done with the project moves out. This is the latest trend in the business environment.

7. Focus on Key Players

Again as already discussed this is a part of the talent management strategy where the businesses target the key players rather than the not so important players and their focus is on retaining them. This will help the organisation in succession planning.

8. Increasing use of Technology and Business Intelligence

Organisations are increasingly looking to technology to enhance performance and fill skills gaps. As a result HR is also using technology for organisation's advantage. This can provide the organisation a competitive edge and lowers the cost of HR operations. The development of HR technologies is helping to transform HR into a decision science with a measurable impact on business results. This creates new roles for HR professionals and the imperative to develop strong HR technology competencies.

The wide range of impact of technology on HR can be clearly viewed on the HR functions such as:

- Recruitment
- Training & development
- Performance management
- Payroll & attendance records

Businesses are widely deploying Business Intelligence in HR for executing extensive manpower assessments, preparing account reports, employee performance reports, evaluating wages, staffing, available jobs and termination rules. This helps HR make strategic decisions and align them with the corporate goals.

Economic Factors

There have been several changes in the global economy as compared to earlier centuries. Some of them are as follows:

1. **Globalisation:** Globalization refers to the increasing unification of the world's economic order through reduction of barriers to international trade as tariffs, export fees, and import quotas.

The goal is to increase material wealth, goods, and services through an international division of labour by efficiencies catalyzed through international relations, specialization and competition. It describes the process by which regional economies, societies, and cultures have become integrated through communication, transportation, and trade. Globalization is caused by four fundamental forms of capital movement throughout the global economy. The four important capital flows are:

➢ Human Capital (i.e., Immigration, Migration, Emigration, Deportation, etc.)

➢ Financial Capital (i.e., Aid, Equity, Debt, Credit & Lending, etc.)

➢ Resource Capital (i.e., Energy, Metals, Minerals, Lumber, etc.)

➢ Power Capital (i.e., Security Forces, Alliances, Armed Forces, etc.)

After the world war many committees and associations have emerged with focus on free global trade.

2. **Monetary Policies:** Monetary policy is the process by which the monetary authority of a country controls the supply of money, often targeting a rate of interest for the purpose of promoting economic growth and stability. The official goals usually include relatively stable prices and low unemployment. Monetary policies of various countries change significantly according to the prevailing economic situation.

3. **Explosion in Stock Markets:** With the advent of free trade and globalisation across the world, there has been a significant change in stock markets of various countries. Due to availability of capital for companies due to portfolio investments and FIIs there is an explosion in stock markets.

4. **Trade in Commodities:** Since the advent of internet and online trading in 1990s, commodities also entered in the virtual trading market. With the entry of commodities like gold, silver, platinum etc the power of safe heaven asset is slightly lost from dollar. Safe heaven asset is the one which is expected to grow in rates with time. Dollar is considered as safe heaven but due to anticipation of a double dip recession, it is losing its appeal as safe heaven.

5. **Growth of Unemployment in Developed Countries & Employment in Developing Countries:** The prices of factors of production are rising continuously in countries like U.S.A and European countries. Companies tend to outsource their manufacturing and service base to developing countries due to which there is a growth of unemployment in developed countries & employment in developing countries.

6. **Growth of Inflation in Developing Countries:** Due to growth of employment in developing countries and shift in focus of major MNCs there is a growth of inflation. Apart from that various economic policies like free trade, globalisation, etc also have an impact on inflation.

7. **Great Divide (GDP Growth Rate):** There is a great divide in the growth rate of various countries. Developed countries are growing at a very slow rate or can be said as stagnant economies whereas the developing countries are growing at a faster rate.

8. **World Economy is More Powerful than Individual Nations:** It has been said, "US sneezes the world freezes". But the saying is not entirely true in the current era. Today the world economy is more powerful than individual nations, and the same was seen in the 2008 recession when the impact of American recession was not much felt by India.

Business Imperatives Driven by Changed Economic Climate

These thrusts of activities are critical to arriving at stated objectives in the business. These are the drivers of business and the principles by which the business acts and thinks, not the actions it takes.

1. **Need to Operate across National Boundaries:** With the advent of globalization, a business firm needs to expand its operations across the national boundaries in order to gain competitive advantage and sustain its business.

2. **Shift Manufacturing and Service Bases:** Outsourcing of service base as a cost reduction procedure by the organization is getting increasingly prevalent.

3. **Cost is a Major Issue and Optimizing Cost is Very Important:** Companies now-a-days retain the core department such as R & D and outsource the non-core ones. This again acts as a cost reduction benefit to the company.

4. **Ensuring Presence of Emerging Markets like China, India, Brazil etc.:** Developing markets such as China, India and Brazil are hot seats for FDIs' and FIIs'. Multinational companies are realizing the market potential of these countries and are expanding their market base to these nations.

5. **Quality Assurance is Significant:** Due to increased global competition, companies are now focussing extensively on quality to sustain their business in the global scenario. Today customers are entitled to choose from a variety of options available in the market, therefore, to maintain market sustainability compromising on quality has to take a setback.

    > Today customers are entitled to choose from a variety of options available in the market.

6. **Competitive Business Strategy Needs to Be Reassessed Continuously:** Any business strategy gains obsolescence over a period of time. Therefore, there needs to be a drive for constant innovation and upgradation of the business strategy continuously.

7. **Need to Focus both on Top Line and Bottom Line Growth:** Achieve bottom line growth through innovative business strategies which may be decreased in expenditures/ raw materials or various combinations including exceptional items (one time expenditures) which can reduce the cost of the business, rather than only focussing on the gross sales and revenue of the company which results in merely top line growth of the company.

    > Today the options available are endless in the market; therefore, the business imperatives should seek a balance between their pricing strategy and quality offered.

8. **Need to Balance Pricing Decisions and Quality Offerings:** Compromising on quality based on reduced pricing decisions can retard the business growth. Today the options available are endless in the market; therefore, the business imperatives should seek a balance between their pricing strategy and quality offered.

9. **Integrating Emerging and Unique Services and Applications in Business:** Aligning innovation in the current scenario with the business strategies to sustain a competitive edge in the market.

10. **Need to Differentiate between Innovation and Manufacturing Headquarters:** There needs to be a distinction between the R&D department and the manufacturing unit of the organization. Generally, companies prefer keeping their R&D department in their home country whereas other services are outsourced. This helps in increased efficiency of their business as well as reduced cost.

HR Imperatives Driven by Economic Environment

With the various changes in the macroeconomic variable there has been significant strategies developed by the corporate. Any strategy developed makes an impact on the HR policies and practices. Some of the HR imperatives are:

1. **Increase Focus on Manpower Management:** There has been a significant increase in focus on manpower management. Practising good manpower management or Human Resource Management (HRM) enables managers of an enterprise to express their goals with specificity, increasing worker comprehension of goals, and provide the necessary resources to promote successfully accomplishment of said goals.

2. **Innovative Flexibility in Work Environment:** Flexibility in work environment brings a culture of creativity and innovation in the work culture. In today's competitive environment, innovation plays a major role in bringing a core competency for the company in market.

Example: Microsoft's focus on creativity and innovation can be clearly seen in its work culture.

3. **Increased Focus on Learning Culture:** There has been an increased focus on employees. Due to this reason organisations are focusing on development of skills. Training and development is now an integral part of HR department.

4. **Increased Focus on Strategic Recruitment:** There has been a clear focus on recruitment strategy to be in line with business strategy. The hiring process should focus on our core competency and should strengthen it.

5. **Change Management:** Today organisations take any change very seriously. With the growth in education among employees and

workers, any change cannot be neglected as it plays a significant role in organisation's working.

6. **Managing Budgets Efficiently & Meeting Biz Expectations:** There should be a proper budget allocation for Human Resources. Human resources should be given a particular importance in the budget allocation. The approach considering human resources as a cost centre is now shifting and the perception has been changing significantly.

7. **Growth & Expansion:** There has been an expansion in every businesses and industry. Global trade and functions seek proper attention on HR. The policies should be in line with such growth.

> **Example:** Diversified Workforce now is covered under HR policies as a part to welcome growth and expansion.

8. **Expectation Management:** There should be proper management of employee expectation because employees are premium assets of the business.

> **Example:** With the growth in inflation, every employee expects a dearness allowance which should be taken care of.

Social Factors

Social change refers to an alteration in the social order of a society. This change is facilitated by the interaction between various other macro environment factors. This change can be measured on the basis of the following criteria:

- **Social Relations:** Social relations focus on the behaviours and needs, those that primarily concern themselves with how people organise and make meaning of their world and their relationships within it.
- **Social Institutions:** A social institution is a complex, integrated set of social norms organized around the preservation of a basic societal value. In short-hand, the five basic institutions are called the family, government, economy, education and religion.
- **Social Behaviour:** It is behaviour directed towards society, or taking place between, members of the same species.

> **Social Networking:** It is the practice of expanding the number of one's business and/or social contacts by making connections through individuals.

To summarize, when taken Social changes as a whole in consideration, we thus note following outcomes:

1. **Demographic Alteration:** The demographic alterations have been the significant changes that have happened in the society. The countries, like India, which have seen a swing towards younger population, have seen a growing need to address the conversion of a potential workforce to a dynamite talent pool. For filling the skill gap as the IBM started IBM Drona and IBM Great Minds Challenge training programs where the brightest brains are trained in the graduation for the required KSA's at workplace. Whereas, countries like Japan and Canada, that have seen a sharp drop in the birth rates, are struggling with low workforce participation and are increasingly becoming more and more dependent on the immigrant population. As the ageing population is increasing there should be a policy of hiring older people with required experience and KSA's. The firm ASDA in UK started applying this policy where it attracts and tries to retain the older population.

2. **Work Force:** The diversity in workforce observed is comparatively more diverse than the previous years. The workforce diversity in terms of nationality, gender, ethnicity, differently-abled people, etc, is more pronounced in the some workplaces.

3. **Growth of Income & Income Disparities:** As India is ranked as 4th country for having highest purchasing power we can easily observe that the disposable income with individuals is comparatively higher than the previous years. At the same time the divide in the income group is also increasing.

4. **Rise in Educational Levels:** The average level of education has risen. Along with the education the levels of awareness has also increased tremendously.

5. **Greater Global Citizenship (Social Relationships have Altered):** Today the youth especially feels more a global citizen then being limited to a region or a nation. The social media has played a huge role in the same. This also has meant greater mobility and transparency.

6. **Change in Family Structure:** Alternation of family structure from traditional joint family systems to nuclear families and introduction of DINK Group- 'Double Income No Kids'.

7. **Pressure Group:** Social pressure groups are being created for human rights, consumer behaviour, social groups etc.

8. **Equality Concept:** Equality concept strongly growing not only in the organizations but also in the society.

Here are some instances from the recent past that underline the social changes:

Example 1: Haagen-Dazs & Honeybee Preservation
Honeybees are disappearing at an alarming rate — and that's bad news for the global food chain. Haagen-Dazs decided to create a micro site to raise awareness about the issue: "Honey bees are responsible for pollinating one-third of all the foods we eat, including many of the ingredients that define our all-natural ice creams, sorbets, frozen yogurt and bars." Again, smartly tying it back to the company's core mission, the company is donating a portion of proceeds from its Haagen-Dazs honeybee brand to research on the topic, and it launched a modest Twit cause campaign through the Help Honeybees hash tag, raising $7,000 in two days last November ("Bee Buzz generated: 643,748 tweets").

Example 2: Donut Don'it
The international donut brand Donut Bakers in Nevada and Ohio branches have implemented a system where in, whenever the fresh donuts come out of the oven the computer automatically tweets and updates facebook status to inform the customers that fresh donuts have just being baked. This enhances the brand awareness and the public relations. During slack period through the social networking sites, they publish discounts to attract consumers. Thus, it is not only about creating an extensive network but it is about making effective utilization of the available network to maximize profit as well as brand visibility.

Example 3: Harley Davidson Riders Club
Earlier companies did not encourage customers having same or similar products to interact with each other but now Harley Davidson riders club created by Harley Davidson has been an outstanding example promoting the brand through consumer interaction. Thus Harley Davidson transforms brand to icon.

Business Imperatives Driven by Changed Social Context

The business imperatives as a result of the social changes can be captured as:

1. Need to alter offerings (products, services, jobs) keeping demographic realities in mind.
2. Need to innovate new product designs and service offerings.
3. Need to cater to aspirations of middle-class.
4. Need to integrate social media in marketing.
5. Need to have flatter and flexible organizations.
6. Need to integrate diversity management.
7. Need to let employees engage with clients/customers and other stakeholders using communication mediums, socializing and networking.
8. Need to understand and manage impact of social groups and peer groups on business.
9. Need to have greater transparency in business disclosures and offerings.
10. With social context becoming more dynamic, there is a need to anticipate the future trends.

HR Imperatives Driven by Social Context

Companies like IBM having equality policies in their manual under which homosexuals, third gender and under-privileged people are treated and recruited with equal rules and procedures. IBM has even received awards for respecting the diversity. The Hispanic, blacks, homosexuals and third gender are treated with same respect and motivated to participate more in the organization.

Example: Levi-Strauss is a company that did engage in a purposeful Socio-cultural change process. In 1985, a group of minority and women managers requested a meeting with the CEO, complaining of discrimination. The CEO convened a three-day facilitated retreat at which white, male managers engaged in intense discussions with minority and female managers. These discussions revealed that there were, indeed, hidden attitudes in the organization that were in conflict with its espoused values. Since that time, Levi-Strauss has worked hard to generate Socio-cultural change. The company developed an "Aspiration Statement" including desired beliefs, attitudes, and behaviour. The statement specifies the company's commitment to communication, ethical management practices, employee empowerment, and recognition for those who contribute to the mission of the company. Employees at all levels also participate in training sessions on leadership, diversity, and ethics. Employee evaluations are based partially on how well they support the "Aspiration Statement."

Overall the HR imperatives driven by the social changes and consequent business imperatives are as follows:

1. **Social Recruiting:** The Society for Human Resource Management (SHRM) reports that the number of companies using social networking sites, including Linked in, Facebook and Twitter, to recruit increased from 34% in 2008 to 56% in 2011. In addition, the number of companies who don't plan to use social recruiting dropped from 45% to 21% during the same time period.

2. **Creative Jobs:** The organizations in order to extract maximum from the dynamic ideas of the GEN Y and are coming up with very creative jobs and job profiles. The jobs that are pretty unconventional in nature are slowly but steadily catching the attention.

3. **Creative Work Culture:** Attitude towards work is now changing as the Gen Y is looking for more challenging options and have alternatives because of the vast market for skilled and knowledge workers.

Example: Google: Right from the employee, space is provided to celebrate creative error of the month. It has made to ensure that it satisfies the creativity in every employee.

4. **Train the Graduate Student:** To make sure that the talent is not drained, the companies now believe in imbibing the skills in the prospective employees even before they join the company.

5. **Outsource Talent and Technology:** To make sure the companies use the resource effectively and efficiently, the companies believe in specialization using core competencies. Thus the companies work on their respective core competencies and outsource the rest from the companies having the respective core competency.

6. **Diversity Management:** Diversity is determined by the following factors:
    - Where do the employees come from?
    - How much do they earn?
    - How do they look physically?
    - Age group
    - Beliefs and traditions

- Level of education
- Tastes, preferences
- Gender
- Attitude and values concerning work.

All these factors either divide employees or unite employees.

Managing diversity can be defined in the present context as follows:

- Recognizing in a very positive way, those groups of people who share common characteristics and those who have different characteristics.
- And hence work on involving them as part of the organization, as a member of the organization culture thus respecting the differences and work towards a common goal which requires the expertise of the people across the globe at different levels.

Thus managing diversity is critical to ensure smooth functioning in every organization. This can be imbibed in the workplace culture only by implementing well thought measures to bring the people to work together. This, no doubt requires HR policies facilitating the needs of the business.

7. **Participative Management:** The power distance is slowly reducing thus the employees are being involved in the process of decision making. It's about taking inclusive and collective decisions.

Cultural Factors

Culture

Culture is composed of the societal forces affecting the values, beliefs, and actions of a distinct group of people.

The cultural changes on a broad level may be described as following:

1. **Mindset Change:** People have become more broad minded and more acceptable in nature and also more tolerant towards different cultures.

2. **Woman Participation:** The participation of women is being encouraged in organizations. They are taking up important roles and their contribution is being recognized.

3. **Diversity in Terms of Work Force:** The organizations are employing people from all over the globe to ensure, they have the best talent onboard, rather than restricting themselves to a particular location.

4. **Orientation (Collective to Individualistic):** The workforce is now self-oriented more than collective.

5. **Multilingual Acceptance:** Acceptance towards other languages has increased.

6. **Emergence of Online Communities:** Various online communities have emerged primarily due to the social media revolution. Such communities are transnational and virtual.

7. **Emergence of Aspirational Culture:** The Gen Y especially is an aspirational generation. It aspires for better quality of life, better amenities, better technology & gadgets, better standard of living, better jobs & career, financial freedom, better access and no-nonsense culture.

8. **Decrease of Shelf-life of Relationship:** The lifelong relationship culture is fast losing its sheen and it is replaced by a culture where every relationship comes with a shelf-life. This can be seen in the society as well as in the organizations.

9. **Increase of 'Other' Cultural Influence:** With people becoming more and more connected and the communities becoming more and more virtual and global, the influence of the 'other' culture can be felt more and more. The emergence of the metro-sexual breed is a result of such influence.

Business Imperatives Driven by Changed Cultural Environment

1. **Cross-cultural Management:** With multi-cultural interactions becoming more and more imminent, the need to understand, appreciate, educate and create awareness about cross-cultural issues is a business imperative.

2. **Presence on Social Networking Websites:** Social networking websites are the new communities of change. Companies are increasingly realizing the need to connect with people through such sites in order to appreciate better the cultural nuances.

3. **Connecting with Stakeholders through Social Networking Platform:** The social networking sites also provide a platform to connect with the other stakeholders.

4. **Implementing Tools that Help to Sustain Diverse Communities:** Businesses need to implement tools that appeal to multi-cultural

Social Marketing: Companies are increasingly realizing the need to connect with people through such sites in order to appreciate better the cultural nuances.

sensibilities and help in sustaining the diverse communities. Many companies have come-out with commercials that have a global appeal and they have appealed to the youth rather than to a single culture. This is also true in the case of products and brands.

5. **Need to Innovate and Design an Offering on a Continuous Basis (Aspiration):** Change is the order of the day. People are looking for newer designs, newer products etc. Sustaining this mindset requires the companies to innovate at a rapid pace and on a continuous basis. Dell for example has introduced laptops with changeable cover-designs. So no more the boring laptop anymore. Everyday you could have a new laptop, without really changing anything but the top lid cover. So you can match the laptop design to your mood, your dress or simple with your friend's laptop.

6. **Customisation and Personalisation:** Driven by the increasing individualistic orientation, the companies have realized the need to offer customisation and personalization services, even to non-premium customers. So there are companies which let you design your own teas, coffee mugs, etc., then there are companies which let you come-out with your own flavour of chips (Lays) or noodles (Maggie, Nestle) etc. E-bay and Amazon provide an option of customized product and services to their customers.

7. **Balancing Standardization and Customisation:** If customisation caters to the growing individual sensibilities, then standardization augurs good for efficiency. Companies are learning how to balance between the same. One of the companies which has done that wonderfully is Mc Donald's, that very much pioneered the entire concept of chaining fast-food outlets based on its ability to achieve custom-standardization, which very much refer to their ability to standardize the back-end (process) and customize the front-end (offerings). Hence in India you have Mc Aloo Tikki, Mc Paneer, etc.

> Most companies try to innovate their products and services to suit their women customers.

8. **Recognizing Women as an Important Decision Maker and as New Aspirational Customer:** The kind of freedom, empowerment and expression that women have found and are continuously seeking makes them powerful new set of aspirational customers. Catering to such customers becomes a business imperative. Most companies are trying to innovate their products and services to suit their women customers.

9. **Uniform Quality Offering Across Globe:** Connected world has meant that quality awareness is uniform around the world. Companies are almost forced to offer similar quality products around the world.

HR Imperatives Driven by Cultural Context

1. **Decentralised Policies:** Empowered, multi-cultural workforce has necessitated the decentralisation of the policies. Companies are adapting to policies according to the different cultures, legality, working hours, e.g., US hourly, India Monthly, holiday policy.

   Companies are adapting to policies according to the different cultures.

2. **Social Networking Platforms:** Engaging employees e.g., HLL intranet blog "Your Say" where employees can post comments, views on recent policies, company procedures, organization practices etc. Moreover they get the response within two consecutive working days for their respective posts.

3. **Innovative Policies and Practices e.g., IBM, LG, Infosys and JW Marriot:** Innovative policies and practices for example IBM flexi time policies, LG bonus five times a year, Infosys-ESOP(Employees Stock Option Programme) JW Mariott- six days off per month.

4. **Customized Policies e.g., Accenture:** Customized policies for e.g., Accenture's compensation restructuring policies. Companies come up with policies that the employees can customize to suit their needs. Modification of variable pay.

5. **Recognizing Women Workforce:** IBM's Diversity workforce with a fixed percentage of women employee ratio. Mind Tree provides crèche facility for women with kids. HLL has job sharing facilities wherein women who have returned after the maternity leave can share their job with other co-workers as they are not allowed too much stress during that period. LG has global mandate to hire more women.

6. **Uniform Value Sharing across Globe:** 'Uniform value sharing across globe' Spirit of WIPRO lays down certain values which are to be followed uniformly throughout the globe and is not subject to change according to the countries and cultures.

7. **Quick Changes in Roles:** Quick change in roles- due to emergence of aspirational workforce, Scope Intl (Backend Process of Standard

Chartered) has adopted a policy of quick change in roles in every two to three years either vertically or horizontally.

8. **Idea Sharing:** Aircel's CEO and Head HR flies frequently to different locations to meet employees across the country. He holds town hall meetings to check the pulse of employees.

Legal/Regulatory Factors

The changes in the legal/regulatory climate can be seen as:

Table 3.1:
Legal/Regulatory Factors

	Then	Now
1.	Highly regulated market (majorly domestic players).	Less regulated markets after Liberalization, Privatization and Globalization (LPG).
2.	Very difficult to get a license for starting up a new venture.	Starting up a new venture is not difficult but running them smoothly is a challenge because of many regulations by the government.
3.	Employees were not empowered.	Employees are aware of their rights and are empowered.
4.	Women did not enjoy the same legal rights as men.	Women enjoy equal legal rights as men, like-voting, wage discrimination, gender discrimination, and employment opportunities.
5.	Consumers did not have much power or rights.	Consumers have more power (formation of consumer courts and consumer rights forums).
6.	Jurisdiction was rigid in terms of the lifestyle of citizens.	Jurisdiction has become more liberal in terms of the lifestyle of citizens (laws for the protection of rights of third gender).

Business Imperatives Driven by Changed Legal/Regulatory Climate

In light of the changes in the legal/regulatory environment businesses face the following imperatives:

1. **Flexible in Corporate Governance and Expansion:** As a result of globalization, businesses now have the opportunity to expand beyond their national boundaries and adapt to the type of regulations followed in that particular country.

2. **Foresight of Legal Changes:** For setting up any kind of business in other nations, the business shall be much aware about the legal/regulatory aspects.

3. **Employment Terms (Talent Philosophy):** Employee rights vary from country to country and it depends on the talent philosophy of the organization how they treat their employees.

4. **Implementation of Laws:** Only understanding the laws is not important, the degree to which they are implemented needs to be known.

5. **Know Your Customer Rights:** The businesses have to understand the rights that customers enjoy in a particular nation. However globally there is a surge in consumer rights and businesses must become cognizant of the same.

6. **Leverage of Legal Rights:** The degree to which the people of the country can leverage the use of their legal rights should be known and understood.

7. **Transparency of Information:** The kind of information that is required to be exhibited in one country as a legal right may not be the same for any other country.

Overall these business imperatives could be articulated as:

1. Ease of Trade

The change in legal frameworks regarding International Trade has led to increased freedom for countries to look beyond their own boundaries and form trade relations with each other. Liberalization and Privatization policies led to increased flexibility in the trade and labour laws, which in turn encouraged cross-boundary business. For example, in India, pre-liberalization era mandated about 129 approvals for the initiation of an Import or Export business, whereas now the count of approvals required has come down to a reasonable and convenient number of just 25, for the same.

> Liberalization and Privatization policies led to increased flexibility in the trade and labour laws, which in turn encouraged cross-boundary business.

2. Restructuring

➤ of Legal Frameworks

The structure of all legal frameworks, global as well as domestic, have undergone a transformation with the aim of making them more direct, organized and specific. This helps in not only covering loopholes, but also to make them easier to be followed.

➤ of Business Processes

The business processes too have gone through a transition making them more organised, better managed, cost-effective and more adaptable to the changing legal scenarios universally. For example, prior to 1995, India had about 18 different acts for regulating food standards and safety, which were disorganized and mostly ineffective, as they provided many loopholes amongst them. But in 1995, the Food Safety Act came into being, which consolidated all these 18 acts under it, hence, providing a single window for all approvals as regulated by the Ministry of Food Processing. Again in 2006, Food Safety and Standards Act, 2006, (No. 34 of 2006) was enacted from 23 August 2006. This act meant to consolidate the laws relating to food and to establish the Food Safety and Standards Authority of India for laying down science based standards for articles of foods. In 2011, Food Safety and Standards Rules were enacted (w.e.f. 5th August 2011) and leter Food Safety and Standards Regulations, 2011 were enacted (w.e.f. 5th August 2011).

3. Security

➤ of Privacy

In a world which is getting smaller, preserving personal space and privacy of individuals is becoming a major concern. Countries around the world are trying to come up with laws to contend with this problem.

➤ of Agreements

Universally applicable laws have ensured their uniformity and acceptance around the globe, hence making agreements and contracts safer.

Example: Google has paused its Street View project in India, due to objection raised by Central Government, and Ministry of Defence. The company has confirmed that they have decided to stop Street View cars. So the legal aspect of each country may vary which should be taken care of.

(**Source:** http://www.medianama.com/2011/06/223-google-street-view-bangalore-police)

4. Parity

> **for Nations**

The WTO has brought all the nations to an equal platform, irrespective of them being a Developed, Transition or Developing Economies. It has provided the Third World countries with the opportunity to indulge in trade practices with the more economically powerful nations of the world.

> **for Organisations**

The legislation of any nation decrees all its laws to be equally applicable to all businesses within it. The various Trade and Labour laws are mandatory for organisations to be part of global trade.

> **Example:** Indian laws currently allow **100%** foreign direct investment (FDI) only in wholesale retail. Current foreign direct investment regulations **do not permit global multi-brand retailers to enter India directly**. At present, **51 per cent FDI** is allowed but only for **single-brand** outlets. **Wal-Mart** cannot enter the **Indian market directly** because current regulations pertaining to foreign direct investment only allow "single-brand" retailers such as Nike or Gucci to own 51 percent of their business operations in India. There is a continuous discussion and representation to ease-up FDI in multi-brand retail.

> **for Workers**

In India, the Labour laws provide for equal opportunity for all citizens, men as well as women, and the constitution endeavours to provide "equal pay for equal work" for both.

HR Imperatives Driven by Legal Environment

The HR response in the face of changed legal/regulatory environment and the altered business scenario should be-

1. **How to align the organizational strategy with the regulatory framework?**
    a. Aligning individual goals to organizational goals.
    b. Take necessary steps required in order to sustain at that point of time.

2. **How to tabe proactive measures to adapt to the dynamic legal/regulatory environment?**

In 1991 when economy was going through a critical phase, there was stagnation in the economy and government controls and protections were lifted.

Example: From April 1994 to April 2001, Tata Steel reduced its workforce by downsizing 38% (from 78,669 to 48,821) employees. One-third of them left due to normal attrition and the rest were due to early separation or the voluntary retirement scheme offered to them. But then also they maintained the profits. Tata Steel took the measure of Downsizing when they realized that it would be difficult for them to sustain in the coming time. So they took this step to cut their workforce by about 38% even when the company was doing well.

3. **How the top management should support the implementation of changes?**

At the time when Tata Steel had to downsize, Dr. Irani, called up a meeting for the top officials and communicated to them the plan. He put forward an idea of "Internal Communications Campaign" through which they would get their employees into confidence by telling them the goals of the company and to have the line managers support them. They also stressed on the fact that don't give fabricated figures to the employees, rather, have an open and transparent communication with them.

4. **How to get Awareness about employee empowerment according to demographics?**

As per the changing demographics there has been a vast change in the legal obligations which differ from one country to another country even though the organization is same.

5. **How to ensure that the HR regulations in the organization are in complete accordance with the country specific legal laws?**

As per the laws of Indian Industry, the textile division of the well-known Group has the following rule in place: The company must give workers a day off for rest on Sunday. If in case of emergencies or urgent need workers are called to work on a Sunday, the company must give the workers a day off within the next three days [i.e., Wednesday at the latest]. Failure to abide by this will be viewed as a serious violation.

6. **How to simultaneously organize HR regulations of all the branches of the organization located in various countries?**

This is a challenge for companies like HSBC bank, which has branches all over the world. The structure and regulations of each branch is based on a lead bank in respective regions. HSBC markets itself as "The World's Local Bank".

7. How to manage HR strategies to address legal and security concerns in a country or region?

Facebook recently got into a controversy regarding the "auto-tagging" of photos through face-recognition technology. Many people especially in the U.S. voiced concerns of their privacy being intruded upon. The U.S. Congress passed an order directing the company to inform the users via e-mail about the new system and the option of opting or not opting for the feature being enabled on their accounts. EU is also looking into this issue.

Technological Factors

The technological environment has perhaps undergone the greatest and fastest transformation world-wide. Technology is into everything and firms that have not been able to keep pace with the same have been forced to exit the business. Consider this for an example - EMI pioneered the innovation of the CT scanner in 1972. Despite a strong market position in early years, by 1977, EMI was forced to exit the scanner business. Primarily, it was because of the company's failure to establish source of competitive advantage and also its failure to build integrated market sensing, design, manufacturing, delivery and service capability.

More than three decades later the scenario is even more competitive with respect to technology. The one who are thriving are those who have combined technology and hence innovation in their business processes and the ones who have failed to do so are either struggling or have closed-down. Contextually, the changes in the technological environment can be captured as under:

Technological Factors

Technological factors influence a business in a major way. It affects the business ability to produce, to sell, expand, and demand.

Many of these technological factors include machinery, workers, and benefits. If you don't have machinery you cannot produce, if you don't have workers you cannot sell, and if you do not have benefits you will not expand.

Table 3.2: Technological Factors

Then	Now
Technology limited to niche areas	Highly technology-intensive
Slow pace of Technology-pace slow	High rate of technological obsolescence
Limited Tech-club.	Everybody has technology
Longer developmental cycles	Speed of development is the key
Technology itself was a USP.	Speed of execution and application determines edge

Competing on technology has led to the creation of knowledge-based organizations.

Technological climate has changed drastically into a highly techno-competitive climate. Competing on technology has led to the creation of knowledge-based organizations and has seen huge resources being allocated to creation, management and strategic use of the knowledge. Today competing on technology is not enough. There is a need to compete on technological applications which are directed towards client's or customer's specific needs. And there is a need to do that continuously. In short, it calls for the organizations to be innovative in whatever they do.

The need to be innovative has also led the organizations to think what it takes to become innovative in the first place.

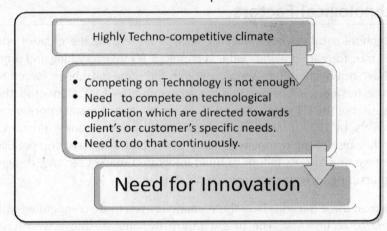

Figure 3.3: Technology Factors

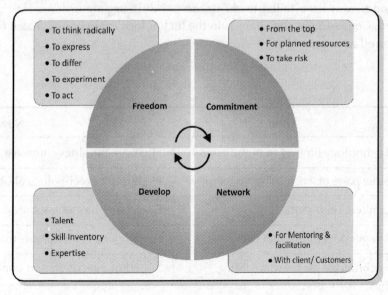

Figure 3.4: Innovation Pizza

The innovation pizza has four slices, which primarily tells us what an organization needs to be innovative:

Slice 1 – Freedom: Organizations have to provide freedom to its employees to:
- Think radically;
- Express and differ without fear;
- Experiment and to act.

Slice 2 – Develop: Dedicated resource and time is required to develop:
- Skill inventory,
- Expertise,
- Talent.

Slice 3 – Network: Organization should allow its employees to network:
- For mentoring & facilitation amongst themselves.
- With client/customers for idea.

Slice 4 – Commitment: And finally strong unwavering commitment shall be required:
- From the top;
- For planned resources; and
- To take risks (tolerate failures).

HR Imperatives Driven by Technological Context

1. How to connect with Business and Organizational Strategy?

Consider these two statements:

A. Based on Aon Hewitt's research, more the 60% of HR's time is transactional, administrative in nature. In addition, HR is often not included.

B. Up to 70 percent of a company's market value can come from intangibles such as its human capital, its brand, and its culture.

These statements make it amply clear that although HR can contribute immensely in adding value to a company, its place is often obscure and non-strategic. There is a need to connect with business and organizational strategy to:
- Understanding true state of technology readiness.
- Align HR efforts with business goals.

> HR can contribute immensely in adding value to a company.

- Build high performance workforce.
- Achieve high ROI (Return on Investment).
- Transform HR from a cost-centre to an investment-centre.

Example: Take Microsoft for example. 'Microsoft has become a place in recent years where little ideas get lost in the shuffle. For a company that's expected to generate about $70 billion in annual sales, an idea that might lead to a $10 million a year business, or even $100 million a year one, can quickly slip through the cracks.' Microsoft launched an initiative called '*garage*' to ensure that such idea do not slip and to spark innovation in the organization once again. Microsoft has recently opened up a new 60,000 square foot facility in Redmond, Washington that it is calling the Garage. Sprinkled around the building are new 'pods,' temporary work spaces where teams of two, three, or five employees can set up shop to collaborate on projects for weeks at a time. The two-year-old program helps incubate those side projects that employees want to dive into but can only find time for at night and over weekends. The Garage gives workers access to tools such as a soldering bench, a laser cutter and a 3D printer. It offers instrumentation for testing prototypes. The Garage hosts Web applications. But maybe most important, it connects workers to colleagues, with similar interests or needed skills, something that can be challenge at a company with nearly 90,000 employees.

'*Garage*' has tinker forums, science fairs, garage weeks etc. to encourage show-casing of various prototypes under development and hence infuse a sense of competition amongst various employee groups. The '*Garage*' pay-offs have already started to come in the form of special apps for women, instant messaging conversation translator, Microsoft shuttered pioneer studios etc.

2. How to Create Non-threatening but Accountable Systems?

Technology is always leveraged by an innovation culture in the organization, which in turn is only possible when people have freedom to think radically and express the same; freedom to differ; freedom to experiment; freedom to act. Non-threatening but account-able systems always **'pull'** people to –

A. Create,
B. Contribute, and
C. Captain.

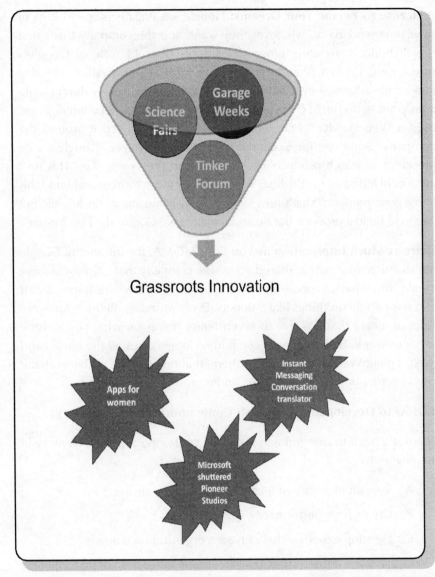

Figure 3.5:
Grassroots Innovation

Google is one such company that has been able to pull people to create by creating non-threatening yet accountable systems. Google has identified them as the rules of innovation at the company. Some of them are:

Ideas Come from Everywhere: Google has this great internal list where people post new ideas and everyone can go on and see them. It's like a voting pool where one can say how good or bad you think an idea is. Those comments lead to new ideas.

A License to Pursue Your Dreams: Google lets engineers spend 20% of their time working on whatever they want, and the company trusts that they'll build interesting things. After September 11, one of Google's researchers, Krishna Bharat, would go to 10 or 15 news sites each day looking for information about the case. And he thought, why don't I write a program to do this? So Krishna, who's an expert in artificial intelligence, used a Web crawler to cluster articles. He later emailed it around the company. Some senior executives like Marissa Mayer, Google's vice president of search products got the mail and they were like, 'This isn't just a cool little tool for Krishna. We could add more sources and build this into a great product.' That's how Google News came about. Krishna did not intend to build a product, but he accidentally gave Google the idea for one.

Share as Much Information as You Can: MOMA, the intranet of Google has so much information shared across the company that employees have insight into what's happening with the business and what's important. It also has people do things like Snippets. Every Monday, all the employees write an email that has five to seven bullet points on what you did the previous week. Being a search company, Google takes all the emails and make a giant Web page and index them. It allows Google to share what it knows across the whole company, and it reduces duplication.

3. How to Develop and Replenish Contemporary Skill Inventory?

There is a need to develop and replenish contemporary skill inventory in employees to -

A. Remain in a state of technology readiness always.

B. Create high-performance work systems.

C. Develop expertise that pervades organizational needs.

D. To out-wit the competition, by accelerating speed of development and execution.

Take for instance CISCO. Cisco Systems is one of the largest network companies in the world with annual revenues of over US$20 billion. Headquartered in the U.S.A., the company has 225 sales and support offices in 75 countries. For years, its training programs were managed independently at each different unit, resulting in redundant and unequal programming. To streamline, expedite and improve the quality of the training programs, the Company developed the Cisco Learning Network

(CLN). CLN training contents are developed using multimedia technologies and stored in a centralized database. The employee selects either a full curriculum or individual modules and takes an assessment test. E-learning programs can be provided in two ways: (1) in scheduled delivery, at fixed time and place using three platforms: multicasts (videos that are sent over the network to desktops), virtual classrooms, and remote laboratories, or (2) on-demand, for individuals who have particular needs using web-based on demand content, CD-ROM, and remote labs. The CLN system promotes significant savings of time away from work - it was observed that CLN courses reduced the time that the sales-employees spent away from their customers by up to 40 percent.

4. How to Build Entrepreneurial Environment?

Amazon.com CEO Jeff Bezos said that at Amazon the entrepreneurial mindset pervades the organization and he wants each and every employee to fulfill his/her responsibilities with an entrepreneurial perspective. *"We have entrepreneurs at every level. Everyone must look for and find ways to do their work better than it's ever been done before and to do that as often as possible."* The entrepreneurial mindset means that every employee thinks himself or herself as an entrepreneur and does things the better next time, whenever he does that again. If a firm needs to have a technological edge, it has to transform itself into an innovation incubator and for that it is paramount to have an entrepreneurial mindset. Take 3M for instance which has over 60000 products selling worldwide has survived on the mantra of 'Grow and Divide'. They have encouraged and celebrated the spirit of entrepreneurship in the organization. Then there is BMW which celebrates 'most creative error of the month' or there is a TATA that has something like 'dare to try'. In both these initiatives those efforts of employees are celebrated that may have failed but in the process provided a great learning for the future.

> The entrepreneurial mindset means that every employee thinks himself or herself as an entrepreneur and does things the better next time, whenever he does that again.

New Age HRM Roles

The change in the macro-environmental variables has dictated change in the way people are managed in organizations. This in turn calls for the new age HR leaders to don new roles to fulfill the new HR imperatives.

> The new age HR leaders play new roles to fulfill the new HR imperatives.

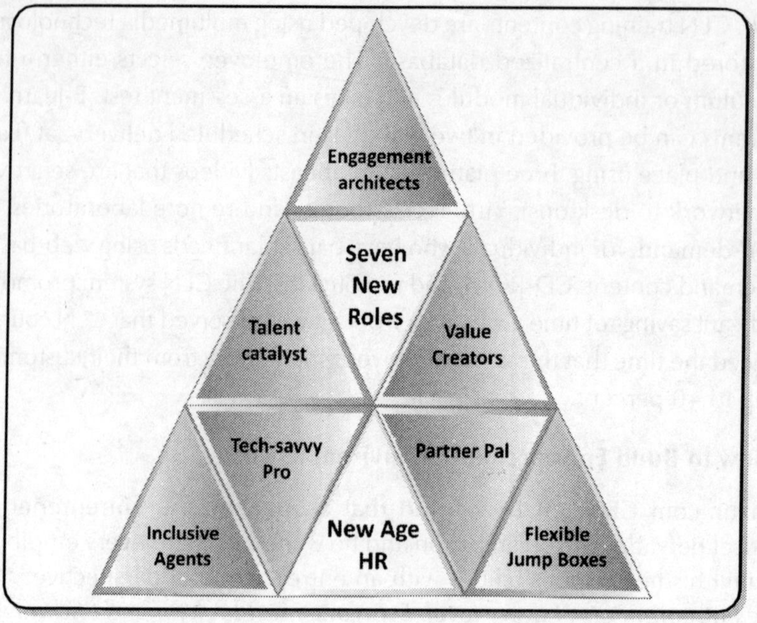

Figure 3.6:
New Age HRM Roles

[Pyramid diagram showing Seven New Roles of New Age HR: Engagement architects, Talent catalyst, Value Creators, Tech-savvy Pro, Partner Pal, Inclusive Agents, Flexible Jump Boxes]

The seven new roles envisaged for the modern day HR manager are:

1. **Flexible Jump Boxes**: Jump boxes help in explosive jump and speed training. Modern day HR calls for change and quick adaptation. As flexible jump boxes HR leaders are expected to:

   a. Bring structural changes in the organization to create non-threatening yet accountable systems.

   b. Bring greater transparency in HR operations.

   c. Create flexible and challenging jobs that can fuel innovation.

   d. Create sustainable HR policies that has common framework but customized offerings for its internal customers (employees).

   e. Ability to manage aspirations of people through role-rotation, early responsibilities, early leadership roles, etc.

   f. Devise HR strategies to address legal & security concerns in a country/region.

2. **Partner Pal**: No HR leader today can afford to stay aloof from the business and the people. HR leader has to be like a partner-pal with people and with the business & the strategy. Only then HR can appreciate the true state of business and understand the strategic directions, to align HR policies and efforts.

Flexible Jump Boxes
Modern day HR calls for change and quick adaptation.

Partner Pal
HR leader has to partner with people and business to be effective.

3. **Tech-savvy Pro**: Technology has pervaded organizations. This permeation has dictated creation of smarter, quicker and efficient systems. As a tech-savvy pro, the HR leader is expected to:

   a. Integrate technology with HR systems.

   b. Integrate Social-media applications in HR.

   Tech-savvy Pro
   HR leader is expected to integrate technology and social media.

4. **Inclusive Agents**: Today the workforce is more diverse then it used to be anytime before. HR leaders are supposed to become inclusive agents to:

   a. Manage diversity and cross-cultural management.

   b. Making organization conducive for women and recognizing women workforce for their contributions.

   Inclusive Agents
   HR leaders have to manage diversity and recognize contribution of women.

5. **Value Creators**: Process efficiency is not enough anymore. Value-creation is equally important. That value-add may be small yet is significant. HR leader must act like value-creators and add value through:

   a. Manpower acquisition (exploring newer avenues like temp-hiring, social media recruitment, hiring, outsourcing, outsourcing talent, etc.).

   b. Total reward concept rather than mere compensation.

   c. Continuous audit of HR processes and improvement of the same.

   Value Creators
   HR leader must act like value-creators.

6. **Talent Catalyst**: Today every organization has severe dearth of talent. Right kind and number of talent is required to speed-up the progress of any organization. HR leaders are expected to act as talent - catalyst to:

   a. Nurture and manage talents.

   b. Develop and replenish contemporary skill-sets in people and build their competencies.

   c. Develop competency-based performance management systems.

   Talent Catalyst
   Nurturing, developing & managing talent and developing competency based PMS are challenges modern day HR leaders confront.

7. **Engagement Architect**: Finally, today any HR leader is expected to create true engagement for all its employees and create entrepreneurial mindset among them. The employees become virtual owners of their processes and eliciting voluntary behaviour towards achievement of organizational goals is key.

   Engagement Architect
   HR leader is expected to create true engagement & an entrepreneurial mindset among employees.

Essay Questions

1. Discuss in detail the 'New-Age HRM Model' and show relationship between macro environment, business environment and HR imperatives.

2. Describe the 'Innovation-pizza' and discuss the HR imperatives dictated by the change in technological environment.

3. What are the seven new roles of HRM of the new age HRM? Discuss each with an example.

Application Questions

1. "The nature and scope of human resource management has undergone serious transformation." Articulate this statement in light of HR practices of a firm.

2. Compare and contrast two organizations from the same industry in terms of their HR practices and state which one is more suited to perform the new age HRM roles.

Bibliography

(n.d.). Retrieved from The Seattle Times: http://seattletimes.nwsource.com/html/reweb/2015264786_facebooks_photo_taggingfeature_allows_for_auto-detection_of_fac.html

2006, from http://www.usatoday.com/money/industries/food/2005-03-10-mcd_x.htm

Vroom, V. (1964). *Work and Motivation*. New York: Wiley.

Boamah, N.A. (2009). Secondary Mortgage Market (SMM): Is it Right for Financing Housing in Ghana? *Journal of Science and Technology*, Vol. 29, pp 17-27.

Boulton, C., & Davis, Z. (2011, June 17). *Regilatots Blast Facebook over face Recognition*. Retrieved from Tech Week Europe: http://www.eweekeurope.co.uk/news/regulators-blast-facebook-over-face-recognition-31945.

Brueggeman, W.B., and Fisher, J. D. (2001). Real Estate Finance and Investments, McGraw-Hill, Irwin.

Cox C (1985) Further Evidence on the Representativeness of Management Earnings Forecasts. Account Rev 60:692–701.

Easton P., Zmijewski M. (1989). Cross-sectional Variation in the Stock Market Response to Accounting Earnings Announcements. J Account Econ 11:117–142.

Francis J., Schipper K. (1999). Have Financial Statements Lost Their Relevance? . J Account Res 37:319–352.

Francis J., Schipper K., Vincent L. (2002a). Earnings Announcements and Competing Information. J Account Econ 33:313–342.

Francis J., Schipper K., Vincent L. (2002b). Earnings Disclosures and the Increased usefulness of Earnings Announcements. Account Rev 77:515–546.

Gelb D., Zarowin P. (2002). Corporate Disclosure Policy and the Informativeness of Stock Prices. Rev Account Stud 7:33–52.

Gompers P., Metrick A. (2001). Institutional Investors and Equity Prices. Q J Econ 116:229–259.

Hirst E., Koonce L., Venkataraman S. (2006). Management Earnings Forecasts: A Review and Framework.

McDonald's may outsource drive-thru order-taking. (2005). *USA Today*. Retrieved March 10.

Mishkin S.F. (2006). The Economics of Money, Banking and Financial Markets. Eighth Edition, Pearson Education Inc.

Nickell, S. (2002). "Monetary Policy Issues: Past, Present, Future", Speech at Business Link and the Coventry and Warwickshire Chamber of Commerce, Leamington Spa, June 19th, 2002.

Pahwa, N. (2011, June 23). *Google Street Views Stops Driving In India Bangalore Police*. Retrieved from Media Nama: http://www.medianama.com/2011/06/223-google-street-view-bangalore-police.

Sacks, P., Merrill, S., and Rabenhorst, C., (2003). "Developing Secondary Mortgage Markets in Southeast Europe: Assessment of the Mortgage Markets in Romania", UI Project 06940-001, January 2003.

Tushman, M. L., & Anderson, P. (1986). Technological Discontinuities and Organizational Environments. *Administrative Science Quarterly, 31*, 439–465.

Tuttle, B. (2011, June 09). *EU Regulators Looking into Facebook's New Auto Tagging feature*. Retrieved from TMC Net.com: http://www.tmcnet.com/topics/articles/184114-eu-regulators-looking-into-facebooks-new-auto-tagging.htm.

Working paper, University of Texas at Austin Kim O., Verrrecchia R. (1991). Trading Volume and Price Reactions to Public Announcements. J Account Res 29:302–321.

Chapter 4

Human Resource Planning

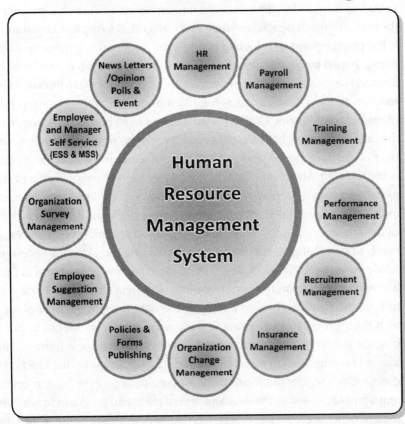

Outline

Introduction

Human Resource Function

Human Resource Planning

Factors Affecting Human Resource Planning

Demand Forecasting

Supply Forecasting

Markov Analysis

Sample Exercises on Markov Analysis

Essay Questions

Application Questions

Bibliography

Key Terms

Human Resource Function

International Labor Organization (ILO)

Markov Analysis

Qualitative Methods

Labour Market

Supply Forecasting

The Macro Environmental Factors

Introduction

International Labor Organization (ILO) defines human resource planning as – *"the process by which management ensures that it has the right personnel, who are capable of completing those tasks that help the organization reach its objectives. It improves the forecasting of human resources needs and the projected matching of individual with expected vacancies."*

Human Resource Function

In leading firms today, the role of the human resource function is growing with the realization that people and their costs are critical to organizational success. If the planning and development of human resources is guided by strategic plans, shaped by organizational needs, and closely integrated with both short-term and long-range company objectives, the importance of the human resource function to corporate success will be demonstrable, and recognized by top management (Manzini, Gridley). Management must be able to guarantee that the organization will have the right number and the right kind of people at the right place and time (Alpander, 1980). Acute social and economic strains are liable to occur whenever plans do not pay enough attention to the need for jobs, and popular support, which is so necessary in carrying out a plan, is not forthcoming as a result (Mouly). Human Resource Planning has been defined as the management process of "analyzing an organization's human resource needs under changing conditions and developing the activities necessary to satisfy these needs" (Walker, 1980). A standard and more traditional definition was applied to human resource planning: "Planning for the corporation so as to have the right numbers of people at the right time, at the right place and with the right skills." It is a simple definition, but not so simple to put into practice as many human resource and business planners know (Burack, 1985). Viewed broadly, human resource planning can be defined as the function that coordinates the identification of the organization's future human resource requirements, oversees the development of plans and programs to fulfill those requirements, and evaluates the results (Hestwood, 1984). Some of the current approaches to human resource planning derive, in part, from an overemphasis on the goal of integrating human resource and strategic plans, rather than on using human resource planning to build a competitive edge. This does not imply that the integration should not occur, merely that the integration alone is not sufficient to provide organizations the competitive edge which follows effective human resource plans (Ulrich). To be effective, an HRP program must

> Human Resource Planning has been defined as the management process of "analyzing an organization's human resource needs under changing conditions and developing the activities necessary to satisfy these needs"

meet several objectives: be integrated with strategic plans, estimate human resource demand, estimate current supply, determine any discrepancy between the two estimates, and develop programs to resolve such discrepancies (Gatewood, Rockmore). Viable programs on human resource planning depend on a clear understanding of planning and human resources. Failure to appreciate their scope has led to the development of programs that have best achieved only modest success (Lopez, 1981).

Human Resource Planning

Human Resource Planning is much broader and more profound than its predecessor, manpower planning. First, a human resource plan includes all employees. Second, it must encompass consideration of both casual and end-result variables that describe and define the state of an organization's human resources. The casual variable consists of factors over which management has control. The end-result variable consists of the effects of these factors on people, which lead to the achievement of organization goals (Lopez, 1981). Planning for the right numbers at the right place and time will continue to be important; however, human resource planning will become more concerned with training potential job applicants, attracting them, and managing a workforce that is highly diverse in terms of backgrounds, needs, sex, age, country of origin and values (Schuler). Human resource planning is directly tied to strategic business planning. Strategic business plans define steps that the organization will take to meet the demands of the future. Human resource plans assure that the right number and the right kind of people become available at the right time and place so that organizational needs can be met (Alpander, 1980). Everyone talks about the weather, but no one does anything about it. Likewise, the subject of human resource planning (HRP) continues to command a very prominent role in articles, seminars, and conventions; yet in terms of practice, very few seem to be doing anything about it (Hoffman, Wyatt, Gordon). Human resource planning professionals need to evaluate their own skills and values in relationship to these roles and determine what they lack and what they are interested in or have the orientation for. If they are technically oriented, they need to either develop managerial and change-based skills or work with existing or new employees in the development of a strategic human resource planning function (Strauss, Burack, 1983). Responsibility for planning and management of resources rests clearly with line management at all organizational levels.

Human Resource Planning

"Process to ensure right personnel in organization capable of completing tasks & meeting objectives. Involves forecasting HR needs & matching of individual with expected vacancies." (ILO)

Human Resource Planning

"Planning for corporation so as to have the right number of people at the right time, the right place and with the right skills."
(Burack)

Responsibility to support managers in the development and implementation of such plans resides with a variety of staff groups at division, branch and corporate levels (Rush, Borne, 1983).

Key Elements of HR Planning

A good human resource plan shall be derived from the strategic plan of organization. There are three key elements of human resource planning:

- Forecasting labor demand.
- Forecasting labor supply (both external and internal).
- Analyzing the 'gap' and developing HRP programs to fill these gaps.

Implications of HR Planning on Organisation

Human Resource Planning programs have primarily three implications on any organization -

    a. Cost implications

    b. Talent implications

    c. Organizational Readiness

Efficiency comes through better manpower utilization.

a. Cost Implications: HRP programs help organization to save on cost considerably by bringing in efficiency and preventing wastage of human resource. Efficiency comes through better manpower utilization. Efficiency also comes through identification of the right number and type of people well in advance so as to seize & maximize opportunities that lie for the organization.

b. Talent Implications: Today talent is required at every level of the organization. A well oiled HRP program shall help in identification of such talent both internally and externally. Such HRP programs would also focus on acquiring and preparing such talent for the future through skill enhancement, succession planning, leadership-development etc.

c. Organizational Readiness: Today competitive edge of a firm is determined by its state of readiness to cope-up with changes in the future. These changes could be in terms of technology, customer preferences, market dynamics, industry or external environment. Having said that, a firm's ability to cope with such changes and hence its state of readiness is determined by dynamism of its HRP programs.

Factors Affecting Human Resource Planning

Multiple factors affect human resource planning of a company. Broadly these factors can be grouped under three heads:

1. The macro environmental factors,
2. The micro environmental (industry specific) factors, and
3. Company specific factors.

The Macro Environmental Factors

The macro environmental factors could have impact in the way a company does its human resource planning.

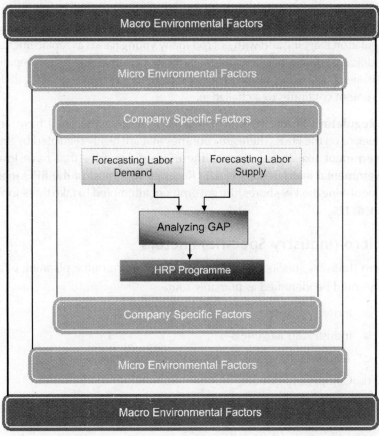

Figure 4.1: Macro Environmental Factors

a. Economy : The prevailing economic conditions have an influence over human resource planning. An economy (like India) with high GDP growth rate, a huge growing market shall mean more jobs (demand). While presently troubled economies like US (very recently lost its AAA credit rating), Greece with high debt load, very low GDP growth facing double dip recession may mean lesser jobs (demand) and more separation programs.

b. Labour Market: The availability of labor, labor participation rate into the workforce, skill levels and skill availability of the labor, all have direct or indirect impact on human resource planning.

c. Demographic Factors: The demographic factors like average age of the working population, gender-mix etc have an impact. For example India and Japan face two different challenges, when it comes to their demographics. India will soon have the largest youngest population of the world, in the age group of 18-35 years. This means more and more Gen Y in the workforce. Companies would need to incorporate their development and ready-employability at all levels. Whereas in Japan most of the working population is ageing and with not too many young hands as replacements (traditionally Japan has been a low birthrate country by choice) keeping their ageing workforce updated on latest technology etc and delaying their retirement continues to a challenge.

d. Regulatory Framework: The regulatory-framework shall have an influence on the HRP. There are countries that are highly regulated by the government like India whereas there are economies that have low governmental interference like US. Recently with most of the BPO jobs relinquishing the US-shores, the government attempted to take these jobs back to US.

The Micro (Industry Specific) Factors

The Micro (Industry specific) factors affecting human resource planning of a company could be identified as primarily four –

   a. Industry growth
   b. Industry attractiveness
   c. Technology
   d. Competitive climate

a. Industry Growth: In the Indian context, most of the industries have shown a very healthy growth over the past decade or so, driven largely by the strong consumer demand in the domestic market. This has in turn fuelled the demand for human capital in majority of the sectors. The Fig. 3.3 to 3.8 attempt to capture the kind of growth that some industries in India have noticed over the last decade.

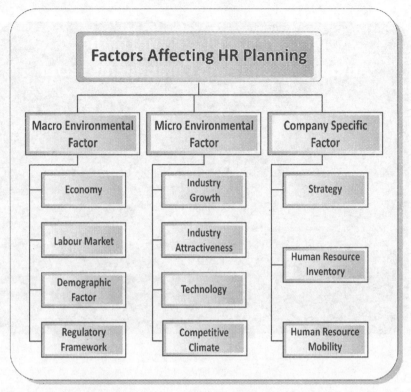

Figure 4.2:
Factors Affecting HR Planning

b. Industry Attractiveness: Some industries like IT, Retail have been able to attract more talent because they have become relatively more attractive because of their growth prospective, their practices, and their offerings, etc. There have been others who are strong string to attract manpower.

Example: Manpower Shortage in Construction Industry
One such sector is Construction and engineering sector, that faces an acute shortage of skilled manpower for the booming construction industry in the country. Based on the country's economic growth about 58.28 million person would be employed in the infrastructure sector by 2022. Out of the projected requirement, 80 per cent belong to worker category. Construction industry loses many of its B.Tech (civil) graduates reportedly to IT-industry because of its more attractive offering.

Example: Manpower Shortage in Garment & Textiles
Similarly one more industry which has struggled to attract enough manpower recently has been the Garment Industry in India. The industry which primarily depends on female workers has failed to attract them in the recent past and factors like low-pay packages, long working hours, constant work pressure and harassment at work stations are cited to be the primary causes. The booming retail activity in the country has added to the woes of garment industry, which has attracted many workers from this sector. Hence we see the attractiveness of a particular industry plays an important role in attracting manpower (supply) and fulfilling the demand.

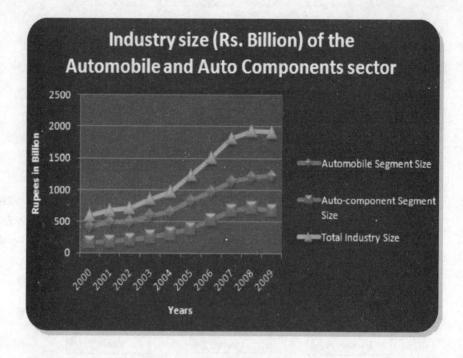

Figure 4.3: Industry Size of the Automobile and Auto Components Sector

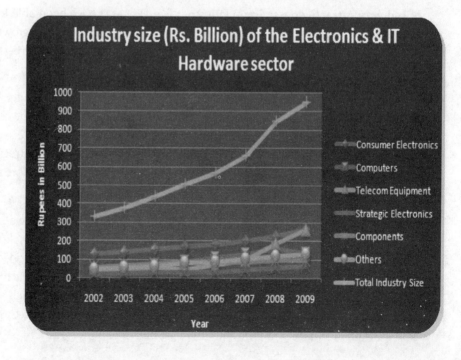

Figure 4.4: Industry Size of the Electronics & IT Hardware Sector

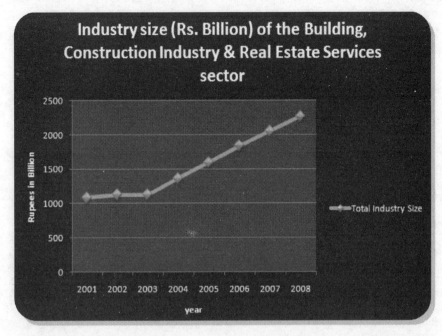

Figure 4.5: Industry Size of the Building, Construction Industry & Real Estate Services Sector

Figure 4.6: Exports of Leather and Leather Products from India (US $ million)

Figure 4.7:
Industry Growth & Size of Organized Retail

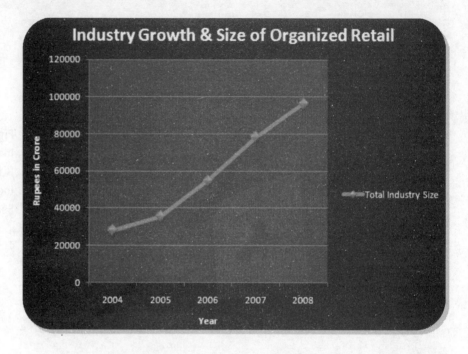

Figure 4.8:
Insurance Segment-Growth in Insurance Premium (2002-2008)

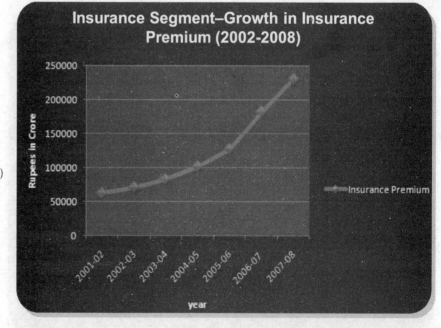

c. Technology: Technology has today pervaded virtually into every industry. We live in a knowledge economy and almost everything is driven by technology. This has in turn necessitated development and replenishment of new skill-sets in people. Employability has become a factor, only because today almost every industry looks at the readiness of the people entering their companies in terms of technology. This has impacted the demand of human resource making it more 'type' dependent rather than being number-driven, as in the past.

d. Competition Climate: The phenomenal growth that most of the industries have seen in India has meant a cut-throat competition in most of the industries of market-share and market-leadership. Today most of the companies are trying to see that as much as their bottom-line grows, their top-line grows as well. Such competition has translated in to a similar competiveness for attracting and acquiring human resources. Talent is the barometer of any company's success today and ability to attract them in large numbers and to do that continuously determines the edge.

The Company Specific Factors

The company-specific factors affecting the Human Resource Planing of a Company include:

a. Strategy
b. Human Resource Inventory
C. Human Resource Mobility

a. Strategy: The strategy of any firm plays an important role in designing its human resource planning programs. Way back in 2005, when Bharti-Airtel decided to outsource activities like IT, software etc and focus on marketing as its core, it changed the HRP of the company forever. The focus then was to build an excellent marketing team and garner the maximum market-share. And, the company was pretty much successful in such efforts. Companies like Titan that are growing and expanding have also been forced to enlarge their HRP programs. A company which has grown from profits of 10 crores to about 1000 crores in less than 10 years, with total revenues touching the 9000 crore mark, the company has required large number of people of various skill-sets, at a rapid pace.

> **Example:** When it forayed into the eye-care business (Titan Eye+) then its demand for optometrist has seen a spurt. However their shortage in the market and competitive pressure from other eye-care chains has meant that it has modified its HRP program so as to include training the new campus pass-outs and catching-them-early.

b. Human Resource Inventory: The current human resource inventory of a company has an impact on the HRP programs. Every company tries to ensure diversity in terms of skill-sets, gender-mix etc. The current set of employees is used as the reference set for a company's new demand for human resource.

c. Human Resource Mobility: The human resource mobility both within and outside the firm has an impact on its HRP programs. The internal mobility is primarily due to growth whereas the external mobility is due to attrition. High mobility rates shall mean the need to replenish the human resource loss at a rapid-pace. This mobility or rather the cause of mobility differs from industry to industry.

Example: In IT industry it is because of better salaries, in PR it is because of growth and learning that an employee wants, in ITES it more because of perceived career stagnation etc. Hence though mobility can be captured in terms of numbers always, the reasons for mobility shall also be important for designing the HRP programs.

Demand Forecasting

Demand Forecasting
Assessing present and anticipating future requirement of human resource in an organization

Workforce demand forecasting is done by companies and they employ different methods ranging from qualitative to quantitative methods. The choice of method generally depends upon the size and complexity of the firm. Smaller firms usually have more informal form of human resource planning and hence many times rely on more qualitative methods. Whereas, larger firms usually having multiple departments, levels and higher mobility of workforce both within and outside the firm, generally use more quantitative methods.

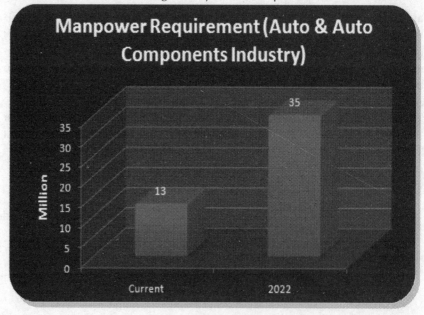

Figure 4.9: Manpower Requirement (Auto & Auto Components Industry)

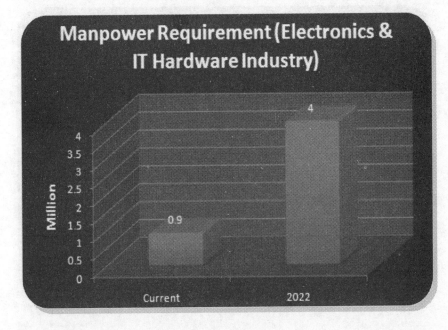

Figure 4.10: Manpower Requirement (Electronics & IT Hardware Industry)

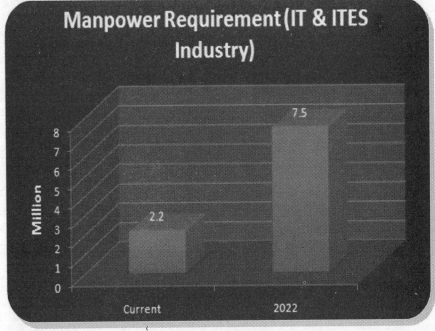

Figure 4.11: Manpower Requirement (IT & ITES Industry)

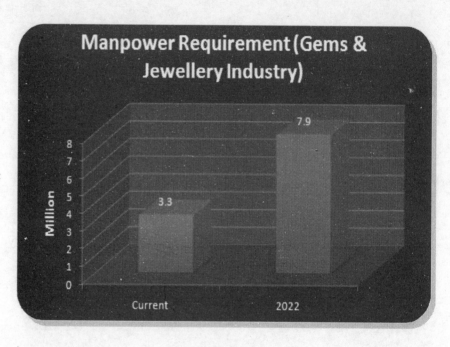

Figure 4.12: Manpower Requirement (Gems & Jewellery Industry)

Figure 4.13: Manpower Requirement (Building, Construction Industry & Real Estate Service)

Figure 4.14: Manpower Requirement (Leather & Leather Goods Industry)

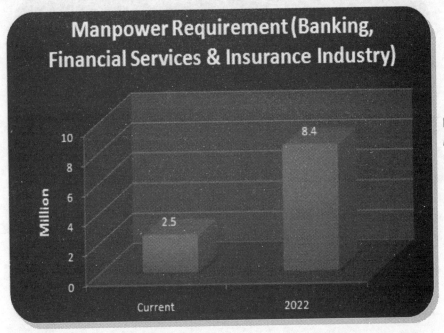

Figure 4.15: Manpower Requirement (Banking, Financial Services & Insurance Industry)

Figure 4.16: Manpower Requirement (Textile & Clothing Industry)

Figure 4.17: Manpower Requirement (Organized Retail Industry)

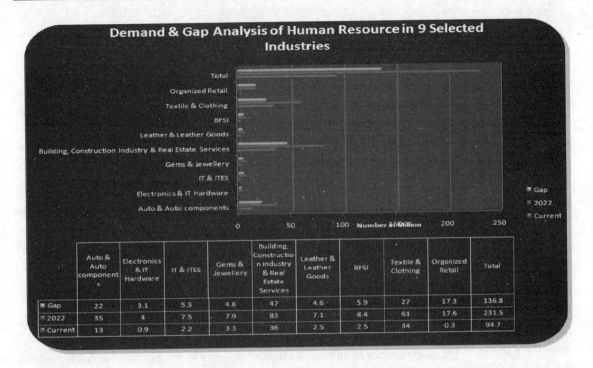

Figure 4.18: Demand & Gap Analysis of Human Resource in 9 Selected Industries

Let us have look at the various qualitative and quantitative methods that can be employed to forecast the demand of workforce:

A. Qualitative Methods

a. Judgemental Methods: Employee and managerial judgement are used to forecast the demand of labour. The approach could differ from choosing to employ only managerial judgement (more of a top to down driven forecasting) to something like using a combination of employee and managerial judgement (more of a down-up driven approach).

b. Delphi Technique: The Delphi technique employs the judgement of the experts. Generally a panel of experts is chosen. They are then polled for their forecasts. The average of such forecasts is then taken as the demand of workforce in that firm.

B. Quantitative Methods

Qualitative methods have their own limitations and hence reliance is more on more hard-data driven forecasts. Two commonly used quantitative techniques are:

a. **Trend Analysis:** In trend analysis first a business factor relevant to human resource needs is chosen, for example sales, production, etc. After this a historical trend of the business factor in relation to number of employees is plotted. The ratio of employees to the business factor provides a labor productivity ratio (for example, sales per employee or units produced per employee etc.). Then such ratios are compared for at least the past five years. Finally, human resources demand is calculated by dividing the business factor by the productivity ratio and projection of human resources demand is done to the target year.

b. **Workload Analysis:** In workload analysis, after considering the workload, the planned man-hours are calculated. Then the productive hours per worker is estimated. The total of planned-man-hours is divided by the productive hours per worker to forecast the demand of workers.

Supply Forecasting

Internal Supply Forecasting

Internal supply forecast essentially draws upon the number of outflows & inflows of human resources.

The internal supply forecast essentially draws upon the number of outflows and number of inflows of human resources in an organisation. Such outflows & inflows have to be mapped for individual jobs. The most commonly supply of labor is Markov Analysis.

Markov Analysis

Markov Analysis

Markov analysis, also known as transition probability matrix or renewal/replacement matrix is a useful way to forecast the internal supply of labour.

Markov Analysis, also known as transition probability matrix or renewal/replacement analysis is a very useful way to forecast the internal supply of labor. No workforce is ever static. Employees are hired, they retire, they are promoted, they resign or are terminated etc. Markov Analysis attempts to project how the current workforce of a firm would look like if the current process of mobility continues. In other words, Markov Analysis does the following:

i. Maps the mobility of people in an organization
ii. Translates such maps into mutually exclusive states. The Organization structure is converted into a matrix. The rows represent the state in Time 1 and the columns represent the state in Time 2.
iii. Determine the probability of movement of people.

Here is a **simple illustration of Markov Analysis**

		JA	JB	JC	JD	JE	JF	Exit
JA	100	0.70	0.20	0.05				0.05
JB	100		0.60	0.15	0.10			0.10
JC	100			0.80	0.05		0.05	0.10
JD	100				0.50	0.25	0.15	0.10
JE	100					0.80	0.20	-
JF	100					0.20	0.70	0.10

In the Matrix given above, there are two time states – time state 1 and time state 2. In time state 1 each of the six jobs – Job A (JA), Job B (JB), Job C (JC), Job D (JD), Job E (JE) and Job F (JF) have 100 incumbents. The rest of the cells show the percentage of people likely to stay in a particular job or likely to move into other jobs or their likelihood to leave (Exit) for example, take the first row. It shows that 70 percent of the people in time state 1 are likely to stay in Job A in time state 2; 20 percent of people are likely to move to Job B, 5 percent to Job C and 5 percent of people are likely to quit in time state 2. Now these percentages are replaced by numbers.

		JA	JB	JC	JD	JE	JF	Exit
JA	100	0.70 (70)	0.20 (20)	0.05 (5)			0.05 (5)	
JB	100		0.60 (60)	0.15 (15)	0.10 (10)			0.15 (15)
JC	100			0.80 (80)	0.05 (5)		0.05 (5)	0.10 (10)
JD	100				0.50 (50)	0.25 (25)	0.15 (15)	0.10 (10)
JE	100					0.80 (80)	0.20 (20)	-
JF	100					0.20 (20)	0.70 (70)	0.10 (10)
		70	80	100	65	125	115	45

Each column is then totaled. For instance, the total of Column A is 70, which means that only 70 people who were in time state 1 are likely to be in Job A in time state 2 as well. There is a likely shortage of 30 people in Job A. The table given below shows the likelihood of people staying in the same jobs in time state 2 as in time state1 and probability of shortage or surplus

	Number of People in Respective Jobs in Time State 2	Shortage/Surplus
JA	70	-30
JB	80	-20
JC	100	0
JD	65	-35
JE	125	+25
JF	115	+15

Job E and F show a surplus of 25 and 15 people respectively. Based on these calculations, the probability of movement of people is determined. Based on such probabilities, surplus or shortage strategies are worked-out. The shortage strategies would include all way to reduce workforce headcount (like not re-hiring for vacant positions, freezing hiring, cross-training resources to improve utilization, retrenching or laying off employees, introduction of VRS etc.) the surplus strategies on the other hand would include everything to increase workforce head count (for example speeding-up hiring process, attracting ex-employees back, providing incentives to delay retirements, skilling people to meet the growing human resource needs, hiring temps etc.)

Company	Staff Cost (Rs. Crores)		% increase	% of Revenue	
	2011	2010		2011	2010
Infosys	14,856	12,093	24	54	53
TCS	13,726	10,879	26	37	36
Wipro	12,687	10,723	18	41	40

Human resource planning helps a firm by not only improving its efficiencies but also by bringing it in a state of dynamic equilibrium; consequently, keeping it in a state of readiness towards human resource and talent needs. Some of the biggest concerns of any firm are – how to efficiently utilize the competencies of existing workforce, how to predict the need of human resource in future, how to gauge possible supply sources and whether they shall be enough or not and finally how to keep human resource cost under control without compromising on their timely and effective availability in the organization. Human resource planning answers all such concerns.

Sample Exercises on Markov Analysis

Exercise 1:
In Madura Private limited, there were five different kinds of jobs named as Job A, Job B, Job C, Job D and Job E. In March 2010 it was observed that 50 people were employed in Job A and similarly 75, 100, 200, 300 in Job B – E respectively. Between March 2010-11, 15% & 20% of those who were doing Job A moved into Job B and C respectively. 5% of Job A incumbents left the job. In the similar manner, in Job B, 10% & 5% of those who were in job B moved to Job A & Job C respectively. 5% of Job B incumbents left the job. Another 5%, 10%, 5%, 10% in Job C moved to A, D, B, E respectively. 10% left the job. 20 % of Job D incumbents also left the job and 20% of those who were in Job E moved to Job C. Lastly 20 % of Job E got better offers and they left the organization.

Question: Find out minimum requirement of new hires to be made for each job in 20011.

Exercise 2:
It is now January 2012. Your task is to predict supply and demand for each job category as of January 2013 and to plan what to do to meet the demand.

- You have 50 HR executives, 20 percent of them are likely to be promoted as senior HR executives and another 10 percent might leave the organization.
- Out of the 30 senior HR Executives 20 percent of them may be promoted as Managers-HR. 10 % of senior HR Executives may leave the organization.
- There are 20 Managers-HR on field. The company is revamping its training department and wants its Managers-HR to join as training managers. At least 50 percent of Managers – HRs are likely to be taken as training manager at Corporate Headquarters.

Since the company is expanding into new cities hence it wants 10 percent more people at every position next year onwards.

Question: Plan minimum number of hires for each position in Jan. 2011.

Essay Questions

1. What is Human Resource Planning? What is its importance and how is it related to other HR functions?

2. What kind of implications do HRP programs have on any organization?

3. Discuss the various factors affecting human resource planning. What kind of manpower shortage does Indian industry face today?

4. What is demand forecasting? Discuss various methods of demand forecasting.

5. What is supply forecasting? Describe 'Markov Analysis' with an example.

Application Questions

1. Solve the Exercise 1 and Exercise 2 given at the end of chapter and write your interpretations.

2. Select a medium sized firm or a SME and do a project on preparing a Human Resource Plan.

Bibliography

Alpander, & Guvenc, G. (1980). Human Resource Planning in U.S. Corporation. *California Management Review, 22* (3), 24-32.

Andrew, O., & Manzini. (1988). Integrating Human Resource Planning and Development: The Unification of Strategic, Operational, and Human Resource Planning Systems; *Human Resource Planning, 11* (2), 79.

Baytos, L. (1984). A "No Frills" Approach to Human Resource Planning. *Human Resource Planning , 7* (1), 39-46.

Bright, W. E. (1976). How One Company Manages its Human Resources. *Harvard Business Review, 54* (1), 81-93.

Burack, E. H. (1986). Corporate Business and Human Resources Planning Practices: Strategic Issues and Concerns. *Organizational Dynamics, 15* (1), 73-87.

Buss, T. F. (1986). Unemployment Rates and Their Implications for Human Resource Planning. *Journal of Economic & Social Measurement, 14* (1), 1-18.

Dyer, L., & Heyer, N. O. (1984). Human Resource Planning at IBM. *Human Resource Planning, 7*(3), 111-125.

Forbes, J., & Benjamin. (1983). Human Resource Planning: Applications and Evaluation of Markov Analysis. *Academy of Management Proceedings*, 287-291.

Hoffman, W. H., Wyatt, L., & Gordon, G. G. (1986). Human Resource Planning: Shifting from Concept to Contemporary Practice. *Human Resource Planning, 9*(3), 97-105.

Huselid, M. A. (1993). The Impact of Environmental Volatility on Human Resource Planning and Strategic Human Resource Management. *Human Resource Planning, 16*(3), 35.

Jack, w. (1984). Human Resource Planning: The Ideal versus the Real. *Human Resource Planning, 7*(2), 67-72.

Kogan, K., & Hawang, N. C. R. (2003). Dynamic Approach to Human Resources Planning for Major Professional Companies with a Peak-wise Demand. *International Journal of Production Research, 41*(6), 1255-1271.

Mills, D. Q. (1985). Planning with People in Mind. *Harvard Business Review, 63*(4), 97-105.

Narahari, N. S., Murthy, & Narasimha, H. N. (2009). System Dynamic Modeling of Human Resource Planning for a Typical IT Organization. *CURIE Journal, 2*(3), 33-45.

Peters, J. W. (1988). Strategic Staffing: A Key Link in Business and Human Resource Planning. *Human Resource Planning, 11*(2), 151.

Rao, V. (1965). Planning For Better Utilization of Human Resources. *Advanced Management Journal, 30*(3), 34.

Stadnyk, R. L., Keefe, J. M., Knight, L., Martin, M. A., & Legare, J. (2011). Key Issues in Human Resource Planning for Home Support Workers in Canada. *40*(1), 21-28.

Strauss, J. S., & Burack, E. H. (1983). The Human Resource Planning Professional: A Challenge In Change. *Human Resource Planning, 6*(1), 1-9.

Ulrich, D. (1986). Human Resource Planning As a Competitive Edge. *Human Resource Planning, 9*(2), 41-50.

Walker, A. J. (1986). New Technologies in Human Resource Planning. *Human Resource Planning, 9*(4), 149-159.

Gatewood, R. D., & Rockmore, W. B. Combining Organizatioal Manpower and Career Development Needs: an Operational Human Resource Planning Model. *Human Resource Planning, 19*, 81-96.

Gilliespie, J. F., Lebvinger, W. E., & Kahalas, H. A Human Resorce Planning and Valuation Model. *Academy of Management Journal, 19*(4), 650-656.

Hestwood, T. M. (1984). Human Resource Planning & Compensation: A Marriage of Convenience. *Human Resource Planning*, 141-150.

Jacobson, W. S. (2010). Preparing for Tomorrow: A Case Study of Work Force Planning in North Caronling Municipal Government. *Public Personal Management, 39*(4), 353-377.

Lopez, F. M. (1981). Toward a better system of Human Resource Planning. *Advanced Management Journal*, 4-14.

Manzini, A. O. Human Resource Planning for Mergers & Acquisition: Preparing for the People Issues that can Prevent Merger Synergies. *Human Rresource Planning, 9* (2), 51-57.

Manzini, A. O. (1984). Human Resource Planning Observations on the State of the Art and State of the Practice. *Human Resource Planning*, 105-110.

Mouly, J. (n.d.). Human Resource Planning as a Part of Economic Development Planning. *International Labour Review*, 107-184.

Munson, J. C., & Murdick, R. G. (1985). The Relational Database for Facilitating HRD. *Human Resource Planning*, 19-27.

Reynierse, J. H., & Harker, J. B. (1986). Measuring & Managing Organizational Culture. *Human Resource Planning, 19*, 1-15.

Rush, J. c., & Borne, L. C. (1983). Human Resource Planning Contributions to Corporate Planning at Ontario Hydro. *Human Resource Planning*, 193-205.

Schuler, R. Scanning the Environment: Planning for Human Resource Management and Organizational Change. *Human Resource Planning, 12* (4), 257-276.

Chapter 5

Job Analysis

Outline

Introduction
What is a Job?
What is Job Analysis?
Primary Actors in Job Analysis
Use of Job Analysis Data
Process Steps in Job Analysis
Data Collection Methods
Job Analysis Interview Format
Instructions for Completing PAQ
Factors to be Considered in Collection of Job Analysis Data
Sample Exhibits of Actual Job Analysis using PAQ
Additional Job Information
Decision Making/Problem Solving
Training for Senior/Middle Level Management
Development Activities
Essay Questions
Application Questions
Bibliography

Key Terms

Compensation
Data Collection Methods
Human Resource Planning
Job Analysis
Job Analysis Interview Format
Job Design
Performance Management
Process Steps in Job Analysis
Recruitment
Selection

Introduction

Job Analysis is a significant step in the entire human resource function, owing to multifaceted use of the data thus obtained from the same.

In this chapter we shall focus on the following:

- What is a Job?
- What is Job Analysis?
- Multiple uses of Job Analysis Data
- Primary actors in job analysis process
- Process steps of Job Analysis
- Data Collection techniques
- Position Analysis Questionnaire (PAQ)
- PAQ used in Arizona State University (ASU)
- Instructions on how to use PAQ-ASU
- Sample Exhibits of actual job analysis using PAQ

What is a Job?

Job
A job is a rational set of tasks & responsibilities almost having the same level of complexity and related set of functions that are performed by an individual or a team.

A job is a rational set of tasks and responsibilities almost having the same level of complexity and related set of functions that are performed by an individual or a team.

A job will always be accompanied by:

- A set of tasks and sub-tasks;
- Duties & responsibilities;
- Supervision and reporting;
- Accountability and authority.

Job-incumbent is the person(s) who accomplishes the job.

What is Job Analysis?

Job Analysis
Job analysis is to understand what the job is all about. It is a planned study of job & job elements, employing a scientific technique.

Job analysis, most simplistically defined is to understand what the job is all about. Precisely job analysis is a planned study and analysis of job and job-elements, employing a scientific technique.

Job analysis data helps to articulate two primary components.

a. **Job Description (JDs):** This clearly expresses the set of tasks, roles and responsibilities of a particular job.

b. **Job Specification:** This expresses what the 'ideal candidate' should be like who can accomplish this job.

Primary Actors in Job Analysis

The primary actors in job analysis process are:

1. The job incumbent himself/herself.
2. The job supervisor.
3. The Human Resource Department.
4. External Analysts (if a company decides to hire external experts or partly outsource this activity).

All these will play role right from initiation to collection & validation of data and to final vetting.

Use of Job Analysis Data

Job analysis data has multiple uses, besides understanding the nature of the job itself.

a) **Human Resource Planning:** Forecasting the demand and supply of workforce is an important foundation function and job analysis data helps in such planning activities.

b) **Recruitment:** Even before a firm starts looking for a candidate or a prospective employee, it should be clear about the purpose behind that search. The purpose is defined by the job and the best answer to that comes from the job analysis data.

c) **Selection:** A reliable, valid selection process could always be able to employ tool and techniques which shall enable selection of the right candidate and vice-versa. One of the most fundamental information to get this right is to first understand what the 'ideal candidate' should be like. The job analysis data provides the answers again.

d) **Fitment:** Person-job fit is best achieved when both are well understood and then matched. The job analysis data is obviously critical in achieving the same.

e) **Performance Management:** Effective setting of performance objectives, key result areas (KRAs) and performance benchmarks is only possible when the job is understood well.

f) **Training**: The job analysis data provides deep insight into the kinds of competencies required to successfully accomplish a particular job. This in turn, when matched with individual employee, helps a firm to identify competency-gaps and training needs.

g) **Compensation**: Job analysis data help identification of 'compensable factors' which not only help in fixing the right compensation for a job but also in maintaining adequate differentials between jobs.

h) **Job Design**: The design aspects of a job are closely related to innovation, efficiency, motivation. Job analysis data is one of the fodders for job design.

Besides these, job analysis data becomes useful in variety of HR functions and activities.

Process Steps in Job Analysis

The process steps in job analysis have been diagrammatically exhibited below:

Figure 5.1:
Process Steps in Job Analysis

Data Collection Methods

The various methods of data collection of job analysis data are:

a) Critical Incident Method: In this method the entire job may not be studied. Only the critical incident and critical behavior expected in that particular job context is recorded.

b) Work Observation: The observation method may be employed to collect job analysis data. It will involve observation of the job incumbent performing the job in the workplace, over a period of time, and recording data

c) Performance Data: The performance data of a worker or workers on a job may be the source of job analysis data.

d) Interview Method: Interview of the job incumbents, supervisors, subject matter experts can also be employed for collecting job analysis data.

e) Questionnaire Method: Questionnaire method is very commonly used for collection of job analysis data.

A Sample of similar questionnaire is given below:

Job Analysis Interview Format

Name of the person Interviewed: ....

Designation (Job Title): ....

Organization: ....

Name of the interviewer: ....

1. What are your primary duties in your current profile?
2. Please provide a summary of your job in terms of different roles that you play.
3. What are your main responsibilities?
4. What machines/equipments are important for your job?
5. What kind of forms or materials do you use?

6. Who are you supposed to supervise and what kind of supervisions are you supposed to give?
7. Whom do you report to?
8. Which kind of working conditions are ideal for your job?
9. Does your job pose any hazard to you? Please elaborate.
10. What kind of safety mechanisms do you adopt to thwart the hazards?
11. What kind of educational qualifications are desirable and essential for your job?
12. How many years of experience and what nature of experience is desirable for your job?
13. Have you received any training for your job? Do you think any training is required?
14. What level of judgment is desirable to make decisions at your level?
15. Do you think your job requires a high level of initiative?
16. Does your job demand high level of physical involvement?
17. How much Communication Skill has a role in your job?
18. Does your job demand any unusual sensory ability?
19. Do you think emotionality has any role in your job?
20. What kind of accountability is important for your job?

More standardized questionnaire includes Position Analysis Questionnaire (PAQ), Management Position Description Questionnaire (MPDQ) etc.

A sample exhibit of a Position Analysis Questionnaire (PAQ) used by the Human Resource Department of a State University is given below, followed by a set of instructions on how to complete this questionnaire to ensure clarity and better understanding.

Position Analysis Questionnaire

Used to document details of position attributes to prepare or update a job description.

Overview and Instructions

Process

- Complete the questionnaire, providing as much detail as possible.
- Sign and route to your immediate supervisor for review ONLY.
- If edits, comments or additional information/explanation is necessary, the supervisor should add information in the supervisor's comment section (provide section references for clarification).
- Supervisor signs and dates document and forwards to Compensation.
- Please be sure to keep a copy of the completed document for future reference.

Compensation will review the questionnaire for completeness and ask follow-up questions if necessary or request a desk interview. A job description will result from this questionnaire.

Preparation

The answers to this questionnaire should describe the various aspects of the work performed; therefore, be as thorough and detailed as possible when completing this questionnaire.

Keep in mind the following questions:

- What is the most important (critical) task performed? (NOT the task that takes up the most time)
- Who do you rely on for information necessary to do your job and why?
- Who do you routinely provide information to and why?
- Are there tasks that must be completed prior to your beginning your job?
- What happens if these tasks are not done?
- Why does your job exist? (This is the 20-second elevator answer.)

Section 1:

General Information

Your Name:

Today's Date (mm/dd/yy):

Current Job Title (system):

Working Job Title (if different):

Department Name:

College/Institute:

Supervisor's Name:

Supervisor's Title:

Job Category:

Length of time in current position:

Length of time with the SU:

Section 2:

Organizational Relationships

In this section, you will identify reporting relationships.

The purpose is to state the position that provides work direction, completes performance reviews and provides guidance, counseling and/or corrective/disciplinary action relative to your position.

For those positions that report to you, it is in the same context.

If you report to more than one position, indicate both and for what purpose.

To whom do you report (title)?

Who reports to you (title)?

Please attach a copy of the current department/unit organizational chart.

Section 3:

Essential Functions (Duties/Responsibilities)

Indicate the **principle duties and responsibilities** performed in this job.

Group your job duties into **major areas** and then list the **associated tasks** in order of importance, beginning with the most important.

Please also indicate the **approximate percentage of time** spent on each task. When

indicating time spent, please state the time reference (% of day, month, quarter or year) appropriate to that task.

Be as descriptive as possible—indicating the desired outcome (or reason) why a specific task is performed. If **additional references or information** may assist in understanding the task, please attach at the end of the document.

% of Time	Major Area(s) of Responsibility

Section 4:

Additional Job Information

Indicate the specific knowledge, skills and abilities your job requires. Think in terms of recruiting to fill a job identical to yours. What background would you expect a successful job applicant to have?

Are there any formal guidelines, regulations, policies or statutes you must follow and understand to perform your job?

I need knowledge of:
I need skill in:
I need the ability to:

Section 5:

Decision Making/Problem Solving

Think about the types of issues your position is held accountable/responsible for completing.

What decisions would you consult or notify your supervisor of before taking action?

What type of issues, concerns or problems come to you to resolve?

List the formal guidelines, technical manuals, regulations, statutes and other policies with which you must comply to perform your job:

What issues would you refer to your supervisor prior to taking action and why?

Please describe the major challenges you consider part of your job duties/responsibilities:

If you supervise others (provide work direction, responsible for performance evaluations, initiate corrective actions or recommend career actions), what issues, concerns or problems are referred to you and what action do you take?

Are you responsible for a budget? ☐ YES ☐ NO

If yes, please describe your participation in the budgetary process.

Section 6:

Working Environment

Describe the physical conditions in which your job is performed on a regular basis (include such items as lifting, pushing, climbing, walking, exposure to different environmental influences as well as estimated percentage of time).

How would you describe the mental and emotional environment under which you regularly perform your job? Examples of situations are helpful to put your job in context.

What type of equipment, tools, instruments, machines or other similar objects are used? Please list and provide approximate time spent:

Section 7:

Minimum Qualifications

Are there any certifications, licenses or registrations required?

Indicate the minimum level of education that would prepare someone to perform this job.

Indicate the minimum number of years of prior experience as well as the type of experience needed to be prepared to perform this job.

Section 8:

Primary Purpose (Position Objective)

In NOT MORE THAN three (3) sentences, answer the following question:

Why does my job exist?

Remember to focus on the end results or outcome of the position. This is your 20-second elevator ride explanation of your job to a stranger, friend or family member.

Signature: _____

Date (mm/dd/yy):

Supervisor's Section

I have reviewed the content of this document and agree with the content as presented.

Signature: _____

Date:

I have reviewed the content of this document and would like to make the following additions/clarifications:

Signature: _____

Date (mm/dd/yy):

> This PAQ is a standard form designed at Arizona State University and has been published as a sample exhibit with due permission from Ms. Carol L. Hurst, Director, Compensation, Office of Human Resources, Arizona State University.

Instructions for Completing PAQ

When conducting a desk audit, the primary purpose is to gather as much data from the job holder as possible using a combination of both visual observation of the job as it is performed at the actual work site as well as a verbal interview of the job holder.

When conducting the audit, keep the following in mind:

1. What is done – this is the "task statement"

2. How it is done – this is the tools, methods, standards by which the task is completed

3. Why it is done – this puts the task in context of the reason for actually doing the task

The purpose for collecting data in such a way to be able to answer each of these items is that ultimately the notes of the desk audit are compiled and then distilled into a finalized job description. It is important that the more detailed the notes taken during the interview, the better to be able to properly classify the jobs (differentiating between levels, scope/breadth of work).

Topics to Cover

1) Describe, in your own words, what is the primary reason or purpose this job exists.

   Note: The incumbent may not be able to articulate this immediately, so it is helpful to save this question for the end…so, to summarize, how would you describe what this job is all about…OR think about how you describe what you do to your friends, significant others, etc.

2) **ADA Stuff:** do you have to lift/pull/push/climb/crawl…what environment is the job performed (standard office environment? Outdoors…if so how much time outdoors…subject to heat/cold/damp/hazardous materials…be sure to capture what type and how often.

Many of these items you can pick up as part of just observing the job...asking to see how the incumbent actually changes out a hard drive (do they have to crawl under a desk? Work in a cramped location?

3) Essential Tasks : These are the task statements of the job description that you want to be sure are identified as essential; how to differentiate between essential and marginal would be picked up from how the incumbent describes the task i.e. on occasion, I may be asked to do XXXX

> **Note:** It is important to understand context of job, type of tasks (how routine, closely/loosely supervised, problem solving/independent decision making etc...remember asking to give examples helps in the understanding of the job.

4) Minimum Qualifications: Have the incumbent state in their own words what does it take to do this job...what do you think...if you were to go on to another opportunity, and you were to hire your replacement, what do you feel is necessary to be successful in this role?

   a. Be sure to ask about any licensing, certifications, etc...again, the incumbent may say that he/she has X...but it is your job to determine if this X is a true minimum qualification or a nice to have

   b. Be sure to break out education, experience...you may need to ask this in several ways as it is important to separate the incumbent from the job; for the job holder, this is sometimes difficult. Be sure to ask type of education, type and quantity of experience

5) Scope/Breadth Dimensions of the Job:

   a. Responsibility for supervision of others...and what type (participates in, initiates action...and what type of action, up to what point is it held at this level of the job and at what point is it passed up the chain of command).

   b. Responsibility for operating/expense budget...again, what type, how extensive and at what point is it passed up the ladder

   c. How does work come to you, is it in meetings, via email, do you come up with work?

   d. What type of things/decisions do you have control/ownership of...and what do you "throw over the wall" to your supervisor for advice, suggestions, collaboration...or ownership?

6) **Reporting Relationship:** Meaning, what position title does this job report to, what position titles report to this job (remember...incumbents change, the job titles may be more stable).

7) **Skills/Competencies:** What other knowledge, skills, abilities do you think are useful, necessary or nice to haves that make you successful in performing your job?

8) **Managers/Directors:** Be sure to cover such items as describe your role/participation in strategic planning, operating budget development/monitoring/reporting, performance and career management of staff.

"Remember that out of the box, the person who is being interviewed will wonder the purpose of doing this exercise. You want to ask each interviewee if they know why you are conducting the interview (the typical response is...yeah, but I'm not really sure) Be sure to be clear that the purpose of conducting the desk audit/interview is to capture information about "your job, how you do it...this is your opportunity to talk to me about everything that you do in your job...all I will be doing is taking notes and occasionally asking a couple of questions to be sure I understand what your describing" You want to put the person at ease, reassure them that this has nothing to do with how well they perform their job, but it is all about describing the job how it is being performed today and be sure it is accurately titled and documented."

Logistics

It is best practice to work through the area administrative support to have that individual coordinate schedules. Provide this person with the parameter of setting at least 1 hour per interview with about 10 minute break between (or take into consideration any travel time between physical locations). Also, be sure to do a touch base with the management person of the group that you're conducting the desk audits (if they are not part of the exercise) so that you give management an opportunity to provide background and insight relative to the jobs studied; take this opportunity to probe for potential/planned organizational shifts, dynamics between staff members which may color (enhance) responses or any other areas/issues that may effect the exercise.

(**Source:** Carol Hurst, ASU, USA)

Factors to be Considered in Collection of Job Analysis Data

1. **Freedom from Bias (exaggeration/hiding of facts):** Respondents at times tend to exaggerate the facts to show the complexity of their jobs and consequently their mastery over the same. Vice-versa few also tend to hide the facts emanating out of their fear as they suspect that the organization may find him/her incompetent. Both exaggeration and hiding of facts will lead to erroneous data and hence care should be taken by the data collector that such bias do not occur.

2. **Allaying Anxiety Respondents:** As told earlier, some respondents look at this activity with suspicion and think that it may be a management's covert strategy which may harm them in the long-run. Allaying all such fears and anxieties is very important to ensure correctness and consistency of data.

3. **Use of Right Data Collection Method:** Choosing a right data collection method is very important in conducting job analysis. Out of the various methods available the method which suits best must be selected and not necessarily the 'best method'.

4. **Recency Impact:** Respondents tend to talk about their job aspects more which have occurred recently or they have been more involved in the recent past, while ignoring other dimensions. Interviewer must ensure that such errors do not occur and guide the respondents in overcoming this bias.

5. **Commitment:** The commitment of the top management, line functions and finally of the HR department is paramount to ensure the success of job analysis.

Sample Exhibits of Actual Job Analysis using PAQ

Exhibit 1: JA of a Senior Manager in India's Premier Commercial Vehicle Manufacturers

Section 1:

GENERAL INFORMATION

YOUR NAME: ABC

TODAY's DATE (mm/dd/yy):

CURRENT JOB TITLE (system): SENIOR MANAGER.

WORKING JOB TITLE (if different): SAME

DEPARTMENT NAME: XYZ MOTORS Pvt. Ltd

JOB CATEGORY: PRODUCTION

LENGTH OF TIME IN CURRENT POSITION: 2 YEARS and 6 MONTHS

LENGTH OF TIME WITH INDICO MOTORS Pvt. Ltd.: 15 YEARS (approx.)

Section 2:

ORGANIZATIONAL RELATIONSHIP

1. To whom do you report?

    - Managing Director

2. Who report to you?

    - Supervisors

Section 3:
ESSENTIAL FUNCTIONS (DUTIES/RESPONSIBILITIES)

Percentage of Time	Major area of Responsibilities
30%	Administrative Stream - Project Management and work planning (Presentation and Communicating plan)
30%	Actual Work Stream - Monitoring the whole production process
20%	Clients care - Making business relationship with clients
20%	Working on a new project of branch extension - Bangalore branch is new, working for its further development.

Section 4:

ADDITIONAL JOB INFORMATION

1. I need knowledge of:
   - Statistical Technique – Linear Regression and Logistics
   - Factor Analysis
   - Domain knowledge about motor parts
2. I need skill in :
   - Software Skills
   - Practical skills of production work to see every things go correct
3. I need ability to :
   - Access information through legal process

Section 5:

DECISION MAKING/PROBLEM SOLVING

1. What things will you take in consideration while performing your job?
   - Client confidentiality
   - All legal binding of Government of India
   - All model should satisfy statistical cut-off specified in technical guideline
   - Know your client policies
2. What issues would you refer to your supervisors prior to taking action and why?
   - Issues related to production and client's requirement because our production is client's requirement specific and number of units changes with every new contract.
3. What major challenges consider the part of your job duties?
   - Getting the assignments ready in due time
   - System Infrastructure and labour availability
   - Changing client requirement
   - Effective management of available resources

4. **While supervising others what issues are referred to you and what action do you take?**

    - Competencies—

    ➢ Lack of technical skills – Through technical training

    - Mind-set

    ➢ If person who reports to you having egoist approach – training and motivations then warning, if require further action

Section 6:

WORKING ENVIRONMENT

1. Describe the physical condition in which your job is performed on a regular basis?

    - Management work in my personal office and monitoring job of production process in the work place.

2. How would you describe the mental and emotional environment under which you regularly perform your job?

    - Working for an automobile part manufacturing company, all other companies are equally competent hence there is a very competitive environment so you should always be on the toes.

    - We are working hard to get an edge over others by technological improvements (Bangalore branch)

    - A sensitive job, if something goes wrong whole name of company will be spoiled

Section 7:

MINIMUM QUALIFICATIONS

1. Is there any certification, license or registration required for this job?

    - Not required

2. Minimum level of education required for the job?

    - PG in Management (MBA)

Section 8:

PRIMARY PURPOSE (Position Objective)

In NOT MORE THAN three (3) sentences, answer the following question: Why does my job exist?

I am solely responsible for management, production function, and growth of the company at Bangalore. I exist just because I am a value enhancer for the business of the company. I am a link between the company and people associated with it in the area assigned to me.

Training Provided by the Organization

As far as training is concerned, the same is provided to the employee according to the type of work expected from them.

Exhibit 2: JA of a Manager-Software Development of a Leading Internet Solutions & Networking Company

Section 1:

GENERAL INFORMATION

Your Name: ABC

Today's Date (mm/dd/yy): 02/12/2012

Current Job Title (system): MANAGER SOFTWARE DEVELOPMENT

Working Job Title (if different): SAME

Department Name:

Head's Name:

Head's Title: DIRECTOR

Job Category: MANAGEMENT

Length of time in current position: 13 YEARS 6 MONTHS

Section 2:

ORGANIZATIONAL RELATIONSHIPS

In this section, you will identify reporting relationships. The purpose is to state the position that provides work direction, completes performance reviews and provides guidance, counseling and/or corrective/disciplinary action relative to your position.

For those positions that report to you, it is in the same context. If you report to more than one position, indicate both and for what purpose.

To whom do you report (title)?

I generally report to the 2ND level manager

Who reports to you (title)?

Engineer, junior engineer, Technician and 6 other staffs

Section 3:

ESSENTIAL FUNCTIONS

(Duties/Responsibilities)

Indicate the principle duties and responsibilities performed in this job. Group your job duties into major areas and then list the associated tasks in order of importance, beginning with the most important.

Please also indicate the approximate percentage of time spent on each task When indicating time spent, please state the time reference (% of day, month, quarter or year).

Be as descriptive as possible indicating the desired outcome (or reason) why a specific task is performed. If additional references or information may assist in understanding the task, please attach at the end of the document.

% of Time	Major Area(s) of Responsibility
50%	WORK
40%	MEETING

Some key responsibilities

1) Working with managers to implement the company's policies and goals.

2) Monitoring the production processes and adjusting schedules as needed.

3) Liaising among different departments.

4) Project delivery to the customers.

Section 4:

ADDITIONAL JOB INFORMATION

Indicate the specific knowledge, skills and abilities your job requires. Think in terms of recruiting to fill a job identical to yours. What background would you expect a successful job applicant to have?

Are there any formal guidelines, regulations, policies or statutes you must follow and understand to perform your job?

I need knowledge of:

1. Project Management
2. Data mining
3. Managing the man power effectively.

I need skills in:

1. Management
2. Planning.
3. Leadership.
4. Communication
5. Strong interpersonal skills; a team player and independent worker.

I need the ability to:

1. Demonstrate ability to manage multiple projects simultaneously, set priorities, identify and address problems, meet deadlines, and stay within budget.
2. Demonstrated effective verbal and written communication skills.
3. Work within the time frame and as per policy and standard procedures of the organisation.

Section 5:

DECISION MAKING/PROBLEM SOLVING

Think about the types of issues your position is held accountable/responsible for completing. What decisions would you consult or notify your supervisor of before taking action? What type of issues, concerns or problems come to you to resolve?

List the formal guidelines, technical manuals, regulations, statutes and other Policies with which you must comply to perform your job:

What issues would you refer to your supervisor prior to taking action and why?

Generally crucial issues of discussions are:-

1. Project/Process duration.
2. Technology upgradation.
3. Monthly Capital shut-down timings.
4. Break-down handling strategies.

Please describe the major challenges you consider part of your job duties/responsibilities:

The major challenges and duties/responsibilities in my job are:- **Challenges**

1. Periodic Technology upgradation
2. Delay in the project.

Responsibilities

1. Relate the operations system to customer/market requirements
2. Delivery of project in time.
3. Creating project according to client need.

If you supervise others (provide work direction, responsible for performance evaluations, initiate corrective actions or recommend career actions), what issues, concerns or problems are referred to you and what action do you take?

Problems are mainly related to delay in project delivery, and I try to direct them in such a way that project can be completed before the time.

Are you responsible for a budget?

- NO

If yes, please describe your participation in the budgetary process.

Section 6:

WORKING ENVIRONMENT

Describe the physical conditions in which your job is performed on a regular basis (Include such items as lifting, pushing, climbing, walking, and exposure to different Environmental influences as well as estimated percentage of time).

The company develops programs and policies to support his employees' work-life integration, and provide a stimulating and inclusive work environment to foster their development.

The physical environment is really very comfortable with all amenities like clean area, the ventilation and temperature are always pleasant, better lighting facility, safe drinking water etc.

How would you describe the mental and emotional environment under which you regularly perform your job? Examples of situations are helpful to put your job in context.

In Cisco Systems, the employees are never kept under stress, working place are not overcrowded, workplace violence does not exists in Cisco.

What type of equipment, tools, instruments, machines or other similar objects are used? Please list and provide approximate time spent:

We are only concerned with the computers and servers to develop our projects in it.

Section 7:

MINIMUM QUALIFICATIONS

Are there any certifications, licenses or registrations required?

1. B.E./B.Tech

Indicate the minimum level of education that would prepare someone to perform this job.

1. B.E./B.Tech
2. 10 years experience as a software engineer

Indicate the minimum number of years of prior experience as well as the type of experience needed to be prepared to perform this job.

1. 10 years experience as a software engineer.
2. Management skill.
3. Planning skill.

4. Leadership skill.

5. Better communication skills

6. Demonstrated ability to manage multiple projects simultaneously.

7. Strong interpersonal skills; a team player and independent worker.

8. Demonstrated effective verbal and written communication skills.

Section 8:

PRIMARY PURPOSE (POSITION OBJECTIVE)

In NOT MORE THAN three (3) sentences, answer the following question:

What is the main purpose of your job?

The main purpose of my job is to manage the colleagues of my department and the primary work is to deliver the multiple projects in stipulated time period.

Signature: _____

Exhibit 3: JA of a Project Manager in a Global Management Consulting, Technology Consulting and Technology Outsourcing Company

Section 1:

GENERAL INFORMATION

- Name: ABC
- DATE – 27th May, 2012
- CURRENT JOB TITLE – Project Manager
- WORKING JOB TITLE – Project Manager
- DEPARTMENT – Technology Services Division
- INSTITUTE – India Delivery Centre (IDC)
- SUPERVISOR'S NAME –
- SUPERVISOR'S TITLE – Program Manager

- ➢ JOB CATEGORY - Financial Software Services
- ➢ LENGTH OF TIME IN CURRENT POSITION – 8 Years
- ➢ TOTAL EXPERIENCE – 8 Years
- ➢ PREVIOUS JOB – None
- ➢ QUALIFICATIONS – Bachelor of Engineering.

Section 2:

ORGANIZATIONAL RELATIONSHIPS

In this section, you will identify reporting relationships. The purpose is to state the position that provides work direction, completes performance reviews and provides guidance, counseling and/or corrective/disciplinary action relative to your position.

TO WHOM DO YOU REPORT?

Mr. Saurabh Bose, Project Manager

WHO REPORTS TO YOU?

A Team of 19 which include –Software developers, Test Analysts and Quality Analysts and a Team Lead.

ESSENTIAL FUNCTIONS

Indicate the principle duties and responsibilities performed in this job. Please also indicate the approximate percentage of time spent on each task.

% OF TIME	MAJOR AREAS OF RESPONSIBILITY
30%	Understanding Customer(FedEx) requirements
30%	Helping team understand the client requirements
30%	Team Meetings (Management/status/planning calls)
10%	Report Writing and Auditing

Additional Job Information

Indicate the specific knowledge, skills and abilities your job requires.

I NEED KNOWLEDGE OF?

I need knowledge of Shipping Services knowledge, the various functionalities of the modules that the team is working on, including past data.

Example: Order generation, shipment etc. It is required in order to understand the customer needs as well as to clear the doubts of team members.

I NEED SKILLS IN?

Software life cycle and application expertise. I need skill to work on and understand the various tools used to execute the functionalities.

Example: Knowledge of oracle apps e-biz suite to use forms and reports for order and invoice generation, DB2 knowledge is essential for data warehousing and Mainframe which is the framework on which the project is built.

I NEED THE ABILITY TO?

Manage teams and training skills. I need the ability to manage team activities smoothly, by ensuring that all members are given work according to their skill and competency. I also need enough leadership abilities to delegate work and to ensure that it is completed on time. Besides the above, I need to have the ability to address team grievances and solve them in a diplomatic way so as to not hurt the feelings of the persons involved. In addition, I need to have good communication skills so as to understand the customer requirements and translate the same to the team members.

Decision Making/Problem Solving

LIST THE FORMAL GUIDELINES, TECHNICAL MANUALS, REGULATIONS, STATUES AND OTHER POLICIES WITH WHICH YOU MUST COMPLY TO PERFORM YOUR JOB.

I must comply with the intellectual property right of the customer, which means that I am not allowed to discuss customer issues outside office or with any person who is not part of the same team. If there are any specific requirements of the customer regarding the work flow or the way in which a certain activity has to be carried out, then that has to be respected and followed by all team members. Apart from these, formal guidelines regarding work ethics, behavior with peers and subordinates, dress code and conduct in office premises are to be very strictly adhered to. There are also a number of policies to be followed which safeguard employee rights and ensure their safety and well being within the work premises. Team management is a major issue, ensuring max productivity with minimal downtime due to various issues.

WHAT ISSUES WOULD YOU REFER TO YOUR SUPERVISOR PRIOR TO TAKING ACTION?

Issues such as promoting a subordinate or firing them have to be referred to my supervisor before taking any action, so that he is aware of the situation and will advise on what action is to be taken. Also, decisions regarding the change of roles of an employee or shifting from one team to another has to be referred to my supervisor. Client handling issues, important status mails must be reported to project managers.

PLEASE DESCRIBE THE MAJOR CHALLENGES YOU CONSIDER PART OF YOUR JOB DUTIES:

The major challenges are with respect to the amount of knowledge that has to be acquired so as to get acquainted with the activities. Another could be imparting this knowledge to new trainees on the team and making them understand the complexities involved. Challenges could also arise when team members don't get along with each other and do not coordinate/communicate or when deadlines have to be met as the work load increases. The responsibilities include being accountable for the team's performance-good or bad, assigning work to the team, monitoring progress and ensuring completion on time. Also management of calls and to balance commitments made to the clients and resource management.

IF YOU SUPERVISE OTHERS, WHAT ISSUES, CONCERNS OR PROBLEMS ARE REFERRED TO YOU?

To keep resources interested and satisfied with his job and role. We have couple of team meetings every week to check on our progress and also to resolve issues, and we also use it to pitch in future plans and projects in the pipeline and pep talks.

ARE YOU RESPONSIBLE FOR THE BUDGET? IF YES, PLEASE DESCRIBE

Yes. Hiring resources, ensuring total resources salary and budget ratio are within the estimated costs. Increments are one of the major areas of costing every quarter. Team outings need to be addressed on a regular basis.

Working Environment

HOW WOULD YOU DESCRIBE THE MENTAL AND EMOTIONAL ENVIRONMENT UNDER WHICH YOU REGULARLY PERFORM YOUR JOB?

It's a very stressful task both mentally - where the deadlines that have to be met, and emotionally because team members need to be pulled to their limits to meet the demands of the customer.

WHAT TYPE OF EQUIPMENT, TOOLS, INSTRUMENTS, MACHINES OR SIMILAR OBJECTS ARE USED?

Desktops and servers connected through LAN/WAN, 4 Databases and finally a simulator.

Minimum Qualifications

ARE THERE ANY CERTIFICATIONS, LICENSES OR REGULATIONS REQUIRED?

Yes

INDICATE THE MINIMUM LEVEL OF EDUCATION THAT WOULD PREPARE SOMEONE TO PERFORM THIS JOB

Minimum level of education would be B.Tech/BE.

INDICATE THE MINIMUM NUMBER OF YEARS OF PRIOR EXPERIENCE AS WELL AS TYPE OF EXPERIENCE NEEDED TO BE PREPARED TO PERFORM THIS JOB

At least 7 years of prior work experience is required in a similar field which includes software development, important decision making, handling a team and its responsibilities.

Primary Purpose

My job exists in order to direct, manage and guide a team responsible for certain client activities, without which there would be a lot of chaos regarding each one's work, responsibilities and duties. In my capacity as a business analyst, I must ensure the team is well trained and has a good understanding of the application. The primary purpose of my job is to ensure the smooth working of my team, motivate them in times of crisis, extend support when they need it and also appraise them for good performance.

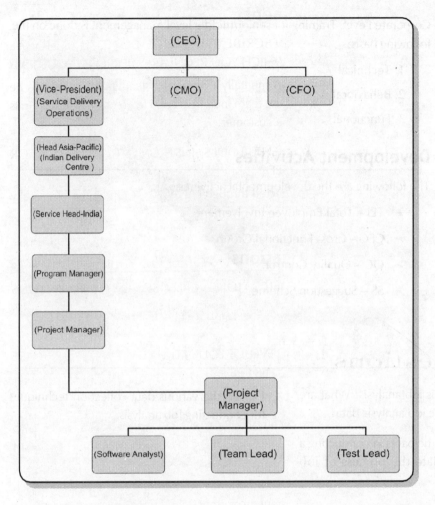

Figure 5.2: Primary Purpose

Training is an on-going process aimed at capability-building of the employees at all levels. Training Program is classified into:

> Skills,

> Knowledge, and

> Behaviour.

Training for Senior/ Middle Level Management

Both external and internal training is given for the executives. Faculty from outside agencies will be arranged for training them. They also get faculty from

Corporate Level. Training for senior/middle level management is done on the following basis:

1. Technical
2. Behavioral
3. Functional

Development Activities

The following are the developmental activities:

- TEI – Total Employee Involvement.
- CFG – Cross Functional Group.
- QC – Quality Control.
- SS – Suggestion Scheme.

Essay Questions

1. What is a job? What is job analysis? What are the various uses of the job analysis data?

2. Who are the main participants in conducting a Job analysis? Elucidate the process of Job analysis.

3. Explain the various data collection techniques for conducting Job analysis.

Application Questions

1. Select a corporate person with 5 or more years of experience and using the PAQ (given in the chapter) interview that person (face to face, telephone or E mail) Use the data to construct a Job Description (JD) and Job Specification (JS) for the position in which that person serves. Validate the JD & JS with the job-incumbent.

   (Hint-Probe well during interview and go down to find details. This shall help in developing robust JD and JS).

Bibliography

Aguinis, H., Mazurkiewicz, M. D., & Heggestad, E. D. (2009). Using Web-based Frame-of-Reference Training to Decrease Biases in Personality-based Job Analysis: An Experimental Field Study. *Personnel Psychology, 62* (2), 405-438.

Banks, M. H., Jackson, P. R., Stafford, E. M., & Warr, P. B. (1983). The Job Components Inventory and the Analysis of Jobs Requiring Limited Skill; *Personnel Psychology, 36* (1), 57-66.

Barisic, A. F., Vaupot, Z., Poor, J., & Szlavicz, A. (2008). Job Analysis and Job Evaluation Systems in the Countries of the Former Yugoslavia. *EBS Review* (24), 83-103.

Conte, J. M., Dean, M. A., Ringenbach, K. L., Moran, S. K., & Landy, F. J. (2005). The Relationship Between Work Attitudes and Job Analysis Ratings: Do Rating Scale Type and Task Discretion Matter? *Human Performance, 18* (1), 1-21.

Cornelius, E. T., Carron, T. J., & Collins, M. N. (1979). Job Analysis Models and Job Classification. *Personnel Psychology, 32* (4), 693-708.

Cucina, J., Vasilopoulos, N., & Sehgal, K. (2005). Personality-Based Job Analysis and the Self-serving Bias. *Journal of Business & Psychology, 20* (2), 275-290.

Felix, L. M., & Gerald, K. A. (1981). An Empirical Test of a Trait-oriented Job Analysis Technique. *Personnel Psychology.*

Garwood, M. K., Anderson, L. E., & Greengart, B. J. (1891). Determining Job Groups: Application of Hierarchical Agglomerative Cluster Analysis in Different Job Analysis Situations. *Personnel Psychology, 44* (4), 743-762.

Hall, D. T., & Heras, M. L. (2010). Reintegrating Job Design and Career Theory: Creating Not Just Good Jobs but Smart Jobs. *Journal of Organizational Behavior, 31* (2/3), 448-462.

Hopwood, J. O. (1935). Job Analysis And Classification in Payroll Administration. *Harvard Business Review, 13* (2), 141.

Jeffrey, C. M., Michelle, D. A., & Kathle, R. (2005). The Relationship Between Work Attitudes and Job Analysis Ratings: Do Rating Scale Type and Task Discretion Matter? *Human Performance, 18* (1), 1-21.

Johnson Jeff W, C. G., Jeff, J. W., & Gary, C. W. (2010). Validating Synthetic Validation: Comparing Traditional and Synthetic Validity Coefficients. *Personnel Psychology,* 755-795.

Jon, p. L., & Randall, D. B. (1978). The Measurement of Perceived Characteristics: The Job Diagnostic Survey versus the Job Characteristics Inventory. *Academy of Management Journal, 21* (1), 123-128.

Jones, A. P., Main, D. S., Butler, M. C., & Johnson, L. A. (1982). Narrative Job Descriptions as Potential Sources of Job Analysis Ratings. *Personnel Psychology, 35* (4), 813-828.

June, W., & Gavriel, S. (2004). The Cognitive Task Analysis Methods for Job and Task Design: Review and Reappraisal. *Behaviour & Information Technology, 23* (4), 273-299.

Kesselman, G. A., & Lopez, F. E. (1979). The Impact of Job Analysis on Employment Test Validation for Minority and Nonminority Accounting Personnel. *Personnel Psychology, 32* (1), 91-108.

Kevin, D., & Jan, J. D. (2010). Match Making and Match Breaking: The Nature of Match within and Around Job Design. *Journal of Occupational and Organizational Psychology,* 1-16.

Kim, S.-Y., & Lee, J.-Y. (2011). A Study on the Development of Korean Academic Libraries' Duty Model Based on the Job Analysis. *Aslib Proceedings, 63* (1), 76-100.

Kwok, L. K., & Oliva, I. K. (2010). Social Cynicism and Job Satisfaction – A Longitudinal Analysis,

Applied Psychology. *An International Review, 59* (2), 318–338.

Levine, E. L., Ash, R. A., Hall, H., & Sistrunk, F. (1983). Evaluation of Job Analysis Methods by Experienced Job Analysts. *Academy of Management Journal, 26* (2), 339-348.

Li, W.-D., Wang, Y., Taylor, P. J., & Shi, K. (2007). A Multilevel Analysis of Sources of Variance in Job Analysis Ratings. *Academy of Management Annual Meeting Proceedings*, p.1-6.

Lopez, F. M., Kesselman, G. A., & Lopez, F. E. (1981). An Empirical Test of a Trait-Oriented Job Analysis Technique. *Personnel Psychology, 34* (3), 479-502.

Luis R, G. M., Ronald, P. C., & Walter, T. W. (1982). A Comparison of the Practical Utility of Traditional, Statistical, and Hybrid Job Evaluation Approaches. *Academy of Management Journal, 25* (4), 790-809.

Marcia, G. K., Lance, A. E., & Barry, G. J. (1991). Determining Job Groups: Application of Hierarchical Agglomerative Cluster Analysis in Different Job Analysis Situations. *Personnel Psychology*, 44.

Mulder, M., Wesselink, R., & Bruijst, H. C. (2005). Job Profile Research for the Purchasing Profession. *International Journal of Training and Development*, 1360-3736.

Oldham, G. R., & Hackman, J. R. (2010). Not What it was and Not What it will be: The Future of Job Design Research. *Journal of Organizational Behavior, 31* (2/3), 463-479.

Safdar, R., Waheed, A., & Rafiq, K. H. (2010). Impact of Job Analysis on Job Performance: Analysis of a Hypothesized Model. *Journal of Diversity Management, 5* (2), 17-36.

Samuel, R., Douglas, H. T., & James, G. G. (1977). Job Scope and Individual Differences as Predictors of Job Involvement: Independent or Interactive? *Academy of Management Journal, 20* (2), 273-281.

Sanchez, J. I., & Levine, E. L. (2009). What is (or should be) the Difference between Competency Modeling and Traditional Job Analysis? *Human Resource Management Review, 19* (2), 53-63.

Schneider, B., & Konz, A. M. (1989). Strategic Job Analysis. *Human Resource Management, 28* (1), 51-63.

Seyin, A. H., & Ibrahim, G. R. (2007, August). Analysis of the Practice of Job Evaluation in the Metal Industry in Turkey. *Int. J. of Human Resource Management*, 1539–1556.

Shetterly, D. R., & Krishnamoorthy, A. (2008). Job Characteristics of Officers and Agents: Results of a National Job Analysis. *Public Personnel Management, 37* (1), 111-131.

Siddique, C. (2004). Job Analysis: A Strategic Human Resource Management Practice. *International Journal of Human Resource Management, 15* (1), 219-244.

Stetz, T. A., Beaubien, J. M., Keeney, M. J., & Lyons, B. D. (2008). Nonrandom Response and Rater Variance in Job Analysis Surveys: A Cause for Concern. *Public Personnel Management, 37* (2), 223-241.

Stetz, T. A., Button, S. B., & Porr, W. B. (2009). New Tricks for an Old Dog: Visualizing Job Analysis Results. *Public Personnel Management, 38* (1), 91-100.

Thomas, N. W., & Daniel, F. C. (2010). The Relationships of Age with Job Attitudes: A Meta-analysis. *Personnel Psychology*, 677–718.

Thompson, D. E., & Thompson, T. A. (1982). Court Standards for Job Analysis in Test Validation. *Personnel Psychology, 35* (4), 865-874.

Wen, D. L., Yongli, W., & Paul, T. J. (1986). Can Raters with Reduced Job Descriptive Information Provide Accurate Position Analysis Questionnaire (PAQ) Ratings? *Personnel Psychology*, 39.

Zhenijao, C., Xi, Z., Leung, L., & Fan, Z. (2010). Exploring the Interactive Effect of Time Control and Justice Perception on Job Attitudes. *The Journal of Social Psychology, 150* (2), 181–197.

Chapter 6

Recruitment

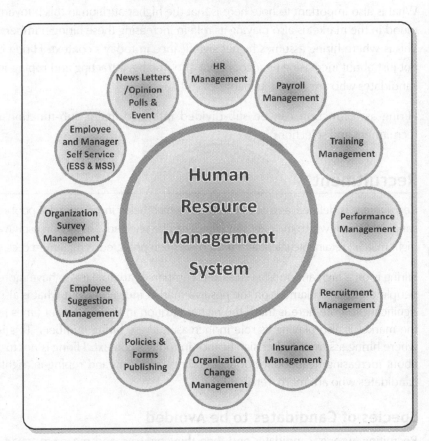

Outline

Introduction
Recruitment
Recruitment Objectives
Various Factors Affecting Recruitment
Sources of Recruitment
Recruitment Process
Recruitment Advertisements – More than a 'Vacancy' Announcement
E- Recruitment Advertisements
Advantages of E-Recruitment Advertisements
SWOT Analysis
Social Media Recruitment
Recruitment Process Outsourcing: Challenges & Opportunities
Talent Acquisition and RPO - The Current State
Defining RPO
What Recruiting Practices Drive RPO Today?
Linking Strategic Priorities and Recruiting Practices
Summary
Essay Questions
Application Questions
Bibliography

Key Terms

Descriptive Statistical Methods
Employability
Employer Brand
Factors Affecting Recruitment
Inferential Statistical Methods
Internal Factors
Political and Social Environment
Technological Environment

Introduction

Confidence in markets, buoyant economy and optimistic growth always boosts hiring. *'Between the quarter ended March 31, 2010 and the quarter ended December 31, 2010, the top 5 IT majors in India –Tata Consultancy Services (TCS), Cognizant, Infosys, Wipro and HCL Technologies – have together clocked a staggering figure of 1,14,038 net additions in terms of headcount. This stands in sharp contrast to the net addition figures of 47,462 in the corresponding year ago period'* (TOI).

What is also important to note here is that the higher attrition in this buoyant mood in the market is also playing its role in increasing these hiring numbers. This is where hiring assumes higher significance in today's context. Hiring is not just about increasing headcount but also finding, attracting and roping-in candidates who are more retainable.

Hiring as a function can be sub-divided into two major sub-functions: recruitment and selection.

Recruitment

Recruitment

Recruitment is defined as a set of activities which helps in preparing a pool of candidates from which the right candidates can be selected.

Recruitment is defined as a set of activities which helps in preparing a pool of candidates from which the right candidates can be selected. The pool must have 'right match', retainable talent and must have been prepared at minimum cost.

Hiring is on a high and most sectors and companies are looking to have more people on-board. Blame it on the positive market indicators. But what is also significant to note here is that - the higher attrition in these buoyant times in the market is also playing its role in increasing these hiring numbers. This is where hiring assumes higher significance in today's context. Hiring is not just about increasing headcount but also finding, attracting and roping-in 'right' candidates who are more 'retainable'.

Species of Candidates to be Avoided

Recruiting 'wrong' candidates and then thinking ways and means to 'retain' them is not going to work. Let us have a look at some 'species' of candidates whom recruiters should give a miss:

    a. **Paper Tigers:** Recruiters generally weed-out the visibly over and under qualified candidates but they often fall into the tarp of 'paper tigers'. These are those candidates who have qualifications and degrees on their resumes however lack real knowledge and skill. They may turn – turtle when it comes to real job performance. Looking at a combination of quality of qualification, nature of experience (rather than experience per say) and individual abilities may be a better idea.

b. **Money Grubbers:** These are candidates who use the new job offers to bargain with their current employers. Such candidates shall always show too much enthusiasm on the package even before the selection process has begun. These money grubbers are better avoided.

c. **Ever-seekers, Never-keepers:** Frequent job-hoppers are a dangerous species as although they may have worth on paper, their loyalties shift over-night. These candidates cannot be trusted.

d. **High-flyers:** Too high-profile candidates (w.r.t., the firm) are never retainable. The seeking firms were never among their aspiring set of companies and hence even if they are selected, these candidates may use the company as a stop-gap arrangement. In other words, there has to be a good match between the background and profile of the candidate and the status of the firm. Few B-tier IT companies faced this problem initially when recruiting from top-notch Indian campuses for whom Silicon Valley was the preferred destination.

e. **Dust-kickers**: It has been very aptly said *'Hire for Attitude, Train for Skill'*. People who are having obnoxious attitude are likely to be problem-creators in organization and seldom add any value despite the fact they may be good performers. Dust-kickers very rarely hit the target; forget about scoring (meeting) goals.

f. **Counterfeits:** Post-hiring reference checks and background verifications are a passe. *Back-channel referencing* is in, where the recruiters pre-qualify executives when they are initially sourcing candidates for a role by speaking to their peers within the same sector. They may also look in the public domain as well, doing a check of blogs, news media sites, social networking sites etc., to familiarize themselves with the candidate. This helps avoid fake candidates completely and avoid the hiring cost.

Back-channel Referencing
The recruiters pre-qualify executives when they are initially sourcing candidates for a role by speaking to their peers within the same sector.

g. **Job Skimmers:** High-nosed candidates and the job skimmers (i.e., those who are not very serious about changing their current jobs but are skimming jobs to see if there is anything worthwhile) are the ones to be approached with caution, as firm may end-up losing money on them since their likelihood of leaving their current jobs may be minimal. Before drafting such candidates into the recruitment pool, their seriousness about job-change must be determined.

With the job market becoming increasingly competitive and the available skills growing more diverse, recruiters need to be more selective in their choices. Poor recruiting decisions can produce long-term negative effects, among them high training and development costs to minimise the incidence of poor performance and high turnover which, in turn not only impacts employee motivation but also hampers the production of high quality goods and services and the retention of organisational knowledge. Worst, the organizations can fail to achieve their objectives thereby losing their competitive edge and their market share (Richardson).

Recruitment Objectives

Recruitment, a precursor to selection has not only been the objective of making itself more productive but also to maximize the efficiency of the selection process. The primary recruitment objectives are as follows:

1. To maximize the pool of applicants so as to provide sufficient choice at the time of selection. However care should be taken to enlarge the pool justifiably and to a feasible level. The pool size should be determined keeping in mind the human resource planning and job-analysis data.

2. To create this pool of applicants at a minimum cost possible. This is not to suggest cutting corners but keeping the cost under control, always keeping an eye on *cost per hire*.

3. To create a pool of applicants who are 'right' and 'retainable.'

4. To ensure that all recruitment procedure adhere to the policy of 'no discrimination' against caste, creed, ethnicity, colour of skin, language, gender etc., and provide an equal opportunity to all.

5. To ensure that the recruitment procedures and steps have clarity, validity and consistency in application.

6. To ensure that the recruitment policy is in line with the legal requirements of the land and also meets the various social obligations of the firm.

7. To train the pool of applicants so as to maximize their chances of selection and hence improve the success rate of the selection process.

8. To retain enough flexibility in the recruitment process so as to take care of the sudden contingent needs arising in the firm due to temporary or permanent unavailability of an employee within the firm.

9. To retain only efficient sources of recruitment and have some way to determine the same.

Example: If the profile of the candidates are being sourced from the consultants then some sort of grading system should be devised by the firm so that it can differentiate those consultant firms that provide best and more reliable matches from those whose matches are poor or the likelihood of the selection and retention upon selection of the candidate provided by them is low.

10. Creating, updating and maintaining a database of all those candidates who applied, solicited or unsolicited in the firm. This helps in present as well and future recruitments as well as to meet contingent human resource needs of the firm.

11. To ensure that recruitment personnel are properly trained and do due diligence in achieving the various recruitment objectives.

Various Factors Affecting Recruitment

The factors that affect recruitment can be broadly classified into External and Internal factors.

External Factors

The factors external to firm affecting recruitment are classified under *external factors*. They are:

1. **Labour Demand and Supply:** Demand and supply situation of labour in the market is bound to have an impact on the recruitment. If the supply of labour is in shortage, the firm tends to look within (internal recruitment) to fulfil its demand. Shortage of labour may also increase the price which a firm is ready to pay to acquire labour from outside.

2. **Employability:** The shortage is always not only in terms of headcount but also in terms of skill-gap i.e., the labour largely lack the skill required in the industry despite being educated. This reflects lack of *'employability'*. Skill shortage puts additional pressure on the recruiting firm to either 'make' their internal resources better for the new roles

or to even launch training programs for their fresh recruits-to-be after the firm identifies them as recruitment source but before the firm contemplates final offers.

3. **Employer Brand:** The image of the firm at large especially in the eyes of the probable candidates has an impact on the recruitment of the firm. Companies with strong *'employer brands'* are able to attract more and better candidates. Hence a strong employer brand has a positive impact on the recruitment function.

4. **Political and Social Environment:** Politically, the state or regional governments are dedicated to increase the prosperity of their state/region. There are companies who enter into MoU (Memorandum of Understanding) with the state/regional governments to reserve 'x' percentage of the total vacant positions for the persons, domicile of the respective state/region. The firms must honour such commitments. Similarly, there are companies whose recruitment is impacted by the social obligation that they feel for themselves.

5. **Technological Environment:** The rate of technological obsolescence in a particular industry has a direct impact on recruitment as the recruitment function must not only find people with new skills but also proactively keep on doing the same. *'New skills'* are not easy to recruit and companies may at several times have a problem with *'employability'*.

6. **Legal Environment:** Legal considerations have to be kept in mind while recruiting for the firm. For example, in India there is *'reservation'* where a particular percentage of the jobs are reserved for the people belonging to the caste of people traditionally left-out in the development process. The government firms must honour the same and private firms have limited impact of the same.

7. **Unemployment Rate:** Higher unemployment rate in a country definitely outs the supply on the surplus side and stimulates a firm to look for cheaper options.

8. **Competitors Strategy:** The companies generally are affected by the recruitment strategy adopted by the competing firms.

Example: When some companies launched training programs for university graduates to improve their skill-levels and hence their employability, other companies also followed the suit.

Internal Factors

The factors specific to the firm are referred to as *internal factors*. They are:

1. **HRP or Not:** Companies who have proper human resource planing in place are able to do a full forecasting and estimation of future demands and supply of human resources. Their recruitment is mostly proactive and targeted at fulfilling future demands.
2. **Size of the Firm:** The size of the firm also impacts recruitment. If the size of the firm is small then the recruitment is mostly 'reactive' in nature where it is mostly targeted towards fulfilling present demands. Smaller size firms also would look for more conservative sources of recruitment rather than the ones which offer more costly ones.
3. **Recruitment Policy of the Firm:** Every firm has its own recruitment policy by which it determines the timing, cost and process of recruitment that it shall follow. For instance, the choice between 'internal' and 'external' sources, e-recruitment or not, temp-hiring or not, 'window shoppers' or planned hires, etc.
4. **Budget:** The recruitment budget of the firm shall decide reach and frequency of recruitment communication. Smaller firms or smaller positions generally tend to have constricted budgets.
5. **Future Plans of the Firm:** The plans of growth/expansion/diversification by the firm are definitely likely to spur-up recruitment.

Sources of Recruitment

A. Internal Sources

Internal sources of recruitment relate to the existing employees of the firm. The company may get recruits for certain positions through transfers, promotions, re-deployment or through succession-panning. All of them shall qualify as *'internal recruits'*.

B. External Sources

The external sources of recruitment may be classified broadly under two types: the traditional and non-traditional sources of recruitment.

   a. **Traditional Sources**: The traditional sources of recruitment include the following:

   i. Recruitment Advertisements: Most common source of recruitment. However, a company decides the reach, frequency and consequently the cost of such ads vis-à-vis the benefits accrued in terms of recruitment.

ii. Employee Referrals: These are candidates who are referred to the companies by their own employees. Generally, the employee-referrals are thought to, safe-bets as they are likely to be good fits both job-wise and culturally as they have been picked-up by their own people. However this source should be guarded from nepotism.

iii. Campuses: Freshers are often recruited from the educational campuses. The companies have an opportunity thus to catch the university graduates young.

iv. Recruitment Consultants: Variety of recruitment consultants flood the market and they provide the firm with variable recruitment options.

v. Employment Exchanges: The Regional employment exchanges may sometimes provide useful database for recruitment.

vi. Leasing Firms: Certain companies may opt for leasing-out employees rather than hiring them. There are firms leasing-out employees to such companies for the time a project or a schedule lasts.

b. **Non-traditional Sources**

i. Boomerangers: These are those workers who used to work for a particular firm sometime back, then left and are now eager to come-back to the fold. This may be a win-win situation for both parties as both would have learnt from each other mistakes and also may have realized each other's value. A boomeranger is likely to be more retainable. However, the firm must definitely check why he/she left the first place before welcoming or calling the employee back. He/she should not have left for any wrongful act or with any blotches on credibility.

ii. Retired not Hurt: These are retired people who have much steam left in themselves. They can help the firm with their rich experience and knowledge. However, a firm should be cautious in testing that they do not come with a heavy baggage of rigidity and self-praise.

iii. Re-entry Workers: These are those categories of workers who used to work before and left due to certain reasons but now with toughening economic situation are eager to come back to work. Again, a good option for the firm but they should check that the commitment is long enough and not a stop-gap arrangement for the employee seeking re-employment.

iv. Students & Housewives: Part-time workers who are eager to make some money in their spare time come in such forms. Not all industries have matches for such employees. BPOs have perhaps the best match.

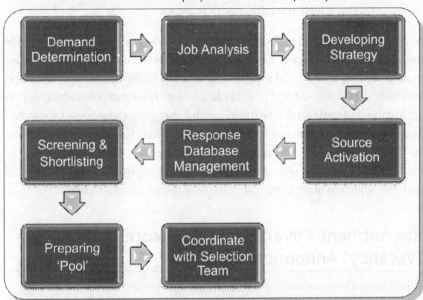

Figure 6.1: Recruitment Function

Recruitment Process

The recruitment process starts with determination of demand and nature of demand of human resource i.e., number and type of people required by the firm. An estimation of the possible sources of supply and also the sufficiency of such sources is done to find out whether the firm can meet its human capital needs or not. Such activities are covered under the broad head of human resource planning (HRP). This is followed by a thorough job analysis. It helps in the preparation of job descriptions (JD) and job specification. An understanding of the job and 'the ideal candidate' form the foundation and this is followed by strategy formulation. Some of the fundamental decisions regarding recruitment are taken during this stage, like:

> Whether to, *make* or to *buy* i.e., whether to hire from internal resource and train them (make) or to hire from external sources (buy)?

> Kind and number of sources to be tapped.

> Desired reach of recruitment communication.

- Desired, mode of recruitment communication.
- Whether to outsource or not?
- When to start the process and by when new recruits are required?
- Whether to tap internet and social media?
- And above all, the recruitment budget.

After this the activation of the source takes place where the formal search for the 'ideal candidate' begins. Once the firm starts receiving responses, a database management is desired and expected to assist in recording, sorting, prioritising and retrieval for present and possibly future use. The candidates are screened against the standards set during the initial phases regarding the 'ideal candidate'. This is a very important stage and all possible misfits based on resumes must be eliminated. Finally, the recruitment team decides on the final 'pool' of candidates to be sent ahead for selection process. Thereafter coordination with the selection team begins, to complete the process of hiring.

Recruitment Advertisements - More than a 'Vacancy' Announcement

"The greatest sin is to think yourself weak"

When Swami Vivekananda went to Chicago for the world religion conference, few knew him in that country. His plain demeanour and simple ways made people perceive him as another saint from the land of snake-charmers and black-magic. With utmost difficulty, he could get few minutes to speak in the conference. He opened his address with "My brothers and sisters of America". The audience immediately broke into applause and the 'man' went on to speak for days. His mesmerising words were able to transform the way Western world, in particular, looked at India. His words made people look at him and at India with a lot of respect.

Communication has that power to transform people's perception and ignite their energies. Mark Antony's famous funeral speech 'Friends, Romans, Countrymen...' in the epic play Julius Caesar by Shakespeare is another classic example of strategic use of communication.

Today, recruitment advertisements have changed from a plain announcement of vacancy to a strategic corporate communication tool. They do much more than merely announcing a vacancy. On careful study, it is found that recruitment advertisements use the marketing principle of 'positioning'.

'Positioning' is defined as an attempt by the marketer to create an 'image' of the product brand or service in the minds of the customer. The same strategy is used to create recruitment advertisements, the only difference being that the marketer is replaced by the recruiter and the target audiences are the prospective applicants/employee for that organisation.

The whole communication strategy revolves around attracting talents in this competitive market, where irrespective of downturns, recession and job-cuts, talent is always at shortage. Four types of 'positioning strategies' are being used in recruitment advertisement:

Career Positioning: The advantage with this type of positioning is that the prospective applicant does not only look at the job at hand, but is also attracted by the career opportunities that a company promises.

Employee Positioning: Through depiction of photographs or interviews of present employees, a kind of image about the kind of people who work for the company and the experiences they had working for the company is created. Right positioning may create an urge among applicants to earn the same identity and profile.

Workplace Positioning: Today's employee does not only look at the job or its remunerative aspects alone. The work culture and workplace environment also plays a critical role in decision-making. This explains the need for workplace positioning.

Corporate Positioning: A famous detergent advertisement of yesteryear depicted a lady quizzing how her friend's sari is whiter than her. Comparison is at the core of human tendencies. When competitive jobs are on offer, candidates often compare the corporate brands and image. Hence corporate positioning plays a crucial role. Not all advertisements use all four positioning strategies. Recruitment advertisements may use one, more or all four; using all seems to cerate maximum impact.

Effective communication has four integral elements, other than just sending the message across — first, the message should be transmitted without distortion; second, the recipient should understand the message (right decoding); third, there must be no misunderstanding; and, finally, the recipient must engage in the action intended by the sender. Retaining all these elements of effective communication, the addition of two more elements — usage (right time, place) and multiplicity (ability to use multiple message for same effect) — makes the communication 'strategic'. Recruitment ads, today, have the same strategic leverage.

Figure 6.2: Recruiting the Right One

Figure 6.3: Mimobile

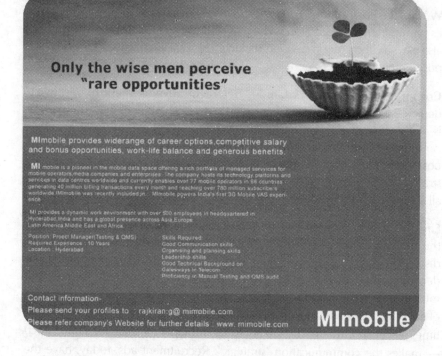

Figure 6.4: Aktwoods

e-Recruitment Advertisements

Companies are focusing on finding more cost-effective ways of conducting operations. Hiring is not untouched by the same. Companies are resorting to cost-effective hiring by using strategies like just-in-time hiring, hiring in relatively small numbers, etc. Experts suggest that during these times of cost-cutting, recruitment advertisements remain a major concern because of the cost associated with them.

This is where, e-recruitment advertisements could perhaps provide an effective solution. e-Recruitment advertisements besides being cost-effective, also have advantages like ease of processing, ability to attract large number of candidates, ease of communication, global presence and speed of the recruitment process. Despite these advantages, opinion is divided on the feasibility of companies using e-recruitment advertisements widely in India due to the limited reach of Internet.

e-Recruitment Advertisements

Recruitment advertisements posted via internet are cost effective and also have ease of processing, ability to attract large number of candidates, ease of communication, global presence and speed.

Advantages of e-Recruitment Advertisements

e-Recruitment advertisements have certain advantages as compared to ads in the traditional media. Some of them are:

Reduced Costs

Research shows that e-recruitment advertisements are 80% cheaper than newspaper advertisements and about 10 times cheaper than hiring consultants. According to a survey by Monster India, a job portal, the average cost per hire using traditional media varies from Rs. 25,000 to Rs. 100000 for senior position. However, the cost of a simple recruitment ad on a site could be just around Rs.1500.

Reduced Time to Hire

e-Recruitment advertisements can be accessed from anywhere, anytime. They are geographically independent, time-zone independent and ensure independent access. The responses can also be immediate. This speeds up the entire hiring process.

Increase Efficiency of the Process

e-Recruitment advertisements can be combined with data warehousing and data mining tools, online screening and testing tools, which increase the efficiency of the process.

Creative Design

e-Recruitment advertisements can be made more graphically rich and more interactive. Sometimes, video clips featuring the company, etc., can also be attached to the e-ad to make it more attractive.

Greater Access

e-Recruitment advertisements provide access to a larger and diverse pool of candidates. Companies looking for global talent can tap a much larger audience.

Flexible and Scalable

Unlike print recruitment advertisements, e-recruitment advertisements are flexible and scalable. The flexible and scalable nature of the Internet gives e-recruitment advertisements this trait as well. Recruiters, hence, can decide cost and reach, based on their needs.

SWOT Analysis of e-recruitment Advertisements

Let us do a SWOT analysis of e-recruitment advertisements in the Indian context:

Strengths

- According to the latest data released by Internet Governance Forum, India as on 31 March 2012 had 121,000,000 (Twelve Crore Ten Lakh) internet users, out of its total population of 118,917,906 (nearly 119 Crore), which is 10.2% of the population. India ranks third in the world in terms of number of internet users.

  (*Source:* www.internetworldstats.com/top20.htm)

- The number of Internet users has grown from about 5 million in the year 2000 to 121 million in March 2012, which is a phenomenal growth.

- Popularity of job sites like timesjob.com; naukri.com; monster.com has increased the visibility of Internet as a medium in the recruitment process.

Weaknesses

- While the number, 121 million Internet users looks huge, it represents only 10.2% of the population, which definitely is very small. In US, around 78.3%, and in Japan 80% of the population uses the Internet).

- The number 121 million users also include occasional Internet users. Hence the number of active Internet users may actually be quite low.

- Indian population is yet to completely consider PC as an item of necessity. While owning a TV, cell phone, fridge etc are considered domestic necessities today, a PC is still treated as luxury. Only about 3% of the Indian households have a PC.

- With just about 7 million broadband connections, India finds no place for itself in the list of top 10 nations in terms of number of broadband connections.

Opportunities

- In emerging markets like India, the average annual growth rates are expected to be between 10-20% in the coming few years. It is also estimated that by 2015, with more than 300 million users, India will be ranked second in the world after China on the parameter of Internet usage.

➤ The recent launch of a translator that can instantly translate an English webpage or document into 47 Indian regional languages will definitely attract many more users.

➤ The number of broadband connections in India may get a huge push with the government deciding to auction radio frequencies to offer 3G mobile services.

Threats

➤ Lack of awareness of Internet as a medium among a large section of the population.

➤ Overall low comfort level with the English language, especially in smaller cities and villages.

➤ The number of cyber cafes in the country has come down due to tightened security measures and thinner profit margins. (IMRB international).

By the above discussion it is clear that Internet usage is expected to increase rapidly in the coming few years. This implies that e-recruitment advertisements stand in good stead as a future option. Currently, however, the time is not opportune for many of the companies to use e-recruitment advertisements exclusively. Only companies in some selected sectors would be benefitted by using this option. A research finding shows that around 90% of the Fortune 500 companies use e-recruitment advertisements.

Companies need to prepare themselves in order to transform their hiring process to include e-recruitment advertisements. This would help in improving the efficiency of the hiring process by increasing visibility, improving speed of reach and hence making it more cost-effective. E-Recruitment methods such as job boards, employer websites, job sites and banner advertisements can complement the existing recruitment methods but not replace these at present.

Social Media Recruitment

Social Media is revolutionising the world in a big way and recruitment is not untouched by the same. Companies are using the Web 2.0 applications including social media/networking sites (Face book, Twitter, Orkut, LinkedIn, MySpace), blogs, podcasts (Podcast Alley, iTunes), video sharing sites (YouTube, Ted, FlickR), mobile apps etc for recruiting people. Social Media recruitment not only widens reach but helps segmentation, targeting and positioning of potential job seekers.

Details are given in the Chapter 19: *Social Media Applications in Managing Human Resources.*

Social Media Recruitment

Social Media Recruitment uses web 2.0 applications including social media/networking sites (Facebook, Twitter, LinkedIn, etc), blogs, podcasts, mobile apps etc for recruiting people.

Exhibit 1: Recruitment Process Outsourcing: Today's Challenges and Opportunities

By Dr. Ross Jones, Human Capital Institute

This article has been authored by Dr. Ross Jones and has been published with permission of **Human Capital Institute.**

About Human Capital Institute

The Human Capital Institute (HCI) is a catalyst for innovative new thinking in talent acquisition, development, deployment and new economy leadership. Through research and collaboration, our global network of more than 130,000 members develops and promotes creativity, best and next practices, and actionable solutions in strategic talent management. Executives, practitioners, and thought leaders representing organizations of all sizes, across public, charitable and government sectors, should utilize all communities, education, events and research to foster talent advantages to ensure organizational change for competitive results. In tandem with these initiatives, HCL's Human Capital Strategist professional certifications and designations set the bar- for expertise in talent strategy, acquisition, development and measurement.

(**Source:** www.humancapitalinstitute.org)

RPO

Recruitment Process Outsourcing (RPO) is the outsourcing of some or most recruiting processes. It includes outsourcing of all recruiting activities for, at least, some levels of employees.

RPO in Today's Economic Environment

The economic climate is changing on a daily basis. To gauge how the ongoing economic crisis will affect RPO over the next two years, we conducted a short follow-up survey of 86 talent acquisition experts working for a wide-range of organizations. We asked them the following three questions:

1. Given the current economic downturn, what trend do you predict for the outsourcing of recruiting practiced in your organization over the next two years?

2. Assuming that your overall recruiting budget will decrease over the next one to two years, what will be the trend for your spending on Recruitment Process Outsourcing (RPO)?

3. Would your organization outsource strategic recruiting practices (e.g., talent strategy development, employer branding, recruitment planning if it results in an increased return on Investment (ROI) for your talent acquisition process?

The responses to the first question on the uncertainty gripping businesses today – both because of the range of responses and because of the fact that the largest group of respondents is the uncertain one.

- 17 percent believe that their outsourcing of recruiting practices will decrease.
- 30 percent will not outsource recruiting practices.
- 14 percent believe that their outsourcing will remain unchanged.
- 6 percent believe that their outsourcing will increase.
- 33 percent are unsure about future trends.

However, many organizations are open to the possibility that RPO, particularly focused on strategic business needs, can be a tool to compete during difficult economic times. The first indication of this comes out of the answers to the second question above—namely that 44 percent of respondents are open to the possibility that even if their overall recruitment budget declines, their organization's investment in RPO may increase. Specifically, while only four percent believe that their RPO budget will increase, 40 percent are unsure about the future of their organization. Again, while highlighting the current uncertainty about what can and will be done in the future, this result points out that many organizations remain open to the possibility of increasing their RPO budget in the future.

Finally, as the figure below shows, the answers to third question indicate that strategic RPO may be the answer for many organizations looking to optimize their investment in talent acquisition. In fact, 78 percent of our respondents who are either using a strategically focused RPO effort now, would definitely use it in the future, or, have not ruled it out. The fact that 52 percent of respondents are unsure if their organizations would move to a strategic RPO, even if it might increase ROI, again points to the uncertainty of today's economic environment. However it also highlights a silver lining – that a vast majority of businesses will remain open to the idea of increasing investments in RPO in general, and strategic RPO in particular if it helps them compete environmental climate of the future.

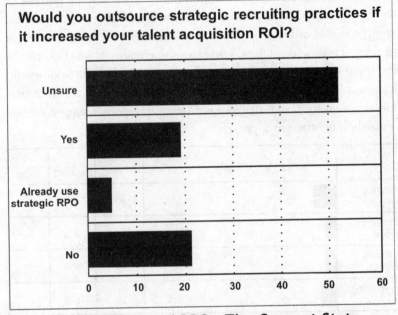

Figure 6.5: Recruitment Process Outsourcing (RPO)

Talent Acquisition and RPO - The Current State

Facing increasing competition for talent and the current economic downturn, many organizations are focusing limited resources on core business needs. As a result, they are outsourcing enemy key recruiting processes (see Figure 6.6) fuelling the growing trend for services and solutions in the market known as Recruitment Process Outsourcing (RPO). During August and September last year, we surveyed and interviewed a wide range of HR professionals, from many types of organizations, to determine:
  ➢ The current state and successes of RPO.
  ➢ The challenges and opportunities facing RPO.
  ➢ The best practices and solutions for implementing a winning RPO program.

Figure 6.6: Does your Organization Outsource Some of its Recruiting Process?

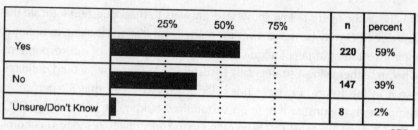

	25%	50%	75%	n	percent
Yes				220	59%
No				147	39%
Unsure/Don't Know				8	2%

n = 375

Defining RPO

What talent acquisition activities are organizations referring to when they say they use RPO? Our study found a general consensus that RPO is the selective outsourcing of some recruiting activities. Results reveal that 73 percent of responding organizations believe that RPO is the outsourcing of some or most recruiting processes, while only 16 percent define RPO as the outsourcing of all recruiting activities for, at least, some levels of employees (see Figure 6.7). Clearly, there is no consensus on the scope of RPO, but the widespread application of RPO on a limited basis suggests a current emphasis on tactical considerations, even though many of our write-in responses suggest a need for a more holistic strategic approach.

Figure 6.7: What Best Describes your Understanding of 'RPO'?

	25%	50%	75%	n	Percent	
Outsourcing ALL aspects of the recruiting process for ALL levels of employees				29	8%	
Outsourcing ALL aspects of the recruiting process for MOST levels of employees				15	4%	
Outsourcing ALL aspects of the recruiting process for SOME levels of employees				15	4%	
Outsourcing MOST aspects of the recruiting process for ALL levels of employees				24	6%	
Outsourcing MOST aspects of the recruiting process for MOST levels of employees				44	12%	
Outsourcing MOST aspects of the recruiting process for SOME levels of employees				28	8%	=73%
Outsourcing SOME aspects of the recruiting process for ALL levels of employees				20	5%	
Outsourcing SOME aspects of the recruiting process for MOST levels of employees				24	6%	
Outsourcing SOME aspects of the recruiting process for SOME levels of employees				134	36%	
Other				38	10%	

n = 371

What are some other definitions of RPO?
(from the 10 percent that chose "other")
➢ *"Outsourcing ANY aspect of the recruiting process for ANY level of employees."*
➢ *"RPO can be an end-to-end solution for all positions, or a service to take over part of the recruitment process, or be confined to just a certain title-type, such as a high-volume title. RPO can be flexible as it needs to be for what the client wants."*
➢ *"RPO can mean any or all of the above options based on business need. Some organizations choose to keep recruiting higher-level positions within the organization, while outsourcing the candidate sourcing, screening and administrative support... up to and some including on-boarding (full life cycle)"*

Why Use RPO?

Now that we know how users define RPO, the next question is: Why do they use RPO? It is unlikely that the decision to turn over parts of such a key talent management process (recruiting) to a third-party service provider is taken lightly. To understand the reasons for this decision, we asked respondents to tell us which of the following were their organizations' reason(s) for turning to RPO:

1. The existence of pressing staffing needs that they cannot meet themselves.
2. The desire to concentrate on their core competencies.
3. A lack of internal HR resources.
4. The high cost of attracting and recruiting new talent themselves.
5. Lack of satisfaction in the new hires they recruited themselves.

While many organizations choose more than one reason for using RPO, Figure 6.8, shows that three stand out: 1) Pressing staffing needs that they cannot meet. 2) Desire to concentrate on core business functions, and 3) Lack of sufficient internal HR resources to do the job. 'The fact that "the existence of pressing staffing needs" is the most important reason for choosing RPO shows that short-term business necessities can be a powerful motivator for action. This is particularly true if those same organizations also lack the internal HR resources needed to deal with their staffing needs, then it is another major reason to outsource.

The other main reason to use RPO, "the desire to concentrate on core competencies," is one example of a driver that is influenced by the organization's long-term business strategy rather than immediate responses to staffing needs. It is certainly likely that many of the organizations that initially choose to use RPO to meet short-term goal will, eventually, embrace it for its ability to solve long-term strategic problems. However, our results show that many organizations are already making business strategy a main reason for using RPO. Later in this chapter we will show how those organizations may also be generating greater benefits as a result of this decision.

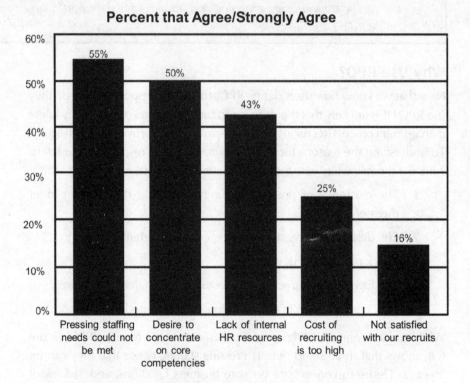

Figure 6.8: Reasons Why Organizations Turn to RPO?

What Recruiting Practices Drive RPO Today?

Before determining the specific recruiting practices included in most RPO programs today, we sought to discover which practices organizations viewed as most critical. Figure 6.9 clearly shows that most organizations agree or strongly agree that all of the major practices presented are important. Even the lowest-ranked practice - permanent hiring services - was viewed by most respondents as 21 critical part of their talent acquisition program. However, our results do indicate that two specific practices, active recruiting and talent strategy development/consulting, are particularly critical to most organizations" talent acquisition processes - see Figures 6.11 and 6.12. These two practices represent the tactical and strategic aspects of recruiting practices, respectively, and they represent the prime components of an effective RPO program.

Figure 6.9:
The Following Activities are Critical to Achieving Your Organization's Talent Acquisition Goals

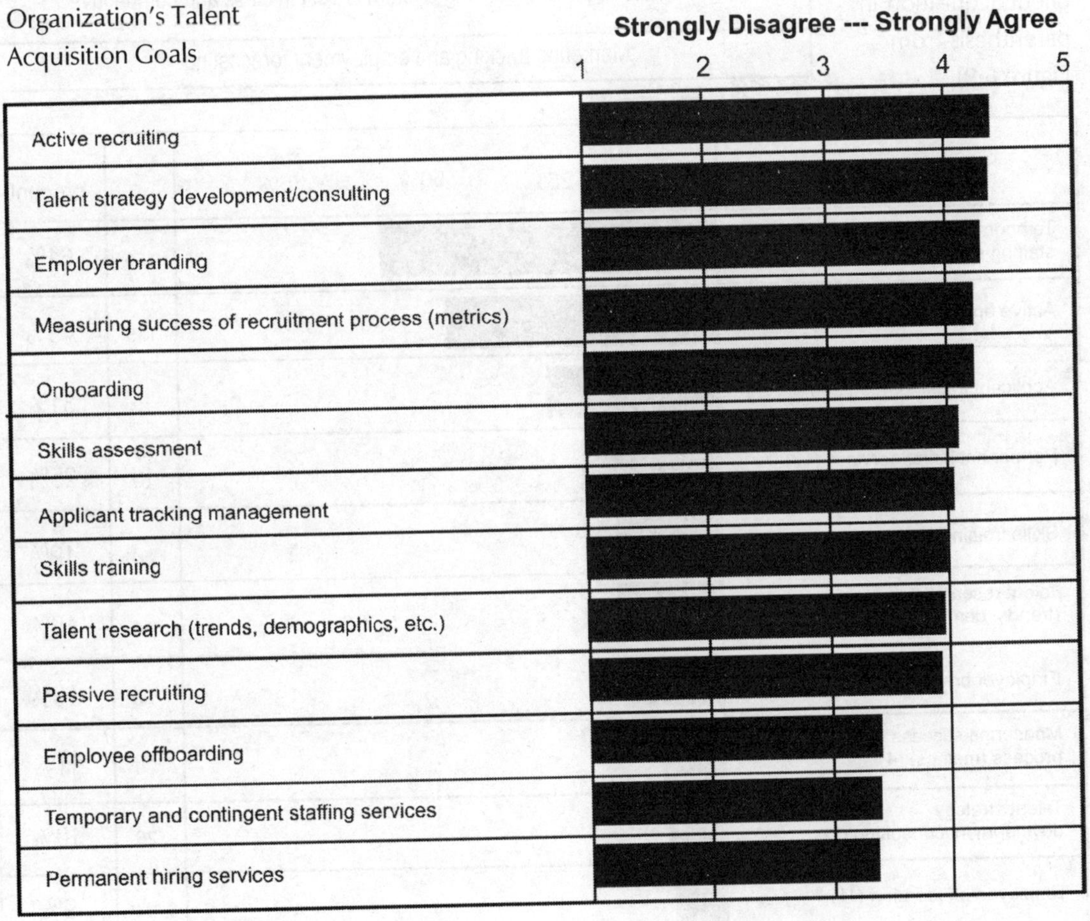

Strongly Disagree --- Strongly Agree
1   2   3   4   5

- Active recruiting
- Talent strategy development/consulting
- Employer branding
- Measuring success of recruitment process (metrics)
- Onboarding
- Skills assessment
- Applicant tracking management
- Skills training
- Talent research (trends, demographics, etc.)
- Passive recruiting
- Employee offboarding
- Temporary and contingent staffing services
- Permanent hiring services

Figure 6.10: Recruitment Parctices Most Likely to be Outsourced (ranking of importance in talent acquisition in parenthesis-from Figure 6.9)

Some Other Critical Activities Related to Organizational Talent Acquisition Goals
As noted by our Survey Respondents
"Alignment with corporate objectives and business strategy"
"Adopting and maintaining a model of continuous sourcing is not only best practice but critical in achieving effective proactive talent acquisition"
"Employee referrals --- good source of applicants"
"Ensuring our Applicant Tracking System is best in class and competitive"
"Marketing tracking and employment forecasting"

	n	precent
Temporary and contingent staffing services (12)	166	61%
Active and passive recruiting (1)	135	49%
Applicant tracking management (7)	84	31%
Permanent hiring services (13)	67	25%
Skills training and assessment (6,8)	51	19%
Talent research (trends, demographics, etc.) (9)	51	19%
Employer branding (3)	50	18%
Measuring success of recruitment process (metrics) (4)	29	11%
Talent strategy development/consulting (2)	26	10%
Employee offboarding (11)	24	9%
Onboarding (5)	19	7%

n=273

In Figure 6.10, the talent acquisition practice that ranks second in its likelihood of being outsourced, active and passive recruiting, was deemed most critical to the success of a talent acquisition proqram (see Figures 6.9 and 6.11). The practice that ranks third in its likelihood to be outsourced, applicant tracking management, is also one of the three practices (along with active and passive recruiting) that makes up the Tactical Recruiting group of practices identified by our analysis.

	25%	50%	75%	n	percent
Strongly Agree				195	53%
Agree				139	37%
Neutral				25	25%
Disagree				5	1%
Strongly Disagree				5	1%
Unable to Rate				5	1%

n = 371

Figure 6.11: Tactical Practice-Active Recruiting (90 percent of respondents agree/strongly agree that this practice is critical to their organization's talent acquisition process).

	25%	50%	750%	n	Percent
Strongly Agree				189	51%
Agree				141	38%
Neutral				26	7%
Disagree				4	1%
Strongly Disagree				7	2%
Unable to Rete				4	1%

n = 371

Figure 6.12: Strategic Practice–Talent Strategy Development/Consulting (89 percent of respondents cite this practice as critical to their organization's talent acquisition process).

Finally, the practice that is most likely to be outsourced, temporary and contingent staffing services, is also another type of tactical recruiting practice. These results highlight the important Tact that RPO today is focused mostly on outsourcing a range of tactical practices, some of which are considered critical components of talent acquisition.

Linking Strategic Priorities and Recruiting Practices

Not surprisingly, our analysis showed a high degree of correlation in the value placed on similar types of recruiting practices, For example, organizations that believe talent strategy development/consulting is very critical also tend to choose employer branding as a very critical recruiting practice. To determine if the 13 recruiting practices could be reduced to a smaller number of key "practice types:" we used a statistical method called factor analysis to assess the pattern of responses from multiple respondents (organizations] to combine various responses into natural groups or components". 'The analysis showed that the 13 recruiting practices belong to the following groups:

Strategy & Analysis

Talent strategy development/consulting, employer branding, talent research, and measuring success of recruitment process (metrics)

> - **Tactical Recruiting:** Active recruiting, passive recruiting, and applicant tracking management.
> - **Skill-based:** Skill training and skill assessment.
> - **Staffing Services**: Permanent hiring services and temporary and contingent staffing services.
> - **Miscellaneous:** Onboarding is part of both the Strategy & Analysis and Skill based groups, while offboarding is unrelated to other practices. Most organizations treat it independently from the more recruitment-focused practices.

As our definitions in Figure 6.7 describes, most organizations view RPO not only as a selective process when it comes to which recruiting practices to outsource, but also when it comes to which level of employees to include in an RPO program Similarly, as with critical recruiting practices, an initial goal of our research was to determine if the recruitment of certain levels of employees is considered more critical in order to understand how well RPO is meeting recruitment of needs of organizations today. As Figure 6.13 shows 59 percent of respondents say that recruitment of upper and middle managers is a very important part of their talent acquisition process - closely followed by executive recruitment (56 percent). Clearly, if an RPO program is to be fully integrated into the talent acquisition process, it needs to be used in the recruitment of these critical employee levels.

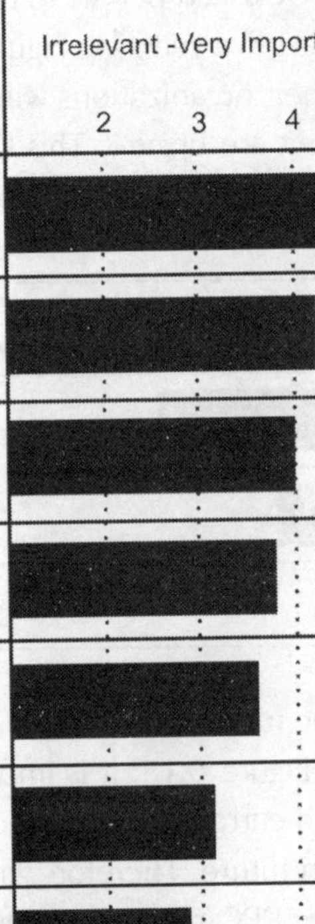

	Irrelevant -Very Important 2 3 4	Irrelevant	Unimportant	Neutral	Important	Very Important
Upper and middle management		6	7	29	101	207 (59%)
Executive		11	16	48	71	192 (56%)
Exempt		22	19	41	122	133 (39%)
Entry-level managers		22	21	73	134	99 (28%)
Hourly		30	36	72	116	93 (27%)
Contract labor		36	58	101	107	31 (9%)
Contingent labor		69	56	97	76	35 (11%)

59 percent of respondents= 207 out of 381 total respondents calling "Upper and middle management" very important to talent acquisition efforts.

56 percent= 192 out of 381 total respondents calling the "Executive" level very important to talent acquisition efforts.

Figure 6.13: Which Levels of Employees will be Most Critical to Your Organization Talent Acquisition Effort over the Next Year?

RPO - Challenges and Opportunities

Results from the survey point to key challenges in the use of RPO in the future. The first challenge is the need to address strategic, rather than tactical, priorities with RPO. Three recruiting practices that comprise the core of a strategic approach to talent acquisition - talent strategy development/consulting, employer branding, and measuring success of recruitment process (metrics) -

currently are the least likely practices to be outsourced. For most organizations, the strategic side of talent acquisition remains in-house. This may simply be an artifact of the still-early stages of RPO implementation: organizations typically begin using RPO by outsourcing tactical practices first and, with growing maturity of the process, will outsource strategic practices later. Our survey results show that those organizations that do move toward a more strategic approach to RPO will reap rewards for their efforts.

A second major challenge facing RPO is the apparent uncertainty about how to use and benefit from it in the future. This uncertainty is evident in the responses we received when we asked people to tell us if their organizations would be using RPO in the next five years. As Figure 6.14 shows, 30 percent of respondents told us that their organizations will not be using RPO in the future and another 2C percent are unsure. This last number, in particular, points to some uncertainty - as well as potential opportunity - for the future of RPO.

Figure 6.14:
Does Your Organization Plan to Outsource Some of Your Recruiting Process Within the Next Five Years?

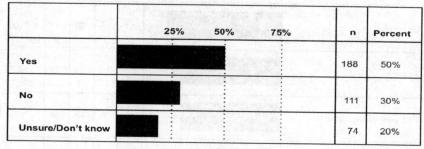

n = 373

Why this uncertainty about the future use of RPO? The main reasons for this reluctance are highlighted in Figure 6.15. It is important to note that these particular results combine both current users and non-users of HPO who say they will not be; using RPO in future. Therefore, most of the 39 percent of organizations that are not using RPO new (see Figure 6.6) presumably chose the "No need to" reason for why they won't in the future. However two other reasons – "too expensive" and "we have not found a company that can provide us with the services we need" - are likely to be key reasons why some potential user of RPO may remain wary.

At the same time it is important to note that 50 percent of respondents say they will use RPO in the future - indicating that many companies are satisfied with their current RPO services. At the end of this report, we will identify the "best practices" that create satisfaction and value between organizations and their RPO service providers. When it comes to turning those "unsure" organizations into RPO users, the challenge, for RPO providers, will be to provide them with those best practices in a cost effective manner.

	25%	50%	75%	n	Percent
No need to - we do a good job of recruiting				95	66%
Too expensive to outsource				26	18%
We don't know which parts of the recruiting process should be outsourced				9	6%
We have not found a company that can provide us with the services we need				14	10%

n = 144

Figure 6.15: Why will Your Organization not Consider Outsourcing Some or All of its Recruiting Processes in the Next Five Years?

Results only include the respondents who state that their organizations will not be using RPO in the next five years.

The third challenge for RPO is one of focus and priority. Organizations consider upper and middle managers as well as executives, as the levels for which recruiting is most important - see Figure 6.13. While executive recruitment is the second most likely employee level to be outsourced, turning to a third-party provider for the recruitment of upper and middle managers occurs less frequently than does the outsourcing contingent and contract workers - two levels of employees for which recruitment is considered a relatively low priority (see Figure 6.16). These results indicate that RPO today tends to be used most for the recruitment of employees on two opposite ends of the spectrum - temporary workers and executives.

The final RPO challenge may also be the greatest opportunity - maximizing the Return on investment (ROI). As with every other business decision, the success of RPO can be measured by its ROI. While organizations use various payment models to invest in their RPO programs, the "fee per hire" model dominates (see Figure 6.17). This is not surprising given the fact that RPO is largely viewed by our survey respondents as a solution to address pressing staffing needs (Figure 6.18). Organizations that are initially turning to RPO to deal with immediate recruiting problems will likely look for a short-term payment model, given the uncertainty of their future RPC needs. However, as those same organizations become aware of the long-term value of RPO (in other tactical and strategic recruiting areas), they will likely move towards longer-term contractual arrangements with RPO service providers, or a combination of payment models (see Figure 6.17).

Figure 6.16:
How Often do You Outsource the Recruiting of Each Level of Employee?

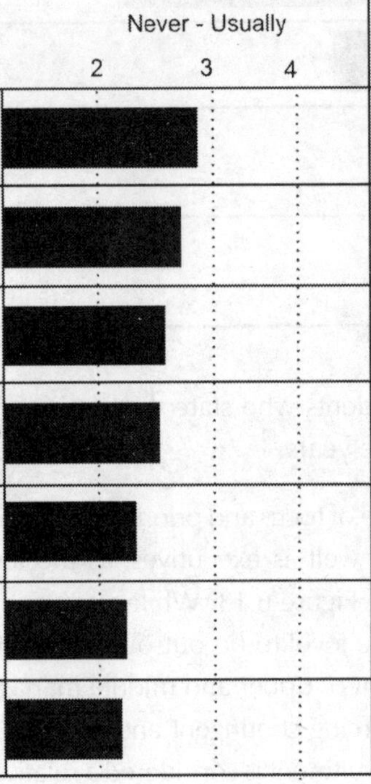

	Never - Usually 2 3 4	Never	Infrequently	Sometimes (but we do most)	Most recruiting is outsourced	Always
Contract labor		86	47	70	86	41
Executive		92	46	79	87	32
Contingent labor		104	51	49	71	43
Upper and middle management		102	58	112	61	14
Exempt		108	85	99	21	9
Entry-level managers		130	81	91	27	7
Hourly		142	82	63	39	9

Figure 6.17:
What Payment Model Does Your Organization Use When Recruiting is Outsourced?

Note: the majority of respondents who chose "Other and/or combination of the above" indicated that they used a combination of fee per hire and short. or long-term contracts for specific levels of employees (e.g., Contingent and/or Executives).

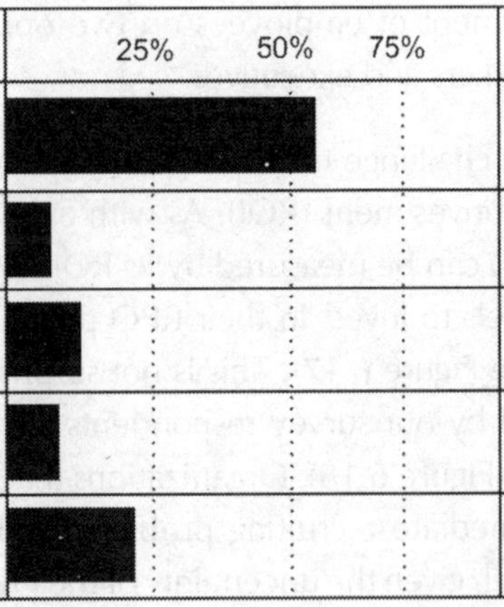

	25% 50% 75%	n	percent
Fee per hire		169	52%
Monthly retainer/management fee		23	7%
Short-term service contract - based on services provided, not number of hires recruited		39	12%
Long-term service contract		25	8%
Other and/or combination of the above		67	21%

n=323

Chapter 6: Recruitment

	Never - Usually 1 2 3	Poor	Below average	Average	Above average	Outstanding
Offer acceptance ratio		5	7	65	85	37
Quality of hire		8	6	70	101	32
Percent of jobs filed		4	18	73	82	39
New hire retention rate		4	16	73	89	23
Staffing efficiency ratio		4	19	69	44	19
Candidate diversity		7	29	81	62	26
Time to submission		5	17	86	55	17
Time to fill		5	33	93	60	24
Cost per hire		6	30	90	58	19

Figure 6.18: How Effective is Your Organization's Current RPO for each of the Following Measures of Recruitment Success?

Figure 6.19: How Would You Rank the Current Return on Investment for Your Organization's RPO?

Note: Only results from organizations currently using RPO.

	25% 50% 75%	n	percent
Poor - the quality of hires and services does not justify the cost of the process		13	5%
Fair - We want the quality and/or cost of the services to improve to continue with RPO provider		60	24%
Neutral - it is a break-even process at the current time		82	32%
Good - RPO has measurably increased the quality of hires and cost effectiveness of recruiting		80	31%
Excellent - RPO is a critical factor in our organization's current and future success		19	8%

n = 254

Regardless of how recruiting is financed, measuring the success of the process is critical to determining ROI - whether for in-house or outsourced recruiting programs. Sixty-four percent of respondents say that they know that their organizations measure some aspects of recruiting success (another 10 percent are unsure). Figure 6.13 summarizes the results for RPO effectiveness, broken down by specific recruiting metrics. Overall, the results display a moderate level of satisfaction with RPO. The vast majority rank their process as "average" or "above average for each metric, with only a few citing "poor" or "below average" satisfaction. However it is also true that relatively few organizations believe that their RPO is doing an outstanding job as measured by any metric. This means that there are definite opportunities for improving RPO effectiveness.

As a bottom line question, we asked respondents to rate RPO impact: is there positive ROI, or is, RPO" a drain on the organization? As Figure 6.19 highlights, the current level of satisfaction with RPO programs leaves room for improvement. In fact almost two-thirds of all organizations (61 percent) rank their current RPO program as being only break-even or worse. In contrast, only 39 percent of organizations currently using RPO think their program is providing a good or excellent ROI.

However, to end the story, we took a deeper look at specific organizations that are experiencing the greatest ROI from their Recruitment Process Outsourcing program. To do this, we differentiated between those organizations that are currently using an RPO approach that outsources talent strategy development/consulting practices (along with other practices that our analysis identified as strategic recruiting practices) and those that aren't" - and looked for how their ROIs differ. The results are striking – see Figure 6.20, Clearly, those organizations that apply RPO to addressing strategic needs in their talent acquisition process are the organizations that are capturing the full value of RPO.

Conclusion

Our study confirms the findings of other recent reports on RPO (Recruitment Process Outsourcing). For most organizations, RPO means the outsourcing of selected recruiting activities for selected levels of employees - the definition used by 73 percent of our survey's respondents, Given that definition, we

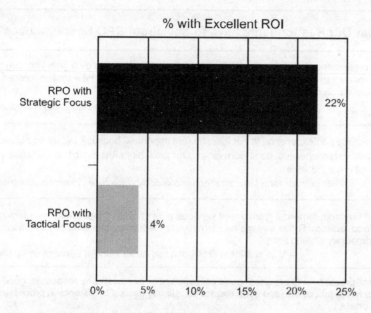

Figure 6.20: Organizations that Apply RPO to Addressing Strategic Needs are Significantly More Likely to Achieve and "Excellent" ROI from Outsourced Recruiting Practices.

found that RPO is an important component of most talent acquisition processes today, with 59 percent of organizations currently outsourcing some or all of their recruiting services.

We identified several important reasons for using RPO, However, the two major ones are distinguishable by their focus on tactical goals - the need to meet pressing staffing needs - and on strategic goals - the desire to focus on core competencies. Clearly, most organizations using RPO today are using it for tactical reasons. However, equally evident is the fact that these organizations that have adopted a strategic RPO approach are the ones that are capturing the most value from the process.

With 50 percent of our respondents saying that they will use RPO in the future and another 20 percent open to the idea, the future of RPO is positive, For those organizations that want to leverage the full potential of RPO to improve the talent acquisition process, and their overall business strategy, it is critical that they consider making RPO a larger part of their talent management strategy. Then, they may be able to join that group of respondents who manage to more fully benefit from RPO.

What Our Respondents have to Say about RPO Best Practices?
" Any organization moving to an RPO should expect to invest its own time in ensuring hiring managers are adequately trained on ho to best work with a new system, process, recruiter, etc. in order to make the relationship work effectively." — Manager in a mid-size retail company
" Knowledge and experience in our industry [are important] because we are so niched. Standard approaches just don't work for us. Our providers must exhibit competence in many different industries..." - HR director for a large healthcare company with offices in seven countries
" I can buy supplemental recruitment services a la carte to supplement my internal team's capabilities. RPOs give me an alternative to the traditional outsource contingency and temporary staffing firms." – Vice president of HR of a mid-size Financial Services company
"[A best-practice RPO provides] good utilization of hr and company resources, good-quality hiring processes, and good metrics on a timely basis. Consistency in processes is important." – Vice President of HR for a large automotive company
"My providers have an understanding of my specific needs and qualifications ...[and the] more personality- and attitude-driven qualities that I would like to see in employees. Will the employee fit in with our corporate atmosphere? My providers can key in to attributes that they have learned from fit in with our corporate atmosphere? My providers can key in to attributes that they have learned from doing business with me for so long." --- HR Director for a small high-tech company
" Great communication!" – Recruiter for a mid-size bank holding company

Summary

Organizations outsource recruitment and hiring practices for many reasons. Some may lack the internal resources to address their talent and acquisition needs. Others may want to focus on core competencies, or to look for a competitive advantage in competing for talent. Whatever the reasons, Recruitment Process Outsourcing (RPO) is a growing practice. Despite this growth, limited information exists on the trends in RPO use, the specific: recruitment practices it includes, and how well it is being carried out.

Survey

To gain a better understanding of today's RPO practices, we surveyed 381 business professionals who have insight about their companies' approaches to RPO. In the survey, we explored current or planned use of RPO, the prevailing definitions of RPO, recruiting practices and employee levels covered by RPO, the business case and drivers, Return on Investment (ROI), and recruiting practices that create the most effective RPO.

Findings

The survey results reveal several trends about the adoption of RPO today, the definition and scope of the practice, and current and future ROI opportunities.

Adoption: More than half of companies utilize RPO.

59 percent of organizations surveyed currently outsource some or all of their recruiting processes.

50 percent say they will use RPO in the next five years. Another 20 percent are unsure.

Scope: The majority of Current RPO Deals Cover Selective Practices for Tactical Needs.

Among users, the most common definition of RPO is the outsourcing of some recruiting activities for some levels of employees, with 36 percent of respondents choosing that specific definition. More generally, 73 percent of respondents accept an RPO definition that includes some form of selected outsourcing of recruiting services for selected levels of employees.

The recruiting service is considered most important to organizations' talent acquisition goals. Active Recruiting, is the second most likely service to be outsourced.

However, RPO practices that focus on strategic talent needs (for example, talent strategy development/consulting) are outsourced less frequently.

ROI: Strategic emphasis correlates with increased RPO value among respondents.

Only 39 percent of organizations rate the ROI for their current RPO program as good or excellent.

In contrast, organizations that use an RPO approach to encompass longer-term strategic needs, such as workforce planning, employment branding and competency management, are significantly more likely to report excellent ROI for their recruitment outsourcing.

An Opportunity for Competitive Advantage

The results of our study indicate a widespread use of RPO to focus on tactical recruiting practices. However, they also demonstrate that those organizations using RPO as a talent acquisition approach to address strategic needs are much more likely to capture the full value of RPO, as evidenced by their significantly greater ROI. The underutilization of this strategic approach today means that there is an immediate opportunity for organizations to adopt RPO to achieve a holistic talent acquisition strategy, increase ROI, and improve competitiveness in today's marketplace.

Organizations typically begin using RPO by outsourcing tactical practices first and, with growing maturity of the process, will outsource strategic practices later. Survey results show that those organizations that do move toward a more strategic approach to RPO will reap rewards for their efforts.

Appendix 1: Methodology and Demographics Methodology

We surveyed 381 people, of which more than 50 percent are Director/Vice President or higher, and over 75 percent work in some area of HR or talent management - see demographic breakdown below. The online survey consisted of 33 questions concerning issues related to RPO use, definition, practices outsourced, payment models used, and overall (and practice-specific) effectiveness. The survey took respondents, on average, about 15 to 20 minutes to complete. The 33 questions on talent branding were divided into six main parts:

1. Current or planned use of Recruitment Process Outsourcing (RPO)
2. User definition of RPO
3. Recruiting practices and employee level included in RPO services
4. Drivers for organizations to use RPO
5. The Return on Investment for RPO
6. Best/worst practices in RPO

For part 6 above, we also conducted nine in-depth telephone interviews with selected survey respondents to gain more information on the success and failure of specific RPO practices.

Chapter 6: Recruitment ◄ 159

A two-step analysis of all quantitative data was carried out:

1) Standard descriptive statistical methods were used to determine the frequencies and/or means (and standard errors) of the current state and future trends in RPO, as well as variation among organizations in RPO practices, payment models and program effectiveness.

2) Various inferential statistical methods (i.e., ANOVA and z-tests) were used to determine whether there are statistically significant differences in the responses for the various groups of respondents, as identified by the demographic shown on the next pages.

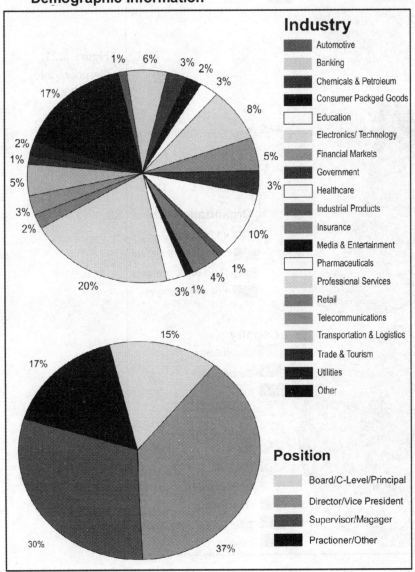

Demographic Information

160 ▶ *Human Resource Management*

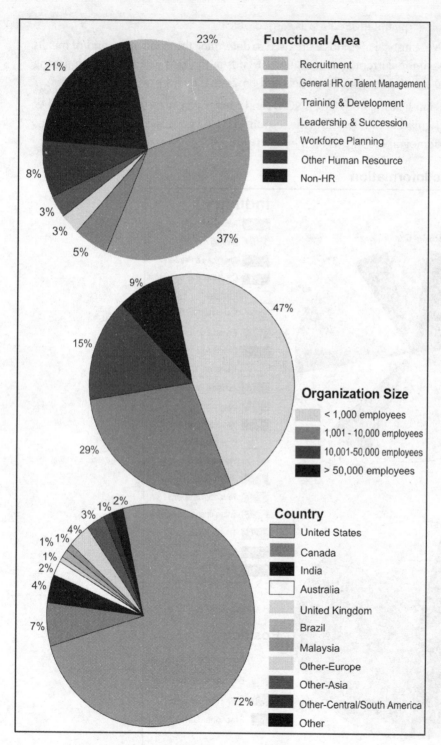

Figure 6.21. Demographic Breakdown

Appendix 2: Factor Analysis of Critical Talent Acquisition Practices

As discussed in the main text, we performed a factor analysis of the 13 talent acquisition practices in order to determine:

1. If the practices could be grouped into logical functional groups.
2. Which groups are most used by RPO today, as well as which groups are underutilized and provide the most opportunity for the future of RPO.

These factor components are a very powerful method to shrink the number of variables to a more manageable level and provide insights unavailable with the analysis of individual variables (e.g., specific talent acquisition practices). More importantly, these groupings often allow us to see patterns in the results that are obscured by the sheer number of original variables. In other words, they allow us to identify new, previously unnamed variables that underlie and drive the variables in our survey.

We were able to group all 13 of the original questions into one of five factors (groups) that explained 70.8 percent of the variation in responses - very high level of explanation. The results show how much the original questions contribute to each of the groups.

The result of the Factor Analysis is striking -

1) **Factor 1** is made up of all the talent acquisition practices associated with talent strategy, metrics and analysis (numbers in red) that are major parts of a strategic RPO. In addition, onboarding is partially included in this group indicating that on-boarding programs play a role in talent strategy, although not as great as the four practices in red. The clear implication is that there is an underlying variable focusing on talent strategy and analysis: of which four specific practices are parts.

2) **Factor 2** is made up primarily of the two skill based practices-skills training and skills assessment (numbers in green), with a significant contribution from on-boarding. This should not come as a surprise since while onboarding includes other important purposes, skill training for new recruits is certainly a major one.

3) **Factor 3** covers the general recruitment practices. They include the major parts of any tactically driven RPO program and consist of the active and passive recruiting practices, as well as the associated applicant tracking management practice (numbers in blue).

4) **Factor 4** includes the two specific hiring services - permanent hiring and temporary/contingent staffing (numbers in pink). This provides evidence that organizations tend to deal with their permanent and temporary hiring needs in a coordinated fashion a positive approach to take!

5) **Factor 5** consists entirely of the employee on-boarding practice and indicates that most organizations do not integrate this practice with their more recruiting-specific practices.

	Factor				
	1	2	3	4	5
Talent strategy development/consulting	.753	.241	.138	-.015	-.095
Employer branding	.736	.172	.185	.003	.189
Talent research (trends, demographics, etc.)	.770	.139	.167	.197	-.023
Measuring success of recruitment process (metrics)	.641	.244	.350	.052	.224
Skills training	.220	.858	.107	.003	.174
Skills assessment	.254	.868	.088	.062	-.017
Onboarding	.446	.513	.195	.021	.316
Active recruiting	.208	.190	.743	.133	-.051
Passive recruiting	.165	-.072	.811	-.016	.048
Applicant tracking management	.228	.240	.661	.118	.224
Permanent hiring services	.225	.002	.011	.804	.154
Temporary and contingent staffing services	-.073	.051	.141	.850	.016
Employee offboarding	.071	.147	.092	.152	.916

Extraction Method: Principal Component Analysis

Rotation Method: Varimax with Kaiser Normalization

a. Rotation converged in six iterations

This reading Exhibit has been authored by Dr. Ross Jones and published with permission of Human Capital Institute.

Essay Questions

1. Differentiate between recruitment and selection.
2. 'Wrong hiring can cost a firm dear' what do you mean by wrong hiring? What type of candidates should a company give a miss?
3. What are the various recruitment objectives? Explain the various factors that affect recruitment.
4. Describe the various stages of the 'Recruitment-process'.
5. Highlight the significance of recruitment advertisements, what are the form positioning strategies used in recruitment advertisements?
6. Why is e-recruitment advertisements used? What are the advantages?
7. Comment on 'Recruitment Process Outsourcing' and its relevance in today's environment.

Application Questions

1. Identify the recruitment sources that the following companies should tap-
   a) A Mobile service company wants to hire temporary field sales officers.
   b) A BPO company hiring for customer care Executives (Voice-Process).
   c) A car dealership hiring for Sales Officers for their showrooms.
   d) A branded chain of eye care retail hiring for optometrists.
2. Choose any recruitment advertisement from any latest edition of a job-supplement and identify the content highlighting the various positioning strategies.
3. Using internet find a company that provides RPO-services. Compare the same with those of another such company.

Bibliography

Adelina, B. M., Gillian, M. A., & Susan, O. (2009). Selling Retailing to Generation Y graduates: Recruitment Challenges and Opportunities. *The International Review of Retail Distribution and Consumer Research, 19* (4), 405-420.

Anna, B. (2006). Graduating Students Responses to Recruitment Advertisements. *Journal of Business Communication, 43* (3).

Anna, S. M. (2003). Recruitment Policy vs. Recruitment Process: Espoused Theory and Theory-in-use. *Academy of Management Best Conference Paper.*

Bayo, M. A., & Angel, O. (2006). Pedro Internal Promotion versus External Recruitment in Industrial Plants In Spain. *Industrial and Labor Relations Review, 59* (3).

David, K. H., & David, H. C. (2009). 22. Field tested Strategies for Physician Recruitment and Contracting, 54:3 May/June. *Journal of Healthcare Management.*

David, S. V., & Douglas, B. S. (2009). Recruitment and Retention of Rural Hospital Administrators: A Multifaceted Approach, Hospital Topics. *Research and Perspectives on Healthcare, 87* (1).

Gary, P. N. (1987). The Effects of Sex and Gender on Recruitment. *Academy of Management Review, 12* (4), 731-743.

Giacomo, S., & Andrea, o. (2008). Recruitment and Selection Services: Efficiency and Competitive Reasons in the Outsourcing of HR Practices. *The International Journal of Human Resource Management, 19* (2), 372-391.

Jack, W. H., Hubret, F. H., William, G. F., & Bernerth, J. B. (2008). The Interactive Effects of Job Advertisement Characteristics and Applicant Experience on Reactions to Recruitment Messages. *Journal of Occupational and Organizational Psychology,* 619-638.

Jack, W. H., Jeremy, B. B., & Neil, T. M. (n.d.). Attitudes at Different Stages of Recruitment: Expectations, Perceptions, and Feedback. *Academy of Management.*

Jared, L. J., & Edward, K. J. (2007). A Revolution in Public Personnel Administration: The Growth of Web-based Recruitment and Selection Processes in the Federal Service. *Public Personnel Management, 36* (3).

Jeremy, B. B., & william, G. F. (2008). 10. Walker H. Jack, Field Hubert S, The Interactive Effects of Job Advertisement Characteristics and Applicant Experience on Reactions to Recruitment Messages. *Journal of Occupational and Organizational Psychology,* 619-638.

Jeremy, T. (2004). How to Increase Diversity through your Recruitment Practices. *Industrial and Commercial Training,* 158-161.

Jerry, N. M. (1978). Discrimination in Recruitment: An Empirical Analysis. *Industrial and Labor Relations Review, 32* (1).

Jian, H., & Christopher, C. J. (2004). Exploring Applicant Pool Quantity and Quality: The Effects of Early Recruitment Practice Strategies, Corporate Advertising, and Firm Reputation. *Personnel Psychology,* 685-717.

Kristin, B. B. (2004). An Exploration of Corporate Recruitment Descriptions on monster.com. *Journal of Business Communication, 41.*

Lisa, B. K., Begun, A. L., & Otto Salaj, L. L. (2009). Participant Recruitment in Intervention Research: Scientific Integrity and Cost-effective Strategies. *International Journal of Social Research Methodology,* 79-92.

Parry, E., & Shaun, T. (2008). An Analysis of the Use and Success of Online Recruitment Methods in the UK. *Human Resource Management Journal, 18* (3), 257-274.

Penny, C. Recruitment and Selection Practices In A Selected Organization. *Journal of Management Practice, 4* (1), 166-177.

Sandra, M. (n.d.). Alternative Recruitment Strategies Case Study on Contract Employment in the Public Service of Trinidad and Tobago.

Sen, I., Arjan, K. V., & Amaresh, D. (2009). Job Recruitment Networks and Migration to Cities in India. *Journal of Development Studies, 45* (4), 522-543.

Staren, E. D., & Unverzagt, D. (2010, June). Optimizing Physician Recruitment. *Physician Executive.*

Tim, D. F., & Guerry, M. A. (2009). Evaluating Recruitment Strategies using Fuzzy Set Theory in Stochastic Manpower Planning. *Stochastic Analysis and Applications,* 1148–1162.

Yakubovich, D. L. (2006). Stages of the Recruitment Process and the Referrer's Performance Effect. *Organization Science, 17* (6), 710-723.

Chapter 7

Selection

Outline

Introduction
Selection Process
Selection Tests
Cold Calling
Sorting the Curriculum-Vitae (CV)
Selection Interview
Reference Checking/Background Verification
Why Verify?
What to verify?
What not to verify?
Where to Verify?
How to Verify?
References
Essay Questions
Application Questions
Bibliography

Key Terms

- Graphology Test
- In-basket Exercises
- Intelligence Tests
- Interest Tests
- Mechanical Aptitude Tests
- O*NET Interest Profiler
- Rorschach Inkblot Test
- Situation Tests
- Thematic Apperception Test

Introduction

Selection

Selection follows recruitment process and involves picking up the right candidates from the pool of applicants shortlisted in the recruitment phase.

Selection follows recruitment in the process of hiring. Selection involves picking-up from the pool of candidates the ones having requisite qualification, experience and ability. The selected ones are termed as hires.

Selection Process

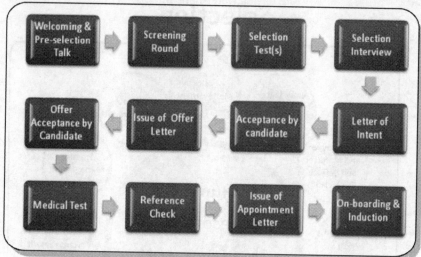

Figure 7.1:
Process of Selection

1. **Welcoming & Pre-selection Talk:** The candidates who have been short listed during the recruitment phase are invited for the selection process on a particular day. The candidates are welcomed and generally companies give a pre-selection talk to the candidates, briefing them about the company, its history and legacy, the job-on-offer etc. Some basic queries and doubts of the candidates can also be cleared during this round.

2. **Screening Round:** If the number of candidates is large, the companies have a screening round that may generally be a written test. This is to effectively weed-out candidates who do not meet basic competency expected by the company.

3. **Selection Test & Interview:** The companies choose an array of selection tools from test to interview and at times have multiple iterations of the same to select the 'right candidate. The various kinds of tests are discussed later in the chapter. The selection interview is also discussed later.

4. Letter of Intent: On satisfaction of the required qualification, experience and competency in the candidate, the company issues a 'letter of intent'. As per the law says, mere intention to do something, is not binding on the parties involved. Implying that, the agreement is not enforceable in the court of law, in the event of eventuality, say if the candidate does not join or if the employer on or before the date of joining dissolves the said position. Therefore, letter of Intent is basically a document illustrating the willingness of the employer to hire the candidate but may or may not turn into successful hiring. This is generally practiced by the firms who are having water-tight and fierce competitors in the market. Generally, it does not carry any compensation/emolument data.

5. Acceptance by the Candidate: The candidate must show in principle agreement and willingness towards the offer made by the company to further continue the process.

6. Issue of Offer Letter: The company then issues an offer letter which has details of the position, compensation, benefits etc., that is being offered to the candidate. The basic terms and conditions of employment are also documented. As per the Contract Act, in offer there is definite intention to enter into legally binding relationship. Offer involves expression of interest by one party to the other, to do or not to do something (Excluding acts of impossible nature or acts which are void ab initio). In an offer letter, the terms of offer are un-ambiguous and definite, with intention to create a legal relationship.

Contract Act, 1872
When one party makes a proposal or offer and the other party accepts it then it is an agreement. An agreement enforceable by law is a contract.

7. Acceptance of Offer by the Candidate: The candidate's acceptance of the offer is again necessary to continue the process. The acceptance may be preceded by some negotiations between the candidate and the company, usually related to salary-aspects. The length and degree of negotiations depends upon the expectations of the candidate and flexibility of the company.

8. Medical Test: Upon acceptance of the offer by the candidate, the companies arrange for a medical examination of the candidate by a registered medical practitioner to ensure the medical fitness of the candidate, especially with regard to the mental and physical demands of the job.

9. Reference Check: Background verification or reference checks are usually done by the company to prevent the chances of having wrong hires on board.

10. Issue of Appointment Letter: On finding the candidate medically fit and upon ascertaining the correctness of the claims made by the candidate during the process of employment about his qualification, experience, reasons for leaving past organizations etc., the company issue appointment letter to the candidate. Generally, the appointment letter is issued to the candidate on the day of joining. Appointment letter is basically, a form of contract between the parties involved viz. employer & employee and involves offer+acceptance+ enforceability by the law. Hence appointment letter qualifies to be a contract.

11. On-boarding and Induction: The new hire is put through a planned on-boarding and induction phase to acquaint him/her about the company, its stakeholders, supervisor, team-members etc.

Selection Tests

Selection tests are of various types. Some of them have been discussed below. Recruiters may use one or more of such tests depending upon the kind of job for which they are selecting the candidates.

Ability/Achievement Tests
It measures how well can the candidate perform tasks in a particular job.

1. Ability/Achievement/Trade Tests: The ability tests measure how well can the candidate perform the tasks in a particular job. In other words, it is a proficiency test of a candidate. Ability test may also be called achievement tests or trade tests. The composition of such tests shall differ from job to job (refer sample exhibit 1) however all such tests shall be directed at confirming the claims of the candidate regarding his/her ability.

Aptitude Tests
They attempt to find out the latent potential of a candidate towards a particular job.

2. Aptitude Tests: All apples are not ripe when they are plucked. Similarly all candidates do not come with prior experience or proven track-record of their abilities. In such cases aptitude tests prove to be very effective. Aptitude tests attempt to find out the latent potential of a candidate towards a particular job; not only in terms of performing it in the future but also learning the same. You cannot teach a hen to dance like a peacock. Without sounding condescending in any way, the fact remains that someone with an aptitude can always be trained but not without that. Aptitude test come in various types:

   a. **Intelligence Tests:** These tests try to measure the overall intelligence of the person to do the job and solve various problems that he/she might encounter while doing the job.

      i. **Verbal Ability Tests:** These tests measure spelling, grammar, ability to understand analogies and follow detailed written instructions.

      ii. **Numeric Ability Tests:** These tests measure basic arithmetic, number sequences, simple mathematics, numerical critical reasoning questions.

iii. **Abstract Reasoning Tests:** These measure and identify the underlying logic of a pattern and then determine the solution.

iv. **Spatial Ability Tests:** These measure ability to imagine shapes in two dimensions or to visualize three-dimensional objects presented as two-dimensional pictures.

v. **Data Checking Tests:** These measure how the speed and accuracy with which one can detect errors in data.

b. **Mechanical Aptitude Tests:** They measure orientation of a person to perform a mechanical job.

c. **Skill Tests:** Such tests attempt to determine whether the skill of the person in doing a particular job is at compilation (just acquired skill) or at automaticity (expertise) level.

3. Situation Tests: Situational tests are thought to be very effective in selection process as they exhibit a candidate's ability to think, ideate, his/her decision-making ability and many-a-times a reflection of their attitude and approach. In situation tests candidates are given scenarios that are close to real-life ones and then tested on how they react to the same. Some examples of situation tests are:

> **Situation Tests**
> These test a candidate's ability to think ideate and decide. Also these help in understanding a candidate's attitude.

a. **Role Plays:** In 'role plays' a group of candidates are provided a situation, usually a problem, which they have to enact and find solutions for the same.

b. **Group Discussion:** A group of candidates are provided a topic on which they are supposed to discuss, explore multiple perspectives and comment. In the process they are expected to develop solution or possible alternatives.

c. **In-basket Exercises:** A candidate is given a series of tasks that he/she has to complete in a fixed period of time, for example, issuing a warning letter, memo, writing to supplier, commenting on a new policy by the company, reviewing requests by some employees, etc. The speed and proficiency with which a candidate deals with each of such items in the basket are recorded and the data is used in selection process.

4. Interest Tests: A candidate's interest towards a particular career or occupation may at times be tested by the employers, since a genuine interest

> **Interest Tests**
> A candidate's interest towards a particular career or occupation may at times be tested by employee using interest tests.

is seen as a precursor to someone doing a good job. The more common career interest tests include:

a. **SDS:** Self Directed Search, also known as SCII - Strong-Campbell Interest Inventory - this is based in part on John L. Holland's six personality types (also known as the Holland Codes).

b. **SII:** Strong Interest Inventory. Based on the Holland Codes this test typically takes about 25 minutes to complete. It is widely used in for educational guidance in relation to career choice.

c. **The Career Key:** A career interest test, also based on the Holland Codes

The **O*NET Interest Profiler** (IP) is a self-assessment career exploration tool that can help clients discover the type of work activities and occupations that they would like and find exciting. Log on to http://www.onetcenter.org/IP.html?p=3

Personality Test

Jobs that are more demanding on the person, may call for a personality test.

5. Personality Tests: Most jobs demand a certain set of personality traits for example a sales person must be extrovert, gregarious, a BPO executive must be type B to avoid early burnout etc. Some employers use personality test to ensure a better candidate-job fitment.

General Awareness Test

A candidate's knowledge about the general economics, social, political, legal environment is tested using such kind of tests.

6. General Awareness Test: A candidate knowledge about the general economic, social, political and legal environment may be tested at times by the employers.

Projective Tests

These tests are designed to test the interpretation that a candidate makes about photos/pictures that he/she is confronted with.

7. Projective Tests: These tests are designed to test the interpretation that a candidate makes about photos or pictures that he/she is confronted with. It is a type of personality test designed to let a person respond to ambiguous stimuli, presumably revealing hidden emotions and internal conflicts. Unlike an "objective test" in which responses are analyzed according to a universal standard (for example, a multiple choice exam), the responses to a projective test are content analyzed for meaning rather than being based on pre-suppositions about meaning. There are a number of different types of projective tests. Some of the best-known projective tests are:

a. **The Rorschach Inkblot Test:** The Rorschach Inkblot was one of the first projective tests, and continues to be one of the best-known. Developed by Swiss psychiatrist Hermann Rorschach in 1921, the test consists of 10 different cards that depict an ambiguous inkblot. The participant is shown one card at a time and asked to describe what he or she sees in the image. The responses are recorded verbatim by the tester. Gestures, tone of voice, and other reactions are also noted. The results of the test can vary depending on which scoring system the examiner uses, of which many different systems exist.

b. The Thematic Apperception Test (TAT): In the Thematic Apperception Test, an individual is asked to look at a series of ambiguous scenes. The participant is then asked to tell a story describing the scene, including what is happening, how the characters are feeling and how the story will end. The examiner then scores the test based on the needs, motivations and anxieties of the main character as well as how the story eventually turns out.

8. Graphology Test: Graphology test is essentially a test of a person's handwriting. The term graphology was first used by a Frenchman Michon in 1875 and has been derived from the Greek words 'grapho' meaning 'I write' and 'logos' meaning 'theory'. Graphology test can tell a lot about the person – his emotions, his ego, his idiosyncrasies, his attitude, perception etc.

Graphology Test
It is a test of a person's handwriting and many reveal his emotions, ego, idiosyncrasies, attitude, perception etc.

The choice of selection test/tests to be employed by the employer in the selection process shall depend upon need, applicability, feasibility and cost to be incurred in administering a test.

Exhibit 1: Sample English Ability Test

1. .... about the organisation?

   A. Asked any questions anyone   B. Were any questions asked   C. Any questions be asked

2. We walked.......................... the entrance of the library.

   A. as far as   B. until   C. till to

3. What time ....yesterday?

   A. you arrived   B. arrived you   C. did you arrive

4. ....his carelessness our work was ruined.

   A. Result of   B. Since   C. Because of

5. His.........................to the problem is that of an administrator.

   A. design   B. review   C. approach   D. detail

6. ....destroys almost as much wheat as rats.

   A. Frost   B. Wet   C. Freeze   D. Hot

7. Even when wheat or rice is .... well, rats find ways of reaching it.

   A. drawn   B. stored   C. heaped   D. mended

Exhibit 2: Sample Aptitude Test

1. In these series, you will be looking at both the letter pattern. Fill the blank in the middle of the series or end of the series.

    1. SCD, TEF, UGH, ___ , WKL

        A. CMN   B. UJI   C. VIJ   D. IJT

    2. B2CD, ___ , BCD4, B5CD, BC6D

        A. B2C2D   B. BC3D   C. B2C3D   D. BCD7

2. In each of the following questions, two statements numbered, I and II are given. There may be cause and effect relationship between the two statements. These two statements may be the effect of the same cause or independent causes. These statements may be independent causes without having any relationship. Read both the statements in each question and mark your answer as:

    (A) If statement I is the cause and statement II is its effect;

    (B) If statement II is the cause and statement I is its effect;

    (C) If both the statements I and II are independent causes;

    (D) If both the statements I and II are effects of independent causes; and

    (E) If both the statements I and II are effects of some common cause.

3. **Statements**

    1. The prices of petrol and diesel in the domestic market have remained unchanged for the past few months.

    2. The crude oil prices in the international market have gone up substantially in the last few months.

        A. Statement I is the cause and statement II is its effect;

        B. Statement II is the cause and statement I is its effect;

        C. Both the statements I and II are independent causes;

        D. Both the statements I and II are effects of independent causes; and

        E. Both the statements I and II are effects of some common cause.

Exhibit 3: Businessballs Handwriting Quick Self-test

Graphology Explanation

Graphology is the study of handwriting, which for hundreds of years has been recognized unique to each individual.

Through the centuries, stating with Suetonius, the Roman historian, scholars like Shakespeare and Walter Scott believed that personality is reflected in the style of writing. The scientific establishment began to compile evidence and theories proving this as early as the 17th century.

Early work in Italy and France was taken forward in Germany, and the basis of today's methods were set down during the 19th and early 20th centuries. This makes graphology a relatively new science, which perhaps explains why many remain sceptical.

The term 'graphology' was first used by the Frenchman Michon in 1875, from the Greek 'grapho' meaning I write, and 'logos' meaning theory.

Graphology is now widely used in field raging from education, recruitment and human resource, to criminal psychology and illness disgnosis.

Further reading on the subject is available in many books including:

What your handwriting reveals?	M Gullan Whur	Awuarian Press
Manual of graphology	E Singer	Treasure Press
Character indicated by handwriting	R Baughan	Upcott Gill
The Psychology of handwriting	R Saudek	Allen & Unwin
P's and Q's	J Meyer	Geoffrey Bles
Self-knowledge through handwriting	H Jacoby	Dent & Sons

At its most complex, graphology is a large and dynamic subject. At its basic level however, it is relatively easy to understand and to begin to apply. Used as a simple guide, graphology can provide useful indicators to the writer's personality, whether you are analysing yourself or those around you.

N.B. Experimenting with analysis is interesting, enjoyable and a good way to learn, but do not to attempt formal analysis of others, particularly staff reporting to you, until and unless you become expert in the use of graphology and preferably receive some certification or accreditation to that effect.

The Basic Features of Handwriting

Write a few sentences freely on a level surface in the space provided.

Now look for and be able to identify the main features of the writing above:

- Size and proportions
- General layout
- Direction of lines
- Degree of connection
- Regularity
- Rhythm (or evenness)
- Degree of broadness
- Speed of writing
- Form of letters
- Covering of space
- Shading
- Angle of writing (slope)
- Right and left tendencies
- Spacing
- Degree of attention
- Pressure
- Decoration/distortion

Now follow the basic analysis process below, which you can use on other samples. The more you practice, the more you become able to analyse without referring to the written guidelines:

Graphology - The Basic Analysis

Is the Sample Valid?: That is, has the style of the writing been affected by any external influences? E.g., an uneven writing surface; an awkward writing position; or written on the move (in a car or train, etc.). You cannot analyse a sample that is not reliable. For the purpose of checking slope and coverage it is more difficult to analyse sample that have been written on lined paper.

Size: There are many aspects to the size of writing and alone it doesn't indicate many things. Size (and especially the relative size of letter parts) needs to be considered along with other factors. There are some simple indicators however. Small writing is generally a strong indicator of a detailed, technical personality. Large rounded and dominant central case letters indicate a friendly and sociable personality.

Letter-word Slope: Is there a consistent slope to the letters and therefore the words int the sample? Check by drawing lines through the up and downward strokes. Backwards slopes indicate an introverted personality; forward slopes are extraverted, upright strokes indicate a personality who is motivated by factors other than people, (i.e., neither extrovert nor introvert). The degree of slope reflects the degree of extraversion or introversion. The degree of consistency of the slope (i.e., parallel strokes) indicates the degree of emotional consistency.

Line Slope: Writing which rises to the right shows optimism and cheerfulness. Sagging to the right shows physical or mental weariness. (This applies to signatures sloping-downwards also.)

Flow: One of the essential indicators, but like any other factor not be used on its own. Generally, restraint is indicated every time the pen leaves the paper, and the converse applies. Gushing, eager, impulsive people have a more continuous flow of writing. Flowing writing has linked letters and sometimes linked words. Artistic and conceptual people who like space and time around them will often have completely separated letters. (It follows that pressure at school on some children to 'write joined-up' - because the common view is that to do otherwise is 'not grown-up'- is unnatural and often counter-productive. In any event continuity of flow does not correlate to intelligence).

Spacing: Space between words indicates social attitude to others. Close words are a sign of sociability. Large spaces between words indicate that the person is comfortable alone, and may even distrust others. Spacing between letters shows artistic spatially aware character, (artists, etc.)

Decoration and Distortion: Don't confuse the two. Decoration is intended; distorted is malformed and unintentional. Both are different to unfinished letters, which is a different indicator. Decoration is generally a sign that the writer wishes to be noticed more than he or she is at present. Malformed letters indicate a variety of things which must be dealt with individually. Unfinished words can be a sign of intelligence and impatience.

The Three Cases - Divisions of Personality

An essential aspect to analyse is the bias of the writing towards upper, central and lower cases. The upper case is the area in which the extended up-strikes are found in the tall letters like b, d, f, h, l, t, etc. The central or middle case is the central region occupied by letters with neither long up-strokes nor long down-strokes, such as a, c, e, m, n, o, etc. Which obviously means that the lower case is the area occupied by the extended down-strokes of letters such as g, j, p, q, etc.

Idealism religion philosophy	**upper**
Imagination logic pragmatism common-snse instinct	**central**
animal appetite physical force	**lower**

The central case contains most of the writing. The upper and lower cases are those which extend above and below the central body of each letter. The three cases represent the three aspects of our personality. If it helps you to assess the relative dominance of the three cases draw a horizontal set of 'tram-line' through some lines of writing to mark the division between the three cases. Look at the relative dominance and extent of each of the cases.

Upper – our 'higher' selves, and thinking about religion and philosophy

Central – our mental and social approach to life

Lower – our physical aptitudes and attitudes

Look where the writing is mainly concentrated, and where the emphasis is, this is where the emphasis of the personality is too. look for any encroachment from upper case to the line above or from lower case to the line below -it's a sure indication that the encroaching case is dominant. Also look at the central case to see if there is an upward or downward pull. An upward pull is best spotted if you see an arched pattern running through the central case. The pull pattern in the central case also indicates the emphasis of the personality.

Some Other Simple Indicators

- Large board upper loops are a sign of emotion.
- Right-pulled lower loops show interest for the good of others.
- Left-pulled upper case shows a fondness for the past.
- Uneven upper loops show changeable satisfaction, or disillusionment.
- Full left-pulled lower loops show physical fulfilment.
- Closed 'e's and other small closed central loops show secrecy.
- 'Stand-alone' or properly formed 's's at word ends show independence.
- Word-end 's's where top of letter is formed into downward right loop show a yieldign or co-operative nature.
- Angular central case is a sign of an interest in ideas rather than people.
- Rounded central case shows interest in people.
- Uncompleted case letters, e.g. 'a's, 'b's etc. (open when they would normally be joined loops) show a casual nature, very open shows propensity to gossip.
- Small writing is generally a sign of technical personality.
- Loops in angular writing show a potentially difficult character.
- 'T' cross strokes connecting a number of 't's with a single line shows speed of through (but not a guarantee of correct thinking).
- Omitted 'I' dots and 't' cross strokes forgetfulness or carelessness.
- Position and style of 'I' dots show different things:
  - Directly above, close to and in line means exacting.
  - Ahead means active and thinking.
  - Flicked shows sense of humour.
  - Behind shows thoughtful.
  - Inconsistent (varying positions) means a distracted mind.

In general you should try to build up a picture of the person you are analysing, using as many different indicators as possible. Also try to use other psychometric tests and systems to build up a multi-dimensional picture, the more perspectives you can use the better.

If this brief introduction interests you then get hold of a book or two on the subject and teach yourself more. It's a fascinating subject and a useful additional way of providing insight into your own personality and those around you.

(**Source:** Alan Chapman 2002-11. Used with permission. Retrieved Businessballs.com (18/4/2011). Not to be sold or published.

Cold Calling

A candidate calling up a company on his own to enquire about the vacancies is known as cold calling.

Cold Calling

Candidates who engage in 'cold-calling' i.e., calling-up the company regarding vacancies must be given through briefing about the job, in case a vacancy exists. This will save time of both the company and the candidate.

They should be briefed about:

- Job
- Deliverables
- KPI
- Responsibilities
- Desirable and essential qualification
- Experience
- Competencies
- Information about working conditions
- Information about working hours

Sorting the Curriculum-Vitae (CV)

Curriculum-vitae is the first claim that the candidate makes about himself/herself and hence is a very important document. But often sorting the CVs becomes quite difficult and wrong candidate start peeping-in or right candidates may be at times ignored. Here are some pointers on how to sort the CVs:

- Seemingly impressive CVs may not be really the right candidates.
- Look for the institution from which degree was awarded and check for genuineness.
- Look for consistency of language. At times certain portions may be very articulate, while others may be poor in grammar. Clearly it is a copy and paste.
- Look for parity in role and responsibilities in past organizations & the salary drawn. At times candidate may have just over-claimed, just to impress.
- Look for overlapping- months in year of experience. They may be faking.

- Also look for the candidates who undersell themselves. They may be high potential ones but may not be good at selling themselves.
- The interviewers must sit with the HR team to ensure consistency in sorting.

Selection Interview

Selection interview is one of the most common selection-tool that is used in most selection process. The success of the interview depends upon a lot of factors. Normally two kinds of errors happen in any selection process including interview i.e., letting the right person 'go' and hiring the wrong person. There are some dos and don'ts that the interviewer must follow to ensure the success of the process. Here are some of them:

Selection Interview
Most Common and important selection tool. Involves face to face interaction between the interviewers and job seeker.

Dos

- What should an interviewer ask the interviewee? What kind of questions will help test the real potential of the person? – These are fundamental questions regarding questions. Normally the interviewer ends-up asking either something that he/she knows very well (sorry this is not the general knowledge test of the interviewer) or something which the candidate does not know (once again this is not an opportunity to find faults). The interviewer should actually ask the candidate what he/she claims to know (CV) and find-out how well the candidate knows that.
- The right candidates have a combination of functional and behavioral competencies & experience. Interviewer must identify what this combination is before the interview.
- Interviewer must also plan areas for probing and areas of assessment.
- Competency-based interviews are more precise as they focus on the kind of skills required.
- Interviewer/ panel must be dedicated singularly to focus on the candidate at the time of conducting the interview. There must not be distractions.
- The panel must meet separately amongst itself and also with the HR. The meeting with HR helps find clarity on job description and job specifications so that the right requirement of the institution is known.

- The panel must also meet amongst itself to set-out the ground rules and to decide amongst themselves on what their approach should be. These meetings are very important.

- And finally, nobody is born as an interviewer but most of us end-up in the joining an interview panel almost like that. One fine day, just out of the blue, one may be asked to be a part of an interview panel and would conduct the interview purely on his/her own understanding and intuition. But that is not done and interviews cannot be successful with this kind of approach. One must undergo some kind of training before being a part of the panel. This training could focus on the right and wrong things done by the interviewer and hence know the dos and also the don'ts while conducting an interview.

Don'ts

Here are some things that any interviewer must not do during an interview process:

- Interviewing in midst of other works (too busy).
- Not reading through the CV of the candidate before the interview.
- Changing certain eligibility criteria's inside the interview room.
- Calling people by adjectives- younger, older, attractive etc.
- Asking personal questions.
- Bringing personal likes and dislikes in the interview and projecting the same on candidate.
- Focusing more on non-important, non-job issues, like about matching hobbies with the candidate.
- Lecturing candidate on what they need to be, what they ought to do in the organization.
- Under-preparing for an interview as much as it holds true for the candidate, it is also true for the interviewer.
- Being pushy as an interviewer does not seem to work. There are interviewers who think that by applying pressure they could be able to find out how a candidate reacts to the same. However they end up testing a person's patience. Such interviewer attitude does not simulate work scenario. They only make the interviewer appear unprofessional.

- Closing the interview in a right professional way is very important. The candidate must not be left in a lurch or given an impression that the organization is doing some favour by offering the job.

How to Avoid Sub-conscious Bias?

- Interview panel must meet before as well as after the interview to avoid subconscious bias.
- Candidate's name should not be used in discussion, instead they must be coded. Names can trigger many sub-conscious affiliations.
- Comparing each candidate to selection criteria makes better sense than comparing them among themselves.
- Interview notes must be specific, descriptive, factual and limited to the selection criteria. Any personal comment may go against the interviewee especially if it is litigated by a disgruntled candidate.
- Over-judging people by their first impression is dangerous.
- Probing effectively makes the process more objective.

Reference Checking / Background Verification

Why Verify?

One of the toughest and biggest challenges confronting human resource professionals today is verifying the background of a candidate. Apart from attrition and non-availability of Skilled manpower, another major problems the IT and ITES companies are facing is the presence of wrong hires on the rolls. 'Wrong hires are those who creep into the company by either using a fake qualification certificate or a fabricated experience certificate and go on to handle a process in which they pretend to have enough skill.' Research suggests that the cost of hiring a wrong candidate is almost 24 times higher than that of a normal candidate. In May 2002, Sandra Baldwin resigned as president of the United States Olympic committee after accepting that she lied about her academic achievements and that her claims of being a Ph.D. from the An US University was all but dissertation incomplete. According to an AOL Jobs Survey, one out of four people say they have lied or embellished the truth on their resume or in an interview to get a job.

Exhibit 4: Cost of the Wrong Hire

ACTUAL COSTS	HIDDEN COSTS
• SEPARATION PAY	• SEPARATION PROCESSING
• ACCRUED VACATION	• LOWER/LOST PRODUCTIVITY
• CONTINUED BENEFITS	DURING INTERIM (PEERS, SUPERVISORS, SUBORDINATES)
• RECRUITING FEES	• LOWER/LOST PRODUCTIVITY
• INCREASED UNEMPLOYMENT TAXES	DURING RAMP-UP TIME
• ADVERTISING/ MARKETING MATERIALS	• RESUME SCREENING
• INTERVIEWING COSTS	• INTERVIEWING TIME/EXPENSES
• ASSESSMENTS	• INFORMAL TRAINING
• CRIMINAL CHECKS/ REFERENCE CHECKING	• MISSED DEADLINES
• MEDICAL EXAMS/DRUG TESTS	• LOSS OF INTELLECTUAL PROPERTY
• RELOCATION EXPENSES	• LOWER MORALE FROM OVERWORK
• TEMPORARY/CONTRACT EMPLOYMENT FEES	• "CHAIN REACTION" TURNOVER
• ORIENTATION MATERIALS	• CLIENT ISSUES FROM TURNOVER
• TRAINING PROGRAMS	• CLIENT LOSS

In calculating the cost of a wrong hire the cost of hiring the wrong candidate, the time for the second candidate to get up to speed, any relocation and severance, the cost of poor productivity by the wrong candidate, etc., all have to be considered. The above exhibit shows the various actual cost and hidden cost items related to a fabricated candidate.

But above all it causes a lot of embarrassment to the firm to find that they had been duped by a crook into making them believe what he wanted them to. The following process of initiating action could get tricky as at times if the concerned candidate is dealing with firm's clients since then the clients have also to be informed about the fraud. This may dent the image of the company in the eyes of the client as being naïve and irresponsible by putting their work in unsafe hands. Then firing a candidate becomes a sensitive issue as it may not only affect the morale of other workers but also could at times lead to serious loss of confidential data.

An effective reference check shall not only weed-away such candidates but shall also do it in a fashion that it is non-intrusive yet fool-proof. We shall discuss how to go about doing the same later in the chapter.

What to Verify?

Virtually everything that the candidate has claimed comes under the umbrella of scrutiny in background reference checks. However the background reference checks may fall under either one of the two categories:

- a) Factual Verification
- b) Qualitative Verification

- a) **Factual Verification:** This involves verification of facts related to the candidate like:
    1) Educational qualification
    2) Past work experience
    3) Criminal background
    4) Identity and address

- b) **Qualitative Verification:** Qualitative verification refers to seeking data about the character, conduct, behavior, work-adeptness, individual attributes, strength, weaknesses etc., about a candidate.

What not to Verify?

Reference checking should not be personal or intrusive. Remember, that person's dignity and personal zone should not be trespassed. Even if the company is outsourcing background verification, clear instruction should be given not to violate such norms. Globally, standard for recruiters is to steer-away from anything mentioned below, related to candidate, spouse or other relatives of candidate:

- a) Age, date, place of birth
- b) Gender
- c) Marital status
- d) No. of children
- e) Race, ethnicity
- f) Native language
- g) Religious preference
- h) Health/physically handicap (unless having direct impact on job/ co works).
- i) Sexual orientation.

Where to Verify?

There are various sources for background verification although primarily ex-supervisors of past-organization (especially the last two organizations) are the target, if the candidate has work experience. However if the candidate is fresher then the last alma mater professors, HOD, are primary target.

The different sources for reference checking would be:

a) **Document Reference:** Documents like address proofs, voter-id cards passport, driving license, educational certificates, job experience letters, relieving letters, fax certificates, work-permits can be used for reference checking.

b) **Professional Reference:** A professional reference is one who has known the candidate in official capacity either as a supervisor, colleague or as a reporting head.

c) **General Reference:** A general reference may be one who may have known the candidate in some other way quite well. A general reference must be in a responsible position and have a strong background.

d) **Faculty Reference:** A faculty reference is from world of academics. Faculty reference comes both the from in from of recommendation letter as well as through telephonic checking.

e) **Third Party Reference:** A third party reference is generally a manpower search firm which may have records about the candidate.

f) **Internet Reference:** With the advent of social-media, blogs, social networking etc., internet has emerged as a major source of background verification.

Exhibit 5: Backchannel Referencing

Background referencing is a fad and backchannel referencing is in. Backchannel referencing involves pre-qualifying the candidate by speaking to peers, searching on public domain, social media, news sites, published sources, etc. Cost saving and targeting only the right candidates emerge as biggest take-aways.

Exhibit 6: National Skills Registry (NSR)

National Skills Registry (NSR) is set-up and managed by NDML (a fully owned subsidiary of National Securities Depository Limited (NSDL) which is the largest securities depository in India) on behalf of NASSCOM (www.nasscom.in). National Skills Registry is a NASSCOM initiative to have a robust and credible information repository about all persons working in the industry. This develops trusted and permanent fact sheet of information about each professional along-with background check reports. NSR is a security best practice for the industry and assures identity security, industry acceptance to honest professionals. It is a web-based system hosting a fact sheet of information about existing and prospective employees of Indian IT & ITeS / BPO industry. This can be used by the IT & ITeS / BPO industry and its clients as a credible source of information about the registered professionals who are being employed or put on client assignments. On one hand NSR improves the global image if the Indian IT/ITES industry and on the other hand it reduces the cost of repetitive background checks on professionals. Considering that NSR is positioned well to serve a process and interest that is common and applicable to all organized, security conscious businesses, NASSCOM and NDML have agreed to extend the benefits of NSR initiative to Banking & Finance industry also.

How to Verify?

The process of verification can be enumerated as follows:

1. **Deciding on Commencement Time for Reference-checking:** It is important to take a call on the commencement time for reference-checking. This is mostly a strategic decision and varies from firm to firm. However within a firm it remains constant for all the positions mostly except in case of very high-profile recruits. Firms can choose to pre-qualify the candidates or begin the reference-checking at the time of sorting the CVs or post-offer or even post-joining of the candidate. The choice of the timing depends primarily on the cost-benefit perception of the company with respect to reference-checks.

2. **Decide on What Needs to be Checked/Verified:** As discussed before, it is important to have a clear idea that what needs to be checked or verified. The degree of verification amongst various menu items may differ from person to person and from role to role.

3. **Decide and Agree upon Code of Ethics to be Followed by the Agency:** The team of reviewers or the agency doing the background verification must decide and agree upon a common code of ethics, so as not to violate the privacy of a candidate's personal and emotional zone. This would also help in keeping the background verification process legally correct.

4. **Check Feasibility of Reference Sources:** At times it may be found that some of the references mentioned by the candidate may not be appropriate or accessible. In some cases it may be very difficult to speak to certain mangers for the purpose of reference checking. In such scenarios some additional references may be requested from the candidate.

5. **Finalize Reference Sources:** After proper analysis of the information to be collected and the quality of information desired, the reference sources are finalized.

6. **Qualify Questions:** The questions to be asked to the references must be jotted down and finalized. Any special question to be asked to the refrences must be drafted after due consultation with the interviewers/supervisors. This enables better reference check and elevates the quality of information.

7. **Obtain Permission:** Before proceeding with the reference-checking, the candidate must be sensitized that process is about to begin and his consent to the same must be taken.

8. **Conduct Reference Check:** The actual process of reference check is then performed through phone, e-mail, letters, social networking sites, etc.

9. **Result Analysis:** The results are then collated and analyzed. The comments of the various references are compared and inferences are drawn.

10. **Report Findings:** The report is then tabled to the appropriate authorities for decision-making and further action, as deemed fit for the case.

Essay Questions

1. Explain the 'Selection Process'. Which are the significant stages of this process, in your opinion? Why?

2. Differentiate between 'Letter of Intent', 'Offer Letter' and 'Appointment Letter'.

3. Describe various types of selection tests. Explain the relevance of graphology tests.

4. Explain 'cold calling'. Should cold calling be taken seriously?

5. Write about selection-interviews. What are the Dos and Don'ts for an interview? How can one avoid rub-conscious bias?

6. 'Reference-check is an important last step in the selection process of a candidate.' Do you agree? Substantiate.

7. What should be borne in mind while during reference-checks? What is back-channel referencing?

Application Questions

Mock-Hiring Drill Project

Divide the class into teams, each team may have 5-6 people. Each team floats a dummy company, on the lines of an existing actual company. The position, for which they have done job analysis in the earlier chapter using PAQ (Chapter 5, Application Question 1), they should engage in the following tasks:

a) Design a recruitment advertisement, advertising that position. Each advertisement is pasted on the class notice–boards. Students can apply in any firm (except their own) for any numbered of jobs that they want. They must apply with their CVs.

b) Each company (team) then screens the applications based on some criterias. These criterias may be watered down for classroom project, however must be documented by the team in advance and shared with the instructor.

c) Each company (team) then takes the screened-in candidates through a pre-decided selection process. The selection tools must have a test & interview, besides any other choosen by the team.

d) The mock-interviews must be done in front of the whole class, who sit as observers.

e) Each company (team) then announces its final list of selected candidates.

f) Each team prepares a detailed report on what they did and their key learnings.

g) Each team should also solicit a written feedback from the candidates in particular as to how they found the selection process.

h) Each team must also take a written feedback from the rest of the class as to what they felt in general about their company Selection Process (especially the interview).

i) Each team must compile all the results and give a detailed presentation.

Bibliography

Androniki, P., Elizabeth, I., & David, W. (1996). The Graduate Management Trainee Pre-selection Interview. *Personnel Review, 25* (4), 21-37.

Barbara, B. W. (2008). Selection And Interview Procedures At A Multinational Company. *Business Communication Quarterly*, 100-102.

Bernard, M., & Stanley, P. (2005). Vice Chancellors for the 21st Century? A Study of Contemporary Recruitment and Selection Practices in Australian Universities. *Management Research News, 28* (6).

Charles, M. (1995). Successful People Selection in action. *Health Manpower Management, 21* (5), 12–16.

Chuel, M. J., & Brian, K. H. (2001). How to Hire Employees Effectively? *Management Research News, 24*.

Cohen, S. L. (1974). Issues in the Selection of Minority Group Employees. *Human Resource Management, 13* (1), 12-18.

DeKay, S. (2009). Are Business-oriented Social Networking Web Sites Useful Resources for Locating Passive Jobseekers? Results of A Recent Study. *Business Communication Quarterly, 72* (1), 101-105.

Derrick, B. F., & Christine, B. L. (1994). Executive Search and Selection Consultancies in France. *European Business Review, 94* (1).

Drysdale, D., Bonanni, C., & Shuttlewood. (2010). Return on Investment for Background Screening. *International Business & Economics Research Journal*, 65-70.

Employers' Selection Methods Inadequate — Disquieting Research Results. (1989). *Management Services, 33* (3), 49-50.

Heather, J., Cliff, L., & Dora, S. (2003). Anticipatory Socialization: The Effect of Recruitment and Selection Experiences on Career Expectations. *Career Development International*.

Hoffmaster, G. (2011). Looking Beyond Reactive Fixes: How Do You Make Talent Acquisition Truly Better? *Journal of Corporate Recruiting Leadership, 6* (6), 3-7.

Holtbrügge, D., Friedmann, C. B., & Puck, J. F. (2010). Recruitment and retention in foreign firms in India: A Resource-based View. *Human Resource Management, 49* (3), 439-455.

Jim, S., & Vanessa, K. (2000). Graduate Recruitment and Selection Practices in Small Businesses. *Career Development International*.

Josefina, T. A. (2010). An Alternative Approach to a Critical Issue in Employment: Identifying and Correcting Potential Disparities in Employee Selections Before They Happen. *Employee Relations Law Journal, 36* (3), 54-64.

Kumar P Aneel, IT Companies Face Problem of Wrong Hires, The Times of India, Oct 9, 2005.

Levinthal, D., & Posen, H. E. (2007). Myopia of Selection: Does Organizational Adaptation Limit the Efficacy of Population Selection.

Administrative Science Quarterly, 52 (4), 586-620.

Lodato, M. A., Highhouse, S., & Brooks, M. E. (2011). Predicting Professional Preferences for Intuition-based Hiring. *Journal of Managerial Psychology, 26* (5), 352-365.

Marieke, V. D., Margo, B., & Sietske, W. (2006). *Employee Relations, 28* (6), 523-539.

Mark, L. A., & Kleiner, B. H. (2000). How to Hire Employees Effectively. *Management Research News, 23.*

Michael, H., & Brian, K. H. (1994). Conducting an Effective Selection Interview. *Work Study, 43* (7), 8-13.

Michael, M. J. (2007). Person-organization Fit. *Journal of Managerial Psychology, 22* (2), 109-117.

Moore, L. F. (1973). Using The Video Tape In Selection Interviewing: A Report of Three Studies. *Academy of Management Proceedings,* 377-382.

Novoa, E. G., Freire, G., Snider, S., & Lane, S. (2009). Strategic Customer Service and Employee Selection. *Allied Academies International Conference: Proceedings of the Academy of Strategic Management, 8* (2), 20-22.

Outsourcing of Recruitment and Selection is Beneficial for an Organization [Individual Analysis of Ten Banks Including Local and Multinational]. (2010). *Interdisciplinary Journal of Contemporary Research in Business, 2* (1), 355-383.

Richard, K. (2003). Trends in Organizations and Selection: An introduction. *Journal of Managerial Psychology, 18* (5), 382-394.

Romanies Michael, The cost of a wrong hire, or doing without, how much is it really costing you? http://www.allbusiness.com/labor-employment/human-resources-personnel-management/11707073-1.html

Samantha, L., & Karen, S. (2010). The Dilemma of Judging Unpaid Workers. *Personnel Review, 39* (1), 80-95.

Schmitt, N. (2007). The Value of Personnel Selection: Reflections on Some Remarkable Claims. *Academy of Management Perspectives, 21* (3), 19-23.

Sharon, I., & Neil, M. (1999). Auditing Recruitment and Selection Using Generic Benchmarking: A Case Study. *The TQM Magazine, 11* (5), 333-340.

Stephen, D., V, N., & Ross, J. (1994). The Role of Personality Testing in Managerial Selection. *Journal of Managerial Psychology, 9* (5), 3-11.

Terpstra, D. E., Kethley, R. B., Foley, R. T., & Limpaphayom, W. (2000). The Nature of Litigation Surrounding Five Screening Devices; (Tam). Spring Vol. 29, Issue 1, p 12p. *Public Personnel Management, 29* (1), 43.

Ullah, M. M. (2010). A Systematic Approach of Conducting Employee Selection Interview. *International Journal of Business & Management, 5* (6), 106-112.

Vieria, M. T., & Valente, E. T. (2009). From Normative to Tacit Knowledge: CVs Analysis in Personnel Selection. *Employee Relations, 31* (4), 427-447.

Wickramasinghe Vathsala, W. (2007). Staffing Practices in the Private Sector in Sri Lanka. *Career Development International, 12* (2), 108-128.

Chapter 8

Reliability & Validity in Selection

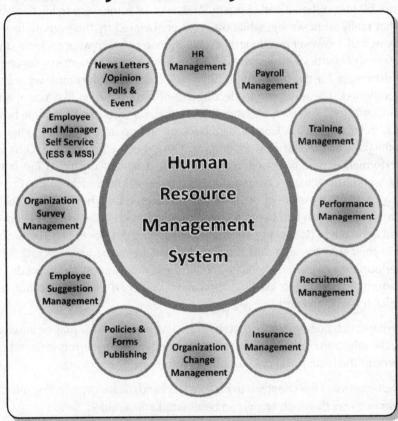

Outline

Introduction

Kinds of Errors in Selection

Reliability

Interpreting Point biserial correlation coefficient (rpbi) values

Validity

Kinds of Validity

Relationship between reliability & validity

Interpreting Validity Coefficients

Essay Questions

Application Questions

Bibliography

Key Terms

Concurrent Validity
Content Validity
Criterion Validity
Face Validity
Internal Consistency

Interpreting Point Biserial Correlation Coefficient (r_{pbi}) Values
Inter-rater Reliability
Parallel-test Reliability

Point Biserial Correlation Coefficient
Rehearsal-effect
Test-retest Reliability
Validity

Introduction

India's recent dominance over the world of cricket has been appreciated and envied equality. When the brand new edition of the T20 world cup started in 2007, India went on to win the maiden tournament. The T20 Indian Premier League (IPL) has already acquired an iconic status all over the world for its big ticket entertainment. So when India was put in the Group C qualifiers for the third edition of the T20 world cup, everybody thought it would be a cake-walk for the Indian team. However to the shock and dismay of millions of cricket-lovers, India crashed-out of the tournament. As usual there were acrimonious cries of utter disbelief and criticism. And as usual some were trying to analyse what really went wrong, while others overwhelmed by their emotions were crying foul. However one thing that was common between what cricket analysts, lovers and fanatics were expressing, was the error in judgement in selecting the Indian team for the tournament. Both 'selection and 'omissions' were being questioned. The wisdom of selecting out-of-form batsman like Yuvraj Singh and 'omission' of in-form big hitter Robin Uthapa was bizarre. Even more bizarre was 'selecting' Piyush Chawla as a back-up spinner to Harbhajan Singh and 'omission' of the star bowler Pragyan Ojha. Both Uthappa and Ojha had performed exceedingly well in the 2010 IPL-3 which concluded just before the world cup. Actually Ojha was adjudged the best bowler of the Indian Premier League -3. The excuse of the selection committee that these players peaked later and selection had been made before that, made little sense. If selections had been made on recent performance then how did player like Yuvraj Singh find their way-through and if selections had been made predicting future performance of players then how could these mechanisms fail to predict the performance of players like Utahappa and Ojha? Then were the selection tools 'reliable' and validated'?

Perhaps such questions in cricket shall remain unanswered or may be answered by the selection committee, however one thing is sure that errors in 'selections' can cost the team's and organization's performance very dearly.

The objective of this chapter is to explore ways and means of perfecting selection tests in a way that such errors can be omitted and avoided.

Kinds of Errors in Selection

Statistically speaking the error can either be systematic or random in nature; where systematic error shall mean those caused by faults in the system or the process whereas random errors would be more related to the usage of the selection tools. However as we just observed, in selection the two main types of errors could be 'selection errors' and 'omission error'.

Selection Errors

Selection errors are those resulting from hiring a 'wrong person'. In such cases success is predicted and failure results. The costs of such errors include the costs of loss (indicating the period for which the wrong-hire worked), cost of training and cost of re-hire, re-training etc.

Omission Errors

Omission errors are those resulting from letting a right person' go and not hiring him/her. The costs of such errors shall primarily be computed on lost opportunity. However it may be impossible to properly estimate the total loss.

Other Errors

Besides attrition and non-availability of skilled human resource, the problem of wrong hires confronts most of the organizations. Wrong hires always mean a wasted cost to the company. It is estimated that the cost of hiring a wrong candidate is always 24 times more than hiring an average candidate. One way to ensure 'correctness' in hiring is to have reliable and robust selection tools.

Reliability

Reliability in selection tools is a precursor to validity. If a test is not reliable, it cannot have validity as well. No two tests are similar. Differences in results may occur due to either candidate specific factors or due to test-specific factors. Candidate specific may include fatigue, monotony, focus, attention-span etc. Test specific factors can be caused by ambiguity in questions; ambiguity in directions/instructions given to examinees for answering the question; ambiguity in scoring pattern or due to incompetence of the rater(s).

Reliability

Reliability of a selection test is the consistency of scores among candidates, when administered different forms of the same test.

However, more the results of two tests are comparable, higher is the reliability of the test. In short, reliability of a selection test is the consistency of scores among candidates, when administered different forms of the same test.

Absolutely identical scores are never possible. But a good selection tool will have high consistency or reliability.

Types of Reliability

Reliability could be of three types:

a) **Test-retest Reliability**: Test-Retest reliability refers to the degree of consistency in scores when a test is administered several times. It is generally represented by coefficient of stability.

The same test is administered on the same set of respondents and the scores are calculated. The correlation coefficient between two sets of scores is calculated. A high correlation indicates high test-retest reliability. Correlation coefficient of 1.0 is a too perfect-case to happen, however coefficient values closer to this value shall indicate high test-retest reliability.

Limitation of Test-retest Reliability

Shorter the time-duration between two tests, higher is the correlation coefficient and longer is the duration between two tests, lower is coefficient value.

There are two effects which are important to consider at this stage. One is the 'rehearsal-effect' and the other is the 'learning-loss' effect.

If the period between two tests is too short the 'rehearsal' effect comes into play i.e., because of the fact that the candidate has practiced the question before, he/she performs better in the test. However if the duration between two tests is too long then the 'leaning-loss' effect comes into play i.e., candidates tend to perform poorly in the second test due to loss of leaning related to isolated concepts or facts. An optimal duration between two tests is about two weeks.

b) **Inter-rater Reliability**: Different raters administering and examining the same test must not produce inconsistent results. The consistency among raters in their observations or evaluation of a test represents inter-rater reliability.

Inter-rater reliability is calculated by calculating the correlation coefficient between the rating/observations of two raters. Again a high coefficient value will indicate high inter-rater reliability.

c) **Parallel-test Reliability**: Suppose 100 questions are made that address the same construct. Then these questions are randomly divided to form two tests. Both these tests are administered on the same candidates. Then a correlation between the results of both the test is established. This is the measure of reliability.

d) **Internal Consistency**: Internal consistency or coefficient alpha (á) measure the consistency of results across various items in a test. In other words each item on a test not only represents a particular domain of interest but also produces consistent results.

The index used to measure internal consistency is *Cronbach alpha*, given by statistician named Lee Cronbach.

Cronbach alpha measures homogeneity between items in a test. It is represented as

$$\hat{a} = \frac{k}{k-1}\left[1 - \frac{\sum_{i=1}^{k} p_i(1-p_i)}{\hat{\sigma}_x^2}\right]$$

Where k = number of items in a test

$\hat{\sigma}_x^2$ = sample variance for the total score

p_i = item difficulty or proportion of examinees who answered items i correctly.

Cronbach alpha expects each item in the test to be a mini-test itself. Large alpha scores will indicate such levels of consistency.

Example 1: Assuming, the number of items in a particular test are 5. The proportion of examinees who answered items 1,2,3,4,5 correctly are 0.5, 0.6, 0.7, 0.8 and 0.9 respectively. The sample variance for total score is 1.74. Calculate the reliability coefficient for internal consistency.

Solution:

Reliability Coefficient for Internal Consistency

$$\hat{a} = \frac{k}{k-1}\left[1 - \frac{\sum_{i=1}^{k} p_i(1-p_i)}{\hat{\sigma}_x^2}\right]$$

$$\hat{a} = \frac{5}{5-1}\left[1 - \frac{0.5(1-0.5) + 0.6(1-0.6) + 0.7(1-0.7) + 0.8(1-0.8) + 0.9(1-0.9)}{1.74}\right]$$

$$\hat{a} = \frac{5}{4}\left[1 - \frac{(0.5 \times 0.5) + (0.6 \times 0.4) + (0.7 \times 0.3) + (0.8 \times 0.2) + (0.9 \times 0.1)}{1.74}\right]$$

$$\hat{a} = \frac{5}{4}\left[1 - \frac{(0.25) + (0.24) + (0.21) + (0.16) + (0.09)}{1.74}\right]$$

$$\hat{a} = \frac{5}{4}\left[1 - \frac{0.95}{1.74}\right]$$

$$\hat{a} = \frac{5}{4}\left[\frac{0.79}{1.74}\right]$$

$$\hat{a} = 0.57$$

What shall the value of 0.57 indicate? Does it indicate a high reliability coefficient for internal consistency? Actually not. To understand interpretation of reliability scores we may use the following table:

Table 8.1: Interpreting Alpha Scores

Reliability Coefficient Values	Interpretation
0.90 and above	Outstanding (very high reliability)
0.80 – 0.89	Good (High reliability)
0.70 – 0.79	Average (Reliability is limited)
Below 0.70	Unreliable tests

For the purpose of selection tests reliability coefficients of 0.90 or more are thought to be reliable. Cronbach's alpha ranges from 0 to 1.0. Higher values (higher reliability) are required in selection tests as they are administered only once on the candidates and results are used to make hiring decisions. Henceforth, it is also important to understand how to improve alpha values. In the previous example, we saw alpha values to be 0.57. This is definitely not good enough. So what do we do about such tests? There are two ways to improve the alpha value:

a) By Altering the Length of the Test

In this method we increase the number of items in a particular test. The percentage of measurement error reduces when number of questions are increased.

To anticipate the change in alpha value as a result of lengthening the test, we use the Spearman – Brown prophecy formula, i.e.

$$\alpha^{new} = \frac{m\alpha^{old}}{1 + (m-1)\alpha^{old}}$$

Where, α^{new} = new reliability coefficient value after increasing the length of the test.

α^{old} = reliability coefficient value before lengthening the test.

m = new test length divided by old test length

Example 2: Assuming in the earlier test (example 1) the number of items are increased from 5 to 10.

Solution:
Then the new reliability estimate will be –

$$\alpha^{new} = \frac{m(0.57)}{1 + (m-1)0.57}$$

m = 10/5 = 2

$$\alpha^{new} = \frac{2(0.57)}{1 + (2-1)0.57}$$

$$\alpha^{new} = \frac{1.14}{1 + 0.57}$$

$$\alpha^{new} = 0.73$$

The new alpha value is 0.73. This is an improvement over the earlier.

But will increase in the number of items in a test, appreciate the alpha value always? To answer this question, few practical considerations are required. One, that the test length cannot be increased too much that in effect becomes incompatible with the time available or with the candidate's ability to take the test. Second, the impact on alpha values is more when a shorter test is lengthened.

b) By Altering the Quality of Question in a Test

The quality of questions determine alpha value to a large extent. A test which has better quality of questions will definitely be more reliable. But how do we know whether a question is a good or poor in terms of quality? What makes a question good?

A question is considered to be good question when it can effectively discriminate between a good candidate and a poor candidate. In other words, a question on a test will be considered of high quality if good candidates are able to answer it correctly whereas the poor candidates are not able to answer the question.

The discrimination of a question is measured by a correlation coefficient known as point-biserial correlation (r_{pbi}). Point-biserial correlation coefficient (r_{pbi}) is the correlation between a candidate's score on a particular question ('1' if he gets it correct and '0' if he gets it incorrect) and the candidate's overall score in a test.

Calculating Point Biserial Correlation Coefficient (r_{pbi})

Point Biserial Correlation coefficient (r_{pbi}) is calculated by using the following formula –

$$r_{pbi} = \frac{M_p - M_q}{S_t} \sqrt{pq}$$

M_p = whole test mean for candidate's answering item correctly (i.e., coded as 1)
M_q = whole test mean for candidate's answering item incorrectly (i.e., coded as 0)
S_t = standard deviation for whole test
p = proportion of candidates answering correctly
q = proportion of candidates answering incorrectly.

Example 3

Let us take a sample data of the performance of 8 candidates in a test having x number of items:

Candidate	Q1	Q2	Q3	Q4... x	Total
Ritwik	1	0	1		50
Anil	1	0	1		48
Sunaina	1	0	1		46
Leena	1	0	1		40
Sumanta	0	1	1		36
Nilesh	0	1	1		31
Veer	0	1	1		28
Shrishti	0	1	1		24

Solution: Total Mean = (50+48+46+40+36+31+28+24) / 8
= 303/8
= 37.9

Standard Deviation

Scores (x)	(x-μ)	(x-μ)²
50	50 − 37.5 = 12.5	156.25
48	48 − 37.5 = 10.5	110.25
46	46 − 37.5 = 8.5	72.25
40	40 − 37.5 = 2.5	6.25
36	36 − 37.5 = -1.5	2.25
31	31 − 37.5 = -6.5	42.25
28	28 − 37.5 = -9.5	90.25
24	24 − 37.5 = -13.5	182.25

$$\text{Standard Deviation} = \sqrt{\frac{\sum(x-\mu)^2}{N}}$$

$$\sqrt{\frac{156.25+110.25+72.25+6.25+2.25+42.25+90.25+182.25}{8}} = \sqrt{\frac{662}{8}}$$

Standard Deviation = 9.09

For Question 1

$M_p = (50+48+46+40) / 4 = 46$
$M_q = (36+31+28+24) / 4 = 29.75$
$p = 0.50$
$q = 0.50$

$$r_{pbi} = \frac{46-29.75}{9.09} \sqrt{0.50 \times 0.50}$$

$$r_{pbi} = \frac{16.25}{9.09} \times 0.50$$

$$r_{pbi} = -0.89$$

For Question 2

$M_p = (36+31+28+24) / 4 = 29.75$

$M_q = (50+48+46+40) / 4 = 46$

$p = 0.50$

$q = 0.50$

$$r_{pbi} = \frac{29.75-46}{9.09} \sqrt{0.50 \times 0.50}$$

$$r_{pbi} = \frac{-16.25}{9.09} \times 0.50$$

$$r_{pbi} = -0.89$$

For Question 3

$M_p = (50+48+46+40+36+31+28+24) / 8$

$M_p = 37.5$

$M_q = 0$

$p = 1.0$

$q = 0.0$

$$r_{pbi} = \frac{37.5-0}{9.09} \sqrt{1.0 \times 0.0}$$

$$r_{pbi} = 0$$

Interpreting Point Biserial Correlation Coefficient (r_{pbi}) Values

Questions with high positive r_{pbi} indicate that candidates with better scores tend to answer it correctly, whereas, candidates with lower scores tend to answer it incorrectly.

Example: In question number 1, the point-biserial correlation coefficient between question 1 and total score is very high (0.89) indicating that it effectively discriminates between a good and a poor performer.

The point-biserial correlation coefficient between question 2 and the total score is – 0.89. This indicates that the question 2 discriminates candidates in an opposite way then the total score do. Questions with negative correlation actually reduce reliability.

The point biserial correlation coefficient between question 3 and the total score is 0. This indicates that this question does not discriminate at all between candidates who are good performers from those who are poor performers. Questions with very small positive r_{pbi} or zero r_{pbi} may in fact reduce reliability.

Validity

Validity is referred as the consistency between the score of a selection test and the quality that it is expected to measure. In other words, validity of selection test indicates that how far inferences made from a test are correct. High validity shall mean that the test measured what it intended to do in the first place.

Kinds of Validity

For selection tests there are three major kinds of validity:

1. **Content Validity**: Content validity measures the degree to which a selection test is a representative of the domain that it intends to cover. A selection test is said to have content validity if it covers what it originally set out to test.

   Example: A test to measure a candidate's knowledge of logical reasoning must not have only verbal or only non-verbal reasoning. It should have a mix of both. There are two types of content validity.

   a) **Representative Validity:** Representation or translation validity is the extent to which an abstract theoretical construct can be converted into a specific practical selection test.

   b) **Face Validity**: If a test appears valid, then it is known as face validity. There is no mathematical way to prove face validity. Common sense is used to test face validity, for example a test of English should have some questions in English language. Face validity cannot assure the validity of a test as the old adage says *'all that glitters is not gold'*.

2. **Criterion Validity**: Criterion Validity is the correlation between the test and criterion variable(s) that have been taken as representative of the construct. Criterion Validity of test will be determined based upon its ability to predict the behavior of a candidate in a specified situation. A criterion variable could be job performance or decision making etc.

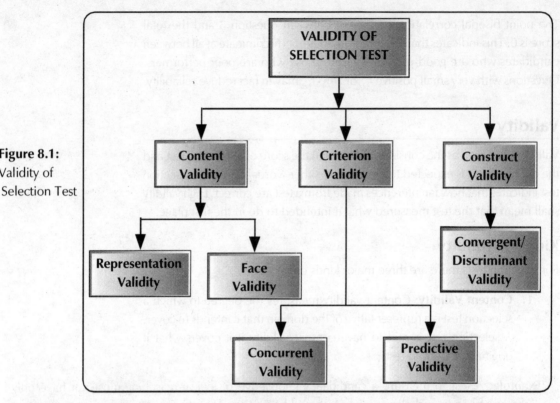

Figure 8.1: Validity of Selection Test

Criterion Validity could be of two types:

a) Concurrent Validity: If current employees are used to measure the criterion validity, then it is called concurrent validity. In this case the test data and criterion data are collected at the same time.

Example: The selection test is administered to a sample of current employees. At the same time, their performance scores in actual job-setting are also collected. Then a correlation is established between them. If the validity is high, then such test may be used for making hiring decisions.

b) Predictive Validity: Predictive validity is measured by administering the test on actual candidates (applicants). Their test data is collected. They are hired irrespective of their performance in the test. Later on their job performance data is collected, which then can be used to establish validity. Predictive validity can be used to perfect a test. Over a period of time the test can be adjusted to improve its validity.

3. **Construct Validity**: A construct is a theory that is being assessed through a test for instance emotional intelligence. A test is said to

have construct validity if it can accurately measure the extent to which the design of a construct (test developed from the theory/construct) measures what theory intends to do.

Construct validity is mostly established over a period of time through a validity of methods like:

a) Convergent/Discriminant (Divergent) Validity

When the measures of a construct that are expected to correlate, do so, then it is said to have convergent validity, and when the constructs that are not expected to correlate, do not, then it is said to have discriminant validity. They together establish construct validity.

In very simple words, convergent validity shows that whether a test measures what it should while discriminant validity shows that whether it does not measure what it should not.

Many times, multi-trait – multi-method matrix may be used to demonstrate construct validity. This method was developed by Campbell and Fiske and it demonstrates construct validity through use of multiple methods like observation, test etc., to measure the same set of traits. The correlations are shown in a matrix and blocks & diagonals have special meaning.

Relationship Between Reliability & Validity

a) If a test is not reliable, it cannot be valid
b) For a test to valid, it should be reliable
c) Every reliable test may not be valid.

In short, reliability is eligibility but not a guarantee of validity.

Validity Coefficient: Validity Coefficient is essentially the coefficient of correlation between a test and a criterion of effectiveness on the job. It compares a candidate's success in a test and success in the job.

Interpreting Validity Coefficients

Selection systems that make use of more than one selection tool have comparability higher validity. Hiring is a very important function and testing validity of selection tools can be a very complex and critical step. Validity coefficient values above 0.35 are thought to be good. Validity coefficient values between 0.21 and 0.35 are likely to be useful. However for hiring tools, validity coefficient values below 0.21 may not be useful.

Great organizations are built with great people. But how do you know that somebody will be an asset for your organization by just looking at them. Finding right hires is one of the toughest jobs that companies confront today. However companies who take their job seriously shall always employ more scientific methods of selection, using more reliable & validated tools and not leave it to chance.

Essay Questions

1. What are the kinds of errors in selection? Why do you think they occur and what are the repercussions?

2. What is Reliability? Describe the various types of Reliability?

3. What does 'Cronbach Alpha' denote? Why is it significant?

4. How do you interpret alpha scores? How can tests with low alpha scores be improved? Discuss the various ways of achieving the same.

5. What is validity? Elucidate various kinds of validity. Is there any relationship between reliability and validity?

6. What is validity coefficient? Is there any relevance of validity coefficient?

Application Questions

1. Divide the class into teams. Each team must have 6-7 members. Each team then designs a dummy selection-test each.

   Specification for designing the dummy selection test

   i) The test must have 10 questions (items) of multiple- choice nature. Each question must have only one correct answer.

   ii) The questions can be made from any subject (read as domain here) studied by the class. However each team must choose a single subject and no two teams must choose the same subject.

   iii) A key for the test must also be prepared for later reference by each team respectively

   The test must then be administered by each team on a sample of 10 students from the class. These students must be randomly selected. The test must be evaluated and scored.

Calculate

1. Sample variance for total score.
2. Proportion of examinees who answered each item correctly, i.e., P_1 to P_{10}.
3. Calculate the 'Cronbach Alpha' value for the test.
4. Check the alpha value for international consistency.
5. In case the alpha value is low, use the -
   A. Spearman-Brown property formula
   B. Point Biserial correlation.

   and note improvement in alpha values. Comment.

Bibliography

Cesare, S. J., & Blankenship, M. H. (1993). A Predictive Validation Study of the Methods used to Eelect Eligibility Technicians. *Public Personnel Management, 22* (1), 107.

Derous, E., & De Witte, K. (2001). Looking at Selection from a Social Process Perspective: Towards a Social Process Model on Personnel Selection. *European Journal of Work & Organizational Psychology, 10* (3), 319.

Dodd, R. W., & Whipple, T. W. (1976). Item Selection: A Practical Toll in Attitude Research;. *Journal of Marketing, 40* (3), 87-89.

H. I., & H. G. (1975). The Impact of Interviewer Training and Interview Structure on the Reliability and Validity of the Selection Interview. *Academy of Management Proceedings*, 231-233.

Johnson, J. W., & Carter, G. W. (2010). Validating Synthetic Validation: Comparing Traditional and Synthetic Validity Coefficients. *Personnel Psychology, 63* (3), 755-795.

Lowry, P. E. (1994). The Structured Interview: An Alternative to the Assessment Center. *Public Personnel Management, 23* (2), 201.

Muchinsky, P. M. (1979). The Use of Reference Reports in Personnel Selection: A Review and Evaluation. *Journal of Occupational Psychology, 52* (4), 287-297.

Terpstra, D. E., Kethley, R. B., Foley, R. T., & Limpaphayom, W. (2000). The Nature of Litigation Surrounding Five Screening Devices. *Public Personnel Management, 29* (1), 43.

Chapter 9

Performance Management Systems

Key Terms

360⁰ Performance Appraisal Method
Annual Appraisal
Balanced Score Card
Checklist Method
Core Responsibilities
Critical Incident Method
Essay Method
Graphic Rating Scale
Individual Contribution Areas
Mid-term Review
Paired Comparison
Ranking Method
The Concept of "fit"
The Performance Management Cycle
Traditional Appraisal Method

Outline

Introduction
Scope of Performance Management
Setting Objectives
Key Result Areas (KRAs)
Core Responsibilities
Individual Contribution Areas (ICAs)
Use of Balanced Score Card (BSC) in Setting KRAs
Anomaly of Assessment
Four Parameters & Cascading Principle
Objective Setting & Cascading Principle
Managerial Role in Setting Objectives
Traditional Appraisal Methods
Doubts on Accuracy of Performance Appraisals
Contemporary Appraisal Methods
360⁰ Performance Appraisal Method
Steps in Annual Appraisal Process
The Appraisal Interview
Essay Questions
Application Questions
Bibliography

Performance Management

Performance Management is creating systems, processes and practices that manage and leverage performance of individuals, teams, work units and consequently of the whole organization in a continuous & sustainable manner.

Introduction

Performance Management is creating systems, processes and practices that manage and leverage performance of individuals, teams, work units and consequently of the whole organization in a continuous and sustainable manner. 'Managing' performance is about planning performance.

Performance management is the process of creating a work environment or setting in which people are enabled to perform to the best of their abilities. Performance management is a whole work system that begins when a job is defined as needed and ends when it's determined why an excellent employee left the organization for another opportunity (Heathfield, 2007). While effective performance management is incredibly difficult, it is also critical to an organization's survival and prosperity. Systematically addressing these critical success factors will ensure consistency and success (Srinivas, 2009). In any organization, employees seek to understand the organization's parameters for those constructs which define productive / unproductive behavior. These constructs will naturally guide evaluations of their own and other's behavior. Constructs are likely to be similar across members of the same cultural community because of their shared experiences and talk (Crockett, 1982). The communication culture of an organization is a major determinant of how effective performance is defined in the organization (Williams, Hummert, 1990).

The concept of "fit" is being widely used in theorising and understanding HRM and management of performance or PMS. Two kinds of fit, widely discussed in HR literature are horizontal (internal) fit which talks about the coherence and consistency in HRM practices and interventions, and vertical (strategic) fit that relates to the relationship and alignment of business strategies and HRM strategies (Khan 2010). High job embeddedness plays a positive role in employee performance (e.g., providing additional resources to the employee) when the quality of leader-member exchange is high, but high job embeddedness plays a negative role (e.g., making the employees feel stuck) when the quality of leader-member exchange is low (Sekiguchi, Burton, Sablynski, 2008). At the individual and aggregated data levels, employee conscientiousness, justice, and organizational identification were positively related to employee in-role performance, extra-role performance toward customers, and extrarole performance toward the organization (Maxham, Netemeyer, Lichtenstein, 2008). Support from an adult individual's family members and friends contributed to his or her creativity at work and (2) that this support made a contribution to creativity over and above that made by support from people inside the workplace who were not family or friends (Madjar, Oldham, Pratt, 2002). Since task performance refers to the specific accomplishment of tasks directly related to the job, it is easier to observe and the supervisor can rely less on abstract categorizations of job performance. In contrast, contextual performance is quite abstract and less well-defined than is task performance. This, together with the fact that contextual performance usually involves behaviors not directly related to the job itself, makes supervisors rely heavily on global and general categorization as a basis to assess the contextual performance of their subordinates (Wang, Law, Chen, 2008).

In short, performance management system in an organization aims to:

- Recognize and differentiate between high and low performance.
- Bring about a feeling of transparency and fairness in the evaluation process.
- Increase the objectivity and accuracy of measurement of performance.
- Increase alignment between individual and organizational goals.
- Increase the performance-reward linkage as well as linkage with other HR systems.

Scope of Performance Management

- The Performance management cycle is mostly aligned with financial year of the company.

Actors in PMS	Roles
Incumbent/Appraisee	• An individual who is assessed as part of the performance cycle. • The key driver of own performance.
Manager/ Appraiser	• An Individual who helps plan performance and assesses the performance of one or more appraises that report to him/her. • Helps manage performance & provides continuous feedback and coaching.
Reviewer	• An individual who is responsible for addressing escalated issues pertaining to the system implementation and would be a skip level employee or the head of Function/Unit. • Will ensure Objectivity, Transparency & Consistency within Function/Unit.

| **Human Resources** | • HR to function as a facilitator in the process.
• HR would ensure adherence to guidelines, support, dispute resolution and modify design aspects to align with organization requirements.
• HR will facilitate the process and ensure sanctity of implementation, process, rigor and quality. |
|---|---|

The performance planning is important because it:

➤ Creates awareness about 'the big picture' i.e., Organization's vision, mission and goals.
➤ Communicates expectations clearly and hence provide role clarity.
➤ Aligns individual goals to organizational goals.
➤ Ensures individual commitment towards goals.

Figure 9.1: Performance Management Cycle (PMC)

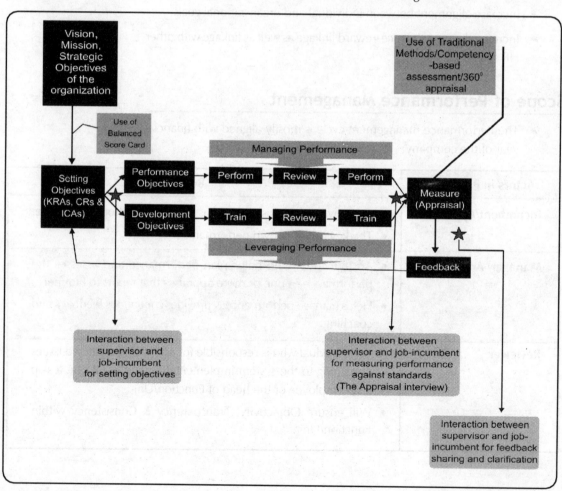

Setting Objectives

The PMS Cycle (refer figure 9.1) starts with setting objectives for each individual employee which of course have to be aligned with the objectives of the respective teams, department units and consequently with the organization as a whole. These objectives could be classified as Key Result Areas (KRAs), Core Responsibilities (CRs) and Individual Contribution Areas (ICAs).

Key Result Areas (KRAs)

Key Result Areas (KRAs) are the identified areas of performance that support the organization's goals which are to be accomplished during the performance year. They should be ideally aligned to function or Business and should be cascaded from the business/Function scorecard.

Core Responsibilities (CRs)

Core Responsibilities (CRs) are on- going tasks or outcomes based on day to day work of an individual and do not have any pre-determined targets at the beginning of a performance period. They may be qualitative or quantitative at times and generally provide opportunity to measure how well the job/ responsibility assigned is performed.

Individual Contribution Areas (ICAs)

Individual Contribution Areas (ICAs) measure the contributions that go beyond the expected realms of performance. They are outcome based and measurable however are not cascaded from the strategy of the business. They could be special projects, developmental activities/lead indicators or other job responsibilities.

Such a performance plan created for every employee must include:

- Setting SMART (Specific, Measurable, Attainable, Relevant & Time bound) goals in consultation with your staff.
- Assigning weightages to KRAs, CRs and ICAs as per the role and structure.
- Defining targets for each KRA that quantifies or verifies the extent of achievement in a given time frame.
- Checking that the targets defined are aligned vertically and horizontally to the goals of the department division & organization, and,
- Developing Action Plan i.e., initiatives to support the goal agreed upon.

Key Result Areas (KRAs)

KRAs are identified areas of performance that support the organizational goals & have to be accomplished in the performance year.

Core Responsibilities (CRs)

CRs are on-going tasks or outcomes based on day to day work of an individual and do not have any pre-determined targets at the beginning of the performance period.

Individual Contribution Areas (ICAs)

ICAs measure the contributions that go beyond the expected realm of job performance. They are outcome-based and measurable.

Use of Balanced Score Card (BSC) in Setting KRAs

Balanced Score Card

A strategic planning and management system used to align business activities to the vision statement of an organization.

Executives the world over have accepted that the measurement systems they have traditionally relied upon are woefully inadequate for the 21st century. They recognize that heavy reliance on financial measures can simply result in short-term, dysfunctional behavior. They have bought into the concept of supplementing their financial measures with non-financial ones and they have invested significant sums in developing more balanced measurement systems as a result (Neely, Najjar, 2006).

Balanced Score Card (BSC) concept was given by Kaplan and Norton. Over the years balanced score card has found several applications. The application of balanced score card in performance management system (PMS) has primarily been in the form of setting objectives and aligning objectives to that of the firm.

Anomaly of Assessment

1. Traditional performance management systems have suffered from certain drawbacks:

    ➢ Performance Appraisals becoming a major part of performance management systems leading to a perception that both can be interchangeably used.

    ➢ Use of too standardized appraisal forms for all positions.

    ➢ Subjectivity in measurement.

    ➢ No measurement of learning objectives.

2. When we assess corporate performance or health, primarily, financial measures are used (balance-sheet, profit loss statement, market capitalization etc.), whereas when we assess performance of individuals in the organization we tend to measure his/her performance on internal processes that he/she is managing or is involved in. The anomaly in assessment is pretty clear. Logically the summation of all individual performances in the organization should be equal to the corporate performance. However how is this possible when we are using different parameters for assessing individual and corporate performance?

Balanced Score Card (BSC) application in PMS aims to overcome all such anomalies in assessment. The discussion to follow shall make it clear as how the same is achieved.

Four Parameters & Cascading Principle

BSC use four parameters that balance various measurement aspects of organizational unit or individual performance:

- Financial Perspective
- Customer Perspective
- Internal Process Perspective
- Learning & Growth Perspective

These four parameters typically follow a cascading principle. It goes like this:

Financial Perspective	What financial objectives must be achieved for maximizing shareholder satisfaction?
Customer Perspective	For achieving these financial objectives what customer needs must be met?
Internal Process Perspective	For meeting these customers needs and financial objectives, which internal process are critical?
Learning & Growth Perspective	For achieving all this, what capabilities need to be built or developed?

Among these four parameters, the Internal Process and Learning & Growth perspectives are like drivers and hence are called lead indicators. Whereas the financial and customer perspectives are more like outcomes and hence are called lag indicators.

Objective Setting & Cascading Principle

The objectives are set around each of these parameters. For example:

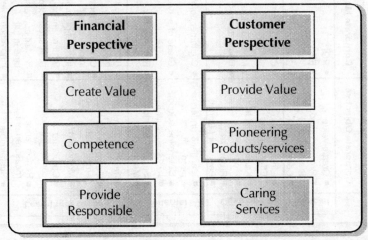

Perspective	Corporate Objective	Corporate Measure	T	A	IS Divisional Objectives	IS Divisional Measures	T	A
Financial	■ Create value ■ Provide responsible leadership ■ Competence	■ ROI ■ EPS ■ Share price	60% US40e $150	50% US30e $100	■ Reduce costs through IT resource optimisation ■ Competence	■ Saving ■ Budget deficit ■ % Certified staff	300M 5% 75%	150M 50% 50%
Customer	■ Efficiency and Effectiveness ■ Knowledgeable ■ Pioneering ■ Proactive ■ Personal / Caring	■ Customer satisfaction survey ■ Meeting SLAs ■ Churn rte	80 95 100	60 80 95	■ Efficiency and Effectiveness ■ Knowledgeable ■ Pioneering ■ Proactive ■ Personal / Caring	■ Internal Customer satisfaction survey ■ Uptime ■ Meeting SLAs ■ Audit report	90% 95% 98% Gr	70% 90% 90% Amb
Internal	■ Identify & understand need ■ Determine solution ■ Provide solution ■ Support solution ■ Manage HR	■ Customer complaint ■ Grade of service ■ Revenue per employee	10% 5% US$	15% 105 US$	■ Identify & understand need ■ Determine solution ■ Provide solution ■ Support solution ■ Manage HR	■ Customer response rate ■ Complaints as a % of users per solution ■ % Resolved time ■ % requests met	80% 105 80 80	60% 15% 70 70
Learning & Growth	■ Training & development ■ Empowering employees ■ Motivation ■ Corporate communication ■ Performance measurement ■ Sustainable competitive advantage	■ Adherence to training program ■ Overall performance improvement ■ Internal promotions ■ Staff retention ■ Staff satisfaction survey ■ % staff appraisals on time in full ■ Innovation rate ■ Brand Equity	1 25% 60% 90% 80% 100% 2	2 -15% +50% 50% 80% 75% 95% 1	■ Training & development ■ Empowering employees ■ Motivation ■ Corporate communication ■ Performance measurement ■ Sustainable competitive advantage	■ # of change to training plan ■ Overall performance improvement ■ Internal promotions ■ Staff retention ■ Staff satisfaction survey ■ % staff appraisals on time in full ■ Innovation rate	1 25% 50% 90% 90% 100% 2	2 -15% +50% 40% 80% 80% 95% 1

Name: XXXXXXXXXXXX **Dept:** Network Planning & Development

Position: Chief Engineer   Individual's Signature: Assessor's Signature:

	Plng & Dev objectives	Plng & Dev Measures	T	A	Actual Score	Rating	Rating	Average Rating	Overall Rating	Average Rating	Overall Rating
Financial	■ Expand Network ■ Manage ITRI ■ Budget & Plan ■ Meet regulatory requirement ■ Provide Quality Service	■ Subscriber Basic ■ Rollout Target ■ Roaming Revenue Inflows (US$) ■ Cost Variance ■ License Obligation ■ Technical compliance ■ Grade of Service: - route 　　　　　　　　　- radio network ■ Dropped Calls	1630C 60% 200C ?? 60% 60% 0.5% 5% 2%	1611C 50% 100C ?? 50% 50% 1% 10% 3%							
Customer	■ Manage Internal Customers ■ Maintain Setubal & high network availability ■ Develop VAS	■ Internal Customer satisfaction rating ■ Meet SLAs ■ External Customer Satisfaction rating ■ Achievement of all graders of service	80% 95% 40% 80%	60% 85% 60% 60%							
Internal	■ Identify & understand need ■ Determine solution ■ Provide solution ■ Support solution	■ Network complaint / subscriber ■ Network complaints resolved on time ■ Usage reports OTIP	x 95% 100%	x 40% 80%							
Learning Growth	■ Training & development ■ Empowering employees ■ Motivation ■ Departmental Communication ■ Performance measurement ■ Keep up-to-date with industry technological trends	■ No of changes to training plan (local) ■ No of changes to training plan (international) ■ Overall performance improvement ■ Internal Promotions ■ Employee Satisfaction rating ■ % minutes of planed meetings ■ % on time in full apparels ■ Benchmark vs. supplier stranded	1 ?? 25% 60% 80% 100% 100% 60%	2 ?? >50% <15% 50% 75% 66% 95% 50%							

T-Target   A-Alarm

Sample Exhibit A: Balanced Score Card (BSC)

(**Source:** ITU/BDT Workshop on HR Management tools and practices (Practicing Balanced Score Card), Sofia, Bulgaria, 26-28 November, 2008.

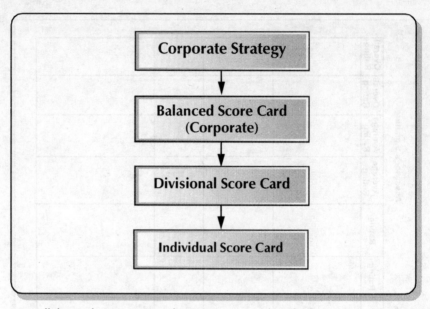

For all these objectives, specific measures are identified. Against each measure a target is set and an alarm is also set to act as check and balance for the objectives and the measures.

The objectives and measures are cascaded down from corporate level to individual level. Since the balanced score card is aligned to the corporate strategy, it provides a natural segway to align individual objectives to corporate objectives.

Managerial Role in Setting Objectives

The process of setting objectives would typically be completed using the following steps:

a) Identifying the KRAs, ICAs and CRs.
b) Preparing a performance plan for the performance period.
c) Submission of the same to manager,
d) Managerial ratification;
e) Approval by the reviewer.

A critical aspect of this phase is the managerial intervention in setting objectives. Here are a few Dos and Don'ts for the managers.

Don'ts
1. Do not set objectives for the employees. Facilitate the process instead.
2. Don't assume. Work on facts.
3. Do not record developmental objectives for the heck of it. Make them count.
4. Do not get caught in fancy phrases or words while recording objectives. Meke them for real.

Dos
1. Prepare well before the interaction, knowing well what the employee has done and what he/she is capable of doing.
2. Ensure that the drive comes from the employees.
3. Probe deeper and find people's aspirations and probe even deeper to see if they really mean it.
4. Align these aspirations to departmental/organizational objectives.
5. Ensure that the objectives are SMART i.e., **S**pecific, **M**easurable, **A**ttainable, **R**ealistic and **T**imely.

Mid-term Review

The Mid-term review or the interim review is an important managerial job that:

➢ Allows for provision of performance plan, if required.

➢ Highlights areas of inputs, guidance, support required by appraise.

➢ Gives feedback & create coaching plan, if required.

➢ Provides document feedback for final year end discussion & evaluation.

The various steps in the mid-term review process are:

a) Self-review by the job-incumbent.

b) Manager reviews the document and provides his own feedback, looks at the possibility of course-correction and even at times revision of mid-year performance plans.

c) Quarterly and mid-year reviews are documented and are later fed into the annual appraisals.

Performance appraisal is a dynamic process that requires a rater to observe and record the employee's performance, responsibilities and contributions to an organization.

Annual Appraisal

Performance appraisals are frequently used in organizations as a basis for administrative decisions such as employee promotion, transfer, and allocation of financial rewards; employee development, including identification of training needs and performance feedback (Decotiis, Petit, 1977). Performance appraisal is a dynamic process that requires a rater to observe and record the performance of others, to pose an evaluative judgment as to the quality of that performance, to provide feedback to the individuals evaluated, and finally to outline developmental opportunities to those same ratees (Murphy and Cleveland 1995). An effective system of evaluating job performance should accurately outline employees' responsibilities and contributions to an organization, motivate employees, and provide valid and important input in personnel decisions (Clausen, Jones, Rich, 2008).

In short annual (year-end) evaluation helps in:

➤ Reinforcing performance excellence within the organization.

➤ Rewarding and recognizing high performance.

➤ Reinforcing organization's priorities and goals.

Traditional Appraisal Methods

1. **Essay Method:** In this method the appraiser (supervisor) writes a description of the employee performance. This method suffers from high degree of subjectivity and possible bias.

2. **Ranking Method:** In ranking method, the supervisor ranks the employee, reporting to him, from best to poorest. However the method is subjective since the criteria that the rater could choose to come-up with the ranking are ambiguous.

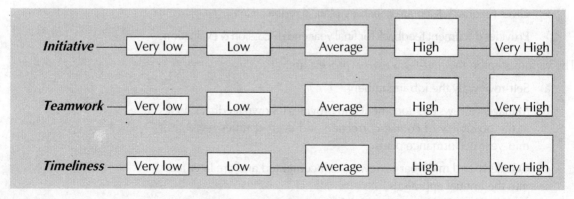

3. **Graphic Rating Scale:** In this method parameters of performance assessment are identified and the supervisor rates the employee on a scale.

Example: Often essay method and raking method may be combined with graphic rating scale to reduce high levels of subjectivity that creeps in the former methods.

4. **Critical Incident Method:** In critical incident method the appraiser records employee's behavior during critical incidents and rates him/her on that basis.

Example: A worker is involved in an accident on the shop floor. Now what are the things that the supervisor on the floor is supposed to do?
   a. Cordon-off the area
   b. Immediately arrange for first-aid
   c. Call ambulance
   d. Inform Management
   e. Inform union leader & take him into confidence
   f. Inform local police
   g. Inform worker's family members and arrange for their transport to hospital
   h. Make sure proper treatment is being given to the worker
   i. Meeting the family members & assuring them of every help
   j. Keeping other workers updated on the development and assuring them of their safety

Problem with this method is that the behavior of the employee has to be noted down as and when an incident happens.

5. **Checklist Method:** In checklist method the rater is given a checklist of all things that an employee must do. Based upon how much of that is achieved, the rater rates the employee.

6. **Paired Comparison Method:** This is more of a group appraisal technique. Each member of the group or team is compared with the other and based on these comparisons, evaluations and rating is done by the rater. The total number of comparisons possible in any group is equal to n (n-2); where n = number of people in a group.

Doubts on Accuracy of Performance Appraisals

Performance Appraisal Effectiveness

It refers to the accuracy of performance observations and ratings as well as the ability of the performance appraisal process to improve the ratee's future performance

Traditional appraisal methods suffer from problems of subjectivity and lack of accuracy. Performance appraisals are an organizational fact of life. Often, however, they are sources of controversy and dissatisfaction within organizations (Williams, Hummert, 1990). Performance appraisal effectiveness refers to the accuracy of performance observations and ratings as well as the ability of the performance appraisal process to improve the ratee's future performance (Lee, 1985). Accuracy in appraising employee performance is a major concern organizations face in their desire to improve their performance management systems. Any attempt to increase accuracy cannot ignore assessors, both from their ability and intention perspectives with respect to appraisals (Diman, Singh, 2007). Some (employees) perceive the PA process as unfair. They noted, for example, that the same PA processes were used for different employees, that there were different degrees of PA training and experience, and follow-up conversations rarely took place (Vasset, Mumburg, Furunes, 2010). The probability that performance is appraised systematically is lower for women than for men. Among those employees whose performance is evaluated by a supervisor, women have a lower probability that this evaluation has an impact on bonus payments (Grund, Sliwka, 2009).

Appraisal politics is defined as constituting those superior's (reviewer's), fellow assessors', and own assessees' behaviours which are informal in nature, and aimed at manipulation or influence on appraisal ratings to achieve their self-serving ends at the cost of assessor's own appraisal goals and interests, and/or at the cost of organizational interests (Diman, Singh, 2007).

Most performance appraisal systems depend heavily on subjective ratings of performance provided by supervisors, peers, subordinates, and job incumbents (Smith, 1986). Despite a heavy reliance on performance ratings, it is generally acknowledged that they are too often contaminated by systematic errors (leniency, central tendency, halo, and contrast errors) (Smith, 1986). The use of rater policies to combine dimensional information into an overall rating explicitly recognizes and deals with important limitations in human information-processing capacity. These include: (a) the inconsistent combination of data on a number of factors into an overall judgment; (b) the lack of insight into the decision rule used to weight and combine the information; and (c) the tendency to change, unwittingly, the combinational rule when used in repeated decisions (Slovic & Lichtenstein, 1971; Slovic et al., 1977).

Contemporary Appraisal Methods

Appraising performance according to the nature of the task, matching task nature with performance appraisal format, and designing training programs to increase observational accuracy may improve performance appraisal systems as well as contribute to successful organizational placement and promotion decisions (Lee, 1985). While no system is perfect, and no system perfectly and reliably measures employee performance, managers need to examine why this established process is so painful for all participants (Heathfield, 2007). To avoid relying on subjective criteria in judging performance, many organizations have adopted a goal setting program in which performance criteria for achievement levels are agreed upon by supervisors and subordinates (Bishop, 1974). Performance appraisals conducted for purposes of employee development are likely to be more accurate than administrative appraisals (Decotiis, Petit, 1977). As performance management systems become more international and increasingly rely on evaluators of different cultural backgrounds there is a greater need for research on how culture influences these evaluators (Brutus, Fletcher, Baldry, 2009). Most senior executives find performance measurement difficult if not threatening, and they're reluctant to engage with it in a meaningful way (Likierman, 2009). People managing performance frameworks are generally not experts in performance measurement (Likierman, 2009). Rater training is an area which has recently shown some promise in improving the effectiveness of performance ratings (Smith, 1986).

> As performance management systems become more international and increasingly rely on evaluators of different cultural backgrounds there is a greater need for research on how culture influences these evaluators.

Modern performance appraisal methods are more objective in their approach and are developmental oriented. Some of the methods that we shall discuss are:

a. Competency based assessment (this is discussed in detail in the next chapter.

b. Balanced score card based appraisals (discussed earlier in this chapter).

c. MBO (Management by objectives) and 360⁰ performance appraisals.

Management by Objectives (MBO)

MBO as a concept was given by Peter Drucker in 1954. The critical and integral part of MBO is setting goals or objectives. The rater and ratee decide the goals for the rate that are derived from the organizational goals. The standards and measures for these goals are decided and the ratee is then assessed based on his/her meeting those goals or objectives.

Goal clarity and communication is very important for the success of MBO based performance appraisal systems. Organizations have so many goals that it is difficult to clearly articulate what the destination is. In some organizations, there are more goals than employees—with each employee having dozens of goals! This would not be such a problem if the goals all aligned neatly with the overall organizational goals. This, however, is rarely the case (Srinivas, 2009). Employees who are ineligible for a reward in the prior period, on average select easier goals in the subsequent period (Webb, Jeffrey, Schulz, 2010).

360^0 Performance Appraisal Method

360^0 performance appraisal method or the 'multi-rater' method was first used by GE (US). 360^0 method allows both vertical and horizontal assessment of an employee's performance, besides the self assessment by the employee. The 'horizontal' assessment includes the peers and family & friends. The 'vertical' assessment includes the superiors, juniors, clients and direct reports.

Merits

1. The 360^0 method attempts to minimize bias and subjectivity in assessment by factoring multi-rater assessments.
2. The method attempts to look at the holistic aspects of a person and hence is developmental in approach.
3. Helps in identifying specific developmental needs.
4. Also gives an impression to the employee the impact that he/she has on the others. Hence it improves self-awareness and creates scope for self-reflection and self-renewal/correction.

Demerits

1. Can fail apart in highly political environments.
2. Can become a tool of venting personal vendetta.
3. The system can be manipulated, in absence of proper implementation.
4. How to make 360^0 work?

The 360^0 method can work provided –

1. High commitment of the top management.
2. Strong buy-in from line-function.

3. Complimented by adequate OD intervention to ensure conducive organizational climate.
4. Asking raters to rate only what they are capable of. In other words the rating sheet for the same employee for different raters has to have some degree of customization.
5. In slowly phasing in the system rather then an immediate introduction.

360° method works big time as a feedback generation mechanisms rather than a standalone appraisal system.

Steps in Annual Appraisal Process

The various steps in the annual appraisal are as follows:

a) Employee complete self-appraisal and submits it to the manager;

b) Manager reviews the same with respect to the KRAs, ICAs and CRs;

c) Manager determines the KRA, ICA and CR score;

d) Manager shares the same with the employee (feedback), discusses the same and clarifies doubts, if any;

e) Manager determines the final performance score of the employee as per the weightage determined for the KRA, ICA and CR at the beginning of the performance period;

f) Manager submits the final score and feedback to the reviewer;

g) The reviewer validates the appraisal by the manager and approves the same;

h) The score is communicated to the employee;

i) Administrative decisions like promotions/demotions, increments/ decrements, reward/punishment are taken;

j) Developmental areas are identified on the basis of the final appraisal score;

k) The final score also becomes a feeder in to setting next year's objectives.

The Appraisal Interview

The manager's or supervisor's role is very important in the appraisal. As a manager it is important to ensure that it is effective and fruitful for both the employee and the organization. Managers should remember that the appraisal interview is a learning and development exercise and it is neither fault-finding one nor a reward-punishment deciding process. PA interviews should not be history-oriented. They should have a future-orientation. Both appraiser and appraisee should prepare in advance for the interview and proper documentation should be done of the process to avoid any ambiguity later.

The various steps of the performance appraisal interview are:

1. Open and set context;
2. Congratulate on good performance;
3. Discuss areas of possible improvements;
4. Offer assistance;
5. Seek input;
6. Respond and clarify;
7. Summarize and close;
8. Document what was discussed;
9. Share document with the employee;
10. Provide feedback;
11. Set action plan and review dates.

Feedback

Feedback is a very important element of the entire appraisal process. Its parallel can be drawn with closing the sales in a sales meeting. Performance evaluation is providing employees with performance feedback. Such feedback should reinforce the link between employee's performance and employer's expectations (Clausen, Jones, Rich, 2008). The performance appraisal is a yearly event. There is always an urgent need for regular and continuous evaluation and feedback of the employees (Khan, 2010). Feedback is a response to an action or situation from one individual (the source) to another individual (the recipient). The information transferred generally regards the recipient and can be essential as motivation or a device to detect errors. Feedback is also important because it gives an individual a sense of competence and provides direction on how to maintain or improve performance (Sadri, Seto, 2011). The feedback should allow the recipient to analyse what should have been done and what can be done differently, rather than focus on what went wrong (Sadri, Seto, 2011).

However feedback is like a double-edged sword. Proper feedback can propel a performance. Similarly, improper feedback can derail an employee's performance and destroy his/her motivation to perform. Feedback could be a positive feedback or a correctional feedback but there has to a right way of conveying the same. Again manager's role is very important to ensure the same.

Manager's Role in Feedback

Manager's role in providing feedback to the employee is significant to his/her receptiveness and probability of acting-upon it. Here are some of the things that managers need to keep in mind while providing feedback:

1. Talk about behaviour and not attitude. Behaviour always has evidence, while attitudes can be more subjective in their interpretation.

2. Remember the whole purpose of feedback is to improve someone's performance. Hence everything has to be done, keeping that in mind.

3. Discuss ways to improve or plug the performance-gaps rather than finding faults.

Conclusion

Performance management systems have been often misunderstood and misinterpreted. Most of the times, they have been equated to year-end appraisals and not seen as an on-going process. Viewing PMS as a continuous process, facilitated by the manager(s) to leverage individual, team and consequently organizational performance is key.

Essay Questions

1. Explain the concept, objectives and scope of performance management.

2. Why is performance planning important? What are the various supervisory interventions?

3. Describe the setting up of performance objectives including KRAs, CRs and ICAs. What is managerial role in setting objectives?

4. How can Balanced Score Cards (BSC) assist in setting performance objectives? Explain the casting principle.

5. What are the various steps in interim review? Why is it important?

6. Describe the annual appraisal process. Explain the traditional appraisal methods.

7. Why are doubts cast on accuracy of performance appraisals? How do contemporary appraisal methods overcome such limitations?

8. Write notes on:
   a) MBO or Management by Objectives
   b) 360 degree performance appraisal Method

9. What are various steps of the appraisal interview? How is the role of manager or supervisor important?

10. 'Performance feedbacks must be specific and timely'. Comment in the light of this statement the importance of performance feedback and the role of supervisor in providing the same.

Application Questions

1. Visit http://www.nytimes.com/2011/03/13/business/13hire.html and study initiatives like 'Project Oxygen' and 'Eight Habits of highly Effective Google Managers'. Comment, how such initiatives led to improvement of managerial performance in managing employee performance.

2. Visit the link http://www.crainsdetroit.com/article/20091109/EMAIL01/911099979/can-a-new-corporate-culture-save-general-motors and study the article 'Can a new corporate culture save General Motors?' by Jeremy Smerd. Comment how performance management process is a company becoming a critical determinant of organizational performance.

Bibliography

Aslam, H. D., & Sarwar, S. (2010). Improving Performance Management Practices in IT Firms of Pakistan. *Journal of Management Research, 2* (2), 1-15.

Broadbent, J., & Laughlin, R. (2009). Performance Management Systems: A Conceptual Model. *Management Accounting Research, 20* (4), 283-295.

Chamberlain, L. (2011). Does Your Performance Management Need a Tune-up? *Strategic Finance, 93* (5), 18-61.

Chan, F. T., Chan, H. K., & Qi, H. J. (2006). A Review of Performance Measurement Systems for Supply Chain Management. *International Journal of Business Performance Management, 8* (2), 110-131.

Colville, K., & Millner, D. (2011). Embedding Performance Management: Understanding the Enablers for Change. *Strategic HR Review, 10* (1), 35-40.

Dervitsiotis, K. N. (2004). The Design of Performance Measurement Systems for Management Learning. *Total Quality Management & Business Excellence, 15* (4), 457-473.

Ferreira, A., & Otley, D. (2009). The Design and Use of Performance Management Systems: An Extended Framework for Analysis. *Management Accounting Research, 20* (4), 263-282.

Furnham, A. (2004). Performance Management Systems. *European Business Journal, 16* (2), 83-94.

Garengo, P., Biazzo, S., & Bititci, U. S. (2005). Performance Measurement Systems in SMEs: A Review for a Research Agenda. *International Journal of Management Reviews, 7* (1), 25-47.

Gimþauskienë, E., & Kloviene, L. (2007). Changes of Performance Measurement System: The Role of Organizational Values. *Economics & Management*, 30-37.

Gimzauskiene, E., & Valanciene, L. (2010). Efficiency of Performance Measurement System: The Perspective of Decision Making. *Economics & Management*, 917-923.

Gruman, J. A., & Saks, A. M. (2011). Performance Management and Employee Engagement. *Human Resource Management Review, 21* (2), 123-136.

Heinrich, C. J., & Marschke, G. (2010). Incentives and their Dynamics in Public Sector Performance Management Systems. *Journal of Policy Analysis & Management, 29* (1), 183-208.

Helm, C., Holladay, C. L., & Tortorella, F. R. (2007). The Performance Management System: Applying and Evaluating a Pay-for-Performance Initiative. *Journal of Healthcare Management, 52* (1), 49-62.

Impact of Performance Measurement and Management Systems. (2010). *Management Services, 54* (3), 8-15.

Kloviene, L., & Gimzauskiene, E. (2009). Performance Measurement System Changes According to Organization's External and Internal Environment. *Economics & Management*, 70-77.

Kolich, M. (2009). Solutions and Recommendations to Address Issues with Company XYZ's Performance Management System. *Performance Improvement, 48* (1), 12-24.

Lee, C. D. (2005). Rethinking the Goals of your Performance Management System. *Employment Relations Today, 32* (3), 53-60.

Medlin, B., & Jr., G. (2009). Developing a Performance Management System at the Community Outreach Agency: A Case Study. *Journal of the International Academy for Case Studies, 15* (2), 93-95.

Norcross, L. (2006). Building on Success [Performance Management System]. *Manufacturing Engineer, 85* (3), 42-45.

Perego, P., & Hartmann, F. (2009). Aligning Performance Measurement Systems with Strategy: The Case of Environmental Strategy. *Abacus, 35* (4), 397-428.

Pulakos, E. D., & O'leary, R. S. (2011). Why is Performance Management Broken? *Industrial & Organizational Psychology, 4* (2), 146-164.

Purwanti, Y., Pasaribu, N. R., & Lumbantobing, P. (2010). Leveraging the Quality of Knowledge Sharing by Implementing Reward Program and Performance Management System. *Proceedings of the European Conference on Intellectual Capital,* 499-503.

Rao, A. S. (2007). Effectiveness of Performance Management Systems: An Empirical Study in Indian Companies. *International Journal of Human Resource Management, 18* (10), 1812-1840.

Rao, T. V. (2008). Lessons from Experience: A New Look at Performance Management Systems. *The Journal for Decision Makers, 33* (3), 1-15.

Salloum, M., Wiktorsson, M., Bengtsson, M., & Johansson, C. (2010). Aligning Dynamic Performance Measures. *Proceedings of the European Conference on Management, Leadership & Governance,* 339-349.

Saltmarshe, D., Ireland, M., & McGregor, J. A. (2003). The Performance Framework: A Systems Approach to Understanding Performance Management. *Public Administration & Development, 23* (5), 445-456.

Schwartz, R. (2011). Bridging the Performance Measurement-Management Divide? *Public Performance & Management Review, 35* (1), 103-107.

Seiden, S., & Sowa, J. E. (2011). Performance Management and Appraisal in Human Service Organizations: Management and Staff Perspectives. *Public Personnel Management, 40* (3), 251-264.

Weng, M. H. (2011). The Application of Balanced Scorecard to Performance Evaluation for Engineering Educational Systems. *International Journal of Organizational Innovation, 4* (2), 64-76.

Wouter, V. D. (2011). Better Performance Management. *Public Performance & Management Review, 34* (3), 420-433.

Chapter 10

Competency Based Performance Management

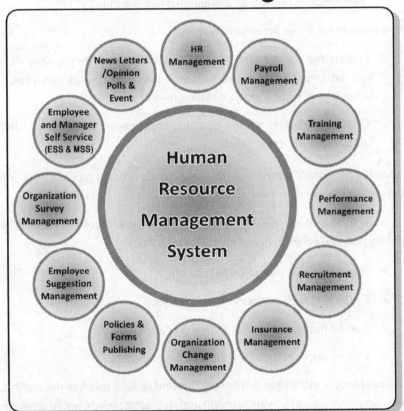

Outline

Competency

Competency and Organizational Strategy

Competency and other HR Processes

Competency Dictionary

Competency Buckets

Preparing Competency Buckets

Accountability

Competency Gap

Types of Competencies

Competency Mapping Process

Functional Competencies

Behavioural Competencies

Functional Competencies

Behavioural Competencies

Functional Competencies

References

Essay Questions

Application Questions

Bibliography

Key Terms

Behavioural Competencies	Competency Buckets	HR Processes
Communication Skill	Competency Dictionary	Individual Development
Competency	Competency Mapping Process	Organizational Strategy
Competency Based Performance Systems	Functional Competencies	Performance Management System

Competency

Competency
Competency is a set of knowledge, skills and attitude required by a person to accomplish a job successfully.

Competency is a set of knowledge, skills and attitude required by a person to accomplish a job successfully. Competencies are always specific to a job, although there could be some generic competencies.

"Competency" is:

> an *underlying characteristic* of an individual.

> *causally related* to *criterion referenced* effective and/or *superior performance* in a job or a situation. (McClelland, 1973).

The definition has three important elements:

- *'Underlying characteristic' means* that the competency is fairy deep and enduring part of the person's personality and can predict behaviour in wide variety of situations and job tasks.

- *'Causally related' means* that a competency causes or predicts behaviour and performance.

'Criterion referenced' means that the competency actually predicts who does what well or poorly, as measured on a specific criterion or standard.

According to Scott Parry (1998), competency is a cluster of related knowledge, attitude, skill and other personal characteristics that:

> Affects a major part of one's job;

> Correlated with performance on the job;

> Can be measured against well-accepted standards;

> Can be improved via training and development.

'A competency is more than just knowledge and skills. It involves the ability to meet complex demands, by drawing on and mobilizing psychosocial resources (including skills and attitudes) in a particular context.

Example: *The ability to communicate effectively is a competency that may draw on an individual's knowledge of language, practical IT skills and attitudes towards those with whom he or she is communicating.'* (OECD, 1997).

Competency and Organizational Strategy

Competency based performance systems are thought to be better as they are connected to the strategy that an organization has chartered for itself. The mission, vision and values drive the strategy of an organization. The strategy execution is then drafted in form of departmental and individual objectives. Such objectives help articulate the nature of various tasks in a job, various kinds of job demands and the challenges that are to be confronted to make the strategy successful. This in turn helps identification of competencies required to perform a job successfully.

Once these competencies are properly defined and mapped, the gaps, if any, can be identified. The competency-gaps are closed with the help of training and development interventions, following the performance takes place. Continuous training, identification of newer competencies and also reviewing the new job demands makes it an iterative process.

Strategy:
The mission, vision and values drive the strategy of an organization.

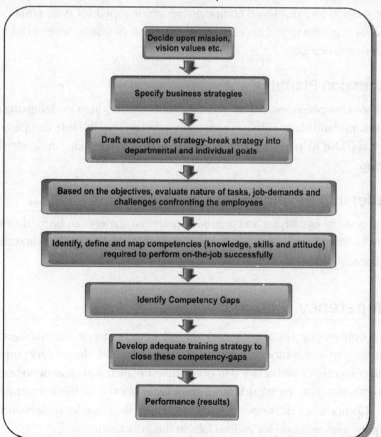

Figure 10.1: Competency and Organizational Strategy

Competency and other HR Processes

The Competency Directory is used as a basis for various HR processes.

Recruitment

This Competency Directory is a tool for short listing and selecting the most appropriate candidate by mapping the role competency with the displayed competencies of the candidates.

Performance Management System

The Role Competencies (both Behavioral and Functional) facilitate the goal-setting and performance evaluation process by making possible for both the appraise and appraiser to define better goals and set measurable performance standards.

Individual Development

If the desired and displayed competencies are mapped for each employee, the areas of improvement are clearly visible, and steps may be taken to address the performance gaps.

Succession Planning

The Role Competencies of a top management role may help in identifying the successors (candidates with a competency set closest to the role competency set). It will also help in grooming potential successors for taking up leadership positions.

Leadership Development

The process of identifying and grooming potential leaders can be made more robust by identifying competencies required for leadership position in various functions.

Competency Dictionary

Competency Dictionary brings more detailed and clear definition for understanding competencies required for various jobs in the organization.

Competency Dictionary

The Competency Dictionary is designed as a resource for managerial, supervisory as well as other employees in the organization. The primary purpose of the competency dictionary is to bring more detailed and clear definition to the behaviors that are important for the organization to achieve its strategic goals. Competency dictionary creates a common language for understanding competencies required for various jobs in the organization.

Each Competency in the dictionary has a definition and a set of behavioral skills called Behavioral Indicators. The Behavioral Indicators are observable behaviors that individuals employ when they are demonstrating a particular Competency.

Competency dictionaries are used by the supervisors as well as by the employees for:

1. Preparation of competency clusters.
2. Preparation of role competency buckets.
3. Creating benchmarks.
4. Developing competencies.

Competency Buckets

The departmental and role competency buckets are prepared from the competency dictionary. The competency buckets are set of competencies required for a specific role. Competency buckets are used by the supervisors as well as by the employees for:

Competency Buckets
Competency buckets are set of competencies required for a specific role.

1. Performance planning: identifying KRA and KPIs and setting performance goals.
2. Setting performance expectations.
3. Managing appraisals.
4. Identifying competency-gaps and developing competencies.

Below given are few examples of role competency buckets of a watch-manufacturing company.

Exhibit 1: Competency Bucket for Head of the Department of Watch Assembly

Competency Bucket for HOD Watch Assemble
- Understanding of pneumatics.
- Understanding of Electronics.
- PLC programming.
- Setting and operating of machines, equipment, instruments, gauges.
- SAP operations/material transactions.
- AUTO CAD.
- Ability to read and understand Engineering Drawings.

- Vendor management - including vendor certification, inbound quality inspection, vendor development etc.
- Ability to conceptualise and communciate the Tooling requirements for new products / changes in existing products.
- Ability to define assemble & disassembly sequence.
- Ability to analyse the defects, identify root cause and rectify / recover the parts.
- Skills in watch inspection/testing standards & international standards.
- Working principles of equipment like witchi, alc 2000, AWRT, WPT10.
- Ability to assemble / disassemble watches.

Exhibit 2: Competency Bucket for Head of the Department of Watch Assembly - Quality

Competency Bucket for HOD Watch Assemble - Quality

- Defect analysis, identifying root cause, recovery.
- Ability to read and understand Engineering Drawings.
- Ability to predict possible complications in New Product assembly, and suggest alternatives.
- Awareness of quality tools and application.
- Awareness of watch assemble & disassembly.
- Setting and operating machines / equipment / instrument / gauges.
- Ability to conceptualise and communicate the Tooling requirements.
- SAP operations / material transactions.
- Skills in watch inspection/testing standards & international standards.
- Ability to define assemble & disassembly sequence.
- Ability to analysee the defects, identify root cause and rectify / recover the parts.
- Skills in watch inspection/testing standards & international standards.
- Working principles of equipment like witchi, Alc 2000, AWRT, WPT10.
- Ability to assemble / disassemble watches.

Exhibit 3: Competency Bucket for Team Member of Watch Assembly

Competency Bucket for Team Member-Watch Assembly

- Understanding of pneumatics.
- Understanding of Electronics.
- PLC programing.
- SAP operations / material transactions.
- AUTO CAD.
- Ability to read and understand Engineering Drawings.
- Vendor performance rating & vendor production, quality establishment.
- Ability to conceptualise and communciate the Tooling requirements for new products / change in existing products.
- Ability to define assemble / disassembly sequence.
- Ability to analyse the defects & identify the root cause.
- Testing and Trouble shooting of watches.
- Working principles of witchi 6000.
- Working principles of A/c 2000.
- Working principles of AWRT.
- Working principles of WPT10.

Exhibit 4: Competency Bucket for Team Member of Watch Assembly - Quality

Competency Bucket for Team Member-Watch Assemble - Quality

- Operating oven tester.
- Operating dynamic tester.
- Operating mega timer.
- Working principles of witchi.
- Working principles of A/c 2000.
- Working principles of AWRT.

- Working principles of WPT10.
- Rectification of defects in watch assembly rejects.
- Use of fixing tools (like stem cutting machines, hands fixing Jig & dial fixing jig).
- SAP operations / material transactions trouble shooting of watches.
- Ability to read and understand Engineering Drawings.
- Vendor management - including vendor certification, inbound quality.
- Ability to assemble & disassemble watches.
- Awareness of watch assemble process.
- Watch inspection standards.
- CAD/CAM.
- Awareness of statistical quality control.

Exhibit 5: Competency Bucket for Team Member of Watch Assembly - Coordination with other Units

Competency Bucket for Team Member-Watch Assemble - Co ordination with other Units.

- Budgeting and planning skills.
- Inventory Management skills.
- Costing.
- Scheduling and Forecasting of materials.
- Ascertaining infrastructural and resource requirements.
- SAP / Material transactions.
- Vendor management- including vendor certification, inbound quality.
- inspection, vendor development etc.
- Ability to read and understand engineering drawings.
- Assembly and disassemble sequence-strapping.
- Ability to conceptualise and communicate tooling requirements.

Comparison between Exhibit 1 and Exhibit 2 tells us how competency buckets differ between departments although the role is similar. Comparison between exhibit 1 & 3 and 2 & 4 show how competency buckets vary across roles. While comparison between Exhibit 3 & 5 shows technical and managerial competencies for the same role.

Preparing Competency Buckets

The preparation of competency buckets typically follows three stages:
1. Sensitization
2. Identification of functional and role competencies

1. Sensitization
- Introduction to Competency – concept, basic terminology, process and outcomes.
- Restating the competency mapping exercise objectives.

2. Identification of Functional and Role Competencies
a. Detail various steps in competency bucket preparation.
b. Identification of functional Groups: if two jobs are approximately 60% identical, they may be put in the same group.
c. Developing laundry list of competencies for each group: all possible competencies are identified.
d. The competencies are then ranked in order.
e. Identify top 80% competencies (max around 20). These form the competency bucket for each Functional Group.
f. Next, from this bucket of competencies, identify relevant competencies for each role.
g. Describe the proficiency level required for each role: (using template for the same).

   1. Not applicable: The competency is not required by the role holder.

   2. Basic: The Role holder has good understanding of the area and basic knowledge of related areas. He uses relevant domain knowledge to complete simple tasks independently or complex tasks with help and/or Guidance.

   3. Proficient: The role holder has in-depth knowledge of the area's processes, systems and procedures and uses it to deliver superior performance.

   4. Advanced: The role holder has functional/technical knowledge and skill to deal with emergent issues and seeks to do a best-in-class application of expertise. He is able to suggest and drive moderate improvements or changes in the process.

   5. Expert: The role holer abreast of cutting edge developments in the field and creates competitive strength by deploying expertise in this specific area. He is able to guide and help others in the area and suggests/is consulted for any major improvements or changes in the area.

Accountability

➢ The functional groups are identified.

➢ The competency bucket for the functional groups is identified by Unit head or his next line of command or both. The unit head may seek verification by one of more people in the functional group.

➢ The functional groups are divided into Roles by Unit head or next line of command.

➢ The role competencies and proficiency levels are identified by next line of command/ role supervisor, as suggested by Unit head.

Competency Gap

Difference between desired (required for job) level and displayed level of competency of a person is called competency gap.

Competency Gap

The difference between the competency of a person and those required for the job is called competency-gap. In other words the difference between desired and displayed level of competencies is called as Competency-gap.

Figure: 10.2: Competency Radar (showing competency-gaps)

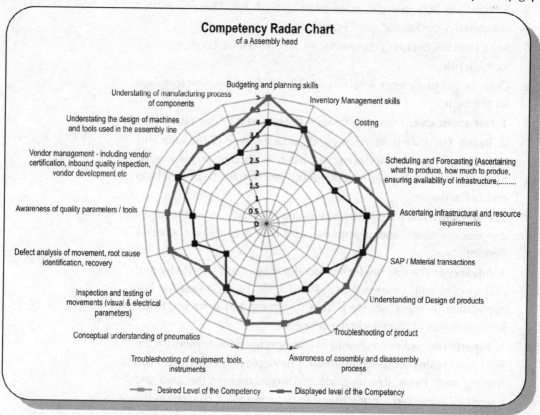

Competency gaps are expected to be closed through effective training and development interventions.

Types of Competencies

Competencies can be classified into mainly two types:

1. Functional Competencies

Functional competencies are set of competencies that are required by an individual to successfully complete a specific job in a particular functional or operational area. *Strategies are formulated to determine the way in which organizations can move from their current competitive position to a stronger one. This can only be achieved by improving specific functional competencies* (Feurer et al, 1994). Client/Customer Service, Consulting/Advising, Data Collection, Equipment Operation, Financial Management – Budget, Information/Records Administration, Planning and Organizing Work etc, are all examples of functional competencies.

2. Behavioural Competencies

Behavioural competencies refer to personal attributes or characteristics (i.e., motives, attitudes, values) that describe how a job or task is performed as opposed to the particulars of the job or task. The behavioural competencies are deep-seated and are not easily developed. They play a significant role in an employee's overall success in his/her job. Building Trust, Building Work Relationships, Judgment, Integrity, Initiative, Resilience, Valuing Diversity etc are all examples of behavioural competencies.

The British Council uses Customer Service Orientation, Flexibility and Team working as behavioural competencies for teacher recruitment. (http://www.britishcouncil.org/teacherrecruitment-recruitment-policy-competencies.htm).

Competency Mapping Process

Competency mapping involves linking roles with relevant behavioural and functional competencies, identifying desired proficiency levels for each role competency (on a scale of 1 to 5) and then matching the job-incumbents (displayed levels) against the proficiency level to identify the competency-gaps. Suitable interventions are then devised to fill these gaps.

Functional Competencies

Functional Competencies are set of Competencies required by a person to successfully complete a specific job in a particular functional or operational area.

Behavioural Competencies

Behavioural competencies refer to personal attributes or characteristics that describe how a job or task is performed as opposed to the particulars of the job or task.

Competency Mapping Process

Competency Mapping involves linking roles with relevant behavioral and functional competencies, identifying desired proficiency levels for each role competency (on a scale of 1 to 5) and then matching the job-incumbents (displayed level) against proficiency level to identify the competency gaps.

The entire process is divided into five steps:

Figure 10.3:
Steps in Competency Mapping

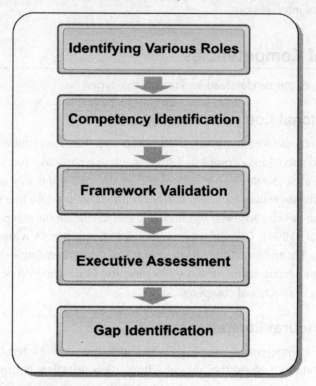

Step 1: Identifying Various Roles

➤ A thorough job analysis identifying various Job roles and responsibilities for the all the Unique roles is done.

➤ A comprehensive role document is developed.

➤ The role document is validated using role-incumbent and the supervisor's inputs.

Step 2: Competency Identification

➤ Various tasks, activities associated with each role are identified.

➤ The immediate Superior/ Head of Department/ any executive appointed by the Head of Department is interviewed to identify various competencies required for each role.

➤ An exhaustive list of all competencies identified for the department *is* prepared which is called the *Competency Bucket*.

Chapter 10: Competency Based Perofrmance Management ◄ 241

- ➢ The identified competencies are categorized as:
  - Behavioral Competency
  - Functional Competency
- ➢ More data is gathered on *Role Competencies.*

Step 3: Framework Validation
- ➢ The Competency Buckets and Role competencies are tabled for an Approval.
- ➢ The feedback on the same is received.
- ➢ The final Competency buckets and Role competencies are prepared.

Step 4: Executive Assessment
- ➢ The final Competency bucket and Role Competency are circulated.
- ➢ The supervisors are engaged to evaluate the employee's Desired and Displayed Proficiency Levels on the various competencies.
- ➢ The RADAR charts for all employees are mapped exhibiting the Desired and Displayed Proficiency Levels.

Step 5: Gap Identification and Program
- ➢ For each employee the competency-gaps are identified.
- ➢ The training needs are consequently identified.
- ➢ Training needs are consolidated department-wise or project-wise and forwarded to the training team for implementation.

Exhibit 6: Competency Mapping of Mr. Thomas Varghese, Senior Consultant (IT)

Mr. Thomas Varghese works as a Senior Consultant (IT) in an Indian IT major. First a detailed job analysis was done using a Position Analysis Questionnaire (PAQ). Based on the data a list of functional and behavioural competencies were identified and defined. The competencies were rated at five levels:

1	Yet to demonstrate
2	Learner
3	Practitioner
4	Leader
5	Expert

Functional Competencies

1. **Project Management:** Planning, development and deployment of IT projects for client organizations.

2. **Budgetary Planning:** Allocation of financial resources.

3. **Competitive Analysis:** Determination of other IT solution players in the global markets, to enhance the company's position.

4. **Performance Evaluation and Metrics:** Evaluating the metrics of project planning, development and deployment for IT solutions.

5. **Value Added Reseller Management:** Interacting and forming ties with Value Added Resellers to gain a competitive advantage.

6. **Knowledge Management:** Interacting and managing knowledge workers in a dynamic work environment.

Behavioural Competencies

1. **Time Management:** Management of time through scheduling of company activities.

2. **Quality Management:** Quality Control/Quality Assurance mechanism implementation.

3. **Team Development:** Management of intra-organizational teams/work groups.

4. **People Management:** Management of the employees in the organization, as per SOP's.

5. **Verbal and Written Communication:** Ability to utilize oral and written communication tools for organizational efficiency.

6. **Language Management:** Managing the various languages required for strategic communication with foreign clients.

Functional Competencies

Competencies	1	2	3	4	5
Project Management	No project planning or deployment possible	Level-1 Project module initiation	Level-2 & 3 project planning, preparation and deployment	Time and Cost escalation management for projects	Strategic partnering with VAR's and affiliates to ensure project completion and deployment according to timelines
Budgetary Planning	No planning of monetary resource allocation	Project wise budget allocation	Unit level budgeting for optimum resource allocation	Budgeting for maximum performance efficiency of project deliverables	2A/2B Asset Management, with focus on movable asset management
Competitive Analysis	Nil involvement in competitive planning	Level-1 competition metrics	Level-2 & 3 competitive metrics	Determining the ideal performance frameworks for strategic partnering	Utilising the 6C framework for determining core competencies, to achieve a competitive advantage
Performance Evaluation and Metrics	Implementation of basic project wise metrics	Level-1 Project development	Level-2 & 3 project mapping and development	Determining unit-wise project deployment requirement & planning	Developing new project planning, development and deployment frameworks
Value Added Reseller Management	No VAR management	Forming ties with initiator level VARS	Forming ties with intermediate level VARS	Forming ties and developing strategic information sharing with the premium VARS	Preparation of VAR selection techniques, in a knowledge management environment
Knowledge Management	Basic levels of interaction with knowledge workers	Initiation of the KM process at the unit level	Knowledge management at the departmental level	Knowledge Management at the line manager level	Knowledge management at the strategic level, partnering with individual unit heads

Table 10.1: Functional Competencies of Mr. Thomas Varghese

Behavioural Competencies

Competencies	1	2	3	4	5
Time and Quality Management	Not responsible for time management or quality control	Basic time management related to project functions	Is responsible for maintenance of time and quality standards in project management	Development of time and quality standards, and implementation of the same in the organization	Developing new methods of time management and Six Sigma Black Belt QC system implementation
Team Development	Not responsible for team control or development	Is responsible for basic team developmental activities like team lunches, trips etc	Cross-functional team development and management	Organizing team performance metrics for intra-organizational efficiency	Strategic Team Development Frameworks, with continuous emphasis on bottom line
People Management	Not a major part of controlling and directing workers	Is responsible for managing various departmental employees	People Management through implementation, analysis and review of employee performance	Development of various cross-functional goals to ensure employee performance	Developing a people Management System using the company Intranet for continuous monitoring
Verbal and Written Communication	Not very adept in communication	Basic written and oral communication for intra-organizational functioning	Slightly improved communication to interact with market intermediaries	Development of communication to foster inter-company interaction for business development	Strategic Communication frameworks for partnering with other businesses
Language Management	Not involved in any form of language management	Is involved in basic language management for intra-organizational functioning	Improved language management to foster team development	Development of different language based competencies for intra-organizational efficiency	Development of language based competencies for partnering with global companies

Table 10.2: Functional Competencies of Mr. Thomas Varghese

The role competency bucket of Mr. Varghese was verified and validated and the desired levels for each competency were decided. Thereafter the supervisor of Mr. Varghese rated him on displayed competency levels, based on which the competency radar chart was created:

Competencies	Desired Level	Displayed Level	Gap
Time and Quality Management	5	5	0
Team Development	5	4	1
People Management	5	4	1
Verbal and Written Communication	5	5	0
Language Management	5	4	1
Project Management	5	5	0
Budgetary Planning	5	5	0
Competitive Analysis	5	4	1
Performance Evaluation and Metrics	5	5	0
Value Added Reseller Management	5	4	1
Knowledge Management	5	4	1

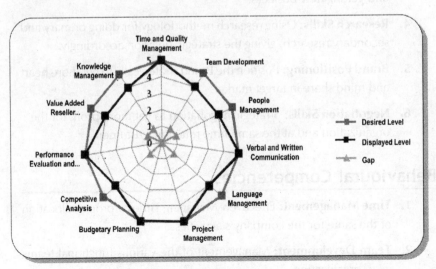

Figure 10.4: Competency Radar Chart of Mr. Thomas Varghese

Exhibit 7: Competency Mapping of Mr. Arnold Hopkins, Director Consultant in a Strategic Consulting Group

Mr. Arnold Hopkins works as a Director Consultant in a strategic consulting group. First, a detailed job analysis was done using a Position Analysis Questionnaire (PAQ). Based on the data a list of functional and behavioural competencies were identified and defined. The competencies were rated at five levels:

1	Yet to demonstrate
2	Learner
3	Practitioner
4	Leader
5	Expert

Functional Competencies

1. **Client Partnership:** Partnering with organization client and keeping two-way communication for current project or future business.

2. **Brand Strategy Planning:** Creating or improving brand equity for the organization client.

3. **Business Development:** Knowledge of building database, prospecting and getting new business.

4. **Research Skills:** Using research methodology for doing primary and secondary research, giving the strategic decision accordingly.

5. **Brand Positioning:** Position the Brand strategically to get more heart and mind share in target market.

6. **Negotiation Skills:** Strategic negotiation to get more profit for the organization and at the same time retaining customer.

Behavioural Competencies

1. **Time Management:** Effectively Managing Time by proper allocation of the same for the company's activities.

2. **Team Development:** Management of the various functional teams in an organization.

3. **People Management:** Management of internal & external employees of the organization.
4. **Communication Skills:** Effective listening, presenting and verbal skills to communicate effectively to all stakeholders.

Functional Competencies	1	2	3	4	5
Client Partnership	Minimal Client Relation	Formation of client relation	Development of Client Networks	Client Servicing	Forming Strategic partnerships with client organizations
Brand Strategy Planning	No involvement	Basic Insights into Brand Planning	Brand Management	Strategic Brand Management	Brand Equity Measurement & Metrics
Business Development	No Business Development	Building Database	Initiate talk with client and follow up for meeting	Developing Business from the leads	New Business Development & Getting Business from Old Clients
Research Skills	Basic Knowledge of research	Knowledge of Primary/ Secondary Research	Knowledge of primary & secondary research	Using Research Methodology while research	Analyzing the research and giving feedback or new initiative
Brand Positioning	Minimal Knowledge	Utilizing Branding Models	Developing Brand Identity Matrices	Analysing Brand Position with relation to Competitor	Strategically Aligning the Brand Mantra with Product Deliverables
Negotiation Skills	No involvement	Basic Insights into Negotiations	Negotiating with Vendors	Negotiation with Business Partners	Strategic Negotiations with Affiliates, with links to Bottom Line

Behavioural Competencies	1	2	3	4	5
Time Management	Not responsible for time management or quality control	Basic time management related to project functions	Is responsible for maintenance of time standards in project management	Development of time standards, and implementation of the same in the organisation	Developing new methods of time management
Team Development	Not responsible for team control or development	Is responsible for basic team developmental activities like team lunches, trips etc	Cross Functional Team Development & Management	Organising team performance metrics for intra-organisational efficiency	Strategic Team Development Frameworks, with continuous emphasis on bottom line
People Management	Not a major part of controlling and directing workers	Is responsible for managing the various departmental employees	People Management through implementation, analysis and review of employee performance	Development of various cross-functional goals to ensure employee performance	Developing a people Management System using the company Intranet for continuous monitoring
Communication Skills	Not very adept in communication	Basic written and oral communication for intra-organisational functioning	Slightly improved communication to interact with market intermediaries	Development of communication to foster inter-company interaction for business development	Strategic Communication frameworks for partnering with other businesses

Competencies	Desired	Displayed	Gap
Time Management	4	4	0
Team Development	3	3	0
People Management	4	5	0
Communication Skills	5	5	0
Client Partnership	5	5	0
Brand Strategy Planning	5	4	0
Business Development	4	3	1
Research Skills	3	3	0
Brand Positioning	5	4	1
Negotiation Skills	4	4	0

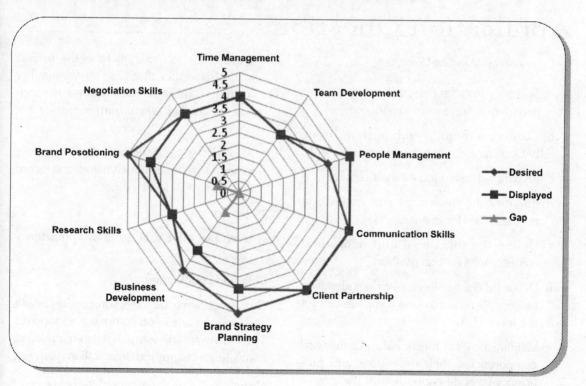

Figure 10.5: Competencies Radar Chart

Essay Questions

1. Define 'competency'. Discuss the relationship between competency and organizational strategy. How is competency linked to various HR processes?

2. Differentiate between competency dictionary and competency bucket.

3. Explain the various stages in preparation of competency buckets.

4. Write short notes on:
   a) Functional competencies
   b) Behavioral competencies
   c) Competency–gap.

5. What is Competency Mapping? Describe the various steps of competency mapping.

Application Questions

1. Competency-Mapping Exercise

   a) Select a corporate person. You know, with minimum 8-10 years of experience.

   b) Conduct a thorough Job analysis, using PAQ, by face -2 - face /telephonic interview.

   c) Prepare a detailed Job Analysis report.

   d) Identify the functional and behavioral competencies for that position

   e) Define the functional and behavioral competencies for that position.

   f) Define proficiency-levels of various identified functional and behavioral competencies for five levels (1-5).

   g) Validate the list of functional and behavioral competencies, their definitions and proficiency-level descriptions with the person –interviewed (Job-incumbent) and also with the course instructor. Update the changes.

   h) Treating the job incumbent as the subject matter expert for that position ask him/her to assign 'desired-level' ratings to each functional & behavioral competency for that position.

   i) Also ask the job-incumbent (Subject-matter expert) to self-rate himself/herself and record the 'displayed- level' ratings.

   j) Record 'gap'

   k) Now, use MS-EXCEL to draw competency radar chart

   l) Report your findings.

2. Go to http://www.businessgyan.com/node/244 and read the article on competency mapping. Trace the relationship between creating competency culture and organizational success.

3. Go to http://www.expresscomputeronline.com/20050131/technologylife01.shtml and read the article on competency mapping. Why competency based HR system is the best HR?

Bibliography

Anitha, N. (2011). Competency Assessment — A Gap Analysis. *Interdisciplinary Journal of Contemporary Research in Business, 3* (4), 784-794.

Bonder, A., Bouchard, C.-D., & Bellemare, G. (2011). Competency-Based Management-An Integrated Approach to Human Resource Management in the Canadian Public Sector. *Public Personnel Management, 40* (1), 1-10.

Bücker, J., & Poutsma, E. (2010). How to Assess Global Management Competencies: An Investigation of Existing Instruments. *Management Revue, 21* (3), 263-291.

Clardy, A. (2008). The Strategic Role of Human Resource Development in Managing Core Competencies. *Human Resource Development International, 11* (2), 183-197.

Dainty, A. R., Cheng, M. I., & Moore, D. R. (2004). A Competency-based Performance Model for Construction Project Managers. *Construction Management & Economics, 22* (8), 877-886.

Greengard, S. (1999). Competency Management Delivers Spectacular Corporate Gains. *Workforce, 78* (3), 104.

Harma, R., & Bhatnagar, J. (2009). Talent Management — Competency Development: Key to Global Leadership. *Industrial & Commercial Training, 41* (3), 118-132.

Huff-Eibl, R., Voyles, J. F., & Brewer, M. M. (2011). Competency-Based Hiring, Job Description, and Performance Goals: The Value of an Integrated System. *Journal of Library Administration, 51* (7/8), 673-691.

Losey, M. R. (1999). Mastering the Competencies of HR Management. *Human Resource Management, 38* (2), 99.

Martone, D. (2003). A Guide to Developing a Competency-Based Performance-Management System. *Employment Relations Today, 30* (3), 23-32.

Murugadoss, S., Kavitha, A. S., & Vasugi, M. S. (2010). An Empirical study on Employee Core Competencies a Proven Tool for an Organization's Success. *Interdisciplinary Journal of Contemporary Research in Business, 2* (8), 120-132.

Scott, J. T. (2005). Management Competencies and Styles. *Concise Handbook of Management: A Practitioner's Approach*, 35-40.

The Definition and Selection of Key Competencies, http://www.oecd.org/dataoecd/47/61/35070367.pdf

Chapter 11

Learning Process & Trainers

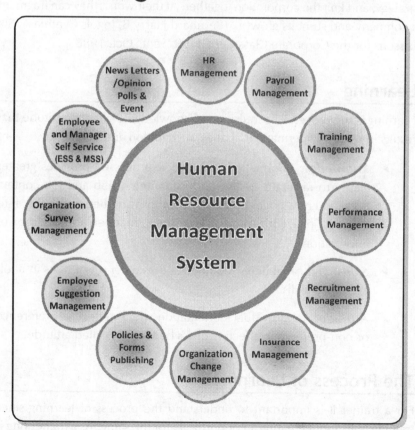

Outline

- Introduction
- Learning
- The Process of Learning
- Learning Styles
- Learning Theories
- The Learning Curve
- Implications for Trainers
- Transfer of Learning
- Essay Questions
- Application Questions
- Bibliography

Key Terms

- Accommodator
- Assimilator
- Converger
- Diverger
- ARCS Model
- Learning Styles
- Reflectors
- Theorists
- Pragmatists

Introduction

T&D is not like the classrooms where as children we learned reading and arithmetic. Second graders do well or poorly as individuals. Children pass or flunk, love school or hate it-which is a great shame for those who do poorly, but only for those who do poorly. In business, individuals and the organization must learn and grow as an integrated whole. Everyone needs common goals and a shared thrill of achievement. Unlike elementary school, the corporate classroom educates the organization, not just the individual. At their best, T&D programs are tools to communicate change, implement strategy, and knit the corporation together. At their worst, they can fragment a company and stunt its growth.' (Bernhard Harry B, Ingols Cynthia A, Six Lessons for the Corporate Classroom, HBR, Sept.-Oct. 1988)

Learning

Learning is the process of acquisition of knowledge, skills and attitude that results in relatively permanent change in cognition & behavior.

Learning

Learning is the process of acquisition of knowledge, skills and attitude that results in relatively permanent change in cognition and behavior.

> **Knowledge:** Information gathered & processed provides greater clarity to facilitate greater understanding of job and job context is called knowledge. Knowledge can provide better visibility into content, procedure and usage (time, manner and degree) of information.

> **Skills:** The capabilities required to execute a set of tasks in a job are called skills.

> **Attitude:** An individual's orientation which reflects a preference or non-preference affecting one's behavior is called attitude.

The Process of Learning

For a trainer it is important to understand the process of learning since training is all about creating an opportunity for the same. As a trainer one is expected to not only make participants feel that it is an opportunity but also ensure that they make most of this opportunity. Besides if a trainer understands how learning actually takes place, he/she can position himself/herself better in terms of planning, resource-development and execution.

Learning Styles

Honey & Mumford (1992) proposed a Learning Style Questionnaire (LSQ) which recognizes four types of learning styles:

   a) Reflectors: Thoughtful, observant, good listeners, think-back on experiences and take time to arrive upon a decision.

   b) Theorists: Rational and objective, they can integrate/assimilate observation into theories that are usually complex but objective.

   c) Activists: Thrive on new experiences and are bored soon by something they have been doing for a while. Many a times act in haste in their quest for change.

   d) Pragmatists: Impatient with theory and comfortable with application, they are practical, no nonsense types. Like to be precise, to the point and are inherently open-minded.

Richard M Felder and *Eunice R Henriques (1995)* proposed five dichotomous learning style dimensions:

   a) Sensing and Intuitive Learners: Sensing learners tend to be 'concrete and methodical' while intuitive learners tend to be 'imaginative and abstract'.

   b) Visual and Verbal Learners: Visual learners prefer the information to be presented in form of pictures, diagrams, flow-charts etc. Verbal learners, on the other hand prefer 'spoken or written explanation' of visual forms. Another third category of learners may be tactile learners i.e., responding to touch, taste & smell.

   c) Active and Reflexive Learners: An active learner will have a natural tendency towards active experimentation. Whereas, a reflexive learner will be oriented more towards observation and reflection.

   d) Sequential and Global Learners: Sequential learners make meaning by absorbing small connected pieces of information. Global learners on the other hand can handle apparently disconnected pieces of information and connect the dots to appreciate their understanding by leaps and bounds.

   e) Inductive and Deductive Learners: An inductive learner first makes observations and then draws conclusions or inferences in form of theory or principle. A deductive learner does complete opposite of the above. He/she first postulates a theory or a principle and then deduces consequences and formulates applications.

Kolb et al (1979) gave a learning style inventory in which they proposed four learning styles:

a) Converger: A converger prefers problem solving through hypothetical deductive reasoning.

b) Diverger: A diverger prefers problem-solving through brainstorming and generation of ideas. A diverger views problem from multiple angles.

c) Assimilator: An assimilator prefers problem-solving through inductive reasoning.

d) Accommodator: An accommodator prefers problem solving through experimentation.

Based on these learning styles, Kolb also suggested for learning cycles i.e.,

i. Concrete experience

ii. Reflective observation

iii. Active conceptualization

iv. Active experimentation

All four cycles are tied into learning styles.

It is clear from the above discussion that learning styles may differ from learner to learner. However there are some truths about learning styles and they are as follows:

I. No single learning style is free from disadvantages. Each learning style has few benefits but at the same time they have few limitations as well.

II. Each learner has a predominant learning style, but he/she learns through other styles too, to some extent.

III. For a trainer understanding the learning style is important to adjust to different training environments.

Learning Theories

Besides the usual learning theories like classical conditioning, operant conditioning etc., we shall primarily focus on two learning theories:
a. Social Learning Theory
b. Adult Learning Theory

a. Social Learning Theory

Social Learning theory was proposed by Bandura. The basic premise of this theory is that any event or consequence in a learning environment is cognitively processed before one learns them so as to influence his/her behavior.

> **Social Learning Theory**
> Any event or consequence in a learning environment is cognitively processed before one learns them so as to influence his/her behaviour.

The Theory states that human beings learn through four steps –
a) **Attention**: Attention to external stimuli (models)
b) **Retention**: Retention of information related to stimuli. Enough motivation for retention must be there.
c) **Reproduction**: Behavioral exhibition of retained stimuli
d) **Reinforcement**: Strengthening / weakening of exhibited behavior based upon consequences.

Application of Bandura's Social Learning Theory for Trainers

In simple words, what can trainer's do to augment the training process with the knowledge of social learning theory:

1) Create Intrinsic and Extrinsic Motivators to Gain Attention: Motivational incentives are important for successful conducting a training program. Keller suggested an ARCS model for motivating trainees:

Attention   **R**elevance   **C**onfidence   **S**atisfaction

The ARCS model can be combined with Gagne's model of nine events of instruction to understand the application of the former –

1. **Attention:** This can be facilitated through first three steps of Gagne's model
   a. Gaining attention (through examples, anecdotes etc)

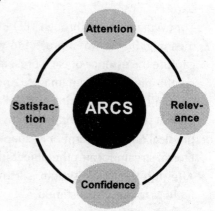

Figure 11.1:
ARCS Model

ARCS Model

The ARCS model is a problem solving approach to designing the motivational aspects of learning environments to stimulate and sustain students' motivation to learn. It provides a good summary of issues to be considered when designing learning materials.

    b. Informing the learner about objective.

    c. Stimulating the recall of pre-requisite learning.

II. Relevance: The next two steps help in creating relevance:

    d. Presenting the new material.

    e. Providing guidance to learners.

III. Confidence – Confidence in trainees can be boosted by executing the next two steps of Gagne's model:

    f. Eliciting performance (from trainees on new knowledge/skill acquired).

    g. Providing feedback (both corrective and appreciative).

IV. Satisfaction: The last two steps of Gagne's model help in creating satisfaction among trainees.

    h. Assessing performance of trainees.

    i. Enhancing retention and recall (of terms, concepts, theories & application learnt in training program).

2) Assist the Trainees in Retention

Retention among trainees can be facilitated by:

    a) Use of symbols, diagrams, pictures etc. It is a kind of symbolic that helps the learner retain the information.

Tom Wuject (2009) through TED BigViz clarified why animation, pictures and graphics create meaning. BigViz was a project in which two visual artists created 650 sketches that tried to capture the essence of each presenter's ideas. This was to help people understand how brain creates meanings from images. And the more we know how brain creates meanings, better we can collaborate, think and collaborate. After our eyes have picked up the visual stimuli, ventral stream of our brain is activated. Ventral stream is the 'what' detector. It clarifies the physical object on term of its shape, size, form etc. Thereafter the dorsal stream is activated. Dorsal stream locates the object in its physical space. In other words, it is 'where' detector. After this the limbic system is activated. Limbic system detects colors, motions etc. It adds feelings to our visual stimuli.

So then what is the point for the trainers? The learning for trainers is 3 fold :

   i. Use images to clarify ideas.

   ii. Create an engagement with these images by making them interactive.

   iii. Make these images persistent to further augment the memory.

   b) Trainers can provide adequate examples to help trainees cognitively organize the information.

   c) Trainers can also simulate job environments in training room/place to help trainee rehearse what they learnt during the training.

b. Adult Learning Theory

The second most important leaning theory which we are going to discuss here is the adult learning theory that is also known as Kolb's adult experiential learning cycle.

Kolb's adult experiential learning cycle specifies four steps through which learning takes place:

   a) *Experiencing:* The stimuli are picked-up by all five senses, in case of trainees primarily through eyes and ear.

   b) *Processing:* Such Stimuli are cognitively processed to create meanings.

   c) *Generalizing:* The learner relates his learning to a higher degree of generalization.

   d) *Applying:* The learner then applies whatever he/she learnt to other elements in the environment.

Adult Learning Theory

Adults primarily learn through experience. They experience, process the stimuli cognitively, generalize and apply their learning other elements in the environment.

Implications of Adult Learning Theory for Trainers

Adult (trainees) learn best when:

   a. They are clear about the agenda of a training program.

   b. Training is linked to actual job scenario.

   c. When there is a chance to rehearse or practice, what they learnt.

   d. When proper, timely and specific feedback is given to them.

   e. Observational learning takes place.

The Learning Curve

Learning especially skill learning follows an S-shaped curve. On y-axis we have a measure of some skill whereas on x-axis we take the number of trials. There is an initial stagnant period, depicting a slow progress at initial stages. Thereafter there is steep increase or a burst of learning which occurs after sometime. And finally there is plateau. The plateau instead of depicting a point of stagnation actually represents a point of stability.

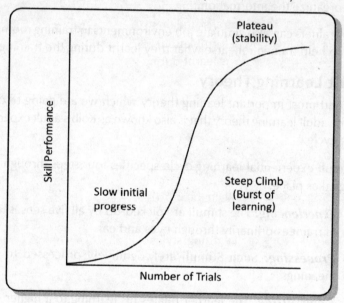

Figure 11.2: The Learning Curve

Implications for Trainers

The learning curve is common for most forms of training. The implications for trainees are as under:

a) Learning-by-doing is the best way of learning.

b) Practice should be incorporated in training.

c) Repeat at times to advance the 'learning burst'.

Conditions for Learning: On an average a human memory retains only 25% of what it learns. According to Dale people generally remember:

- 10% of what they read;
- 20% of what they hear;
- 30% of what they see;

- 50% of what they hear and see;
- 70% of what they say and write;
- 90% of what they say as they do.

Trainers must understand that learning-by-doing is the best form of learning.

Transfer of Learning

One of the biggest challenge confronting most training managers is how to ensure that whatever is imparted in the training room, is translated on to the actual job. Transfer of learning needs involvement (of line managers, right of need formulation) relevance (of the program) and measurement (of how effective it was to apply the KSAs learnt during training in the job).

Essay Questions

1. Define 'Learning'. Briefly explain the process of learning.
2. Discuss various types of 'Learning styles'. Why is it important to understand the process of learning?
3. What is social learning theory? Discuss its implications for trainers.
4. Explain the adult learning theory proposed by Kolb. What are the implications for trainers?
5. What are the various conditions for learning? Explain the learning curve and its implications for trainers. Why is transfer of learning a challenge?

Application Questions

1. Go to -http://www.nationalforum.com/ Electronic%20Journal%20Volumes Calais, %20Gerald%20J%20Haskell's%20tax onomies%20of%20transfer%20of%20 learning.pdf and read the document on 'Haskell's Taxonomies of transfer of learning, implications for classroom instruction'. Reflect.
2. Go to -http://ucsfhr.ucsf.edu/index.php /training/article transfer_of_learning_a_guide _for_strengthening_supervisory_performance / and read the article on Transfer of Learning: A guide for strengthening supervisory performance. Discuss in the group.

Bibliography

Baldwin, T. T.; Danielson, C. and Wiggenhorn. 1997. The Evolution of Learning Strategies in Organizations: From Employee Development to Business Redefinition, *Academy of Management Executive*, 11: 47-58.

Beitz, W., Langner, T., Luczak, H., Muller, T., & Springer, J. (1990). Evaluation of a Compact CAD Course in Laboratory Experiments. *International Journal of Human-Computer Interface*, 2, 111-135.

Bhavnani, S. K., John, B. E., & Flemming, U. (1999). Strategic Use of CAD: An Empirically Inspired, Theory-based Course. *Proceedings of the 1999 Conference on Human Factors in Computing Systems*, May 15-20, Pittsburgh, PA, 183-190.

Brinkerhoff, R. and Apking, A. 2001. *High Impact Learning*. Cambridge, MA: Perseus. Daniel, J. 1998. Can you Get My Hard Nose in Focus? Universities, Mass Education and Appropriate Technology, in Eisenstadt.

Can you Say "Fun CAD Training" (2001). *Design News*, 56, 36.

Compton, P., & Jansen. R. (1990). Aphilosophical Basis for Knowledge Acquisition. *Knowledge Acquisition*, 2, 241–257.

Coury, B. G., & Strauss, R.A. (1998). Cognitive Models in User Interface Design. *Proceedings of the 1998 42nd Annual Meeting of the Human Factors and Ergonomics Society*, 1, 325-329.

Dar-El, E. M., Ayas, K., & Gilad, I. (1995a). A Dual-phase Mode for the Individual Learning Process in Industrial Tasks. *IIE Transactions*, 27, 265-271.

Dar-El, E. M., Ayas, K., & Gilad, I. (1995b). Predicting Performance Times for Long Cycle Time Tasks. *IIE Transactions*, 27, 272-281.

Dutton, J., & Thomas A. (1984). Treating Progress Functions as a Managerial Opportunity. *Academy of Management Review*, 9, 235-247.

Dvorak, P., & Teschler, L. (1993). Climbing CAD's Learning Curve. *Machine Design*, 65, 52-55.

Eisenstadt, M. and Vincent, T. 1998. *The Knowledge Web: Learning and Collaborating on the Net*. London, Kogan Page.

Engelke, W. D. (1987). *How to integrate CAD/CAM Systems: Management & Technology*. New

Forslin, J., &Thulestedt, B. M. (1989). Computer-aided Design: A Case Strategy in Implementing a New Technology. *IEEE Transactions on Engineering Management*, 36, 191–201.

Hofstede, G. (1980). *Cultures Consequences: International Differences in Work Related Values*.

Hulme, D. (1991). *A Comparative Study of the Effectiveness of Different Approaches in Training Overseas Officers in the Fields of Management, Administration and Social Sciences*, British Council, London.

Hunt, J. W. (1986). *Managing People at Work: A Manager's Guide to Behaviour in Organisations*, McGraw Hill, London.

Iqbal, S. (1989). 'Management of Training Awards: Dr. Jekyll or Mr. Hyde?' *Management Education and Development*, 20, 67-76.

M. and Vincent, T. (eds.). *The Knowledge Web: Learning and Collaborating on the net*. London, Kogan Page.

Rutkauskienė, D. and Butkevièienë, E. 2007. Distance Education from the Perspective of Educators: Opportunities and Challenges, in *Advanced Learning Technologies and Applications* Sage, Beverly Hills.

Stamatis, D.; Kefalas, P. and Kargidis, T. 1999. A Multiagent Framework to Assist Networked Learning, *Journal of Computer Assisted Learning* 15(3): 201-210.

Waller, J. and Wilson, J. 2003. E-learning definition [online]. <http://www.odlqc.org.uk/odlqc/

Chapter 12

Employee Training & Development

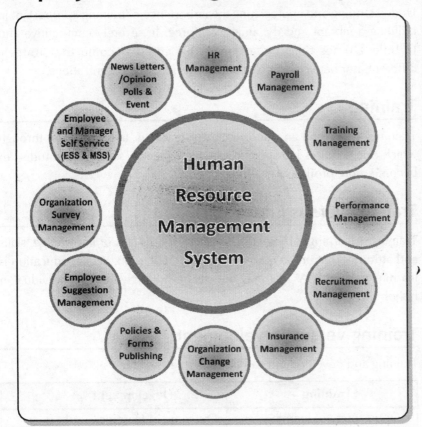

Outline

Introduction
Training
Training versus Education
Training versus Development
Relationship Between Learning, Training, Education & Development
Competency & Competency Gap
The Training Process Model
Training Need Analysis
Approaches to Training Need Assessment (TNA)
Training Plan
Training Methods
Commonly Used Training Methods
Choosing the Right Training Method
Training Evaluation
Return on Investment in Training
Categories of ROI
Practical Issues in ROI Computation
Eassy Question
Application Question
Bibliography

Key Terms

Competency Gap
Job Description
Return of Investment (ROI)
Training Evaluation
Training Need Analysis
Training Need Assessment
Training Plan
Training Process Model
Instructional Design Model

Introduction

It is probably said that defense forces of any nation primarily engage in two types of activities i.e., training and fighting. While war-times or crisis moments need action, peace-times are typically characterized by training that prepares them for such situations. A defense personnel's job is perhaps one of the most challenging ones that demands constant state of readiness to meet any eventuality or crisis. Such demands require regular and intensive training that not only facilitates skill up-gradation but also prevents any skill loss that might happen due to passage of time.

Understanding and appreciating the importance of training is important in building a vibrant and dynamic workforce. In severely competitive and turbulent times that prevail now, this could become the strategic differentiator between successful and unsuccessful organizations.

Training
> Process through which one acquires job specific KSAs (Knowledge, Skills and Attitudes) to become more proficient in a job.

Training

Training is basically an opportunity for learning. It is a process through which one acquires job specific KSAs (knowledge, skills and attitudes) to become more proficient in a job.

Training versus Education

Education
> Learning general KSAs that may directly or indirectly help an individual in his job.

Training is learning job specific KSAs i.e., acquisition of knowledge, skills and attitudes that one requires to do a particular job. While, education is learning general KSAs that may directly or indirectly help an individual in his job.

Training versus Development

Training and development can be contrasted as follows:

Table 12.1: Training vs. Development

Training	Development
Opportunity of learning.	Outcome of learning.
It is time specific.	It is continuous, never-ending life long process.
Every training should ideally result in development.	Development may/may not be because of training. Development can be at times because of non-training factors too.

Development
> Outcome of Learning. may or may not be because of training.

Relationship between Learning, Training, Education & Development

Clarity on such basic concepts is important to later appreciate the various theoretical constructs and the application areas. The relationship between learning, training, education and development can be diagrammatically represented as follows:

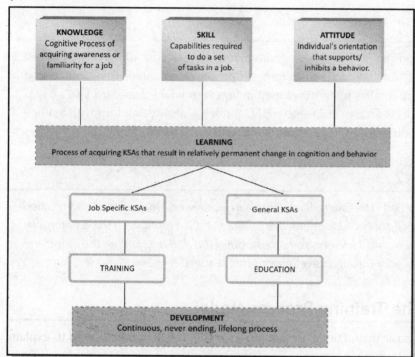

Figure 12.1: Relationship between Learning, Training, Education & Development

Competency & Competency Gap

A competency is defined as a set of KSAs i.e., knowledge, skills and attitude required as a part of a job.

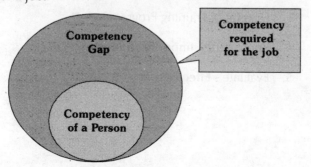

Figure 12.2: Competency and Competency Gap

Competency of a person essentially, is a set of KSAs, required for a job, already present in a person. Competency gap is the difference between the competency required for the job and competency of a person. Such gaps can be narrowed / closed by using training as an intervention. Narrower the competency gap, better are a person's chance to perform on the job.

Reading Exhibit 1

HDFC Standard Life, a private life insurance provider, and Manipal Education recently joined hands to launch First Advantage, a three-month certificate programme in insurance and management. The curriculum has been developed in line with HDFC Standard Life's eight-step structured sales process known as Disha. HDFC Bank has also teamed up with leading business schools to introduce a certification programme in retail banking.

Reading Exhibit 2

Caterpillar recently launched 'The Caterpillar Leadership Framework' through a program called *Making Great Leaders (MGL), a two-day interactive program. MGL emphasized three Caterpillar leadership competency i.e., instil a Vision of success, build the skills to Execute the vision and assure the creation of a Legacy* through developing future leaders.

The Training Process Model

A basic instructional design model – The ADDIE model is used to explain the training process.

1. Analysis – of training needs
2. Design – of training programme
3. Develop – Training Programme
4. Implement – Importing training
5. Evaluate - Effectiveness

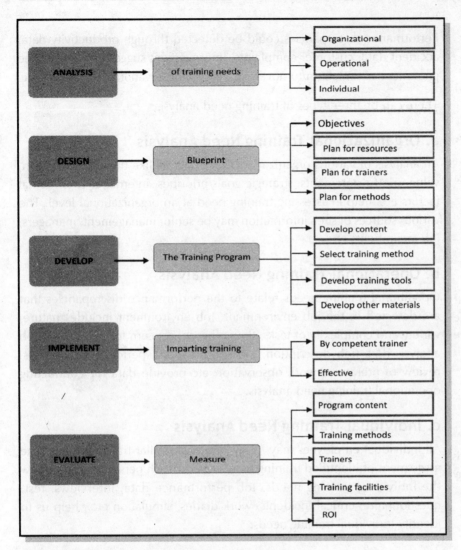

Figure 12.3: Instructional Design Model

Training Need Analysis

Assessment of training need is the first and most important step in designing a training program. Only a proper diagnosis of training needs can ensure effectiveness (relevance, reliability and returns) of a training program.

Training need essentially represent a gap between expected performance standards and present performance standards. The gap between the two may represent a competency-gap. At times the gap between the expected performance and present performance may be because of non-training reasons like supervisor, work environment, office politics etc. However, if it is a competency-gap then it represents a need of training.

Training Needs Analysis

Diagnosis of training needs to ensure effectiveness (relevance, reliability and returns) from a training program.

Performance discrepancies could be detected through productivity data, accident data, customer complaints, improvement suggestions, employee grievances, absenteeism/turnover data, survey/observation of employees etc.

There can be three types of training need analysis:

Organizational TNA
Assessment of training needs at an organizational level.

a. Organizational Training Need Analysis

An analysis of various organizational level factors like the mission, vision, value, motto statements, strategic goals/priorities, internal environmental factors etc. help in assessing training need at an organizational level. The various sources of such information may be senior management, managers, job incumbents etc.

Operational TNA
Training needs that relate to performance discrepancies that are detected in the job environment.

b. Operational Training Need Analysis

Operational training needs relate to the performance discrepancies that are detected in the job environment. Job environment includes nature, variety and complexity of tasks, flow of work, concern for people etc. Job analysis data (job description, job specification), performance records, review of literature, work observation etc provide data for conducting operational training need analysis.

Individual TNA
Unique training needs that an individual may possess.

c. Individual Training Need Analysis

All individual employees may / may not have similar training needs. The assessment of identified training needs against each person helps us know the individual training needs. Job performance data, interviews, test, questionnaire, critical incidents, work diaries, simulation etc., help us to identify individual training needs.

Approaches to Training Need Assessment (TNA)

There could be two approaches to training need assessment:

a. **Proactive TNA:** Approach that involves anticipating performance discrepancies in advance.

b. **Reactive TNA:** Approach that involves responding to the present problems.

An organization must have a proactive training need analysis approach. However, having said that, even if a company has predominantly a proactive training need analysis approach, it will still always have some training needs that shall arise suddenly. Every company should be able to meet such demands also, owing to uncertain and competitive nature of business.

Reading Exhibit 3

HP Skills Gap Analysis helps to assess the critical skills that the organisation will need. HP then creates a detailed training plan to ensure the organisation has the proper training structure in place. Structuring training to business critical areas maximises the efficiency of the training budget. This ultimately encourages skill enhancement for both current and future employees, as well as improvements to business performance and return-on-investment. It also improves staff morale and supports career development.

Reading Exhibit 4

Larsen And Turbo, a leading Infrastructure Company, has established Construction Skills Training Institute(CSTI). Out of every 16000 passouts, 250 are recruited by L&T itself.

Reading Exhibit 5: Proactive TNA by IBM

Anticipated Problem: Around 1.5 million IT-experts will be required by 2012 in India. This would mean a severe shortage of IT-experts for most IT companies including IBM.

BEST (POTENTIAL) BETS: The best bets to meet this scarcity are the students in hundreds of engineering colleges in India. But the problem is that these students only represent a potential source and not an actual one, owing to skill-gaps that exist related to modern IT platform & technologies.

TRAINING AS SOLUTION: IBM decided to impart training (proactive assessment of training needs) as a solution to this looming problem. They came up with two very important programs:

>>**IBM DRONA**

SPIRIT –
a) Train faculty members and empower them with right resources.
b) Collaborate and partner with faculty members.

LOGIC –
a) Faculty members in turn train the students.

b) Faculty members have the longest window of opportunity with the students

>>IBM GREAT MINDS CHALLENGE

SPIRIT –

a) Touch screen kiosks at engineering colleges showcasing technologies and platforms that IBM works on.

b) Self-directed virtual tours of IBM.

LOGIC –

a) To entice the hearts and minds of students towards IBM.

b) Catch them young.

Training Plan

A training plan is like a blueprint for training. Careful planning will not only help the trainers but also the trainees. Generally a training plan will have the following constituents:

a) Period for which planning is done.
b) Financial resources allocated for the program.
c) Takeaways from the program (specific & preferably measureable KSAs).
d) Profile of trainees.
e) Number of trainees.
f) Training method to be employed.
g) Span (duration of the program).
h) Place/location of the program.
i) Trainer(s).
j) Facilities required in training room/place.
k) Facilities required outside training room (e.g., Lodging, boarding of trainees/trainers, etc.).
l) Evaluation model/ technique to be used.
m) Feedback collection and management.

Training Methods

Broadly the training methods could be classified in to:

a) On the Job Training: Training that is given during the job at the job-site itself is known as on-the-job training (OJT)

OJT methods may involve:

    i. Apprenticeships (work-study under trained instructor).
    ii. Shadowing (A senior worker non-intrusively observes a junior worker's work).
    iii. Observational learning.
    iv. Self-directed learning programs.
    v. Demonstration.
    vi. Safety drills (for safety training).

b) Off-the-job Training: Training that is given away from the job location, is known as off the job training.

Commonly Used Training Methods

Simulation

Replicating a real job like situation in the training room is known as simulation. Simulations help in making training content and environment closer to actual job conditions, thereby increasing its relevance. Simulations assist trainees in improving their skills and understand application of their learning

Role Play

Role play is a powerful and significant learning opportunity based on practice (Robinson). The importance of role play as a training method is in the fact that it is a very interactive method and creates greater degree of involvement among participants. Role plays help uncover hidden habits and invites constructive criticism and comments. They enhance practical learning and an opportunity for participants to use their creativity.

Case Studies

Case studies are descriptions of problems in organizations and strategies to deal with those problems. Case study improves the analytical and logical thinking of employees and helps them approach the problem from a unique perspective. It also engages participants in coming out with suggestions and actions required to solve the problem at hand.

Computer Based Training (CBT)

Computer based training (CBT) is high tech training involving delivery of training via CD-ROMs intranets, internet, virtual classrooms etc. CBT may/may not require an instructor's assistance. CBT is interactive and self-paced. It allows multiple iterations and can combine practice. Computer based training can mix audio, video, graphics, animations, text etc to create video simulations or virtual tours and experiences for the trainees.

Reading Exhibit 6: Triage Training (Virtual Training)

'Virtual crisis' is being used to train emergency service workers. It is a part of so called "serious game", an emerging niche in the video game industry. The game 'Triage Training' developed at the University of Coventry (U.K.) in collaboration with the Serious games Institute (SGI) is designed to provide a virtual real-time training to deal with emergencies. The interactive video game takes the trainee through a virtual crisis like a sudden bomb blast on a busy street etc. As chaos ensues the player must quickly fulfill a series of tasks viz. check to ensure victim's respiratory tracts are not blocked, make sure he has a pulse and various other quick diagnosis before moving swiftly to treat other victims, as efficiently as possible. It works in real time and hence if one does not take care of these casualties soon enough, they will die. Pretty scary! However much better than losing actual human lives.

Other methods available for similar training may involve shutting down a city centre for entire day and hence substantial cost and time. Besides multiple iterations may not be possible. Virtual crisis is not only cost effective and non-chaotic but also helps trainee to undergo multiple iterations and improve his/her skill level.

Outbound Training

Outbound Training methods involving adventure camping, trekking etc are mostly used as group/team training techniques in areas of decision making, team building and leadership. The participants are taken to resort or to an adventurous location and are give a series of activities to do that requires them to collaborate and work synergistically.

Reading Exhibit 7: Outbound Training @ Cognizant

Camps at Adventure Zone are a part of Cognizant's Campus Associate Training Program offered to fresh recruits by in-house learning centre of the company known as *Cognizant Academy*. The trainees are divided into teams and participate in sessions of rappelling, rock-climbing, rifle and pistol-firing, running obstacles courses etc., are followed by a process of review with team facilitators. On one hand, the activities test the physical and mental strength, on the other they also help create a sense of teamwork, leadership and collaboration. This translates into building their ability to work as a team on their jobs also.

(**Source:** Business Line)

Reading Exhibit 8: Team Building through Drumming

DRUM CAFÉ founded by Warren Lieberman and originally started at Johannesburg (South Africa) in 1996 is a leading training organization. It trains corporate employees into team building through drumming. Inspired by the experience of communal drumming in Africa and with a strong desire to unite different groups of people in South Africa, post apartheid era, Warren Lieberman developed a global team building and entertainment program, joining with leading motivational speakers, team builder and top-drummers of Africa.

(**Source:** http://www.drumcafe.com/index.asp)

Other training methods include:
- Lectures
- Group discussions
- Self-study manuals
- Games, etc.

Choosing the Right Training Method - The 3-C Model

A training method should not be chosen because it is a more popular method or it has been used by other successful trainers or because one has become too comfortable using a particular method. Imitation or operating within one's comfort zones may not be the right approach in choosing a training method.

Choosing a right training method is very important and right factors should be taken into consideration while making that choice following factors are important for choosing a training method.

Figure 12.4:
The 3-C Model for choosing Right Training Method

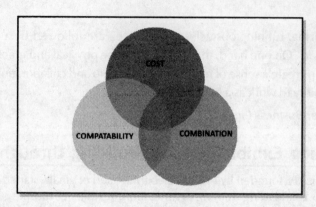

a. Cost: Undoubtedly cost is a major factor while choosing a training method. For every dollar spent on training to be treated as investment rather than cost, the returns must be ascertained. However when we say 'cost' as a factor in choosing a training method, we mean more in sense of cost-benefit. And hence aspects like:

- Size of audience;
- Significance of training program;
- Expected output and business results through that training program are important when calculating the cost.

b. Compatibility: The same shoe does not fit everyone. While choosing the training method compatibility with following is important:

- *Trainee's Learning Needs and Expectations:* It must compliment a trainee's learning needs and fulfill his/her expectations.

For example, an outbound training may be more suitable for a team building training rather than a lecture method.

- *Content:* A training method must do justice to the content of a training program.

For example strategy training can do with some techniques like case-method and creative problem solving.

- *Group Size, Facilities, Duration:* The chosen training method must be compatible to the group size, facilities (like projectors, props, space etc.) available at the training site and with the duration of the training program.

- *Trainer's Skills:* And finally, the chosen training method must match with skills of a trainer.

c. Combination: A combination of training methods must be mostly chosen for the following reasons:
- Variety.
- Balance the different learning styles of trainees.
- Facilitate adult-learning process and 'learning-by-doing'.

Training Evaluation

The resources that a company uses to train its employees are a cost or investment. The answer lies in the fact that how seriously does a company evaluate its training programs. The input resources can only be treated as investment if 'returns' are sought and expected.

> **Training Evaluation**
> Estimating 'benefits' or returns from a training program.

Why Evaluate?

Training evaluation is required for the following reasons:
a) To close performance gaps, effectively.
b) To improve quality of training.
c) To improve returns on training investment.
d) To understand a better evaluation model.

What to Evaluate?

Knowing what to measure is basic to the entire evaluation process. Training activity may require evaluation of:
a) Trainer
b) Training material
c) Training delivery
d) Training perception
e) Facilities, etc.

When to Evaluate?

Evaluation of training should be done:
a) Before the training.
b) During the development of training.
c) After the training.
d) Much-after the training.

a) Before the Training

Training evaluation starts even before the training has actually begun. It helps in:

i. Choosing an appropriate evaluation model.

ii. To check level of preparation on part of trainer/ training department.

iii. To reassess the competency gaps sought to be closed with the training program.

iv. This data (especially of the KSA level of trainees) can help to compare effects of training later.

b) During the Development of Training

Evaluation during the training facilitates:

i. Mid-term assessment, feedback and possibility of course-correction.

ii. Feedback on course material, methods resources and delivery.

iii. Match target audience with all of the above.

c) After the Training

Evaluation of training after the training program helps assess:

i. Change in level, knowledge, skill and attitude.

ii. Degree of application of training inputs on-the job.

iii. Assess whether performance-gaps have been closed.

iv. Measure effectiveness of training w.r.t., organization objectives and training needs.

d) Much after the Training

Real effects of training may be visible only after quite some time has passed after the training. Evaluation of training mush after the training may be undertaken to assess:

i. Change in business results like productivity, sales, reduction in waste/ scraps/ downtime/ re-works/ repairs etc.

ii. Change in business unit's outcomes.

iii. Fulfillment of organization strategic goals.

iv. ROI on amount invested in training.

How to Evaluate?

One of the most commonly used training evaluation method is using the Kirkpatrick's four levels:

Level 1: Reaction

Level 2: Learning

Level 3: Behaviour Application

Level 4: Results (Business Impact)

Level 1 to 4 also shows a progression in terms of difficulty in measurement. In other words level 4 is most difficult to measure and level 1 is simplest to measure. Having said this, the quality of information is best in level 4. Organizations mostly use levels in increasing order of complexity.

What each of these levels measure and how the same is assessed is given in the table 12.2 below:

Kirkpatrick's Levels	What is Assessed?	Tools
Level 1: Reaction	Assess trainee's reaction about the – ➤ Program ➤ Training material ➤ Trainer ➤ Facilities ➤ Lodging/ boarding ➤ Time of training ➤ Method of training	Mostly questionnaires / Reaction forms
Level 2: Learning	Assess change in trainee's ➤ Knowledge ➤ Skills ➤ Attitude	Performance Tests (Use of control group is recommended)
Level 3: Behaviour Application	Assess application of training knowledge on	➤ Observation ➤ Work- sampling

Table 12.2: Kirkpatrick's Four Levels

	the job in terms of – ➤ Frequency ➤ Effectiveness (Cost benefit)	➤ Interview of supervisor/ juniors/ incumbent (control group may be continued)
Level 4: Business Impact	Assess changes in – ➤ Productivity ➤ Quality ➤ Wastage ➤ Scraps ➤ Downtimes ➤ Client satisfaction ➤ Stakeholder satisfaction	➤ ROI scores ➤ CSAT/ ESATscores ➤ Other business performance data

Return on Investment in Training

Return on Investment (ROI) in training is computed using the formulae:

$$\text{ROI in Training} = \frac{\text{Net Benefits (from a training program)}}{\text{Total Cost}} \times 100$$

Cost of training shall include cost of materials, resources trainers, facilities, venue, lodging & boarding cost of trainees etc.

Categories of Return of Investment (ROI)

There are four categories of ROI:

I. **Immediate Returns**: Computation is done 1-2 months after the training program. It is done for trainings like technical training application- specific training.

II. **Delayed Returns**: Computation is done much after the training programme. It is done for training like behavioural training, six-sigma training etc.

III. **Organizational Returns**: Computation of ROI is compared with the objectives/ goals realized by the organization as a result.

IV. **Value Added Returns**: Such ROI is computed to depict the 'value' created as a result of training, for the organization.

Practical Issues in ROI Computation

The computation of (ROI) on training has its own complexities and limitations. There are several reasons for this such as:

1. Does Performance Result in increase of Organizational Revenues/Billing?

This is a very critical question and ideally an improvement in performance due to training must result in increase in billing/ revenues for the organization. However this may not be always possible or visible. In such cases, 'savings' done as a result of training-enabled improved performance must be taken into account.

> **Example:** There may be a clause from the client that in core performance of 'X' level is not achieved, and 'Y' target if not met, may result in penalty. The aversion of the same shall become a saving.

2. Are Improvements Always Quantitative?

The answer is 'no'. Quantitative improvements or benefits accrued as a result of training are easy to compute. But qualitative improvements are difficult to account for.

There can be two kinds of treatment of a qualitative improvement:

a) Conversion of Qualitative Data into Monetary Terms

Qualitative data like decrease in number of customer complaints, defects or reworks can be converted into monetary terms by computing unit costs. In other words let's say we compute the cost of processing one customer complaint in terms of time and other overheads. This multiplied by the number of reduced complaints and benefit as a result of training programme can be computed.

b) Qualitative Data may be Treated as ROI Itself

At times it may be impossible to convert qualitative data into monetary terms. In such cases the same may be taken as ROI e.g., CSAT scores, ESAT scores.

3. Can Effects of Training be Isolated?

On the toughest challenges that a training manager faces is to isolate the effects of training. This may be due to:

a) An individual employee's feeling that improvements in his/her performance are due to experience.

b) A line manager may be reluctant to acknowledge the benefits of training and would rather attribute improvement in performance to his/her efforts and leadership. The line manager's predicament is not unfounded as he/she would also have a contribution in any improvement in performance.

Hence for all practical purposes, reasonable lower-bound on ROI is taken for computational purpose. The objective is not to find out ROI on training in absolute terms. Rather it is an attempt to understand whether ROI on training shows substantial benefits accrued as a result of training or not.

To summarize:

a. ROI on training may be in quantitative form;
b. It may be in the form of savings;
c. ROI on training may be in intangible form;
d. ROI on training is based on conservative estimates;
e. ROI data is primarily indicative in nature.

For a training division of a company to be regarded as an investment centre and not a 'cost center', proper evaluation of training is mandatory. Training involves everyone right from line managers to trainer, trainees.

And relevance of any training program is possible with the involvement of one and all, right from concept to implementation.

Reading Exhibit 9: A Training Need Analysis Sample

A training need analysis sample is given below for the job of Manager-Projects:

Company Profile

XYZ Group is a well organized establishment based in middle-east since 1960. XYZ group deals in all kinds of commercial activities, general trading agencies and import and exports offers after sales and technical support in association with in-house affiliated.

Group of Companies

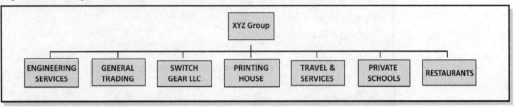

JOB DESCRIPTION	
Job Title	Manager – Projects
Department	Projects & Engineering
Job Function	Project Planning & Execution
Reporting to	Director (Projects & Engineering)
Location	Middle East

Job Summary (with % share of each role)
Planning & estimation (15%)
Bidding in tenders (15%)
Engineering design (20%)
Project execution (35%)
Negotiation and order confirmation (10%)
Commissioning (5%)
Responsibilities & Duties
1. Quality evaluation and pricing for tenders.
2. Design finalization and approval from client and consultant.
3. Reviewing tender documents, preparation of technical submittals and method statements for work involved.
4. Seeking approvals from government organizations to carry out the work.
5. Quality finalization, Compliance verification.
6. Negotiation & Order confirmation with suppliers in coordination with SBU.

7. Detection of bottle-necks in work front.
8. Site mobilization & Project execution.
9. Weekly site visits to monitor progress of work.
10. Project progress presentation before General Manager, Client and Consultant.
11. Pre-commissioning review.
12. Commissioning & handing over.

Description of Type & Extent of Instructions Normally given to Incumbent by Immediate Supervisor

The Manager projects reports directly to the General manager. The instructions given to incumbent are generally over electronic means or in face to face meetings. Giving sole responsibility for actions

AUTHOURITY OF INCUMBENT

The incumbent is authorized by the organization to have complete authority in planning and execution of multiple projects simultaneously. He can make decisions in strategic purchasing from anywhere in the world on sole discretion subject to compliance of client specifications and abiding organizational principles. He is assisted by a team of two senior project engineers, five project engineers and eight site engineers who report to him in a structured pattern. He is authorized to monitor their performance, control, question and take actions to ensure successful project completion in purview of organizational goal achievement.

STANDARD OF PERFORMANCE

The Project Manager is expected to follow the guidelines of performance given below:

➢ Ensure on-time completion of Projects with a maximum tolerance of +2% variations.

➢ Ascertaining Project cost keeping in mind clear profit margin stipulated by the organization.

> Creating a conducive learning experience within the team & promoting efficient training sessions and workshops for collective learning

WORKING CONDITIONS

- The Project Manager is offered an ergonomically designed, well furnished and air conditioned cabin where he is expected to spend over sixty percent of his working hours.
- The incumbent is required to be on-site at least once in a week to evaluate the project progress.
- The profile offered will involve extensive travelling as need arises to meet clients, consultants and suppliers. Organization will take care of his/her daily commutation to office and any other official trip called for.
- The incumbent will be working on a contract basis involving twelve months on-job followed by one month paid vacation.

Working Hours per Week

No. of Working hours per week = 48 hours (8 hours/day x 6 days/week)

JOB SPECIFICATION

Job Title	Manager Projects
Reports to	The Director (Projects & Engg.)

Skill Factors

Description	Minimum Criteria
Education	• Post Graduate in Mechanical Engineering. OR • Post Graduate in Business Administration with Mechanical Engineering as main in graduation.

Experience	• 7 to 10 years of relevant work experience in similar positions handling multifarious projects in utilities & petroleum industry.
Technical Skills	• Proficiency in Mechanical Engg. design software's like ProE, Catia, Autocad, Finite element analysis. • Hands on experience in Primavera Project Planner or MS Project.
Communication	• Excellent articulation skills. Proficiency in making impressive presentations. • Effective comprehension.

Training Requirements

Certified with limited Access Permit to Critical Job Sites
Trained in safety procedures and manuals as stipulated by OSHA

Effort Factors	
Physical Demands	• Pleasing Personality. • Willing to travel extensively.
Mental Demands	• Cognitive Thinking. • Critical Analysis.
Other Factors	
Industriousness	• The role requires persevering determination to accomplish a task.
Judgement	• The incumbent is expected to have excellent cognitive skills to make right judgments with limited information in many cases.

Initiative	• The claimant should have readiness to embark on bold new ventures.
Emotionally	• The person should be emotionally stable with a sound mental state to work in a diverse team.
Schedule Flexibility	• Te titled will have to work on extended working hours to meet project deadlines.
Accountability	• Responsible for all actions of his team and will be answerable to all questions in that regard.

Training Need Analysis & Results

A. **Organizational Analysis of Training Needs**

   ➢ QMS (Quality Management Systems) audit & assessment.

   ➢ OSHA regulations.

   ➢ Basic construction equipment safety standards.

   ➢ Leadership strategies.

   ➢ Integrity and team work among employees.

B. **Operational Training Need Analysis**

   ➢ Design softwares like ProE, Catia, Autocad.

   ➢ Advanced design softwares like Staad Pro & Micro station Power draft.

   ➢ Project Management softwares like Primavera, MS Project

   ➢ Industrial safety standards.

   ➢ Orientation program for employees on fire and safety measures.

   ➢ Pipe line standards like API, ASME etc..

   ➢ Training on Cognitive Skills.

   ➢ Critical data analysis and interpretation.

- Develop & foster negotiation skills.
- Strategic procurement skills.
- Training on Communication skills.
- General training for employees on pragmatics.
- Improving communication skills.
- Learn other languages.

C. **Person Analysis**
- Training on negotiation skills.
- Training on Staad Pro Design software.
- Training to impart strategic procurement skills.
- Training on pragmatics (especially on local language).
- Training to enhance emotionally stability.

Reading Exhibit 10: Training Employees at Titan

Titan Industries Limited (TIL) have institutionalized training as a major intervention throughout the organization aimed at leveraging the performance of its employees to make most of the strategic opportunities that the company comes across. The robust growth and expansion of the company are testimonial to the success of such skill enhancement. Training and Development has been responsible in a major way for the growth of the organization to its current 1 billion USD turnover. It will continue to be a unique enabler for the future growth engine as well, towards a 3 billion USD turnover, over the next five years. Titan, mostly recognized for its wrist-watch brand, has established its strong presence in jewelry (Tanishq), eye-care (Titan eye+), Fast Track (watches & gear accessories) and precision-engineering.

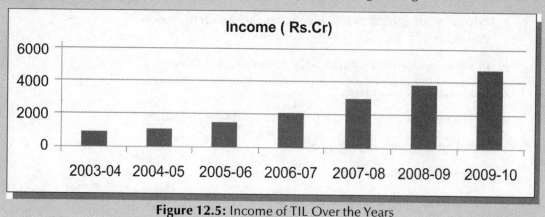

Figure 12.5: Income of TIL Over the Years

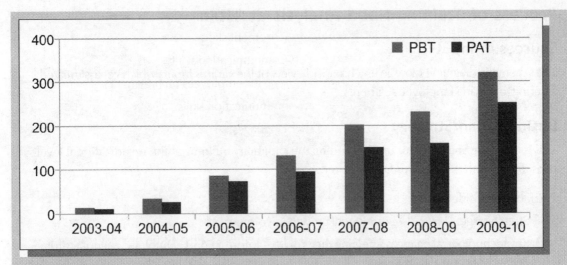

Figure 12.6: Profit of TIL Over the Years

Titan follows a PRAKS model of training. The model depicts major area in which the company provides training. PRAKS stands for:

Physical: Training on physical well-being.

Relation: Training on better inter-personal relationship.

Attitude: Training on better job-behavior and attitudes.

Knowledge: Training to improve job, organizational and market knowledge.

Skill: Training to improve job-capabilities.

Training and Development straddles across all segments of the employee groups and work force, be it the blue collared workforce, or the white collar employee, or the Frontline consumer facing employee or even the temporary staff employed by the company. Totally the company caters to the training requirements to over 7500 strong workforce. The training groups at Titan include:

1. **Retail Service Group**: Includes frontline selling, customer service.
2. **Corporate group**: Leadership development, Capability-building
3. **Sales & Marketing**: New product development, Sales Operation, Distribution penetration, brand management.
4. **Manufacturing**: Technical training, training on various processes like ISO etc.

Process of Training Need Analysis at Titan

Sources of Inputs

The schematic diagram below gives a broadside view of the various inputs which get assimilated, catering to varying Employee segments:

Business Plan/Strategy

This is a key starting point for understanding the capability building at the organizational level considering both the short and the long term needs

The factors considered include

a. Stretch targets in KRA's/exponential growth in volumes etc
b. Key technological changes affecting the growth – Information Technology, Manufacturing Technology and also on
c. Organic and Inorganic growth – May include setting up of new stores/expansion of the retail chain, new format retail chains, newer manufacturing units, possible mergers and acquisitions and so on.

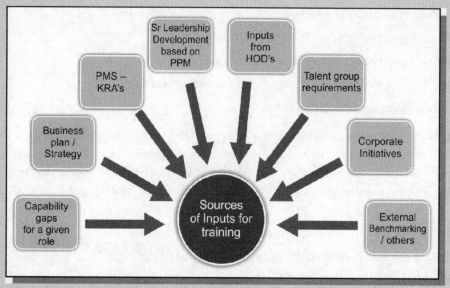

Figure 12.7: Sources of Inputs for Training

The above spans across multiple divisions and business as well as critical support functions.

Some of the critical capability/training needs which have resulted in the recent past based on Long term strategy include - Training on use of plastic technology, Handling multiple luxury brands in a luxury brand out let, Upgradation of IT – SAP and so on.

Senior Leadership Development Based on PPM's

Titan recognizes the role of the leadership team in critically shaping the future of the company. Accordingly there is a three level input identification process and delivery

a. Creation of an overall Individual Development Plan (IDP) with the involvement of the MD/ Head of HR and the Tata Group HR head.

b. Broad need identification as part of Senior Management Performance appraisal along with the MD

c. Self development plans.

These are both specific to a functional need, but mostly generic in nature to address the leadership development, to handle key organizational requirements, steering the company into the future. Programs which support the leadership include Advanced Management Development program at Harvard, Coaching and mentoring certification and so on. Many a times the needs also get thrown up from peer level interactions, Benchmarking with peers outside the company, within the Tata group and outside as well.

Capability Gaps for a Given Role

This is the most important, and is the heart of training needs understanding at the individual role level. A scientific process encompassing a) Functional requirements for a given role b) Behavioral requirements for a given role (based on 14 Tata Leadership Practices) is in place which creates a role map for each individual role across the organization.

The 14 Tata leadership practices comprises of: 1) Managing Vision and purpose b) Strategic Capability c) Dealing with Ambiguity d) Business acumen e) Functional Excellence f) taking ownership g) people Development h) Interpersonal effectiveness i) Building effective teams j) withstanding pressure k) Drive for results l) Customer focus m) Timely decision making n) Innovation management.

Every individual is mapped against these competencies for the role he/she is playing through a process of interviewing techniques and the training/capability gap drawn up for the individual.

A sample of the competency radar for a specific role is given below (figure 12.8)

These are then translated into a training plan and executed. Post which the competency matrices are updated.

Performance Management System/KRA's

The performance Management system at Titan which promotes a Performance Culture is another key source of input for identifying individual training need.

The PMS process, driven annually with a Mid Term Review focuses on the individuals performance and achievements over the KRA's and targets set for the previous year.

The appraisal process combines the goal setting process for the ensuing year. The resultant of this intense process, which includes a feedback on the individual's performance is based on two areas:

1. Performance w.r.t. KRA's
2. Performance on Critical success factors (TLP)

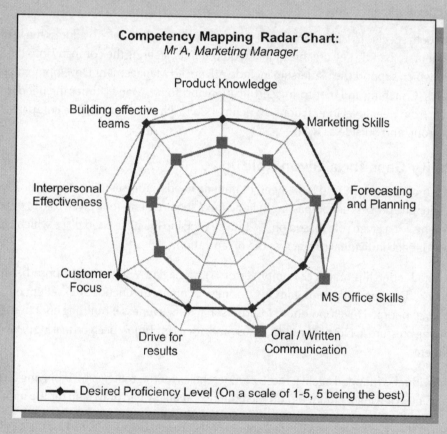

Figure 12.8: Competency Radar

The individuals development needs as a result of this exercise provides inputs on 1) Capability gaps which would have helped the individual perform better b) Feedback on the enablers (TLP) which help in perform better in the new KRA's and goals for the ensuing year. Both these are vital inputs into the Training plan drawn up for the year. Examples of the output which arise would include Execution skills, skills required to perform in a new role, Innovation, problem solving and so on.

Talent Group Requirements

Titan has a very focused and involved Talent Management program. The purpose of this program is to enable identify and build leadership talent for the future.

A detailed performance potential filter is applied, post which all managers go through an assessment centre, which is based on identifying potential for the leadership at the next level.

This process classifies managers as

1) Corporate Resources ie, managers who are capable and have the potential to move to a cross functional role given a specific period of time
2) Functional Resources i.e. managers who are capable of growing within a function

The output of this leads into a set of areas of development at the individual level, which when focused on provides him the necessary capability to develop his leadership potential for likely new roles, across divisions. An Individual development plan (IDP) for each manager in the company is drawn up which focuses on development separately for the Corporate and Functional Resources. For the corporate resources the needs would include Coaching, Mentoring, Advanced Management programs, and Situational leadership and so on. For the Functional Resources programs such as Seven habits, Functional Excellence in respective areas like Supply chain, etc would be the focus.

Corporate Initiatives

As an organization, Titan has several cross cutting initiatives driven across the company. Most of these are driven by Senior Executives which has implications across the company and not necessarily domain specific. Such Interventions or Initiatives necessitate large scale training to take the initiative momentum forward.

Examples of such companywide initiatives would include: Innovation, Theory of Constraints, OHSAS, Information security and so on. The focused training needs arising out of these interventions are driven through Cross Functional teams across the organization, facilitated by the HR function. Development needs are also supported through specific Education interventions such as providing Executive MBA courses, an Education Policy etc.

External Benchmarking/Developments

While all the above inputs are formal mechanisms to understand the training needs, very often the company is also sensitive in understanding what's happening in the external world through constant benchmarking and visits to other companies, fairs and so on both within India and Abroad. Many a times focused training is organized to enhance people knowledge and sometimes skill upgradation, based on suggestion ad inputs from these sources. Examples of such inputs would include Latest in Retail management, Innovation, Business Excellence related programs, Climate Change etc.

Inputs from HOD's: Last but not the least, often the HOD's across functions that monitor performances of both individual as well as their team members would also be an important input provider for Training Need Analysis.

In addition to the formal inputs they provide during appraisal process they do constantly provide inputs to the HR function on focused departmental needs on training. Examples of such would include Team building, Innovation, Technology training specific to that department, niche segment training Ex: Aerospace, Automotive for PED and so on.

All the above TNA inputs culminate into a set of training plans delivered by the HR function as well as core specialists across the organization.

Essay Questions

1. Write notes on:
   a) Training.
   b) Training and Education.
   c) Training and Development.
   d) Relationship between learning, training education and development.

2. Describe briefly the ADDIE (training process) model and the concerns at each stage.

3. 'Assessment of training need is the first and most important step in designing a training program' Why is it so? Explain the various types of training need analysis

4. What are the two approaches of training need analysis? Explain with example. Which approach is better? Can a company choose one of these approaches?

5. Explain a 'training plan' and its importance.

6. Explain briefly the commonly used training methods. What is difference between on-the job training methods and off-the-job training methods.

7. Describe the 3-C Model used for choosing the right training method for a training program.

8. Explain the 'Why', 'What', 'When' and 'How' of the Training Evaluation.

9. Return-on-investment in training is often regarded as the fifth-level of evaluation. Why is it significant? What are the various categories of ROI? Highlight the practical issues in ROI computation.

Application Questions

1. Visit the site http://www.nwlink.com ~donclark/hrd/trainsta.html and read the article 'Learning and Training'. Statistics and My ths How effective is training?' Give a classroom presentation. Explore the other training links on this site.

2. Go the site http://www.astd.org/ prepare a report on the world's largest professional association dedicated the training and development field.

Bibliography

Acemoglu, D., and Pischke, J. 1999. Beyond Becker: Training in imperfect labor markets. *The Economic Journal*, 109: 112-114. American Society for Training and Development: ATSD State of the Industry Report, Executive Summary http://www.astd.org/astd/research/research_reports

Ainsworth, S. E., & Peevers, G. J. (2003). The Interaction between Informational and Computational Properties of External Representations on Problem-solving and Learning. In R. Altmann & D. Kirsch (Eds.), *Proceedings of 25th Annual Conference of the Cognitive Science Society.*

Barrett, A., & O'Connell, P. J. 2001. Does training generally work? The returns to in company training. *Industrial and Labor Relations Review*, 54(3): 647-662.

Bartlett, K. 2001. The Relationship between Training and Organizational Commitment: A Study in the Healthcare Field. *Human Resource Development Quarterly*, 12(4): 335-352.

Bassi, L. & McMurrer, D., (2007). Maximizing Your Return on People. *Harvard Business Review,* March 2007, Reprint R0703H.

Bassi, L., Gallager, A., & Schroer, E. (1996). *The ASTD Training Data Book.* Alexandria, VA: American Society for Training and Development.

Burke, R. J. 1995. Benefits of Formal Training Courses within a Professional Services Firm. *The Journal of Management Development,*14(3): 3-13.

Chapman, B. and the staff of Brandon Hall Research (2006). *PowerPoint to E-Learning Development Tools: Comparative Analysis of 20 Leading Systems.* Published by Brandon Hall Research, Sunnyvale, CA.

Chapman, B. and the staff of Brandon Hall Research (2006b). *Online Simulations 2006: A Knowledgebase of 100+ Simulation Development Tools and Services.* Published by Brandon Hall Research, Sunnyvale, CA.

Chapman, B. and the staff of Brandon Hall Research (2007). *LCMS Knowledgebase 2007: A Comparison of 30+ Enterprise Learning Content Management Systems.* Published by Brandon Hall Research, Sunnyvale, CA.

Clark, Ruth, Chopeta, L. (2004). *Graphics for Learning: Proven Guidelines for Planning, Designing, and Evaluating Visuals in Training Materials.* Jossey-Bass/Pfeiffer.

Colarelli, S. M., & Montei, M. S. 1996. Some Contextual Influences on Training Utilization. *The Journal of Applied Behavioral Science*, 32(3): 306-322.

Delahoussaye, M & Ellis, K. & Bolch, M. (2002). Measuring Corporate Smarts. *Training Magazine*, August 2002. Pp. 20-35.

Eck, A. 1993. Job-related Education and Training: Their Impact on Earnings. *Monthly Labor Review*, 116(10): 21-38.

Frazis, H. J., and Speltzer, J. R. 2005. Worker Training: What we've learned from the NLSY79. *Monthly Labor Review*, 128(2):48-58.

Frei, B. & Mader, M. (2008). *Perspective: The Productivity Paradox.* C/Net News, 1/29/08. Retrieved 3/2/08: http://news.cnet.com/The-productivity-paradox/2010-1022_3-6228144.html?part=rss&tag=2547-1_3-0-5&subj=news.

Georgenson, D. L. (1982). The Problem of Transfer Calls for Partnership. *Training & Development Journal.* Oct 82, Vol. 36 Issue 10, p75, 3p.

Glance, N.S., Hogg, T., and Huberman, B.A. 1997. Training and Turnover in the Evolution of Organizations. *Organization Science*, 8(1): 84-96.

Groen, J. A. 2006. Occupation-specific Human Capital and Local Labour Markets. *Oxford Economic Papers*, 58: 722-741.

Heyes, J., & Stuart, M. 1996. Does Training Matter? Employee Experiences and Attitudes. *Human Resource Management Journal*, 6(3): 7-21.

Kaufman, B., & Hotchkiss, J. 2006. *Economics of Labor Markets* (7th ed.). Mason, OH: Thomson South-Western.

Keller, Fred (1968). Good Bye Teacher. *Journal of Applied Behavior Analysis*

Krueger, A., and Rouse, C. 1998. The Effect of Workplace Education on Earnings, Turnover, and Job Performance. *Journal of Labor Economics*, 16(1): 61-94.

Lincoln, J. R., & Kalleberg, A. L. 1996. Commitment, Quits, and Work Organization in Japanese and U.S. Plants. *Industrial and Labor Relations Review*, 50(1): 39-59.

Liou, K. T., & Nyhan, R. C. 1994. Dimensions of Organizational Commitment in the Public Sector: An Empirical Assessment. *Public Administration Quarterly*, 18(1): 99-113.

Lynch, L. M. 1991. The role of off-the-job vs. on-the-job training for the mobility of women workers. *American Economic Review*, 81(2): 151-156.

McMurrer, D., Van Buren, M., & Woodwell, W., Jr. (2000). *The 2000 ASTD State of the Industry Report.* Alexandria, VA: American Society for Training & Development.

Owan, H. 2004. Promotion, Turnover, Earnings, and Firm-sponsored Training. *Journal of Labor Economics*, 22(4): 955-978.

Chapter 13

Compensation & Benefits

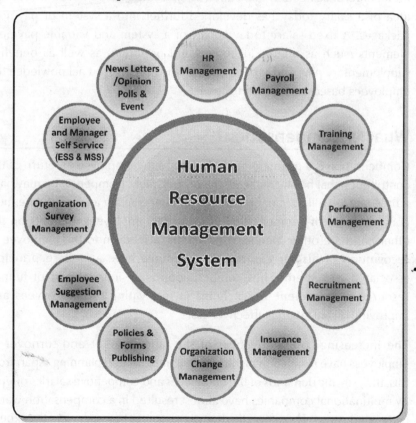

Outline

Introduction
What is Compensation?
Factors Governing Compensation
Objectives of a Compensation System
Components of a Compensation Package
Base Pay Structure
Variable Pay Programs
Benefits
Rewards & Recognition
Pricing the Jobs
Job Evaluation
Compensable Factors
Non Quantitative Techniques of Job Evaluation
Quantitative Methods of Job Evaluation
Factor Comparison Method
Market Pricing/Benchmarking
Pay Fairness (Pay Equity)
What is Behind Pay Differences?
Job Evaluations and Market Consideration
Elements of a Wage Structure
Maintaining a Pay Structure
Essay Questions
Application Questions
Bibliography

Key Terms

Compensable Factors
Compensation
Factor Comparison Method
Gratuity
Job Evaluation
Provident Fund

Introduction

The Roman 'salarium' is derived from the relation between salt and soldier. It means 'be in employment, be on the payroll', but the origin is uncertain. According to the least accepted theory, the word 'soldier' comes from the Latin 'sal dare' (give salt). As a matter of fact, Plinius, a Roman historian, also mentions sea water in his "Natural History" book, 'In Rome, a soldier's salary was originally salt, and 'salary' is derived from this word.' The modern era of industrialization gave birth to the concept of productivity and value-creation. Consequently, any person involved in the process of creating value for an enterprise needed to be adequately compensated or rewarded. The idea of a salary today has developed further into a system of payment packages. A fixed salary today is part of a system and variable payment elements (such as bonus, incentives and premium) as well as benefits, supplementary pay, and others, enables the employer to acknowledge the employees based on their performance.

What is Compensation?

Compensation

Payments made in cash, benefits, reward, etc., to the employee in return of his/her contribution in the organization, with an objective of motivating the employee and improving organizational effectiveness.

Compensation is a payment made in cash to the employee in return of the contribution that he/she makes in the organization. Compensation may have a base pay as well as variable pay components. Salary and wages are most common form of compensation given to the employees. Benefits on the other hand are other then such payments, also given to the employee in recognition of his/her contribution. Benefits have a welfare principle associated with them. Thus compensation is an integral part of human resource management which helps in motivating the employees and improving organizational effectiveness.

The increasing competitiveness of the labor market and turnover of employees have resulted in nightmare in compensation planning. Apart from this, the growing demands of the employees and competitive salaries offered by multinational companies have almost resulted in a compensation war in certain industries. Therefore, the human resources managers and tax experts have to evolve proper compensation planning for High end and qualified employees. The components of compensation have to be devised in such a way that, it focuses on the growing demands of employees while retaining the competitiveness and profitability of the company. Thus Compensation systems are designed keeping in minds the strategic goals and business objectives. Compensation system is designed on the basis of certain factors after analyzing the job work and responsibilities. There are also certain driven factors that are influencing the compensation planning.

Factors Governing Compensation

The various factors governing compensation for a job are:
1. **Industry:** Across industry the compensation for a job may vary and hence for determining compensation for a job it is important to understand the nature of business, a firm is in.
2. **Stage of Maturity:** The stage of maturity of affirm is also important to determine the compensation. Normally, more mature organizations shall have broadbands (defined later in the chapter).
3. **Scale of Operations:** The scale of operations shows the degree of expansion and hence is directly correlated to compensation.
4. **Nature of Customer:** The nature of customer a firm is servicing also impacts the compensation. Bigger customers shall beget more compensation.
5. **Culture:** Finally, the culture of the company also influences the compensation structure.

Example: Companies like Siemens that have performance-based culture have more performance-related incentives. Then there are companies who believe in less cash component and more valuable benefits.

Objectives of a Compensation System

The two primary objectives of a Compensation system are:

1. Equity
Equal pay for work of equal value.
   a. **Internal Equity:** Requires that pay be related to the relative worth of a job so that similar jobs get similar pay.
   b. **External Equity:** Paying worker what other firms in the labor market are paying to any comparable worker. The external equity is established through wage and salary surveys. The various sources of information may be employer surveys, professional agencies, consulting firms, internet, published literature etc.

2. Efficiency

The efficiency in a compensation system entails to:

a. Linking compensation to productivity/ profit/ individual performance.

b. Attracting rewarding, motivating and retaining highly capable and efficient.

c. Maintaining market competitiveness.

d. Ensuring compliance with laws and regulations.

e. Building employer brand.

Components of a Compensation Package

It is important to understand the laws of the land and taxation policy to understand the components of compensation and compensation strategies. Organizations always pay for the work done (job) and less for the individuals. Job is the nucleus for determining compensation. Each organization will have its own way of defining jobs and determining hierarchy of jobs. However for simplicity the components of jobs shall look like:

1. Base Pay Structure (Fixed component);
2. Variable Pay Programs;
3. Benefits;
4. Rewards & Recognition.

Base Pay Structure (Fixed component)

Salaries and wage are the periodic assured payments made to the employees. Salaries are generally paid to the permanent employees on the monthly basis, whereas wages are paid to temporary or contractual workers on the daily basis. Base Pay is the fixed component and generally consists of the following:

Basic Component

Normally 40 percent of the base pay is basic and rest of the base pay falls under various other categories. This breakage is governed by the tax laws of the land. In India, for instance, if everything is given to an employee in the form of basic the whole shall be taxed, whereas if the base pay is broken into sub-components like HRA certain tax-exemptions may be obtained.

HRA (House Rent Allowance)

Calculated as a percentage of basic. HRA limits are fixed by the government and are uniformly applicable. If a company decides to pay more than the limit decided by the company it can however the excess shall be taxed as is the basic. If a company pays HRA component then it must collect proofs of rent-paid (rental receipts) from the employee.

DA (Dearness Allowance)

It is calculated as a percentage of basic. The payment of dearness allowance facilitates employees and workers to face the price increase or inflation of prices of goods and services. The onslaught of price increase has a major bearing on the living conditions of the labor. The increasing prices reduce the compensation to nothing and the money's worth comes down based on the level of inflation. The payment of dearness allowance, which may be a fixed percentage on the basic wage, enables the employees to face the increasing prices.

Leave Travel Allowance

Leave Travel allowance or LTA is paid by certain companies. However again proofs of travel expenses must be collected by the company from the employees.

Mobile Expenses

Medical Allowance/Reimbursements, etc.

Variable Pay Programs

Variable pay programs are generally classified differently for sales and non-sales.

Variable Pay Plans for Sales

Variable pay plans for sales represents a pay-mix that may be a 70-30 or 60-40 or 50-50 plan. Here the 30, 40 or 50 represents the variable portion of the pay and is linked to the targets. Targets could be product-based, territory-based, revenue-based, profitability-based or based on new business creation. However payment of the variable portion does not always follow a linear scale. Supposedly the target is USD 100 million of sales. It is possible that till USD 50 million there may be no variable pay. If the person achieves USD 75 million (threshold level) then he/she may get 50%

of the variable portion growing up to 100% of the variable portion when he/she achieves USD 100 million in sales. Variable pay plans do not come with an upper cap ie., if the same guy exceeds USD100million of sales will he get more than the plan as variable pay? Well the answer is Yes! Generally, a person in a 50-50 plan makes upto 70% or 80% variable pay.

Variable Pay Plans for Non-sales

Such pay plans are for those employees who either are those who need incentives to propel their work or are those whose performance can be improved by giving them incentives like insurance plans, credit cards, mutual funds etc. Generally the variable portion in non-sales is lesser than in case of sales. The variable pay is based on jobs and levels of job. Sometimes such plans may be covered under company-wide plans and the entire variable portion may be broken under employee performance, functional performance (i.e. performance of the function in which that employee works) and organizational performance.

Example: In a 80-20 plan, the 20 may be broken as employee performance (10), functional performance (5) and organizational performance (5).

The various variable-pay components very briefly have been discussed below. The next chapter discusses such plans in detail.

Bonus

Bonus is generally post-facto. The bonus can be paid in different ways. It can be fixed percentage on the basic wage paid annually or in proportion to the profitability. The Government also prescribes a minimum statutory bonus for all employees and workers. There is also a bonus plan which compensates the Managers and employees based on the sales revenue or Profit margin achieved. Bonus plans can also be based on piece wages but depends upon the productivity of labor.

Commissions

Commission to Managers and employees may be based on the sales revenue or profits of the company. It is always a fixed percentage on the target achieved. For taxation purposes, commission is again a taxable component of compensation. The payment of commission as a component of commission is practiced heavily in target based sales. Depending upon the targets achieved, companies may pay a commission on a monthly or periodical basis.

Mixed Plans

Companies may also pay employees and others a combination of pay as well as commissions. This plan is called combination or mixed plan. Apart from the salaries paid, the employees may be eligible for a fixed percentage of commission upon achievement of fixed target of sales or profits or Performance objectives. Nowadays, most of the corporate sector is following this practice. This is also termed as variable component of compensation.

Incentives

Incentive is clearly defined, target-related and upfront. Piece rate wages are prevalent in the manufacturing wages. The laborers are paid wages for each of the quantity produced by them. The gross earnings of the labor would be equivalent to number of goods produced by them. Piece rate wages improve productivity and is an absolute measurement of productivity to wage structure. The fairness of compensation is totally based on the productivity and not by any subjective factor. The GANTT productivity planning and Taylor's plan of wages are examples of piece rate wages and the related consequences.

Sign on Bonuses

The latest trend in the compensation planning is the lump sum bonus for the incoming employee. A person, who accepts the offer, is paid a lump sum as a bonus. Even though this practice is not prevalent in most of the industries, Equity research and investment banking companies are paying sign-on-bonuses to attract scarce talent.

Profit Sharing Payments

Profit sharing is again a novel concept nowadays. This can be paid through payment of cash or through ESOPS. The structuring of wages may be done in such a way that, it attracts competitiveness and improved productivity.

Stock Options

Stock options are given to employees for two primary purposes – one to have long-term interest of the employee and second to link individual performance to organizational performance. Generally stock options may be given under three categories:

a) ESOPs or Employee Stock Options;

b) RSUs or Restricted Stock Units;

c) ESPP or Employee Stock Purchase Plans.

a) **ESOPs or Employee Stock Options:** Suppose an employee is given ESOPS in the following way – 'A', an employee is given 2000 stocks of Rs. 100 (Grant price). He is allowed to sell 50% of the stocks after 2 years and the rest of the stocks after another 2 years. Let's say after two years the price of stock is Rs. 110/- (vested price). Then the employee actually gets only 1000 x 10 = 10000/- rupees only. In such a scenario if the price of the stock fell below 100/- rupees then the employee does not get anything. ESOPs worked well when stock prices were rising continuously. However when share prices started to drop then the relevance of ESOPs declined.

b) **RSUs or Restricted Stock Units:** These are different from ESOPs. When stocks are given to the employees it is deemed at zero value. So whatever is the stock price the employee ends-up making some money. Taking forward the earlier example if after two years the price of stock is Rs. 90/- then the employee still gets 90000/- rupees, on trading his options.

c) **ESPP or Employee Stock Purchase Plans:** This is more like a benefit. When the company is doing well then it gives option to employees to purchase shares on some discount.

Benefits

The benefits could be the one that are legally-mandated ones or the ones that are 'good-to-have' for competitive-edge. The benefits may be monetary or non-monetary, long-term or short-term, free or at concessional rates and may include education, housing, medical, or recreational facilities, provided individually or collectively, inside or outside the organizational premises. The benefits should always be given with a genuine concern for the employees and hence – a) most of the benefits should be broad-based and should uniformly apply to all the employees; and b) must be designed keeping in mind the genuine benefit that it shall provide to the employees.

Example: In HSBC India the biggest benefit that it used to provide was a medical insurance plan that included the employees, their spouses and their kids. However on survey they found that about 70% of their employees were either unmarried or were newly married and had no kids.

This meant that this benefit did not reach majority of the employees. The company tweaked the benefit slightly to include the employee's parents as well. This increased the value of the benefit considerably.

Companies are increasingly taking the employees to a 'total rewards perspective' that involves considering base pay, variable pay, employment benefits and work-life balance together. Despite this the benefits that a company provides to its employees have remained threadbare or minimum owing to the prevailing tough economic conditions. However in future there is chance of the revival of benefits.

Types of Benefits

Benefits may include:

Paid Time off (also referred to as PTO)

It is earned by employees while they work. They may be a) holidays (governed by the law), b) Leaves (governed by the shop and establishment act) like Casual Leaves, Sick Leaves, Earn or privilege leaves, etc.

Insurance Programs

The insurance programs may include health insurance, life insurance, personal accident insurance, disability insurance, family-health insurance, etc.

Fringe Benefits

Fringe benefits include a variety of non-cash payments that are used to attract and retain talented employees and may include educational assistance, flexible medical benefits, child-care benefits, and non-production bonuses (bonuses not tied to performance). These may include:

  a) Company cars

  b) Paid vacations

  c) Membership of social/cultural clubs

  d) Entertainment tickets/allowances.

  e) Discounted travel tickets.

  f) Family vacation packages.

  g) Reimbursements: Employees, depending upon their gradations

Fringe Benefit

An employment benefit given in addition to one's wages or salary. These commonly include health insurance, group term life coverage, education reimbursement, childcare and assistance reimbursement, cafeteria plans, employee discounts, personal use of a company owned vehicle and other similar benefits.

in the organization may get reimbursements based on the Expenses incurred and substantiated. Certain expenses are also paid based on expenses incurred during the course of business. In many cases, employers provide advances to the employees for incurring certain expenses that are incurred during the course of the business. Some examples are:

a) Travel expenses;

b) Entertainment expenses;

c) Out of pocket expenses; and

d) Refreshments expenses.

h) Sickness benefits/pregnancy: The increasing social consciousness of corporate had resulted in the payment of sickness benefit to the Employees of companies. This also includes payments during pregnancy of women employees. The expenses incurred due to injury or illness are compensated or reimbursed to the employees. In certain companies, the death of an employee is compensated financially. Companies are also providing financial benefits to the family of the bereaved employees covering these cost through appropriate insurance policies like, Medical and life insurance.

Social Security

Social security benefits are aimed at protecting employees against all types of social risks that may cause undue hardships to them in fulfilling their basic needs. Such benefits have a welfare objective and refer to all such services, amenities and facilities to the employees that improve their working conditions as well as standard of living of the employees and their families.

In India, the social security is generally governed by the state and is provided through the five Central Acts:- (i) The Employees' State Insurance Act, 1948; (ii) Employees' Provident Funds & Miscellaneous Provisions Act, 1952; (iii) The Workmen Compensation Act; (iv)The Maternity Benefit Act; and (v) The Payment of Gratuity Act. The social security besides medical facilities, compensation benefits and insurance coverage to the employees, also include the retirement benefits i.e., those relating to the provident fund and gratuity provisions.

Provident Fund (PF)

Provident Fund contributions are determined in India by the Employees Provident Fund and Miscellaneous Provisions Act, 1952. The act provides for the social security, pension fund and deposit-linked insurance fund for the employees. The Employee Provident Act is a kind of social security legislation that covers three schemes:

a) Provident Fund (PF)

b) Pension Scheme (PS); and

c) Employee Deposit-linked Insurance Scheme (EDLI)

The PF Act is a central act and the government can set up a central board, an executive committee, state board, appellate tribunals, officers etc. to implement the Act. Under Section 6, 6A and 6C, the PF fund gets contributions from both the employer and the employee. In case of EPS and EDLI contributions are generally made fully by the employer. EPS also gets contributions from the central government.

Gratuity

Gratuity is also a type of retirement benefit paid to an employee. Gratuity is linked to the number of years of service and is paid only to employee upon separation only if he/she completed five years of service in the company.

Gratuity payments are determined by the Payment of Gratuity Act 1972. Under section 4 of the act – Gratuity shall be payable to an employee on the termination of his employment after he has rendered continues service for not less than five years:

a) On his superannuation, or

b) On his retirement, or

c) On his death or disablement due to accident or disease:

Provided that the completion of continuous service of five years shall not be necessary where the termination of the employment of any employee is due to death or disablement.

Provided further that in the case of death of the employee, gratuity payable to him shall be paid to his/her nominee, or if no nomination is made, to his heirs, and where any such nominee or heir is a minor, the share of such minor shall be deposited with the controlling authority who shall invest the same for the benefits of such minor in such a bank or financial institution, as may be prescribed, until such minor attains majority.

Gratuity is calculated by using the following formulae:

Case A (where employee is covered under the Payments of Gratuity Act)

Gratuity = Last drawn salary x 15/26 (number of years of service*)

Case B (where employee is not covered under the Payment of Gratuity Act)

Gratuity = Last drawn salary x 1/2 (number of years of service*)

*rounded off to nearest full year e.g., 20 years 10 months, 25 days = 20 years

Gratuity Ceiling

A ceiling (upper limit) of Rs 10 lakh applies to the aggregate of gratuity received from one or more employers in same or different years. Death-cum-retirement gratuity received by employees of central or state government and local authorities is exempt without limit.

Table 13.1: Contrasting PF and Gratuity

Provident Fund	Gratuity
Contributions from both employer and employee.	Contribution only from employer.
Employee becomes eligible for PF from the day of joining.	Eligible only after 5 years in a single organization.
The PF act applies to any company having 20 employees or more.	The payment of Gratuity Act applies to any company having 10 employees or more.
PF is transferable to new company.	Gratuity is not transferable.

Reading Exhibit 1: HSBC (USA)

HSBC (USA) provides benefits to its employees under following heads:

1. Health Care

a. Medical, Dental and Vision Plans (for eligible full- and part-time employees and their spouses, children and opposite or same-sex domestic partners)

b. Flexible Spending Accounts (tax-free health care, commuter expense and dependent care flexible spending accounts).

c. Insurance, Disability and Long-term Care Programs

2. Work/Life Balance

a. Adoption Assistance (HSBC pays up to $5,000 toward eligible adoption expenses for each adopted child).

b. Child Care Centers

c. Time Off Program (TOP)

d. Company-paid Holidays

3. Financial Security

a. Sharesave (offers employees the opportunity to buy shares of HSBC Holdings plc stock at a 20 percent discount, without brokerage fees or commissions).

b. HSBC - North America (U.S.) Retirement and Savings Program.

c. HSBC - North America (U.S.) Tax Reduction Investment Plan and Trust 401(k)

d. The HSBC - North America (U.S.) Retirement Income Plan and Trust

4. Employee Services (Locations and availability vary)

a. Concierge Services (such as dry cleaning, a cafeteria, movie passes, a gift shop, postal services, photo finishing services, ATMs and discounts to entertainment destinations).

b. Merchant Discounts (All employees can take advantage of discounts and special promotions offered by national and local merchants, including savings on furniture, jewelry, cell phone plans, travel programs and tours, and health club memberships).

Rewards & Recognition

At the end of the day we are all human beings and like to compete and do better than others. This creates a natural urge to be rewarded and recognized. While designing the rewards and recognition plans the 'why' and 'what' kind of people to be covered in such plans needs to be answered. Generally the rewards and recognition pyramids looks like –

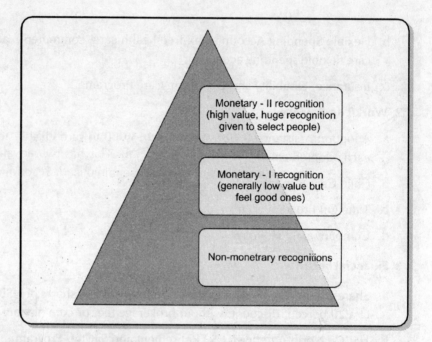

Figure 13.1:
Rewards & Recognition Pyramid

Pricing the Jobs

Pricing the jobs simply means determining the compensation for a particular job. Job evaluation is the process by which the relative worth of various jobs in an organization is determined. The relative worth signifies two things i.e. how much a job deserves to be paid and where does it stand in comparison to other jobs in the organization. Job evaluation serves the following objectives:

1. It helps in setting standards of pricing the jobs in the organization. The same set of standards shall be used to evaluate different jobs in the organization.

2. Since the same standards are applied in all the jobs in an organization, the inequities and inequalities amongst various jobs can be minimized.

3. Job evaluation also helps to distinguish closely-linked jobs in an organization.

4. Often specialization results in hundreds of similar jobs in an organization. Job evaluation also helps to eliminate unnecessary specialization that might have resulted from long time functioning of the organization.

5. It helps an organization to know various jobs in detail and also appreciate their relative importance. Hence an organization can understand which jobs are critical.

6. New jobs are assimilated in the earlier set of jobs in an organization, with ease.

7. Job evaluation technique impersonalizes the basic price determination a job. This has two advantages – one bias for an individual would be minimized. Second, a job is not important or unimportant because of the individual who occupies the position.

Success of job evaluation hinges on the degree of acceptance of this process from the employees. Such buy-ins can be created by communicating and involving the employees in this very important process. A job evaluation committee is identified and that committee does the actual job evaluation.

Job Evaluation

Job Evaluation
Process of determining the relative worth of various jobs in an organization.

Job evaluation is a process of determining the relative worth of various jobs in an organization. It involves ranking different jobs on the basis of various compensable factors and then assigning a pay grade to that job. In short, job evaluation process helps in determining price for a job relative to other jobs in the organization.

Reading Exhibit 2: Hay Group Spectrum - Job Evaluation for a New Generation

Hay Group is a global management consulting firm that works with leaders to transform strategy into reality. Many organizations, including more than half of the world's largest companies, rely on Hay Group's job evaluation methodologies. Some Hay Group clients have successfully used job evaluation to help with job design, talent development and performance management for over 25 years. Realizing that many organizations actually miss out on the real value of understanding their work by only applying job evaluation to reward and very often take a fragmented approach to analyzing work, using one job evaluation methodology for reward decisions, another for talent management &sometimes even a third for structuring work, the Hay Group created the *Hay Group Spectrum* – a unique offering that builds upon the job evaluation methodology to connect jobs, people, structure, pay and performance in an organization.

Figure 13.2:
Hay Group Spectrum

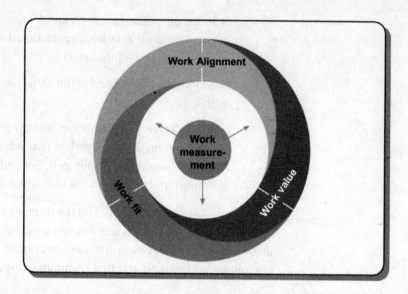

(The Hay Group Spectrum and related information to Hay Group Job Evaluation methodology has been published with the permission of Hay Group. More information is available on http://www.haygroup.com/in/services/index.aspx?id=30147)

Hay Group Spectrum enables an organization to answer four critical questions:

➢ **Work measurement**: Do you know how, where and why work is done?

➢ **Work alignment**: Does your structure fit with your strategy?

➢ **Work fit**: Do you have the right people in the right roles?

➢ **Work value**: What is each role really worth to your organization?

Compensable Factors

Compensable Factors

Factors in particular jobs which should be compensated for they directly or indirectly contribute in successful completion of those jobs, are called compensable factors.

Factors in a particular jobs which should be compensated for they directly or indirectly contribute in successful completion of that particular job are called compensable factors.

Compensable factors help in determining worth of various jobs. Generally, in an organization compensable factors are identified and defined by the assigned job evaluation committee.

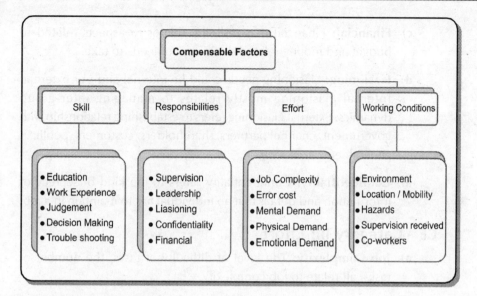

Figure 13.3: Compensable Factor

CF - Category I: Skill

a) **Education:** Education refers not only to the qualification possessed by an individual but also the kind of knowledge that he/she has about the job.

b) **Work Experience:** This refers to the number of months or years a person has spent doing similar or related jobs.

c) **Judgment:** Judgment relates to the level of independent discretion required in a particular job.

d) **Decision Making:** Every job shall require the incumbents to take some decision. These decisions will vary in frequency, complexity, importance and risk.

e) **Trouble Shooting:** This relates to the individual's requirement of solving problems related to job.

CF - Category II: Responsibility

a) **Supervision:** This factor relates to the kind of supervision that an individual is required to give to the people working with him or under him.

b) **Leadership:** This relates to initiative that an individual needs to take in doing his/her job. Besides the degree to which he needs to guide and facilitate his/her team members.

c) **Financial:** Financial responsibility relates to aspects related to budget and money related decisions on needs to take.

d) **Liasioning:** Liasioning needs could be internal and / or external. Internal Liasioning mostly relates to managing inter-group dynamics. External Liasioning refers to establishing relationship with government, channel partners, shareholders, customers, public in general, etc.

e) **Confidentiality:** Confidentiality refers to the kind of secrecy of information and details that an individual has to maintain in a job.

CF - Category III: Effort

a) **Job Complexity:** The level of difficulty of tasks, the number of tasks, all relate to job complexity.

b) **Mental Demand:** This relates to the kind of analytical thinking, inductive and deductive reasoning, logic & rationale required in a particular job.

c) **Physical Demand:** This relates to demand from an individual in terms of physical effort and strain for accomplishing a job.

d) **Emotional Demand;** Every job demands some kind of emotional demand from the incumbent. However certain jobs could be emotionally draining. Hence emotional quotient demands shall vary from job to jobs.

e) **Error Cost:** If the job incumbent commits an error while doing his/her job, how serious the consequences would be?

CF - Category IV: Working Conditions

a) **Environment:** This relates to general ambience at workplace, ventilation, lighting, hygiene, & sanitation level, humidity etc.

b) **Location/Mobility:** The hospitable or inhospitable location of the workplace, the general terrain, and the degree of travel that is required for accomplishing a job.

c) **Hazards:** The kind of hazards that work and workplace pose because of the nature if job & the risk to the job incumbent as a result of the same.

d) **Supervision Received:** The kind of supervision that a person receives from his /her supervisors also relates to working conditions.

e) **Co-workers:** This relates to the kind of co-workers that a person is expected to work with, their ingenuinity and the kind of support that he gets from them.

Non-quantitative Techniques of Job Evaluation

Ranking Method

In this method a job is ranked related to other jobs in an organization. First, detailed information about various jobs in an organization is obtained, then jobs are grouped based on their similarity and difference. Thereafter the compensable factors are selected, after which the jobs are ranked.

Job/ Ranks	Salary (Per Month)
Area Manager	Rs. 24000 p.m.
Store Manager	Rs. 18000 p.m.
Assistant Store Manager	Rs. 14000 p.m.
Store Executives	Rs. 11000 p.m.
Billing Clerks	Rs. 9500 p.m.
Packaging and baggage boys	Rs. 8000 p.m.

Table 13.2: Example of Job Ranking at XYZ Books & Music Store

Job Classification Method

In job classification method the committee groups similar jobs together in groups or classes based on the amount or degree of compensable factors that they contain. These groups or classes then help in determining the value of different jobs.

Job classes could at times be prepared on the basis of their difficulty level like

1. Very simple tasks.
2. Simple tasks directive in nature.

3. Simple task but difficult process.
4. Tasks calling for judgment by individual.
5. Regular tasks with accountability.
6. Non-regular tasks.
7. Complicated tasks requiring specialization.
8. Creative, entrepreneurial tasks.

Quantitative Methods of Job Evaluation

Point Method

Point method of job evaluation is used widely and consist of the following steps:

A. **Identifying Compensable Factors for the Benchmark Jobs:** Benchmark jobs are those that are commonly found in the market.

B. **Assigning Point Values to Compensable Factors:** There after the job evaluation committee determines the relative weight-age of various compensable factors and assigns point values to them.

Table 13.3: Compensable Factors, Weightage and Point Values

COMPENSABLE FACTORS	Weight-age (%)	DEGREE 1	2	3	4	5	Min pts	Max pts
Skill								
Education	7.43	20	40	60	80	100	20	100
Work Experience	5.57	15	30	45	60	75	15	75
Judgement	4.46	12	24	36	48	60	12	60
Decision Making	4.46	12	24	36	48	60	12	60
Trouble Shooting	3.71	10	20	30	40	50	10	50
Responsibilities								
Supervision	3.71	10	20	30	40	50	10	50
Leadership	5.57	15	30	45	60	75	15	75

Financial	5.57	15	30	45	60	75	15	75
Liasioning	4.46	12	24	36	48	60	12	60
Confidentiality	5.20	14	28	42	56	70	14	70
Effort								
Job Complexity	6.69	18	36	54	72	90	18	90
Mental Demand	7.43	20	40	60	80	100	20	100
Physical demand	3.71	10	20	30	40	50	10	50
Emotional demand	4.46	12	24	36	48	60	12	60
Error cost	3.71	10	20	30	40	50	10	50
Working Conditions								
Environment	5.57	15	30	45	60	75	15	75
Location / Mobility	4.46	12	24	36	48	60	12	60
Hazards	5.57	15	30	45	60	75	15	75
Supervision received	4.46	12	24	36	48	60	12	60
Co-workers	3.71	10	20	30	40	50	10	50

C. Collecting Job Information: Detailed information about the jobs is obtained using job analysis techniques. Tools like Position Analysis Questionnaire (PAQ), MPDQ etc. may be used for this purpose. The job description and job specification reports help in understanding the job & the ideal candidate better.

D. Rate Each Job using Point Table: Each job is then rated using the point table and the total points are calculated.

E. Plotting Points & Wage Rate: The points of the benchmark jobs so obtained are plotted with the market wage rates for these jobs. The Point values of benchmark jobs are taken on X-axis and market wage rates for these jobs are taken on Y-axis.

A line of best fit is drawn from the plot through use of scattergram. This line is known as the wage trend line, drawn using a statistical technique known as least squares method of regression.

Point values of other jobs can be plotted on this line and pay-rates can be obtained. The employer has a choice of being the best-paymaster, average pay master or pay-at-par with the market. It all depends on employer's compensation philosophy. There are companies who deliberately want to be at par or average pay master because they offer very good benefits and culture.

		Education	Work Experience	Judgement	Decision Making	Trouble shooting	Supervision	Leadership	Financial	Liasioning	Confidentiality	Job Complexity	Mental Demand	Physical demand	Emotional demand	Error cost	Environment	Location / Mobility	Hazards	Supervision received	Co-workers
Area manager	Degree	3	3	4	4	3	3	4	4	4	3	3	3	2	3	4	3	3	2	2	2
	Point	60	45	48	48	30	30	60	60	48	42	54	60	20	36	40	45	36	30	24	20
Store Manager	Degree	2	2	3	4	4	3	3	2	3	2	2	2	3	3	3	3	3	3	2	3	3
	Point	40	30	36	48	40	30	45	30	36	28	36	40	30	36	30	45	36	30	36	30
Asst. Store Manager	Degree	2	1	2	3	3	3	2	2	3	2	2	2	3	3	2	3	3	2	3	2
	Point	40	15	24	36	30	30	30	30	36	28	36	40	30	36	20	45	36	30	36	20

Table 13.4: Point Values of Jobs and Pay Rates

Factor Comparison Method

Factor Comparison method is another quantitative approach for job-evaluation. It uses wages of the existing key jobs, which provide standard against which all other jobs are compared. The factors used for analysis and evaluating jobs are: (1) skill, (2) mental effort, (3) physical effort, (4) responsibility, and (5) working conditions. A composite score is obtained for all factors. The jobs under consideration are evaluated using factor-by-factor in relation to the key jobs on job comparison scale. Then each job is evaluated and compared with other jobs in terms of each factor. Pay is then assigned by comparing the weights of the factors required for each job, i.e., the present wages paid for key jobs may be divided among the factors weighed by importance. All other jobs are compared with the list of key jobs and wage rates are determined.

Job	Hourly Rate	Factor 1	Factor 2	Factor 3
Area Manager	Rs. 100	Rs. 50/-	Rs. 30/-	Rs. 20/-
Store Manager	Rs. 75/-	Rs. 45/-	Rs. 20/-	Rs. 15/-
Asst. Store Manager	Rs. 50/-	Rs. 25/-	Rs. 15/-	Rs. 10/-

Market Pricing/Benchmarking

Market pricing or benchmarking is a comprehensive and time-consuming process. Generally market pricing/Benchmarking is done through salary surveys, done by third party like Mercer, Hewitt, Hay group etc. Market pricing/ benchmarking helps companies to know the wage-rates prevailing in the market, for the benchmarked jobs.

The market pricing or benchmarking is done through following steps –

i. Defining the jobs (Job analysis)

ii. Deciding the job families. Similar jobs in the same family

HR Job family (Let us say for example) may look like –

A3 – HR Head

A2 – HR Manager

A1 – Sr. HR Executive

A – HR Executive

All job families put together form a job architecture.

iii. Identifying a third party for carrying out the salary surveys.

iv. Matching the job analysis information with the standard job-descriptions available with the third party and deciding appropriate scale of each job.

v. Choosing the benchmark companies. Generally for each job-family separate set of benchmarking companies are chosen. The benchmarking companies for respective job-families are:

➤ Companies from where one hires; or

➤ Companies to which one losses people

At times when bidding for a project, benchmarking companies are close competitors.

vi. Survey & sharing of information – the third-party consultant conducting the survey operates on strict confidentiality and does not disclose any company-specific information to the client-company. Then how is the information shared? Let me give you an illustration. Let's say Company XYZ has given a list of ten companies C1, C2, C3,........C10 to the third party consultant, for the previously mentioned HR job family. The third party consultant shall have pay information of all ten companies for the jobs within the family. However it will not share company-specific information like company C1 pays Rs. 16000/- to job scale A1 and so on. However it will give only aggregate data like lowest, highest, median, percentile salaries of a particular job to the client.

Let's Say

		Median Salary
A3	HR Head	50000 INR
A2	HR Manager	35000 INR
A1	Sr. HR Executive	22000 INR
A	HR Executive	15000 INR

For each job then pay range or band is worked-out by:

vii Determining Pay Grades – The existence of thousands of pay-rate shall be cumbersome and also irrelevant as they shall not differ significantly. Hence point range are developed for job classes and plotted against the average pay rates. This helps in determining pay grades.

viii Banding – Banding means further collapsing pay-grades into few levels called as bands. In broad banding the number of the job bands are less and hence people spend more number of years in each job band, whereas in narrow banding the vice-versa is true.

Reading Exhibit 3: Internal Wage Structure

Jobs that call for creativity, autonomy, analysis, and personal growth may provide the best motivator of all: intrinsic rewards. Such satisfaction originates from within the worker. An intrinsically motivated worker does not obtain his motivation from external stimulation provided by the employer. An overemphasis on external rewards may be responsible for elimination of internally originated ones. There are personal and organizational objectives that simply cannot be realized through pay.

On the down side, intrinsic motivators, as wonderful as they may appear, are not equally found among all workers, nor do they always motivate the type of performance you may desire. Pay can be a powerful management tool often consider pay as a measure of individual achievement and social status. The importance of pay, then, ought neither be over or underrated.

To be effective, pay must be tied to performance. While incentives (Chapter 8) can yield the clearest link between performance and pay, they are not suitable to all jobs. In this chapter we will look at wage structures, or time-based pay. Even though its relationship to performance may not be as salient as incentive pay, time-based pay can also motivate increased worker performance.

Pay issues covered in this chapter include (1) pay fairness; (2) what is behind pay differences; (3) job evaluations and market considerations; (4) elements of a wage structure; and (5) maintaining a pay structure.

(**Source:** *An Article by Mr. Gregorio Billikopf, U C Davis, University of California*)

Pay Fairness (Pay Equity)

In a casual survey I conducted, workers said that they expected wages to: (1) cover basic living expenses, (2) keep up with inflation, (3) leave some money for savings or recreation, and (4) increase over time.

Workers also become concerned later in their careers about supporting themselves during their retirement years. Personnel who have lived in farm provided housing will find it especially difficult to afford payments on a new home after they retire. Although beyond the scope of this work, farmers may want to look into retirement and tax deferred plans to cover some of these future needs.

Even if a farmer devises a wage structure to satisfy these expectations, worker dissatisfaction may arise if either internal or external equity principles are violated. Simply put, internal equity refers to the relative fairness of wages received by other employees in the same organization. External equity is fairness relative to wages outside the organization. Depending on the type of work and location, tests of external equity may involve comparisons with other farms or even nonfarm corporations.

Employees will act to restore equity if they perceive an imbalance. In evaluating the fairness of their pay, employees balance inputs (e.g., work effort, skills) against outcomes (e.g., pay, privileges). Workers may experience guilt or anger if they feel over or undercompensated. The greater the perceived disparity, the greater the tension. Employees may seek balance in the following six ways:

(1) Modify input or output (e.g., if underpaid, a person may reduce his effort or try to obtain a raise; if overpaid, a person may increase efforts or work longer hours without additional compensation);

(2) Adjust the notion of what is fair (e.g., if underpaid, a worker may think himself the recipient of other benefits – such as doing interesting work; if overpaid, an employee may come to believe he deserves it);

(3) Change source of equity comparison (e.g., an employee who has compared himself with a promoted co-worker may begin to compare himself with another worker);

(4) Attempt to change the input or output of others (e.g., asking others not to work so hard or to work harder);

(5) Withdraw (e.g., through increased absenteeism, mental withdrawal or quitting);

(6) Forcing others to withdraw (e.g., trying to obtain a transfer for a co-worker or force him to quit).

The issue of fairness is critical to compensation administration and most every phase of labor management. Generally, workers and managers agree, in principle, that wages should take into account a job's (1) required preparation, responsibility, and even unpleasantness and (2) performance differences and/or seniority. Less agreement exists about the relative importance of each of these factors. Challenges in applying differential payment stem from subjectivity in the evaluations of both jobs and workers.

Equity considerations influence the satisfaction of the workforce. Within a broader view, the stability of a nation may be affected when the contributions of any segment of society are either greatly exaggerated or undervalued.

What is Behind Pay Differences?

Philosophical differences affect judgments employers make about their wage structures. Some think all members of a society should receive enough income to meet their necessities. Such employers may base pay more on the needs than on the contributions of the individual worker. To some, all jobs contribute equally to farm productivity and, therefore, all employees should be compensated equally. By this standard, pay differences are based on how well a job is performed rather than what job is performed. In a contrasting system the nature of the job—besides the quality of performance—is an important part of how pay differences are set at the ranch.

All employees should be compensated equally.

In making pay decisions at the farm, you have much flexibility within the constraints of the law, labor market, and local norms. The choices you make will affect employee recruitment, retention, satisfaction and performance.

Alan, a former Farm Bureau president, was asked by his workers why irrigators were paid less than tractor drivers. After considering the question, Alan concluded these wage differences among his workers were rather arbitrary. He decided to start paying everybody the same hourly rate. Another grower, Cecilia, increases wage rates as employees move up the job ladder from general laborer to irrigator, to supervisor, and so on.

What do Alan and Cecilia gain or lose from their respective approaches? The single rate Alan has settled on is fairly high. He has raised lower wage jobs to the level of better paying positions, rather than the reverse. His total wage bill is probably higher than it need be, but it is buying him a relatively content work force. Simplicity is one advantage of this approach. Alan does not have to adjust rates for employees when they work outside of their usual assignments—which is often.

Most farmers require flexibility in employee assignments. Individuals are called on to wear several hats and use a variety of tools in their jobs. On a livestock ranch, a worker who is digging fence post holes and fixing corrals today, might be herding cattle tomorrow, pouring cement the next day, and entering herd data into a computer next winter.

Despite the practical advantages of paying everyone identical rates, more skilled workers may resent being paid the same as others. Cecilia forgoes the simplicity of Alan's method in hopes of using pay as a tool to attract, retain, and motivate qualified employees.

> Workers may resist taking on tasks outside their normal routine.

Paying different wages for different jobs, however, tends to make people more sensitive to job boundaries. Workers may resist taking on tasks outside their normal routine. On her ranch, Cecilia handles this by paying her workers their regular rates when they perform lower paid jobs. When employees perform more highly classified tasks—which is not often—she pays them extra.

When several positions receive a similar assessment, they can be combined to create a pay grade. To simplify, we will mostly speak of pay grades, but it is understood that pay grades may sometimes consist of a single position.

> An occasional chance for a manager to milk the cows may underscore the importance of the job.

Of course, pay is not the only factor that affects workers' resistance to taking on tasks outside their normal duties. Employees quickly sense when lower paying jobs are not as valued by management. An occasional chance for a manager to milk the cows may underscore the importance of the job, and also serves as a good reminder of what the employee does.

Once you decide whether persons holding different jobs should be paid different rates, the next question is whether pay rates should vary for workers performing the same job (e.g., tractor driver). If so, what factors could determine pay differences within a job?

Since abilities and actual performance vary remarkably among individuals, even in the same type of job, individual differences can be acknowledged if each job has a rate range (as in Figure 13.4). Higher rates or "upper steps" in the range could be given to employees with longer seniority, merit (i.e., better performance evaluations), or a combination of the two.

Establishing rate ranges requires careful consideration. The relationships careful consideration. The relationships between grades and ranges have symbolic and practical consequences. A person at a top step within a pay grade, for example, may earn more than a person in a higher pay grade,

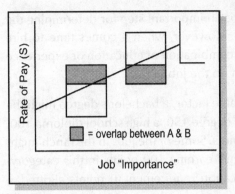

but at a lower step (Figure 13.4). Whether and how much overlap to build into a pay structure is discussed later in this chapter.

While not recognizing differences in the importance of positions, Alan could also establish rate ranges (not pictured here) within his flat wage line. Like Cecilia, he would need to consider the basis for pay differences with a given job.

Figure 13.4: Pay grades can have rate ranges. Each pay grade is represented by a rectangle. rate ranges by the height of the rectangle

Job Evaluations and Market Consideration

You can arrive at appropriate wages for positions on your farm on the basis of two main management tools: (1) job evaluations (based on compensable factors such as education, skill, experience, and responsibility), and (2) the going rate (or market value) of a job.

Job Evaluation

A farmer such as Cecilia who pays different rates for different jobs usually first classifies the jobs on her ranch. Through a job evaluation she rates the jobs on the farm according to their relative "importance." Each job might be given its own rate, or jobs of comparable importance may be grouped or banded into a single wage classification, or pay grade.

Job evaluations compare positions in an organization with respect to such factors as education, responsibility, experience and physical effort. Figure 13.5 shows a sample job evaluation. In it, for instance, much more value is given to responsibility and education than to physical requirements. The supervisor in this example would earn about twice what an equipment operator would.

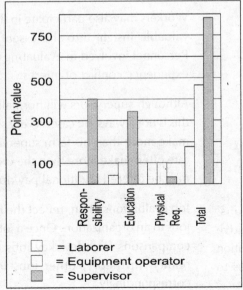

Figure 13.5: Compensable Factors

Figure 13.5 uses education as a compensable factor. You may prefer to think in terms of what combination of experience and education would qualify a person for the job. This is an important step for determining the value of the position to be filled. However, when it comes time to hire someone, you may not care what combination of education or experience an applicant has as long as he can do the job.

If education is used as a compensable factor, a bachelor's degree might be worth 200 points, a junior college degree 150, a high school diploma 100, and an elementary diploma 50 points. Some of the jobs in the ranch might require a high school diploma, thus earning 100 points in this category, while others might have no education requirement.(0 points allotted) - regardless of the educational qualifications of the person who may actually apply. Similar ratings of jobs would be made for responsibility and other factors worth compensating.

> For job evaluation a detailed list of compensable factors needs to be articulated.

You decide how much weight to allot various compensable factors and how to distribute points within each job. For the job evaluation to be useful, a detailed list of compensable factors needs to be articulated. (The job analysis created during the selection process can help.) You can test the job evaluation by comparing a few jobs you value differently. Does the tentative evaluation match your expectations? If not, are there any job factors missing or given too much or too little value?

Workers may also participate in the process of evaluating jobs and can add valuable insight into the essential job attributes for various positions. Personnel involved in evaluating their own jobs, nevertheless, are likely to experience conflict of interest.

Although supervisors will normally make more than those they supervise, this is not always the case. A very skillful welder or veterinarian will probably make more than his farm supervisor. Some workers harvesting at a piece rate often make more than the crew leaders supervising them. Supervisors may be offered additional pay during labor-intensive periods.

> Job evaluations, reflect the relative value or contribution of different jobs to an organization.

Job evaluations, then, reflect the relative value or contribution of different jobs to an organization. Once a job evaluation has been completed, market comparisons for a few key jobs need to be used as anchors for market reality. In theory, other jobs in the job evaluation can be adjusted correspondingly.

Market Considerations

In practice, results of job evaluations are often compromised—or even overshadowed—by market considerations. Labor market supply and demand forces are strong influences in the setting of wages. No matter what your job evaluation results may indicate, it is unlikely you will be able to pay wages drastically lower or higher than the going rate.

Supply and demand factors often control wages. When there are many more pickers than available jobs, for instance, the going wage decreases. If few good livestock nutrition specialists are available for hire, they become more expensive in a free market. The market may also influence the migratory patterns of farm workers, for example, whether a worker stays in Mexico or travels to Texas, Florida or Oregon.

Of course, the market is not totally free. Legal constraints affect wages (e.g., equal pay, minimum wage). Labor groups, in the form of unions, can combine forces to protect their earnings. They may prevent employers from taking advantage of a large supply of workers. At times wages are driven so high that corporations cannot compete in a broader international market. Some professional groups can also impact the market. By limiting acceptance to universities, a limited supply of available professionals is set.

> Legal constraints may prevent employers from taking advantage of a large supply of workers.

To establish external equity, employers need information about what other employers pay in the same labor market. While some employers are content to lean over the fence and simply ask their neighbors what they pay, others conduct systematic wage and salary surveys.

Wage surveys need to describe jobs accurately as positions may vary widely even for jobs with the same title. Surveys should seek information about benefits given employees (e.g., farm products, housing). Of course, there are other "intangible benefits such as stability, the prestige of the position or the institution [and] the possibility of professional development." Surveys need to consider the number of workers per farm in a given classification. Wages on a farm employing many employees affect the going rate more than one with few. In some cases, farmers may compete for labor within a broader labor market. When compensating mechanics or welders, for instance, you may have to check what those in industry are paid.

An important pay decision is whether one will pay the going market rate. Those who pay at or below the market may have difficulty attracting workers. Further, they may find themselves training people who leave for higher paid positions. Merely paying more than another farm enterprise, however, does not automatically result in higher performance and lower labor costs. Even when well paid, workers may not see the connection between wages and their performance. Farmers who pay too much may find it difficult to remain competitive. Furthermore, there are other factors valued by employees besides pay, such as working for an organization that values their ideas and allows them to grow on the job.

Reconciling Market & Job Evaluations

In wage setting, it is usually more beneficial to reconcile market information and job evaluation results than to singly rely on either. Unique jobs are more appropriately priced on the basis of job evaluations. You may depend more heavily on the job market for common jobs.

In most cases, farmers have freedom to satisfy both job evaluation and the market. Where the market pays a job substantially less than a job evaluation does, however, you can either pay the higher wage, reconsider job evaluation factors, or pay the reduced wage. The farmer has fewer viable options when the market would pay a higher wage than the job evaluation.

Elements of A Wage Structure

Wage structures, we have said, help illustrate many of the decisions you can make about pay. We have already introduced most of the elements of a wage structure (review Figure 13.4) and will revisit them here.

Wage lines reflect wage differentials between jobs The steeper the wage line slope, the greater the differences in pay between jobs. In Figure 13.6, two farm enterprises pay their lowest level job the same. From this point on, wages for one farm rise at a steeper rate.

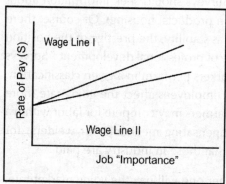

Figure 13.6: Wages may begin at the same level but rise steeper at one farm.

Wage lines also reflect the overall pay level of the organization. Figure 13.7 illustrates two farms whose differential between the highest and lowest paid job are the same despite the differences in the total wages paid.

The number of pay grades (job groupings sharing the same wage levels) and the scope of rate ranges may vary. Rate ranges are represented by the height of a pay grade, that is, the difference between the lowest and highest pay within the grade. For example, the minimum and maximum salaries for tractor drivers might be $10 and $14 per hour, with a potential $4 pay range.

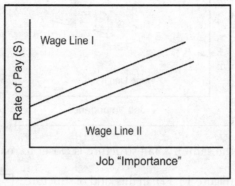

Figure 13.7: Pay differential maintained.

The more pay grades, the finer the distinctions between jobs. Alternatively, broadbanding is the use of fewer pay grades with larger rate ranges. Broadbanding allows employees to step out of very narrow or rigid job descriptions. Broadbanding may result in significant differences in jobs going unrecognized, and pay equity concerns may arise.

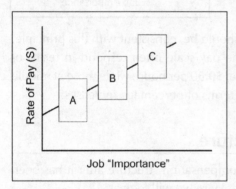

In organizations with few pay grades, it may be that there are taller rate ranges within each grade (Figure 13.8). This allows room for pay increases within a grade.

Figure 13.8: Few pay grades (broadbanding), with taller rate ranges.

Where many grades exist (Figure 13.9) workers may also obtain an increase by moving from one pay grade to another (i.e., being promoted) as they are by getting a raise within their grade. Some farms may have few grades and short rate ranges, also.

There tends to be more overlap where a pay grade slope is flatter (Figure13.10), or with larger rate ranges. We shall return to overlapping

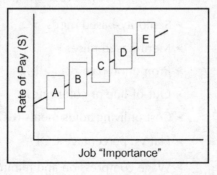

Figure 13.9: Many pay grades with shorter rate ranges.

Figure 13.10:
Flatter slopes lead to increased overlap.

Note: Wage Line II is a Flatter than Wage Line I, and thus contains more overlap.

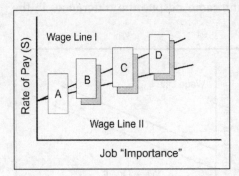

Figure 13.11:
A Fan Type Structure

rate ranges once more, as we discuss pay as a function of employee promotions.

Up to here—for simplicity—we have depicted wage structures containing equal rate ranges for all pay grades (i.e., the differential between the starting and top wages within each pay grade are the same). A fan structure is closer to reality.

(Figure 13.11). In this kind of structure the rate ranges are comparatively taller for jobs at higher pay grade classifications. To someone earning $9 an hour, an increase of 50 cents an hour would be significant. To someone making $40 an hour, the 50 cent raise would not be nearly as meaningful.

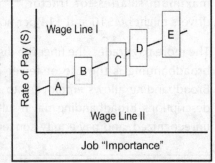

When asked how large pay raises should be, consistent with this principle, employees at the lower end of the pay scale often respond in terms of specific dollar amounts (for example, $0.50 per hour), while those at middle and higher levels tend to speak in terms of percentage increases.

Maintaining A Pay Structure

Maintaining pay equity within a compensation structure after it has been developed is an ongoing challenge. Here we will look at:

- Seniority-based raises
- Merit-based raises
- Promotion pay
- Out-of-line or color rates
- Cost of living adjustments (COLAs)
- Flat vs. percentage COLAs
- Wage compression and minimum wage.

Employees traditionally progress within a grade on the basis of merit and/or seniority. Decisions about pay increases should be fair, sound, and well communicated to workers.

Seniority-based Raises

Systems providing periodic raises regardless of evaluated merit may be based on the assumption that ability grows with time on the job, which simply is not always true. Many companies use pay increases to reward workers for "belonging" and for their length of employment with the farm. As long as worker performance meets minimum standards, they continue to receive periodic raises.

Personnel value the certainty of seniority-based pay, and workers' needs for increases in pay through time are served well. Seniority-based pay also promotes continuous service and may reduce turnover.

Employers who give raises on the basis of seniority value the maturity and experience of senior workers, but they are sometimes relieved when senior workers leave. In some instances, senior workers cost organizations disproportionately higher wages and benefits (e.g., longer vacations) than their contribution to the organization. This is not a reflection on the senior employee, but rather, on a system that undervalues the new employee with the promise that in due time, new personnel will be able to earn greater amounts.

In order to avoid having employees climb the pay scale too quickly, smaller but more frequent pay increases may be given early in an employee's career. Increases later on are given at a slower pace. These increases, without being overpaid, must be large enough to motivate employees to stay.

Merit-based Raises

Merit wage increases are designed to recognize improved worker performance and contribution to the organization. In theory, in a merit system workers earn wage increments proportional to their performance. As with the seniority system, however, once someone climbs to a given wage level his wages are rarely reduced. Incentive pay plans can solve the problem of giving "permanent" raises based on present and past performance.

Incentives, however, can have a disrupting effect on an internal wage structure. Employers who use incentive pay systems for some jobs and not others may find workers in some lower "value" jobs earn more than those in higher level ones. Companies sometimes abandon their incentive programs or expand them to cover more jobs.

Where pass/fail merit reviews are conducted at specified time-service intervals—and where employees tend to pass—the process may be viewed as a "glorified seniority system." Length of employment and wages are closely correlated within each job category. In such a system workers would experience the same positive and negative benefits of a seniority system.

Managers may feel unduly constrained when given a choice between recommending a worker for a full step raise or nothing. To deserve no raise an employee must have performed quite poorly. If the choices were even slightly expanded to include half or quarter steps (e.g., half step, step and a quarter), managers may be more likely to reward workers commensurate with their performance.

Whenever performance reviews affecting raises are given at specified time intervals, merit systems automatically include a seniority factor. Alternatively, performance reviews for raises could be triggered by other events, such as specific performance accomplishments, or skill acquisition (skill-based pay).

Some workers may merit faster advances to the top of the pay scale than others. Unfortunately, employees who advance too quickly may not have any further economic increase to look forward to, and experience a feeling of stagnation. The only growth may mean trying for a promotion—or a job elsewhere.

In order to avoid having employees climb a merit scale too quickly, upper levels of the scale must be harder to achieve. Also, if the merit system incorporates seniority (i.e., performance reviews are triggered by time spent on a given pay step) reviews need to take place less frequently as people move up the pay scale.

It turns out, then, that there are fewer differences than expected between seniority and merit based pay systems. In order to fully take advantage of merit based pay, it is critical that employees understand how they will be evaluated. That is where the negotiated approach to performance appraisal can play a key role along with the more traditional appraisal.

Promotion Pay

How much of a pay increase should accompany a promotion? If there is a pay structure policy, the boundaries of such a decision already exist. A tall rate range or steep wage structure may permit room for larger wage increases after raises or promotions. The wage differential will also depend on the height of rate range occupied by the employee within the present pay grade, as compared to the height in the grade promoted to. Obviously, a greater pay increase will accompany those promotions where the employee moves up more than one pay grade.

Any time there is an overlap between jobs, some workers in a lower grade may earn more than some workers on the adjacent higher grade. If workers are seldom promoted from one grade to another, this structural characteristic rarely creates a dilemma.

> If workers are seldom promoted from one grade to another, this structural characteristic rarely creates a dilemma.

When workers move from one grade to another, difficulties may arise. There might be some pay overlap between the jobs of "assistant mechanic" and "mechanic." Consider an assistant mechanic who, because of many years of work, has reached the top of his scale and makes more than a journeyman mechanic who has been working for a couple of years. The journeyman mechanic is likely to tolerate the wage discrepancy because even though the assistant is earning more temporarily, due to seniority, in time the wages of the journeyman are likely to surpass those of the assistant, due to the higher potential earnings in the journeyman's pay grade.

The challenge arises when this assistant mechanic, who has topped out in his grade, decides to seek a promotion to mechanic. The assistant is unlikely to want to start at the bottom step of the mechanic scale where he would be making less than in his previous job.

One solution would be to start the assistant mechanic at a higher step level in the mechanic grade. But if the newly promoted mechanic ended up with higher pay than the more experienced journeymen, questions of internal equity may be raised. Both employees are now performing exactly the same job but the one with less experience (although more overall seniority) is earning the same as or more than the other. This pay equity situation may become even more pronounced when the accomplished mechanic has to help train the one who just obtained the promotion.

> if the newly promoted mechanic ended up with higher pay than the more experienced journeymen, questions of internal equity may be raised.

You may help employees manage career and development plans to avoid losing pay when obtaining a promotion. They will have to apply for promotions early enough in their careers as not to lose the potential economic advantage. Another possibility is to give the promoted employee a one-time lump sum, or pay adder, to make the transition into the temporarily lower paying job more palatable.

Another promotion pay consideration is the inherent risk of failure in the new position. The greater the risk of failure a promoted employee faces in a new position, the larger the wage increase should be.

The greater the risk of failure a promoted employee faces in a new position, the larger the wage increase should be.

Out-of-line or Color Rates

Sooner or later you will encounter situations where jobs are paid more or less than their actual worth in the labor market. Different "color rates" are commonly used by compensation specialists to indicate particular out-of-line pay relationships (Figure 13.12): red and green illustrate either over or under compensated jobs—when compared to current worth.

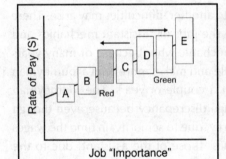

Figure 13.12: Red and Green Rates

Although the colors imply the farmer loses money with the first and gains with the latter, both situations can be quite costly. If out-of-line rates are not corrected speedily, both internal and external equity will be disturbed.

Red rates (so called because they represent overpaid jobs). If rates are allowed to stay out of proportion to the rest of the farm jobs, other workers may feel mistreated. Also, the wage bill will likely be higher than it need be. When red-grade rates are cut abruptly, workers may experience difficulty meeting their financial obligations. Smoother alternatives include combinations of freezing raises until internal equity is reached; exerting efforts to transfer workers to higher paying jobs are consistent with present wages; or even adjusting rates downward immediately while giving workers a lump sum (or several) to offset the downward adjustment.

Green rates (underpaid jobs). Green-grade rates can be brought up into line immediately in one or two steps. A grower may attempt to cut labor costs with green rates, but the benefits may be short term as it will be difficult to retain valuable workers.

Two likely green-grade indicators are (1) increases in turnover (with employees seeking better paying jobs); and (2) feeling forced to start inexperienced new workers up near the middle of a pay grade. If the latter approach is taken, no sound basis for pay differences among workers may remain.

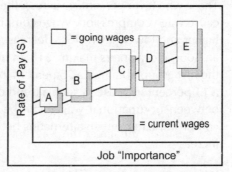

Figure 13.13: Current Wages have Failed to Keep up with Market Reality.

Of course, it is possible an employer does not have a green-grade rate problem, but rather, her whole wage structure may have failed to keep up with the market (Figure 13.13).

Cost of Living Adjustments (COLAs)

Inflation can have especially devastating effects on a worker's ability to make ends meet. We have seen how farmers whose pay structures fall below market values may have difficulty attracting and retaining personnel. Some corporations (and often union contracts) stipulate a COLA based on the Consumer Price Index (CPI). The index is supposed to reflect cost-of-living changes. The prices of common commodities purchased by most consumers are observed and compared.

While the CPI can be a useful tool, some observers feel the list of common articles used to come up with the index is not so common. The greatest challenge posed by the CPI is that it acts independently from labor market wages. In doing so, it may exaggerate and perpetuate inflation. Instead of using the CPI, farmers may prefer to monitor changes in the labor market through periodic wage surveys. Geographical transfers—especially international ones—may involve upward or downward COLAs to reflect substantial differences in cost-of-living requirements.

Flat vs. Percentage COLAs

COLAs may be given in terms of flat dollar amounts or percentage increases. Those who argue in favor of flat increases feel workers at the lower end of the earning scale need the COLA increases more than those at the higher end. Across-the-board percentage increases, they contend, have the effect of "further widening the gap in already disparate incomes" between the haves and have-nots. Some even feel it would be fair to give greater increases to those who make less.

Those who favor percentage across-the-board increases allege flat increases cause wage compression. Wage compression means differentials between higher and lower paying jobs decrease. For instance, if workers making $8 an hour and workers making $18 an hour both get a $2 an hour increase, the first group obtained a 25 percent increase while the second group only a 11 percent increase. If such a trend continues, proportional differentials between occupational wages can be all but eliminated. A conceivable compromise may mean alternating between giving straight and percentage increases.

Wage Compression & Minimum Wage

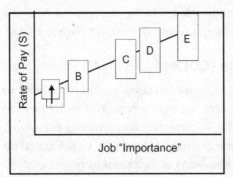

Figure 13.14: Sample wage compression

Increases in the minimum wage can also cause pay compression in agricultural enterprises paying at, or near, the legal minimum. For instance, if starting hourly wages for irrigators and hoers are $8.15 and $7.20, respectively, a new minimum wage of $8.00 would bring both to essentially the same starting wage (Figure 13.14).

In order to avoid raising the complete wage structure a farmer may, without raising the top wage, make minor adjustments all along the wage structure. Although one pay grade would not take the brunt of the wage compression, this approach may create pay compression throughout the organization.

Summary

This reading exhibit focused on internal wage structures, the framework for establishing and maintaining pay relationships in a farm organization. An important feature of a well-designed pay system is the provision for rewarding performance achievements with increased pay, either within the present job or through a promotion.

Pay is an important work reward for most people. Workers expect their wages will: (1) cover their basic living expenses, (2) keep up with inflation, (3) leave some money for savings or recreation, and (4) increase over time.

Farmers can set wages based on (1) job evaluations, and (2) market values. In practice, results of job evaluations must often defer to market considerations. Once wages are set, pay structures must be continually evaluated to assure competitiveness in attracting, retaining, and motivating personnel.

(Published with permission of Mr. Gregorio Billikopf, U C Davis, University of California)

Essay Questions

1. What are the key aspects to be kept in mind during compensation planning? Explain various factors that govern compensation.

2. What are the two main objectives of a compensation plan? List the main components of a compensation package.

3. Explain the various sub-components of the base pay structure (fixed component).

4. Classify the variable pay programs, and explain the difference between those for sales versus non-sales. Why do we need variable pay programs?

5. Write short note on:
   a) Bonus
   b) Commissions
   c) Incentives
   d) Sign on Bonuses.

6. Why are stock option given to employees? Differentiate between ESOPs, RSUs and ESPP.

7. Briefly describe the 'Benefits' given to employees as part of their compensation package. How can effectiveness of benefits offered to employees be enhanced?

8. Explain 'Provident Fund' and 'Gratuity'. What is the difference between the two?

9. 'Rewards & Recognitions need not always be monetary, – Is it true? Corroborate.

10. What is job evaluation? What are the various objectives of Job evaluation? Explain the Hay group spectrum for job evaluation.

11. What are compensable factors? Discuss the various categories of compensable factors.

12. Explain the various non-quantitative and quantitative techniques of job evaluation, with special emphasis on point method.

13. Explain the concept of 'Pay Equity'. What is behind differences in pay? How can pay-equities be maintained?

14. What are COLAs? Explain flat versus percentage COLAs.

Application Questions

1. Go to http://www.intel.com/jobs/usa/bencomp/compensation.htm, http://www.intel.com/jobs/usa/bencomp/stock.htm and http://www.intel.com/jobs/usa/bencomp/benefits.htm and study the various components of cash compensation, stock options and benefits being offered to its employees in US. Also study the Employee Cash Bonus Program (ECBP). Prepare a report/presentation.

2. Go to and study the Real Rewards of Nestlé USA's http://www.nestleusa.com/nirf/cm2/upload/81C7DAEC-D955-4170-83F2-1E97F0FB8AFE/RealRewardsBroch_FINAL.pdf.— a comprehensive package for salaried employees that includes competi-tive pay, comprehensive benefit programs as well as world-class learning and development opportunities.

3. Go to http://www.towersperrin.com/tp/getwebcachedoc?webc=HRS/USA/2007/200710/TRE_Employee_Value_1004.pdf and read the Tower Perrin's concept of Total Rewards.

4. Study the salary survey report summaries on India from the year 2000 to 2010 available on world wide web and comment on –
   a) Salary hikes rates over the years;
   b) Industry salary trends;
   c) Executive compensation;
   d) Salary hikes versus retention.
   e) Prepare a presentation/report.

5. Go to http://www.ssa.gov/ - explore the website and the prepare a report on the social security benefits offered to employees in US. Compare them to those offered in India.

Bibliography

Albrecht, C. (2009). Moving to a Global Sales Incentive Compensation Plan. *Compensation & Benefits Review, 41* (4), 52-57.

Alsop, R. J. (2011). Special Issue: Benefits & Compensation. *Workforce Management, 90* (9), 3.

Baker, P., Moderson, M. J., & Wechter, K. A. (2011). Eleven Things to Know About Employee Benefits and Executive Compensation. *Employee Benefit Plan Review, 65* (11), 25-30.

Benest, F. (2008). The Role of Benefits in Winning the War for Talent. *Benefits & Compensation Digest, 45* (6), 42-45.

Blostin, A. P. (2004). The National Compensation Survey: a Wealth of Benefits Data. *Monthly Labor Review, 127* (8), 3-5.

Brose, D. A. (2011). Workers' Compensation: Determining When It Is Truly the "Exclusive Remedy". *Employee Benefit Plan Review, 65* (10), 25-29.

Browne, M. J., & Trieschmann, J. S. (1991). Salary and Benefit Compensation at American Research Universities. *Journal of Risk & Insurance, 58* (3), 513-524.

Butler, R. J., Gardner, B. D., & Gardner, H. H. (1997). Workers' Compensation Costs When Maximum Benefits Change. *Journal of Risk & Uncertainty, 15* (3), 259-269.

Compensation & Benefits News. (2011). *HR Focus, 88* (11), 13.

Compensation Benefits & Compensation Digest. (2006). *43* (10), 46-49.

Davolt, S. (2006). Total compensation. *Employee Benefit News, 20* (6), 32-36.

Dema, R., Diamond, L., Germano, L. C., Koutter, D. J., Miller, R. J., Neumark, A. E., et al. (1995). Compensation & Benefits. *Journal of Accountancy, 179* (3), 86-88.

Ellig, B. R. (1983). What's Ahead in Compensation and Benefits; *Management Review, 72* (8), 56.

Greene, M. R. (1963). Fringe Benefits or Salary. *Journal of Marketing, 27* (4), 63-68.

Halperin, R., & Tzur, J. (1985). Monetary Compensation and Nontaxable Employee Benefits: An Analytical Perspective. *Accounting Review, 60* (4), 670.

Harvey, M. (1993). Designing a Global Compensation System: The Logic and a Model. *Columbia Journal of World Business, 28* (4), 56-72.

Jensen, H. H. (1982). Analysis of Fringe Benefits for Nonmetropolitan versus Metropolitan Employee Compensation. *American Journal of Agricultural Economics, 64* (1), 124.

Leininger, J. (2007). Recent Compensation and Benefit Trends in China. *China Business Review, 34* (4), 28-30.

Liebtag, B. (1986). Compensation. *Journal of Accountancy, 162* (5), 80-90.

Macintyre, D. M. (1953). Workmen's Compensation and Private Benefit Programs. *Industrial & Labor Relations Review, 7* (1), 63-72.

Murray, M. L. (1985). Workers' Compensation—A Benefit Out of Time. *Benefits Quarterly, 1* (2), 8-15.

O'Connell, K. (2007). The Importance of Strategically Designed Compensation Plans. *Benefits & Compensation Digest, 44* (9), 20-25.

Paul, R. J. (1976). Workers' Compensation — An Adequate Employee Benefit? *Academy of Management Review, 1* (4), 112-123.

Paul, R. J. (1990). Workers' Compensation-An Adequate Employee Benefit Now. *Journal of Economic & Social Measurement, 16* (1), 1-17.

Pauly, M. V., & Rosenbloom, J. (1996). sing a Total Compensation Approach for Wage and Benefits Planning. *Benefits Quarterly, 12* (1), 47-55.

Purushotham, D. P. (2009). Compensation and Benefits: Theory to Practice. *Proceedings of the Northeast Business & Economics Association,* 177-179.

Purushotham, D. P. (2010). The Impact of Current Economic Climate on Compensation and Benefits Issues. *Proceedings of the Northeast Business & Economics Association,* 547-549.

Schiemann, W. A. (1987). The Impact of Corporate Compensation and Benefit Policy On Employee Attitudes and Behavior and Corporate Profitability. *Journal of Business & Psychology, 2* (1), 8-26.

Setting & Managing Compensation: What Law Firms Need to Know Now. (2006). *Compensation & Benefits for Law Offices, 6* (2), 1-11.

Shenenberg, T., & Smith, D. (1999). Certifying Compensation and Benefits Management competencies. *Human Resource Management, 38* (2), 161.

Sperling, R., & Hicks, L. (1998). Trends in Compensation snd Benefits Strategies. *Employment Relations Toda, 25* (2), 85-99.

Sullivan, J. F. (1972). Indirect Compensation: The Years Ahead. *California Management Review, 15* (2), 65-76.

Ternberg, E. (2009). Voluntary Benefits Can Expand Options. *Benefits & Compensation Digest, 46* (8), 30-32.

Thickens, T. P. (2006). Executive Compensation and Benefits Reporting. *Journal of Financial Service Professionals, 60* (3), p. 21-22.

Tibbetts Jr, J. S., & Donovan, E. T. (1989). Compensation and Benefits for Startup Companies. *Harvard Business Review, 67* (1), 140-147.

Weathington, B. L., & Tetrick, L. E. (2000). Compensation or Right: An Analysis of Employee Fringe Benefit Perception. *Employee Responsibilities & Rights Journal, 12* (3), 141-162.

Williams, M., McDaniel, M., & Ford, L. (2007). Understanding Multiple Dimensions of compensation satisfaction. *Journal of Business & Psychology, 21* (3), 429-459.

Woodbury, S. A. (1983). Substitution Between Wage and Nonwage Benefits. *American Economic Review, 73* (1), 166.

Wudyka, D. J. (2006). Ten Common Questions about Compensation Programs. *Benefits & Compensation Digest, 43* (5), 1-15.

Zou, L. (1997). Incentive Roles of Fringe Benefits in Compensation Contracts. *Journal of Economics, 65* (2), 181-199.

Hewitt. (2009, February 20). *India to See Single-Digit Salary Hikes:* Retrieved from http://www.bpowatchindia.com/bpo_industry_report/hewitt_research/february-20-2009/india_to_see_single-digit_sal_hikes.html

Hewitt. (n.d.). *Times of India.* Retrieved from India Tops Salary Hike in Asia: http://articles.timesofindia.indiatimes.com/2005-11-24/india-business/27849448_1_salary-hewitt-associates-hike.

Hewitt, A. (n.d.). *India Inc may give 10.6% salary hike in 2010.* Retrieved from Live mint.com: http://www.livemint.com/2010/03/04174442/India-Inc-may-give-106-salar.html.

Hewitt, a. (n.d.). *India to See 12.9% Salary Hike in 2011.* Retrieved from The Economic Times: http://articles.economictimes.indiatimes.com/2011-03-08/news/28668737_1_salary-hike-double-digit-salary-increases-junior-manager.

India GDP - real growth rate. (n.d.). Retrieved from Indexmundi.com: http://www.indexmundi.com/india/gdp_real_growth_rate.html.

India Inc Gets Lowest Salary Hike: Hewitt survey. (n.d.). Retrieved from Financial Express: http://www.financialexpress.com/news/india-inc-gets-lowest-salary-hike-hewitt-survey/34425/2.

India Shines with Highest Average Pay Hike. (2008, Feb 20). Retrieved from The Economic Times: http://articles.economictimes.indiatimes.com/2008-02-20/news/27723424_1_highest-average-salary-double-digit-largest-economy.

Indian Firms Witness High Attrition Rate Despite Downturn. (n.d.). Retrieved from Silicon indiaa.com: http://www.siliconindia.com/shownews/Indian_firms_witness_high_attrition_rate_despite_downturn-nid-62287.html.

Modest Salary Hikes. (2002). Retrieved from The Hindu: http://hindu.com/2002/02/08/stories/2002020800391300.htm.

Modest salary hikes projected in. (2002). Retrieved from http://economictimes.indiatimes.com/modest-salary-hikes-projected-in-2002/articleshow/27346541.cms.

Modest Salary Hikes Projected in 2002. (n.d.). Retrieved from The economic times: http://economictimes.indiatimes.com/modest-salary-hikes-projected-in-2002/articleshow/27346541.cms.

Nair, A. (2010, Dec). *Attrition Rate May Go Up 25% in 2011 with Sefty Hikes.* Retrieved from The Economic Times: http://articles.economictimes.indiatimes.com/2010-12-23/news/27588783_1_attrition-rate-salary-hikes-salaried-class.

Salary hike: India beats China. (n.d.). Retrieved from http://www.rediff.com/money/2004/nov/08pay.htm.

Chapter 14

Performance-based Compensation

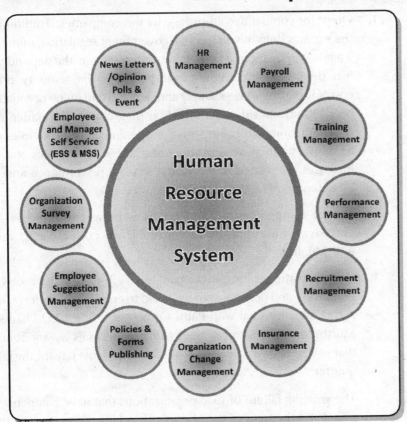

Outline

Introduction

Performance-based Pay/ Variable Pay

Types of Performance-based Pays

The Payment of Bonus Act, 1965

Reading Exhibit -1

Reading Exhibit -2

Reading Exhibit-3

Profit Sharing

Gainsharing

Essay Questions

Application Questions

Bibliography

Key Terms

Employee Stock Options
Incentive Piecework
Individual Incentive
Payment of Bonus Act
Performance Bonus
Performance-based Pay
Piecework Plan
Profit Sharing
Variable Pay

Introduction

What do the organizations pay their employees for? Do they pay them for the time that they spend in the organization? Do they pay them for their inputs? Do they pay them for their skills? Or do they pay them for their performance? There is an argument in support of each of them and another to counter as well. However over the recent years most of the arguments have been in the favour of performance and skill-based pay.

The factors that have played a role in the shift towards performance-based pay are:

1. Quest for competitive advantage by the companies: Traditionally the pay was determined through government regulation, minimum wage determination, unions, labour contracts etc. the pay and pay-hike determinants considered various factors like seniority, profit, cost of living, manpower supply and demand and union negotiations but seldom considered individual or group performance as a determination factor. But with the opening up of economies and to gain a competitive edge the enterprise's pay systems and pay increases are related to individual or team performance and can be determined by the output.

2. Nature of negotiations, and relations between employer and employee have gradually shifted from collective to more individualistic.

3. Compensation being increasingly used as tool to motivate employees and hence had to be linked to employee's performance. A day after his deal with Patni Computer, iGate CEO Phaneesh Murthy provided a mega treat to his employees by announcing that each iGator would get 125% of their variable pay for the latest quarter.

4. The growing failure of such organizations that have compensated people on the basis of their hours of working rather than on their output. In India most the government organizations are an excellent example of such policies.

In its global executive pay trends 2011, Mercer predicted that the executive salaries in Asia may soon surpass those in the US. The top management salaries in Asia have crossed those in Europe and Mercer anticipates that by

2013, these could even cross US levels. The average pay increase across Asia, except for Japan, was 7 per cent, whereas in Western Europe and North America restrained by debt crisis and weak economy the average pay hike it was barely 2-3 per cent.

The reasons attributed to narrowing of pay-gaps between Asia-Pacific regions are:

(a) Resurgence of equity-linked pay at mid-management levels in smaller organizations that have not yet run into dilution pressures. Although at senior levels, Mercer finds that pay has risen disproportionate to performance, and it feels that going forward this could lead to greater pay governance, increased scrutiny by boards on compensation structures and remuneration benchmarks with more emphasis on performance as criteria for reward.

(b) Leadership Shortages and inflation.

(c) Weak economic conditions prevailing in Western Europe and North America.

Performance-based Pay/ Variable Pay

Performance-based pay is also called as Variable pay. Variable pay is used to recognize and reward employee contribution towards company productivity, profitability, or some other metric deemed important. Variable pay is awarded in a variety of formats including profit sharing, bonuses, holiday bonus, deferred compensation, cash, and goods and services such as a company-paid trip etc.

Types of Performance-based Pays

Performance pays range from individual to team-based and organization-based. Some of the types of performance pays are:

    a) Merit Pays/Increments

    b) Incentives

        i. Individual Incentives

        ii. Gain Sharing

        iii. Profit Sharing

        iv. Employee Stock Options (ESOPs)

Except the first one, the rest are group incentives.

c) Performance bonus.

Merit Pays/Increments

These are the most primitive form of performance pays and come generally in the form of cyclic increments. They have limited effectiveness for some very obvious reasons:

- Most of the times, it becomes a victim to the kind of performance-appraisal mechanism that a company uses.
- Such systems can be subjective and can fall prey to organizational politics.
- Since these increments get merged with the salary, their impact is very limited.
- Over a period of time, such increments may become a norm and hence may change their texture from merit-based to annual norm.

Individual Incentives

Individual incentives are lump sum payments like sales commission, worker incentives etc., based on standard piece-rate system or standard hour system. Individual incentive plans include Piece-work Plans, Management incentive plans, etc.

Piecework Plans: Incentive Piecework is a type of incentive program whereby the employee is paid based on each unit of output. Employees are paid a certain rate per unit times the number of units produced. Piecework incentive programs work because they give the opportunity for the worker to earn over and above their hourly rate. Incentive systems usually have higher productivity levels than measured daywork systems. Generally, piecework systems will generate about 125% productivity levels compared to measured daywork systems that usually generate about 80% of normal productivity. Piecework incentive systems are declining in popularity due to the fact that it requires constant administration as well as industrial engineers and/or industrial engineering technicians to maintain the system.

(**Source:** Industrial Timestudy Institute).

Management Incentive Plan: The Management Incentive Plan generally applies to the senior executives with a significant level of responsibility within the organization. The Incentive Plan contains both an annual and a long-term incentive element. The Incentive Plan, therefore, ensures that a sizeable portion of total remuneration of the executives is dependent on achieving demanding business performance measures aligned with the Business Plan goals and, as a result, provides a strong incentive for the participants to successfully deliver them.

Generally there is a pre-decided formula for calculating such incentives.

1. **Halsey & Rowan System:** Both Halsey and Rowan system reward a worker if he/she finishes his/her work before the standard time. A additional bonus is added and the total incentive is higher.

2. **Barth Variable Sharing System:** Barth Variable Sharing System uses a standard formula to calculate the incentive based on standard hour system.

$$\text{Incentive} = \sqrt{xy} \times a$$

   where, x = standard hours, y = hours used by the worker, and a = wage rate per hour

3. **Taylor's Differential Piece-rate System:** According to Taylor's Differential Piece-rate System, higher than the standard piece-rate is to be applied if the output is equal to or more than the standard output and less than the piece-rate if the output is below the standard.

4. **Merrick Differential Piece-Rate System:** According to Merrick differential piece-rate system, straight piece-rates are paid up to 83% of the output. A bonus is payable on any output more than the same. The bonus however varies depending upon whether the output is at par or above-par of the standard output, the latter being more than the former with a higher differential piece-rate.

Gain-sharing & Profit-sharing

Gain-sharing and profit-sharing are group incentive plans. The former is based on the gains made by the organization in any aspect, which could be in the form of better outputs, sales, or even optimization of inputs, less wastage, less down-time, low incidence of re-works, increased client satisfaction etc. The latter on the other hand is share given to the employees in the profits made by the company.

Gain-sharing is considered to be more holistic by many experts as they feel it leads to all-round growth and development of the company rather than only bottom-line driven growth. The flip-side to gain-sharing however is that many times payments may have to be made even when the profits are low.

Profit-sharing on the other hand is clearly a share in the profits and hence it is easier to convince the employees on the payments made to them. This however could run into problems as it can make people overtly profit-oriented and hence take them away from contributing more than their immediate work. Besides profit-sharing may regard only employees working in revenue-generating centres of the company while others in support and facilitating function may also be making commendable contributions which may go unrecognized.

Employee Stock Options (ESOPs)

> An ESOP is a kind of employee benefit plan, similar in some ways to a profit-sharing plan.

Employee Stock Options or ESOPs are plans that give employees the right to buy specific number of shares of the company at a fixed price within a certain period of time. Many companies use Employee Stock Options Plan (ESOP) to compensate, retain and attract employees. ESOPs are long-term instruments and hence the gain of such options is realized by an employee only when he/she sticks to a company for 4-5 years. ESOPs work well both for the benefit of the company as well as for the employee because of three reasons:

a. The value of ESOPs can be significantly higher than a person's annual income/investible funds. Although such gains depend on the hierarchy however even for other employees, the proportion would increase significantly over a 3-5 year time-frame.

b. ESOP is an investment that does not require cash commitment (from the company) till an employee wants to exercise his options. The appreciation in option value happens even without investing funds or taking market risk.

c. There is no downside risk for this component. If the stock price is below the exercise price the employee can defer his/her exercise and if it is still not high enough he/she can allow the options to lapse without any cash investment.

Experts even say that the best time to grant options is during recession. It works for the company as it does not have to grant too many options. It also works well for the employee, since his downside risk is lower. This will also suit the shareholders as the dilution is lower.

According to N. R. Narayana Murthy of Infosys, the company has given away Rs.50,000 crore (at current stock prices) of stock options to its employees since inception. IBM completing 100 years of its existence in 2011, decided to celebrate the same by announcing $1,000 stock bonus to every employee, a move that reportedly forced other multinational and Indian tech firms to dole out more incentives to check attrition. IBM employs nearly 1,28,000 staff in India. In India, barring the top 40 executives, IBM announced ESOPs for all its employees. IBM employees were offered what is called restrictive stock unit (RSU), an agreement under which the employees will be promised returns on the stocks awarded without actually owning them.

> An agreement under which the employees will be promised returns on the stocks awarded without actually owning them.

At a time when other competitors were preparing to fight the talent war, many saw IBM's move as one to retain and woo new talent. As other tech firms prepare to cope with rising demand for outsourcing, India is fast becoming the battleground to hire the most and retain the best performers. The same year, Bennett, Coleman & Co planned to give stock options to employees in preparation for a potential initial public offering in India in the next two years. In Chennai, the 100-year-old, $3 billion Murugappa Group with 29 companies, some of them unlisted, should have been among the last to experiment with stock options considering that it belongs to an old-world industrial group managed by three generations of family members. But in 2007, the otherwise conservative group chose the ESOP way to new age attract professionals. The group felt a need to adapt quickly as their conventional products like bicycles were being perceived by customers as lifestyle products. The group came up with the Stock Appreciation Rights Scheme (SARS), similar to stock options but involving a cash bonus rather than shares. SARS is based on the valuation of the unlisted company, derived from profitability ratios and the price-to-earnings multiple prevailing in the stock market for the relevant industry.

> SARS is based on the valuation of the unlisted company.

In March 2011 India's leading producer and exporter of aluminium, Nalco became the first public sector company to initiate action for Employee Stock Options (ESOPs), for offering its share to its employees. The ESOPs are planned to be issued to the executives of the company as part of payment of dues to them under Performance Related Payment (PRP), a component of revised pay package. The ESOP-scheme is expected to considerably improve performance and involvement level of the employees in the company.

Tax implications on ESOPs differ from country to country. For India in the year 2009 there was major change in taxation of ESOPs with the same coming under the ambit of FBT (Fringe Benefit Tax) and the onus shifting on the employees to pay the tax. However in case if an employee decides to hold the shares for more than 12 months from the date of exercise, it will be a long term capital asset and the capital gains will be fully exempt from tax. In general capital gains taxes are calculated based on three factors. Buy & Sell Date, Buy & Sell price and holding period.

ESOPs are excellent incentive tool to motivate and retain staff, however it must be remembered that the company should match the objective of granting ESOPs with the compensation objectives of the individual. The objective of ESOPs are long term capital gains, however if the employee's objective is short-term cash gain, then ESOPs shall not be rewarding for the employee. In other words, the company must choose wisely the set of employees who must receive ESOPs. The rest may be granted other form of incentives. The objective of any incentive is to spur performance of the employee and the organization. If the same is not achieved, there is no point in granting such performance-based incentives in the first place.

Performance Bonus

Money is recognized as a motivator by many companies and they use performance bonus as a supplemental payment in addition to the salary to prop-up the performance. In 2010, Indian Railways had given 77 days salary to all its employees in the form of productivity-linked bonus to all its non-gazetted employees. In the year 2011, Indian railways decided to pay 78 days salary as bonus to all its non-gazetted employees. The decision benefited 12.61 lakh non-gazetted Railway employees. The financial implication of payment of 78 days Performance-linked Bonus (PLB) to railway employees has been estimated at Rs 1,098.58 crore. This has been the highest PLB payment ever to be made by the Railways. Payment of PLB to eligible railway employees is made each year before the Dusshera holidays. Performance-linked Bonus (PLB) is based on the productivity indices reflecting the performance of the Railways and its payment is expected to motivate the employees for working towards improving the same in future.

The California Public Employees' Retirement System, the largest U.S. public pension, paid its investment officers $4.4 million in performance bonuses in the year 2010, a 33 percent increase from the previous year. Calpers earned 20.7 percent in the year ending June 30, its best performance in 14 years, as stocks and private-equity holdings rebounded from losses in 2008 and 2009. Bonuses are based on investment performance over a three-year period.

(**Source:** Bloomberg)

Vedanta controlled Bharat Aluminum Company Limited (BALCO) announced an annual bonus for it employees in September 2011, paying about 12% more as compared to last year. The company has only a single slab of bonus and each employee right from company's top executive to the worker received Rs 27,700 as bonus. Decision to this effect was taken after the final round of meeting with the representatives of trade union and company management. In 2010, the employees received INR 24,500 as annual bonus.

The Indian Postal Department in the year 2010 paid 60 Days PLB (Productivity Linked Bonus) to its employees. The maximum ceiling was @ 3500 for Regular Employees; 2500 for GDS; and 1200 for Casual including Temporary Status Casual Labourers.

The Payment of Bonus Act, 1965

The payment of Bonus in India is determined by the Payment of Bonus Act, 1965. The Payment of Bonus Bill having been passed by both the Houses of Parliament received the assent of the President on 25th September, 1965. It came on the Statute Book as The Payment of Bonus Act, 1965. Since then many amendments have been made to this act. As Payment of Bonus (Amendment) Act, 2011, all employees who are getting wages/salary not more than Rs. 10,000 are eligible for bonus. The Act provides for the payment of bonus to persons employed in certain establishments on the basis of profits or on the basis of production or productivity and for matters connected therewith. This Act extends to the whole of India and applies to:

  (a) Every factory; and
  (b) Every other establishment in which twenty or more persons are employed on any day during an accounting year.

The available surplus in respect of any accounting year shall be the gross profits for that year after deducting any amount by way of depreciation, any amount by way of development rebate or investment allowance or development allowance and any direct tax which the employer is liable to pay for the accounting year in respect of his income, profits and gains during that year.

Tata Steel announced in September 2011 that it will give an annual bonus of 18.5% of salary/wages of all its unionized employees for the year 2010-11. Close to 30,155 employees were paid annual bonus, the total payout on account of which was approximately Rs 171 crore. What is fascinating about the Tata Steel example is that they have decided to pay their employees bonus despite the fact that they do not come under the ambit of the Payment of Bonus Act, 1965. A company's press release said it all – "Since all employees of the steel company are drawing salary/wages higher than the limit laid down in the Payment of Bonus Act, 1965, no employee is eligible for bonus under this Act. However, respecting our old traditions, the company is going to pay bonus to all employees in the unionized category."

(**Source:** The Hindustan Times)

That is the true essence of bonus payments. Truly wise companies are not really worried even if they have to pay bonus without being dictated by the Act, although it is undoubtedly like a guide to employers to share the surplus generated.

The flip-side of bonus payments is that many times such payments can be politically motivated rather than being linked closely to productivity. In January 2011, one state government in India announced Pongal bonus for government employees and pensioners, costing the exchequer Rs. 277 crore. All Government servants in 'C' and `D' Groups received bonus equal to 30 days salary with an upper limit of Rs 3,000 and 'A' and `B' category employees a special bonus of Rs. 1,000. Pensioners and family pensioners received Rs. 500 as Pongal gift. Yet again in August 2011, the another state government decided to raised the Durga Puja bonus, that it is granting since 2000-01 financial year, to Rs 2,100 from Rs 1,000 of employees earning up to Rs 20,000 a month and doubled the ex-gratia for pensioners costing the exchequer over Rs 127 crore. How far these bonuses will help raise employee productivity is not ascertained.

Bonus should always help generate more business which could be read in the form increased productivity, top-line or bottom-line growth, new ideas and innovations etc. The additional profits created as a result, should become the funding source of bonus. Any other approach to payment of bonus shall result in drain of organizational resource and shall always be read by employees as entitlements.

Reading Exhibit 1

Performance Pay Hits Peak at India Inc, Writankar Mukherjee, The Economic Times

Indian executive salaries got a shot in the arm as companies showered one of the best performance-linked bonuses to employees this year. The buoyant mood is reflected in almost all the top companies, of which recorded double-digit growth rates in sales and profits in 2010-11. Consequently, some of them doled out more than 100% of the target variable pay, and the sky was the limit for top performers.

Korean electronics major Samsung has given employees variable payout of around 150-250% of the target amount, while competitor LG has given 200-700% of Basic pay as bonus based on performance.

Hindustan Unilever (HUL) made headlines earlier this month after it paid its highest bonus in recent years (between Rs 20 lakh-40 lakh), to managers after a two-year freeze. Pharma major Sanofi Aventis has given 110-128% of the target variable incentive, about 5-6% higher than last year. The Essar group has provided employees with a 100% variable payout, and as much as 125% to top performers, while Schneider Electric has given an average variable payout of around 130%, compared to about 90% last year. Dabur, Godrej Consumer Products and Future Group are also considering hefty payouts. Headhunters say this trend of sizeable payouts is an indication of a more performance-oriented compensation culture coming into India Inc.

Performance Pays

	% of Target Variable Pay
Samsung	150-250%
Sanofi Aventis	110-128%
Schneider Electric	130%
Essar Group	All: 100%
	Top Performance: 125%
MTS	150%
	For mid-level managers
Mahindra Satyam	All: 100%
	Top Performers: 120%

LG employees received 200-700% of basic pay as bonus, Dabur, Godrej Consumer Products, Future Group all considering hefty payouts

(**Source:** The Economic Times, May 31, 2011)

Reading Exhibit 2

Cognizant's compensation performance milestones to its top executives point to strong growth in the year 2012.

Performance Milestones

The company's compensation committee granted the awards (in the table) of performance units to the top five executive officers.

\	TOP FIVE	
Name	Designation	No of performance units
Mr Francisco D'Souza	President and Chief Executive Officer	95,400
Mr Gordon J. Coburn	Chief Financial Officer	44,700
Mr Rajeev Mehta	Chief Operating Officer Global Client Services	37,800
Mr R. Chandrasekaran	President and Managing Director, Global Delivery	30,300
Mr Steven Schwartz	Senior Vice-President General Counsel and Secretary	9,060

The units will be subject to certain performance milestones and continued service requirements. All or a portion of the units shall vest based on the level of achievement of the revenue milestone set forth below:

0 per cent of the units, which are awarded, shall vest up on achievement of 2012 revenue of less than $7,243,000,000

50 per cent on achieving revenue of $7,243,000,000

100 per cent on achieving $7,525,000,000 and

200 per cent on achieving $8,087,500,000.

(*Source:* Business Line, Dec. 1, 2011)

Reading Exhibit 3

Gainsharing or Profit Sharing: The Right Tool for the Right Organization (Robert L. Masternak-2009)

Many people who confuse Profit Sharing and Gainsharing view them as being one in the same. I find that many companies that install a Profit Sharing have selected the wrong tool and quickly become disappointed that they have been unable to foster a change in behaviors and to drive organization performance. The purpose of this chapter is to explain the similarities in Profit Sharing and Gainsharing, their differences, the primary purpose for both system, and why Gainsharing is often the better tool. The chapter begins with a fairy tail about a farmer's well founded intension gone a rare. The story may be familiar to some and may proof to be insightful to others.

Story

Once upon a time there was a farmer in the land of Michigan who held his workers in high regard. He appreciated their dedicated service during the hot and dusty summer days and the cold and dampness of the November corn harvest. He respected their efforts and wished to recognize them for their part in the farm's success. He knew that without them he would not have been able to enjoy the prosperity and pride that he had in his highly successfully farm. He had often thought about ways he could recognize them for their efforts. Yes, it was true that he had the annual harvest feast, but that did not seem to be enough.

He had heard of another successful farmer in an adjacent land who had recently installed a profit sharing plan in order to share the financial gains with his workers. So the farmer went there for a visit and then came home to put together his own, very simple and understandable profit sharing plan. Basically, the farmer calculated his total revenue from a variety of sources, including the sale of grains, livestock, land leasing, and produce sales at the local farmer's market. From his revenue, he subtracted all expenses including: the cost of seed, fertilizer, labor, fuel, attorney fees, insurance, depreciation, etc. His result, he called "the bottom line." Then in turn, he designed a formula to share a portion of the profit pie with his workers. He announced the good news of the newly designed profit sharing plan at his annual year-end feast and handed out bonus checks to the workers equal to 6% of their annual pay. The average check amounted to $1,200, ($20,000 annual compensation x 6%). The workers were delighted with the unexpected bonus and rejoiced in the farmer's generosity.

The farmer explained to his employees that there would be more of the same next year, if the farm continued to prosper. The workers' spirits were high, and they eagerly looked forward to the second plan year.

In year two, the farmer made a strategic decision to plant his entire farm in corn, since the price of corn in that land had skyrocketed to $3.00 per bushel, a record level. The farmer foresaw a great opportunity for increasing production and resulting profits. The farm hands worked especially hard planting, fertilizing, cultivating, and irrigating the corn. As a result of their labors that fall the corn harvest yielded a new record, 200 bushels per acre. The extra irrigation and cultivation had paid off! Unfortunately, other farmers also had decided to place all their land in corn as well. That season's corn production all over the land was at a "bumper year" level. As a result, the selling price plunged to $1.00 per bushel, and the farmer's profits fell to half of the previous years. At the annual harvest feast the farmer passed out the bonus checks, this time only 3% of compensation. His people were greatly disappointed, but after all, some money was better than nothing. The workers forgave the farmer and looked forward to a better third year.

In year three, the farmer made several strategic business decisions. He acquired more land and decided to boost productivity by investing in a new John Deere tractor. He bought a new truck as well. The tractor was the largest and newest on the market, and he thought it would most likely lead to higher land productivity. The truck was a "4 by 4" with a leather interior and all the added accessories. He knew that the truck was excessive, but after all, he had worked so hard all those years and knew the fancy truck was something he very much deserved. He rejoiced when the bank offered an attractive low interest rate on three loans for the land, tractor, and truck. As luck would have it, however, the new loans had several strings attached, including a variable rate and prepayment penalties. In addition more workers needed to be hired to help with the cultivation and harvest that year, and the spring planting had been especially hectic.

The old workers enjoyed driving the beautiful, new tractor and managed to do some added cultivation. The new workers weren't as nearly impressed, since they had never once experienced the discomfort and excessive noise of the older, retired model.

By the end of that fateful year, corn production doubled the previous year's level. The workers grew excited because they had never seen so much corn. Unfortunately, during the course of the year interest rates had taken a dramatic turn. The truck and tractor loan had initially been at only 2%, but during that year the loans soared to 12%. The new variable rate on the land was so excessive that the farmer had to refinance to a fixed rate, resulting in sizable prepayment penalties and costly refinancing charges. He talked to the workers about some of these problems, but they weren't that interested. Their focus was on better corn yield, cultivation, and irritation.

By the end of that disastrous year, profitability had tumbled to "break-even." The farmer's investments had had a devastating effect! At the annual harvest feast, the workers eagerly looked forward to the announcement of the bonus results, but the farmer said, "Woe is me; I have bad news." Instead of checks, the farmer handed out a copy of the dismal financial results. All of the workers were extremely disappointed. The new workers were especially unhappy. They had been told so many good things about the farm from the human resources manager when they had first been hired. All the workers bitterly complained about the farmer's extravagant purchases and poor financial decisions. They were especially unhappy when they saw the farmer driving his new fancy truck. Employees claimed they had no control over the farmer's shortsighted decisions. Attitudes and level of trust declined. Some workers even became bitter and resentful, grumbling and plotting against their hapless employer.

The Moral of the Story

There are many lessons to learn from the farmer's story. The farmer's intentions were very noble, but the results lead to an undesirable outcome. The farmer failed to thoroughly consider what he was trying to accomplish by installing a profit sharing plan. What was the farmer's purpose for the plan? What did he want to accomplish? Was the objective to drive operating performance (yield) or to help instill in the workers the concept of "common-fate?" Was he primarily interested in providing a monetary reward to motivate employees in their efforts, or was he more interested in providing a benefit to recognize loyalty and service. Also, the farmer failed to consider the appropriate rewards system for the culture, growth, and demographics of his workforce. The farm had grown considerably, adding a number of new workers. Unfortunately, the farm had gotten so large that the farmer didn't even have the opportunity to meet many of them. Perhaps, he should have talked to more than one neighboring farmer before he jumped into profit sharing. He had heard about a few farmers in other counties who had Gainsharing plans for their workers. However, he didn't take the time to investigate the Gainsharing concept, thinking that profit sharing was basically the same. Employees have an opportunity to earn a financial reward under both approaches. However, the farmer didn't recognize that that was where the similarity ends. If he had researched the history and evolution of both approaches and their intended propose, he might have avoided his ill-fated good intentions.

Profit Sharing

History

Profit sharing certainly is not a new concept. One of the first documented profit sharing plans in the United States was introduced in 1794 at New Geneva, PA, Glass Works. At the time the company was recognized by the Secretary of the Treasury under Presidents Jefferson and Madison as applying "the nation's fundamental democratic principles to an industrial operation. However, profit sharing arrangements were far from prevalent until the end of the Civil War. As America became more industrialized, profit sharing begin to grow through the 1920's. Profit Sharing companies held the belief that sharing profits would unite workers and management in the pursuit of the same common goal. In addition, profit sharing was offered as a means to discourage unionization, but after the Depression through the 1930's many of these profit sharing plans were discontinued.

After World War II there was a rebirth of profit sharing. Most of these plans were deferred compensation plans driven by the desire to avoid a tax on excess income that had been imposed during the war. In other words, companies would place a portion of the profits aside to fund employee retirement plans. This was especially popular among private, "family" owned companies that saw employees as an extended family. The concept was also one of "common fate." In good times a family would be able to share more, in the bad times, less. Employees often spent their entire working career with the same company. There was mutual loyalty on both the employer's and employees' behalf.

In the late 1980's some companies attempted to deviate from the deferred compensation nature of Profit Sharing. In other words, Profit Sharing was viewed as incentive compensation rather than a benefit plan. One of the best documented examples was at Dupont's fibers division which employed approximately 20,000 people. The plan's designers intended to develop a "program to reward employee contributions, in the belief that sharing the rewards as well as the risks of the division's financial performance would help the business succeed in the market place." The complex arrangement focused on "world-wide after-tax operating income and established a "Compensation Target Rate" and a "Variable Element Rate."

Basically, DuPont's new pay concept was that employees would place a portion of their normal base compensation at risk. In return employees had the opportunity to more than offset the "at-risk" monies through a year-end bonus. On the other hand, if profitability was significantly below targeted levels employees would loss the monies "at-risk." The plan could yield a bonus of up to 12 % of salary in an exceptional year. In a bad year an employee could loss as much as 6% of salary. The new "pay-at-risk" system would enable the company to better manage costs by moving to more of an "ability to pay" approach. In addition, the thinking was there would be less work force pressure for base salary adjustments. The theory was that since employees would be sharing in the profits, they would feel and act more like stakeholders. The result would lead to changes in behaviors and work habits, resulting in even more profits.

When the plan was rolled out in 1989, DuPont employees saw a modest bonus after the first year. However, the second year saw rapidly declining profitability. Profits had declined due to a number of unforeseen business conditions, two of which were the rapid increase in raw material prices and the erosion in the final product's selling price. Profits were "squeezed." As a result employees lost the portion of their base pay that was placed at-risk. The employee loss represented approximately 4% of compensation. DuPont experienced a significant rise in employee discontent. Some felt that they were "hoodwinked." A company executive commented, "Employees were not ready for such a program. Employees felt it was fine when they were getting money back, but thought it was not fair when no bonus was paid." As a result the program was quickly abandoned.

The flaw in the "pay-at-risk form of profit sharing" was that employees were asked to put a portion of their pay in jeopardy over something they had little or no control, profitability. In addition DuPont is a large, world-wide organization. Obviously, the sense of employee ownership and identity toward a very large corporation often is found to be less than in a small family-owned company. People have more difficulty trusting the financial data. Clearly most DuPont employees didn't like putting their base pay at "risk" in exchange for the opportunity to share in the profits. Many would say they "preferred to lose money at the casino; at least they would have had some fun and excitement in doing so."

In more recent times, "cash," profit sharing plans have been installed where no "pay-at-risk" is involved. These plans are designed to include all employees including hourly and salaried, non-exempt employees, not just executives and managers. In other words, all employees have an opportunity to share in the profit pie by having an opportunity to receive a year-end cash bonus.

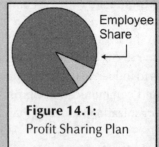

Figure 14.1: Profit Sharing Plan

When profits are up, "I get more." If profits are down, there's no consequence. Companies that install these plans hope to enable employees to share in the organization's success, to motivate workers to improve profits, and in turn to act in the best interest of the company.

Unfortunately many companies that have a "cash" profit sharing plan find that workers view the system as an entitlement. People are happy when they get a bonus and are upset when they don't. Employees feel that when they receive a profit bonus they "earned it." When they don't, "it's the company's fault." In lean years, the employee response is too often complaining, whining, and mistrust in the company.

What would the farmer have learnt from these experiences?: The clear and simple issues are that for most organizations Profit Sharing plans provide very little or no "line-of-sight" in terms of what employees do and what they are paid. The general employee population has little understanding of how they directly impact a broad financial measure of profitability. Even those who have an understanding of the financial data find their efforts insignificant in relationship to key management decisions and external market conditions. To make matters worse, some may feel that the company may manipulate the numbers in order to take advantage of tax regulations or influence the investment community. These feelings are further exaggerated in large multi-location organizations where employees are distanced from top management. Also these multi-site organizations may calculate profit company-wide rather than on a location-by-location basis.

So should the farmer further consider Profit Sharing? It depends on the objective. If the focus is to share the organization's success and to reinforce a sense of ownership, then profit sharing might be the appropriate answer. However, the farmer needs to clearly understand the result will most likely be in terms of impacting employee attitudes rather than driving behaviors. This is especially true in organizations that have an absence of a high degree of employee involvement.

If Profit Sharing is the route, should it be a compensation system or should it be designed to be used as a benefit plan, a method to help finance employee retirement years? In most cases history has demonstrated that the farmer may be better served to incorporate Profit Sharing into a retirement scheme. In doing so, employees would see their retirement security grow in tune with the company's growth and prosperity. In other words, both employee and employer would share in a "common-fate." This would certainly satisfy the objective of sharing in the organization's success. The plan would give employees more of a long term outlook and strengthen the sense of identity and ownership. On the other hand, if the farmer's objective is to influence not only attitudes but to change behaviors, in terms of teamwork, involvement, and communications, profit sharing most likely will be the wrong answer, particularly if the organization has more than a handful of employees.

Gainsharing

History

Today many people view Gainsharing strictly as a bonus or group incentive plan. However, it is much more than a compensation plan. It helps drive a change in the culture. Employees feel that they are more valued and respected. As a result, people develop a higher sense of teamwork, ownership, and identity. People are more engaged which leads to a higher level of performance. There are four relatively simple principles for understanding why Gainsharing works. All four are incorporated in the strategy used to install and maintain a successful plan. The four principles address equity, identity, involvement, and commitment. The four principles are interrelated and mutually reinforcing.

In order to fully understand the concept, one must examine its roots. The Gainsharing concept dates back to the 1930's when a labor leader, Joe Scanlon, preached that "the worker" had much more to offer than a pair of hands. The premise was that the person closest to the problem often has the best and simplest solution. Moreover, if the worker is involved in the solution, most likely he or she will make the solution work. Scanlon is often credited for developing a system that promotes involvement in the workplace through employee ideas and suggestions.

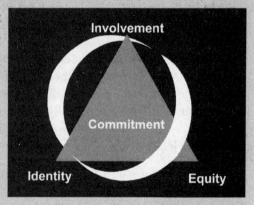

Figure 14.2: Gainsharing

Basically, employee teams are formed to solicit and review suggestions from other members of the workforce. The teams are permanent groups that meet on a regular basis to discuss ideas and suggestions. The teams are given limited spending authority to approve and implement suggestions. Suggestions that are approved by a team, but are beyond their spending authority, are advanced to a higher level in the organization for final approval.

The involvement structure not only is intended to encourage participation but also is meant to enhance two-way communications regarding company goals and objectives. The idea system helps foster respect and cooperation. In other words, if employees feel their ideas are listened to, are given prompt feedback, and see their ideas promptly implemented, they will feel that they are respected.

Unlike a traditional suggestion system, Scanlon's system does not provide individual monetary rewards for improvement ideas. The thinking is that the review, investigation, and implementation of employee's ideas are truly a collaborative effort. Suggestion systems that pay individual awards based on the projected savings from the idea promote behaviors in which employees may conceal their improvement suggestions rather than freely share and collaborate with others to advance the idea. Originally, the Scanlon approach didn't have

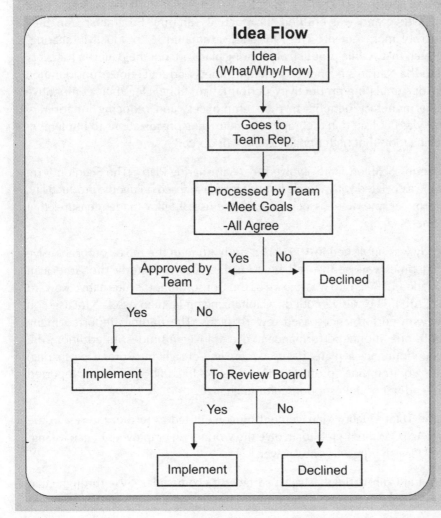

Figure 14.3: Idea System

an employee bonus component. However, a few years after the plan's initial implementation, Scanlon devised an organization-wide bonus formula that provided a more frequent and line-of-sight measurement system than profit sharing. The idea system and other improvement efforts drove the performance measures, and in turn gains (savings) generated through the measurement formula are shared with everyone in the organization. Basically the Scanlon philosophy says, "As we work together to improve the operations, everyone shares financially in the savings."

The Scanlon Plan became known as "a frontier in labor-management cooperation." Scanlon went on to work at MIT to help other labor leaders and managers. As a result the Scanlon message gradually began to spread. In the 1950's Scanlon developed a group of disciples including Frederick Lesieur and Carl Frost. As companies moved forward with the concept, interest in academic and government circles grew. One of the earlier studies was done by the General Accounting Office and was entitled 'Productivity Sharing Programs; Can they Contribute to Productivity Improvement?' The 1981 study examined 36 "productivity sharing" firms. The GAO reported that "while productivity sharing plans are not the panacea for every firm in the solution to the Nation's economic problems, they warrant serious consideration by firms as a means of stimulating productivity performance, enhancing their competitive advantage, increasing monetary benefits to their employees, and reducing inflationary pressure." The report was published in the hope of encouraging organizations to implement performance-enhancing tools that better engaged the workforce.

As time passed, the term "Scanlon Plan" evolved to "Gainsharing Plan". The Scanlon term mistakenly had become associated with a single bonus formula focused on people productivity. The "Gainsharing" term became more associated with the use of tailor-made measures that still focused on the line-of-sight.

Another hallmark study was published in 1992. The study, (one of the most comprehensive studies up until that time) was sponsored by WorldatWork (Formerly the American Compensation Association). The group was known as the Consortiums for Alternative Reward Strategies Research (CARS). The study entitled, "Capitalizing on Human Assets," focused on 2,200 organizations with performance-based reward plans. The findings reported many positive results in both operational performance and employee attitudes. In addition, the study reported better performance in plans that used more line-of-sight measures (Gainsharing) than plans using only "a bottom-line" profit-sharing measure. In addition the study reported that successful plans lead rather than support cultural change.

In the mid-1990's, the Total Quality Management movement led to further interest in the Gainsharing concept. As TQM attempted to involve the workforce, employees began asking; "What's in it for me?" Gainsharing was one answer.

More recently, interest in Gainsharing has again surfaced as companies cycle through Lean Manufacturing and Six/Sigma initiates. An important point is that all of these improvement initiatives are nothing more than tools to better engage the workforce and to promote involvement. Simply put, these tools are an extension to what Scanlon had preached in the 1930's.

Unfortunately, many of today's companies that study Gainsharing see the concept as an incentive, thinking that if you simply put a carrot in front of people, you will put "fire in their belly." These organizations focus on the bonus/incentive side of Gainsharing, and may lack the understanding and appreciation of the cultural and employee involvement origins of the concept. They believe that a bonus system lacking employee involvement, will somehow miraculously lead to a positive result. The problem is that they are putting the cart in front of the horse, the incentive in front of the involvement.

Line-of-Sight & Measurement

After focusing on the cultural and employee involvement heritage of Gainsharing it is appropriate to turn to the bonus/incentive side. Basically, to provide Gainsharing's incentive an organization measures performance through a pre-determined formula which, in turn, shares the savings with all employees. The organization's actual performance is compared to baseline performance (often a historical standard) to determine the amount of the gain. The gains and resulting payouts are self-funded based on savings generated by the measurement formula. Some plans may utilize broad financial measures that closely resemble profit sharing. However, it is more common to find Gainsharing companies that utilize more narrow operational measures such as productivity, quality, customer service, on-time delivery, and spending. Typically gainsharing plans have multiple measures. In order for a gain to occur, the performance pie must improve.

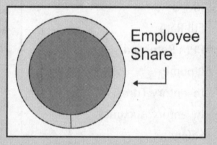

Figure 14.4:
Detamining Amount of Gain

As the pie expands, the greater the improvement (gain), and the more financial benefit for the company and employees. The key point is that there must be an improvement before any sharing occurs. A critical point is that since gains are typically measured in relationship to a historical baseline, employees and the organization must change in order to generate a gain.

A multi-measure system is commonly used which is referred to as a "family of measures" approach. Basically the "family of measures" approach uses 3 to 6 drivers of performance. Examples of measures are listed below.

Examples of Operational Measures
Productivity
Equipment efficiency
Cycle time
Yield
Shrinkage
Scrap
Rework
Spending
On-time Shipments
RMAs
Fill Rate
PPM Returned
Uptime
Inventory Turns
Inventory Accuracy
Safety
Schedule Attainment
Energy Usage
Customer Complaints
Service Satisfaction
Spending
Credits
Collections

The drivers are measured, and gains and losses are calculated for each respective measure. The gains and losses are shared for each measure and then aggregated into an employee distribution pool.

It's very important to point out that employees do not have 100% control of any measure. No matter what the measure: productivity, cycle time, yield, spending, or on time delivery, there are always outside factors that will influence the result. The point is that employees have more control of operational measures than profitability.

However, unlike Profit Sharing and depending on the Gainsharing plan's design, employee payouts can potential occur even during periods of profitability decline. Companies with this type of Gainsharing model argue that even though profits may be down, profits would have further declined if not for the savings generated from the gainsharing measures. In this example the company is sharing "savings" and not necessarily "profits."

Family of Measures

Another line-of-sight feature of Gainsharing relates to employee eligibility. All employees at a site are generally included in the plan, including hourly, salaried, and managers. The objective is to improve the line of sight by having the plan applied to employees "housed under the same roof."

On the other hand, a Profit Sharing plan may exclude lower level or hourly employees, or profit bonuses may be paid out on a hierarchical basis. In other words, the bonus payout percentage is reduced as the Profit Sharing cascades down the organization. The end result could divide the workforce and create feelings of inequity rather than build teamwork and the sense of unity. On the other hand, Gainsharing plans are designed to distribute gains based on an equal percentage of pay or cents per hour worked.

Another Gainsharing line-of-sight enhancement is that Gainsharing is always paid in the form of a cash bonus. Gainsharing's intent is to be based on the "pay-for-performance" concept as compared to a "benefit/deferred compensation plan." In addition the frequency for possible

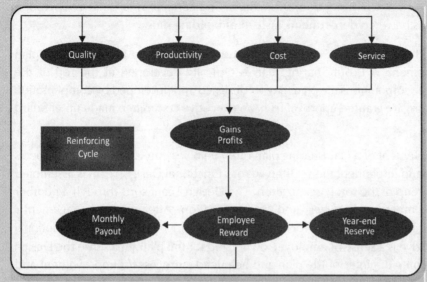

Figure 14.5: Housed Under the Same Roof Plan

payout is greater for Gainsharing than Profit Sharing. The payout of Profit Sharing plans is typically an annual arrangement.

On the other hand, Gainsharing typically has the potential for a monthly or quarterly payout opportunity. A gain and resulting payout is best described as a score rather than a bonus. Since everyone in the organization is typically included, the score is a "team score" as compared to an individual one. The score helps give a common focus for employees on measures they can influence and control. Therefore, Gainsharing works best in work environments that require collaboration between individuals, work groups, and departments.

Another important feature regarding Gainsharing is that typically a portion of the employees share is placed in a year-end reserve account that is paid to all the eligible participants at the end of each plan year. In periods of deficit performance, the employees' share of the loss is deducted from the annual reserve account. In other words, employees will see consequences for worse performance and longer-term thinking is reinforced. If at the end of the plan year the reserve is negative, a company will typically absorb the loss and start the next plan year at zero. The reserve concept helps further develop a sense of employee identity and ownership to the organization. For example, if a company measured scrap and shared 50% of the gain and 50% of the loss (through the reserve) in a sense employees would own 50% of the financial value of the scrap. Obviously, the sense of ownership would drive many new behaviors.

Unlike Profit Sharing in multi-site operations, Gainsharing is typically site specific. The measures and resulting gains are specific to the facility rather than gains being aggregated from multiple locations and in turn distributed across the organization. Again the concept is to increase controllability and the line-of sight. On the other hand, unlike group incentives, Gainsharing typically measures across department/units/functions. The concept is to build cooperation and communications between departments instead of building silos.

Another distinction between Profit Sharing and Gainsharing relates to the method of plan design and development. A Profit Sharing plan is typically developed at the top of the organization. In larger corporations the plan may be designed and developed by compensation executives who in turn are granted approval from an executive committee made up of board members.

However, the development of a Gainsharing plan often involves employees in many aspects of the plan's design and implementation. Often a cross-functional Design Team is assembled that mirrors the makeup of the total organization. The Design Team sorts through a number of issues related to measures, policies, and communication. After upper management's approval, the Design Team is responsible for conducting all employee kick-off and promotional meetings. The objective is a sense of employee ownership for the plan. In a sense the Design Team members become disciples of the plan and help lead a process for improvement and change.

So should the farmer consider installing a Gainsharing plan rather than profit sharing? Again, the same question must be asked. What is the objective? If the farmer's objective is to drive organizational change by influencing attitudes and behaviors, then Gainsharing may be the right answer. However, the farmer needs to have the horse in front of the cart. He needs to understand that Gainsharing is an employee "involvement system with teeth." Simply instituting some type of bonus formula is not enough. A second question; "Should the farmer consider a broad financial measure of performance or more narrow operational measures?" All other things being equal, the use of more narrow, "line-of-sight" measures will more likely yield significant changes in behaviors which in turn generate positive results. The use of a broad financial based measure is much more dependent on the level of employee involvement in the organization at the time of the plan's implementation. In other words, "How open is the company's communication? How knowledgeable are employees about the business conditions? What is the level of trust? How much baggage is the organization carrying from its past? A Gainsharing plan that uses a broad financial measure such as profitability, EBIT, or ROI may be a success if the organization can answer "yes" to the following questions:

➢ Is there a high level of company commitment to the concept of sharing?

➢ Are employees afforded regular training both in terms of skills and individual development?

➢ Is communication ongoing?

➢ Are the financial results openly shared?

➢ Does the company practice open book management?

> Are managers willing to admit mistakes?
> Is the workforce highly engaged?
> Are people at all levels involved in some decision making?
> Do employees have a strong understanding of how they influence profitability?
> Do people identity with the business?
> Does the company demonstrate loyalty to the workforce?
> Do employees view themselves as stakeholders?

If the answers are "yes", then measuring and sharing profits may work. If not, then it's best to have a plan that focuses on operational more "line-of-site" measures. Otherwise, the organization will find itself in the same position as the generous, but disappointed farmer.

	Gain Sharing	*Profit Sharing*
Purpose	To drive performance of an organization by promoting awareness, alignment, teamwork, communication and involvement.	To share the financial success of the total organization and encourage employee identity with company success.
Application	The plan commonly applies to a single facility, site, or stand-alone organization.	The plan typically applies organization-wide; companies with multiple sites typically measure organization-wide profitability rather than the performance of a single site.
Measurement	Payout is based on operational measures (productivity, quality, spending, service), measures that improve the line of site in terms of what employees do and how they are compensated.	Payout is based on a broad financial of the measure organization's profitability.

Table 14.1: Gain Sharing vs. Profit Sharing

Funding	Gains and resulting payouts are self-funded based on savings generated by improved performance.	Payouts are funded through company profits.
Payment Target	Payouts are made only when performance has improved over a historical standard or target.	Payouts are typically made when there are profits; performance doesn't necessary have to show an improvement.
Employee Eligibility	Typically all employees at a site are eligible for plan payments.	Some employee groups may be excluded, such as hourly or union employees.
Payout Frequency	Payout is often monthly or quarterly. Many plans have a year-end reserve fund to account for deficit periods.	Payout is typically annual.
Form of Payment	Payment is cash rather than deferred compensation. Many organizations pay via separate check to increase visibility.	Historically profit plans were primarily deferred compensation plans; organization used profit sharing as a pensionplan. Today we see many more cash plans.
Method of Distribution	Typically employees receive the same % payout or cents per hour bonus.	The bonus may be a larger % of compensation for higher-level employees. The % bonus may be less for lower level employees.
Plan Design & Development	Employees often are involved with the design and implementation process.	There is no employee involvement in the design process.

Communi-cation	A supporting employee involvement and communication system is an integral element of Gainsharing and helps drive improvement initiatives.	Since there is little linkage between what employees do, and the bonus, there is an absence of accompanying employee involvement initiatives.
Pay for Performance Plan versus Entitlement	Gains are generated only by improved performance over a predetermined base level of performance. Therefore, Gainsharing is viewed as a pay-for-performance initiative.	Profit sharing often is viewed as a entitlement or employee benefit.
Impact on Behaviors	Gainsharing reinforces behaviors that promote improved performance. Used as a tool to drive cultural and organization change.	Little impact on behaviors since employees have difficulty linking what they do and their bonus. Many variables outside of the typical employees control determine profitability and the bonus amount.
Impact on Attitudes	Heightens the level of employee awareness, helps develop the feeling of self worth, builds a sense of ownership, and identity to the organization.	Influences the sense of employee identity to the organization, particularly for smaller organizations.

(***Source of Reading Exhibit:*** by Robert L. Masternak (2009), Published with permission of Masternak & Associates, Ohio www.masternak.com)

Essay Questions

1. Explain the concept of performance based-compensation. What are the factors that have caused a shift towards performance-based compensation?

2. Explain-
   a) Merit pays/ Increments;
   b) Individual Incentives.

3. Differentiate between Gain-sharing and Profit sharing.

4. What are Employee Stock Options or ESOPs? Why are they offered? Do they work?

5. Discuss the Bonus Plan, in light of the Payment of Bonus Act, 1965. Provide Examples. Do bonus payments work?

Application Questions

1. Go to http://www.tata.com/company/Articles/inside.aspx?artid=Z0JoHe2e4gw= and study the Performance Ethic Plan' (PEP) of Tata Steel, recommended by management consultants McKinsey & Company. What is PEP, what were its main objectives and why was this required?

2. Explore:
   a) http://articles.timesofindia.indiatimes.com/2012-01-10/job-trends/30610921_1_chief-executive-tim-cook-apple-ceo-steve-jobs
   b) http://money.cnn.com/galleries/2011/technology/1111 gallery.top_paid_tech_executives/index.html
   c) http://www.minyanville.com/dailyfeed/2012/01/10/why-tim-cook-did-not Study the kind of stock-options or bonuses offered to the CEOs. How far do you think the same is justified?

Bibliography

Brencic, V., & Norris, J. B. (2010). On-The-Job Tasks and Performance Pay: A Vacancy-Level Analysis. *Industrial & Labor Relations Review, 63* (3), 511-544.

Coates, E. M. (1991). Profit Sharing Today: Plans and Provisions. *Monthly Labor Review.*

Executive pay packets in Asia could soon overtake those in US: Mercer. (n.d.). Retrieved from Business Line: http://www.thehindubusinessline.com/industry-and-economy/article2526070.ece

Industrial timestudy institute. (n.d.). Retrieved from Incentive Piecework Standard: http://industrialtimestudy.com/incentive.html

Larkin, I., Pierce, L., & Gino, F. (2010). The Psychological Costs of Pay-for-Performance: Implications for the Strategic Compensation of Employees. *Working Papers — Harvard Business School Division of Research*, 1-44.

Lesieur, F. G. (1958). The Scanlon Plan A Frontier in Labor-Management Cooperation, Cambridge: *The MIT Press*.

Management Incentive plan statement. (n.d.). Retrieved from http://www.networkrail.co.uk/browse % 20 documents regulatory%20 documentsregulatory%20compliance%20and %20reporting management%20incentive%20plan%20statement/mip%20statement%2007-08.pdf

Masternak, R. L. (1991). Gainsharing Programs at Two Fortune 500 Facilities: Why One Worked Better. *National Productivity Review.*

Masternak, R. L. (2003). Gainsharing: A Team-Based Approach to Drive Organizational Change. Scottsdale. *WorldatWork*.

Masternak, R. L., & Michael, C. A. (2005). Gainsharing and Lean Six Sigma – Perfect Together. *WorldatWork Journal*.

Masternal, R. L. (1997). How to Make Gainsharing Successful: The Collective Experience of 17 Facilities. *Compensation & Benefits Review.*

Mcadams, J. L., & Hawk, E. L. (1992). Capitalizing on Human Assets: The Bench Mark Study, Scottsdale: ACA.

Menguc, B., & Barker, A. T. (2003). The Performance Effects of Outcome-based Incentive Pay Plans on Sales Organizations: A Contextual Analysis; *Journal of Personal Selling & Sales Management, 23* (4), 341-358.

Mitlacher, L. W., & Paul, C. (2009). Performance-based Pay Systems for Teams: Explaining the Design of Performance-based Pay Systems for Teams from an Expanded Agency Theory Perspective. *International Journal of Business Performance Management, 11* (3).

Monks, M. (2011). Performance-based Pay, without Fear of Defection. *American Banke, 176* (48), 1-2.

Murthy, P. (2011, January). *i Gate employees to get 125% of variable pay*. Retrieved from The Economic Times: http://articles.economictimes.indiatimes.com/2011-01-12/news/28425469_1_igate-global-solutions-ceo-phaneesh-murthy

O'Donnell, M. (1998). Creating a Performance Culture? Performance-based Pay in the Australian Public Service. *Australian Journal of Public Administration, 57* (3), 28.

Risher, H., & Smallwood, A. (2009). Performance-based Pay at NGA. *Public Manager, 38* (2), 25-29.

Rusaw, C. (2009). Professionalism under the "Performance-based Pay" Reform: A Critical Assessment and Alternative Development Model. *Public Personnel Management, 38* (4), 35-54.

Sautter, K. M., Bokhour, B. G., White, B., Young, G. J., Burgess Jr, J. F., Berlowitz, D., et al. (2007). The Early Experience of a Hospital-based Pay-for-Performance Program; Vol. 5. *Journal of Healthcare Management, 52* (2).

Sturman, M. C., Trevor, C. O., Boudreau, J. W., & Gerhart, B. (2003). Is it Worth it to Win the Talent War? Evaluating the Utility of Performance-based Pay. *Personnel Psychology, 56* (4), 997-1035.

Tepp, M., & Poomann, M. (2006). Impact of Pay-for-Performance on Work Motivation of Sales Personnel: A Case of Information Media Firms. *Working Papers in Economics, 19* (144), 77-88.

Walker, J. (2010). The Use of Performance-based Remuneration: High versus Low-growth Firms. *Australian Accounting Review, 20* (3), 256-264.

Chapter 15

Workplace Health & Safety

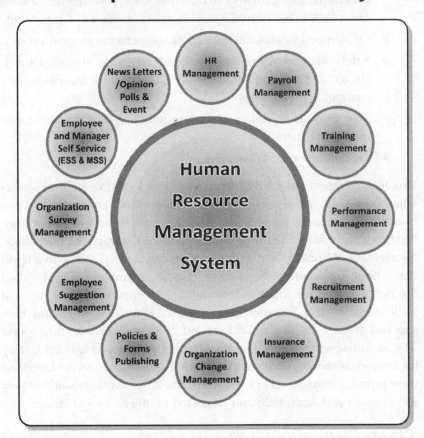

Outline

Introduction
Accidents/Industrial Disasters
The Ten Worst Worldwide Mining Disasters
Four Levels of Safety Interventions
Legal Angle
Some other Acts
Workplace Violence
Growing Menace
Essay Questions
Application Questions
Bibliography

Key Terms

Factories Act, 1948
Growing Menace

Industrial Disaster
OSHA, 1970

Women's Compensation Act, 1923
Workplace Violence

Introduction

Workplace health and safety is one of the prime issues concerning the state of mental, physical and emotional well-being of the employees. The issues concerning workplace health and safety are:

- General hygiene, cleanliness, sanitation, proper ventilation of the workplaces, free of Allergens – causes of allergic reactions, biological agents like bacteria, virus, parasites and fungi, carcinogens – cancer causing agents, mineral dusts causing cancers and respiratory disease, vegetable dusts causing asthma, allergic reactions and cancers, toxic chemicals and agents causing neurological and reproductive disorders, cancers and poisoning.
- Uncramped workplaces with adequate personal space & privacy.
- Safety of workplaces against threats like fire, electrical short-circuit, and training employees of safety aspects and emergency routines and responses.
- Safe workplaces, adequate safety policy against accidents and industrial disasters.
- Prevention of workplace violence.

Usually such aspects are hard to detect because it looks like regular business when viewed from a distance. Recently when a CNN crew travelled to a brick kiln in Ponneri, Tamil Nadu — it was hard to believe it was once buzzing with activity. The firing chamber was cold, storage chambers dark. Neatly stacked bricks glistened in the harsh sun. Earlier, acting on a tipoff that a brick kiln used bonded labour, a local government official, called the police and representatives from a human rights group, International Justice Mission (IJM). Together, they raided the kiln. What they found there shocked them. Expecting to find around 200 people inside, they found 514, including women and children. They had been working at the factory for around six months under a brutal, oppressive regime. All the labourers were from the north, most of them from Orissa. The workers said that they were beaten with rods, belts and subjected to other forms of abuse.

Accidents/Industrial Disasters

Most accidents and industrial disasters happen due to four main reasons:

1. Managerial: The managerial reasons for such accidents include lack of top management commitment to safety, lack of safety guidelines & policy,

Lack of awareness on safety by the management, lack of safety drills and training educating employees on such issues, lack of attention on basic workplace environment etc.

2. Technical: At times accidents may be because of technical glitches or because of use of old, outdated technology. Periodic checks and audit may prevent such incidents.

3. Behavioural: 'The Ostrich's Phenomena' is very common amongst workers, supervisors and managers, alike. The ostrich digs its head deep into the sand and presume that no one is looking at it and assumes that no ones can see it as well. The truth lies somewhere between theses presumptions and assumptions. Similarly tendency to overlook warning signals, procrastination of safety aspects to be addressed at the workplace, many times becomes a reason for accidents.

4. Ethical: Cost-cutting at the cost of safety is rampant at some workplaces, heavily compromising with the health and safety of the employees as well as of the public-in-general.

Some of the Worst Industrial Accidents & Disasters

March 10, 1906: Courrières Mine Disaster in Courrières, France

A dust explosion, the cause of which is not known with certainty, devastated a coal mine operated by the Compagnie des mines de houille de Courrières (founded during 1852) killing 1,099 workers, including children, in the worst mine accident ever in Europe.

1932-1968 Minamata Disaster

In May 1956, four patients from the city of Minamata on the west coast of the southern Japanese island of Kyushu were admitted to hospital with the same severe and baffling symptoms. They suffered from very high fever, convulsions, psychosis, loss of consciousness, coma, and finally death. Soon afterwards, 13 other patients from fishing villages near Minamata suffered the same symptoms and also died. As time went on, more and more people became sick and many died. Doctors were puzzled by the strange symptoms and terribly alarmed. It was finally determined that the cause was mercury poisoning. Also at that time, cats began to exhibit bizarre behavior that sometimes resulted in their falling into the sea and dying, in what residents referred to as *cat suicides*.

The Chisso Corporation, a fertilizer and later petrochemical company, was found responsible for polluting the bay for 37 years. Mercury was in the waste product dumped into Minamata Bay on a massive scale by a chemical plant. The mercury contaminated fish living in Minamata Bay. People ate the fish, were themselves contaminated, and became ill. It is estimated that over 3,000 people suffered various deformities, severe mercury poisoning symptoms or death from what became known as Minamata disease. The local flora and fauna also got severely affected. The people who survived faced social rejection for many believed that the disease was contagious.

Bhopal Gas Tragedy, 1984

One of the largest industrial disasters in India, on record. A runaway reaction in a tank containing poisonous methyl isocyanate caused the pressure relief system to vent large amounts to the atmosphere at a Union Carbide plant. Estimated 20,000 people perished in the accident. The disaster caused the region's human and animal populations severe health problems till date.

Chernobyl Disaster 1986

Reactor four of the Chernobyl Nuclear Power Plant in Ukraine suffered a catastrophic power increase, leading to explosions in its core. The accident occurred during an experiment scheduled to test a potential safety emergency core cooling feature, which took place during the normal shutdown procedure. The catastrophic accident was caused by gross violations of operating rules and regulations. The personnel disconnected a series of technical protection systems and breached the most important operational safety provisions for conducting a technical exercise. The operator error was probably due to their lack of knowledge, as well as lack of experience and training. At the time of the accident the reactor was being operated with many key safety systems turned off. The ensuing steam explosion and fire killed up to 50 people with estimates that there may be between 4,000 and several hundred thousand additional cancer deaths over time. For the next 150 years, areas around Chernobyl have been declared as unfit for inhabitation and comes under the Chernobyl Exclusion Zone. The Chernobyl Exclusion Zone, covering portions of Belarus and Ukraine surrounding Prypiat, remains poisoned and mostly uninhabited. Prypiat itself was totally evacuated and remains as a ghost town.

Kader Toy Factory Fire in Thailand, May 10, 1993

A fire started in a poorly built factory in Thailand. Exit doors were locked and the stairwell collapsed. An estimated 188 workers were killed, mostly most of them young women from impoverished rural families, died in the blaze. Another 469 were injured; many seriously and permanently, after they were forced to leap from second, third and fourth floors of the buildings to avoid being burnt to death.

'Hundreds of workers were packed into each of the three buildings that collapsed. There were no fire extinguishers, no alarms, no sprinkler systems and the elevated walkways between the buildings were either locked or used as storage areas. The buildings themselves were death traps, constructed from un-insulated steel girders that buckled and gave way in less than 15 minutes. Those who attempted to flee through the narrow ground floor exits found them jammed shut' (Symonds, 2003).

Besides the ILO report indicates that there were incidents of fire before in this location that were summarily ignored. The fire in August 1989 destroyed three buildings and all associated machinery and equipment. A small fire erupted late at night in a storage area on 13 February 1993. All these warnings were not heeded to and no safety aspects were reviewed. The production of toys and meeting order deadlines was clearly given more priority over safety of workers.

Explosion at SHAR Complex in Siharikota 2004

Thirty-six killed in an explosion in the SHAR complex in Siharikota. SHAR is India's premier space research station.

The Ten Worst Worldwide Mining Disasters

As Measured by Casualties

By far the worst mining safety record belongs to China. Even today, hundreds (if not thousands—the secretive Chinese government does not reveal figures) die every year in Chinese mining accidents.

1. April 26, 1942, Honkeiko Colliery, China

In what is probably the worst mining disaster of all time, 1,549 miners died in a mine operated in Japanese occupied Manchuria. China has a horrible history of mine safety. . The Japanese also likely are culpable in this accident: the Chinese were treated as sub-human slave labor by Japanese.

2. March 10, 1906, Courrieres, France

1,100 died in a coal dust explosion.

3. November 9, 1963, Omuta, Japan

An explosion in a coal mine killed 447.

4. October 14, 1913, Senghenydd, Wales, UK

The worst of the Welsh coal mining diasters killed 438 men and boys

5. January 1, 1960, Coalbrook, South Africa

437 casualties.

6. June 6, 1972, Wankie, Rhodesia

A coal mine explosion kills 427.

7. May 28, 1965, Dhanbad, India

375 miners die in a coal mine fire.

8. December 27, 1975, Chasnala, India

A coal mine explosion, followed by flooding kills 372.

9. December 12, 1866, Barnsley, England, UK

361 casualties.

10. December 6, 1907, Monongah, WV

361 casualties. The worst mining disaster in US history is said to have provided the origins of the first Father's Day celebration. A woman named Grace Clayton asked her church to hold a Sunday memorial for the fathers lost in the mine. The commemoration was held in a church in Fairmont, West Virginia.

(*Source:* http://www.epicdisasters.com)

Qinghe Special Steel Corporation Disaster 2007

A ladle holding molten steel separated from the overhead iron rail, fell, tipped, and killed 32 workers, injuring another 6 workers.

Chilean Mining Accident 2010

This accident happened at San José copper–gold mine, located deep in the Atacama Desert. 33 men were trapped 700 meters (2,300 ft) underground and about 5 kilometers (3 mi) from the mine's entrance via spiraling underground service ramps. The mixed crew of experienced miners and technical support personnel subsequently survived for a record 69 days deep underground before their rescue. '*On Oct. 13, 2010, 33 miners who had been trapped underground for more than two months all returned to the surface after a successful rescue operation that inspired Chile and riveted the world*' (New York Times). Chile implemented a comprehensive plan to both nurture the workers during their entrapment and to rescue the miners from the depths. It required the expertise of the United States' NASA space agency and more than a dozen multi-national corporations, besides the Chilean government efforts to rescue the miners. Many believed that the medium-sized gold and copper mine, 500 miles north of Santiago, had become the epitome of unsafe mining practices and it was an accident waiting to happen. *'Miner unions had continuously accused the San Jose mine for its faulty safety measures, but the company attracts workers with higher than average salaries and benefits'* (Global Post).

Deep-water Horizon Oil Spill in the Gulf of Mexico 2010

11 oil platform workers died in an explosion and fire that resulted in a massive oil spill in the Gulf of Mexico, considered the largest offshore spill in U.S. history.

Fukushima I Nuclear Accidents 2011

The Fukushima Daiichi nuclear power complex was central to a falsified-records scandal. Testimony by Dale Bridenbaugh, a lead GE designer, purports that General Electric was warned of major design flaws in 1976. The safety records appear falsified. However the jury is still out on the same and nothing can be said conclusively on this accident.

Four Levels of Safety Interventions

The four levels of workplace safety interventions are:

1. **Intervention at the Managerial Level:** The various components of managerial interventions include:

    a. Assessing workplace safety aspects and possible threats or hazards.

    b. Drafting safety policy.

    c. Safety policy implementation & follow-up on a regular basis.

    d. Safety Training & drills on a periodic basis.

    e. Legal & statutory compliance

    f. Workload assessment

    g. Equipment and maintenance audit.

2. **Technological Interventions:** The technological interventions refer to technology-audit and ensuring that better technologies are used and employed in the organizations that enhance safety aspects.

3. **Behavioural Interventions:** Making safety at workplace a way of life rather than a periodic inspection issue is the real challenge.

Anything and everything that an employee or a manager does must be in line with the safety practices. Safety should become everyone's agenda rather than being an enforcement issue. Zero tolerance for any unsafe practice or unsafe act, zero procrastination of safety aspects, prioritizing safety over everything are some of the desired behaviour from employees especially from managers.

4. **Ethical Interventions:** In this era of competition, market volatility and uncertainty there may be sometimes a tendency to cut-corners when it comes to safety issues. No such steps must be permitted that endangers lives of the employees or of any other member of the society due to operations of an organization.

Legal Angle

Some of the act in India that ask factories and other establishments to comply to industrial safety and accident/disaster prevention as well compensation in case of occurrence are discussed below:

The Factories Act, 1948

'An Act to consolidate and amend the law regulating labour in factories. Whereas, it is expedient to consolidate and amend the law regulating labour in factories.'

This act secures safety, health, welfare of the employees, regulates their working hours, ensures their annual leaves with wages, and provides for additional protection from hazardous processes, additional protection to women workmen and prohibition of employment of children.

Health issues covered under the acts include:

1. Cleanliness
2. Disposal of wastes and effluents
3. Ventilation and temperature
4. Dust and fume
5. Artificial humidification
6. Over-crowding
7. Lighting

8. Drinking water
9. Latrines and urinals
10. Spittoons

Safety Issues are discussed under the following heads:
1. Fencing of machinery
2. Work on or near machinery in motion
3. Employment of young persons on dangerous machines
4. Striking gear and devices for cutting off power
5. Self-acting machines
6. Casing of new machinery
7. Prohibition of employment of women and children near cotton-openers.
8. Hoists and lifts
9. Lifting machines, chains, ropes and lifting tackles
10. Revolving machinery
11. Pressure Plant
12. Floors, stairs and means of access
13. Pits, sumps, openings in floors, etc
14. Excessive weights
15. Protection of eyes
16. Precautions against dangerous fumes, gases, etc
    a. Precautions regarding the use of portable electric light
17. Explosive or inflammable dust, gas, etc
18. Precautions in case of fire
19. Power to require specifications of defective parts or tests
20. Safety of buildings and machinery
    a. Maintenance of buildings
    b. Safety officers
21. Power to make rules to supplement stability.

The act also specifies provisions relating to **Hazardous processes**:
1. Emergency standards
2. Permissible limits of exposure of chemical and toxic substances
3. Worker's participation in safety management
4. Right of workers to warn about imminent danger

Welfare issues discussed under this act:
1. Washing facilities
2. Facilities for storing and drying clothing
3. Facilities for sitting
4. First-aid appliances
5. Canteens
6. Shelters, rest-rooms and lunch-rooms
7. Creches
8. Welfare Officers.

The Factories Act also specifies working hours for adults, overtimes, overlapping shifts, holidays, employment of young persons, annual leaves with wages etc. The act also has some special provisions related to exemptions, certain kinds of accidents, diseases etc.

The Act is applicable to the premises wherein:

(i) 10 or more workers are employed with use of power

(ii) 20 or more workers are employed without the use of power

(iii) Less than 10 workers, if activity is notified by the State Government.

Some Other Acts

THE MINES ACT, 1952 (As modified upto 1983) - An Act to amend and consolidate the law relating to the Regulation of labour and safety in mines.

THE DOCK WORKERS (SAFETY, HEALTH AND WELFARE) ACT, 1986

An Act to provide for the safety, health and welfare of dock workers and for matters connected therewith. "Dock work" means any work in or within the vicinity of any port in connection with, or required, for, or incidental to, the loading, unloading, movement or storage of cargoes into or from ship or other vessel, port, dock, storage place or landing place, and includes:

i) Work in connection with the preparation of ships or other vessels for receipt or discharge of cargoes or leaving port;

and

ii) Chipping, painting or cleaning of any hold., tank, structure or lifting machinery or any other storage area in board the ship or In the docks.

"Dock worker" means a person employed or to be employed directly or by or through any agency (including a contractor) with or without knowledge of the principal employer, whether for remuneration or not, on dock work.

This act shall not apply to any ship of war of any nationality.

Workmen's Compensation Act, 1923

The Workmen's Compensation Act, aims to provide workmen and/or their dependents some relief in case of accidents arising out of and in the course of employment and causing either death or disablement of workmen. It provides for payment by certain classes of employers to their workmen compensation for injury by accident. The employer of any establishment covered under this Act, is required to compensate an employee who has suffered an accident arising out of and in the course of his employment, resulting into:

(i) Death;

(ii) Permanent total/partial disablement;

(iii) Temporary disablement, whether total or partial; or

(iv) Who has contracted an occupational disease.

OSHA, 1970

The **"Occupational Safety and Health Act of 1970"** enacted by the Senate and House of Representatives of the United States of America states that – "To assure safe and healthful working conditions for working men and women; by authorizing enforcement of the standards developed under the Act; by assisting and encouraging the States in their efforts to assure safe and healthful working conditions; by providing for research, information, education, and training in the field of occupational safety and health; and for other purposes."

Workplace Violence

Workplace Violence

"Workplace violence could be physical or psychological, anything at place of work that may fall under homicide, rape, kicking, biting, punching, harassment, including sexual, and racial abuse, bullying, mobbing, victimising, leaving, offensive messages, name-calling or deliberate silence".

(ILO)

In a tragic incident, the DGM (operations) of Graphite India Ltd – Powermax Steel division, was killed when some suspended workers staging 'dharna' outside the plant at Bolangir (Orissa) stopped his car and allegedly set it on fire. This is not an isolated incident of violence by employees against employee(s).

In a similar case, in September 2009, the Vice President (HR) of an auto manufacturing company was killed by a group of sacked workers in his cabin in the company's unit about 20 km from Coimbatore. Earlier, in September 2008, at Greater Noida, the CEO and Managing Director of Cerlikon-Graziano Transmission India Pvt Ltd was killed by the agitating workers.

All such incidents fall under the category of 'Workplace violence'. This, however, is just the tip of the iceberg. Many such incidents go unreported and don't make news headlines. The discussions below focus on various types of workplace violence and means to prevent and contain the same.

Awareness: What exactly is workplace violence? Is it only homicide?

Most of the times, workplace violence is equated with only physical assault. However, the ILO has a much broader description. Workplace violence could be physical or psychological, anything at place of work that may fall under homicide, rape, kicking, biting, punching, harassment, including sexual, and racial abuse, bullying, mobbing, victimising, leaving offensive messages, name-calling or deliberate silence. Greater levels of awareness are required in organizations, both amongst managers and workers.

Growing Menace

Any violence that happens related to work is categorized under workplace violence. Most of the times the perpetrators are co-workers; at times they may be customers, irate public etc. Workplace violence has pervaded global borders, work settings and occupational groups. About 30 personnel from the rank of Assistant Commissioner of Police to constable were booked by Delhi Police on sexual harassment charges in the past three years. The ILO report says some workplaces and occupations have become high-risk and women are especially vulnerable.

In March 2011, the simmering discontent among suspended workers of Graphite India Ltd's Powmex steel division, a private steel factory in Orissa's Bolangir district took a nasty turn today when a group of sacked workers burnt alive a 60-year-old deputy general manager of the company. Radheshyam Ray, DGM (Operations) of, was about to leave the factory at Turla in Titlagarh for lunch when the incident took place.

This is not an isolated incident. In many cases the lack of evidence makes it difficult to pinpoint the accused. In a shocking incident in the year 2006, during the student elections at Madhav College in Ujjain, some members of a student union allegedly manhandled Professor Sabharwal. He died following the assault. This lead to a widespread outrage, however all the accused were acquitted by the court in 2009 for lack of evidence.

In another sensational case of homicide however with huge mass-support the accused were brought to the law. On November 19, 2005 IOC sales manager S. Manjunath, an IIM Lucknow graduate, was killed-on-duty, for exposing a racket in sale of adulterated fuel. While working for the Indian Oil Corporation (IOC) in Lucknow, he had ordered two petrol pumps at Lakhimpur Kheri to be sealed for selling adulterated fuel for three months. When the pump started operating again a month later, Manjunath decided to conduct a surprise raid around November 19, 2005. On the same night, he was shot dead in Gola Gokarannath town of Lakhimpur Kheri. The murder of Manjunath, had resulted in nationwide outrage, with IIM alumni, student groups, NGOs, rights groups, and the media campaigning for justice.

What is even more worrisome is that many times the incidents become so common and so little is done to contain them that employees, especially women are often left traumatized; however for the fear of rebuke or social condemnation they keep quiet. But there are few who speak-up. One of them was a senior Indian Administrative Service (IAS) female officer named Rupan Deol Bajaj who filed a complaint against the super cop K.P.S.Gill for, in 1988, "patting" her indecently at a party where he was alleged to be drunk. In August 1996, Gill was convicted under Section 354 (outraging the modesty of a woman) and Section 509 (word, gesture or act intended to insult a lady), generally summarized as sexual harassment. Gill was sentenced to pay a fine of Rs 2 lakh, be imprisoned rigorously for 3 months and simply for 2 months, and finally to serve 3 years of probation. The apex court, Supreme Court of India upheld the conviction in July 2005, but the jail sentences were reduced to probation. The victim had declined to accept the monetary compensation, and the court ordered that it be donated to women's organizations. Justice finally came after 17 long years.

Pratibha Srikanthmurthy, a BPO employee in Bangalore was raped and killed while on her way for night-shift duty in December 2005. The prime accused: Shivu alias Shivakumar, substitute cab driver who picked her up from home. After 5 years in 2010, the cab driver who collected BPO employee Pratibha Murthy for work on that fateful night was found guilty of raping and murdering her by the fast-track court in Bangalore. The case had raised a huge storm and questions were asked about the security of women employees especially in BPOs. In 2005, when the case happened, NASSCOM, the apex body of software and BPO industries, had voiced its concern over the incident and said it would continue its dialogue with the police for "conducive" law and order and also improve the industry's internal system for safety and security of employees, especially women.

In 2010, a disgruntled employee went on a shooting rampage Tuesday at a beer distribution firm- Hartford Distributors in Manchester, Connecticut, killing eight co-workers before turning the gun on himself. The shooter, who local media reports said had been called in by managers for a disciplinary hearing, was found dead some 40 minutes later after shooting a total of 10 people then himself.

Vice-President (HR) of Pricol Ltd., an auto component manufacturing company, Roy George was murdered by a group of sacked workers on Sept. 22, 2009. Pricol Limited hit by the slump in the automobile industry, posted its first annual loss in 32 years last fiscal. It also posted loss in the April-June quarter of 2009. Company employees have been on strike for the past two years over pay and other disputes.

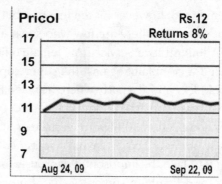

Figure 15.1: Pricoll Hit by Slump in Automobile Industry

The Rs. 614-crore-company reportedly announced shifting its production to its facilities in the north citing continued labour unrest at its Coimbatore plants. The company also sacked 42 employees for indiscipline, including preventing capacity utilisation of the factory and stopping other workers from carrying out their duties. The employees were allegedly removed after they ignored repeated warnings and show-cause notices and the company accused them of 'persistent slow-going' tactics.

The workers allegedly barged into the Pricol premises and attacked employees, including Roy George. The human resources V-P was trying to initiate a dialogue with the agitating workers to bring operations back on track after the union made various demands. A group of workers attacked him with iron rods in his cabin in the company's unit at Periyanaickanpalayam, about 20 km from Coimbatore on Ooty road and 500 km from Chennai. They also damaged a computer, one laptop and a few other things like mirrors and tables. Roy George succumbed to his injuries later in a hospital.

A young SpiceJet air hostess was molested by a senior pilot in the cockpit of a Delhi-bound flight. The incident took place on Sept. 4, 2007 soon after the flight took off from Kolkata. The pilot allegedly called the air hostess into the cockpit and molested her. The incident happened when the co-pilot went out of the cockpit to relieve himself. It was then that the captain called the air hostess and molested her. The accused pilot, having past history of similar complaints, was sacked by the private airline. The pilot's contract with the company was terminated after the internal committee found him guilty.

Reading Exhibit: Top of Form

9 Most Common Myths About Workplace Violence that Put Your Company at Risk

By: Jeffrey M. Miller

While we can't do much about what people believe in general about the world around them, we can take personal responsibility for what we believe ourselves - especially when our beliefs center around our own personal safety, and the safety of those we're responsible for. This article explores the most common myths about workplace violence and how these unfounded beliefs actually serve to perpetuate and aggravate the problem of violence in the workplace.

Myth #1: Workplace violence incidents are rare.

Unfortunately, we can find ourselves living in a bubble of complacency. And, unless we're shaken out of our sleepwalking state by a terrifying news story, we tend to not notice less horrific things around us.

While it is true that the number of murders occurring from a workplace violence attack have lowered over the past few years, we shouldn't be limiting our focus to just homicide. In fact, according to OSHA, there are over 1 million reported incidents of assault each year, just in the United States alone. And, since it's estimated that only about half of all incidents are ever reported, that the total is closer to 2 million. And, this doesn't include the approximately 1,000 homicides and 51,000 sexual assaults!

Myth #2: It will never happen here.

I call this the "Ostrich Syndrome." You know, the belief that, "If I bury my head in the proverbial sand, I can make danger disappear." The truth is that workplace violence can happen in any business, at anytime, and anywhere. And, it does. In fact, I've consulted with executives, business owners, and employees from, not only the US, but also Canada, Germany, England, France, Japan, and Thailand. And...the story is the same: Today's workplaces are the most violent environments in which you can find yourself.

Myth #3: Postal employees have more to worry about than I do.

Unfortunately, due to a few incidents which occurred decades ago, the post office and its employees have garnered a much undeserved reputation for violence. Even the phrase, "going postal," is still popular after nearly four decades of its creation. The reality is that only about 3% of all incidents occur within all government agencies - combined!

In fact, post office employees, as with any government workers, are probably some of the "least" likely to encounter violence in the workplace. While occupations like nursing and other healthcare, teaching, and psychiatric counselors have some of the highest incidents.

Myth #4: Workplace violence is a guy thing and women shouldn't worry about it.

Murder is the number one cause of death for women killed on the job. And, as I said before, this is paled by the 13,000 rapes, 51,000 sexual assaults, and about 35% of the 600,000 simple assaults that occur in American workplaces every year. In other countries, like India, the Middle East, and the East, the percentages are even higher.

Men may perpetrate more of the attacks involving the use of guns, but women share the field almost equally when it comes to being the attacker and the victim. In addition, over 65% of all non-fatal workplace assaults occur in nursing homes, hospitals, residential care facilities, and other social service environments - places where women make up the vast majority of the work force.

Myth #5: Security guards and metal detectors will prevent workplace violence.

As a former police officer, I learned very quickly that security measures can do little to stop a determined perpetrator of a crime. It doesn't matter if we're talking about a burglar, a rapist, murderer, or even a terrorist - the newest threat to workplace safety.

In fact security guards and detection devices can do little more than cause an attacker to think more creatively. And, even if they do prevent the outsider from entering your company, they can do little to stop current or former employees, friends, family members and visitors that would have both knowledge of your facility, and a reason to be there in the first place.

Myth #6: The only cost we'll have to worry about is attorney fees.

Over the years, I've had the opportunity to speak to my share of human resources managers, administrators, and executives about the need for a workplace violence prevention plan and crisis response training program in their facility. In that time, one of the most disturbing comments that I've ever heard was, "that's what our attorney's are for."

Not only can your attorney's, or the police for that matter, "not" take away the damage, injuries, death, and destruction that can occur, but their fees will be the least of your problems. The true cost of workplace violence incidents are estimated to be between 55 and 2 million US dollars every year. Costs associated with your company's recovery in the post-event aftermath include not only attorney's fees, but also lost work time, the effects of negative press and public image, property repairs, increased insurance premiums, and fines or judgments entered in favor of any plaintiffs suing you for liability. To give you an idea about just one of these areas, OSHA reports that American companies pay for over 1,700,000 sick days annually due to lost time resulting directly from violence in the workplace.

In many cases, the financial strain resulting from just one incident has put more than a few companies out of business for good.

Myth #7: He just "snapped." We can't prevent it because there are no warning signs.

Reports show that in 80% of all incidents of workplace violence, the assailant gave warning signs that went unheeded. In all of the programs that I teach, regardless of whether we're talking about basic self-defense, street survival for law enforcement professionals, or workplace violence prevention and defensive tactics, "awareness" heads the list and is the easiest and most successful means for surviving a workplace violence attack.

The reality is that managers and employees alike can learn to anticipate, assess, and even manage the risk from internal causes by identifying, monitoring, and addressing employees who exhibit high-risk behaviors and characteristics before they can escalate into actual violence.

While not all situations can be prevented, and this is where a good, solid, self-defense and attack avoidance program comes in, early awareness and action can save property, lives, money, guilt and the embarrassment which can arise out of knowing that action "could" and "should" have been taken to prevent or minimize it.

Myth #8: We have insurance to cover the cost of damages.

Most workers and managers, as well as business owners wrongly believe that they are covered completely by whatever insurance coverage is in place to protect the company. When, in fact, supervisors, managers, and others in an authority or leadership position can be held personally responsible and sued in civil court for their actions or failure to act, and the conduct of others over which they had authority.

And, while most companies carry some sort of liability coverage, you may find that your insurance policy may have clauses that exclude damages from certain types of actions. Like hospitals, universities, and other open, "porous" entities, your company can be left holding the proverbial "bag" in the case of injuries, damages, or harm that comes to visitors, guests, and family members caught in the cross-fire of an event but who are not actually employees of your company.

Myth #9: We have a workplace violence prevention policy so we're safe.

In light of all the evidence, most companies still do not have workplace violence plans, policies, or training programs. I have found that those who do, are still missing critical elements from these plans and leaving themselves open to the same or greater liability issues that their plans were supposed to eliminate in the first place.

(Published with permission of Jeffrey M. Miller, Shidoshi, Founder & Director - Warrior Concepts International (Self-Protection & Personal Development), Sunbury, Pa)

For more information log onto: http://www.warrior-concepts-online.com

Action: Workplace violence needs to be tackled with immediacy and toughness. There are, however, two hurdles. The first one is of 'reporting'. Many incidents of workplace violence go unreported or are reported very late (after the damage has been done) primarily due to fear of repercussion and lack of awareness.

A well-known Indian women wrestler-turned-model, had recently alleged that she also had been the victim of sexual advances and said the problem is far more of corrupt federation officials who demand favours from men and women for inclusion in the team. She also moved Delhi high court over selection in Commonwealth Games and had claimed that the federation president had told her that he will never pick her and had demanded a hefty amount to pick her in the squad. However, she did not find support from her teammates, who stood by the federation and its officials. A statement signed by as many as 30 members, including top women wrestlers among others, supported the selection trial and termed the complainant the victim as undisciplined, irresponsible and frustrated.

The second problem is absence of a strong legislation to deal with all forms of workplace violence. In such a scenario not all organizations do enough to curb such incidents. Most of the incidents, discussed earlier in the chapter, where justice has been delivered, have been the sensational ones wherein there was immense public or peer pressure. But not all incidents have this magnitude of public support. We definitely need more teeth both in terms of legislation and reporting. Countries such as Canada have drafted legislation to deal with workplace violence.

Prevention: An even more important aspect is prevention of workplace violence since once an incident happens, considerable damage is done. Understanding causative factors, the psychological and behavioural patterns of people engaging in workplace violence may help prevention. But this requires considerable research and study.

For instance, in a yet another shocking incident in the year 2010, minutes after a woman was suspended and escorted from her job at the Kraft Foods plant in Northeast Philadelphia, she returned with a .357 Magnum and opened fire, killing two women and critically injuring a third co-worker. Hiller, 43, the accused, is said to have had a history of run-ins with co-workers and management. It is high time the government and organizations paid attention to preventing/dealing effectively with workplace violence.

Essay Questions

1. What are the common issues concerning the health and safety of employees?

2. What are the four main reasons attributed to industrial accidents?

3. In light of worst industrial accidents & disasters that have occurred, which one(s) of the reasons cited in the answer 2, do you think is the prime reason behind such accidents?

4. Describe the four levels of managerial safety interventions.

5. Explain how each legal act listed below contributes to ensuring industrial safety:

    a) The Factories Act

    b) The Dock Workers (Safety, Health and Welfare) Act

    c) Workmen Compensation Act

    d) Occupational Safety and Health Act (OSHA)

6. What is workplace violence? Discuss the key issues related to workplace violence, with relevant examples.

7. What are the various myths associated with workplace violence? Why are they myths?

Application Questions

1. Go to http://www.wst.tas.gov.au/ click on the various hyperlinks and 0repare a report on the workplace safety standards at Tasmania.

2. See the YouTube video - http://www.youtube.com/watch?v=umFMwdsGai4 and search for similar information on the website and make a presentation on the workplace violence legislation in Canada.

Bibliography

Baker, G. (2011). Business first, Safety Always. *NZ Business, 25* (2), 24-28.

Boone, J., Van Ours, J. C., Wuellrich, J.-P., & Zweimüller, J. (2011). Recessions are Bad for Workplace Safety. *Journal of Health Economics, 30* (4), 764-773.

Campeau, M. (2011). Updates on Workplace Health and Safety Regulations. *HR Professional, 28* (1), 39-42.

Cantor, D. E. (2008). Workplace Safety in the Supply Chain: A Review of the Literature and Call for Research. *International Journal of Logistics Management, 19* (1), 65-83.

Ceniceros, R. (2009). Workplace Safety is about People's Lives. *Business Insurance, 43* (44), 6.

Chapman, J. A. (2007). Safe Workplaces: A Key Issue for Quality of Working Life. *Employment Relations Record, 7* (1), 25-35.

Chhokar, J. S. (1987). Safety at the Workplace: A Behavioural Approach. *International Labour Review, 126* (2), 169.

Christian, M. S., Wallace, J. C., Bradley, J. C., & Burke, M. J. (2009). Workplace Safety: A Meta-analysis of the Roles of Person and Situation Factors. *Journal of Applied Psychology, 94* (5), 1103-1127.

Credo, K. R., Armenakis, A. A., Feild, H. S., & Young, R. L. (2010). Organizational Ethics, Leader-Member Exchange, and Organizational Support: Relationships With Workplace Safety. *Journal of Leadership & Organizational Studies, 317* (4), 325-334.

Curington, W. P. (1986). Safety Regulation and Workplace Injuries. *Southern Economic Journal, 53* (1), 51.

Davis, M. E. (1980). The Impact of Workplace Health and Safety on Black Workers: Assessment and Prognosis. *Labor Law Journal, 31* (2), 723-732.

Eckhardt, R. F. (2001). The Moral Duty to Provide Workplace Safety. *Professional Safety, 46* (8), 36.

Foulke, J., & Edwin, G. (2010). Strategies to Improve Workplace Safety. *South Carolina Business, 31* (5), 4.

Grenny, J., & Maxfield, D. (2011). Five Crucial Conversations that Drive Workplace Safety. *Professional Safety, 56* (8), 24-26.

Hilyer, B., Leviton, L., Overman, L., & Mukherjee, S. (2000). A Union-Initiated Safety Training Program Leads to Improved Workplace Safety. *Labor Studies Journal, 24* (4), 53-66.

Huang, Y.-H., Chen, P. Y., Rogers, D. A., & Krauss, A. D. (2003). Role of Workplace Safety: A Revisit of the Relationship between Job Satisfaction and Employment Status. *21* (3), 251-256.

Huang, Y.-H., Leamon, T. B., Courtney, T. K., Chen, P. Y., & DeArmond, S. (2011). A Comparison of Workplace Safety Perceptions among Financial Decision-makers of Medium- vs. Large-size Companies. *Accident Analysis & Prevention, 43* (1), 1-10.

Huang, Y.-H., Leamon, T. B., Courtney, T. K., Chen, P. Y., & DeArmond, S. (2007). Corporate Financial Decision-makers' Perceptions of Workplace Safety. *Accident Analysis & Prevention, 39* (4), 767-775.

Järvis, M., & Tint, P. (2009). Innovations At Workplace: An Evidence-based Model for Safety Management. *Business: Theory & Practice, 10* (2), 150-158.

Kramer, D. M., Wells, R. P., Bigelow, P. L., Carlan, N. A., Cole, D. C., & Hepburn, C. G. (2010). Dancing the Two-step: Collaborating with Intermediary Organizations as Research Partners to Help Implement Workplace Health and Safety Interventions, *36* (3), 321-332.

Long, T. (2010). Workplace Violence can Put your Company at Risk. *EHS Today, 3* (6), 22-23.

Lorenzo, O., Esqueda, P., & Larson, J. (2010). Safety and Ethics in the Global Workplace: Asymmetries in Culture and Infrastructure. *Journal of Business Ethics, 92* (1), 87-106.

Makin, A. M., & Winder, C. (2009). Managing Hazards in the Workplace Using Organisational Safety Management Systems: A Safe Place, Safe Person, Safe Systems Approach. *Journal of Risk Research, 12* (3/4), 329-343.

Markiewicz, D. (2011). Workplace Safety as a Public Health Issue. *Industrial Safety & Hygiene News, 45* (4), 20.

Maxfield, D. (2010). Workplace Safety is the Leading Edge of a Culture of Accountability. *EHS Today, 3* (6), 39-44.

McGuire, C. (2011). Implementing Safety and Security in the Workplace. *Safety Compliance Letter* (2526), 1-3.

OSHA Photo Contest Highlights Workplace Safety & Health, (2011). *Professional Safety, 56* (6), 37.

Parboteeah, K., & Kapp, E. (2008). Ethical Climates and Workplace Safety Behaviors: An Empirical Investigation. *Journal of Business Ethics, 80* (3), 515-529.

Robertson, R. E. (2006). Workplace Safety and Health: OSHA Could Improve Federal Agencies' Safety Programs with a more Strategic Approach to its Oversight. *GAO Reports,* 1.

Ryan, D. (2009). Safety Perception Survey. *Professional Safety, 54* (12), 22-27.

Safety Leadership. (2011). *Professional Safety, 56* (9), 42-49.

Schultz, G., & Arunachalam, R. (2011). Predict & Prevent Workplace Injuries. *Industrial Safety & Hygiene News, 45* (6), 64-66.

Silvestre, J. (2010). Improving Workplace Safety in the Ontario Manufacturing Industry. *Business History Review, 84* (3), 527-550.

Sinclair, R. R., Martin, J. E., & Sears, L. E. (2010). Labor Unions and Safety Climate: Perceived Union Safety Values and Retail Employee Safety Outcomes. *Accident Analysis & Prevention, 42* (5), 1477-1487.

Wallace, J. C., & Vodanovich, S. J. (2003). Workplace Safety Performance: Conscientiousness, Cognitive Failure, and their Interaction. *Journal of Occupational Health Psychology, 8* (4), 316.

Walters, D. (1987). Health and Safety and Trade Union Workplace Organisation – A Case Study in the Printing Industry. *Industrial Relations Journal, 18* (1), 40.

Warrack, B. J., & Sinha, M. N. (1999). Integrating Safety and Quality: Building to Achieve Excellence in the Workplace. *Total Quality Management, 10* (4), 779-785.

Workplace Safety 100 Years Ago. (2011). *Safety Compliance Lette* (2524), 1-6.

Workplace Safety and Disaster Management. (2010). *Law Office Management & Administration Report, 10* (8), 1-10.

Workplace Safety Oversight must be Strengthened, (2011). *EHS Today, 4* (7), 13.

Workplace Violence Takes a Deadly Toll. (2009), *EHS Today, 2* (12), 17.

Chapter 16

Industrial Relations

Outline

Introduction

Theoretical Approaches to Industrial Relations

Roles of Industrial Relations

Trade Unions

The Trade Unions Act, 1926

Labour Acts

The Minimum Wages Act, 1948

Payment of Wages Act, 1936

Workmen's Compensation Act, 1923

Equal Remuneration Act

Employee State Insurance Act, 1948

Payment of Gratuity Act

Payment of Bonus Act

The Shops and Establishments Act

The Maternity Benefit Act, 1961

The Industrial Disputes Act, 1947

The Factories Act, 1948

Apprentices Act, 1961

Future of Industrial Relations in India

Essay Questions

Application Questions

Bibliography

Key Terms

Trade Unions

The Trade Unions Act, 1926

Labour Act

The Minimum Wages Act, 1936

Workmen's Compensation Act, 1923

Employee State Insurance Act, 1948

Introduction

India has witnessed a spate of strikes and agitations in the last few years. Over the past few years, there have also been other labor incidents at MNCs in India. In January 2006 there was an 18-day lockout at the Toyota unit in Karnataka following unrest over recognition of the trade union. In September 2008, Lalit Kishore Chaudhary, CEO of Italian MNC Graziano Transmission India, was battered to death outside his factory gates by dismissed workers. There was a violent strike, too, at the Honda Motorcycles and Scooters unit close by. Honda Motorcycles is a wholly-owned unit of Honda of Japan, which also has a joint venture in Hero Honda. There was three-week strike in April-May 2009 at the Nestle India plant in Uttarakhand over the dismissal of two probationers. There have been problems at Hyundai Motors, culminating in a strike in June, 2010 at its unit in Sriperumbudur (40 kilometers, or 25 miles, from state capital Chennai), which was later resolved with the company agreeing to take back 67 workers who had been fired for "gross misconduct." In July 2010 it was Nokia India's turn. Once again, the issue was settled with the management taking back the 60 suspended workers. At auto parts supplier Pricol, in which Denso Corp. of Japan has a 12.5% equity stake, a human resources manager was killed last September after an attack by workers. Pricol had dismissed about 35 workers at its Coimbatore factory, citing indiscipline. And more recently, in 2011 strikes at Maruti Suzuki Manesar plant in Haryana over non-recognition of new labour union and on disciplinary issues, strike at Bosch plant at Bangalore over outsourcing of ancillary activities, the one-day Coal India strike serving as a threat for future conflict between the employees and the management reportedly over compensation issues have not been good news for India Inc., especially, for growing tribe of MNCs who have invested heavily in India.

For those who think Industrial Relations is out of vogue, a reality check is definitely called-for. Industrial relations is many times also called labour relations or employment relations. It is called labour relations primarily because industrial relations emerged during the period of industrial revolutions. The name employment relation comes from the fact that the discipline covers more than the unionised workers.

Industrial relations is relationships between management and employees.

'A sound industrial relations system is one in which relationships between management and employees (and their representatives) on the one hand,

and between them the State on the other, are more harmonious and cooperative than conflictual and creates an environment conducive to economic efficiency and the motivation, productivity and development of the employee and generates employee loyalty and mutual trust' (ILO).

The primary participants in the Industrial relations systems are employers, employees and the government. Employers are creators of jobs and reserve privileges of designing the conditions of employment in their respective organization. The employees are the job-seekers, seeking better conditions of employment. The government acts as a regulatory authority being the law maker and enforcer.

Theoretical Approaches to Industrial Relations

Systems Model Approach

The systems model approach was suggested by John Dunlop in the 1950s. According to Dunlop- "Industrial relations system consists of three agents – management organizations, workers and formal/informal ways they are organized and government agencies. He proposed that three parties—employers, labor unions, and government— are the key actors in a modern industrial relations system. He also argued that none of these institutions could act in an autonomous or independent fashion. Instead they were shaped, at least to some extent, by their market, technological and political contexts. Hence according to Dunlop, industrial relations is a social sub system subject to three environmental constraints- the markets, distribution of power in society and technology, each of them more or less intimately affects each of the others so that they constitute a group of arrangements for dealing with certain matters and are collectively responsible for certain results."

The two main participants in the system are the employees and the employers. Basically three approaches define their dynamics and relationships. The first approach is the Unitary approach, where the management and union are seen as one cohesive unit, who work together towards a common goal of creating better organizational environment.

Industrial Relations

"A sound industrial relations system is one in which relationships between management and employees (and their representatives) on one hand, and between them & the state on the other, are more harmonious and cooperative than conflictual and creates economic efficiency and the motivation, productivity and development of their employee and generates employee loyalty and mutual trust".

(ILO)

Figure 16.1:
Theoretical Approach to Industrial Relations

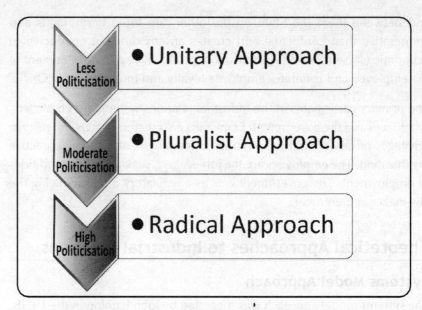

The Pluralist approach is the second approach that has management and union as two separate entities. The management assumes a command and control orientation, whereas, the union assumes itself as the protector of employee rights through collective bargaining. The third and the final approach is the Radical approach. The radical approach has management and union approaching each other with suspicion. The management looks at union as a problem-creator and a roadblock. The union looks at management as a threat. The obvious outcome is conflict.

As one progresses from Unitary approach to radical approach there is a definite increase in politicisation. The increase in politicisation leads to a more and more confrontation. The Unitary approach is ideal, the Pluralist approach is the practical reality and the radical approach the least desirable.

Roles of Industrial Relations

The Industrial relations has various roles –

1. To develop a theoretical perspective as to what should be ideal relationship between the employer and the employee.
2. To develop an ethical climate that discourages commoditisation and exploitation of human element in the organization.
3. To develop a legal framework that defines the rules and conditions of employment.

4. To minimize industrial conflicts and work towards resolution.
5. To promote growth and industrial harmony.

Trade Unions

Trade Union is an organization formed by employees or workers. Various features of a trade union are:

- It is formed on a continuous basis.
- It is a permanent body and not a casual or temporary one.
- It is formed to protect and promote all kinds of interests – economic, political and social-of its members, with economic interests being the dominant interest.
- It achieves its objectives through collective action and group effort.

The formation and governance of trade unions comes under the Trade Unions Act, 1926. This act is important because other labour laws such as the Industrial Disputes Act, 1947 (IDA), and the Industrial Employment (Standing Orders) Act, 1946 (IESOA), define a labour union to mean a union that has been registered under the TU Act.

Trade Unions
Trade Union is an organization formed by employees to protect & promote economic, political & social interest of its members, through collective action and group effort.

Labour Acts

There are several acts under the Labour Acts in India, which can be grouped under the following headings broadly:

- Laws related to industrial relations
- Laws related to wages
- Laws related to working hours, conditions of services and employment
- Laws related to deprived and disadvantaged sections of the society
- Laws related to equality and empowerment
- Laws related to social security
- Laws related to labour welfare
- Laws related to employment and training
- Other laws

Table 16.1:

List of Various Central Labour Acts

	Laws Related to Industrial Relations
1	The Trade Unions Act, 1926 The Trade Unions (Amendments) Act, 2001
2	The Industrial Employment (Standing Orders) Act, 1946 The Industrial Employment (Standing Orders) Rules, 1946
3	The Industrial Disputes Act, 1947

	Laws Related to Wages
1	The Payment of Wages Act, 1936 The Payment of Wages Rules, 1937 The Payment of Wages (AMENDMENT) Act, 2005
2	The Minimum Wages Act, 1948 The Minimum Wages (Central) Rules, 1950
3	The Working Journalist (Fixation of Rates of Wages) Act, 1958 Working Journalist (Conditions of service) and Miscellaneous Provisions Rules, 1957
4	The Payment of Bonus Act, 1965 The Payment of Bonus Rules, 1975

	Laws Related to Working Hours, Conditions of Services and Employment
1	The Factories Act, 1948
2	The Dock Workers (Regulation of Employment) Act, 1948
3	The Plantation Labour Act, 1951
4	The Mines Act, 1952

5	The Working Journalists and other Newspaper Employees' (Conditions of Service and Misc. Provisions) Act, 1955 The Working Journalists and other Newspaper Employees' (Conditions of Service and Misc. Provisions) Rules, 1957
6	The Merchant Shipping Act, 1958
7	The Motor Transport Workers Act, 1961
8	The Beedi & Cigar Workers (Conditions of Employment) Act, 1966
9	The Contract Labour (Regulation & Abolition) Act, 1970 The Contract Labour Regulation Rules
10	The Sales Promotion Employees (Conditions of Service) Act, 1976 The Sales Promotion Employees (Conditions of Service) Rules, 1976
11	The Inter-State Migrant Workmen (Regulation of Employment and Conditions of Service) Act, 1979
12	The Shops and Establishments Act
13	The Cinema Workers and Cinema Theatre Workers (Regulation of Employment) Act, 1981 The Cinema Workers and Cinema Theatre Workers (Regulation of Employment) Rules, 1984 The Cine Workers' Welfare Fund Act, 1981.
14	The Dock Workers (Safety, Health & Welfare) Act, 1986
15	The Building & Other Construction Workers (Regulation of Employment & Conditions of Service) Act, 1996
16	The Dock Workers (Regulation of Employment) (inapplicability to Major Ports) Act, 1997

	Laws Related to Equality and Empowerment of Women
1	The Maternity Benefit Act, 1961
2	The Equal Remuneration Act, 1976

	Laws Related to Deprived and Disadvantaged Sections of the Society
1	The Bonded Labour System (Abolition) Act, 1976
2	The Child Labour (Prohibition & Regulation) Act, 1986
3	The Children (Pledging of Labour) Act, 1933

	Laws Related to Social Security
1	The Workmen's Compensation Act, 1923 The Workmen's Compensation (Amendments) Act, 2000
2	The Employees' State Insurance Act, 1948
3	The Employees' Provident Fund & Miscellaneous Provisions Act, 1952 The Employees' Provident Fund & Miscellaneous Provisions (Amendment) Act, 1996
4	The Payment of Gratuity Act, 1972 The Payment of Gratuity Rules
5	The Unorganised Woekers' Social Security Act 2008 The Unorganised Workers' Social Security Rules 2008

	Laws Related to Labour Welfare
1	The Mica Mines Labour Welfare Fund Act, 1946
2	The Limestone & Dolomite Mines Labour Welfare Fund Act, 1972

3	The Beedi Workers Welfare Fund Act, 1976	
4	The Beedi Workers Welfare Cess Act, 1976 The Beedi Worker's Welfare Cess Act Rules, 1977	
5	The Iron Ore Mines, Manganese Ore Mines & Chrome Ore Mines Labour Welfare Fund Act, 1976	
6	The Iron Ore Mines, Manganese Ore Mines & Chrome Ore Mines Labour Welfare Cess Act, 1976	
7	The Cine Workers Welfare Fund Act, 1981	
8	The Cine Workers Welfare Cess Act, 1981	
9	The Employment of Manual Scavengers and Construction of Dry latrines Prohibition Act, 1993	

	Laws Related to Employment & Training	
1	The Employment Exchanges (Compulsory Notification of Vacancies) Act, 1959 The Employment Exchanges (Compulsory Notification of Vacancies) Rules, 1959	
2	The Apprentices Act, 1961	

	Others	
1	The Fatal Accidents Act, 1855	
2	The War Injuries Ordinance Act, 1943	
3	The Weekly Holiday Act, 1942	
4	The National and Festival Holidays Act	
5	The War Injuries (Compensation Insurance) Act, 1943	
6	The Personal Injuries (Emergency) Provisions Act, 1962	
7	The Personal Injuries (Compensation Insurance) Act, 1963	
8	The Coal Mines (Conservation and Development) Act, 1974	

9	The Labour Laws (Exemption from Furnishing Returns and Maintaining Register by Certain Establishments) Act, 1988
10	The Public Liability Insurance Act, 1991

(*Source:* http://labour.nic.in/act/welcome.html)

The Trade Unions Act, 1926

"An Act to provide for the registration of Trade Unions and in certain respects to define the law relating to registered Trade Unions." Any combination, whether temporary or permanent, formed primarily for the purpose of regulating the relations between workmen and employers, or between workmen and workmen, or between employers and employers, or for imposing restrictive conditions on the conduct of any trade or business, and includes any federation of two or more trade unions. It extends to the whole of India. THE TRADE UNIONS (AMENDMENT) ACT, 2001 ACT NO. 31 OF 2001 [3rd September, 2001] was enacted as — an Act further to amend the Trade Unions Act, 1926.

Pre-requisites for registration of trade union:

➢ There should be at least 10%, or 100 of the work-men, whichever is less, engaged or employed in the establishment or industry with which it is connected.

➢ It has on the date of making application not less than 7 persons as its members, who are workmen engaged or employed in the establishment or industry with which it is connected.

Mode of registration of Trade Union is as under:

Any 7 or more members of a trade union may, by subscribing their names to rules of the Trade Union and by otherwise complying with the provisions of this Act with respect to registration, apply for registration of the Trade Union under this Act.

The Minimum Wages Act, 1948

An Act to provide for fixing minimum rates of wages in certain employments. Where as, it is expedient to provide for fixing minimum rates of wages in certain employments.

In unorganised sector, where labour is vulnerable to exploitation, due to illiteracy and having no effective bargaining power, minimum rates of wages are fixed/revised both by Central and State Governments in the scheduled employments falling under their respective jurisdictions under the provisions of this act. Wages means all remuneration capable of being expressed in terms of money, be payable to a person employed in respect of his employment or of work done in such employment. It includes house rent allowance, medical attendance, or other amenity or service excluded by Pension/Provident Fund, travelling allowance, gratuity.

The main provisions of the minimum wages act are:

- The rate fixed can be revised periodically but it should not exceed a time interval of five years.
- The rate can be fixed on Time work basis (minimum time rate), Piece work basis (minimum piece rate), minimum rate of remuneration as a security for workers receiving a piece rate wage (guarantee time rate) and for the overtime work done (overtime rate).
- Minimum wage rates are not the same all over the country. It differs for different employments, different class of work in the same employment, adults, adolescents, children and apprentices and different localities.
- Rates can be fixed on basis of hour, day or month, or even larger period.

Payment of Wages Act, 1936

Payment of Wages Act is an Act to regulate the payment of wages to certain classes of employed persons.

The main provisions of the Payment of Wages Act are:

- Every employer shall be responsible for the payment to persons employed by him of all wages required to be paid under this Act.
- It applies in the first instance to the payment of wages to persons employed in any factory, railway, either directly or through a subcontractor.

- Every person responsible for the payment of wages shall wage periods in respect of which such wages shall be payable. No wage period shall exceed one month.

- If any person is terminated by the employer, the wages earned by him shall be paid before the expiry of the second working day from the day on which his employment is terminated and all payments of wages shall be made on a working day.

- Every employer shall maintain such registers and records giving such particulars of persons employed by him, the work performed by them, the wages paid and deducted to them.

- All wages shall be paid in current coin or currency notes or in both; however the employer can get a written authorisation from the employee and can pay him by cheque or deposit in his account.

- Wages can be deducted in the form of fines (cannot exceed more than three percent of the wages), damage or loss (either by neglect or default of the person) or deduction for service provided by the employer.

Workmen's Compensation Act, 1923

The Workmen's Compensation Act, aims to provide workmen and/or their dependents some relief in case of accidents arising out of and in the course of employment and causing either death or disablement of workmen. It provides for payment by certain classes of employers to their workmen compensation for injury by accident. The employer of any establishment covered under this Act, is required to compensate an employee who has suffered an accident arising out of and in the course of his employment, resulting into:

(i) Death;

(ii) Permanent total disablement;

(iii) Permanent partial disablement, or

(iv) Temporary disablement, whether total or partial; or

(v) Who has contracted an occupational disease.

The following come under the category of dependants:

- Widow, minor legitimate or adopted son, an unmarried legitimate or adopted daughter, or a widowed mother.
- If wholly dependent, son, daughter who has attained the age of 18 years.
- A parent other than widowed mother.
- Minor illegitimate son, unmarried illegitimate daughter.
- Daughter legitimate or illegitimate or adopted if married and a minor or if widowed and a minor widowed daughter in law.
- A minor child of a predeceased son.
- A minor child of a pre-deceased daughter where no parent of the child is alive.
- A paternal grandparent, if no parent of the workman is alive.

Equal Remuneration Act [Act 25 of 1976 Amended by Act 49 of 1987]

An act to provide for the payment of equal remuneration to men and women workers and for the prevention of discrimination, on the ground of sex, against women in the matter of employment and for matters connected therewith or incidental thereto.

The Equal Remuneration Act was enacted to give effect to the provision of Article 39 of the Constitution of India which contains a directive principle of equal pay for equal work for both men and women. The Act provides for the payment of equal remuneration to men and women workers for the same work or work of a similar nature and for the prevention of discrimination on the ground of sex against women in the matter of employment.

The Act provides for the payment of equal remuneration to men and women workers for the same work or work of a similar nature.

The main provisions of this act are:

- No employer shall pay to any worker a remuneration (whether payable in cash or in kind) at rates less favourable than those at which remuneration is paid by him/ her to the workers of the opposite sex in such establishment for performing the same work or work of a similar nature.

> No employer shall, while making recruitment for the same work or work of a similar nature, or in any condition of service subsequent to recruitment such as promotions, training or transfer, make any discrimination against women except where the employment of women in such work is prohibited or restricted by or under any law for the time being in force.

Employee State Insurance Act, 1948

"An Act to provide for certain benefits to employees in case of sickness, maternity and employment injury and to make provision for certain other matters in relation thereto."

The Act has been enacted primarily with the object of protecting workers and their dependents, in the organised sector, in contingencies, such as Sickness, Maternity and Death or Disablement due to an employment injury or occupational hazard.

The ESI Act 1948 applies to:

> Non-seasonal Factories using power in and employing ten (10) or More persons.

> Non-seasonal and non-power using factories and establishments employing twenty(20) or more persons.

> Employees of the Factories and Establishments in receipt of wages not exceeding Rs.7500/- per month are covered under this Act.

> The sum payable to the contribution by the principal employer in respect of an employee and employer.

Payment of Gratuity Act

The Payment of Gratuity Act is a social security enactment. It is derived from the word 'gratuitous', which means 'gift' or 'present'. However, having being enacted as a social security form, it ceases to retain the concept of a gift but it has to be seen as a social obligation by an employer towards his employee. This act has been discussed in more detail in Chapter 13.

Employees' Provident Funds & Misc. Provisions Act, 1952

The Act has been enacted to provide for the institution of Provident Funds, Pension Fund and Deposit Linked Insurance fund for the employees in factories and establishment. It aims at savings of employees and to provide financial support after retirement in the form of Pension. It also provides for pension benefit to the nominee in case of death of member while in service irrespective of length of membership & pension to the member in case of permanent disablement while in service. This act has been discussed in more detail in Chapter 13.

The Industrial Employment (Standing Orders) Act, 1946

The Act is applicable to every industrial establishment in which one hundred or more workmen are employed. The Government can, however, apply the provisions of the Act to any industrial establishment employing less than one hundred persons.

"Standing Orders" means the rules of conduct for workmen employed in industrial establishment relating to matters like attendance, leave, misconduct, etc., enumerated in the Schedule appended to the Act. "Model Standing Orders" means the standing orders prescribed by the Central Government or a State Government for the purpose of the Act to serves as a model. They provide a pattern of the rules of conduct relating to the various matters specified in the Schedule appended to the Act.

The Payment of Bonus Act

This act to provide for the payment of bonus to persons employed in certain establishments on the basis of profits or on the basis of production or productivity and for matters connected therewith. The payment of Bonus in India is determined the the payment of bonus act, 1965. The Payment of Bonus Bill having been passed by both the Houses of Parliament received the assent of the President on 25th September, 1965. It came on the Statute Book as The Payment of bonus Act, 1965. Since then many amendments have been made to this act. This act has been discussed in more detail in Chapter 14.

The Shops and Establishments Act

This act was enacted to provide statutory obligation and rights to employees and employers in the unorganized sector of employment, i.e., shops and establishments. It is a state legislation and each state has framed its own rules for the Act. The act is applicable to all persons employed in an establishment with or without wages, except the members of the employer's family, however the state government can exempt, either permanently or for a specified period, any establishments from all or any provisions of this Act.

The main provisions of this act are:

- Compulsory registration of shop/establishment within thirty days of commencement of work.
- Communications of closure of the establishment within 15 days from the closing of the establishment.
- Lays down the hours of work per day and week.
- Lays down guidelines for spread-over, rest interval, opening and closing hours, closed days, national and religious holidays, and overtime work.
- Rules for employment of children, young persons and women.
- Rules for annual leave, maternity leave, sickness and casual leave, etc.
- Rules for employment and termination of service.

The Maternity Benefit Act, 1961

"An Act to regulate the employment of women in certain establishments for certain periods, before and after child-birth and to provide for maternity benefit and certain other benefits."

The purpose of this act is to provide healthy maintenance of pregnant women employee and her child. The various cash and non-cash benefits that a pregnant lady is liable to receive from her employer, under this act are:

Cash Benefits:
- 84 Days leave with pay.
- A medical bonus of Rs. 1,000/- (As Per latest Amendment)
- An additional leave with pay up to one month
- In case of miscarriage Six weeks leave with average pay.

Non Cash Benefits:
- Light work for 10 weeks (6 weeks plus 1 month) before delivery.
- 2 Nursing breaks of 15 Minutes until the child 15 months old.
- No discharge or dismissal while on maternity leave.
- No charge to her disadvantage while on maternity leave.
- Leave for Miscarriage & Tubectomy Operation.

The Industrial Disputes Act, 1947

"An Act to make provision for the investigation and settlement of industrial disputes, and for certain other purposes."

The act provides clarity on the following types of disputes that could occur between employer and employee:
- Settlements and Awards
- Strikes
- Lockouts
- Lay-off
- Retrenchment
- Closure

This act has not only helped the judicial system resolve several cases that have been raised by employees and employers alike but also provides a machinery for investigating and settling disputes through works committees, conciliation officers, boards of conciliation, courts of enquiry, labour courts, tribunals and voluntary arbitration.

The Factories Act, 1948

(The Factories (Amendment) Act, 1954, 1976, 1987)

'An Act to consolidate and amend the law regulating labour in factories. Whereas, it is expedient to consolidate and amend the law regulating labour in factories.'

This act secures safety, health, welfare of the employees, regulates their working hours, ensures their annual leaves with wages, and provides for additional protection from hazardous processes, additional protection to women workmen and prohibition of employment of children.

Apprentices Act, 1961

'An Act to provide for the regulation and control of training of apprentices and for matters connected therewith.'

The Apprentices Act, 1961 was enacted to regulate and control the programme of training of apprentices and for matters connected therewith. The Act makes it obligatory on part of the employers both in public and private sector establishments having requisite training infrastructure as laid down in the act, to engage apprentices in 254 groups of industries covered under the Act.

Future of Industrial Relations in India

The recent spate of labour strikes in India have put a huge question mark on the future of Industrial Relations in this country. The Maruti Strikes was perhaps the most talked about. The spate of labour strikes at the Manesar plant of the auto manufacturer left it with a 60 percent plunge in its quarterly profits. There were strikes at Bosch Plant at Bangalore, at Coal India; not so long ago at General Motor's India Ltd. (GM) Halol plant located in the western Indian state of Gujarat. 'According to the Indian Labor Bureau, over five million working days were lost in 2010 as a result of strikes and lockouts in the country. The most intense strikes occurred in the south-eastern state of Andhra Pradesh; in the eastern state of West Bengal; Himachal Pradesh and Rajasthan located in the north; and in Tamil Nadu and Kerala in the south' (Kumara, 2011).

It would not be wrong to say that the Industrial relations in India is at cross-roads. Employment relations need to be looked from a larger perspective of 'Unitary Approach' both by the management and by the trade unions. The restoration of the 'psychological contract' and an 'engagement-led approach' is the answer, if India were to really compete with countries like China.

Essay Questions

1. Is IR relevant in current times? What is a sound industrial relations system? Who are the primary participants in the industrial relations system?

2. Discuss the theoretical approaches to industrial relations. What are the various roles of IR?

3. What is a Trade Union? Discuss the Trade Unions Act.

4. What are the various heads under which labour acts can be grouped in India? Also list major Industrial Acts.

5. Write notes on the following Labour Acts in India-
   a) The Minimum Wages Act
   b) Payment of Wages Act
   c) Workmen Compensation Act
   d) Equal Remuneration Act
   e) Employee State Insurance Act
   f) Payment of Gratuity Act
   g) Employee Provident Funds and Miscellaneous Provisions Act.
   h) The Industrial Employment Act
   i) The Payment of Bonus Act
   j) The Shop and Establishment Act
   k) The Maternity Benefit Act
   l) The Industrial Disputes Act
   m) The Factories Act
   n) Apprentices Act

6. Comment on the future of Industrial Relations in India.

Application Questions

1. Go to –
   a) http://www.guardian.co.uk/society/2011/nov/30/strikes-public-sector pensions-impact
   b) http://www.bbc.co.uk/news/uk-england-london-15947818

   Watch the videos -
   a) http://www.youtube.com/watch?v=tW1J1aBX1zU
   b) http://www.youtube.com/watch?v=bH4d7AAuySk&NR=1&feature=fvwp
   c) http://www.guardian.co.uk/society/video/2011/nov/30/cameron-miliband-public-sector-strike-video

   If necessary browse through similar material and analyze the 2011 strike by over 2 million public sector workers in U.K. over pensions. Note the political overtones, the contentious issue, impact and negotiations.

Bibliography

(n.d.). Retrieved from Indian Export Import Portal: http://exim.indiamart.com/ssi-regulations/shops-establishments-act.html

(n.d.). Retrieved from SC judgements: http://www.scjudgments.com/updates/law.aspx?ls=38

Clarke, L., Donnelly, E., Hyman, R., Kelly, J., Mckay, S., & Moore, S. (2011). What's the Point of Industrial Relations? *International Journal of Comparative Labour Law & Industrial Relations*, 27 (3), 239-253.

De silva, S. R. (n.d.). Elements of a Sound Industrial Relations System. Retrieved from http://www.ilo.org/public/english/dialogue/actemp/downloads/publications/srseleme.pdf

Employees Provident Fund and Miscellaneous Provisions Act. (n.d.). Retrieved from http://www.legalissuesforngos.org/main/other/EPF.pdf

Employees's State Insurance Act 1948. (n.d.). Retrieved from Cite HR: http://www.citehr.com/64713-employees-state-insurance-act-1948-ppt.html

Gopinath, M., & Krishna, H. (n.d.). Employee State Insurance ; for a Handful of Contribution, a Bagful of Benefits. Retrieved from http://www.ccsindia.org/ccsindia/interns2003/chap6.pdf

Jacob, A. (2010, June 10). Hyundai Faces Persistent Labour Strikes in India, Plans to Shift Part of i20 Production to Turkey. Retrieved from http://paultan.org/2010/06/10/hyundai-faces-persistent-labour-strikes-in-india-plans-to-shift-part-of-i20-production-to-turkey

Jr, W., & M. S. (1966). Corporate Industrial Relations Research—Dream or Reality? *Academy of Management Journal*, 9 (2), 127-135.

Katz, H. C., Kochan, T. A., & Weber, M. A. (1985). Assessing the Effects of Industrial

Relations Systems and Efforts to Improve the Quality of Working Life on Organizational Effectiveness. *Academy of Management Journal,* 28 (3), 509-526.

Kranthi, K. (2011, March 23). GM India Workers Launch Wildcat Strike in Gujarat. Retrieved from http://www.wsws.org/articles/2011/mar2011/gmin-m23.shtml

Labor Backlash: Multinationals Feel the Heat of Worker Dissatisfaction in India. (2010, July 29). Retrieved from knowledge.wharton: http://knowledge.wharton.upenn.edu/india/article.cfm?articleid=4505

Management Shops and Establishments Rules Need to be Updated, made Uniform. (n.d.). Retrieved from Livemint.com: http://www.livemint.com/2008/04/14014744/Management—Shops-and-establi.html.

Overdorf, J. (2011, November 7). Shiva's Rules: Union Strikes Threaten India Inc. Retrieved from http://www.globalpost.com/dispatch/news/regions/asia-pacific/india/111106/union-strikes-india-economy-labor-maruti-suzuki.

Pyman, A., Holland, P., Teicher, J., & Cooper, B. K. (2010). Industrial Relations Climate, Employee Voice and Managerial Attitudes to Unions: An Australian Study. *British Journal of Industrial Relations,* 48 (2), 460-480.

Sen, R. (2011). Multinationals & Industrial Relations in India. *Indian Journal of Industrial Relations,* 46 (3), 367-383.

The Employees' Provident Fund and Miscellaneous Provisions Act, 1952. (n.d.). Retrieved from https://www.lkncon-sultants.net/beta/f1.asp

The Employees' Provident Funds and Miscellaneous Provisions Act, 1952. (n.d.). Retrieved from Employee's Provident Fund Organization, India: http://epfindia.nic.in/legel_provision.htm

The Role of the State in Industrial Relations. (2010). *Seoul Journal of Business,* 16 (2), 95-125.

Ther, S. M., & Nimalathasan, B. (2011). Industrial Relations In China: Lessons for Bangladesh. *Global Management Review,* 5 (3), 54-61.

Trade Unions Movement in India. (n.d.). Retrieved from http://www.slideshare.net/hemangitawde147/trade-union-ppt

Vikas, S. (2011). Industrial Relations In Bric Nations: A Study. *Asia Pacific Journal of Research in Business Management,* 2 (6), 135-157.

Workers Compensation Amendment Act 1993. (n.d.). Retrieved from http://www.legislation.qld.gov.au/LEGISLTN/ACTS/1993/93AC048.pdf

Workmen's Compensation Act. (n.d.). Retrieved from http://www.ngosindia.com/resources/wcact.pdf

Workmen's Compensation Act 1923. (n.d.). Retrieved from http://www.slideshare.net/tkjainbkn/workmens-compensation-act-1923-991548.

Chapter 17

Women Workforce & HR

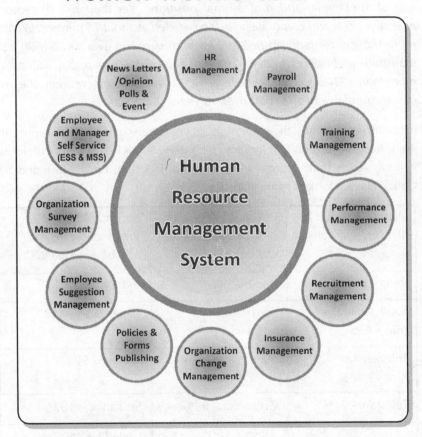

Outline

Introduction
Unequal Worlds
Work-life Imbalance
Sexual Harassment & Physical insecurity
Pay Discrimination & Glass Ceiling
Work Stress
Women Resource
Essay Questions
Application Questions
Bibliography

Key Terms

- Accounting
- Education Index
- Human Resource Accounting
- Sexual Harassment
- Unequal Worlds
- Women Resource
- Women Workforce
- Work Stress
- Work-life Imbalance

Introduction

The idea of dedicating a chapter on Women and the much needed HR response to the same does not stem from the perception that women are in anyway lesser employees but from the fact that despite the all-round brilliance of women it is still very much a man's world and the odds are loaded in all possible ways against women. This is true even for the most developed countries of the world like US.

'Women have long constituted roughly half of US workforce and just over half of managerial and professional positions. Yet their rise to senior-executive posts and corporate boards has stalled at about 15 percent. What's more the gender pay gap persists. Women earn, on average, $4600 less than their male peers in their first post MBA job – a gap that widens to more than $31000 as their careers advance. Without intervention, the lost pay accumulates to $431000 over 40 years '(Lang, 2011).

In countries like India the general social conditions of women is a worry in itself. In some aspects like literacy, secondary school enrolment etc. India features lower than countries like Rwanda, Pakistan, Bangladesh and Sri Lanka. Have a look at some statistics:

Table 17.1: Women Literacy Secondary School Enrolment, and Age at Marriage in Different Countries

Women Married by 18 (20-24 age group)	Women Literacy (15-24 age group 2005/2008)	Secondary School Enrolment (Girls per 100 boys) (2005/2008)
India – 47%	India – 74%	India – 88
South Central Asia – 45%	Iran – 96%	Bangladesh – 112
Sub-Saharan Africa – 38%	Bangladesh – 76%	Bhutan – 99
Pakistan – 24%	Sri Lanka – 99%	Sri Lanka – 102
	Libya – 100%	Canada – 98
	Tunisia – 96%	US – 100
	Kenya – 93%	Austria – 96

(**Source:** The Times of India, New Delhi Edition, 13-11-2011)

Women Economically Active (15+ age group)	Presence in Parliament (2010)
India – 33%	India – 11%
Bangladesh – 59%	Afghanistan – 27%
Sub-Saharan Africa – 61%	Pakistan – 22%
	Bangladesh – 19%
	Nepal – 33%

Table 17.2: Women Presence in Parliament

(**Source:** *The Times of India, New Delhi Edition, 13-11-2011*)

The percentage of women married by the age of 18 in India is higher than Sub-Saharan Africa and Pakistan; the literacy rate of women in India is worse than Iran, Libya, Kenya; the secondary school enrolment of girls in India is worse than Sri Lanka, Bhutan (Table 17.1); more women are economically active in Sub-Saharan Africa than in India; and, Indian women have lesser presence in Parliament than those in Nepal, Pakistan, Afghanistan (Table 17.2).

Even in the UN Human Development and gender Inequality study India performs no better. In terms of Gender Inequality India ranks lower than countries like Rwanda, Pakistan, Bangladesh and Zimbabwe, who rank much lower to India when it comes to overall Human Development Index (Table 17.3).

Country	Human Development	Gender inequality
India	134	129
Pakistan	145	115
Rwanda	166	82
Bangladesh	146	112
Zimbabwe	173	118

Table 17.3: Human Development & Gender Inequality

(**Source:** *The Times of India, New Delhi Edition, 13-11-2011*)

Such statistics are worrying and go on to further point that women who make it to the corporate world have not got things on platter and had to really work against a lot of odds to reach where they have. This doesn't take anything away from their male counterparts but for them the social conditions and settings are different, expectation are different and odds are much less. If this is not enough reason to write this chapter, study after study has indicated that having more women as employees in organization has contributed to high gains for the organizations. Consider this blog post:

Studies by the RAND Corporation and Catalyst, among others, show a clear and positive correlation between the percentage of women board directors in a company's past and the percentage of women top executives in its future. The Catalyst blog (Posted by Ilene on September 29th, 2011, http://www.catalyst.org/blog/tag/fortune500) states the following findings:

➤ More diversity, more innovation.
➤ More women, fewer problems.
➤ More women, stronger corporate ethics.
➤ More women, more effective problem-solving.
➤ More women on top, more women in pipeline.

Unequal Worlds

Women in our society have fought and come along way however they still do not find this world equal to what a man finds in this planet. Although such inequities can be found in all walks of life, the ones that I have attempted to discuss here are the ones faced by the working women.

Work-life Imbalance

The work-life imbalance of women is very high. The domestic responsibilities remain the primary responsibility of women. This does not mean that men do not help in domestic chores but please mark the word 'help'. This seldom gets better than that. And for a moment if you thought that such trends prevail in only countries like India then think again. As per the McKinsey report (2007) 'Women Matter', 'an average European women spends about four and a half hours on domestic work as opposed to men who give little more than two and a quarter.' In the words of the famous women entrepreneur and CEO of Biocon Kiran Shaw Majumdar: *"I do enjoy the work I do, but find most of my time goes towards activities like conferences and award ceremonies. I have come to accept that I am a prisoner of work. Conferences take so much of my time. And award ceremonies are*

particularly tiresome. I try to take some days off, at least twice a year." In her own words she is not able to play golf anymore, which used to be her favourite non-work activity.
(**Source:** *Outlook Business*)

Sexual Harassment & Physical Insecurity

The U.S. Equal Employment Opportunity Commission (EEOC) has defined sexual harassment in its guidelines as - Unwelcome sexual advances, requests for sexual favors, and other verbal or physical conduct of a sexual nature when:

- Submission to such conduct is made either explicitly or implicitly a term, or
- Condition of an individual's employment, or
- Submission to or rejection of such conduct by an individual is used as a basis for employment decisions affecting such individual, or
- Such conduct has the purpose or effect of unreasonably interfering with an individual's work performance or creating an intimidating, hostile, or offensive working environment.

Sexual harassment may be categorized under following types of harassments:

- Verbal harassment: namely comments that have sexual overtones, or personal remarks that are humiliating and of a sexual nature.
- Psychological harassment: namely behaviours that cause the woman mental anxiety, such as, for example, insistence on accompanying the respondent, phone calls at odd hours, stalking/following the respondent, staring and sending obscene sms/text messages.
- Sexual gestures and exposure.
- Unwanted touch and embraces.
- Rape, attempted rape or forced sex.

The "Workplace Sexual Harassment Survey" carried out in 2010, by the Centre for Transforming India, a non-profit organization in the Information Technology and BPO/KPO industries has claimed that nearly 88% of the female workforce in Indian Information Technology and business process outsourcing and knowledge process outsourcing (BPO/KPO) companies reported having suffered some form of workplace sexual harassment during the course of their work. Close to 50% women had been subjected to abusive language, physical contact or been sought sexual favours, These statistics are scary and worrying.

(**Source:** Southasia.oneworld.net)

One of the biggest problems in case of sexual harassment is lack of awareness. The survey found that that 60% of the respondents were not aware of the workplace sexual harassment policies of their organizations. Around 10% were only partially aware. This posed a hurdle in getting a redressal.

Another problem is lack of reporting or the fear of reporting. As many as 47% employees did not know where to report, while 91% did not report for fear of being victimized. What is even worrying is that it was found that in nearly 72% of the incidents the perpetrator was a superior.

Pay Discrimination & Glass Ceiling

Wide ranges of pay-disparities still exist in many industries between male and female workers. Some statistics discussed earlier in the chapter is an indication in itself. At the same time, it is alleged that still in many companies a sort of glass-ceiling exists when it comes to women leaders. Female employees are considered less favourably compared to male workers when it comes to the senior and top positions in the company. Globally women represent more than 40 percent of workforce. Despite this most organizations have this typical glass-ceiling which results in them getting discriminated which is done covertly, most of the times.

A very recent newspaper report alleges a globally reputed IT firm of unfairly overlooking a female employee for the role of managing director in a firm. Ms. Ayres who worked at this firm for 15 years was seen as an outstanding candidate to become GM of its "Small Medium Enterprise & Partner group". But the role was allegedly handed over to Mr. Frazer, a GM at this firm, even before Ayres could finish her interview. It is also alleged that the company paid over one million sterling pounds to silence Ayres.

Work Stress

In a survey conducted by Kenexa Research Institute, an HR advisory firm based in the US, while women at work deliver the same results as men, across occupations, women experience "unreasonable" stress than men do. The survey sampled some 29,338 men and women were surveyed from India, China, Brazil, Russia, America, Britain, Australia, Canada, Denmark, Finland, France, Germany, Italy, Japan, Mexico, the Netherlands, Spain, Sweden and Switzerland and found that across roles, more women experienced unreasonable amount of stress than men did. Some of the key stressors in women were:

- Payment parity,
- Equal opportunities,
- Career growth,
- Fair performance assessment,
- Work-life balance,
- Doing exciting work,
- Having a respectful manager.

(**Source:** *The Times of India*)

Women Resource

By engaging women on equal terms, organizations and societies shall do no favour. Such efforts shall bring them growth and sustainability. The World Development Report 2012 (Gender Equality & Development) says that – 'Gender equality is all about smart economics, as it can have a huge impact on productivity and economic efficiency...For an economy to be functioning at its potential women's skills and talent should be engaged in activities that make best use of those abilities.'

The human resources of the organizations have to evolve into truly valuing the 'women resource'. In doing so following issues are of key importance:

1. Equal work, equal pay;
2. Women Leadership development;
3. Supportive family policies
   a. Parental Leaves
   b. Day-care
   c. Pregnancy care

4. Anti-sexual harassment policy;
5. Flexible Work Option
   a. Flexible work-timings
   b. Work-from-home
   c. Job-Sharing
   d. Career-breaks & re-entry issues
   e. Part-time work
6. Physical security of women; and,
7. Networking, Counseling and mentoring.

We now look at few examples of companies who have formulated some of the above mentioned practices, both in letter and spirit.

Exhibit 1: IBM India

IBM started the 'equal-work, equal-pay policy' much before the Equal Pay Act, came into existence. A letter issued by Watson Sr., the legendary leader of IBM, in 1935 stated, "Men and women will do the same kind of work for equal pay. They will have the same treatment, the same responsibilities, and the same opportunities for advancement." Since then IBM's management always made efforts to find out the specific needs of its women employees and provided women-friendly facilities accordingly. IBM India's specific initiatives include:

Indian Women's Leadership Council (IWLC): Indian Women's Leadership Council (IWLC) is a part of this Diversity Council and it brings in the required focus on gender diversity for the entire organization, to 'attract, retain and grow' women talent.

IBM's Taking the Stage Program: IBM's leadership development program for women employees, it shows female employees how to project an aura of leadership whenever they speak at work.

Tailor-made Training Programs: IBM India recently announced the launch of custom-made training programmes, christened *TechAcme* and *SalesElan*, for its potential women leaders in technology and sales to create an accelerated leadership pipeline in these two segments traditionally dominated by men. According to India Women Leadership Council (IWLC), IBM India, the move has been prompted by the attitude of young women who are becoming more adventurous in moving to new roles and aims to increase the leadership pool of women in technology by 20% and in sales by 15% in the next 18 months through these programmes. TechAcme and Sales-Elan will complement the firm's succession programme for women in general management that started in 2009. Technology leadership programme. TechAcme will focus on women in technical functions such as architecture and database administration, while SalesElan will be a multi-tier programme across all levels and business units. SalesElan- which will add to the existing Sales Eminence programme for building basic selling skills.

Family Policies: IBM has one of the best of childcare/dependent care services. It provides 156 weeks of job-protected parental leave and a full menu of child-care services.

Grievance-Addressal System: IBM takes any allegations of sexual harassment in nature very seriously. IBM insists on a non-discriminatory workplace and do not tolerate harassment of any type.

Flexibility in Work: The work-life flexibility options (work from home, flexi-timings, part-time options, etc...) are provided. Flexible working options include job-sharing, term-time working, compressed hours and sabbaticals.

Exhibit 2: Ernst & Young

Ernst & Young (EY), one of the largest professional services firms in the world and one of the "Big Four" accountancy firms, along with Deloitte, KPMG and PricewaterhouseCoopers (PwC), was placed among the top 50 places in the Where Women Want to Work awards for 2007. The firm was also named as one of the 10 Best Companies for Working Mothers by *Working Mothers* magazine in 2006.

Some of its exemplary initiatives for women employees are as follows:

- Flexible work environment i.e., work from home option is provided (both for part time and full time women employees).

- Family friendly benefits wherein paternity leaves are provided to the husband to take care of their wife during motherhood.

- **'Ashray'** a crèche facility provided by the company to take care of the kid while their mother is at work.

- If any of the female employees is working late at the company, for security reasons the company makes sure that a security guard is accompanying the employee till their home premises.

- A program named **'Promoting change developing and advancing women'** – which promotes systematic change for women by working through the firm's business units to foster local innovation and ownership.

Exhibit 3: American Express, India

American Express, India has taken initiatives for the women employees to balance their work life balance and provide them more opportunities to grow. In American express 43% employees women, and the company is employee sensitive provide flexi timings to the employees. The company has program called '**Pregnancy Care**'. This programme takes care of needs and queries for the entire nine-month period. The programme helps in understanding what body may go through during this period and provides the pregnant women employees with books and written material provided, discount coupons for tests, along with newsletters that keep informing on a regular basis. If a woman employee is in the programme, company also send reminders for periodic check-ups and tests.

Exhibit 4: Hindustan Unilever Limited (HUL)

HUL takes extraordinary initiatives towards retaining more women employees. Various initiatives have chalked out as parts of its HR Policy are discussed below:

Day Care Facility: HUL realized that most women professionals are forced to take a career break for personal reasons, getting the personal professional life balance back can be quite difficult. It becomes an absolute necessary for the mothers to take care of the child in this crucial stage. This made HUL to come up with the concept of Day Care Facility within the office premise.

Work for Home Facility for Women: After the maternity period women employees in HUL have a privilege to work from home for the next few years.

Job Sharing Facility: This is a new concept developed at HUL where two women can share a particular task of women employees who returns from the maternity leave. They could work when ever convenient and do a particular task jointly. This initiative was also taken considering the fact of the difficulties that a women employees faces after the maternity stage.

Diversity: HUL aggressively pursue the target of increasing the proportion of women in management cadres. They have a number of gender-friendly policies such as Maternity Benefit, Career Break, Flexi-working, Agile Working from remote location, Sabbaticals, Part-time work and Career Breaks.

Career Break Facility: Hindustan Unilever Limited allows its employees (both men and women) to take long career breaks. Such breaks can be availed for more than twice during the employee's career span and the total duration of the break(s) extends up to five years.

Exhibit 5: Taj Group of Hotels

At Taj, diversity is promoted not just in the situation where in people from different cultures are encouraged to work together, but also when people of both the genders. Hence Taj has formulated policies which promote the employment of women, especially in the organization.

- Taj was first company in the hotel industry to employ women in areas other than housekeeping. It promotes the concept of employing graduate women and expanding their career-path within the organization.

- Taj has extremely stringent anti-sexual harassment policies aimed at providing a safe and work-oriented organization culture for women.

- The concept of flexi-timings and optional career paths are provided for women who have multiple priorities like family and motherhood.

- Taj also promotes its women employees to take sabbaticals, so that its women employees can study further while still being on the pay-roll.

- Other than this, Taj has features like day-care centres and crèches for women employers who have infants or small children to take care.

- Taj also provided a leave of absence for the pregnant women employees with pay during their absence.

Taj is also known for taking care in the development and empowerment of all the women who are affiliated in to the organization. Some of the measures are listed below:

- Most of the linen used in Taj group's chain of Jiva spas is a major source of income for women who would otherwise be marginalized. Aura Herbal Wear that supports Indian NGOs working with under-privileged women is Taj's partner in this venture. These women are taught various skills such as designing and stitching garments, to make them self-reliant.

- Most of the Jiva spa specialists use towels stitched by women from Himmat, a group started to support the community of minority women who are left to fend for themselves and their children after the communal riots of Ahmedabad, Gujarat.

- Aura Herbal Wear also supports Apang Manav Mandal, which educates and trains physically-challenged girls.

- Taj also supports the renowned and traditional silk weavers of Varanasi who thread all the sarees worn by the women employees of Taj Group of Hotels. It helps the weavers financially and aids in keeping the craft alive.

Exhibit 6: PepsiCo

PepsiCo is firmly committed to leveraging the power that its talented women associates bring to the company Some of the initiatives at PepsiCo that support women workforce are:

- **'Women's Inspiration Network (WIN)'** the global online women's networking portal where women are asked to "share their stories of inspiration" for a chance to become a "correspondent" for PepsiCo.

- **'BlogHer'** - PepsiCo's partnered with the world's largest women's bloggers conference **'BlogHer'**.

- **'Women of Colour-Multicultural Alliance'** serves as a strategic support and resource group focused on attracting, retaining, and developing women of colour in the middle and senior management ranks at PepsiCo mainly Alaskan, African, American-Indian, Asian-Hispanic etc.

- **'Power Pairs'** a program that builds authentic relationships and advancement opportunities for women of colour through facilitated dialogues with immediate and skip-level managers; a national leadership development conference; and regional networking events.

Exhibit 7: Marriott International, Inc.

At Marriott, women hold many powerful jobs from president of a major operating division to global leader of sales and revenue management, as well as responsibility for some of the most profitable hotels. Marriott International Inc., through extensive internal research, created a three-pronged approach: improving the career planning and promotion process, creating career development tools to encourage networking and mentoring, and providing increased support for work/life balance.

Marriott organizes a 2 day Women Leadership Conference, once every 6 months, to introduce the initiative and to foster a dialogue concerning women's leadership opportunities at Marriott. It has a custom-made Leadership Development Talent Inventory process for women, which includes a thorough personal assessment, extensive feedback, executive coaching, a workshop, and the creation of a personal development plan. This process allows women control over their own careers and the latitude to move throughout the businesses at Marriott. Other facilities, like, child care, elder care, flexibility, relocation assistance, mentoring, and networking are offered to make the life of its employees, especially women employees on whose shoulders rests the major responsibility of family-care, much simpler and engaging. No wonder, Marriott International, Inc. was ranked by Working Mother magazine as one of the 2011 Working Mother 100 Best Companies.

Exhibit 8: Deloitte

Deloitte's WIN: Deloitte launched a major initiative for women, the Women's Initiative (WIN), some 18 years ago for the Retention and Advancement of Women, that has helped the company to find the intellectual capital to meet aggressive growth targets. Launched in 1993, WIN addressed two related issues: a high rate of female attrition and underrepresentation of women in leadership positions. The unique components of WIN include a broad range of leadership and development programs. 'National Women as Buyers' workshops address the distinctive communication and decision-making styles of women, while regional career development programs prepare Deloitte's women for advancement at all levels. The Women's Initiative has fueled significant increases for women in leadership: women's representation as partners, principals, and directors has risen from 6 percent in 1995 to 22 percent in 2009, and representation of women senior managers has increased from 23 percent to 36 percent in the same timeframe.

Exhibit 9: Accenture

Accenture has created unique programs to support our women in their career development and progression, including:

- **Vaahini:** Accenture has a women's networking forum, Vaahini, a formal community of all women employees to enable them to share experiences, create opportunities to learn and grow as well as to empower them to drive change. Several programs have been launched under the Vaahini banner, ranging from workshops on self-defence, domestic violence and financial planning to effective parenting, child abuse, harassment at the workplace as well as lesbian and gay's issues.

- With the objective of nurturing and developing women leaders, in addition to its leadership development offerings, focused initiatives such as Developing High Performing Women Managers, Women Mentoring and Sponsorship Programs and Mentoring Circles are being designed and executed to enable women at all levels with networks, sponsors and advocates to accelerate growth and development of women leaders as well as to provide consistent coaching and guidance to women to achieve success personally and professionally.

- It has flexible work arrangements that support the unique needs of professionals in the workplace, encouraging a balance between work and personal priorities.

- Through Maternity Returners Program, it helps ease the transition for new parents back into the workforce by providing career guidance and support for finding ideal re-entry roles.

> In its endeavour to enhance health and well-being of its employees and provide organisation support to specific segments such as parents and expecting women, its wellness rooms are fully equipped with private space for nursing for new mothers. Multiple workshops and free counselling on 'Effective Parenting', regular gynaecologist visits, free women's health camps are some of the examples of initiatives we have undertaken to support our people.

> It ensures highest level of transport safety and security to its women employees through measures such as a dedicated 24/7 emergency helpline, security escorts and dedicated medical cabs for expecting mothers.

Essay Questions

1. Comment on the general state of Women in India. What is the relevance?

2. In your opinion, do women employees add value to the organization they work? Explain with examples.

3. What are the various inequities that women face in the organizations? Why do these inequities exist?

4. How can such inequities might be addressed? Explain with examples.

5. Discuss initiatives of IBM in promoting women workforce.

Application Questions

1. Study the links –

   a) http://www.economist.com/blogs/daily chart/2011/11/working-women

   b) http://collegetimes.us/10-surprising-statistics-on-women-in-the-workplace/ and, comment on the state of women employees at workplaces, at large.

2. Go the http://www.eowa.gov.au/ and study the Australian government's initiatives for promoting equal opportunity for women in the workplace agency.

3. Go to the link http://www.ey.com/Publication/vwLUAssets/Women_of_Africa/$FILE/\Women%20of%20Africa%20final.pdf and the read the document on 'Women of Africa: A powerful untapped economic force for the continent'

Bibliography

(n.d.). Retrieved from Accenture: https://microsite.accenture.com/moving_forward_india/why-accenture/Pages/Focus-on-Women.aspx.

(2010, July 22). Retrieved from Women suffer more stress at work: http://articles.timesofindia.indiatimes.com/2010-07-22/bangalore/28287797_1_work-stress-fewer-women women-fight.

(2011). Retrieved from NAFE Top 50 Companies: http://www.workingmother.com/nafe-top-companies-female-executives/2011-nafe-top-50-companies-0.

A Touch of Caring. (2011, May). Retrieved from Tata Review: www.tata.com/pdf/tata_review_may_11review_touch_of_caring.pdf.

Anahita, M. (2011, Nov). Some lessons from Rwan. Retrieved from The Times of India.

Carrer Opportunities for Women. (n.d.). Retrieved from Accenture: http://uscareers.accenture.com/us-en/working/overview/diversity/women/Pages/index.aspx.

Catalyst. (n.d.). Retrieved from http://www.thefreelibrary.com/Catalyst+Gives+Bayer,+Fannie+Mae,+and+Marriott+Prestigious+Catalyst...-a081820582.

Catalyst Study Shows Sponsorship is Key to Women's Success. (2011). Retrieved from http:/www.catalyst.org/press-release/190/catalyst-study-shows-sponsorship-is-key-to-womens-success.

Developing and Advancing Women. (2003). Retrieved from www.catalyst.org:: http://www.catalyst.org/publication/110/ernst-young-llppromoting-change-developing-advancing-women.

Dhar, A. (2010, Nov 15). India: 88% Women Victims of Sexual Harassment at Workplace. Retrieved from http://southasia.oneworld.net/todaysheadlines/india-88-women-victims-of-sexual-harassment-at-workplace.

Ernst & Young Ranks among the Top 10 on Working Mother Magazines 100 Best Companies. (2008). Retrieved from www.ey.com: http://www.ey.com/US/en/Newsroom/News-releases/Media-Release-23-09-08DC.

HUL Allows Women to Work from Remote Locations, if their Roles Mermit. (n.d.). Retrieved from The Economic Times: http:/economictimes.indiatimes.com/quickiearticleshow/5658357.cms.

Lukovit, K. (2011, July). PepsiCo Ramps Up BlogHer Event Partnership. MediaPost News.

Paramita, C. (n.d.). Sexual Harrassment in Workplace. Retrieved from http://www.popcouncil.org/pdfs/wp/India_HPIF/001.pdf.

PepsiCo, Inc. – Women of Color Multicultural Alliance. (2007, January). Catalyst.

Puri, S. B. (2010, January 11). Companies Roll Out Women-friendly Initiatives to Retain Female Staffers. The Economic Times.

Saumya, B. (2011, November). IBM to Incxrease Women Execs by 20%. Retrieved from IBM: http://timesofindia.indiatimes.com/tech/careers/job-trends/IBM-to-increase-women-execs-by-20/articleshow/10676409.cms.

Shaw, K. M. (2010, Jan). Work Life Balance foe Women. Retrieved from Outlook Business: http://business.outlookindia.com/article.aspx?263508.

Singh, N., & Zachachariah, R. (2010, March 8). The Times of India. Retrieved from Companies Offer Flexi Options to Retain Women Employees: http://articles.timesofindia.indiatimes.com/2010-03-08/india-business/28131679_1_women employees-flexi-work-women-professionals

Weaving a New Life, (2008, November). Retrieved from http://www.tata.com/ourcommitment/articles/inside.aspx?artid=/1gZ8FEhnhM.

Women and Marriott: Partners for the Future. (2002, Jan). Retrieved from Catalyst: http://www.catalyst.org/publication/121/marriott-international-incwomen-and-marriott-partners-for-the-future.

Chapter 18

Human Resource Automation, Audit & Accounting

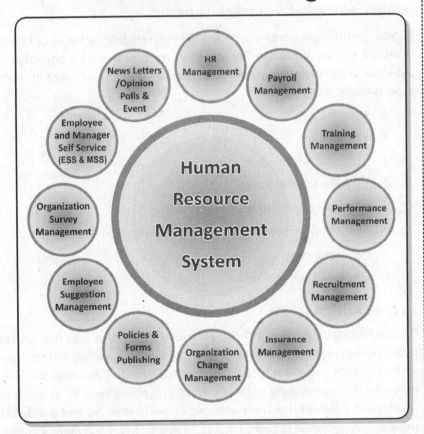

Outline

Automation
Benefits & Pitfalls of Automation
Audit
Rationale of Audit
Approaches to Audit
Sample HR Audit
Accounting
Methods of Calculating HRA
HRA at Infosys
Education Index
Is HRA useful?
Arguments against Human Resource Accounting
Future of Human Resource Accounting
Essay Questions
Application Questions
Bibliography

Key Terms

Accommodator
Assimilator
Converger
Diverger
Honey & Mumford
Learning Styles
Richard M Felder and Eunice R Henriques

This chapter delves on three topics i.e., HR Automation (HRIS), Audit and Accounting. Although these three topics are varied but they all are futuristic in nature when it comes to managing human resources and also qualify for extensive exploratory research.

HRIS

"Systematic procedure for collecting, storing, maintaining, retrieving, and validating data needed by organization about its human resources, personnel activities and organization unit characteristics."

Automation

The automation of human resource management relates primarily to Human resource information System (HRIS). **Kovach et al** defined "HRIS as a systematic procedure for collecting, storing, maintaining, retrieving, and validating data needed by organization about its human resources, personnel activities, and organization unit characteristics."

Basically, HRIS represents a marriage between traditional forms of human resource management and information technology. The objective of automation is to make processes faster, cheaper and more efficient. It covers aspects like:

1. Payroll
2. Work Time
3. Appraisal performance
4. Benefits Administration
5. HR management Information system
6. Recruiting/Learning Management # Training System
7. Performance Record
8. Employee Self-service

Payroll Automation

Payroll processing is one of the most common iterative jobs that an HR personnel has to perform. It involves considerable time, energy and resource with very little value-addition. The American Payroll Association (APA) estimates that automation reduces payroll processing costs by as much as 80 percent, much of that from reducing errors in invoices and paychecks (*Inc.com*). Automation of payroll makes the system faster and more accurate. Good payroll software should be able to maintain detailed records with clear audit trails, keep a track of sick and vacation days, keep up to date with tax law changes, analyze payroll expenses and employee productivity and must comply with the financial regulations of the land. Some example of payroll software are Mentis from Benett technologies, Beehive from Beehive HCM, Ascent Payroll from Eilisys, Paysoft from Opel Systems And Consultants Pvt. Ltd. (OSAC), Wings Payroll from Wings etc.

Performance Management Automation Systems

Automated performance management system must be flexible, robust, user-friendly and cost-effective. They must have built-in features like pre- and post-tests, skills tests, performance review & assessments, certification tests, course evaluations, surveys, 360 degree feedback, training needs assessments and readily adaptable to meet current and evolving company needs. Some examples of automated performance management systems are Halogen eAppraisal™, a web-based employee performance and talent management application from Halogen Software, ReviewSNAP™ from ReviewSNAP™ is a division of Applied Training Systems, Blue from eXplorance etc.

Recruitment Automation Systems

Recruitment automation systems are the need of the hour for HR professionals considering that hiring has become an all-round activity in most companies because of continuous attrition. The hiring can at times be very tedious process. Automated recruitment systems not only help in saving time & money spent on hiring but also help in-maintaining strong database of candidates, in preliminary screening and also in matching the requirements of the organization with the profile of the candidates. The automated recruitment system helps in making the process much more efficient by removing loads of paperwork and replacing the same with smart software capable of maintaining thousands of records and also helpful in retrieving the same intelligently. Automated recruitment systems also provide better visibility into a company's present and future resource demands and supply trends. Hence these systems also help in talent management. Examples of some recruitment systems are Resource Datamine, an end to end automated recruitment solution, promoted by NetEdge Computing solutions, IDS's Recruiter from Information data Systems, Akken Staffing™ from Akken etc.

Employee Self-service Systems

The employee self-service systems automate & streamline paper and labor-intensive processes and enables managers and employees to view and update their own data (address change, emergency contact, etc.), including online leave request and approvals, give employees quick and easy access to general company information including directories, news bulletins, stock or financial information, holiday schedules, temporary schedule changes/office closings, and any merger, acquisition or rightsizing news etc. Examples of ESS are Justlogin, SelfSource™ from Auxillium West, Deltek time and expense software from Deltek etc.

Benefits & Pitfalls of Automation

According to Society for Human Resources Management - "60% – 80% of an HR staff time is tied to repetitive administrative tasks. Much of this time is spent answering employee & manager questions and gathering information for reports." Automation helps HR to get rid of the repetitive administrative tasks that it has to do, making it free to engage in strategic HR issues that benefit the organization more and bring more value to the business. "Software and technology still hold the key to increased productivity and efficiency–it can save employee's time, help them work smarter, and require less peoplepower" (Workforce Management).

However over-automation may have its own pitfalls more so if it completely take-away the human interface where it is required most. For instance, in a software major when the performance appraisal system was being automated, the employees made a request that everything except the feedback from the supervisor should be automated. They would prefer to discuss their performance feedbacks with their respective supervisors rather than discover the same through an automated response. Care should be taken not to over-automate and desist from taking 'human' out of 'human resource management'.

Human Resource Audit

"Involves devoting time and resources to taking an intensely objective look at the company's HR policies, practices, procedures and strategies to protect the company, establish best practices and identify opportunities for improvement"

Audit

Human Resource Audit is essentially evaluating the various HR practices and processes in an organization against the set standards. *'An HR audit involves devoting time and resources to taking an intensely objective look at the company's HR policies, practices, procedures and strategies to protect the company, establish best practices and identify opportunities for improvement'* (SHRM, India).

'A Human Resources Audit is a comprehensive method (or means) to review current human resources policies, procedures, documentation and systems to identify needs for improvement and enhancement of the HR function as well as to ensure compliance with ever-changing rules and regulations' (Strategic HR Inc.).

The HR audit shall include evaluating:

1. Job Analysis
2. Recruitment
3. Selection
4. Performance Management
5. Performance Appraisals
6. Performance Feedbacks
7. Competency Mapping
8. Training Process
9. Compensation
10. Rewards Management
11. Benefits Management
12. Employee Relations
13. Workplace Safety
14. Best Practices
15. Managerial performance
16. Supervisory Performance
17. Leadership at various levels
18. HR Business Partner Role
19. HR Strategic Initiatives
20. Legal HR issues.

Rationale of Audit

A very famous watch-manufacturing company ventured into eye-care business. They needed, besides other staff, optometrists at every eye-care retail outlet, across the nation. A good optometrist is a vital link between the company and the customers. Many times it is the optometrist who coverts a potential to an actual customer. The company had a very good hiring team in place and was confident that it would be able to hire very able personnel for their eye-care division as well. Their primary targets would be various students graduating from different optometrists colleges in India. They had been following these processes for quite some time for their watch-division. The company went ahead with its plan of expansion. Later, when the hiring team visited the colleges to hire optometrists, to their dismay they found that most of these graduates were not employable. They had requisite knowledge but did not have very high level of skill that would be required in this profession. They had hardly any time to train them now. Left with no option, they hired optometrists from competitors at a very high market price. Obviously the acquisition cost went-up that was least expected when the company was expanding into a new business. In retrospect they should have 'audited' their hiring process in light of the new business and seen whether they needed to incorporate any changes. This would have forewarned them about the real state of talent demand and supply situation and they could have organized some pre-hiring training for the various graduating optometrists. This way they would have not only been able to keep their hiring cost under control but would have also been successful in sowing a greater degree of loyalty among their new recruits. A timely audit would have saved the company a lot and made their process more efficient.

The rationale of the audit hence can be outlined as:

- Audit increases the efficiency of the HR team.
- It helps in saving a lot of cost.
- Helps in achieving internal and external benchmarking.
- Helps in compliance issues to various quality initiatives in the company.
- Helps in legal compliance.
- Improves managerial performance.
- Improves supervision and leadership at all levels of the organization.
- Helps to retrospect and reflect upon various practices from a practical stand-point.
- Audit extends HR business partner's role and helps it make quantifiable contributions in business.
- Helps in making the HR department more effective and credible.

Approaches to Audit

Legal Approach to HR Audit

The audit of performance or conformity consists of .making an inventory of the social situation of the company, considering the labor law norms and regularly verifying the company's compliance with the applicable regulations (*Antona,1993*). Concern about labor risks has created a function within HRM with the purpose of altering working conditions by identifying the risks that could stem from them and implementing necessary preventive measures. Such preventive activity could fit perfectly into the legal approach of HR, although the effort that the company can make in this sense can go beyond the application of the existing risk prevention laws' (*Olalla, Castillo, 2002*). Hence the legal approach is primarily focused on the company's legal compliance to various labour legislations and acts.

Benchmarking Approach

The benchmarking approach to HR audit is primarily oriented towards continuous improvement in HR systems, policies and processes to deliver more value to the employees. Such benchmarking can be done internally as well as externally. The internal benchmarking shall compare the HR practices of the company against its own standards, whereas in external benchmarking the same is compared with the best-in-class practices in the industry.

Strategic Approach to HR Audit

In strategic approach to HR audit the relevance of the HR practices, systems and processes is seen with respect to the strategic objectives of the fir. How much do they these systems and practices contribute to furthering the business objectives of the firm? 'The strategical audit of HR helps assure that the HR programs are aligned with the Company's long-term objectives. In this way, the HR function is becoming a source of competitive advantage and is ceasing to be considered as a specialized and unrelated function that incurs high costs to the company' (*Olalla, Castillo, 2002*).

Reading Exhibit 1: Sample HR Audit

Employee Communications & Documents

- **Employee files:** Are employee files organized appropriately? Are confidential files, such as those containing health information or I-9 forms, kept separate?

- **Employee handbook or employment policies:** Is there an employee handbook/manual? Is it current and legally compliant?

- **Employee communications:** Is there an employee newsletter/e-mail? Is there a complaint/grievance process in place? Are employee surveys ever conducted? Are exit interviews done? Is the information acted upon?

- **Legally required posters:** Has a review of the poster requirements been done? (If not, check http://www.dol.gov/elaws/.) Are the appropriate posters available for employees to see?

Recruitment, Employment and Selection

- **Recruitment processes and sources:** How does the company find applicants? Who conducts the interviews? Have interviewers been trained?

- **Selection processes:** Are hiring processes and decisions documented? Are background investigations and reference checks being done?

- **Necessary forms, applications, etc.:** Is the employment application legally compliant focusing only on job-related data collection?

New Hire Orientation

- Is there a company new-hire orientation? Do departments do orientations? Does management follow up with new hires to check on how they are doing in their new jobs?

Compensation & Wage Administration

- **Consistent pay standards:** Is equal pay provided for equal work?

- **Time management:** Is there an attendance policy and procedure?

Benefits

- **Paid time off:** Is there a policy regarding paid time off?

- **Reward and recognition:** Is there an employee recognition and/or reward program?

Employee Training & Development

- **Employee training:** What kinds of training are provided?
- **Supervisory/management training:** Are regular supervisory training courses available?
- **Employee development:** Do employees receive career counseling or feedback?

Performance & Behavior Feedback Processes

- **Coaching and discipline:** Is there a progressive discipline process/policy in place?
- **Performance appraisal:** Is there a performance appraisal process? Are supervisors trained on how to coach and administer discipline?

Termination

- Termination forms and processes: Are terminable offenses documented? Are there written termination procedures? Is there a rehire policy?

Human Resource Responsibilities

- Administration: Is someone designated to be responsible for human resource management? Is there a HR manager and/or an HR department? Are HR responsibilities carried out by employees in other departments? Are any HR responsibilities outsourced? Are individuals responsible for HR administration regularly trained in HR-specific competencies?

(**Source:** HR One Source)

Another sample of HR Process Audit can be seen on -http://www.competitiveedgehr.com/Img/pdf/1361.pdf

Accounting

Mr. Narayana Murthy, Chairman Emeritus of Infosys once said that - "Our assets walk out of the door each evening. We have to make sure that they come back the next morning." In many ways what Mr. Murthy said made sense. The asset that daily moves out of the organization premises every evening is the human resource. And, an organization that attaches value to this precious asset shall always ensure that these assets come-back secured every morning. It is accentuated that the human element is the most important element in any corporate enterprise. However without truly determining the actual value of human resource, how can one even try to secure the same? The need for Human Resource Accounting arises because the organizations can actually find out how valuable an individual is, as

Human Resource Accounting

"HRA is the process of identifying and measuring data about human resources and communicating this information to interested parties."

the intellectual assets of a company are often worth three or four times the tangible book value. Human Resource accounting (HRA) denotes this process of quantification/measurement of the Human Resource.

The American Accounting Association's Committee on Human Resource Accounting (1973) has defined **Human Resource Accounting** as "the process of identifying and measuring data about human resources and communicating this information to interested parties".

Chronology of Research in Human Resource Accounting	
Mid 1960s	Initiation of work on Human Resource Accounting. Hermanson attempted incorporating employees into formal financial statements and coined the term 'Human Asset Accounting'
1965	Models for estimating the financial utility of personnel selection and downsizing, by Cronbach and Glaser, and Naylor and Shine using a concept named 'Utility Analysis'.
1968	Brummet et al fir the first time used the term 'Human Resource Accounting'
1998	Grojer and Johanson came up with 'Human Resource Costing and Accounting' (HRCA) marrying both Human Resource Accounting and Utility Analysis.
1999	Lynn concluded that managing intangible assets is fundamentally a management accounting issue
2002	Tayles et al. stated that management accounting has a natural affinity towards human capital

Table 18.1: Chronology of Research in Human Resource Accounting

Methods of Calculating HRA

Basically HRA can be calculated through two methods—cost-based analysis and value-based analysis.

Cost Approach

The cost-based approach focuses on the cost parameters, which may relate to historical cost, replacement cost, or opportunity cost. The cost component entails from the time the recruitment begins and ends when the employer terminates the services of the employee. The cost of acquiring talent, engaging, training and remunerating is calculated at various levels.

Economic Value Approach

'The value of an object, in economic terms, is the present value of the services that it is expected to render in future. The value-based approach suggests that the value of human resources depends upon their capacity to generate revenue. Similarly, the economic value of human resources is the present worth of the services that they are likely to render in future. This may be the value of individuals, groups or the total human organization.' The method for calculating the economic value of individuals may be classified into monetary and non-monetary methods.

Under the economic value approach, we shall discuss the **Lev and Schwartz Model** employed by Indian organizations. According to this model, the value of human capital embodied in a person who is 'y' years old, is the present value of his/her future earnings from employment and can be calculated by using the following formula

$$E(V_y) = Ó P_y(t+1) Ó I(T)/(I+R)^{t-y}$$

where, $E(V_y)$ = expected value of a 'y' year old person's human capital

T = the person's retirement age

$P_y(t)$ = probability of the person leaving the organisation

$I(t)$ = expected earnings of the person in period I

r = discount rate

The basic theme of Lev, Schwartz model is to compute the present value of the future direct and indirect *payments* to their employees as a measure of their human resource value. Companies adapt this model to their practical requirements by making necessary alterations, assumptions and use different discount rates for ascertaining the present value of future cash flows.

Few organizations, that recognize the value of their human resources, and furnish the related information in their annual reports in India, are: Infosys, Bharat Heavy Electricals Ltd (BHEL); the Steel Authority of India Ltd. (SAIL), the Minerals and Metals Trading Corporation of India Ltd. (MMTC), the Southern Petrochemicals Industries Corporation of India (SPIC), the

Associated Cement Companies Ltd., Madras Refineries Ltd., the Hindustan Zinc Ltd., Engineers India Ltd, the Oil and Natural Gas Commission, Oil India Ltd., the Cement Corporation of India Ltd. etc.

Table 18.2: HRA by Various Companies in India

Organization	Introduction Year	Model	Discount Rate (%)
BHEL	1973-74	Lev & Schwartz	12 %
ONGC	1981-82	Lev & Schwartz	12.25%
MMTC	1982-83	Lev & Schwartz	12%
SAIL	1983-84	Lev & Schwartz	14%
NTPC	1984-85	Lev & Schwartz	12%
Infosys	1999	Lev & Schwartz	12.96%

(**Source:** indianmba.com)

This method of accounting is basically oriented towards measuring changes in the employees' value rather than employers' gains from the employees. Unless the employees' payments are directly linked to employee productivity or the company performance, the changes in the value of employees will not reflect the changes in the employees' contribution.

HRA at Infosys

Infosys has estimated the value of its human resources of 91,187 employees, including both delivery and support staff at Rs 98, 821 crore for fiscal 2008. This represented a growth a 72 per cent growth over the previous year's Rs 57, 452 crore, when the company had a headcount of 72,241 employees. The IT major has used the Lev and Schwartz model to compute the value of its human resources.

The evaluation is based on the present value of the future earnings of the employees and on the assumptions that employee compensation includes all direct and indirect benefits earned both in India and abroad. It also considered the incremental earnings based on group/age and discounted the future earnings at 13.32 per cent (14.97 per cent in the previous year), the cost of capital for computing the HR value.

Education Index

The company reported a substantial jump in the education index of its employees for fiscal 2008 at 2,51,970 up from 2,03,270 in the previous year, reflecting the rising quality of its employees. The average age of the Infosys employees stood at 26 years in FY07, the same as in the previous years.

Is HRA Useful?

The issue of Human Resource Accounting has always been debated hard and there have been arguments both in favour and against regarding its practical utility and effectiveness.

Argument in Favour of Human Resource Accounting

The various arguments favouring human resource accounting are:

1. HRA helps to justify human resource as assets in an era of knowledge-based economy.
2. Attaches numerical monetary-equivalent to the true-value of human assets in an organization.
3. Facilitates HR decision-making. HRA provides the HR professionals and management with information for managing the human resources efficiently and effectively. Such information is essential for performing the critical HR functions of acquiring, developing, allocating, conserving, utilizing, evaluating and rewarding in a proper way. These functions are the key transformational processes that convert human resources from 'raw' inputs (in the form of individuals, groups and the total human organization) to outputs in the form of goods and services.
4. It also helps the management to understand the long-term cost implications to such decisions. HRA indicates whether these processes are adding value or enhancing unnecessary costs.
5. HRA helps institutional investors in making a more informed financial decision.
6. Finally, in an era where performance is closely linked to rewards and, therefore, the performance of all groups/departments/functions needs to be quantified to the extent possible, HRA helps in measuring the performance of the HR function as such.

Arguments against Human Resource Accounting

As far as the statutory requirements go, the Companies Act, 1956 does not demand furnishing of HRA related information in the financial statements of the companies. The Institute of Chartered Accountants of India too, has not been able to bring any definitive standard or measurement in the reporting of human resources costs.

Some of the limitations to human resource accounting are:

1. Absence of demonstrated usefulness (*Rhode et al.*).
2. Lack of evidence of HRA from financial viewpoint.
3. Lack of commonly accepted norm regarding intangible assets.
4. Inconclusive links between HRA, KM processes and organizational performance.
5. Lack of industry standard and hence every industry has to devise its own standard.

Future of Human Resource Accounting

The future of human resource accounting shall be strongly determined by the research that is done in this field. Considerable research is required in this area to sort-out various anomalies that exist in its practice. For the time-being it serves certain advantages but has less practical utility.

Reading Exhibit 2: Thoughtful HRIT Strategy and Preparation: Indispensable Precursor to HCM Solution Adoption

Human resource costs represent a significant portion of the total operating expenditure of a business. In the current competitive business scenario, companies driven by intense cost pressure realize that the workforce represents a largely unexploited source of competitive advantage. Better management of human capital is seen as a key strategic and competitive differentiator for organizations to excel. Appreciating this, organizations often view the combination of HR business and technology transformations as one of the key strategic initiatives.

HCM solutions are key enablers of such transformation initiatives. Companies embarking on the adoption of new HR applications or to augment the existing automation in specific HR functions, or seeking to obtain more value from the current solution must have an insightful HRIT strategy and prepare themselves well in advance for better business value realization.

This paper highlights some of the key points to be considered in an HRIT strategy and the functional aspects of people preparation in the adoption of a package-enabled HCM solution.

HRIT Strategy: Points to Ponder

Clear strategic goal definition

Goals and business drivers - Lack of clarity on the business goals to be achieved through the HRIT strategy and lack of cognizance of key drivers of system implementation are the major pitfalls in HRIT strategy implementations. Since the decision to adopt an HCM solution is with the expectation of solving a business problem or with the aim to gain a competitive edge in the market, the definition of the central theme of the HCM solution and the business drivers are the essential building blocks of the HRIT strategy. Some of the common themes of an HCM solution are: empowerment of employees, providing 'single-truth' of human resource information, supporting the growing organization size or offering quality and consistency in human resource services across geographical boundaries and cultures.

Metrics - It is important to define pertinent HR key performance indicators and metrics in key processes or transaction areas. This will serve as a means to measure the accomplishment of the desired result as an outcome of the HCM solution.

Some examples of HR metrics are: Cost to hire, Time to fill, ROI on recruitment spend, Employee turnover, Training effectiveness and Compensation as percent of revenue unit (e.g. Labor Cost of Sales). It is also important to define a process for continuous measurement and improvement of pertinent HR Key Performance Indicators and Metrics to constitute a feedback mechanism for the HRIT strategy.

Alignment of automation priorities to match the goals: Phased system enablement

Prioritization of HR processes that need to be system-enabled to match the strategic goals is important to achieve incremental and quick wins from the business perspective. Balancing the needs of individual units or functions and prioritizing the processes that need to be system-enabled in order to meet the corporate goals is a challenging proposition. Involving all the key stakeholders in the early stages of this decision is critical to get early buy-in and support in order to execute the HCM solution strategy. Addressing stakeholder concerns and expectations at the outset significantly increases the likelihood of widespread acceptance of the process and system adoption.

With time and money being the key constraints in most strategic initiatives, identification of processes that need to be covered by each phase of the HCM solution business release is imperative. In addition to this, the definition of high-level scope for each of the identified processes in a specific business release will provide clarity on the HCM solution roadmap to the different stakeholders and process owners. Generally, organizations automate transaction and effort-intensive HR operations and administration functions, prior to the rest of the processes. However, depending on the criticality of the process and its impact on strategic goals, industry characteristics and expected business value, HRIT strategists may prioritize the automation of specific tactical and strategic HR processes in the initial business releases.

An illustration: A large retail company with customer service focus will typically prioritize automation of HR operations and administrative functions to bring in process efficiency. Simultaneously, given the fluctuating workforce demand-supply situation in the retail industry, a recruitment management system and/ or a workforce scheduling and optimization system will also find a place in the first business release of its HR process automation roadmap to optimize the recruit-hire-deploy cycle time. Whereas, in the case of a knowledge-based

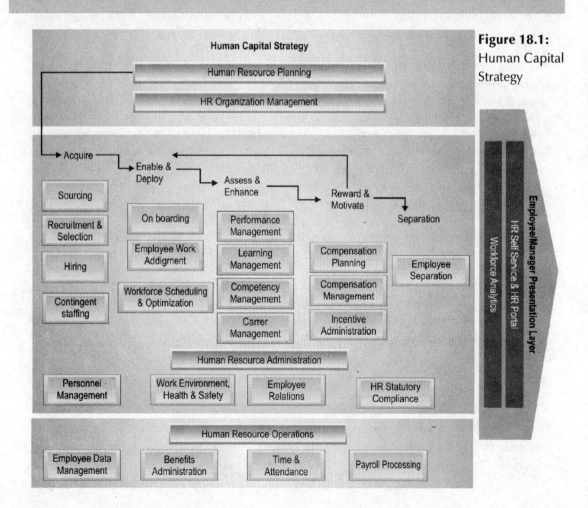

Figure 18.1: Human Capital Strategy

telecom services and product company, in addition to automation of operations, a well-established competency-based talent management system will also be given high priority in order to gain a competitive advantage.

A sample of a phased HCM Solution implementation roadmap is given in Figure 18.1.

In-house versus Outsource

Having decided on the automation priorities, the next concern encountered by every HR & IT strategist is - 'Inhouse or Outsource?'. Traditionally, non-core yet critical HR processes like payroll processing, benefits processing, employee data management have been outsourced by buyers. In recent years, companies are further broadening their footprint of HR outsourcing footprint to include core tactical and strategic functions such as recruiting (including planning), compensation planning and administration, and learning management.

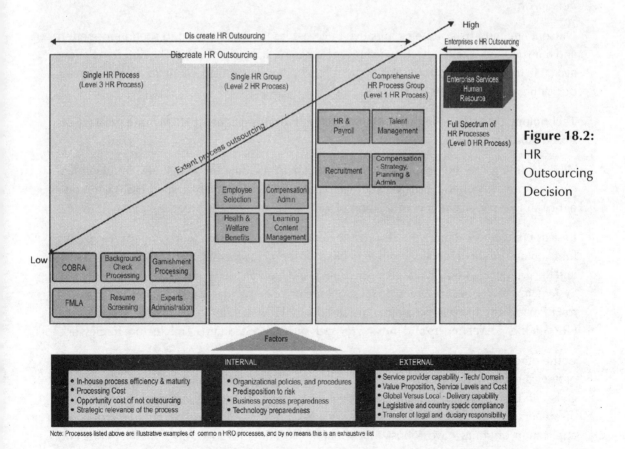

Figure 18.2: HR Outsourcing Decision

Note: Processes listed above are illustrative examples of common HRO processes, and by no means this is an exhaustive list

As far as the outsourcing models are concerned, apart from resorting to the hosted application services, companies also have the option to choose either discrete outsourcing or Enterprise outsourcing models. Over the last few years, companies have progressed from outsourcing transaction-intensive processes like COBRA and background check processing in isolation to outsourcing groups of related processes, like health and welfare benefits, contingent worker management, attendance and leave administration. Some of the companies opt to outsource entire processes or significant portions of a comprehensive process, for example, HR & Payroll, Benefits, and compensation administration and planning.

Even though the process outsourcing footprint is expanding, most companies still favor lower-cost Discrete outsourcing options over the comprehensive Enterprise HR outsourcing. Companies are doubly cautious when contemplating to outsource the complete HR function due to apprehensions of losing the in-house expertise and control and the strategic risk of disruption of service. Many are inclined to adoption of automation of services as opposed to outsourcing.

Outsourcing must be a strategic initiative that enables the organization to spend more effort and time on specialized strategic functions of human capital management. The different options available for outsourcing and some of the typical factors for consideration in the outsourcing decision are shown in the Figure 18.2.

Technology Decision - Single HCM Suite (on ERP or mid-segment HCM Suite) vs Best-of-Breed Solutions

While defining the HRIT strategy, many companies including the global and multinational corporations deliberate on the technology platform for the globally unified HCM solution - either an ERP package or a combination of well-integrated bestof-breed solutions.

Best-of-breed applications typically provide depth and robustness in functionality on a specific function or a group of functions within HR like Performance Management, Applicant Tracking and Recruitment System, Workforce Scheduling and Optimization, and Learning Management System. In general, best-of-breed applications are on open standards architecture as compared to ERP packages that rely on proprietary standards. However, in the recent days most of the ERP vendors are gearing up and moving towards the Open Standards Architecture framework.

At the other end of the spectrum, an ERP package is capable of bringing together all aspects of the value chain. Out-of-the-box data and process integration, standard user interface, and global and multi-language capabilities provide leading ERP packages an edge over the best-of-breed solutions which are packaged with extended features in specific functions. ERP application offerings have robust functionalities in administrative functions like core HR, benefits administration as well as good processing capabilities in operational areas like Payroll and Time and Attendance Processing. With the advent of web-based architecture and with the increasing importance of the HR function in the market, ERP applications are now covering the entire spectrum of the HR function, particularly in the areas of Recruitment, Talent Management, Learning Management, and self-service. However, best-of-breed players in Human Capital Management solutions market have the 'early-mover' advantage in some niche areas.

The decision to choose the best-of-breed solution for a specific process or process group may depend on the some of the factors given below:

- Nature of the process - centralized or decentralized.
- Ability of the specific HR function to create a competitive edge in the market and its direct relevance to corporate goals.
- Robustness in product functionality.
- Long term approach towards deployment of shared services.
- Total Cost of Ownership of the application.
- Organization maturity and/ or process maturity.

Generally, most companies adopt a mixed bag approach, i.e. implementation of a single global HCM solution for most of the normal HR life cycle processes and operational areas. This is done on either an ERP package or a mid-segment HCM suite product and its functionality is supplemented with best-of-breed packages in specialized HR functions where there is a strong need to gain a competitive edge with either industry-specific solutions or mature processes and best practices. This approach is gaining prominence in the market as both ERP and best-of-breed products move toward the service-oriented architecture framework.

When a company's processes and/or business requirements are so unique that they cannot be fulfilled by either best-of-breed applications or ERP packages without major customization or product extensions, the company may resort to custom developed software solutions provided it is convinced about the strategic relevance of the process and wants to retain the processes in an 'As-Is' state. After the organization carries out diligence on the above aspects, the downstream steps of its HRIT strategy will include package evaluation and selection, business case preparation, and vendor selection.

Aspects of Preparation
Functional Preparation

Before an HCM solution implementation, performing a reality check on functional preparedness and initiating a rationalization exercise in pertinent areas will provide an opportunity to the HR process owners to align themselves to the HCM solution business drivers and goals. This phase will set the platform to incorporate best-in-class practices, and to bring in process efficiency with an aim to shred some of the non-value adding legacy practices. Undermining the significance of this phase can have an exponentially negative effect on benefit realization, solution implementation, user acceptance and adoption, and hence may not be fitting with the overall corporate strategy. The functional preparation is typically a two-step process:

Step 1: Readiness assessment for solution enabled transformation

In the human resource function, components of such assessment include, but not limited to, core functional framework (e.g., competency framework in case of talent management), key structural elements (e.g., organization structure, departments, jobs, grades), key organizational HR policies, and business processes relevant to the scope of HCM solution.

Step 2: Rationalization exercise

As an outcome of the readiness assessment, necessary corrective actions or rationalization initiatives pertinent to the solution implementation are initiated and the execution timelines of the same are mapped to the HCM solution implementation timelines.

Preparation of People

Preparing people is an important precursor to successful HCM solution adoption - be it in-house HCM system implementation or HR process outsourcing. Preparing stakeholders at different levels in the following areas can pave the way for success:

1. Companies are often entrenched in practices acquired over many years which may not be optimal given the change in the ecosystem. One of the biggest barriers to the adoption of an HCM solution is the resistance to relinquish old, ineffective business processes and policies. Management commitment and involvement coupled with appropriate intervention strategies combine to overcome these constraints.

2. Traditionally, HR has been perceived as a record-keeping and data-intensive function; the nature of information recorded and stored is given more importance as compared to the strategic importance of the HR function. Hence it is important to reinforce the HR function's relevance in the accomplishment of the overall organization's goal to the

pertinent stakeholders involved in the HR IT transformation exercise. It is also vital to note that HR includes many business processes and policy-intensive sub-functions. Hence orientation towards business processes, role based information needs and workflow will contribute to a large extent towards the conceptualization of an optimal HCM solution.

3. HR is about managing Human Capital in the organization and typically an HCM solution has an impact or a perceived impact with a larger audience in the organization. This makes change management a very vital component in the implementation of HCM solution. Such solution implementations may include change of processes and practices, and institutionalizing such changes is a key pre-requisite for successful adoption of an HCM solution. In managing change it is imperative to appreciate the fact that managing change is a continuous journey.

Conclusion

An HCM solution can be a vital enabler for HR transformation initiatives. In order to realize maximum value from an HCM solution and to achieve successful adoption of such solutions by different stakeholders, it is important to have a thoughtful HRIT strategy, supported by structured preparation and a detailed Change Management plan.

Permission

This article has been printed as a reading exhibit with permission of Mr. Sriram Ramanujam, the author of this article and a certified SPHR and PMP, is a Senior Consultant with the Enterprise Solutions group at Infosys. He has worked with several HCM solution implementations in different capacities.

Essay Questions

1. What is the significance of automation of HR systems? What are the main objectives behind it?

2. Discuss:
   a) Payroll Automation
   b) Performance Management Automation Systems
   c) Recruitment Automation System
   d) Employee Self-service System.

3. Is automation a boon or bane for HR systems? Comment.

4. What is HR audit? What does it include? What is the rationale of audit?

5. Discuss the legal, Benchmarking and strategic approach to HR audit?

6. Define Human Resource Accounting. Highlight the chronology of research in HR accounting.

7. What are the various approaches used for conducting Human Resource Accounting?

8. Which HRA method is most commonly used? Explain with an example.

9. Is HRA useful? Substantiate with examples. What is the future of HRA?

Application Questions

1. Go to the document http://www.hrinformationsolutions.com/images/Cost Savings In Automating HR And Benefits.pdf and study the *'Cost Savings in Automating HR & Benefits'*.

2. Find out more on HR accounting by studying some research papers at –
   a) http://www.eurojournals.com/ejefas_21_05.pdf
   b) http://www.smsitlucknow.com/journals/vol1(2)/P131-133.pdf
   c) http://www.ipublishing.co.in/ajmr vol1no1/sped12011/AJMRSP1021.pdf

Bibliography

Borbidge, R. How to Conduct a Human Resources Effectiveness Audit. Point Richmond, CA: Jacob-Cameron Publishing Company. 1998.

Boudreau, J.W. (1998). 'Strategic Human Resource Management Measures: Key Linkages and the People Vantage Model'. *Journal of Human Resource Costing and Accounting*, 3: 2, 21-40.

Cascio, W.F. (1998). 'The Future World of Work: Implications for Human Resource Costing and Accounting'. *Journal of Human Resource Costing and Accounting*, 3: 2, 9-19.

Fischer, R. (1995). HRIS Quality Depends on Teamwork. *Personnel Journal,* 74(11), 9-11.

Flamholtz, E.G. (1974). Human Resource Accounting, Encino, CA: Dickenson.

Gallo, J. and P. Thompson. "Goals, Measures, and Beyond: In Search of Accountability in Federal HRM." *Public Personnel Management.* 29:2 (Summer, 2000), 237-248.

Greengard, S. (1995). When HRMS goes Global: Managing the Data Highway. *Personnel Journal,* 74(6), 90-98. Retrieved June 14, 2007, from EBSCO Online Database Business Source Complete.http://search.ebscohost.com/login.aspx?direct=true&db=bth&AN=9506151054&site=ehost-live

Grojer, J-E. and Johanson, U. (1998). 'Current Development in Human Resource Costing and Accounting: Reality Present, Researcher Absent?' *Accounting, Auditing and Accountability Journal,* 11:1, 495-505.

h&AN=9512036730&site=ehost-live

Huselid, M. (1995). 'The Impact of Human Resource Management Practices on Turnover, Productivity, and Corporate Financial Performance'. *Academy of Management Journal,* 38: 5, 635-672.

Johanson, U. (1999). 'Why the Concept of Human Resource Costing and Accounting does not Work'? *Personnel Review,* 28: 1/2, 91-107.

Ngai, E. & Wat, F. (2006). Human Resource Information Systems: A Review and Empirical Analysis. *Personnel Review,* 35(2), 297-315.

Rao, T. V. HRD Audit: Evaluating the Human Resources Function for Business Improvement. Response Books, Sage India, New Delhi. 1999.

Retrieved June 14, 2007, from EBSCO Online Database Business Source Complete. http://search.ebscohost.com/login.aspx?direct=true&db=bt.

Targowski, A., & Deshpande, S. (2001). The Utility and Selection of an HRIS. *Advances in Competetiveness,* 9(1), 42-57.

Travis, W. (1994, January). Personnel Computing: How to Justify a Human Resources Information System. *Personnel Journal*, 11-14.

Turner, G. (1996). 'Human Resource Accounting – Whim or Wisdom?' *Journal of Human Resource Costing and Accounting*, 1, 63-73.

Walkey, F. H., and McCormick, I.A. (1993). 'FACTOREP: A Pascal Programme to Examine Factor Replication'. Publications in Psychology No. 29, Victoria University of Wellington, Wellington, New Zealand.

Hagood, W., & Friedman, D. (2002). Using the Balanced Scorecard to Measure the Performance of your HR Information System. Public Personnel Management, 31(4), 543. Retrieved June 14, 2007, from EBSCO Online Database Business Source Complete.http://search.ebscohost. com/login.aspx?direct= true&db=bth&AN=9004413 &site=ehost-live.

Chapter 19

Social Media Applications in Managing Human Resource

Outline

Introduction
Social Media Recruitment
Reference Checks
Networking & Communication
Essay Questions
Application Questions
Bibliography

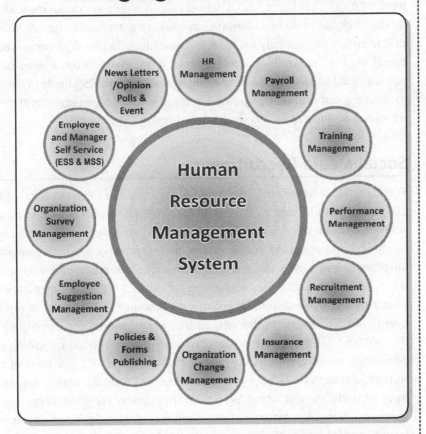

Key Terms

Buzzword

Commonwealth Bank

Networking & Communication

Recruitment

Reference Checks

Social Media Applications

Introduction

Radio took 38 years to reach 50 million users; television took 13 years, internet took 4 years, i-pod took around 3 years to reach the same figure... Facebook added 100 million users and i-phone users touched 1 billion in just about 9 months. India currently has 8 million active facebook users, which is 2 percent of the total users worldwide. Social Media is in big time... no questions asked. According to a report, out of the 425 million active internet users worldwide, in the age bracket of 16-54 years, 394 million people watch video-clips posted on internet and 346 million people read blogs. Blogs, wikis (that allow users to create, share and edit content on internet pages), podcasts, social networking sites etc., are popular on social media. A global study by Lodestar Universal, a media buying agency, shows that firms are increasingly using tools like widgets (a chunk of code which brings in "live" content – advertisements, links, images from a third-party site without the website owner having to update) and RSS feeds (a format of sending–out frequently updated content such as blog entries and news headlines to subscribers) to work and communicate.

Social Media Recruitment

Social media recruitment is the next big thing on the cards. In May – June 2010 survey conducted by Career Builder, a global leader in human capital solutions, among approximately 2500 employers, revealed that one-quarter of the companies used social media to recruit and research potential employees. The survey also revealed that employees would prefer company pages on social media sites containing job-listing, FAQs on organizations, career-paths, work-culture, employee-testimonials, pictures of company events video of a day on the job, awards & recognition etc. According to the 2010 social media recruiting survey by Jobvite, social recruiting has become a mainstream channel for companies. Over 83 per cent of the respondents say they either use or plan to use social media. Many companies have already started using Web 2.0 application for their recruitment purposes. Web 2.0 is actually a term given to the second generation internet based services which is different from the first generation static websites with little interaction. Web 2.0 applications include social media/networking sites (Facebook, Twitter, Orkut, LinkedIn, MySpace), blogs, podcasts (Podcast Alley, iTunes), video sharing sites (YouTube, Ted, FlickR), mobile apps etc. Social Media recruitment not only widens reach but helps segmentation, targeting and positioning of potential job seekers. They also increase the accuracy of profile searches. The finding, screening and validating of applicants can be done online and with high precision. Companies are using Boolean strings, with operators like 'AND', 'NOT', 'OR' to pin-point profile searches from social media/networking sites. For example Boolean strings like Intitle: resume AND "10 years experience" Insite: LinkedIn will provide resumes of candidates only with 10 years of experience, only from LinkedIn. Companies are also using decoders for geek code (created by Robert Hayden in 1993) to optimize candidate profile searches. Recruiters can reach such candidates using social media that they could never imagine otherwise. Some companies are also using an Oracle based recruitment tool – '*i*-recruitment model.

Social media recruitment is a low cost recruitment tool with high return on investment. Using social media recruitment, job opportunities can be made "portable" so that anyone can post, direct message or update their status across major social media platforms. Some Companies are also using **'location based social networking sites'** like Foursquare, Gowaila, Loopt for a range of applications including recruitment (building relationship with potential candidate). Location based social networking sites ('lo-so-networks') allow users to "check-in" at venues using mobile devices, allowing people in their network to know about their location at any given moment of time. Although at present the recruitment function using 'location-based social networking sites' are not strong enough. They are seen with huge future potential. Some of these 'location based social networking sites' are reportedly tying-up with search engines to power recruitment. Actually using social media for recruitment is a PR tool itself for the company. The future application of location based social networking sites are seen in the form of their use as engagement tools, orientation (induction) etc.

With more than 1.5 million content pieces shared everyday on face book alone, social media is revolutionizing the way we link and communicate. Recruitment which is essential a process of linking and communicating to potential job seekers, cannot remain untouched from this revolution. A sequel to the highly successful social media in recruitment conferences (July 2009, April 2010) came in the form of 'First Mobile & Video in Recruitment Conference organized in London in Sept. 2010 (http://www.socialmedia inrecruitment.com/). These conferences are adding value in terms of popularizing and creating more awareness about application of social media in recruitment. The conference provide a common platform to corporate recruiters, recruitment agencies, recruitment advertising agencies, job boards and recruitment industry suppliers to congregate & deliberate.

Social media recruitment will soon be a *buzzword*. The future is even more exciting when Web 3.0 the next generation web hits the recruitment scene. The searches will become ultra-refined and interface will be so easy that even a moron will be able to use it. Social media recruitment is the future of hiring

Reference Checks

Many companies are increasingly using social media like twitter, facebook, linkedin etc. for performing reference checks on employees. They are looking for aspects like:

> - Employees who have maligned their previous employers.
> - Too much use of social media during office-hours.
> - Indecent comments, pictures or posts.
> - Falsification of qualification or job history details.
> - Use of drugs or substance-abuse
> - Racial comments or abuse by candidates

Recently an online reputation research was commissioned by Microsoft and was conducted by Cross-Tab between December 10 and 23, 2009, in France, Germany, the United Kingdom, and the United States. Approximately 275 recruiters, human resources (HR) professionals, and hiring managers, and about 330 consumers interviewed in each country.

This study explored the attitudes of consumers, HR professionals, and recruiters on the subject of online reputation. Specifically, it examined the impact of online reputation on hiring and how people manage their online reputation.

Some of the study's findings include:

> - The recruiters and HR professionals surveyed are not only checking online sources to learn about potential candidates, but a majority of them also reported that their companies have made online screening a formal requirement of the hiring process.

- About 70% of the U.S. recruiters and HR professionals surveyed, have rejected candidates based on information they found online. The percentages were however not equally high from the U.K. and Germany although they too report the same trend.

- Recruiters and HR professionals surveyed report being very or somewhat concerned about the authenticity of the content they find.

- In all countries, recruiters and HR professionals say they believe the use of online reputational information will significantly increase over the next five years.

- Positive online reputations matter.

Networking & Communication

In-house social networking platforms have done what above-normal salary hikes have not been able to do – control attrition. It is reported that the company-social networking platforms have helped engage employees better and reduce attrition (in some cases by about $1/3^{rd}$). Cognizant's Facebook-like platform – Cognizant 2.0 or C2, Wikis & Justask at Tata Consultancy Services, Channel W and My Wipro World at Wipro Technologies, Ideabank of BankWest, Australia are few but very strong examples of a new trend where companies have started to embrace social networking by their employees, to their advantage, rather then regard the same as threat and create barriers to curb it.

The Commonwealth Bank has recently deployed a new intranet which focuses on social networking and collaboration. Earlier the bank's intranet was inconsistent, lacked updation, was non-collaborative and was micro-managed. But now, powered by Web2.0 tools, the bank's intranet is more collaborative using blogs, podcasts and vodcasts. Employees can even do a bit of micro-blogging. One of the immediate benefits has come in the form of reduced travel expenses because of the collaboration.

Another company powering in-house social networking using Web2.0 tools is Procter & Gamble (P&G). P&G has about 138,000 employees spread in more than 160 countries of the world. The company views them as 'countless ideas and expertise'. P&G aims to connect all of that by encouraging employees to use the social networking at work.

Some of the common advantages of in-house social networking are:

1. Connect with others and communicate.
2. Share ideas without intervention or permission.
3. Kick-off discussions.
4. Spearhead special interest groups.
5. Integrate workflows across varied skills, locations and business units.
6. Enhance cohesiveness and collaboration among workgroups.
7. Provide platform for asking questions openly.
8. Discover new knowledge and create knowledge-repositories.
9. Identify talent within the organization.
10. Eliminate manual tracking of projects.
11. Bridge-gap between personal computing and work-computing experiences.
12. Engage the Gen Y (the restless millennials) and reduce attrition.

Essay Questions

1. What is social media recruitment? Why is it considered the next big thing on the cards?
2. What are 'location-based social networking sites'?
3. How can social media help is conducting reference checks on employees?
4. What do Cognizant 2.0 or C2, Wikis & Justask at Tata Consultancy Services etc. help in? Elaborate, with more examples.

Application Questions

1. If you have a account on linkedin.com then click on the job hyperlink and explore and explain the kind of services that it offers to the job-seekers and recruiters. Do you know anyone who has found a job through LinkedIn Interview that person and record his/her experiences?

2. Go to http://mashable.com/2011/10/23/how-recruiters-use-social-networks-to-screen-candidates-infographic/ and learn how Recruiters Use Social Networks to Screen Candidates.

3. Read the articles in the links –
   a. http:/ www.financialexpress.com/news/importance-of-social-media-in-recruit-ment/815754/0
   b. http://www.forbes.com/sites/drewhansen/2011/11/12/social-media-transform-recruiting/
   c. http://www.readwriteweb.com/biz/2011/07/linkedin-social-job-hiring-grows.php
   d. http://digitallife.today.msnbc.msn.com/_news/2012/01/17/10175765-job-hunters-still-not-careful-on-social-media study?chromedomain=lifeinc and high-light the future of social media recruit-ment.

4. Go to the link http://linkhumans.com/blog/how-to-use-social-media-to-recruit-deloitte-case-study and read **Deloitte case Study** on How to use social media to recruit?

Bibliography

Banks Lisa, BankWest Sees Success with in-House Social Networking, July 30, 2010, http://www.cio.com/article/601359 Bank West_Sees_Success_with_in_House_Social_Networking

Barone Lisa, Are you performing social media background checks? September 1, 2009, http://smallbiztrends.com/2009/09/social-media-background-checks.html

Can Location-Based Social Networking Be Used for Recruitment and Retention? http://socialmediarecruitment.com/blog/2010/08/11/can-location-based-social-networking-be-used-for-recruitment-and-retention.

Goldberg Stephanie, Young Job-seekers Hiding their Facebook Pages, March 29, 2010, CNN, http://edition.cnn.com/2010/TECH/03/29/facebook.job-seekers/index.html

Heathfield Susan M. Use LinkedIn for Recruiting Employees, http://humanresources.about.com/od/recruiting/a/recruit_linked.htm

http://www.socialmediainrecruitment.com/

More than one-third of employers use social media to promo their organizations, find new CareerBuilder survey, http://www.prnewswire.com/news-releases/more-than-one-third-of-employers-use-social-media-to-promote-their-organizations-finds-new-careerbuilder-survey-100967334.html.

Online Reputation in a Connected World, http://www.marketingtecnologico.com/ad2006/adminsc1/app/marketingtecnologico/uploads/Estudos dpd_online% 20reputation%20research_overview.pdf

Rai Archana, Companies Heed the Online Message, http://www.livemint.com/2008/08/03235151/Companies-heed-the-online-mess.html

Sachoff Mike, More Employers Using Social Media to Promote their Companies, Aug. 18, 2010, http://www.webpronews.com/node/55509/print

Swanborg Rick, How Procter & Gamble Got Employees to Use Social Networking at Work, Aug. 24, 2009, http://www.cio.com/article/500363How_Procter_Gamble_Got_Employees_to_Use_Social_Networking_at_Work

Wortham Jenna, More Employers Use Social Networks to Check Out Applicants, August 20, 2009, The New York Times, http://bits.blogs.nytimes.com/2009/08/20/more-employers-use-social-networks-to-check-out-applicants/

Iyer Srvidya, Mishra Pankaj, Inhouse Social Networking Platforms Keep Flock Together, The Economic Times, Sept. 13, 2010.

Reji John LinkedIn, Facebook can Help you Get a Job Jul 20, 2010, Mumbai Financial Chronicle, http://www.mydigitalfc.com/opportunities/linkedin-facebook-can-help-you-get-job-955.

Chapter 20

Talent Management

Outline

Is Talent Management an 'Oxymoron'

Who is a Talent?

Who owns & drives Talent Management?

Talent Management – Priorities or Prescription

Talent Management in a Bust Economy

Talent Management: The New HRM Approach

Essay Questions

Application Questions

Bibliography

Key Terms

Corporate Talent

Critical Talent

Functional Talent

Oxymoro

Six Sigma Framework

Talent Management

Is Talent Management an 'Oxymoron'?

Deliotte 2009 year report 'Managing Talent in a Turbulent Economy' came-out with some interesting findings on how executives around the world are planning and managing their workforces in extremely challenging economic environment. The findings clearly showed that senior executives around the globe being well aware about the severity of the economic crisis, placed the need to have experienced talent and strong leadership at the top of their strategic talent list, in order to navigate through rough waters. 'Companies around the world are focused on retaining the critical talent they have while attracting seasoned leaders. Companies also recognize the urgency of managing their workforce headcount and costs while maximizing their utilization of talent'. However much to our surprise, we also find the report indicating a large percentage of the companies doing very little to integrate workforce planning into all levels of their planning process.

A survey of human resources executives from 40 companies around the world, sometime back in 2005 by Douglas A Ready and Jay A Conger indicated that virtually all of them had an insufficient pipeline of high potential employees to fill strategy management roles.

A survey by Institute for Corporate Productivity (i4CP) showed that more than 75 percent of the companies they surveyed don't have an agreed upon definition of talent management.

So what is Talent Management? Is it a mere 'oxymoron', a messy set of practices or a more organized effort to drive company's strategy through talent stimulus?

Some have defined talent management as the process of getting 'right people in the right place at the right time for the right cost'. Then what happens to the issue of identifying, attracting, engaging this talent in the first place and later to the issue of retaining this talent.

The objective of this chapter is to provide a more objectives assessment and practical understanding of Talent Management and emphasize how it has grown to become the new face of managing human resource strategically.

Who is a Talent?

Before we even try to understand the entire gamut of Talent Management, it is pertinent to decipher that after all who is a talent in the organization?

Marcus Buckingham and Curt W. Coffman in their work 'First break All the Rules' (Simon & Schuster 1999) argued talent to be a 'celebrated excellence' or a 'recurring pattern of thought, feeling or behavior' that can be productively applied. They tend to disagree with the former idea of talent that suggests it to be some sort of secret gift bestowed on selected few. Instead they opined that every role required talent and hence a 'recurring pattern of thought, feeling or behaviour' that is productive in nature will be required for each role and a person who exhibits the same must be called a talent.

The emphasis here has been on the word '**recurring**', Extending this concept further into organizations will make us believe that an effective '**hiring filter**' (*refer to Figure 20.1: The Talent Pipeline*) would be able to separate the grain from the chaff and induct people who exhibit similar recurring productive behavior, in the organization. The strength of the 'hiring filter' will depend upon many factors like reliability and validity of the selection tools used, linkage of hiring with other functions & business strategy etc.

However an effective 'hiring filter' will ensure that we have no below average or poor performers in the organization, once the performance filter is applied. This assumption is not unfounded since below average or poor performers are as much a reflection on the organization's hiring effectiveness as much it is on a candidate's incompetence. This would be in other words again test of the strength of our 'hiring filter.'

Talent

"... recurring pattern of thought feeling or behaviour that can be productively applied."

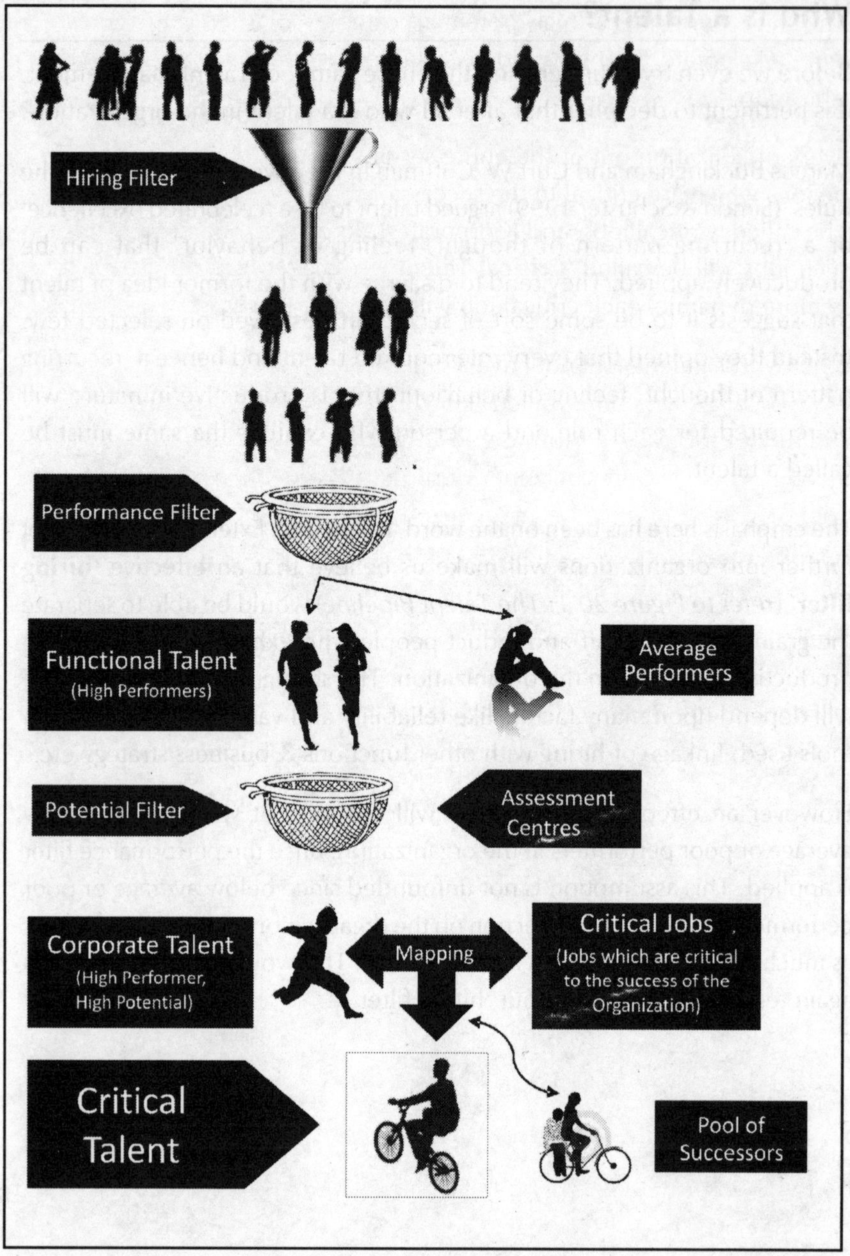

Figure 20.1:
The Talent Pipeline

- Hiring Filter
- Performance Filter
- Functional Talent (High Performers)
- Average Performers
- Potential Filter
- Assessment Centres
- Corporate Talent (High Performer, High Potential)
- Mapping
- Critical Jobs (Jobs which are critical to the success of the Organization)
- Critical Talent
- Pool of Successors

Functional Talent

High performers in every role identified through application of performance filters are known as functional talent.

Once the 'Performance Filter' has been applied, the 'high performers' in every role will be identified. These 'high performers will be called **'Functional Talent'**. But whether they remain as mere 'Functional Talent' or graduate to a higher state will depend upon the 'Potential Filter' largely depicted by Assessment Centers. The higher state of functional talent would be the 'high performer', 'high potential' category or simply **'Corporate Talent'**. 'Corporate Talent' would be suitable for different roles across the organization.

In every organization out of the entire set of various jobs there would be some jobs which are critical to the success of the organization. These jobs will be called 'Critical jobs' and 'Corporate Talent' that can be mapped on to such jobs will be called **'Critical Talent'**. To make this 'Critical Talent' base more dynamic, each critical job will have a pool of successors.

In other words 'talent' will not have a single definition in the organization. There would be something called 'Functional Talent' to which everyone including the 'average performers' will try to graduate. However every 'Functional Talent' won't become 'Corporate Talent' and similarly every Corporate Talent cannot be mapped on to a 'critical talent' category. However at any given time all would remain viable in the organization in some or the other way. Organizations hence must evolve systems to manage these differently. In other words, there cannot be a one 'common way' of appraising, appreciating, developing, engaging and retaining all these different types of 'talents'. This is a common mistake that most companies make. For instance, having a same five-pointer appraisal rating mechanism for all and sundry. Such systems will only create perceptual distortion and more significantly talent wastage, by and large.

Management Guru Late C.K Prahalad's n=1 strategy of serving customers work for firm in terms of treating its employees. It implies treating every employee group as a 'unique entity' and not trying to fit everyone in same size. A firm's constant endeavour to bring things at 'par' will ensure better convergence

Who Owns & Drives Talent Management?

Strategic Management of human resources in any firm has to take the shape of managing various kinds of talents at different levels in the firm. Mere operational maintenance issues have to be clubbed with the strategy map of the firm and it will be critical for the leaders in the firm to deliberate what kind of people will be required by the firm in future to actualize this road-map. Here is where talent management takes the centre stage of this entire corporate wagon-wheel.

Corporate Talent
Functional talents who also have high potential & would be suitable for different roles across the organization are known as Corporate Talent.

Critical Talent
Corporate talent that can be mapped to the 'critical jobs' in the organization are known as Critical Talent.

Critical Jobs
In every organization out of the entire set of various jobs there would be some jobs which are 'Critical' to the success of the organization. Such jobs are called 'Critical Jobs'.

A critical question is then who owns this humongous activity? Is it the sole responsibility of the human resource department or Talent Management department? No *iota* of common sense will suggest the answer in affirmation. The truth is that all business leaders and managers own talent management activities. And an even bigger truth is, that line functions contribution in such activities should be greater. Then who drives talent management activities in a firm? If you ask this question to anyone, chances are that a majority group will echo 'top management' as a vocal answer. Sadly, much to the disappointment of many, the true driver of talent management is the learning, training and development function. This is not a common practice though; but then everything that is 'popular' is not 'correct' and all that is 'correct' is not always 'popular'. Galagon Pat (2008) argued that 'if talent management centers around competency development, it is logical that the learning and development function would play a leading role... such firms identify their talent requirements and either buy those capabilities in the marketplace or build them through learning, development, performance feedback & coaching and succession process.' This is not to suggest at all that top management commitment is not required but a firm's greatest need has to be people who can steer it successfully through its strategy road. And hence all its resources and energy must be focused on 'making' or 'buying & developing' people and transforming them into a 'talent'. This 'making' or 'developing' activity must draw its inputs from other HR domains. This thorough integration is true gamut of managing people strategically and managing talent effectively.

Infosys Technologies, ranked number one continuously by various employer surveys in India, has built a magnificent 'Global Education Centre in Mysore that is being touted as the world's biggest training centre. The centre is a mini city in itself, spectacular by any measure of corporate monuments, houses food courts, swimming pool, basketball courts, tennis courts, laundromat, trainee quarters and can train around 14000 employees in a year. Every new recruit has to go through this grind of very demanding training schedule at this centre, which can last up to several months. The company strongly believes in a meritocracy that embeds and values skills in its people, which in turn ensure Infoscions a financially secure future. Incidentally Infosys remains perhaps the first among handful of Indian companies to account the value of its human resources.

At Edward Lifesciences, the global leader in the science of heart valves and hemodynamic monitoring talent management initiatives begun even before the company came into its existence in the year 2000, when it spun off as an independent company from Baxter Healthcare. Two years prior to this, the company's president of cardio-vascular unit Mike

Mussallem and Mckinsey & Co. identified 'critical positions' in the company. The 'critical positions' had four unique features.

a. These positions were those that were critical to attaining the corporation's business imperatives.

b. The critical positions were identified across the length & breadth of the company and not limited to the selected top echelons of the management.

c. The critical positions were identified by position and not by personality. In other words a lousy person doing an important job could not disqualify a position or a smart person doing a menial task could not qualify a position to be called critical.

d. Considering the highly volatile medical device industry, the critical positions were time specific and may change over a period of time.

The talent management activities were finely woven in company's business strategy. The strategic imperative drove the key operating drivers which in turn drove the objectives that each person set around himself.

Once the critical jobs had been identified *(refer to Figure 20.2)*, right talent was identified for such positions. Each critical talent was also supported by a pool of two successors. The development of the high potential employees was centered around the personnel objectives set in line with the operating drivers, in turn in tune with the firm's strategic imperatives. The 2008 year sales of Edward Lifesciences touched $1.24 billion spread roughly across 100 countries.

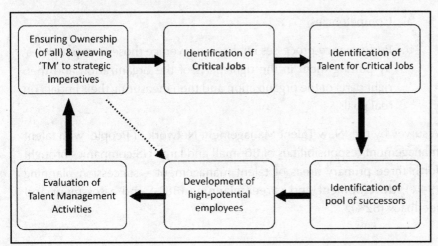

Figure 20.2: Talent Management at Edward Lifesciences (Reindl Rob, T+D, Feb. 2007)

Talent Management – Priorities or Prescription

The institute for Corporate Productivity (i4CP) identified nine areas of talent management:

a. Leadership Development
b. Succession Planning
c. Career Planning
d. Performance Management
e. High Potential Employee Development
f. Learning and Training
g. Competency Management
h. Retention
i. Professional Development

Can these areas of talent management be generalized for all firms? Are these nine areas the total gamut of talent management? The answer to both these questions is 'no'. More and more research has shown that talent management for most firms is a matter of priority. Neither this is an exhaustive list of various areas of talent management nor these areas equally apply to every firm. For instance, for many firms' identification and acquisition of talent remains an issue of grave concern.

The i4CP research also showed that 'most companies concentrate on at least two areas of talent management –

a. Competencies
b. Performance processes i.e. how to leverage those 'competencies' by putting them in the right parts of the organization and then right parts of the organization and then measuring their impact on real goals.'

A survey by the 'New Talent Management Network of People' with talent management responsibilities of 80 small and large US companies brought forth three primary areas of talent management – succession planning (94%), development and career planning (88%) and assessment and feedback (82%).

Talent Management is more about priorities that a firm faces in terms of its talent requirements to realize its strategic objectives.

Talent Management in a Bust Economy

Managing Talent in a downturn is also a matter of priorities. The Deliotte report (Feb. 2009) had an interesting finding related to the current strategic issues as perceived by the industry. Industry expert's around the world felt that playing defense and offence both were necessary to tide over tough economic conditions.

Playing defense was essential to tide over the 'present' (downturn economy) which primarily included:

- Cutting and managing costs (61%)
- Acquiring, serving and retaining customers (56%)
- Managing human capital (27%)

However playing offence was critical for 'tomorrow' (recovery & beyond) which mainly included:

- Developing new product and services (26%)
- Investing in innovation, research and development (13%)
- Expanding into global and new markets (12%)

Other issues included:

- Improving top and bottom-line performance.
- Addressing risk and regulation challenges.
- Capitalizing on M&A/ divestiture/ restructuring.
- Leveraging Technology.

Interestingly these strategic issues had different priorities across different industries (refer to Table 20.1).

Table 20.1 Strategic issues in Downturn (Industrywise)

Rank	Consumer/ Industrial Products	Life Sciences/ Health	Technology/ Media/ Telecom	Energy/ Utilities	Financial Services
1	Acquiring/ Serving/ retaining customers	Cutting and managing costs	• Acquiring/ Serving/ retaining customers • Cutting and managing costs (2 way tie)	Cutting and managing costs	Cutting and managing costs
2	Cutting and managing costs	Managing Human Capital	Managing Human Capital	Acquiring/ Serving/ retaining customers	Acquiring/ Serving/ retaining customers
3	Developing new products and services	• Developing new products and services • Investing in Innovation/ R&D (2 way tie)	Developing new products and services innovation / R&D (3 way tie)	• Capitalizing on M&A/ divestiture/ restructuring • Managing Human Capital • Investing in	Improving top and bottom line performance

(**Source:** Deliotte Feb. 2009)

Such prioritization of strategic issues across different industries is clearly reflected in the way talent management is approached by different industries differently, in a downturn. For instance executives surveyed by Deliotte differed in terms of areas of increased focus on reducing costs and employee headcount:

> 52% of executives surveyed said that their company planned to restructure jobs to lower costs and increase efficiency. In fact a majority of industry executives surveyed in Financial Services (56%),

Technology/Media/Telecom (54%) and Life sciences/ Healthcare (52%) reported that they planned to restructure jobs to lower costs and increase efficiency in the times ahead.

- 39% of executives said that their company planned headcount reduction to lower costs.
- 35% of executives said that their company planned bonus reduction as a cost cutting strategy.
- While 31% of executives said that their company planned hiring part-time employees to lower costs and increase efficiency. More than 40% executives surveyed in the Asia Pacific region expect to increase the hiring of part-time employees to reduce costs compared to 29% in the Americas and 23% in EMEA. The industry which emerged as most likely to hire part-time employees was technology/ Media/ Telecom and the one that was least likely to do so was Financial Services.

Some other areas of increased focus on reducing costs were:
- Promoting early retirement (28%)
- Benefit reduction (23%)
- Using offshore or outsourced employees (21%)
- Salary reduction (18%)
- Retirement contribution reduction (15%).

Similarly, Training & Development- emerged as one of the high priorities of executives in recessionary conditions. In every region roughly six out of ten surveyed participants said training & development and retention are a priority now will be so for some time. Large majorities of executives agree in every industry.

The areas that emerged of increased focus on training and development were:
- High potential employee development.
- Leadership/ Management Development.
- Job Specific: sales, customer service.
- Regulatory, security and risk training.

- On-boarding and orientation.
- Job specific Operations.
- Job specific, IT, Finance, HR.

Interesting however, preference for these areas were not same and different across industries. For instance, executives surveyed working in Consumer/ Industrial Products, Technology/Media/ Telecom and Financial Services sectors lead the way when it comes to investing in the development of corporate leaders and high potential employees. Life Sciences/ Health care and Financial Services companies also place a high priority on regulatory, security and risk training.

Recession many-a-times is a trigger for quality. This appears to be the trend in recruitment whether it is in the process or in the method. 40% of executives report that they will try to attract more critical talent with hard-to-find skills, while 30% report they are looking to bring in more critical leaders. Similar trend continues across corporate recruitment, where a downturn creates a buyer's market for experience and leadership. Recruitment in a recession is not a priority; however most companies surveyed wanted to focus on hiring experienced professionals. The high degree of un-certainty reduced campus hires. There is also a strong need for increasingly using sophisticated business tools to project headcount and labour supply. However Deliotte found in its survey that most companies are not making use of important planning tools or are utilizing them to only a limited extent. Only 49% of human resource professionals used forecasting tools such as predictive models to project HR demand and supply. Current use of forecasting tools is in the following areas:

- Workforce Planning
- Recruiting
- Retention
- Workforce transition
- Leadership Development
- Workplace safety

These areas were again not same in terms of priority in usage of forecasting tools across industries. Uniformly however there was a need to increase use of forecasting tools.

Asia/Pacific executives surveyed by Deliotte were likely to increase the use of workforce analytics in the times to come as compared to their international counterparts. Consumers Industrial Products and Life sciences/Healthcare were likely to lead among industries

Talent Management: The New HRM Approach

Talent Management activities are no longer stand-alone activities in any firm. They have to be integrated at all levels to make talent process efficient and effective and to build talent factories. This is why managing Talent in any firm has grown to the proportion of strategic human resource management.

Talent Wheels

Douglas A. Ready and Jay A Conger (2007) proposed the 'functionality' and 'vitality' wheel. Mapping talent process on these wheels shall give true picture of the state of human resource effectiveness.

'Functionality refers to the processes themselves, the tools and systems that allow a company to put the right people with the right skills in the right place at the right time.' In short, it encompasses rigorous talent processes that support strategic and cultural objectives. Functionality wheel maps a firm's talent process in 8 areas:

 i. Sourcing
 ii. Assimilation
 iii. Development
 iv. Deployment
 v. Performance Management
 vi. Rewards
 vii. Engagement
 viii. Retention

If functionality is about focusing one's company's talent management processes to produce certain outcomes, vitality is about the attitudes and mindsets of the people responsible for those processes – not just in human resources but throughout the line, all the way to the top of the organization.

In simple words, vitality refers to the emotional commitment by management that is reflected in daily actions.

According to Ready and Conger, vitality of a company's talent management processes is a product of three 'defining characteristics': –

i. Fostering Commitment
ii. Building Engagement
iii. Ensuring Accountability

Ready and Conger advocated mapping the talent pool, line management, HR/talent staff and the top executives team on all these three defining characteristics.

Process	Talent Benchmark Metrics			
Define				
Company Standards	Productivity	Unwanted Turnover	Reduce Costs increase profits	
Measure				
Accurate Statistics	Competencies	Limitations	Improvable Weaknesses	
Analyze				
Errors & Improvements	Best Job Fit	Career Potential	Levels of Engagement	
Improve				
Repeatable Process	Selection & Assignment	Career Path	Recognition & Compensation	
Control				
Process & measures	Accurate Assessment Measure	Development & training	Succession Planning	

Figure 20.3: Six Sigma Framework Applied to Talent Management

(**Source:** Stevens P Howard, Total Quality Management Now applies to Managing Talent, The journal for Quality & Participation, Summer 2008)

Identifying weaknesses in functionality and vitality can help a company its talent management agenda among industries.

This further corroborates that talent management has become the new face of managing human resource strategically.

To sum up the discussions Howard P. Stevens (2008) proposed a Six Sigma Framework applied to Talent Management *(refer Figure 20.3)*.

Bringing quality to various human resource functions is the need of the hour for any firm to withstand competitive battlegrounds. This book is set on similar agenda as it moves through complex issues and explores how integration of talent management issues could result in better and more strategic management of human resource.

Essay Questions

1. Is talent management an 'Oxymoron'? Comment.
2. Define 'Talent'. Explain the 'talent-pipeline'. How does Prahlad's n=1 strategy apply to managing talents?
3. Who owns and drives talent management in a firm? Corroborate with examples.
4. List on the nine areas of talent management identified by the institute of corporate productivity (i4CP). How do these areas apply to different companies?
5. Discuss in detail talent management in a recessionary economy. What are the priorities? Elaborate with examples.
6. Explain the 'functionality' and 'vitality' wheels of Talent Management.

Application Questions

1. Go to http://www.adb.org/documents/information/knowledge-solutions/primer-on-talent-management.pdf and read the article 'A Primer on Talent Management'.
2. Go to http://www.haygroup.com/ca/downloads/details.aspx?id=27570 and the read the talent management case study on Novartis. Discuss within group.

Bibliography

A Simpler Way to Determine the ROI of Talent Management. (2004, December). HR Focus.

Altman, W. (2008, March). Engineering & Technology. Turning in the Talent.

Bhushan Ratna, Yum: To Serve calorie food, The Economics Times, Oct 23, 2009.

Brockett, J. (2007, June). Engage Execs to Develop Fitting Talent. NEWS Conference Report, Talent Management, CIPD, London.

Cappelli, P. (2008, March). Talent Management for 21st Century. *Harvard Business Review*.

Cappelli, P. (2009). A Supply Chain Model for Talent Management. People & Strategy, 32 (3).

Chuai, P. I. (2010). Talent Management as a Management Fashion in HRD: Towards a Research Agenda. Human Resource Development International, 13 (2).

Fernando, K. V. (2008). Aligning Recruitment to Talent Management Efforts. The Association for Strategy & Leadership Professionals.

Forman C David, Talent Metrics, *Leadership Excellence*.

Forman, D. C. (n.d.). Talent Metrics- Measure What Matters. *Leadership Excellence*.

Galagan, P. (2008, May). Talent Management- What it is, who owns it, and why should you care? T+D.

Galagon Pal, Talent Management – what is it; Who Owns it and why should you care?; T&D, May 2008.

Hills, A. (2009). Succession Planning – or Smart Talent Management. Industrial and Commercial Training, 41 (1).

Howard, S. P. (2008). Total Quality Management Now Applies to Manaéiné Talent. *The Journal for Quality & Participation*.

Kevin Vince Fernando, K., & Fernado, K. V. (2008, April). Aligning Recruitment to Talent Management Efforts. The Association for Strategy & Leadership Professionals.

Loiselle, S. (n.d.). Trends in Human Capital Management.

Managing Talent in a Turbulent Economy: Playing both Offence and Defense, Feb 2009, *Deliotte Report*.

Managing Talent in a Turbulent Economy: Playing both Offense and Defense. (2009, February). *Deloitte Report*.

McCauley, C., & Wakefield, M. (2006). Talent Managementin the 21 Century: Help Your Company Find, Develop, and Keep its Strongest Workers. *The Journal for Quality & Participation*.

Ogden, G. (2010, March). Talent Management in a Time of Cost Management, *Healthcare Financial Management*.

Preece, P. I. & Chuai, X. (2010). Talent Management as a Management Fashion in HRD: Towards a Research Agenda, I. *Human Resource Development International*, 13 (2), 125–145.

Ready A Douglas, Conger A Jay, Make your Company Talent Factory, Harvard Business Review; June 2007.

Reindl Rob, Growing Talent at Edward Life sciences, T&D, Feb 2007.

Reindl, R. (2007, February). Growing Talent at Edward Lifesciences. T+D.

Stevens P Howard, Total Quality Management Now applies to Managing Talent, *The Journal for Quality & Participation*, Summer 2008.

Stevens, H. P. (2008). Total Quality Management. Now Applies to Manaéiné Talent. *The Journal for Quality & Participation*.

Talent Management Is Now a CEO Responsibility. (2006, August), hrfocus.

Threading the Talent Needle: What Global Executives are Saying about People and Work, Deliotte Report.

Threading the Talent Needle-What Global Executives are Saying about People and Work Deloitte Report.

Valerie, G., & Hirsh, W. (2008). Talent Management: Issues of Focus and Fit. *Public Personnel Management*, 37 (4).

Chapter 21

Employee Engagement

Key Terms

- Employee Engagement
- Engagement Model
- Engagement Trends
- Job Involvement
- Multi-channel Communication
- Work-life Imbalance

Outline

- Introducing Employee Engagement
- Three Entities of Engagement
- Is Employee Engagement More than Job Involvement?
- Why Engagement?
- Engagement Models
- Levels of Engagement
- Building Blocks of Engagement
- Breathing Offices
- Collaborate
- Empower
- Communicate
- Work-life Balance & Engagement
- Work-life Balance Myths:
- Impact of Work-life Imbalance
- Towards Greater Work-life Balance
- Measuring Employee Engagement
- Essay Questions
- Application Questions
- Bibliography

Employee Engagement

Bonding an employee rationally as well as emotionally, so as to elicit maximum productivity, involvement & contribution & retaining him/her by creating happiness as an output.

Introducing Employee Engagement

Engagement at work was conceptualized by Kahn (1990) as the 'harnessing of organizational members' selves to their work roles. In engagement people employ and express themselves physically, cognitively and emotionally during role performances.

Employee Engagement can be defined as the level of commitment and involvement as employee has towards his/her organization and its values.

OR

'It is the degree to which an employee is emotionally bonded to his/her organization and passionate about his/her work.'

Three Entities of Engagement

i. Employees as unique entities in terms of their skills, abilities, attitudes & aspirations.

ii. Employers in their role to create condition of engagement

iii. Relationship, trust and communication between employees across levels.

Is Employee Engagement More than Job Involvement?

Engagement is thus viewed as an antecedent to job involvement wherein a deep sense of identity with individual job role sets-in.

Job involvement is defined as the degree to which the job situation is central to the person and his or her identity. Job Involvement is a cognitive or belief state of psychological identification. Thus job involvement results from a cognitive judgment about the ability of a job to satisfy the needs.

Engagement differs from job involvement as it is concerned more with how an individual employee views himself/herself during the performance of his/her job. Engagement is thus viewed as an antecedent to job involvement wherein a deep sense of identity with individual job role sets-in. Besides engagement is also about emotional connect.

Why Engagement?

Various Research show strong Correlation of Employee Engagement with Employee Commitment & Financial Performance of the company. Better Engagement leads to:

- Better employee performance.
- Higher employee commitment & discretionary efforts.
- Employee less likely to be a source of inventory shrinkage.
- Higher operating income, net income, profits & EPS for the firm.
- Higher annual growth rate for the firm.
- Lower staff turnover, higher customer satisfaction & loyalty.

Engagement Models

1. **IES Model:** Recognizes factor at work, individual factors and work-life factors as contributors to engagement.
2. **Blessing White's Engagement Model:** Blessing White's engagement model focuses both on the individual contribution to the company's success as well the personal satisfaction that he/she derives from his/her role.
3. **The Zinger Model:** David Zinger attempts to balance Organizational inputs, leadership inputs and individual (self) inputs in creating and fostering engagement. According to Zinger, to achieve full engagement, efforts must come from organizations, leaders and employees.
4. **AMMA's Four Quadrant Model of Employee Relations and Organizational Effectiveness:** AMMA, the sole national employer association representing the employee relations and human resource management interests of Australia's onshore and offshore resource sector and associated industries proposed this model to assess the impact of employee engagement on workplace performance.

Levels of Engagement

Blessing White Anexi has classified employees in 5 categories depending upon their levels of engagement:

(i) 'The Engaged'
- Engaged employees are among their high contributors.

- Bring forth discretionary effort to work.
- Take initiatives.
- Have the ability to influence, motivate and lead other groups
- They are thought to be more retainable.

(ii) Almost Engaged
- Almost Engaged Employees rank medium to high on both contribution and satisfaction.
- They may perform at a very high level although they are not consistent.
- May have deep impact on performance in the event of their leaving the organization.
- Highly employable by competing firms.
- Can get de-motivated and performance level can plunge.

(iii) Honeymooners and Hamsters
Both Honeymooners and hamsters are medium to high on satisfaction but low on contribution. Honeymooners are newly hired employees who do not have a clue on how they can contribute effectively to the organization. Hamsters are old-timers contributing little to the organization, although they may perceive themselves to be effective contributors. Hamsters are however unlikely to leave the organization.

(iv) Crash & Burn
- Crash & Burn are medium to high in contribution but low on satisfaction.
- Disillusioned and potentially exhausted.
- Can contribute but have grown bitter with the company & colleagues primarily due to lack of personal satisfaction.
- Critical & vocal in airing disillusionment.
- 'Flight' or 'with drawl' tendency is exhibited.
- Can become disengaged, in isolation.

(v) The Disengaged

- Disengaged are both low in contribution and satisfaction.
- Minimize contribution while try to remain afloat.
- Very bitter & Skeptical of their organization.
- Disconnected and disenchanted.
- Majority of them may not have started in this fashion but may have grown to this state.

Employee Engagement is not easy to attain but even more difficult to sustain. Organizations and leaders must try to create engagement in their firms; maintain and appreciate the same in terms of engagement levels; and finally sustain high levels of engagement consistently over a period of time.

Building Blocks of Engagement

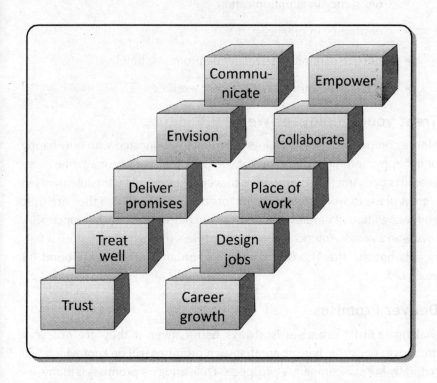

Trust

Building trust is fundamental to building engagement, yet it often fails to gain precedence among employee – strategies. Employee feel more engaged when they work in a safe, cooperative environment. "Safe", in this context means that employees trust one another and are able to quickly resolve conflicts when they arise.

Leaders play an important role in building trust but the role of peers must not be totally discounted.

Some of the trust building behavior could be:

- Transparency in operations.
- Timely information sharing.
- Unbiased attention.
- Tolerance for failure.
- Consistency in communication.
- Consistency in practices.
- Not over-committing. Delivering promises, timely.
- No finger-pointing & fault-finding exercises.

Treat your Employees Well

Among all factors/elements in a great place to work, two of the factors never changed and they are trust and recognition of employees.

How a company treats its employees is directly connected with how happy or unhappy customers/clients of that company feel. Fortune magazine every year lists best American companies to work. Among all factors/elements in a great place to work, two of the factors never changed and they are trust and recognition of employees. And yes, such firms were highly successful. While an average American company lasts less than 20 years before it fails or gets bought, the 100 best companies, on an average, are around 85 years old.

Deliver Promises

Making realistic promises is always better, even if they are not very attractive; because chances are that such promises will be kept which will naturally boost a company's prospects. Delivering on promises is many–a–times an implementation issue. Hence involvement of line-function from design to delivery of such promises is critical. And lastly, promises that a company makes to its employees get tested when tough-times prevail such as recessionary conditions or mergers & acquisitions.

Envision
Vision of an organization remains as a lofty well-crafted and well articulated statement of the founder until and unless the same is broken-down to the level of even an average worker in a company so that even he can know what he must do to actualise the vision. This process is known as envisioning, where 'vision' becomes a part of everybody. Eg. Royal bank of Canada's 'Client-first Initiative'

Career Growth
Most employee engagement surveys put career development opportunities as one of the top-most priorities for the employer. Managers must develop career development checklists.

Design Jobs
A good job design must be linked to the strategic choices of the firm. Job design identifies:

- What work must be performed?
- How it must be accomplished?
- Where it must be done?
- Who must do that work?

Place of Work
Expectation on nature of workplace has undergone serious transformation. 'Gen Y and Workplace Annual Report-2010' shows that workplace plays a significant role in not only attracting and retaining the Gen Y but also help improve productivity and creativity. ILO emphasizes on safe & non-hazardous workplaces play an important role in affecting the psyche of workers. According to 'WISHA' The work-related musco-skeletal disorders (WMSDs) account for 40% class of injury claims in the office e.g., Carpel Junnel Syndrome. There is a strong need for office Ergonomics.

Collaborate

In a globalized world that we live in today, the issue of 'collaboration' among employees working in various teams (at times virtual teams) across cities, countries and continents has become very significant. McKinsey & Company's report on "Mapping the value of employee collaboration" (2006) corroborates the same.

Exhibit 1: Engagement through Idea Sharing and Team Participation @ Titan

Employee Involvement and engagement does not restrict itself to mere job and work. It also transcends and manifests itself in the manner in which every employee participates in larger organizational Initiatives' and provides suggestions, as well as builds effective teams. Employees at all levels do participate in a wide variety of initiatives which either bring to the fore an individual creative mindset (Through Suggestion scheme – IDEA +, Kaizens) or participation in Small Group Activities (SGA). In addition to these, they also participate in larger organizational initiatives as a team member, to either accomplish a task or, solve problems. These include participation in CFT's (Cross Functional Teams) leading or participating in new/challenging assignments and so on. The company truly believes and recognizes the fact that employee participation in these initiatives not only creates a sense of belongingness but also encourages them to contribute to larger organizational purposes beyond routine work. Hence the benefits are immense. Today most of Titan's employees are a part of one or many of the above initiatives. The company has more than 200 SGA's, more than 100 CFT's and also more than 5000 Kaizens in place, which only keeps increasing year on year!

(Case excerpt[1])

Empower

Empowerment should not only be a decorative word. It means instilling a feeling of true sense of ownership among employees and includes creating systems and designing work pressures & structure, integrating empowerment as a part of policy, process & procedure is important, since implementation is the key. Informal Networks, comparing networks to human body- the formal structure is only the skeletal framework, while informal network add meat, veins and muscles to the same. Informal networks engage employees to the organization. However to make informal networks following should be kept in mind-

- Informal networking should be left to chance.
- Over-reliance may be counter-productive.
- Grapevine management is the key.

---

[1] Excerpt from case 'Titan's Turnaround using Engagement as a Cornerstore of its Strategy' from – Sengupta Debashish, Ramadoss S., Employee Engagement, Biztantra (2011).

Communicate

Communication is the key. Rightful integration of communication is important linkage of communication and social-learning skills. There is a need to focus on evolving forms of communication.

Work-life Balance & Engagement

Work life balance is essentially an individual's ability to strike equilibrium between one's professional and personal life. Absence or lack of work life balance can rattle the most resilient and in the long-run can have an impact on performance and longetivity of employees. This is why work life balance is an engagement issue. Attainment of work life balance is not possible without the active participation of the employer and employee. Hence engagement through better W/L balance calls for a more concentrated effort.

Exhibit 2: People Philosophy at Taj Hotels

1. You are an important member of the Taj family.
2. We endeavor to select, retain and compensate the best talent in the industry.
3. We reward and recognize quality customer care based upon individual and team performance.
4. We commit to providing you with opportunities for continuous learning and development.
5. We abide by fair and just policies that ensure your well-being and that of your family, the community and the environment.
6. We commit to regular and formal channels of communication, which nurture openness and transparency.
7. We strongly believe that you are the Taj.

(Case excerpt[2])

Exhibit 3: Multi-channel Communication @ TCS

In a large and growing organization communication is not only a huge challenge but also an opportunity in itself to closely engage the employees. TCS ensures that all employees are met on a one-on-one basis or in groups through regular connect sessions referred to as 'Lets Talk' sessions, 'Dialogue sessions', 'Cliques', 'Town Hall Meetings', 'Coffee with HR', etc. Cliques are regular session by HR to meet the employees on the floor, once in a fortnight, to update the people about policies, new recruits and other information. Let's Talk is a program wherein the employees can choose to meet anybody in the organization to talk and HR organizes

---

[2] Excerpt from the Case – 'Taj Hotels – Pioneers in Engagement'

> such meetings. Town Hall Meetings are like open forums where senior leaders come and meet employees en-mass. People can ask questions, tell what they feel about their role, satisfaction or talk about any other issue. There are dedicated HR professionals for each of the accounts/projects who take care of engaging an employee through several channels. Communication has such a high focus that employees are overwhelmed with information about happenings in the company, how well the company is doing, new policies, employee benefits, etc.
>
> (Case excerpt[3])

Work-life Balance Myths

- **Myth 1:** Work-life imbalance is only at managerial level (It is at all levels).
- **Myth 2:** Work-life imbalance increase with the income level of an employee (has little to do with income levels).
- **Myth 3:** Work-life imbalance are higher in developed economy (In developed as well as developing economies).

Impact of Work-life Imbalance

Three independent researches, i.e., Attitudes in American Workplace Survey, Audrey Tsui's Asian Study of Wellness Decline and MDRA & Outlook Business show that the cost of rising prosperity is pretty high:

- Increased 'pulls and pressures'.
- Direct impact on work-life balance.
- Work time includes travel time.
- Chronic fatigue & work stress.
- True for larger as well as smaller organizations.
- Rise in incidents of yelling, crying screaming etc.
- Rise in anxiety related ailments.
- Long working hours, excessive workload, weekend duties, inadequate physical activity & unhealthy lifestyle are cited as reasons.
- Impacts both family and non-family domains
- Skewed WLB leads to higher absenteeism, turnover, sickness and lessen commitments, productivity and efficiency.
- *Karoshi-* death due to overwork.

---

[3] Excerpt from the Case – 'TCS – Engagement through Performance-based Learning Culture' from the book – Sengupta Debashish, Ramadoss S., Employee Engagement, Biztantra (2011).

Towards Greater Work-life Balance

A greater work-life balance leading to a higher engagement can be achieved through Positive culture and supportive supervisor.

- Training supervisors (People often do not leave their organizations, they leave their supervisors)
- Job sharing
- Flexi work hours
- Flexible work week
- Telecommunicating – Choosing right telecommunicatting options
  - Occasional
  - Temporary
  - Permanent
- Flexibility in day to day management
- Onsite support services.
- Flexi leave options
- Family's day out.

Measuring Employee Engagement

Measuring the true state of employee engagement in any organization is both a need and an opportunity. Measuring engagement levels in an organization is more diagnostic in nature.

Commonly used Methods

- Dedicated employee engagement surveys.
- Opinion surveys
- Other techniques

Gallup Q. 12

12 questions arranged in four categories:

- What do I get?
- What do I give?
- Do I belong here?
- How can we all grow?

USAID 26- item Measurement Tool

- Adapted from Gallup and other questionnaires.
- Primarily designed for international public healthcare professionals in poor countries.
- Can be administered to all categories of working with varying levels of qualifications.
- 26 questions arranged in six categories:-
  - Belief in job and organization
  - Belief in ability to succeed
  - Relation with my colleagues and my supervisor
  - Professional advancement
  - Support and recognition
  - Influence in decision making

DDI's E3

- 20 survey items arranged in six categories:-
  - Align efforts with strategy
  - Empowerment
  - Teamwork and collaboration
  - Development plans
  - Support and recognition
  - Satisfaction and loyalty

Engagement Trends in India

Engagement levels in India have gradually improved since 2001 demonstrating greater commitment among employers for creating a better and more challenging workplace. Best employers in India show visibly higher scores on employee engagement compared to rest of the companies. Aspirations of Indian workers are no different from that of global workers. Career aspirations ride supreme in a dynamic and growing economy like India and companies that have shown better ability to manage the same have better reported higher engagement levels.

Challenges Ahead

Some of the engagement challenges ahead for the companies are:

- To ensure higher levels of engagement.
- To ensure more consistent levels of engagement across all levels of organization.
- To close the gender differences in engagement levels by creating women friendly work places.
- To create more career development opportunities for employees.
- To ensure fair and dignified treatment to employees, even in worst times.
- To bond closely with the employee's families.

This chapter is an excerpt from the 2011 best-selling book - Employee Engagement authored by Dr. Debashish Sengupta & S. Ramadoss, Sr. V.P. & CHRO – Titan.

The **Table of Contents** of the book read as –

Foreword ix
About the Authors xi
Acknowledgements xiii

Chapter 1: Demystifying Employee Engagement 1
Chapter 2: Inequalities in Gender Engagement at Workplaces 21
Chapter 3: Building Blocks of Engagement 31
Chapter 4: Life @ Work 55
Chapter 5: Lens of the Service Marketer 75
Chapter 6: The Extended Honeymoon 87
Chapter 7: Measuring Engagement 107
Chapter 8: Best Practices and Benchmarking in Employee Engagement 119

Business Case 1: Taj Hotels: Pioneers in Engagement 129 _(**Case[2]**)_
Business Case 2: Titan's Turnaround using engagement as a cornerstone of its strategy145 _(**Case[1]**)_
Business Case 3: TCS - Engagement through Performance-based Learning Culture 167 _(**Case[3]**)_
Business Case 4: Engaging Employees the Oliver Wyman Way 175
Business Case 5: Who let the baby out? 179
Business Case 6: Google - Ideas above Hierarchy 183
Business Case 7: Bharti Airtel: The Engagement Tone 187
Business Case 8: Titan's Employee Engagement – Survey findings by Gallup 191

Essay Questions

1. What is employee engagement? Which are the three entities of such engagement? Is engagement required?

2. Explain briefly the various models of Employee Engagement.

3. What are the various levels of engagement? List the characteristics of each level.

4. List and explain the various building blocks of employee engagement. Exemplify.

5. What role does work-life balance play in creating engagement? Delve on the various myths of work-life balance and provide rationale argument.

6. How can employee engagement be measured? What is the current state of engagement in India?

Application Questions

1. Go to http://www.infosys.com/socialedge/resources/Documents/employee-engagement-platform.pdf and read the *'Infosys Socialedge Employee Engagement Platform.'*

2. Go to http:/ articles.economictimes.indiatimes.com/2011-04-05/news/ 29384472_1_employee-engagement-myths-bright-future and read the article *'3Cs of employee engagement: Career, competence and care'*.

3. Go to the link http:/ articles. economictimes. indiatimes.com/2011-12-16/news 30525071_1_women-professionals women-employees-indian-women and read the article *'Companies need to classify their women employees and engage with them accordingly'*.

4. Go to the link http://www.thehindubusinessline.com/opinion/article 2347571.ece and read the review on Employee Engagement.

5. Go to the link http://www.thehindubusinessline.com/opinion/article1153519.ece and the article *'The Myth of Engagement'*.

6. Go to the link http://www.thehindubusinessline.com/todays-paper/tp-opinion/article 1029992.ece and read the article on *'Employee Engagement'*.

Author's Blog on Employee Engagement http://www.peopleengagement.blogspot.com/

Bibliography

Atchinson Chris, How to Build a Super Staff, Profit, *Toronto*, May 2010, Vol. 29, Iss.2, pg. 30.

Attitudes in American Workplace, http://www2.themarlincompany.com/MediaRoom/PollResults.aspx.

Bailey Eileen, Compressed Work Week, 2008, http://smallhomebusiness.suite101.com/article.cfm/compressed_work_week.

Benthal Paul R., Measuring Employee Engagement (white paper), DDI, MMIV.

Best Employers in Asia 2007, http://www.rediff.com/money/2007/apr/17best.htm.

Bhattacharya Saumya, Bid for Breakfast with your Boss, November 13, 2009, http://businesstoday.intoday.in/index.php?option=com_content&task=view&issueid=77&id=13205&Itemid=99999999&sectionid=25.

Bird Jim, Work-life Balance – Doing it Right and Avoiding the Pitfalls, *Employee Relations Today*, Autumn 2006, Vol. 33 No. 3.

Buckingham Marcus, Coffman Curt (1999), First, Break all the Rules, Simon & Schuster, ISBN: 0684852861.

Busch Kira, Trust Begins at Home – Netflix's Approach to Building Customer Relationships, http://www.darden.virginia.edu/corporate-ethics leading_practices_Trust_Netflix_Customer_Relations.htm.

Callahan Shawn, Schenk Mark, White Nancy, Building a Collaborative Workplace, Anecdote white paper, www.anecdote.com.

Castellano Willams G., A New Framework of Employee Engagement, Centre for Human Reource Strategy (CHRS) whitepaper, The State University of New Jersey.

Castellano William G., A New Framework of Employe Engagement, www.chrs.rutgers.edu.

Colvin Geoff, The 100 Best Companies to Work for 2006, Treating Employees Well, these Firms are Thriving, January 11, 2006, http://money.cnn.com/magazines/fortune/fortune_archive/2006/01/23/8366990/index.htm.

Employee Engagement – A Lifetime of Opportunity, an Analysis of the Employee Engagement Experiences of AMMA Members Using the Four Quadrant Model of Employee Relations and Organizational Effectiveness, AMMA Sept. 2007.

Employee Engagement and Talent Management, www.watsonwyatt.com.

Engaging the Employee, A Kenexa Research Institute Work Trends Report 2008.

Fleming John H, Asplund Jim, Human Sigma (2007), Gallup Press, New York, ISBN: 978-1-59562-016-3.

Fox Adrienne, Raising Engagement, HR Magazine, Alexnadria, May 2010, Vol. 55, Iss. 5, pg. 34.

http://www.oestrategies.com/papers/white_paper_on_EE_engagement_&_brand.pdf

Kurlekar Advait, Engage to Gain Drive Business Results through your Engagement Program, Sept. 2007, www.kpconsulting.in.

Lawrence Lucie P., A Critical Link to Employee – commotted to Emplotyee Engagement Avnet takes action, watsonwyatt.com/strategyatwork.

Leadership Opportunities – Increased Bottom Line Results through Improved Staff Engagement, Hewitt.

Macleod David, Clarke Nita, Engaging for Success – Enhancing Performance through Employee Engagement, www.bis.gov.uk.

Mahoney Manda, How your Employees and Customers Drive a New Value Profit Chain – Q&A with James Heskett and W. Earl Sasser, March 31, 2003, http://hbswk.hbs.edu/item/3405.html.

Morgan Lloyd, Driving Performance and Retention through Employee Engagement, Corporate Leadership Council 2004, www.lloydmorgan.com.

Seijtts Gerard H., Crim Dan, What Engages Employees the most or, The Ten C's of Employee Engagement, *Ivey Business Journal Online*, March/April 2006.

The Employee Engagement Equation in India, HRAnnexi AblessingWhite, 2008.

Wellins Richard S., Bernthal Paul, Phelps Mark, Employee Engagement; the Key to Realizing Competitive Advantage, DDI MMV.

Working Today: Understanding What Drives Employee Engagement, the 203 Towers Perrin Talent Report, www.towersperrin.com.

http://davidzinger.wordpress.com.

Chapter 22

Strategic Management of Human Resource in Organizations

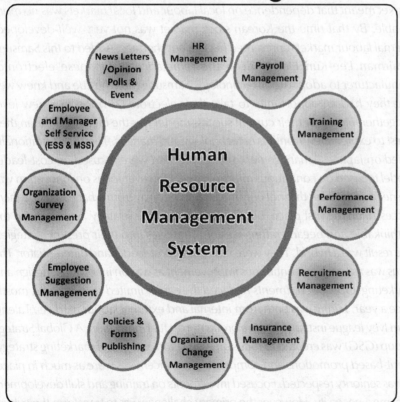

Outline

Business Byte

HRM Effectiveness and Business Success

Strategy & Strategic Managment

Types of Strategies

Strategic Management Process

Strategic Human Resource Management

Approaches to Strategic Human Resource Management

HR Strategies

Essay Questions

Application Questions

Bibliography

Key Terms

Technical HRM

Strategic HRM

HRM Effectiveness

Competitive Strategy

Cost Leadership

Corporate Strategy

Business Byte

Samsung Electronics Corporation's transformation from a small low-cost electronics manufacturer to a sophisticated global electronics brand has been a fascinating story. The future of the company pretty much depended on such a transformation. Driven by changes in the environment, the business transformation was catalyzed by a parallel internal transformation of human resource function. The business strategy was well complemented by the HR strategy. It was early 90s and the environment was fast changing. Political, economic, social, technological, regulatory environment was fast-changing. Globalization footprints were reaching Korean shores. Weak external capital market, coupled with underdeveloped labour market meant that dependence on local labour and local markets was no more tenable. By that time the Korean stock market was not very well-developed. Internal labour market represented huge talent shortage. Added to this Samsung Chairman Lee-Kun Hee noticed the reluctance of Japanese electronics manufacturer to adopt digital technology. Samsung took the cue and knew well that they had an opportunity to take their electronic division to a new level altogether. However their current success model was the biggest barrier in their quest to explore new frontiers of technology and markets. They had traditionally relied on Japanese management philosophy and were focused on cost-leader model focused on continuous improvement. However focus on innovation was the need of the hour that not only meant turning away from what had made them successful in the first place, but also a change in the strategy. Samsung did the unthinkable and began grafting western strategies into their present strategies. The result was a hybrid. They were now both a cost-leader and differentiator. The focus was as much on continuous improvement as was on innovation, design and marketing. Open recruitments replaced the earlier limited recruitments, mostly once a year. Hiring was both from internal and external labour markets. Talents from Ivey league institutions were brought-in to fuel innovation. A Global Strategy Group (GSG) was created to focus on innovation and global marketing strategy. Merit-based promotions and compensation & incentives were as much in place, as was seniority respected. Focused investments on training and skill development became a necessity. However the primary challenge was to transform the culture of the company and the senior leadership led none other than the chairman himself played a major role in the same. By the turn of the decade, Samsung was a force to reckon with in the global electronics market, beating Japanese manufacturer by miles. Few years down the line, Samsung beat Apple in smartphone sales. Today Samsung boasts of the cutting-edge electronic technology and rivals the best in the business.

HRM Effectiveness and Business Success

The resource view of a firm suggests that human resource of a company can be 'leveraged' to gain competitive advantage (Barney1991). Research has also supported and exhibited a strong linkage between HRM effectiveness and business success. One such study done in the SME sector in Pakistan showed that the supply chain management success was activated by the success of HRM practices. Organizations that employed sophisticated HRM practices achieved greater success with their supply chain management process (Khan, Taha, Ghouri, Khan, Yong, 2013). This is turn played a major role in the success of the SMEs. Another study done among large scale manufacturing firms in Malaysia showed a positive relationship between HR's business partner role and HRM effectiveness (Mohd.Yusoff, Baharom, 2010). The study indicated that a progressive change in the role of HR department improved the effectiveness of HRM in the organizations.

> Organizations that employed sophisticated HRM practices achieved greater success.

HRM is important for organizational success.	Barney, 1991; Jackson & Schuler, 2000; Pfeffer, 1994
HRM practices have a role to play in ensuring sustained competitive advantage of a firm.	Gerhart & Milkovich, 1992; Huselid, 1995; Macduffie, 1995;
HRM helps in the improvement of organizational performance.	Becker andGerhart (1996)
Alignment of HRM with business strategy help a firm achieve better outcomes.	Becker and Huselid (1998), and Dyer & Reeves (1995)
Positive Relationship between HRM activities and productivity & quality of a firm.	MacDuffie (1995)
Positive Relationship between HRM activities and operational performance.	Youndt et al(1996)
Positive Relationship between six underlying HRM practices on business performance, namely training and development, teamwork, compensation /incentives, HR planning, performance appraisal, employee security and improved business performance of a company.	Lee & Lee, 2007
Positive relationship between HRM activities and employee productivity, firm's flexibility and quality performance.	Chang and Chen, 2002; Ahmad and Schroeder, 2003; Kuo,2004 Sang, 2005

Table 22.1: Selected Research Evidence on Positive Relationship between HRM Effectiveness and Business Performance

Positive relationship between seven HRM practices such as employment security, selective hiring, use of teams and decentralization, compensation/incentive contingent on performance; extensive training, status difference and sharing information and operational performance.	Ahmad and Schroeders (2003)
HRM is a part of the overall strategy of the firm	Myloni et. al. (2004)

>The Strategic HRM effectiveness helps to make the workforce inimitable or difficult to copy.

HRM effectiveness is comprised of Technical HRM effectiveness and Strategic HRM effectiveness. Technical HRM activities include recruitment & selection, performance management, compensation and benefits management and training. Technical HRM effectiveness helps companies to hire unique talent and equip them with unique skills. Strategic HRM on the other hand involve activities like innovative job designs, team building, talent management, empowerment & participation of employees, employee engagement, building flexible workforce and high-performance work systems etc. The Strategic HRM effectiveness helps to make the workforce inimitable or difficult to copy. While technical HRM effectiveness requires HR people to have high occupational skills and expertise; Strategic HRM effectiveness requires a concerted effort by the HR, Line and the Leadership – HR needs to align to business needs and add value to business, Line managers need to own HR responsibilities and involve in all aspects of managing their teams and finally, the leadership needs to have a strong commitment and involvement so as to impact both design and policy. Specifically with respect to the HR function, while for technical HRM effectiveness professional capabilities of HR people were enough, for ensuring Strategic HRM effectiveness business-related capabilities are needed (Schuler, 1992).

Strategy & Strategic Management

>Operational excellence is often doing activities better than one's competitors.

Strategy has often been confused with operational excellence. Michael Porter in a 1996 article in *HBR* outlined the difference between operational excellence and strategy (Porter, 1996). Operational excellence is often doing activities better than one's competitors. Hence aspects like total quality management, benchmarking, time-based competition, outsourcing, partnering, reengineering, change management have come into place. Although these have helped company improve its efficiency, cut costs, reduce wastage and defects etc., they may not have always helped the company improve its profitability or market share. The reason has been the absence of a clearly drawn and executable strategy. Strategy is doing activities different than those of rivals, consistently and those that help a company to outperform its rivals. As Michael Porter call it rightly – Competitive Strategy.

Michael Porter's competitive strategy theory meant that a company can beat its competition by devising a strategy and executing it in a manner to garner maximum market share and profits. He suggested five competitive forces (Clayton, 2015) that will determine how a company's product or service would fare with respect to its competitors:

Michael Porter's Theory of Competitive Strategy

1. **Entry:** If the entry barriers are low, then it is easy for the new players to enter the market and pose competition. Key questions then are:
   a. How easy is it for new 'players' to enter the market?
   b. Do new entrants face significant barriers like high capital requirement for entry by the new players, high cost of switching by the customers etc., or do they expect sharp opposition from existing competitors?

2. **Threat of Substitution:** If there are easy and many substitutes available for a product then the competition is tougher and wider. Tea for instance today faces competition not only from within the industry but from other beverages like coffee, soft drinks etc.

   Key question:
   a. Are there other products and services that can easily substitute a company's goods?

3. **Bargaining Power of Buyers:**
   Key questions:
   a. Are a small number of buyers responsible for a large portion of sales?
   b. Do their purchases represent a large portion of their costs?
   c. Can they easily switch suppliers, or go into the same business themselves?

TQM, Benchmarking time-based competition, outsourcing, partnering, reengineering, change management have come into place. Although these have helped company improve its efficiency, cut costs, reduce wastage and defects etc.

According to Porter five forces that drive competition are:
1. Existing competitive rivalry between suppliers.
2. Threat of new market entrants.
3. Bargaining power of buyers.
4. Bargaining power of suppliers.
5. Threat of substitute products (including substitute products).

Affirmative answers to the above question would mean that buyers will command huge influence over price and would be a challenge to retain. This might weaken the competitive position of a company.

4. **Bargaining Power of Suppliers:**

   Key questions:

   a. Does a company have multiple suppliers?

   b. Are there substitutes that it can use?

   c. Is it easy to switch suppliers?

   d. Is the company a relatively important customer?

   Few and unique suppliers will always increase the bargaining power of the suppliers.

5. **Nature of Current Competition:**

   Key question:

   a. How intense is the rivalry among the firms you compete with?

   Degree and nature of competition may differ depending on the relative strength of the competitors and also on the kinds of strategy that they are putting-in place.

Types of Strategies

Regardless of the nature of a business firm, there are three kinds of strategies – Corporate Strategy, Competitive/Business Strategy and Functional Strategies.

Corporate Strategies

Corporate Strategy deals with the overall firm and deals with markets and businesses that a firm will operate. '*Corporate strategy is typically decided in the context of defining the company's mission and vision, that is, saying what the company does, why it exists, and what it is intended to become.*' There are generally three broad types of corporate strategies – Growth, Stability and turnaround/Retrenchment.

Growth: Company decides to grow, either externally or internal. While internal growth happens through expansion of operations, increasing range of products or services and/or acquiring new set of customers; external growth generally happens though mergers and acquisitions.

Corporate strategy is typically decided in the context of defining the company's mission and vision, that is, saying what the company does, why it exists, and what it is intended to become.

Stability: A company decides to maintain status quo situation for the reasons – one it may not see any significant new opportunity in the environment and second, that it might see it profitable to keep doing what it is already doing and hence just wants to be better the same.

Turnaround/Retrenchment: A company either wants to streamline or reduce its operations. The need may arise because a company may find more threats than opportunities in the environment and the company may feel the need to consolidate.

Competitive Strategies

Michael Porter suggested three generic strategies to cope-up with these five 'competitive' forces: Cost Leadership, Differentiation and Focus.

Cost Leadership: A company tries to minimize its cost and keep it lower than other competitors. Improving efficiency and utilization of man, machinery and other resources becomes primary concern. By doing this the company is also able to offer the same product at a lower price than anyone else in the market. Walmart, Big Bazaar, D-Mart, Southwest Airlines, Indigo airlines are all examples of cost-leaders.

Differentiator: A company tries to create a unique product or a service that no one else offers in the market. Creativity, innovation, R&D, market research are the focal points and where the company makes maximum investments. Apple, Louis Vuitton, Mercedes are examples of companies that have adopted differentiation as their strategy.

Focus: A company decides to focus on the needs of a particular set of customers and/or on a particular geographical area and/or on a particular segment of the product line. At times companies may have a mixed or hybrid strategy.

> **Example:** At times to cater to different markets or to different income group customers, company may become a focused cost-leader or a focused-differentiator, and sometimes even become both a cost-leader and a differentiator.

Functional Strategies

Functional strategies are at the functional or ground level and help to achieve the objectives set at corporate and business level. Each function devises its own strategy aligned to the company corporate and business strategy; hence we have HR strategy, Finance Strategy, Marketing Strategy, Production Strategy, IT Strategy etc.

An HR manager strategically plans his responsibilities of staffing, setting policies, compensation and benefits, retention, training, employment laws, and worker protection.

Strategic Management Process

The strategic management process has five distinct stages – Goal-setting, scanning the environment, strategy formulation, implementation of the strategy and strategy evaluation.

Goal-setting: The business goals and plans are drawn from the overall vision and mission of a company. Vision essentially is where a company wants to reach or what it wants to achieve, whereas mission defines how it wants to reach that point or achieve what it wants to.

Scanning the Environment: Environment is dynamic and keeps altering. The environmental factors such as political factor, economic factors, socio-cultural factor, technological factor, environmental factor and legal/regulatory factors define the environment and shape a organizations' strategy.

Strategy Formulation: A organization formulates strategy to further its vision and mission while dealing with the competitive forces and the external environmental factors. Strategy is formulated at corporate, business and functional level.

Strategy Implementation: If strategy formulation is a complex process, the execution or implementation is even more critical and difficult. The execution of strategy is done as a set of various action plans and involves the participation of various actors that includes senior leadership, managers, employees, channel partners and other stakeholders.

Strategy Evaluation: The successful execution of a strategy is evaluated by success of the business plan and achievement of the business objectives of the firm. In short term, it means fulfillment of business targets; while in the long-term in means delivering superior value to customers consistently and to all other stakeholders.

Strategic Human Resource Management

The primary objective of the HR function, like all other functions in the organization is to add value to business. Strategic human resource management is managing people in a manner that helps in achieving business goals by effectively supporting and servicing the business strategies. The key considerations are:

- How do people need to be managed to achieve the business goals and fulfill customer needs?
- What do people managers need to do the same? How should they behave?
- What HR strategies need to be formulated to achieve the business strategies?
- What role does the HR department, other than functional expertise?
- How will the HR practices, policies and process be impacted?

Strategic Human Resource Management, hence, has four implications (Hendry, Pettigrew, 1986):

a) Use of planning;

b) Clear and comprehensive approach of design and management of employees based on HR strategy and driven by 'philosophy'.

c) Congruence between HR activities, policies and business strategy; and

d) Treating employees as 'strategic resource' of the organization that helps latter in achieving competitive advantage.

Approaches to Strategic Human Resource Management

1. **Resource-based Approach:** The resource based view believes that a strategic fit between the firm's resources and opportunities must be achieved so as to deploy and use the resources in a manner to provide competitive advantage to the organization. Employees are treated as resource and using the resource-based view it is believed that managing them strategically will help the organization do better and outperform the rivals.

   Employees are treated as resource and using the resource-based view, it is believed that managing them strategically will help the organization do better.

2. **Strategic Fit:** The concept of strategic fit believes in vertical and horizontal integration. Vertical integration aligns the HR strategy with the business strategy and also makes the former an integral part of the latter. Vertical integration helps in building a rationale for every HR action or policy, since directly or indirectly the same helps in the furtherance of the business strategy. It is also called External fit. Horizontal integration implies that various HR strategies are aligned so that there is congruence and they have a cumulative positive effect on business. This is also called Internal Fit.

   Vertical integration aligns the HR strategy with the business strategy and also makes the former an integral part of the latter.

Marginal notes:
- Universalistic approach aims to transform the traditional human resource practices into a limited set of "correct" HR procedures and policies.
- Strategy of the organization is considered as the primary contingency variable.
- HR strategies are formulated to actualize the SHRM objectives.

3. **Universalistic Approach:** Universalistic approach aims to transform the traditional human resource practices into a limited set of "correct" HR procedures and policies (Delery & Doty, Aug. 1996), like decentralization of decision-making, selective hiring, job security, better pay etc.

4. **Configurational Approach:** This approach believes that firm's performance and effectiveness of the strategic human resource management practices are linked and synced. HR practices strategized and executed will have a direct impact on the performance of the company. The approach is based on the understanding that a single good HR practice will not have made difference to the company as much as a bundle of HR practices will do.

5. **Contingency Approach:** Contingency theories have suggested that the interaction of the independent variable and dependent variable is different for different levels of critical contingency variable. Strategy of the organization is considered as the primary contingency variable. Hence the impact of the HR strategy on the performance of the organization will depend upon the interaction of the former with selected theory of a firm's strategy (Venkatraman, 1989) (Van de Ven, Drazin, 1985).

HR Strategies

The purpose of strategic human resource management is to differentiate the human capital of the company with all other firms and consequently to manage it in a way to make them a source of competitive advantage. HR strategies are formulated to actualize the SHRM objectives. HR strategy may be overarching or more specific. Overarching HR Strategy is more firm-wide and represents the overall direction of the HR strategies. Google for instance, has completely data driven HR strategy. All HR decisions and plans are based on data analytics. In short, Google's HR is more data-driven then relationship-driven (Sullivan, 2013). Specific HR strategies like talent management, workforce planning, are directed towards achieving specific objectives.

Essentially HR strategy ask the 'Why' question in whatever is done in terms of managing people, keeping always in mind that the answer must help business and customers.

Example: When Samsung decided to focus on innovation, design and marketing then it changed it hiring strategy from 'closed' to 'open' and from limited recruitment, once a year pattern to recruitments all the year round. This meant that it recruited from outside Korea, bringing in western talent from Ivey league business schools to fuel their new business focus on innovation, design and marketing. The result was tremendously gainful for Samsung. General Motors for instance has a clearly defined talent management strategy. The company that has seen some very tough times lately plans to rejuvenate its innovative streak, develop exciting car platforms by its renewed focus on talent. Flipkart, the e-commerce giant in India has a PMS strategy built around meritocracy. The core of its review system is 'what' and 'how' (Ballakur, 2012). 'What' refers to what did the employee do? What were the achievements and the impact of the employee? The 'how,' on the other hand, looks at the way the employee went about making the impact. The latter is embedded in the value system of the company - ownership, innovation, responsiveness, honesty and team spirit. Flipkart also uses a 360-degree feedback process as part of the performance review. This means that every employee's review has inputs from self-review, peers, managers and the employee's direct manager.

In essence the HR strategy's alignment with the business strategy and corporate strategy should mean more value to business, improvement in its performance and henceforth its competitive position.

Essay Questions

1. What is relation between HRM effectiveness and business success?

2. What is a strategy? Outline the various five competitive forces that affect any company.

3. What are various types of strategies? Discuss the strategic management process.

4. Explain strategic human resource management. What are the various approaches to strategic human resource management?

5. Briefly explain HR strategy. What is the difference between overarching and specific HR strategies?

Application Questions

1. Explore:
   a) http://articles.timesofindia.indiatimes.com/2012-01-10/job-trends/30610921_1_chief-executive-tim-cook-apple-ceo-steve-jobs
   b) http://money.cnn.com/galleries/2011/technology/1111gallery.top_paid_tech_executives/index.html
   c) http://www.minyanville.com/dailyfeed/2012/01/10/why-tim-cook-did-not Study the kind of stock-options or bonuses offered to the CEOs. How far do you think the same is justified?

Bibliography

Ahmad, S., & Schroeder, R.G. (2003). The impact of Human Resource Management Practices on Operational Performance: Recognizing Country and Industry Differences. *Journal of Operations Management*, Vol. 21, No. 1, pp. 19.

Ballakur, A. (2012, December 25). Chief People Officer, Flipkart. (V. Ramnani, Interviewer)

Barney, J.B. (1991). Firm Resources and Sustained Competitive Advantage. *Journal of Management*, 17, 99-120.

Becker, B. & Gerhart, B. (1996). The Impact of Human Resource Management on Organizational Performance: Progress and Prospects. *Academy of Management Journal*, 39, 779-801.

Becker, B.E. and Huselid, M.A. (1998). High-Performance Work Systems and Firm Performance: A Synthesis of Research and Managerial Implications. *Research in Personnel and Human Resource Management*, 16, G.R. Ferris (ed). Greenwich, CT: JAI Press.

Chang, P.L., & Chen, W.L. (2002). The Effect of Human Resource Practices on Firm Performance: Empirical Evidence from High-tech Firms in Taiwan. *International Journal of Management*, 19(4), 622.

Clayton, J. (2015). The Five Stages of the Strategic Management Process. Retrieved from Small Business Chron: http://smallbusiness.chron.com/five-stages-strategic-management-process-18785.html

Delery, J. E., & Doty, D. H. (Aug. 1996). Modes of Theorizing in Strategic Human Resource Management: Tests of Universalistic, Contingency, and Configurational Performance Predictions. *The Academy of Management Journal*, Vol. 39(No. 4), pp. 802-835.

Delery, J.E. & Doty, D.H. (1996). Modes of Theorizing in Strategic Human Resource Management: Tests of Universalistic, Contingency and Configurational Performance Predictions. *Academy of Management Journal*, 39(4), 802-835.

Dyer, L., & Reeves, T. (1995). HR Strategies and Firm Performance: What Do we know and where do we need to go? *International Journal of Human Resource Management*, 6(3), 656-670.

Gerhart, B. & Milkovitch, G. B. (1992). Employee Compensation: Research and Practice, Dunnette, M. & Hough, L. (Eds). Handbook of Industrial and Orhanisational Psychology, Consulting Psychologists Press, Palo Alto, CA, 3, 481–569.

Hendry, C and Pettigrew, A (1986) The practice of Strategic Human Resource Management, *Personnel Review*, 15, pp 2–8

Hendry, C and Pettigrew, A (1990) Human Resource Management: An Agenda for the 1990s, *International Journal of Human Resource Management*, 1 (3), pp 17–43

Jackson, S. E. & Schuler, R. S. (2000). Managing Human Resources, A Partnership Perspective, Southern-Western College Publishing, London.

Khan, N. R., Taha, S. M., Ghouri, A. M., Khan, M. R., & Yong, C. K. (2013). The Impact of HRM practices on Supply Chain Management Success in SME. *Scientific Journal of Logistics*, 9(3), 177-189.

MacDuffie, J.P. (1995). Human Resource Bundles and Manufacturing Performance: Organisational Logic and Flexible Production Systems in the World auto Industry. I Backer, B. & Gerhart, B. (1996). The Impact of Human Resource Management on Organizational Performance.

Mohd.Yusoff, Y., & Baharom, H. S. (2010). HRM Effectiveness within the Role of HRM Department at the Large Companies in Malaysia. *International Journal of Business and Management Science, 3(1)*, 1-16.

Myloni, B., Harzing, A.-W. K. & Mirza, H. (2004). Host Country Specific Factors and the Transfer of Human Resource Management Practices in Multinational Companies. *International Journal of Manpower*, 25(6), 518 – 534.

Pfeffer, J. (1998). Seven Practices of Successful Organisations. *California Management Review*, Vol. 40, No. 2, pp. 96-124.

Porter, M. (1996, November). What is Strategy? Retrieved from HBR: https://hbr.org/1996/11/what-is-strategy

Schuler, R.S. 1992. Strategic Human Resource Management: Linking people with the needs of the business. *Organizational Dynamics,* 21(1): 18-32

Sullivan, J. (2013, Februrary 25). How Google Became the #3 Most Valuable Firm by Using People Analytics to Reinvent HR. Retrieved 01 14, 2015, from ERE.NET: http://www.ere.net/2013/02/25/how-google-became-the-3-most-valuable-firm-by-using-people-analytics-to-reinvent-hr/

Van de Ven, A.H., & Drazin, R. 1985. The Concept of Fit in Contingency Theory. In L. L. Cum- mings & B. M. Staw (Eds.), *Research in Organizational Behavior*, vol. 7: 333-365. Green- wich, CT: JAI Press.

Venkatraman, N.1989. The Concept of Fit in Strategy Research: Toward Verbal and Statistical Correspondence. *Academy of Management Review,* 14: 423-444.

Youndt, M.A. Snell, S.A., Dean, J.W. & Lepak, D.P. (1996). Human Resource Management, Manufacturing Strategy and Firm Performance. *Academy of Management Journal,* 39(4), 83

Lee, Feng-Hui, & Lee, Fzai-Zang. (2007). The Relationships between HRM Practices, Leadership Style, Competitive Strategy and Business Performance in Taiwanese Steel Industry, Proceedings of the 13th *Asia Pacific Management Conference*, Melbourne, Australia, 2007, 953-971. 6-866.

Chapter 23

International Human Resource Management

Outline

Introduction

Strategic View of International HRM

Human Resource Strategies & Roles in a Multinational Company

International HRM Activities

Reading Exhibit

Essay Questions

Application Questions

Bibliography

Key Terms

International HRM

International Staffing

IHRM Roles

IHRM Strategies

Parent-country National

Host-country National

Introduction

International human resource management bears both functional and strategic resemblance to human resource management. Functionally it performs almost the same set of activities as human resource management – recruitment, selection, performance management, compensation, training, industrial relations, career management etc. Strategically international HRM is closely linked to the business strategy of the organization.

Hence international human resource management can be defined as the set of activities involved in hiring, managing performance, compensation, training and relations with employees hired to manage internal operations of a company, with a view to ensure the success of their international business and strategies.

International human resource management differs from domestic human resource management primarily in terms of the complexity associated with managing people across national boundaries. International human resource management deals with at least three types of employees based on their country of origin:

Parent-country Nationals (PCNs): Employees belonging to the country where a company's headquarters are located are called as parent-country nationals or home country nationals.

Host-country Nationals (HCNs): Employees belonging to country where the company has set up a subsidiary or a manufacturing facility are called host-country nationals.

Third-country Nationals (TCNs): Employees who work in the home or host country facility of the company but are not nationals of either are called third-country nationals.

International HRM also means dealing with issues related to different countries, expatriation, repatriation, cross-cultural issues etc.

Dowling (1999) attributed to six factors that differentiate international from domestic HRM (Gomes, 2012):

1. Wide range of HR activities.
2. Need for a broader perspective.
3. More Involvement in personal life of the employee.
4. Responsiveness to changes in staffing requirements as international strategy changes.

International human resource management is the process of procuring, allocating and effectively utilizing human resources in a multinational, while balancing the integration and differentiation of HR activities in foreign locations.

International human resource management is a set of activities involved in hiring, managing performance, compensation, training and relations with employees hired to manage a company's international business.

5. Higher risk exposure.
6. More external influences.

Strategic View of International Human Resource Management

"*The amount of time and energy needed to successfully merge two sophisticated organizations is more likely to resemble the planning and execution of the invasion of Normandy, accompanied by the resultant clash of cultures from many elements attempting to work together towards one end. This corporate failure to consider and plan for the long-term consequences can result in financial problems, loss of employee loyalty, lowered employee morale and reduced productivity.*" Rita Salame, founder of Key Strategy, aptly outlined the complexity of mergers and acquisitions in her seminal research work – '*Why do mergers fail? What can be done to improve their chances of success?*'.

Much of the business today is international in nature thanks to the firms roots of globalization around the world. 'The fast-expanding boomlet in mergers and acquisitions spans from pharmaceuticals to the industrial sector, with General Electric (GE) negotiating to buy Alstom (ALO:FP), a French power and transportation company, for $13 billion. Much of the activity is coming out of Europe, where the $149 billion worth of acquisitions in the first quarter amounts to 60 percent more than in 2013. That's a bigger year-over-year increase than in North America (18 percent) or Asia (41 percent). Across the globe, $939 billion of deals have been proposed or completed since the start of 2014, according to Bloomberg data' (Summers, 2014).

Success of international business deals and strategy largely depends upon the successful management of human resource across the boundaries. McKinsey report states – "Plenty of attention is paid to the legal, financial and operational elements of mergers and acquisitions. But executives who have been through the merger process now recognize that in today's economy, the management of the human side of change is the real key to maximizing the value of a deal" (Kay & Shelton, 2000).

In other words, international human resource management not only determines the success of across-boundary business forays of companies but also helps them to bring-in more effectiveness in their initiatives and create more value.

> Success of international business deals and strategy largely depends upon the successful management of human resource across the boundaries.

Rita Salame identified the top 8 reasons for failure of any merger deal (Salame, 2006):

1. Lack of communication.
2. Lack of direct involvement of human resources.
3. Lack of training.
4. Loss of key and talented employees.
5. Loss of customers.
6. Corporate culture clash.
7. Power, politics.
8. Inadequate planning.

> Communication by leadership and human resource may make or break the confidence of the people and consequently their decision to stay or leave.

A closer look at the reasons enumerated by her makes it very clear that at least 6 of the 8 reasons mentioned by her are directly concerned with people and hence the manner in which they are managed. In a merger scenario employees may experience lot of uncertainty about their future in the company. Communication by leadership and human resource may make or break the confidence of the people and consequently their decision to stay or leave. Similarly, involvement of HR in pre-merger, during-merger and post-merger stages is significant to ensure the success of such forays. This enables them to assess the impact of every decision on employees and keep the people agenda alive to other business leaders. Most of the times though HR is involved very late, only in the post-merger stage.

KPMG in its remarkable report – Post-Merger Integration of People stated that – "*Financial advisors may guide merger managers in broad areas in which merger synergies may be realized, but the success of a merger or an acquisition depends more on getting the people equation right. Thus, it is vital for the organizations to be mindful of people issues right from the design stage to the implementation stage. However, when it comes to due diligence most activities relate to the tangible assets such as financial structures, IT systems, or intellectual property, leaving out the intangible assets such as organizational capital, relational capital, cultural fitment and human resources. Thus the critical issue here is to have a comprehensive yet tailored approach to Post-Merger People Integration. Mismanagement of post-merger people integration may lead to employee disengagement, key talent attrition, goal misalignment, culture misalignment and litigations. Thus may adversely affect the realization of merger synergies.*"

Type of M&A	Key People and Organization Related Implication
Growth	Senior management team expected to make discrete changes in performance goals. Some new entrants may join top team. Expected administrative efficiencies in term of common support functions. Process and systemic integration may be considered in specific areas depending on the requirement.
Synergy	Top teams to collaborate on key areas of synergy. Other areas are left intact.
Diversification	Loosely coupled management teams. Expected administrative efficiencies in terms of common support functions. Joint reporting to the holding company/corporate office. Separate identities and logos.
Horizontal & Vertical Integration	Integrated top teams. Merged administrative systems in terms of common support functions. Tightly coupled core processes. Single corporate identity. Better partnership working. Pooled resources.
Defensive Measures	If managed well, it may lead to greater commercial strength.

Table 23.1: People Issues in Mergers (KPMG, 2011)

Research after research has revealed that managing internal HR issues is critical to the success of a global organization. Another McKinsey report clearly states – "*Consider the impact of mergers and acquisitions: high-profile public events that typically involve redundancies and relocations. In fact, when mergers fail, it's often because of the loss of critical talent. The attrition rate among executives in merged entities is twice that elsewhere, and can stay so for up to a decade after the event. The impact on a business can be severe; for instance, in the year following a merger, sales in the target company typically dip by between 5 and 8 percent. Getting retention and motivation right during change efforts is crucial for long-term business performance, but it can save a lot of money in the short run too.*" (Cosack, Hourihan, Lawson, & Merschen, 2010)

Retention and motivation right during change efforts is crucial for long-term business performance.

Human Resource Strategies & Roles in a Multinational Company

> IHRM practices are tailored to the specific characteristics and needs of the MNC and its environment.

Human resource strategies and roles in a multinational company (MNC) have high degree of context-specificity. Context, in other words, plays a very important role in determining the kind of HR strategy and the type of role that HR plays consequently. The HR roles in a multinational firm are determined by the international HR strategy, which in turn is determined by the internationalization strategy that the company is following.

Internationalization Strategies

> MNC's global strategy must be carefully translated into specific IHRM objectives and goals.

Multinational companies go global for different reasons. However all of them do so to gain competitive advantage. For the same they follow varying internationalization strategies as their reasons for going global may vary, their stage of development may be different from one another and they may have different capabilities as well as limitations.

The various types of internationalization strategies can be (Perlmutter, 1969) (Bartlett & Ghoshal, 1989):

1. **Ethnocentric:** The MNC follows a global strategy. The control is centralized at the headquarters of the parent company and subsidiaries resemble the former.
2. **Polycentric:** The MNC follows a multi-domestic strategy. The control is decentralized and the subsidiaries follow the local practices.
3. **Geocentric/Regiocentric:** The MNC follows a transnational strategy. The headquarters as well as subsidiaries follow the worldwide or regional standards.

Hence subsidiaries may have different roles depending upon the classification.

International HR Strategies

> Adaptive HR strategy means there is low consistency with rest of the company, whereas there is high consistency with the local environment.

Depending on the kind of internationalization strategy being followed by the multinational company, the international HR strategy can of three types (Taylor, Beechler, & Napier., 1996.):

1. **Adaptive:** Adaptive HR strategy means there is low consistency with rest of the company, whereas there is high consistency with the local environment. MNC having polycentric or multi-domestic internationalization strategy generally have adaptive HR strategy.

2. **Exportive:** There is low consistency with the local environment. The HRM systems of the subsidiaries are strongly integrated with those at the parent headquarters. MNC having ethnocentric or global strategy are the ones that have exportive HR strategy.

3. **Integrative:** There is high degree of integration of subsidiaries with the parent HRM systems, with some flexibility to incorporate certain local practices. Transnational MNCs are governed by integrative HR strategy.

> MNC having ethnocentric or global strategy are the ones that have exportive HR strategy.

International Human Resource Management Roles

The HR strategy and the degree of internalization determine the role or roles that HR assumes upon itself. Various international human resource management roles (Evans, Pucik, & Barsoux, 2002) (Sparrow, Harris, & Brewster, 2003) (Novecevic & Harvey, 2001) suggested by various researchers are:

1. **Champions of Processes:** This roles encompasses –
   a. Building commitment of the senior leadership.
   b. Training managers.
   c. Monitoring HR processes.

2. **Guardian of Culture:** This includes –
   a. Supervision and management of implementation of global values and systems.
   b. Ensuring future leaders are sensitive and equipped to deal with global challenges.

3. **Effective Political Influencer:** It means –
   a. Understanding internal labour market where a subsidiary is located.
   b. Managing the internal labour market for the global managers.

4. **Network Leadership:** It includes –
   a. Building strong internal and external networks.
   b. Keeping abreast with latest trends and developments.
   c. Mobilizing resources to staff project teams effectively.

5. **Builder:** This includes –
   a. Articulating various International HR management basics.
   b. Developing basic internal HR management practices at the beginning of internalization.

6. **Change Partner:** This means –
   a. Continuously calibrating human resource management practices as the external environment changes.
   b. To enable the MNC to be agile in terms of its HR practices to meet the challenges of the environment and cash-on the business opportunities.
7. **Navigator:** It encompasses –
   a. Competency development of the people and developing a competent organization.
   b. Balancing between long-term and short-term plans and goals.
   c. Balancing between global integration and local responsiveness.
   d. Balancing between change and status quo in an global environment.

International HRM Activities

Managing human capital is undoubtedly the most challenging task for any manager and for the human resource department. The knowledge-based economy and knowledge workers have meant that a lot is at stake when it comes to managing people. The internationalization puts additional challenges and issues in managing employees. The complexity is far greater and issues are many times delicate since expatriation often means relocation of the employee's family as well. The focal areas of priority of HR also changes with the stage of internationalization.

International HRM involves employees of three countries – parent country or the home country, host country and third country.

There are three major international HRM activities – Procure, Allocate and Utilize. In effect these three major activities of IHRM cover all the six activities of domestics HRM i.e, HR planning, Employees Hiring, Training and Development, Remuneration, Performance Management and Industrial Relations. International HRM involves employees of three countries – parent country or the home country (where a company's headquarters might be located), host country (where company's subsidiary may be located) and third country (Other countries that may be sources of labour or finance). Accordingly there are three country nationals as employees:

Parent Country Nationals (PCNs): A parent country national is an employee who is working in a country other than that of origin.

Host Country Nationals (HCNs): Employees who are nationals of the country where a subsidiary is located are called host country nationals.

Third Country Nationals (TCNs): Third country nationals are employee hired from 'other' countries and belong neither to the country of origin of the company or countries where its subsidiaries are located or its area of operations.

Internationalization hence gives rise to an Expatriate. An expatriate (often abbreviated to 'expat' or sometimes 'ex-pat') is a person 'temporarily or permanently residing in a country and culture other than that of the person's upbringing or legal residence'. In other words, somebody who isn't from 'around here'.

International Staffing

Staffing is a challenging function. Finding the right set of people has never been easy. However when it comes to international operations, the complexity of staffing increases many folds. Deciding on the mix of local employees to expats is not an easy decision to make. Several factors may impact the same. Then cost is another major consideration. Cost of finding an international employee and hiring that person if often very high. Such cost aspects demand even more careful consideration and selection. Errors in selection could be tremendously costly for the firm. Expat compensation and tax laws are huge consideration in international staffing. Tax treaties between certain countries ease income tax obligations of an expat. Such treaties may make it easier to hire from certain countries, while it may difficult to hire from others since the compensation may not work out in the favour of the expat. Environmental factors may also affect international staffing. Political environment may change with government regimes and may favour or dis-favour expat movement (see reading exhibit – 'Nitaqat')

The selection process for international assignment should provide the candidate with a realistic picture of life, work and culture to which he or she might be sent, because most expatriate failures occur due to cultural adjustment problems, not difficulties with job or technical skills.

Cultural Challenge

Difference in national cultures of expats poses a challenge in hiring and assimilating international staff. A lot of pre-departure training for the expats is focused on cross cultural training. Cultural fitment of the expats plays a important role in the success of the projects and international assignments. Multi-national companies often develop hiring strategy (see reading exhibit: 'Glocal Hiring') and training interventions to cope up with this cultural challenge.

Geert Hofstede work on cultural dimensions is an authoritative repository on national cultures and how cultures differ across countries. Hofstede defines six cultural dimensions to qualify a national culture (Hofstede, Cultural Dimensions). A comparison across these dimensions also helps distinguish

Cross cultural sensitivity is required in conducting business and negotiations in different countries. Adjustment of the spouse is closely related to adjustment of the expatriate.

one national culture from the other. The cultural dimensions according to Hofstede are:

1. **Power Distance Index (PDI):** The degree to which the less powerful members of a society accept and expect that power is distributed unequally.

2. **Individualism versus Collectivism (IDV):** Preference for a loosely-knit social framework in which individuals are expected to take care of only themselves and their immediate families. The opposite of individualism is collectivism.

3. **Masculinity versus Femininity (MAS):** Masculinity side of this dimension represents a preference in society for achievement, heroism, assertiveness and material rewards for success, whereas femininity, stands for a preference for cooperation, modesty, caring for the weak and quality of life.

4. **Uncertainty Avoidance Index (UAI):** The degree to which the members of a society feel uncomfortable with uncertainty and ambiguity.

5. **Long-term Orientation versus Short-term Normative Orientation (LTO):** Cultures low on this dimensions, for example, prefer to maintain time-honoured traditions and norms while viewing societal change with suspicion. Contrastingly, those high on this dimension have a more pragmatic approach: they encourage thrift and efforts in modern education as a way to prepare for the future.

6. **Indulgence versus Restraint (IND):** Indulgence stands for a society that allows relatively free gratification of basic and natural human drives related to enjoying life and having fun. Opposite of indulgence is restraint.

The Hofstede center (http://geert-hofstede.com/countries.html) helps to understand how each nation features on these six dimensions and hence can give a very definitive picture of its national culture. It also lets users compare two national cultures (also see exhibit: Map of National Cultures).

Hofstede's work established a major research tradition in cross-cultural psychology and has also been drawn upon by researchers and consultants in many fields relating to international business and communication. It continues to be a major resource in cross-cultural fields. It has inspired a number of other major cross-cultural studies of values, as well as research on other aspects of culture, such as social beliefs.

Reading Exhibit 1: 'Nitaqat'

The recent labour reforms in Saudi Arabia will not trigger a major reverse migration to India.

Saudi Arabia, the world's biggest oil producer and exporter and a fast-growing economy, has an estimated nine million 'legal' expat workers out of which there are more than two million Indians working in the kingdom. Plus, at least two million illegal workers who do not possess valid papers. Non-Saudis make up nearly 40 per cent of the country's total estimated population of 290 million. That percentage is a big worry for the government.

What is NITAQAT?

The Nitaqat is a carrot-and-stick incentive programme for companies and businesses to hire more Saudis across a spectrum of jobs. It categorizes firms into four colour ranges: blue (premium), green, yellow and red. For example, if a company has 40 per cent Saudis on its under-500-member staff, it is in the blue (premium) category and will enjoy privileges in importing foreign manpower. If the company has only 12-39 per cent Saudi staff, it will be in the green category and its hiring privileges will be fewer. If a company's Saudi employees' percentage is only 6-11 per cent, it will fall in the yellow range, and hence will need to do some extra hiring to fall in line with the Nitaqat. If the percentage is between 0 and 5, the company is in real trouble: for instance, its foreign staff's work permits would not be renewed. Meaning: the company will have to fold up. A firm should have at least one Saudi employee, if it has under 10 employees, otherwise, it will fall into the red category. In April this year, there were 2.25 lakh firms and business entities that did not have a single Saudi employee. Expats from India working for 'red' companies will have to leave. Where possible, they can move to 'green' and 'blue' companies if jobs are available. The Saudi government has relaxed 'sponsorship' rules so that workers in the red companies can seek a transfer without the permission of the sponsor (current employer). Several thousand Indians have made use of this provision.

It's Political, Too

In a country with one of the highest unemployment rates in the world, particularly educated unemployment, Nitaqat looks quite fair. But, it is also a political tool — aimed to forestall a likely 'youthquake' in the wake of the Arab Spring. "Nitaqat is more political than economic," says the filmmaker and former CPI(M) MLA P.T. Kunhimohammed, who anchors a weekly TV programme that handles non-resident Keralite (NRK) issues. "It shows the Saudi authorities are worried over unemployed youths' frustrations. At the same time, in a pan-Arab sense, it hints at the assertion of the Arab self."

Effect on India

How do the Nitaqat and the drive to flush out illegal expats impact India? Thousands will return. Already, some 70,000 people, mostly blue-collar workers, have applied for the Emergency Certificate from the Indian embassy — the highest number of 26,000 is from those hailing from Uttar Pradesh.

Indian policymakers have looked at the impact of Nitaqat only in terms of job loss, reverse migration and remittances. Indians in Saudi Arabia are not workers only, they are investors and job providers, too. There is a large community of small and tiny entrepreneurs (who often run their businesses technically in the names of Saudis.) This community will take a hit.

(Source: The Hindu Business Line) (BASHEER, 2013)

Reading Exhibit 2: 'Glocal Hiring'

Prompted by global expansions in regions such as South-East Asia, Latin America, the US and Africa, several large Indian companies including Godrej, Aditya Birla and Wipro, among others, are hiring talent from global business schools as well as graduate colleges. This hiring is also aimed at finding more appropriate cultural fitment, candidates with greater understanding of local market and also because local talent would have long-term career plans in the region and make retention easier for a company.

"For the last couple of years, we have been getting interns from global business schools from where we keep some. Next year, we may target hiring talent from global institutions in one or two regions like South East Asia and the US, where we have significant presence," says Santrupt Misra, CEO, Carbon Black Business, and Director, Group Human Resources of the Aditya Birla Group. Last year, the group hired 5-6 candidates from global schools. "The hiring from overseas is purely driven by business requirements," he said.

Others like Godrej Consumer Products (GCPL), too, have similar plans this year led by business interest in overseas regions, hiring students from ethnic business school students from regions such as Africa, South-East Asia and Latin America. Such hiring is aimed at empowering the local teams and maintaining ethnicity of business.

Wipro has a Global Campus Programme which hires candidates from global business schools based on business requirements. The company, which has hired from business schools in the Americas and the UK over the past 24 months, is increasing its hiring numbers from international campuses in keeping with its business and client requirements. Separately, the company has initiated a Global Top 100 programme, under which it will hire graduates every year from leading global business schools. The new hires will then be posted across businesses and geographies at Wipro to give them the necessary exposure to varied intersections of business and culture.

A couple of months earlier, Indian IT major Infosys announced that it plans to hire at least 200 from overseas B-schools this year in order to create a global talent pool in line with their business requirements. Infosys this year is looking to visit top schools like Harvard, NYU Stern, Geogia Tech, Yale Kellogg, Booth, Wharton, UCLA in the US, London Business School, Insead, Rotterdam School of Management. Campus recruitment in the US is mostly business graduates for the client engagement side or business consulting side. We are working on our strategy to increase the diversity of our workforce by bringing in people at various levels in geographies we operate," says Srikantan Moorthy, SVP and Group Head HR at Infosys. The company did not hire from global business schools in previous four years.

"Today, the skill we need to build is 'understanding our customer', and culture is a key factor. With this programme, we will be able to acquire this understanding and help percolate the same across the organisation," says Govil.

The Mahindra group conducts a need assessment every year that determines the number it hires from global campuses.

Source: (The Economic Times) (Bhattacharyya, 2014)

Reading Exhibit 3: Map of National Cultures (Hofstede, Practical Applications of Hofstede's Cultural Dimensions, 2013)

International Labour Relations

The trade unions across countries differ in terms of their strength and relevance. Equally management philosophy of companies may be different in different countries, resulting in different management approaches, rules and policies. Cultural differences between the management and the workers also exist. Such variables at times may lead to conflict and labour unrest. The strike by 1,700 workers at the Manesar Honda Factory near New Delhi at the end of May 2005 escalated to riots in which up to 700 people were injured, saw motorcycle production drop by more than 75% to 400 units per day, cost Honda, the Japanese auto manufacturer, a reported 3 billion yen (US$26,8 million) (Frost, 2005). International labour relations require thorough understanding of labour laws of the land, difference in cultures and expectations and union movement in that nation.

International Compensation

Executives who craft compensation and benefits programs for global companies must take into account not only the economies of countries in which they do business, but also cultural and managerial norms that may differ wildly from those at home. Expat compensation issues are –

Currency: Relative strength of a currency has an impact on expat compensation. Generally if an expat is coming to nation whose currency is stronger than his/her nation of origin then he/she stands to gain in a big way.

Inflation: Inflation levels prevailing in nation where an expat is going on assignment also impacts compensation. Generally international compensation seek to cover inflation so as to not to put the expat employee in any sort of disadvantage compared to nation of residence.

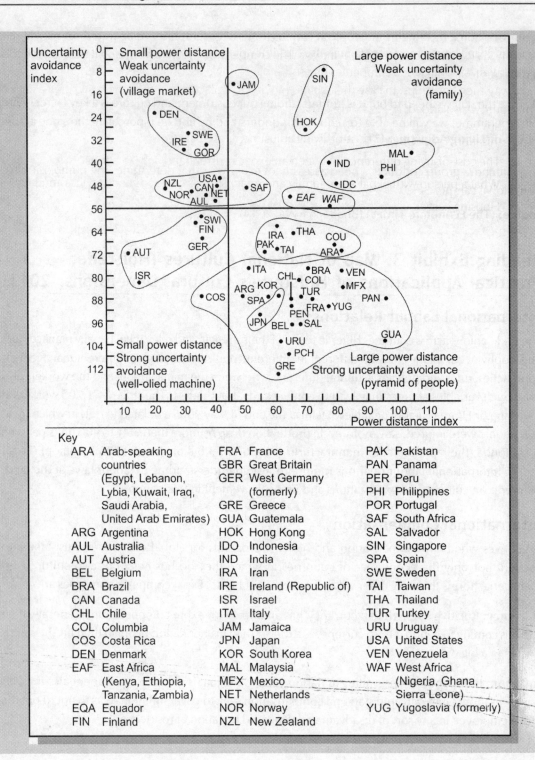

Foreign Service Premiums: For an expat moving to another country to take up an assignment means taking himself and many times also his family out of comport zone and replanting themselves in an alien nation. Hence companies pay something known as foreign service premium to ward-off in a way such hardships. In case the expat is moving to a place that is difficult to live then a location premium is also added.

Cost-of-Living Adjustment: Cost-of-living adjustments are based on:
- The cost-of-living difference between an expat's current and new locations.
- What a person with expat's size family and salary spends on goods and services annually.
- Housing costs.

Housing Allowance: rentals in some countries are very expensive. Housing allowance is an important benefit. Family size and corporate rank determine the size of one's housing allowance.

Tax Assistance: Income tax laws and requirements differ from one country to another. Tax treaties are also not consistent. Expats are given tax assistance by the companies so that compensation can be structured tax-effectively

Mobility Pay: Mobility pay is paid to expat as an incentive to change assignment.

Spousal Assistance: If the spouse of the expat is working then companies take care to provide assistance to the spouse so that he/she can find a suitable job in the country where the employee is relocating. This is done to avoid spousal dissatisfaction and unhappiness over his/her career affects the expat's effectiveness in the international assignment. Spousal assistance also covers help with visa issues and getting the family settled in the new location.

Education: Companies also provide assistance and allowance to take care of expat's children education in a new country.

Security: Owing to global terrorism threats and ethnic violence in some countries, companies often provide additional security to expat and his/her family members.

Extra Paid Time off to Return Home: Expats who go on a long-term assignment are often paid extra time off to return home so that they can occasionally visit their near and dear ones back home.

Repatriation Assistance: Upon completion of their assignment when expats return back to their home, the process is known as repatriation. Repatriation can often be stressful much the expatriation process. Coming back to familiar settings, absence of newness and novelty can bother the expat. Often families may find it difficult to adjust back home, being now more in touch with foreign nation practices and culture. Kids may find it difficult to adjust in schools. Companies provide repatriation benefits to ease an employee and his family adjustment in their home country.

Health and Safety of Expatriates

Health and safety standards differ from one country to another. Laws and regulations governing health of workers and workplace safety also vary. Countries in which such laws and their implementation are weak expats may face hardships, poor health provisions and shabby or dangerous working conditions. Many times such workers are hired by agencies that later absolve from their responsibility when workers face hardships. Hundreds of workers from poor countries in South Asia continue to be exploited reportedly in Qatar. Qatar quest for hosting the 2022 World Cup Football event has been marred by accusations of these poor labours. They continue to put to inhumane conditions of work and living. Lucky ones survive this torture and manage to send some precious money home that keeps their stoves burning. And the unlucky come back home in coffins. Hundreds of labour have died due to poor and stressful working & living conditions. These workers mainly hired through some local agencies are driven by extreme poverty to take up such risky employments. Take Nepal for instance, 25% of the population continues to be below the poverty line. Nepal remains one of the poorest countries in the world, with a Human Development Index of 0.463, placing it 157th out of 187 countries listed in the United Nations Development Programme's Human Development Report 2013. The industry in Nepal is in poor state and most are making huge losses. Unemployment rate is high and underemployment is rampant. The direct impact of such poverty is on the family of the workers and primarily on children. 2/3rd of Nepal children are severely deprived and 40% of them live in absolute poverty. Malnutrition continues to be a major problem among kids. No wonder workers from these nations risk their lives in search of some money and livelihood for themselves and their families (Guardian, 2014).

Essay Questions

1. What is international human resource management?
2. What is strategic view of international human resource management?
3. What do you understand by Human Resource Strategies and their role in a multinational company?
4. Explain international human resource management roles.
5. What are the various international human resource management activities?
6. Explain international compensation.
7. Discuss international staffing. What are the cultural challenges that come in the way of international staffing?

Application Questions

1. Go to —
   a. https://www.youtube.com/watch?v=n2ZAmwpwMFg
   b. https://www.youtube.com/watch?v=eUdTlqGba5I
   c. https://www.youtube.com/watch?v=rOH-ndjMTEk

   and discuss in the group.

2. Go to —
   a. https://www.youtube.com/watch?v=wdh40kgyYOY and read matter on Geert Hofstede on culture.
   b. https://www.youtube.com/watch?v=LBv1wLuY3Ko and discuss cross cultural issues in International HRM.

Bibliography

Bartlett, C. A., & Ghoshal, S. (1989). *Managing Across Borders: The Transnational Solution.* Boston: Harvard University Press.

BASHEER, K. P. (2013, June 30). *Saudi Arabia's Nitaqat blues.* Retrieved from thehindubusinessline: http://www.thehindubusinessline.com/opinion/saudi-arabias-nitaqat-blues/article4866385.ece

Bhattacharyya, R. (2014, April 4). *Indian companies like Godrej, Birla, Wipro and others hiring talent from global business schools.* Retrieved from ET: http://articles.economictimes.indiatimes.com/2014-04-04/news/48866639_1_godrej-industries-ltd-godrej-consumer-products-local-talent

Cosack, S., Hourihan, N., Lawson, e., & Merschen, J. (2010, May). *How do I retain and motivate my key people during organizational change?* Retrieved from McKinsey: http://mld.mckinsey.com/downloads/centers/How_do_I_retain_and_motivate_my_key_people_during_organizational_change.pdf

Evans, P., Pucik, V., & Barsoux, J. (2002). *The global challenge. Frameworks for International Human Resource Management.* New York: McGraw-Hill.

Frost, S. (2005, August 9). *The Honda strike in India.* Retrieved from CSR-Asia: http://www.csr-asia.com weekly_news_detail.php?id=4373

Gomes, S. (2012). *International Human Resource Management*. Retrieved from XISSPM: https://xisspm.files.wordpress.com/2012/02/chap-2-concept-of-ihrm.pdf

Guardian. (2014, July 28). *Qatar's World Cup 2022 workers: 'We may as well just die here'*. Retrieved from The Guardian: https://www.youtube.com/watch?v=I0EsOFDA6uM&x-yt-ts=1422411861&x-yt-cl=84924572

Hofstede, G. (2013, January 27). *Practical Applications of Hofstede's Cultural Dimensions*. Retrieved from https://laofutze.wordpress.com/2010/01/08/applications-of-hofstedes-theories/

Hofstede, G. (n.d.). *Cultural Dimensions*. Retrieved from Geert Hofstede: http://geert-hofstede.com/dimensions.html

Kay, I. T., & Shelton, M. J. (2000, November). The People Problem in Mergers. *The McKinsey Quarterly*.

KPMG. (2011). *Post-merger Integration of People*. Retrieved from KPMG: https://www.kpmg.com/IN/en/IssuesAndInsights/ArticlesPublications/Documents/Post%20Merger%20People%20Integration.pdf

Novecevic, M. M., & Harvey, M. (2001). The changing role of the corporate HR function in global organizations of the twenty-first century. *International Journal of Human Resource Management.*, 12(no. 8), 1251-68.

Perlmutter, H. V. (1969). The Tortous Evolution of the Multinational Corporation. *Journal of World Business,* 4(1), 9-18.

Salame, R. (2006, January). *Why Do Mergers Fail? What can be Done to Improve Their Chances of Success?* Retrieved from Key Strategy: www.key-strategy.com

Sparrow, P., Harris, H., & Brewster, C. (2003). *Towards a New Model of Globalizing HRM. 7th Conference on International Human Resource Management.* Ireland: University of Limerick.

Summers, N. (2014, April 24). *The 2014 M&A Boom: Almost $1 Trillion and Growing.* Retrieved from Bloomberg Businessweek: http://www.businessweek.com/articles/2014-04-24/the-2014-m-and-a-boom-nearly-1-trillion-and-growing

Taylor, S., Beechler, S., & Napier., N. (1996.). Toward an Integrative Model of Strategic International Human Resource Management. *Academy of Management Review,* 21(no. 4), 959-85.

Part II

BUSINESS CASES

Cases

Case Study 1

Chink in the Giant!

E-Tech Solutions was started a few years back is now a burgeoning global leader in 'next generation' IT and consulting with offerings spanning business and technology consulting, application services, systems integration, product engineering, custom software development, maintenance, re-engineering, independent testing and validation services, IT infrastructure services and business process outsourcing. Today E-Tech Solutions has a global presence with over 80 offices and development centres in India and around the world, over a lakh employees and revenues in excess of US$ 5 billion. This has been possible primarily due to inspiring leadership, a culture of innovation and a people-centric approach that the company prides in possessing.

The company has long been known for its best HR practices and has been one of the most sought after employer among the Indian students. Some of its initiatives like employee learning initiatives have been path-breaking and a role-model for others to emulate. It has been continuously on the list of best employers nationally and globally.

Despite all these laurels, of late the company has come under a volley of criticism for some of its HR policies. The chinks first appeared when after consecutively being ranked No. 1 in the year 2008 and 2009 as the best employer, the crown slipped to 5th position in the year 2010. The primary reasons cited for this slip were growing scale, inadequate competition, growing competition from multi-nationals, slow promotions of the employees and the HR-lag. It was perhaps getting harder for a company with over 80000 employees to be agile with people practices as smaller rivals. Of late, it has also been slow to communicate emerging company philosophy to employees. The emergence of MNCs in India has dented its reputation as among the best pay masters. Employees feel that their careers are slowing-down as the organization is growing in size. E-Tech Solutions has yet to put in place a comprehensive HR policy to deal with a global organization.

Were these chinks in the giant's amour? Experts were divided on the opinion and felt that E-Tech Solutions will be able to put these concerns behind with a robust HR response. After all E-Tech Solutions has always focused on HR very strongly that is reflected in its practices. Interestingly, according to E-Tech Solutions's filing in 2008, its human resources head took home the highest salary and bonus among all the Board of Directors of the company, including Chairperson and Chief Executive Officer.

One of its recent HR initiatives has come under tremendous criticism. The initiative which essentially is a career architecture that aligns talent management activities with client priorities, business focus and employee aspirations has been designed with the help of a consulting firm. It is considered to be a platform that defines roles, competencies and proficiency requirements while linking career movement to performance and business focus and was created with an idea of mapping positions with experience and skill levels.

At E-Tech Solutions many felt that previously positions and promotions were often given arbitrarily, based on the bargaining power of the employee. This led to a lot of client-discontent and problems in the projects. The objective of this initiative was to focus on people with deep domain knowledge, capable of adding high-value o the business. What made it controversial amongst employees of E-Tech Solutions was the fact that it was implemented with retrospective effect, which meant all existing employees will be reassessed based on the new standards. This led to the demotion of a large number of employees. Some were even demoted two levels. Although, the salaries were protected, but loss of positions created a big grouse against the company's HR policies. The discontent spilled-over on blogs and media. Some of the prime areas of discontent were: How can a company find a person good for a position earlier and later find the same person unfit?

It was largely felt that it will now be tougher for the employees to move-up in their careers. Many even alleged that employees in higher positions were not at all affected. Others criticized the initiative for discounting earlier experience in multiple other verticals and considering tenure in a particular vertical in which an employee currently is in. With many alleging it to be a disguised cost-cutting tool, E-Tech Solutions has a challenge in front of itself in clearing the perceptions of the people but also in arresting this growing discontent.

Questions

1. What do you think is wrong with E-Tech Solutions? Do you think there is some sort of HR-lag?

2. Evaluate & comment on the latest HR initiative at E-Tech Solutions. Is the HR justified in introducing this initiative? How can the discontent among employee be contained?

3. How can E-Tech Solutions, a company that was known for its HR practices, regain its earlier glory? Suggest measures for the same.

Case Study 2

No Time to Holiday

Sean Davis has been having a dream-run ever since he got an opportunity at the top-most engineering college in the country. He passed-out with honors and then went on to do his masters in business administration from another premier school. He got the best offer during the campus placements. Reflecting upon all that Sean looked-out of his 16th floor Nariman Road office window and remembered how hard he had worked to realize his dreams. Now he was working with one of the best investment banks in the world. He had worked hard and his achievements in the past five years justified his credentials in every possible way. He was leading the bank's operations in the entire Asia-Pacific. Although it meant lots of international travel and communication over phone and mails, but he enjoyed his assignments. Sean worked not less than 16-17 hours a day. He took conference-calls on weekends and was virtually connected 24 hours to his job. He was drawing a hefty salary & perks.

Sean's personal life though was a bit strained especially after his marriage almost two years back. His wife, a working lady herself, was quite bewildered by her husband's aggressive pursuance of his career. They hardly met or more appropriately hardly met each other awake. Sean used to leave the house before his wife Tina could wake-up and would return after she had retired for the day. Even on Sundays most of the time, Sean was on conference calls and hence many plans had to be unceremoniously shelved at the last moment. Those included their picnic-plan with close friends, a movie or a two and Tina's friend's marriage reception-party etc. Tina was however a very sensible and understanding girl and did not complain much and always hoped things shall get better. They had not been to a single decent holiday together since their marriage and Tina had been urging Sean to plan one, since the last 6 months. Sean had been promising, planning and postponing the trip. Finally when he saw that Tina was very upset by his behaviour, he booked a three day-four nights holiday-package through a reputed travel agency for Singapore.

The day they were booked to leave, Sean had a series of meetings. They almost missed the flight. It was only after a bond-like cab driver showed his histrionics on the road that they could catch their flight, after the final call for boarding had been announced. Tina was really exhausted by the run but heaved a sigh of relief as they were finally on a holiday. She thought that whatever might have happened they would at least have 3-4 days together without any work hassle. Besides the lack of quality-time that they were spending together, Tina was also worried about the impact of such a work-life on Sean's health.

They reached Singapore and were lodged-up comfortably in one of the finest hotels of the land. The next day early morning they started their city-tour trip. However throughout the day, Sean kept getting calls. During their transfers from one spot to the other in the city he would be checking his mails on his tablet. Tina felt lonely and irritated. This trend continued throughout their holiday and finally their holidays ended in a quarrel. Although Sean felt a little guilty about his behaviour, but he thought Tina should have been a little more understanding. On the other hand, Tina felt let-down.

"Others goof off work, Indians, says new study, goof off holidays." The latest study by Expedia, an online travel firm, shows interesting stats reflecting Indian behaviour towards vacations:

Indians leave 20 percent of their vacations unused. 29 percent of Indians couldn't plan their holidays due to work pressure.

- Fifty-three per cent of Indians regularly check in on their emails and work status even during vacations.
- 28 per cent Indian respondents said they would prefer getting paid for unused vacations.

The study concluded –

- Europeans and Brazilians treat holidays as necessity.
- Japanese and Koreans treat holidays as rare treasure (since they hardly get it).
- And Indians view holidays with guilt habit.

Another survey by Regus (2011) also suggested the same trend amongst Indians –

Sector	Mfg. & Production	Consultancy & Services	Retail	ICT	Media & Marketing
Voluntarily working during Xmas & New Year	66%	69%	86%	75%	56%
Working in office during Xmas & New Year	54%	56%	71%	52%	41%

The statistics is alarming and shows that a very high majority of people in India are working during their holidays. Is it having an impact on their health and personal lives? From an organizational view-point is it leading to quick burnout and drop in productivity-levels? Is it affecting their 'engagement' with their work and with the organization? Interestingly, the same survey also indicates that not much work is actually done by the staff working during holidays.

Sector	Mfg. & Production	Consultancy & Services	Retail	ICT	Media & Marketing
Staff working during Xmas & New year tend not to get much actual work done.	43%	40%	19%	43%	35%

Questions

1. Do you think Sean's behaviour towards his work is affecting his personal life? Is it his ambition or the organizational competitive pressures – who should be blamed for this state?

2. Do you think Sean's case is just an extension of a larger problem prevailing in this country? Comment. How can the same be corrected?

Case Study 3

Why Indian Firms go Wrong when Hiring US Sales Teams?

For Indian organisations aspiring to sell their products and services in the US, one of the most competitive markets in the world, the first big step is to hire seasoned sales professionals locally. The bad news is that six out of 10 such hires seem to go terribly wrong. These mistakes are extremely expensive and set organizations back by millions of dollars and many valuable years and even threaten their global ambitions. So what can Indian organizations learn from these huge mistakes?

In my mind, culture is a good place to start though there is a lot beyond culture that we must pay attention to.

Assertiveness and Modesty

In the book Cultures and Organizations - Software of the Mind by Geert Hofstede and Gert Jan Hofstede, the distinction they draw between American and Dutch employers and job applicants has interesting lessons for us in India.

According to their research, "American job applicants, to Dutch eyes, oversell themselves. Their CVs are worded in superlatives, to demonstrate their outstanding qualities. During the interview they try to behave assertively, promising things they are unlikely to realise — like learning the local language in a few months."

"Dutch applicants, in American eyes, undersell themselves. They usually write modest, short CVs. They are careful not to be seen as braggarts and not to make promises they are not absolutely sure they can fulfil. American interviewers know how to interpret American CVs and they tend to discount the information provided. Dutch interviewers, who are accustomed to Dutch applicants, tend to upgrade the information."

The Hofstedes thus explain that when the applicant comes from a culture where being assertive is encouraged and the employer comes from a culture

where being modest is encouraged, the potential for cross-cultural misunderstanding is high.

In their article, 'Culture and the Self - Implications for Cognition, Emotion and Motivation', Hazel Rose Markus of the University of Michigan and Shinobu Kitayama of the University of Oregon, point out that western culture promotes the need to be independent, private, unique, express oneself, promote one's own goals, be assertive and so on. In contrast, they see that for people in the East the concept of self is all about being connected to the social context, being flexible, fitting in, occupying one's proper place, promoting others' goals, adjusting oneself to others, having restraint and being indirect.

Read together, these two pieces of research confirm that one of the primary reasons for our failure is to do with the cultural orientation towards self-worth, assertiveness and modesty. It has been my personal experience that many Americans communicate articulately, present themselves assertively and share their opinions in a manner that gives the Indian interviewer the mistaken impression that the American is senior, competent, has an expansive business sense and will therefore deliver. On the other hand, given Indian interviewers' modesty, we seldom challenge, confront or dig deeper to understand or verify the facts.

Setting Expectations

Edward T. Hall, an anthropologist and author, did pioneering work on intercultural communication and used context as an important means of understanding cultural differences.

Hall looks at context as being either 'high' or 'low' and maintains that in a high context culture, it is important to have a contextual knowledge of that culture to understand the true meaning of what is said. On the other hand, in a low context culture, no contextual knowledge is needed.

Hall found that in a high context culture, things get done based on one's relationships with people, whereas in a low context culture things get done by following procedures and attention to a goal.

It has been my experience that in defining the roles and goals and stating expectations with sales professionals in the US, Indian organisations tend to be somewhat indirect, global and vague. While they may, for instance, spell out the targets clearly, they may never reach agreement on the strategies to be pursued to achieve the targets.

As a result, Indian employers may expect the salesperson to understand the true strengths of their organisation and its unique value proposition and on that basis take the ownership to evangelise it to US customers, but may not clearly spell out the preferred sales process, the right target customers, provide clear product- or service-related information, clear discount policies, transparent sales commission plans, travel budgets, reporting systems, review systems and so on.

So, while Indian employers expect their American sales professionals to go beyond rigidities and think out of the box when it comes to sales tactics, they do not meet the employee's expectation in terms of well established, formal guidelines to close the sale.

Other Problems

Added to this are the usual issues such as the American employee's lack of proper orientation to the organisation's culture and way of working, cultural gaps that affect their ability to get support from their Indian colleagues, people practices that do not reflect local sensitivity, misplaced expectations about work-life balance and so on.

Having made a few attempts and burnt a lot of cash, many Indian organisations quickly give up and reconcile themselves to sending a "known devil from India" to get the job done. This, to my mind, is not a sustainable solution.

The true difference between being multinational and becoming global lies in our ability to recognise the diversity issues and learning to bridge them effectively by establishing a successful mechanism to attract, select and retain talent from every country in culturally appropriate ways. What is also clear is that if Indian organisations wish to do business globally, they must have a work culture that is low context, where the need for Indian contextual knowledge is minimal and everything is explicit.

(**Source & Permission:** *The case is based upon an article by Mr. Ganesh Chella in The Hindu Business Line and has been reproduced with requisite consent from the author.*)

Questions

1. Where do you think Indian firms generally goof-up when it comes to hiring sales personnel from US? Suggest a remedy for the same.
2. Do you think such problems exist only in recruiting sales people, given the nature of the job or do you think the problem is more endemic? Substantiate.

Case Study 4

Selection Blues

Selection Process is an excellent opportunity for the companies to build a positive image of a responsible corporate citizen. However, unfortunately selection process is most awfully managed by most of the companies. *Confusion at selection site, no clear information to the interviewees regarding the interview time, test schedule etc., long waiting hours, making candidates wait in full public glare, no proper arrangement of refreshments for the waiting candidates, lack of information regarding the timing of declaration of result etc.,* are some of the common sights.

What Harry went through during the early part of my career is a testimony to the acrimonious experiences that most of the candidates undergo. It was a walk-in for an executive position in a reputed multi-national organization. The walk-in was arranged in Lucknow and the reporting time was 9:00 a.m. Harry reached around 8:00 a.m. thinking that the since it is an walk-in the processing of the application (submission etc.) will start at least a hour earlier then the scheduled interview time. But to his surprise nothing happened till about 10:00 am. Their staff kept on coming till about 9:30 a.m. By 10:00a.m., a crowd of about 350-400 people had built outside the office. There was no arrangement for seating of the candidates. Leave alone that there was no arrangement to stand even. Most of the candidates were standing on the road. Even the hiring company was not expecting a large turnout and was a little taken-aback by the huge pouring. Confusion prevailed as candidates scorched in heat and dust. The candidates were randomly put through several rounds of group discussions and around 10-15% of the candidates were short listed for the interview. During the interview Harry found most of interviewers either appearing least interested or a bit hostile. After few questions Harry was asked what could he do for the firm. Before he could answer, the interview board asked him if could hold his ears and do sit-ups. Harry was taken aback but thinking of the situation that he was in, Harry even did that! It was very embarrassing and self-denigrating act. There hardly appeared any rationale of that strange demand by the interview board. After his interview, like so many other candidates, Harry was left in the lurch, with no information. They kept waiting till all the interviews were over. This went on till late evening. At around 10:00 p.m. the result was announced. Ten candidates had been short-listed for the final interview, including Harry. Final Interview? Yeah! You guessed it right; it was at that time that they came to know that all this was supposed to be the preliminary round. All ten of them who had been short-listed were asked to appear in the final interview a day after in Delhi. It was an end of a long day; a day Harry had spent with no food, very little water and with lots of dust and heat.

Harry's reporting time for the final interview was 9:30 a.m. As per his habit, he reached the interview place at around 8:45 a.m., good 45 minutes ahead of schedule. The anxiety and the overnight journey had forced him to take just two bread toasts and a cup of tea in his breakfast. The candidates were asked to wait in a basement room. The room was quite dingy and had almost no ventilation. They kept on waiting and waiting… again…! When it was good three hours they were told that the zonal manager had missed his flight and the interviews could be delayed. In the same breath they were also told that the he could arrive at any time and immediately after that the interviews shall begin. Harry kept on waiting like his other counterparts and because of the uncertainty regarding the time of commencement of the interview and out of fear of missing it out, they did not go anywhere out of the room; not even to have their food. They kept waiting for a little over 14 hours. The interview began at 1:00 a.m. and Harry's turn came at around 1:30 a.m. Harry thought in his mind that had they informed the 'Guinness People', they could have perhaps registered a new world record for waiting time. Being a fresher, however, Harry was hardly in a position to say this 'no' to an MNC.

It is shocking why some companies would do this! Selection process can be used as an excellent public relation tool. The candidates, who come to any organization, arrive from all walks of the society and irrespective of whether they get selected or rejected, if they have a nice experience, they talk high about the company. Selection process can also be a first step in the engagement process of the selected candidates. Employees do recall their first encounter with their present company and if that experience is a good one it definitely urges them to stay longer.

Questions

1. Do you think what Harry experienced is common to most candidates who go through the selection system? What reasons do you attribute to such experiences?
2. Interview someone you know who had similar experiences while appearing for a selection interview. Analyze and narrate. Could the organization have done something better?
3. How can you make the selection process an enjoyable experience for the candidate as well? List the dos and don'ts.

Case Study 5

Faulty Appraisals

Puneet works as a Project Manager in ITECH Corporation, a 150 year old technology company. The company offers various technology based solutions in a broad-range of areas to a wide-array of industries including telecommunications, banking, retail, automobile, logistics, aerospace, media and advertising etc. Puneet works in ITECH's Hyderabad-based facility in India.

Puneet a computer engineer from one of the premier engineering colleges of the country has been working in ITECH for the last 1.5 years. His total work-life of 11 years is filled with rich experiences. He brings all that into his work coupled with his dedication and ingenuity. He reports to the global Delivery head Mr. Nataraj Srinivasan. 19 other project Managers like Puneet also report to Mr. Srinivasan.

Puneet has been a high-performer through-out and has been trusted by his seniors for challenging responsibilities. One year back he was assigned to his current project. At a time when he took over there were lots of issues in the project. The client was high on discontent and the project contract to be renewed the corresponding year was wide-open to competition. At such a juncture last year, Punnet was asked to take over the reins of the project. He had dual challenges: one to sort-out the issues in the project and second and more difficult one, to retain the project & the client. Puneet's whole-hearted devotion, his excellent leadership qualities and his strong technical understanding had his team rallying behind him and in a year he was able to bring the project on track.

The annual appraisal interview had just concluded and Puneet was crestfallen. The ratings by his supervisor Mr. Srinivasan had left him with a huge sense of discontent and displeasure. Actually ITECH had a 65% weightage on the KRAs or the core job responsibilities and 35% weightage on the ICAs or the individual contribution areas other than the core job. Punnet's focus on reviving the troubled project saw him scoring very high on the KRAs, however that left him hardly with any time to focus on contributing other than his core job responsibilities. Hence his overall rating had taken a hit. He tried to rationalize this with his supervisor. However Srinivasan expressed his helplessness as he had to operate within the 'system' ITECH also had a policy of comparative rating and forced distribution. This meant that, supposedly, 10 team members were reporting to a person X, then X would have to rate some 20% of the team members with A- rating, some 50% of the members with B-rating, 10% as C-rating and the rest 10% as D-rating, where A was the highest and D would mean PIP (Performance Improvement Program). Puneet's overall rating among 20 project managers was C and he was distraught at the logic and felt cheated. He lamented the fact that he took up the challenging troubled project on insistence of the management.

His hopes with the 360-degree feedback system of the company had also been dashed. ITECH had a system whereby the appraise could choose his/her 360-degree ratees. Puneet had made honest choices and had got a reasonably good feedback. However he later came to know that some his fellow PMs had hand-picked the 360-degree ratees and had received 'fixed' feedback. Comparatively, Punnet's feedback was more conservative and this also did not go in his favour.

Puneet could not see any motivation to continue in his current project and even in his current organization.

Questions

1. Do you think there is something wrong with the appraisal mechanism at ITECH Corporation or do you think Puneet is becoming too paranoid?

2. Do you think $360°$ degree feedback systems are just a fad that fall prey to organizational politics or is there some merit in such a system? Provide adequate rationale for your answer.

3. Assuming yourself to be the HR head of the company, suggest improvements, if any, in the appraisal process.

Case Study 6

Appraisals at Hexagon Foods

Hexagon Foods pink slipped 54 executives in a single day. The company, faced with soaring costs and hyper-competition, cracked the whip on under performers. The move was criticized by some of the managers who felt such large scale laying-off of people would have demoralizing effect on the people. However Mr. Sanjay Rathi, the CHRO of the company believed that the company was justified in taking this step.

At Hexagon Foods, this was a part of the ongoing performance management process, which differentiated the outperformers, performers and under-performers. Each year, under-performers (usually 20 to 30) were put on a performance improvement plan and progress was consistently and carefully monitored. In those cases, where the level of performance continued to be below the acceptable benchmark and there was no noticeable improvement, employees are transitioned. Hexagon Foods had sharpened performance parameters for the staff for the past couple of years, differentiating them into "outperformers, performers and under-performers" and rewarded the top performers with bonuses as high as 150%, something not very common in the industry.

Hexagon Foods decided to let go executives who had underperformed in two out of the last three years. All 54 employees, including some managerial staff, who had been asked to leave were being given their salaries for the next two months, but also asked to go on leave immediately. These employees were from the manufacturing, sales, packaging and quality control teams, and comprised roughly 2.5% of the company's total strength of around 2,000.

Some of the sacked employees felt the development came as a surprise and were also critical of the way they were suddenly asked to leave. A senior management team accompanied by the Human Resource team had come down to Mumbai and asked the employees to put in our resignations. The only explanation that was given was that this decision was taken in light of their performance. Most of the employees who were asked to leave had not received any salary-hike in the last two years.

Industry experts believed that companies like Hexagon Foods are bound to get tougher on performance expectation from employees with increasing competition in the marketplace. Hexagon Foods has been facing stiff competition from MNCs as well as some regional players. The $ 1.029 billion Hexagon Foods has been growing at strong double digits every year for the last four-five years. It has consistently stepped up brand investments as well to support and maintain its market shares.

Most companies in the same industry follow a performance appraisal system where employees are segmented into different levels of delivered performance every year. Those who fall in the lowest bracket are usually mentored for a certain period of time to upgrade their performance. However, the level of strictness observed in weeding out the bottom 1-2% employees may vary from company to company. But no company openly confesses to following a policy of laying off under-performers. Some companies have in the past followed performers practices of "outplacing" surplus employees based on their interests. The attrition rate in the industry is around 20% and there is a severe war for talent.

Questions

1. In your opinion, do you think such segmentation of employees makes the appraisal mechanism more effective? Support your views with logic.
2. In a scenario of talent shortage and talent-war do you think such policies will be helpful? Why?

Case Study 7

The Skills Gap in Canada

The knowledge requirements of Canadians' jobs are growing rapidly. Changes in production technologies and in the nature and organization of work in general have fuelled the demand for workers equipped with solid literacy and numeracy skills. Despite the successes of Canadian schools and post-secondary institutions in producing graduates with such skills, a gap remains between the demand for workers with strong literacy and numeracy skills and the supply of Canadians who possess them.

The Demand for Skills is Increasing

The rising level of competition facing Canadian firms, changes in production technologies, and changes in the nature and organization of work are all driving increases in the knowledge intensity of jobs in Canada. Foreign outsourcing has reduced the domestic demand for unskilled workers, thereby increasing the relative demand for skilled workers. The growing prominence of information–communication technology *industries*[1] has also fed the demand for skilled workers who can thrive in a knowledge-based economy.[1]

Between 1991 and 2003, the number of businesses in Canada grew by 12%, fostering an 8% increase in the number of workers. There was a related rise in the demand for skills over the same period: as the number of high-knowledge businesses increased by 78%, the number of medium-knowledge businesses increased by 14% and the number of low-knowledge businesses fell by 3%.

Canadian Workers have not kept up with the Growing Demand for Skilled Labour

Various educational indicators show that Canadians are better educated than ever before. For example, high school dropout rates have been steadily

---

[1] Industries are categorized as high, medium or low-knowledge on the basis of research and development measures (e.g., the ratio of R&D personnel to total employment) and human capital measures (e.g., the ratio of workers with post-secondary education to total employment). a list of industries and their knowledge intensity classifications can be found on p. 18 of Kanagarajah (2003).

declining across Canada. In the early 1990s, the Canada-wide dropout rate was 16%. In recent years, that rate has fallen to 10%.[2] During the same period, more and more Canadians enrolled in post-secondary education. Between 1990 and 2005, the proportion of Canadians with at least some post-secondary education increased from 42% to 57%.

There is also evidence that Canada's elementary and secondary schools are providing a solid foundation for the skills needed in the workforce. Based on *PISA*[2] scores, Canadian 15-year-olds rank among the top industrialized nations in reading, science, mathematics, and problem-solving skills.

However, there are other indications that the Canadian labour force does not have adequate skills to keep up with demand as high-knowledge industries play a progressively larger role in Canada's economy. The data from the 2003 Adult Literacy and Life Skills Survey (ALL) indicate that 40% of Canadian adults do not have literacy skills at "the level considered by experts as a suitable minimum for coping with the increasing demands of the emerging knowledge society and information economy." A comparison of the 2003 results with those of the 1994 International Adult Literacy Survey (IALS) indicates that the average level of literacy skill remained virtually unchanged, despite the fact that the average quality and duration of education rose rapidly over that same period.

This lack of progress may reflect a phenomenon best described as *skill loss*[3]. In other words, individuals can lose skills that they once had—through

---

[2] The Programme for international Student assessment is a survey of 15-year-olds conducted every three years in 41 industrialized countries. Pisa tests students' reading, math, science, and problem solving skills and is designed to determine whether students in these countries are well prepared to meet the challenges of the future as they reach the end of their compulsory education.

[3] Literacy skill, as measured by IALS/ALL, decreases with increasing age among Canadian adults. As a group, younger Canadians have better literacy skills than their older counterparts. Canadians aged 26 to 45 scored 20 points higher than those aged 46 to 65 on the 2003 ALL. As well, 53% of those in the older age group scored below the level considered adequate, while 38% in the younger group scored below this level.

This age-related decrease in skill has two causes:
1. Generation Effects. Older generations had lower initial levels of skill when they entered the labour force. As Canadians become more highly educated, succeeding generations enter the labour force with higher and higher initial levels of skill.
2. Skill Loss. Some Canadians experience skill loss over the years following their entry into the workforce. As a result, some older Canadians have lower levels of skill than was previously the case.

Skill loss accounts for approximately 60% of the differences in Prose Literacy between 35- and 65-year-old Canadians. The remaining age-related differences can be attributed to generational effects (see Figure 1).

forgetting and lack of use. This skill loss may account for the finding that average Canada-wide levels of adult literacy have not increased even though educational attainment has improved.

Detailed analyses of the 1994 IALS and the 2003 ALL reveal that many adults appear to have lost considerable skill—ranging from 5% to 25% of the skill they possessed in 1994, depending on their province of residence, their socio-economic status and their level of educational attainment. In general, skill loss is higher for individuals with lower educational attainment or who have occupations requiring fewer skills. At their worst, these losses are equivalent to losing the average literacy skills gained through three years of schooling.

Canada is unique in having developed a tool to monitor the demand for literacy, numeracy and a range of other skills for each of the occupations in our national system of occupational classification. The Essential Skills profiles make it possible to compare the skills needed to fulfill job requirements with the skills that Canadian workers actually possess and thereby identify any skills gaps. For example, the Canadian Trucking Human Resources Council compared the literacy skills required by truck drivers (as described by the Essential Skills profile) with the skills available in the current truck driver work force (as measured by IALS). It concluded that there is a gap between the skills required to understand documents needed for the job, such as the Transportation of Dangerous Goods Act, and the available level of skill. Comparisons across a number of different industries indicate that similar gaps exist for a broad range of occupations.

These findings point to the existence of a growing skills gap in Canada's labour market.

Implications of a Skills Gap

The skills gap is a problem for individual Canadians and for the country as a whole. For individuals, differences in literacy and numeracy skills are associated with large differences in employability and wage rates, particularly in occupations that demand high levels of knowledge and skill. Other analyses of IALS data have shown that skill—independent of educational attainment—has a large effect on earnings. These findings suggest that literacy and numeracy skills are economically important and one of the key determinants of economic inequality. In other words, skill creates economic winners and losers as employers select and reward workers with the required skills, leaving behind those without.

On a larger scale, a country's long-term economic success is largely dependent on the literacy skills of its population. Detailed analyses of IALS and ALL data show that a large proportion of differences in economic growth between countries and between provinces can be attributed to differences in average literacy and numeracy skills. Thus, unmet labour-force demand for solid literacy and numeracy skills—the skills gap—limits Canada's economic potential.

The skills gap reduces the competitiveness of Canadian firms, largely by limiting rates of technical, process and organizational innovation upon which productivity growth depends. Large numbers of adults with low literacy levels limit the rate at which technologies that increase productivity can be adopted.

Age-related changes in literacy skill can be attributed to skill loss and generational effects.

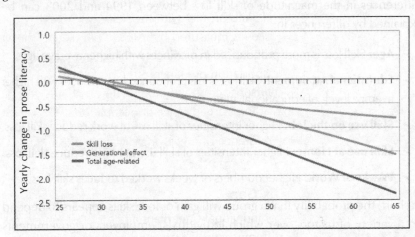

Figure 1: Skill Loss and Generational Effects

(**Source:** Cartwright, F. (2006). *The relative effects of cohort and skill loss on age-related differences in literacy.* Unpublished manuscript, Canadian Council on Learning.)

The skills gap also plays a less direct role in the economic fortunes of individuals and of the country. There is a strong link between individual physical health and literacy levels: more literate adults have fewer spells of illness, their illnesses cost less to treat and require less recovery time. Thus, not only do higher literacy rates contribute to personal quality of life, these findings also suggest that low literacy levels impose greater societal costs by increasing the demand for health services and the expense and duration of treatment. There is also a strong relationship between literacy and the receipt of social transfers; low skilled individuals are far more likely to receive these benefits.

Lessons in Learning: Increasing Skill Levels among Canadian Adults

Many of Canada's competitors have recognized the need to increase the level and equitable distribution of adult literacy and numeracy skills. The U.K., Sweden, Ireland and the Netherlands have all increased their level of investment in adult skills, including literacy and numeracy.

Canada needs to develop a coordinated strategy designed to close the literacy and numeracy skills gap. Such a strategy should take into consideration the factors relevant to skill loss. Analyses suggest that skill loss is greater among adults whose parents are from lower educational backgrounds. Additionally, a significant fraction (75%) of the inter-provincial differences in the magnitude of skill loss between 1994 and 2003 can be explained by differences in:

- **Age:** Skill loss is more pronounced in provinces with higher average ages.
- **Educational Attainment:** Skill loss is less pronounced in provinces with higher average levels of educational attainment.
- **Skill use on the Job:** Higher intensities of skill use at work reduce skill loss.
- **Skill use at Home:** Higher intensities of skill use at home reduce skill loss.
- **Weeks of Work:** Higher numbers of weeks worked reduces skill loss.

In short, the probability that a group will gain or lose skills appears to depend on a variety of factors over which individuals, employers or governments may be able to exert some control. Post-secondary education, the amount of reading on and off the job, and stable employment all appear to have an impact on the stock of literacy skills in the population.

Progress toward closing the skills gap can be made by increasing the average skill levels of graduating students, ensuring that fewer students leave the system with inadequate literacy and numeracy skills. The provincial and territorial governments are working together through the Council of Ministers of

Education to develop coordinated strategies to achieve this goal. Progress can also be made by encouraging larger numbers of Canadians to take courses to improve their skills.

Individuals can help to raise the level of adult literacy by evaluating their own learning needs and investing in their own adult learning.

Employers can help to raise the level of adult learning by providing higher levels of workplace training. Ironically, employers are more likely to provide additional training to employees who already have higher levels of education. Employers need to recognize the benefits of fostering better skills for individuals with a wide range of skills and educational backgrounds. For example, employers should be aware that employees are motivated to take training in order to perform more effectively in their current jobs. According to CCL's Survey of Canadian Attitudes toward Learning, released October 2006, 69% of Canadians reported this to be the case, compared with less than a third who reported it was for more money or a better job.

Educational institutions can develop and disseminate effective curricula and diagnostic tools, and create institutional mechanisms for the rapid transmission of skills training best practices. For example, Bow Valley College has developed the Test of Workplace Essential Skills (TOWES), which uses real-world workplace tasks to measure text reading, document use and numeracy. This tool allows employers to identify specific skills gaps among their employees. This information can be used by employers and training providers to develop workplace training programs. It can also be used to foster relationships between employers and community colleges so that programs can respond to specific skill shortages.

Governments also have a range of strategies at their disposal. They can use public awareness campaigns to encourage behavioural change (i.e., participation in and provision of training). They can employ tax incentives to encourage individuals to participate in adult learning and to encourage businesses to offer training. They can also use tax incentives to encourage businesses to acquire skill-intensive technologies—Canadians who work with these technologies will be more likely to acquire and maintain strong skills. Governments can also eliminate tax disincentives to the adoption of technologies requiring high levels of skill.

Investments in skill development will foster economic growth more effectively when a large proportion of the labour force—rather than a small number of highly talented individuals—benefits from additional skills training.19 Canada's efforts to close the skills gap must include the broadest possible cross-section of Canadians.

Published with permission of Canadian Council on Learning

(**Source:** Canadian Council on Learning, The skill gap in Canada: The knowledge intensity of Canadians' jobs is growing rapidly) (Lessons in Learning – Ottawa: December 21, 2006, www.ccl-cca.ca)

Questions

1. Why do you think Canadian workers have not kept up with the growing demand for skilled labour?

2. What are the implications of skill-gap on Canadian Economy? Evaluate the role of various entities in closing such skill-gaps.

3. Do you think similar skill-gap exists in India? How can the same be mitigated? Study some steps taken-up by the government and the industry in closing the skill-gaps. What role does academia have in reducing the skill-gap?

References

1. Yan, B. Demand for Skills in Canada: The Role of Foreign Outsourcing and Information-Communication Technology (Ottawa: Statistics Canada, 2005). Catalogue no. 11F0027MIE – No. 035. Accessed Nov. 9, 2006.

2. Bowlby, G. and K. McMullen. Provincial Drop-Out Rates – Trends and Consequences (Ottawa: Statistics Canada, 2005). Catalogue no. 81-004-XIE. Accessed Nov. 9, 2006.

3. Statistics Canada. Labour Force Survey – Historical Review (Ottawa: 2005).

4. Statistics Canada and OECD (2005). Learning a Living: First Results of the Adult Literacy and Life Skills Survey (Paris and Ottawa: OECD and Statistics Canada, 2005). Statistics Canada, Catalogue no. 89-603-XIE. Accessed Oct. 26, 2006.

5. Willms, D. Variation in Literacy Skills among Canadian Provinces: Findings from OECD PISA (Ottawa: Statistics Canada, 2004). Catalogue no. 81-595-MIE. Accessed Nov. 21, 2006.
6. MacLeod, C. Essential Skills Needs Assessment of the Trucking Industry. (Canadian Trucking Human Resources Council, 2002). Accessed Nov. 27, 2006.
7. Willms, D. and T.S. Murray. Gaining and Losing Skills over the Life Course (Ottawa: Statistics Canada, unpublished).
8. Statistics Canada and OECD. Literacy in the Information Age: Final Report of the International Adult Literacy Survey. (Paris and Ottawa: OECD and Statistics Canada, 2000) Accessed Nov. 21, 2006.
9. Statistics Canada and OECD. Learning a Living (2005). Statistics Canada, Catalogue no. 89-603-XIE.
10. Johnston. Adult Literacy and Economic Growth (Wellington: New Zealand Treasury, 2004). Working Paper 04/24.
11. Green, D. and W. Riddell. Literacy, Numeracy and Labour Market Outcomes in Canada (Ottawa: Statistics Canada, 2001). Catalogue no. 89-552-MIE. Accessed Nov. 9, 2006
12. Coulombe, S., J.F. Tremblay and S. Marchand. Literacy Scores, Human Capital and Growth Across 14 OECD Countries (Ottawa: Statistics Canada, 2004). Catalogue no. 89-552-MIE. Accessed Nov. 21, 2006.
13. Coulombe, S. and J.F. Tremblay. Human Capital and Canadian Provincial Standards of Living (Ottawa: Statistics Canada, 2006). Catalogue no. 81-552-MIE. Accessed Nov. 21, 2006.
14. Rudd R., I. Kirsch, and K. Yamamoto. Health Literacy in America, (Princeton: Educational Testing Service, 2004).
15. Statistics Canada and HRDC. Reading the Future: A Portrait of Literacy in Canada. (Ottawa: Statistics Canada and HRDC). Statistics Canada, Catalogue no. 89F0093XIE. Accessed Nov. 21, 2006.
16. Murray, T.S. The Assessment of Adult Literacy, Numeracy and Language at the International Level: A Review (Washington, D.C.: National Academies of Science, 2003).

Case Study 8

The Best Archer

In the ancient Indian epic Mahabharata, Guru Dronacharya has been regarded as the greatest teacher & trainer of all times. Dronacharya was well-versed in *Vedas, Upanishads, Yoga's* and meditation. But when it came to archery skills, Dronacharya was regarded as an ultimate authority.

His disciples included *Pandavas* as well as *Kauravas*. Out of all his disciples, Arjuna was his favorite one, since he exhibited immense perseverance & concentration. Arjuna gradually emerged as the best archer. Dronacharya's lavish praise for Arjuna and preferential treatment of his favourite disciple made Dronacharya and Dushasana very jealous & bitter. One day these two Kaurava brothers expressed their unhappiness openly to Guru Dronacharya.

As a reply to this criticism, Guru Drona decided to test the best archer among Kauravas & Pandavas. Guru Drona placed a wooden bird on the branch of a tree. The bird was partly hidden by foliage. The eye of the bird was painted prominently. The test was to hit the bird's eye. First he called the eldest of them all, Yudhistara to try his archery skills. As Yudhistra took aim with his bow & arrow, Guru Dronacharya asked him "O' Yudhistra, can you tell me, what can you see?"

Yudhistra replied innocently – "Guru Drona I can see you, people around me, the tree, branch, foliage and the bird."

Guru Dronacharya asked him to step aside as he was sure he will miss his target. Similarly he asked each one of them including Duryodhana, Bheem, Nakul and all of them gave similar replies.

Then he asked Arjuna to step-in and take aim with his bow and arrow. Guru Dronacharya asked Arjuna – "O' Arjuna, what can you see?

Arjuna replied – "*Gurudev* I can see the bird's eye."

Guru Drona further asked – Arjuna can you see only bird's eye? Can't you see all of us, the tree and things around you?

Arjuna replied – No Guru Drona I cannot see all these things. I can see the bird's eye.

Dronacharya was thrilled with Arjuna's concentration and approach to archery. He then explained that why he considered Arjuna his best disciple. Everyone was convinced by the answers but the seeds of jealousy became stronger in the heart of Dushasana & Duryodhana.

Eklavya was a son of tribal and he also wanted to learn archery skills. He approached Guru Dronacharya but the latter refused as he was the son of a tribal. However Eklavya did not give up and in the jungle practiced his archery skills. He constructed one statue of Guru Drona and considered him as his trainer. Eklavya's love for archery and his concentration & determination made him a excellent archer, even better then Arjuna.

This was discovered by Guru Drona and his disciples including Arjuna when they accidently stumbled upon Eklavya, while they were roaming in the jungle. While others were in praise for Eklavya, Arjuna grew very jealous of him. Guru Dronacharya could not tolerate this, as he wanted his favourite disciple Arjuna to be the best archer.

Guru Dronacharya asked for *'Guru Dakshina'* – the offering that a disciple makes to his teacher, from Eklavya. Guru Drona asked for the right thumb of Eklavya as *'Guru Dakshina' (reward for the teacher or Guru form the disciple)*. Everyone was shocked, but Eklavya like a true disciple, cut his right thumb and placed it upon the feet of his Guru.

As a result Eklavya could never again shoot an arrow and Arjuna went on to become the best archer of all times.

Questions

1. Evaluate Guru Dronacharya's competencies as a Trainer.
2. Identify the short comings of Guru Dronacharya. How do you think these short comings had an impact on his trainers?
3. In light of this case, highlight why training the trainer is important?

Case Study 9

Bharti Airtel Trains for Customer Service

The mid of August 2008 saw the launch of iPhone in India, amidst much fanfare. Launched initially in India by Bharti Airtel and Vodafone Essar, the smart phone was priced at premium. The lower version of iPhone 3G was priced at Rs. 31000 and the higher version with more memory was priced at Rs. 36000.

Faced with a pre-registration of over 2 lakh customers is for the 16 GB phone, Airtel worked overtime in ensuring iPhone's availability. Bharti Airtel launched iPhone simultaneously in 65 cities across India with some of the stores open past midnight to cater to enthusiasts & early birds.

But Airtel had some other concerns besides ensuring accessibility and availability of iPhone. iPhone was one of the most advanced handsets ever introduced, in the mobile telephony market. With features like voice control, inbuilt digital compass, cut-copy-paste options between applications, spotlight searches, accessibility features to assist users who are visually or hearing impaired like voice-over screen reader, zoom features, white on black display options, mono audio, Internet tethering, Voice memos, Nike + iPod sensor, stock market updates, You-Tube access, remote wipe (in case of iPhone is misplaced) etc. made this phone a technological masterpiece.

However to make this masterpiece deliver a truly world class experience, the features of iPhone must be well-understood by the customers. This became all the more necessary since Airtel planned to bundle data plans with the iPhone.

True to its smart marketing strategy and excellent market focus, Airtel conducted special training programs for thousands of sales & service employees. They were extensively trained in sales & service of device that included 5 days of training for service and 2 days on sales.

Questions

1. Comment on Airtel's strategy of using training for better customer service.
2. To what extent do you think service-gaps can be closed by focusing on employee training? Elaborate with examples.
3. Narrate any experience of yourself as a customer where you think the sales/service employee who interacted with you could have done better with some training.

Case Study 10

Training for Safer Roads

India received another dubious distinction when the World Health Organization revealed in its first ever 'Global Status Report on Road Safety' that – more people die in road accidents in India than anywhere else in the world, including the more populous China. According to World Health Organization (WHO), road fatalities have taken the shape of an 'epidemic' and will become the fifth largest killer by 2030. Maximum deaths due to road accidents happen in developing low and middle income countries (almost 90%).

In India the statistics are scary enough to send a chill down the spine:

Around 14 people died every hour on Indian roads with annual toll touching 1.27 lakh in 2009. This was nearly 80 per cent more than the road accident casualty toll of China where 70,000- odd people died during the corresponding period. Around 10 years ago a WHO report had stated that India will see an annual escalation of over 3 per cent in road accident deaths till 2040.

(**Source:** http://www.goimonitor.com/taxonomy/term/148)

India's record in road deaths has touched a new low, as toll rose to at least 14 deaths per hour in 2008 against 13 the previous year. The total annual deaths due to road accidents has crossed 1.18 lakh, according to the latest report of National Crime Records Bureau (NCRB).

(**Source:** Times of India, 24 Feb 2010)

Over 30,000 more people died in road accidents in India in 2010 as compared to the previous year.

(**Source:** Times of India, 12 May 2011)

According to a note being jointly prepared by the Union health ministry and the ministry of road highways and surface transport, an estimated 1.6 lakh were killed in road accidents last year. In 2009, 1.25 lakh were killed.

(**Source:** Times of India, 12 May 2011)

India's killer roads have been registering an increase of almost 8% in the number of road accidents every consecutive year, according to an IIT-Delhi report. National Crime Records Bureau (NCRB) says that 1.3 lakh people died and over 4.7 lakh were injured on the country's highways and side-roads last year. And the World Health Organisation predicts that road accidents will rise from its present position as India's ninth biggest killer to number three by 2020. Clearly, road accidents will

be the new epidemic that doctors and town planers will have to address sooner than later.

(**Source:** Times of India, 9 November 2011)

Biggest victims of road mishaps are occupants of trucks & lorries followed by two wheelers. The states leading in terms of death due to road mishaps are Andhra Pradesh (12%) followed by Maharastra & Uttar Pradesh (11% each). (NCRB)

The main contributing factors in this alarming rate of deaths due to road accidents in India are speeding (major factor), drinking-driving, low use of helmets, seat-belts etc.

Life is precious and loss of the same due to road accidents is almost criminal considering that most of these deaths can be avoided. Countries like U.K. have drastically brought down number of deaths due to road accidents with only 3298 deaths reported due to road mishaps in UK in the year 2006.

Compliance of road safety norms, higher awareness of traffic rules & more vigilant traffic surveillance are key to reducing road mishaps & resulting deaths. The two major stakeholders in ensuring the above are the drivers & traffic police personnels.

'Traffic and Road Safety Institute' in Bangalore has taken an unique training initiative. The trainees are traffic police personnel, cutting acrossrank & file, right from ACP to constable. Trainees also include errant drivers of Bangalore Metropolitan Transport (BMTC) and Karnataka State Road Transport Corporation (KSRTC).

The trainees are imparted basic knowledge of signals, road markings and new technology like how to handle Blackberry devices. What is unique about this training is methodology which has been adopted for imparting these skills. Real time audio-visuals are streamed into the training norms from the Traffic Management Centre (TMC). The gridlocks, accidents and other road user behaviours captured on surveillance cameras are used as training material. These training materials & methodology help the trainiees understand the causes of traffic problems, accidents & ways to minimize/avoid them, much better compared to theoretical inputs.

Another state-of-the art centre, complete with all modern training facilities & equipments is slated to come-up in a couple of years.

The country's largest car maker Maruti Suzuki rums Institute of Driving, Training and Research (IDTRs) and Maruti Driving School (MDS) as a part of its corporate social responsibility. Currently, with two IDTRs in Delhi and 47 MDSs across the country, the company plans to set-up 8-10 new IDTRs and 110 MDSs by 2010, and in the process aims to train around 5 lakh people in next three years. Usually the driving school are set-up through commercial dealers network.

These institutions impart training on various courses on driving, traffic rules and other safety aspects like safe driving practices.

All this is a part of Maruti Suzuki National Road Safety Mission – To train 500,000 people in driving in next 3 years – "Gratitude to India on completion of 25 years".

Unveiled in Dec 2008, under this mission the company will:

Train 500,000 people in safe driving practices in next 3 years across India. While utilizing the existing 2 institutes of driving Training and research (IDTR) in Delhi & 47 Maruti Driving Schools (MDS) across the country the company will enter into partnerships with state governments for more IDTRs and with its dealers for more MDS. Of the 500,000 people to be trained, atleast 100,000 will be people from under privileged section of society, who are keen to take driving as a profession. The company will continue to support to government and industry in their efforts for road safety. Maruti Suzuki has already trained around 450,000 persons in safe driving practices in past few years.

Questions

1. Analyze the role of training in reducing road accidents and deaths caused by same.
2. Do you think initiatives mentioned in the case will alone be able to reduce road accidents in India? Analyze critically.
3. Do you think Public-Private Partnership in training on safe driving practices will pay dividends? Opine.
4. Identify some other areas/problems in society or organizations where training can act as a successful intervention.

References

1. India leads world in road deaths: WHO, The Times of India; Aug 17, 2009. http://timesofindia.indiatimes.com/news/india/india-leads-world-in-road-deaths.
2. Practicals of Traffic cops; The Times of India; Aug 25, 2009.
3. Maruti's 2010 roadmap has more driving schools, research institutes; Business Line, Aug 19, 2008.
4. http://www.marutisuzuki.com/Maruti-suzuki-national-road-safety-mission.aspx.

Case Study 11

Compensation Woes of Engineering Faculty

Ambrish had been working in the College of Electrical Engineering (CoEE) in UBS Engineering College as an Assistant Professor since the past 4 years. Prior to joining UBS he has served in faculty position in another college for another 4 years. He had emerged to be an outstanding teacher and was in high demand amongst the students. Ambrish was not only technically very sound, but also had an excellent pedagogy. His examples in the class were always practical. This was because he always chose to keep his teaching close to industrial application, by keeping himself updated. Students were literally hooked to Ambrish's classes & he had to spend a good time with the students after the class also clearing the doubts that they had in subjects taught by other professor's too. Ambrish was happy with his job but he was not so much happy with his salary. Regular but paltry increments every year had not helped his salary to increase much. Ambrish was however recognized by the HOD of Electrical Engineering College as a faculty having immense potential to excel in academics in future. His peers & senior were silently appreciative as well as jealous of Ambrish's achievements and popularity among students.

The salary issue became a little more worrying for Ambrish after he got married. His responsibilities & hence expenses were increasing. He was straining to make both ends meet. He discussed the issue with HOD, who assured that he would do something about. However after the annual increments were done with, all Ambrish got was an extra-increment for his outstanding performance. Each increment in the scale that Ambrish was placed meant an addition of only Rs. 275/- to his basic pay. Ambrish was in the pay scale of 8000-275-13500. Ambrish was disappointed and he passively started considering a job change that his wife had been prodding him for long.

The College of Electrical Engineering was also facing some issues with the student satisfaction with some newly appointed faculty members. Most of the new joinees had 2-3 years of experience. The students were having lots of doubts in the subjects taught by them. But with a severe shortage of Engineering faculty in the country and hardly any doctorate faculty in the stream, finding faculty had been a uphill task for the CoEE as had been for other colleges.

One day while casually glancing through the newspaper in the reception he found a sheet of paper that contained the salary details of the faculty and staff in the CoEE. Employees at UBS were not expected to discuss their salary details with their colleagues. He wondered how could that sheet be lying there loose. Few days back lots of documents were being prepared for the visit of the officials from the apex technical board that provided affiliation to the college. May be this paper slipped out of the numerous bundles of files that were being readied for the visiting team Ambrish thought in his mind. Out of curiosity, he glanced through the paper and the contents shocked him. The new faculty members who had joined the college, and were atleast 3-4 years junior to him were getting almost equal salary as he was drawing. Ambrish was quite disturbed and confronted the HOD with the document that he had accidentally bumped into. The HOD accepted the fact and said the details on the paper were true, however this had happened because the current set of faculty had been hired on the present market-rate. Ambrish found this argument weak and enquired why then his salary was not increased proportionately? The HOD told him that had he been hired now, he would also have got the same rate. Ambrish wondered whether it was his fault that he had been loyal to CoEE and had been working there for the last 4 years?

Ambrish was completely disillusioned, although the HOD assured him that he shall put-up his query and request to the administrative board of the college. Ambrish had little hopes. Within a month Ambrish found a much better paying job in a competing engineering college with additional perks & benefits. He resigned from his job at CoEE in UBS College of Engneering and all later attempts to retain him failed. The students were appalled at the loss of such a good faculty and although Ambrish maintained a dignified silence on reasons for his leaving, the rumor-mill was going agog. Already suffering from some very average-quality teaching from other faculty, the students were up-in arms against the UBS management.

Questions

1. Was the UBS management justified in its compensation policy? Opinionate with rationale.
2. What impact do such compensation policies have on motivation & retention of the talented employee?
3. How far do you think the dilemma of paying the new recruits as per the market-rate and non-correction of the salaries of the older employees can be addressed? Give your suggestions.

Case Study 12

ESOPs in GMT Bank

GMT Bank was one of the earliest in the banking sector to experiment with employee stock options. It launched a scheme as early as 2001, starting with the unreserved objective of covering all employees, based on performance.

When GMT Bank first designed the Employee Stock Ownership Plan (ESOP) scheme, there was much debate about how broad-based it should be. The bank chose to include all employees except the poorest performers. The belief was based on the findings of various surveys that showed that GMT Bank was below its competitors on cash performance bonuses. Also, the bank did not have an aggressive variable pay plan. So, the management decided ESOPs would be a good way to compensate employees, even at lower levels.

At first, employees didn't take well to the new plan. But when the stock price started climbing, they saw the point and embraced the scheme.

However, over the years, the scheme has undergone changes, teaching the bank an important lesson: Not everybody in the organization wants ESOPs and even for those who do, the current market price is an important consideration.

The first major change came in 2004. GMT Bank had been accounting the difference between the price at which options were granted and the prevailing market price as an expenditure on the books and noticed that they were taking a hit. So, the company changed the formula for pricing the options. It switched from the 52-week average to the previous day's close as the basis for the grant price. This helped the company eliminate its accounting expenditure, and also wiped out the arbitrage the employees enjoyed between the two prices.

The next year dealt a bigger blow to ESOPs. The government brought them under the ambit of Fringe Benefit Tax (FBT). Any difference between the fair market value and the vesting price came to be taxed at 33.99 per cent. The industry was enraged at what it saw as an unfair levy, but the government did not budge. At GMT Bank, the management decided to pass on the FBT burden to employees, taking advantage of a clause in the tax laws. This and the new pricing formula had a telling impact on the popularity of ESOPs.

Employees have exercised far fewer options from 2005 to the present than they did in the first four years of the plan. In April 2004, more than three million options were exercised, up from one million at the start in April 2001. However, in April 2007, that number had dropped to less than 3 lakhs. The amount of wealth created had exceeded Rs. 90 crore in April 2004, but had dropped to just Rs. 10 crore in the same month three years later. The year 2008 saw a big shift in GMT Bank's ESOP strategy. In April, the company decided to narrow the scope of the plan to only employees in the middle management and above. Staff in the lower rungs was excluded. There were two reasons for this. Previously, the company was growing at an exponential rate, but growth slowed down and they could not give options to everyone anymore. Also, lower level employees appreciate a cash bonus more than an ESOP. The bank had looked at the ESOP plan as a long-term wealth creating exercise, but the employees didn't.

GMT Bank is now toying with ideas such as restricted stock units. These options may result in cash outflow and is forced to explore options for better compensation of employees.

Questions

1. Weigh the merits and demerits of the ESOPS. Are they suitable for all types of employees?

2. Why do you think GMT Bank is toying with the idea of other kind of stock options?

3. Illustrate the example of any other company that gives stock-options to its employees. What advantages do you think it has been able to derive through such variable-pay option?

Case Study 13

Sexual Harassment at Simon Logistics

Pavithra was working with Simon Logistics for the last five years as an administrative executive. She was polite and a very diligent worker. She had been having really tough adjusting with her new boss Mr. Jeet Bhasin. Bhasin had recently joined Simon Logistics and had replaced the outgoing & very affable Administrative Head Mr. Rajesh Garg. Jeet Bhasin was a loud gregarious fellow and had earned good amount of disliking & ire from most of his subordinates in the last six months that he had been with Simon. Pavithra had on several occasions rebuffed his unwelcome advances. Bhasin had made offensive verbal remarks against Pavithra and some other female executives on more than one instance. One day, Bhasin summoned Pavithra to his cabin to give her dictation. While taking dictation Pavithra noticed that Bhasin had displayed "pornographic material" on his computer. Before she left the office, Bhasin also made some "offensive and intimidating" remarks. Pavithra shared this incident with her colleague, named Peter Samuels. Samuels had been an outperformer himself and also reported to Bhasin. Samuels was trusted by everyone in the office and Pavithra told him of her agony to seek his advice. Samuels suggested that she speak to Mr. Roy Thacker who was the Vice-President – Administration and to whom Bhasin reported. Pavithra brought the concerns to the notice of Roy Thacker, who declined to act or take the matter to Jeet Bhasin and asked her to speak to HR instead. She also spoke to HR head and although he assured her of taking 'some' steps but nothing concrete happened on ground. Bhasin somehow came to know of this reporting by Pavithra and his animosity towards her grew in the days to come. A week later Bhasin handed Pavithra a 'indecent' photo with 'explicit nudity'. Bhasin wanted Pavithra to incorporate the image in a presentation warning employees about the dangers of drinking. Pavithra was so upset that she went home. She put-in her papers the very next day. Samuels tried to speak to Bhasin about Pavithra but he shot back saying that "If she doesn't like it, she can quit. One clown doesn't stop no show." After quitting her job, Pavithra consulted her lawyer and filed a law-suit against Bhasin and Simon Logistics accusing 'victimization and sexual harassment'.

When the case came up for hearing Bhasin told Samuels that he "was in trouble" and that his involvement in the case "would be detrimental to his career. However Samuels testified and told the court that he repeatedly warned his superiors that women in the office were being sexually harassed or discriminated against, but that his concerns were ignored. Pavithra won the case and Simon Logistics had to pay ₹10 Lakhs as damages.

After this Samuels found the work environment "hostile" in which he was "demeaned," "treated differently from other employees" and denied promotions because of his willingness to speak out. His performance reviews were consistently positive until then, when Bhasin gave him his lowest score, after a series of incidents in the department and was denied a promotion. A month later, Bhasin called Samuels into a conference room and informed him "that he was being terminated as a result of his poor performance."

Samuels was shocked, although he had been sensing trouble ever since he testified. Only a year back, Samuels had received a congratulatory letter from the HR, along with a silver cuff-links. He had at least once expressed his alarm — both about the treatment of female staff in the office and his fear of retaliation to Mr. Roy Thacker.

Questions

1. Why do you think people like Jeet Bhasin continue to engage in dastardly act of sexual harassment? What role did Roy Thacker play in the entire episode?

2. Do you think the monetary compensation awarded to Pavithra by the court shall solve her problems? Would it deter people like Bhasin in the future from doing a similar act?

3. If you were Samuels, what would you do?

Case Study 14

Strike at Spark Automotives & Precision Engineering

Spark Automotives & Precision Engineering is a leading supplier of technology and services, and has a strong presence in the country at numerous locations in diverse industry segments. Spark Automotives & Precision Engineering set up its manufacturing operations in 1974, and has grown over the years. Spark Automotives & Precision Engineering employs about 15000 employees in India, and in business year 2010 achieved total consolidated revenue of over 4237 crores. Techno-Automotive division is the largest business segment of Spark Automotives & Precision Engineering in India, supplying to the local automotive industry, and exporting components overseas. Spark Automotives & Precision Engineering is an expert for all drive, control and motion technologies.

The employees association of Spark Automotives & Precision Engineering Ltd, accused the management, back-tracking on several issues, one of them being ancillarisation. The worker's association had demanded that the company should not go ahead with ancillarisation and a written settlement to this effect be signed before the Labour Commissioner. The management on its part claimed that the decision to outsource was taken after several meetings with its labour union.

The main bone of contention between the management and the labour union seemed to be the issue of sub-contracting function. Employees claimed that without their knowledge, several machines were taken away from the Spark Automotives & Precision Engineering facility and given away to sub-contractors. Workers not only feared change of jobs and the possible loss of wages, but also protested against the disrespect shown to the official document. The workers were opposing ancilliarisation and outsourcing of production, and the Management's "illegal shutdown" of the another plant sometime back. The union also alleged that the management has been 'illegally' employing women, trainees, administrative staff and other workers from Spark's other units to continue production.

The stand-off between the management and its workers took a turn for the worse when the union members prevented company officials from entering the factory. The strike continued for over two weeks and was finally called-off after the government order referred the issue for adjudication to the Industries Tribunal. The three issues referred for adjudication were — 1. outsourcing and ancillarisation, 2. the tool down strike and plant shutdown, and 3. the loss to employees due to the shutdown — and has given the parties six months to resolve the issue.

Questions

1. Do you think the management is justified in ancilliarisation and outsourcing of production? Why?

2. 'The strike and preventing company officials from entering the premises by labour unions is vindicated'. Do you agree or disagree. Why?

3. How can the issue be resolved?

Case Study 15

Strike at Maruti Suzuki India

Maruti Suzuki India was crippled by a strike in June 2011 that lasted a whopping 13 days. The strike at Manesar Plant of Maruti resulted in a production loss of 13400 cars and a revenue loss of Rs 460 crores for the company. Besides, Maruti Suzuki scripts took a dip at the Bombay Stock Exchange (BSE).

Workers Demands

Some 2000 of the 3000 workers at the plant went on a strike. The striking workers demanded the formation of separate independent Union for the Manesar Plant employees, alleging that the company had forced some staff to sign document to affiliate themselves with the Union at Gurgaon plant- the 'Maruti Suzuki Kamgar Union'. The striking workers believed that the existing 'Maruti Suzuki Kamgar Union' was a management backed union that did not know about the real problem of the workers.

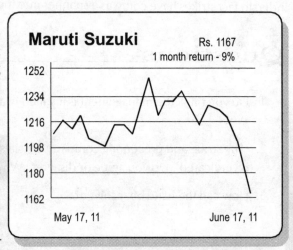

Management Stand

The management of Maruti Suzuki India maintained that there was no need of a sound union. The company's management declared the strike as illegal and sacked 11 workers who were said to be prime-movers behind orchestrating the strike.

Deadlock

The stand-off between the company's management and the striking workers resulted in a deadlock, with talks between the two parties failing to resolve the issues. The company's facility at Manesar that produces its best-seller hatchbacks and sedans like Swift, Swift Dzire, A-star and SX4 was hit hard.

The Manesar plant is the only one amongst Maruti's production facility that produces diesel models, some of which have long waiting periods. Rising petrol prices pumped up demand of diesel models.

Spill-over Effect

With no signs of resolution of the deadlock between the management and the workers, the stir threatened to 'spill' over to other companies, in that location. The workers in neighboring automakers and around twelve ancillary units joined the protest and threatened similar action at their companies, expressing solidarity with the striking workers of Maruti Suzuki India. In fact strikes have come as a spanner into the otherwise fast growing industrial belt of the country. The last 18 months saw disputes hitting other auto-company plants in the vicinity like Honda's Daruhera plant, HMSI's Manesar factory, Rico Auto's Gurgaon plant and Sunbeam Auto's Gurgaon plant. It is said that some companies are contemplating setting up facilities in other cities due to volatile industrial relations in the region. Workers of over 60 unions served notices to their respective management threatening tool-down for expressing solidarity with Maruti workers. This proposed tool-down was called off only after appeal from the state government.

Compensation Woes

The real problem of workers at Manesar plant seems to be pointing towards compensation woes of the contractual workers. About 85% of Maruti's 3000 workers at Manesar are contract workers, who are paid around Rs 6000 – 7000 per month, a third of the remuneration given to the permanent workers. However the company's HR maintains that it pay Rs 11000 – Rs 12000 per worker to the contract from whom the labor is sourced and it has no control over how much they pay to the labour. Around half of the workers at Maruti are contractual labours.

Governmental Intervention

With the strike entering seventh day, the state government of Haryana passed prohibitory orders on the on-going strike at Maruti Suzuki's Manesar plant. The matter was referred to the local labor court and industrial tribunal for adjudication. Under section 10(1) of the Industrial Dispute Act 1947, once the matter is under judicial scrutiny no party can prejudice the reference in the court by acts such as strikes and lock-outs. The court had to decide on four legal points – whether the strike is justified or not; if it is legal what relief can be granted; whether termination of 11 workers was justified; and if the termination is illegal what relief can be granted. The AITUC supported strike by the workers.

Tripartite-talks & Compromise

Several rounds if tripartite-talks were held between the management, worker's representatives and the government. Meanwhile there were accusations and counter accusations by both parties on retracting their stands. Finally a compromise was reached. The Maruti Suzuki's management decided to reinstate 11 sacked employees, however conduct internal enquiries, into their cases. The management would take action against those found guilty; however no one would lose his job. Instead of enforcing no work-no pay rule of eight days salary cut for every single day of the strike, the MSI management decided to deduct one days salary for each day of the strike. The strike was called-off. However confusion continued to prevail over the existence of the proposed new union, with contradicting claims from the parties. The management maintained on 'no second union' rant, section of workers still claiming new union and government taking a neutral stand.

Company	June 2011	May 2011	% Change
Maruti Suzuki	70020	72812	-4
Hyundai	30402	27366	11
Tata Motors	21993	27811	-21
Mahindra	16053	13316	21
Ford*	9145	8483	-8

*Includes exports

Sales Toll

Rising petrol prices, higher borrowing cost and a host of other factors have hit most car manufacturers hard and the sales have plummeted for most in June 2011, compared to last year. In case of Maruti the strike added to the list of factors that ultimately took a toll on the cars sales.

De-risking Indian Operations

Maruti Suzuki India had shifted production of Swift, Dzire and other diesel variants to its Manesar Plant from the parent Gurgaon plant in 2009. This was done to keep-up pace with the growing demand of diesel cars in wake of rising petrol prices. However the strike at Manesar plant forced it to rethink its strategy of total reliance on a single plant for producing all diesel variants. The company for the first time contemplated shifting production of its diesel hatchback & sedan variants partly to Gurgaon plant. Although because of factors like high cost and longer time duration, the transition shall not be easy, however the company wished to explore several possibilities in the future to de-risk Indian operations by increasing production facilities.

Wisdom at the End of Tunnel

After being hit by incessant strikes last year and suffering big blows on car sales in 2011, Maruti Suzuki seems to be back in reckoning after claiming the top three car brands positions in 2012, in terms of sales this year. The top three car brands by sales in India (2012) are Maruti Alto, Maruti Swift and Maruti Wagon R. Wagon R has pushed Hyundai i10 to number four position. Maruti is now expecting its news Dzire to razzmatazz the competitors even more.

So what turnaround the company's fortunes? Diesel version of Swift, Wagon R? Possibly…but that could have happened last year as well. That did not happen because the production was halted several times at its Manesar plant, in the northern part of the country, due to strikes. Infact Maruti had to ultimately shift some of its Swift Diesel production to its Gurgaon plant. The bookings of the diesel versions at the dealers were running into long pending list and things were hardly working for the company. The original demand of the striking workers at the Manesar plant was formation of a separate union than the existing Maruti Udyog Kamgar Union (MUKU). The workers at the Manesar plant felt that the exiting union was primarily interest representation of the workers at Gurgaon and hence they demanded a separate union that could address to their concerns, one them being wage-hike. The management of the company opposed the new union formation tooth and nail and the deadlock continued for several weeks.

Interestingly the new union has now been formed by the workers at Manesar plant and the company's management has not helped the workers register their new union but also has recognized the same. The union is also planning to take-up wage revision with the management. The present wage of workers at Manesar plant is around Rs. 18000/- per month that includes Rs. 8000/- as incentive. The resulting peace has presumably altered the sales figures of the company.

What led to this sudden change of heart on part of the company's management? But then what was the logic in opposing the new union in the first place, if later the company were to accept it, in fact help forming it? Second, if it was a fair demand then why did the management oppose it?

Surely, they realized that such a stand was not only being detrimental for the company in the form of low sales but more importantly they were losing the advantage to the competitors like Hyundai etc., but the Maruti story clearly shows:

1. People, and not anything else, are the real competitive advantage for a company. That is not to suggest that employees have an infinite right to demand but the legitimate needs & demands must also not be negated.

2. HR myopia is most damaging for any company. The workers with their union at Manesar plant shall always remember the 'struggle' more than the management's help in getting them register. Had the company realized it in the first instance itself not only the loss could have been avoided but bad PR and bruises on employee engagement could also have been avoided.

Questions

1. How far do you think are the worker's demands are justified? Also analyze the management's stand in this case.

2. Strikes lead to major losses. At a time when car sales are not looking-up, do you think Maruti can afford losing-out on the demand of diesel variants? Do you think the strike could have been avoided?

3. Do you think such strikes are spoiling the name of India as a labour-intensive country or the nation is in need of labour reforms?

Reference

- Workers on strike at Maruti's Manesar plant, June 4, 2011, articles.economictimes.indiatimes.com.
- Maruti sacks 11 employees at Manesar; Production hit, *Business Line*, June 7, 2011.
- Maruti stock drops as strike at Manesar plant continues, articles.economictimes.indiatimes.com, June 7, 2011.
- Strike at Maruti's Manesar plant enters fourth day, *Business Line*, June 8, 2011.
- Will not give into demand for second union: Maruti, *Business Line*, June 9, 2011.
- Strike at Maruti's Manesar plant enters sixth day, economictimes.indiatimes.com, June 9, 2011.
- Maruti Stir threatens to spill into neighborhood, *The Economic Times*, June 10, 2011.
- Maruti strike: Haryana clamps prohibitory orders, *Business Line*, June 11, 2011.
- Union plans tool-down in Gurgaon-Manesar as Maruti strike continues, *Business Line*, June 12, 2011.
- Worker's strike: Maruti inches towards compromise, *Business Line*, June 13, 2011.
- Maruti inches towards compromise formula to consider new union formation, *Business Line*, June 13, 2011.
- No headway in Maruti talks; strike enters 10th day, *Business Line*, June 14, 2011.
- Khan Henna, A thousand angry men, *Business Line*, June 15, 2011.
- Tool-down postponed on Haryana CM's appeal, *Business Line*, June 15, 2011.
- Chauhan Chanchal Pal, Philip Lijee, Maruti likely to shift Swift, Dzire production to old unit, *The Economic Times*, June 16, 2011.
- Swaminathan Padma, Maruti strike called off, but has it dented India's image, in.finance.yahoo.com/new, June 17, 2011.
- Maruti Suzuki scrip jumps over 3 pc on bourses in early trade, in.finance.yahoo.com/news, June 17, 2011.
- Strike at Maruti ends, production to resume today, *Business Line*, June 18, 2011.
- June car sales skid on costlier loans, fuel price hikes, *Business Line*, July 2, 2011.

Case Study 16

Air India Strikes

Air India Pilots union announced a strike in May 2012, which led to cancellation of several flights. Air India's pilots members of IPG (Indian Pilots Guild) took mass sick leave to protest the management decision to provide Boing-787 Dreamliner training to pilots from Indian Airlines. As the Air India management tried to minimize the disruption and operate the maximum flights possible, several flights were cancelled or delayed and the normal working was seriously disrupted for several weeks. The employees demanded pay parity, better working conditions and a CBI enquiry for huge loss. While, the Air India management declared the strike illegal and derecognized the Indian Commercial pilots' association (ICPA) besides sealing its offices in Delhi and Mumbai.

Air India, the state-owned flag carrier is the oldest and the largest airline of India. It is a part of the Indian government-owned Air India Limited (AIL) which is renamed as Air India Ltd. The airline operates a fleet of Airbus and Boeing aircrafts serving various continents. Its corporate office is located at the Air India Building at Nariman Point in South Mumbai. It is the 16th largest airline in Asia. Air India has two major domestic hubs at Indira Gandhi International Airport and Chhatrapati Shivaji International Airport.

It was founded in the year 1932 by J.R.D. Tata. In August 1953, the Indian air transport industry was nationalised to provide safe, smooth and economic air travel to the people. It involved eight warring airlines with different work cultures, horrendous safety record, disastrous financial conditions because of cut-throat competition and inefficient management in some. Thus come into existence Indian Airlines Corp and Air India Ltd to operate domestic and international long haul services. The nationalisation was also expected to spur growth, promote economic activity, rush assistance in times of natural calamities like flood, famine and earthquake, foster national integration and, above all, serve as the second line of defence in the event of war with another country. In 2007, Air India and Indian Airlines were merged along with their subsidiaries to form Air India Limited. Senseless merger of the two wings of the airline took loss figures to Rs. 7,200 crores (72 billion) by March 2009. This was followed by various restructuring plans which were not at all effective. Due to strike the revenue loss was estimated at around Rs. 300 crore. Even the state-run oil companies – the Indian Oil Corporation, the Bharat Petroleum Corporation Ltd. and the Hindustan Petroleum Corporation refused to supply fuel to the bleeding carrier.

When India woke to an era of liberalization of economic policies in 1991, it was least prepared for competition. Air India has a bloated workforce. In May 2012, it had a strength of 26,851 employees, including 1543 pilots.

> The Indian Pilots Guild on 23 May 2012 alleged that the Air India management was responsible for financial irregularities to the tune of Rs. 4,324 crore. Speaking to reporters at a press conference, Tauseef Mukaddam, IPG spokesman said that underutilisation of aircraft was due to lack of planning. The pilots, under the banner of Indian Pilots Guild (IPG), were agitating over the rescheduling of Boeing 787 Dreamliner training and matters relating to their career progression. Mukaddam said that the management deployed aircrafts on loss making routes and introduced routes before doing market research. On 9 May 2012, the high court had restrained over 200 agitating pilots from continuing their "illegal strike", reporting sick and staging demonstrations, a day after the airlines management sacked 10 pilots and derecognised their union.
>
> (**Source**: The Economic Times)
>
> On 23 May 2012, Air India filed a contempt petition against striking pilots in the Delhi High Court on grounds that the agitators have failed to comply with its previous order restraining them from undertaking the stir. Filing the petition through counsel Lalit Bhasin, Air India management said despite the court's restraint order, several opportunities were given to the striking pilots to resolve their issues but they failed to settle the matter. A contempt notice was issued to Air India pilots. The notice said that the pilots have to reply by July 13 and if they don't join work, they'll continue in contempt till then. If their contempt is upheld after they file their reply on July 13, court will inflict punishment of three months civil imprisonment. Earlier in the day, Air India management had filed a contempt petition in the high court against the striking pilots on the ground that they have failed to comply with the court's earlier order restraining them from undertaking the stir.
>
> (**Source**: IBN live)
>
> It faces uphill challenges to tackle a bloated cost structure, a difficult task given a workforce that is heavily unionized. Air India has to secure a massive debt and operational overhaul if it is to survive in a market growing at 20 percent a year. Besides of course to lure customers and grab lost market share. The huge debt running into billions of dollars won't be easy for Air India to clear and it would need to cut unprofitable routes and create a new plan that would focus on a hub-and-spoke route model.

Questions

1. 'Poor HR management, planning & strategy have been largely responsible for the pathetic state of the national carrier'. Do you agree? Substantiate.
2. 'The strike by Pilots on compensation issues is reflection of larger disengagement'. Opinionate.
3. What HR strategies would you propose to turnaround the fortunes of Air India? You can also study the best-in-class HR practices from other airline, particularly national carriers.

Case Study 17

Women Participation in Workforce

At 34.2 percent, India's rate of female participation in the labor force is the lowest of any of the BRIC countries, according to U.N. statistics. Women make up 42 percent of college graduates in India, yet even those with diplomas are expected to let their careers take a back seat to caring for husband, children, and elderly parents. The Center for Work-Life Policy, a Manhattan think tank, conducted a study in the year 2010 on the challenges Indian women face in the workplace, and found that in fact, gender disparities at Indian companies grow more pronounced in management's upper ranks.

Who is to be held responsible for such low participation of females in the workforce? Many blame the organization for being inflexible and un-empathetic towards women. Some critics even put some organizations in the bracket of being biased towards women and as the cliché goes for women there is a glass-ceiling at the top. During the India Economic Forum-2009, Indra Nooyi, chief executive officer, PepsiCo spoke about her own personal experiences as a woman employee. She said, "The resume of a successful woman looks impressive but no one knows the heart aches and breaks that go in its making and as a woman I understand what other working women like me go through." There are some who put the blame on managers and point to the fact that most of them either berate women colleagues or do not let them decide at all. Male managers, many feel, do not come-out honest towards women colleagues, a trait that women do not appreciate. Others think that that the women employees themselves are to blame for such a dismal rate of women participation in India. A primary research conducted on 1,140 women professionals shows 'career orientation' being the key factor, Indian women can be segmented into: a) Career Primary, b) Career and Home and c) Home Primary. They approximate into a distribution of 19%, 58% and 23% of women in the workforce — data which requires more authentication and individualization to each workplace. The second and major category (Career & Home – 58%) seems to causes maximum heartburn to talent managers. High attrition, lethargy in managerial evolution and low engagement are some key issues. The study finding indicates that a stressor at home forces the woman to work. Once it is removed, she quits. While at work, she seeks flexibility, templatised work with little goal pressure and prefers to remain an individual contributor life-long. Hence the study feels that companies should not waste their energies on this category and instead focus on the first category of female employees that is those belonging to the 'Career Primary'.

Despite this blame-game, several companies have taken wonderful initiatives for their women employees. CSC has not only flexible hours for women but they have also launched an exclusive website for its women employees called Planet W. The site acts as a discussion forum to exchange ideas and get useful tips on diverse issues. Google has taxis on call for employees, a particular draw for women who may need to rush home to care for a sick family member. German drugmaker Boehringer Ingelheim, mindful that families frown on young women traveling alone, will pay for an employee to bring her mother along on longer trips.

Tata lead in many ways the business scenario in India. They are truly the captains of the Indian Industry. When it comes to the issue of women equality & diversity as well they are miles ahead of others. They provide a beckon of light to those women who are talented and want to make a successful career. Tata SCIP is a career transition management programme for women professionals who have taken a break of 1-8 years for any reason, and wish to re-enter the professional space. The programme provides opportunities for such women to take on flexi-hour assignments with various TATA group companies. For all those aspiring women out there looking for respectable second career, TATA SCIP is the answer. Talk about a pioneer in India, in terms of engaging the hugely talented women workforce in this country, Tata's are leagues ahead. Here is a snapshot of various initiatives of Tata Group of companies in India and away –

Tata Consultancy Services (TCS)	High women participation rate (30.3%) Women occupy 11% of senior management positions Encourage women to take-up top leadership roles not only in India but in all 42 countries that it operates.
Tata Motors	Started a initiative called '*Tata Motor's Diversity Pudding*' to increase the percentage of women in workforce (present

	only 3.5%)The trim line of Tata World Truck in Jamshedpur is completely managed by womenTrain women to undertake physical tasks such operating dumpers, bulldozers, overhead cranes and loco operatives. The initiative is called '*Tejaswini*'
Tata Capital, TCS, Titan, Tata Indicom, Tata Teleservices	Flexibility in roles, Job-rotation across businesses, practices and functions
Taj Hotels	Women make-up almost half the employee-size

Some women who have been in top roles across Tata Group (2011)

(*Source:* ET)

1. Simone Tata, Chairperson, Trent
2. Ritu Anand, VP & deputy global head of HR, head global talent management, TCS, India
3. Deborah Hadwen, CEO, TCS, Australia
4. Delna Avari, Product Head, Tata Motors
5. Veetika Deoras, Deputy VP (brand Marketing), Tata Captal
6. Jia Maheshwari, DGM Tata Reality & Infrastructure
7. Sohini Thakur, Head of Business HR, Tata Steel
8. Jyoti Narang, COO, Taj Hotels
9. Deepa Harris, Senior VP – Marketing & Sales, Taj Hotels
10. Renu Basu, Head – Sales, Taj Hotels
11. Suma Venkatesh, Director Development, Taj Hotels
12. Mridula Tangirala, Director – Operations, Tajsafaris
13. Ashrafi Matcheswala, GM, Taj Group
14. Ritu Chawla, DGM, Taj Krishna, Hyderabad

While there have been some companies in India that have similar stories to share, yet there have been very few who have been able to emulate what Tata group has been able to do in terms of engaging the female employees.

Questions

1. Who do you think is responsible for such low participation of females in the workforce?
2. Evaluate the practices of the Tata Group towards women employees and come-out with a broad set of suggestions to increase the participation of females in the workforce and increase their engagement levels.

References

- Kaushal Ranjana, Corporates open gates for women employees, *India Today*, New Delhi, November 28, 2009.
- Saundarya Rajesh, Companies need to classify their women employees and engage with them accordingly, *The Economic Times*, Bangalore, Dec. 16, 2011.
- Srivastava Mehul, Keeping Women on the Job in India - Companies are using family-friendly perks to hold on to female workers, *Bloomberg Business Week*, March 3, 2011.
- Subramanian, Ravi, How should managers deal with women employees at work? *The Economic Times*, Bangalore, March 8, 2011.
- Vijayraghavan Kala, Philip Lijee, A Fair Advantage for Women at Bombay House, *The Economic Times*, Bangalore, December, 21, 2011.

Case Study 18

Automating to Match Scale

India is the fast becoming the preferred destination of the world. Being one of the very few growing economies of the world, India commands considerable clout in the world of business, today. Some of the Indian companies that have led this growth story in this country are Infosys and Reliance. Such prodigious growth has meant that a large number of applicants from within the country wanted to apply in such companies. Besides the company lesser known outside the country wanted to build awareness about themselves abroad. Such challenges necessitated automation of HR processes.

Infosys started this with automating its hiring process. Not only could its leverage its presence and proportion through automation but it could also make the hiring process much more efficient. The online submission & screening of applications, online testing and database creation of potential & aspiring candidates. Millions of candidates from all over the world could access and apply to Infosys through a single window. The success of the automation of the hiring process encouraged Infosys to automate other HR processes. All internal HR systems were shifted onto the company's intranet in the period of 2000-2002. Elements of web 2.0 also appeared in the intranet that enabled employees to interact virtually with the HR and the top management.

Reliance Communications or RCom, part of the Anil Dhirubhai Ambani Group (ADAG), is India's second-biggest mobile phone services firm with some 92 million customers. Being in the fast growing telecom business, Reliance Communications, or RCom, has seen customer demand soar as at other phone firms. Such demand has meant growth in employee base and with that the complexities have also grown in acquiring, keeping, maintaining, developing, appraising and compensating them. The automation of HR processes in RCom, a company of 53,000 employees, helped to reduce the burden, off-loading HR from a lot of repetitive jobs. This not only ensured that the HR processes became more efficient and effective but also meant that the valuable time of HR was freed for focusing on strategic employee issues like communication & engagement.. Every event in an employee's lifecycle is managed on the company's Intranet through its portal, MyWorld. It captures a potential's interest to work at RCom, does regular reviews, productivity tracking, training and even exit interviews.

Job rotations both at RCom and between it and ADAG, for instance, are driven by daily postings. Even in the middle to senior levels, managers have moved to ADAG's direct-to-home television, Big TV, and employees are encouraged to make such movements. Employee interest is kept high in the portal with ADAG Chairman Anil Ambani and other top executives blogging on it.

Questions

1. How far do you think automation has helped in Infosys & RCom? Count other advantages of automation.
2. Do you think automation of HR systems means dehumanizing human management systems? Articulate with strong rationale.

Case Study 19

Employee-voices on Social Media

About a year back, Kimberley Swann, a 16-year-old was fired from Ivell Marketing & Logistics, a product development and sourcing company, for describing her job as 'boring' on Facebook. Miss Swann working as an office administrator found her job of filing, stapling, shredding hole-punches and scanning paper as wasteful and monotonous and so she let out steam by sharing the same with her friends on Facebook. She was given marching orders from the Ivell premises.

Should employees criticizing their organizations or employers on social networking sites be seen as a problem or symptom to a bigger problem? Some companies are reportedly contemplating a social media policy. Such policies seek to impose restrictions on its employees' tweets, blogs and other social media messages. The defaulters face warnings, or even termination. But the question is: Will this quell employees' voices on the social media? Again, in the age of ubiquitisation of social media, can such restrictions really make a difference? Should companies try to gag such voices or should they make an attempt at finding out the reasons behind such disenchantment?

In another incident, a women employee, who had posted a negative comment about her boss on her Facebook page from her personal computer on personal time, was reportedly suspended and then fired for her Facebook postings because the posting violated the company's internet policies. In a landmark legal action regarding employees online postings, the National Labor Relations Board (NLRB) filed a complaint against the women employee's company, a Connecticut ambulance company, that fired a worker because of what she posted on Facebook.

The National Labor Relations Board (NLRB) is the federal agency in US that administers the National Labor Relations Act, the primary law governing relations between unions and employers in the private sector. The NLRA protects workers who form, join, support, or assist labor unions, and protects groups of workers (two or more employees) who engage in protected concerted activities without a union seeking to modify their wages or working conditions. The National Labor Relations Act protects both non-union and union employees against employer and union discrimination based on union-related activities.

According to the NLRB, "An NLRB investigation found that the employee's Facebook postings constituted protected concerted activity, and that the company's blogging and internet posting policy contained unlawful provisions, including one that prohibited employees from making disparaging remarks when discussing the company or supervisors and another that prohibited employees from depicting the company in any way over the internet without company permission." The financial terms of the settlement were not disclosed. The company, is also reportedly changing its blogging and Internet use policies in ways that will no longer prohibit employees from talking about work online, even if such talk constitutes what the company called online badmouthing.

Most companies are however very apprehensive about letting their employees speak freely on social media sites. A 2011 survey by Robert Half Technology, that interviewed 1400 CIOs (chief information officers) of companies with over 100 employees, reveals the following results with regard to using social networking sites at work:

- 31% of companies prohibit all access (down from 54% in 2009)
- 51% of companies permit access for business purposes only (up from 19% in 2009)
- 14% of companies permit access for limited personal use (down from 16% in 2009)
- 4% of companies permit any access for personal use (down from 10% in 2009)

This is in completely in contrast to the growing tribe of employees using social media at their workplaces. According to a recent survey by global Internet content security provider Trend Micro, the percentage of employees visiting social networking sites at the workplace globally rose to 24 per cent this year from just 18 per cent in 2008, even as more companies are restricting access to such Web sites. According to Nielsen research, social network traffic grew by 43% from June 2009 to June 2010.

But can companies really control what employee say on social media? Can a social media policy help? Can the same social media, which is becoming a cause of concern for some employers unable to contain the voices of dissention of their employees, could become a strength for them if the word 'spread' changed to positive?

Many experts feel that it is not the social medial policy of gagging employee voices that will work, instead trust is the operative word. In an article Jeannette Paladino quoted IBM's Jon Iwata, SVP, Marketing & Communications saying –"Communications, points out the company can't control what employees say. This scares the heck out of CEOs who don't trust their employees to do the right thing. But as Iwata points out, the same policies that apply to an employee who might give away company secrets in a bar apply to the employee who is posting a tweet. IBM isn't afraid of social media because, as Iwata says at the conclusion of the video, "employees can be trusted."

If a video on YouTube has made a local taxi-driver of Varanasi a celebrity, and if an engaging Facebook account has made some popular foreign (Starbucks, Coca-Cola, Skittles) and Indian (Vodafone Zoo Zoos, Fastrack, Tata Docomo) brands garner a huge following, then there must be more to social media than being a negative publicity tool.

Many experts feel that it's time that companies started identifying how they can leverage social media to connect and better engage with their own employees. Also, companies must try to address 'real' problems by doing a root-cause analysis, rather than quell dissent on the social media. Additionally, they must also provide for internal communicable platforms that allow for a dialogue between the firm and its employee constituents.

The content generated from such platforms can then be used as a feedback tool to better internal processes. It would bode well for companies to look at social media as an opportunity rather than a threat. Infosys for instance after burning its fingers with a social media policy, launched a facebook version of internal blog called the Infy Bubble. Infy Bubble', is supposedly a platform for disgruntled Infoscions to vent on. The site mirrors Facebook and allows employees to connect across borders with colleagues as well as bicker about anything they want.

Questions

1. Do you think it is possible to curb the voices of employees on social media in this era of social networking? How far do you a social media policy for the employees shall help?

2. Can companies use social media to connect & communicate with employees better?
3. The growing incidence of usage of social media at workplace, is it a matter of concern to employers?

References

- Cohen Jeffrey L., 31% of companies block employees from using social media, July 28, 2011, http://socialmediab2b.com/2011/07/company-block-employee-social-networ/

- Dell Jolie 'O', Employee fired over Facebook comments settles law suit, Feb. 9, 2011, http://mashable.com/2011/02/08/facebook-employment-speech-lawsuit/

- Doyle Alison, National Labour Relations Board (NLRB), http://jobsearch.about.com/od/employmentlaw/g/nlrb.htm.

- Dyle Alison, Fired for Facebook, http://jobsearch.about.com/od/employeerights/a/fired-for-facebook.htm.

- Paladino Jeannette, Companies need to trust their employees as brand advocates, http://writespeaksell.com/can-employees-be-trusted-as-brand-advocates-using-social-media.

- Sengupta Debashish, Titus Ray, Policing social media isn't a smart policy, *Business Line*, Aug. 17, 2010.

- Social Work? More companies permit social networking on the job, Robert Half Technology Survey reveals, May 26, 2011, http://www.prnewswire.com/news-releases/social-work-more-companies-permit-social-networking-on-the-job-robert-half-technology-survey-reveals-122650448.html.

- Stroud Jim, How to build employee engagement using social media? May 2, 2011, http://www.therecruiterslounge.com/2011/05/02/how-to-build-employee-engagement-using-social-media/

- Swaminathan Padma, Infosys gives its employees 'a voice', July 12, 2010, http://in.finance.yahoo.com/news/Infosys-gives-employees-voice-yahoofinancein-2281851788.html.

Case Study 20

On-boarding at Taj Hotels

The Indian Hotels Company Limited (IHCL) and its subsidiaries are collectively known as Taj Hotels Resorts and Palaces and are recognized as one of Asia's largest and finest hotel company. Incorporated by the founder of the Tata Group, Mr. Jamsetji N. Tata, the company opened its first property, The Taj Mahal Palace Hotel, Bombay in 1903. The Taj, a symbol of Indian hospitality, completed its centenary year in 2003.

Taj Hotels Resort and Palaces comprises more than 60 hotels in 45 locations across India with an additional 15 international hotels in the Malaysia, United Kingdom, United States of America, Bhutan, Sri Lanka, Africa, the Middle East and Australia.

Spanning the length and breadth of the country, gracing important industrial towns and cities, beaches, hill stations, historical and pilgrim centers and wildlife destinations, each Taj hotel offers the luxury of service, the apogee of Indian hospitality, vantage locations, modern amenities and business facilities.

Taj Hotels Resorts and Palaces is part of the house of Tatas which is renowned for conducting its business in value oriented, ethics driven business practices. Historically, the house of Tatas recognized for pioneering social welfare, business ethics and corporate social responsibility in the country. In the present business context, it has translated to a firm set of values and commitment to ethical business practices which is present across all group companies. The Taj has a detailed code of conduct guidelines, which is applied across all businesses and is integral to the way we operate. With ethical business practices and strong sense of values underpinning the way our organization operates, it is essential that we aim to hire candidates with the right value and culture fit. The endeavor is to hire individuals who would contribute to the organizations growth within the boundaries of ethical business practice and without compromising on personal integrity.

One of the key components of the Taj as an employer brand is its value driven practices. All recruitment criteria emphasize the requirement of high levels of personal and work ethic. From hiring at campus recruitment programs to sourcing of board level executives, the organization emphasizes on this attribute as a prerequisite for prospective candidates and the same is clearly enunciated in the campus presentations, position guidelines and mandates provided to search agencies.

The Selection process of external candidates includes behavioral aspects to determine the ethic and culture fit in the organization. Also every candidate goes through a detailed background check including both professional and personal dimensions, which provide inputs for the final selection. There are other mechanisms which support hiring of candidates with the right culture fit. For example the organization prefers to hire external candidates through its internal employee referral program called 'Vibes'. Taj believes that its employees are advocates of its unique culture and automatically refer candidates who are a good culture fit in the Taj.

Welcoming New Associates

The process of engaging and welcoming a prospective employee to Taj begins much before the selection of the candidate. The organizations selection processes are designed to make all prospective candidates feel welcome and get a taste of the warm Taj culture. It is a common practice for interviewees to be shown around parts of the hotel and have an insight into their intended place of work. Interviewees are encouraged to have a meal in the staff dining room and interact with the associates present there. Post selection this is followed by regular interactions with the HR SPOC. In the campus selection processes, where normally there is gap of 4-5 months before joining, the interaction is kept alive by sharing happenings, new initiatives and other points of interest.

On the day of joining, the associate is received by the HR on arriving at the hotel and begins the institutionalized orientation process of "TAP ME" – The Taj Acculturation Process for Managing Excellence. TAP ME is applicable to all new joinees across levels and across all hotels. The day begins with the HR SPOC explaining the "dos and don'ts" and continues into a 15 day long process during which the inductee is exposed to the organization's work practices, norms and policies. A welcome letter with the candidate's photograph is placed on notice boards across the hotel to enable other employees to identify the new member of the family. As part of the process, the new joinee is introduced to the senior leadership team of the hotel within two days of joining. The other aspects of TAP ME include orientation to the code of conduct practices, mandatory certifications including fire safety, first aid etc., and familiarization with the history and culture of the organization.

Besides this individual hotels develop customized initiatives which are added on to the standardized TAP ME for greater effectiveness. One example is the "The Orange Club" where new joinees are given orange badges to distinguish them from the older employees. Other aspects of the scheme focus on providing support during the initial phase and a 60 day review by the HR SPOC to ensure that the associate is settling well in the new assignment. The other example is "Red Carpet" where the associate goes through a series of interactions with the senior management until completion of the first six months. Post TAP ME, when the new joinee joins the workplace, he/she is attached to a 'Buddy' – a colleague from the same department, who provides guidance and assists the new incumbent to get acquainted with the norms and practices of the workplace.

Questions

1. Taj Hotels believe that - "A delighted employee leads to a delighted guest". How far do you think such belief is true? What lessons can be learnt from the Taj-way of welcoming new employees?

2. 'Early engagement of employee goes a long way in keeping them enthused & engaged for a long time'. Comment on this statement.

3. Study the response of employee of Taj Hotel during the Mumbai terror attack from the web media and draw parallels to the on-boarding practices at Taj.

Case Study 21

YUM – Increasing Footprint through Effective Talent Management

Yum is a $16 billion Kentucky – based company and the owner of famous restaurant chains like KFC, Pizza-Hut and Taco Bell. With over 35000 restaurants worldwide and in keeping with its aggressive growth plans, the company needs to develop large number of managers as quickly as possible.

At one time Yum opened two KFC restaurants everyday in China. This required a strategic planning for talent to be available to match this scale. Yum made it a point to prepare enough restaurants managers at a rapid pace and this became a key part of their talent strategy. Such initiatives of Yum bore fruits. Globally, during the period of recession (July – September 2009), when the same-store sales were flat, the company still recorded a 18% jump in profits, primarily due to its strong sales in China.

In India, as well, Yum is following the same strategy. 'While a same store sale of KFC in India is growing at 7%, those of Pizza-Hut are growing at over 20%.' The parent company is planning to invest an additional $ 100-120 million in the Indian operations in terms of direct equity by 2015. The company has already invested $100 million in opening around 200 restaurants in the country. Currently there are 140 Pizza Hut stores in 35 Indian cities and 55 KFC stores across 12 cities. Yum India is working towards an overall restaurant footprint of 1000 by 2015 in 62 cities. Effective management of talent will be key to actualize such ambitions growth targets. In line with its vision of being a 'fine dining company that feeds the world', the parent company wants to make Yum India a billion dollar company. The company does not believe in running the business with expatriates and considers local management as key. Yum believes localization to be a western brand with an Indian heart. For instance, close to 60-70% sales of Pizza-Hut is vegetarian. Availability of local talent and talent preparedness is important to match both the scale and the style. The global Chairman and CEO of Yum, David C Novak believes that not only India has been a tremendous source of talent in the past but will continue to be an exporter of talent in the future.

Bench planning has been the cornerstone of Yum's talent strategy. The company has continuously focused on 'what are the critical roles and who's ready? And what kind of development experiences are required to set the future leaders up for continued success. Yum University and global learning services is dedicated towards building leaders by transitioning them for next roles, which mean a rising star (talent) can quickly gain real-time experiences in key operational & business skills.

Questions

1) How do you think Yum prioritized its talent management strategy to post higher profits in a downturn?

2) Do you think Yum will be able to replicate its performance in India as it did in China?

3) How is the identification of 'critical roles' key to talent planning?

Case Study 22

Indian Problem, Singaporean Solution – Will it Work?

What happens when most of the employees receive outstanding ranking (9 or 10 out of 10) from their supervisors?

What happens when these ranking are given without even a face-to-face meeting between the appraise and the appraiser?

What happens when most employees feel that Performance Appraisal (PAR) system is neither fair nor objective?

What happens when despite high performance ratings received by the employees, their department's performance shows decline?

It's enough indication that something is fundamentally flawed in the system or the system itself is flawed. That's what the Department of Personnel and Training (DoPT) has come to a conclusion regarding the PAR of the Civil Service officers under various ministries. All the above symptoms discussed above were visible.

DoPT suggests embracing a Singaporean model that is stated to be far more fair and rigorous. The proposed system will hold the supervisors more accountable for the ratings that they give to the rates and necessitates them to support their ratings with evidences. The proposed system also recognizes the fact that promotions are not only a outcome of past performance but also dependent on the Current Estimated Potential (CEP) or simply the officers' expected performance in the higher role. The CEP will allow accelerated promotions to deserving officers and links the pace of promotions to an estimation of the highest level of work an offence can competently handle before his retirement and considers the official's intellectual qualities, result orientation and leadership qualities for appraisal.

The diagnosis of a faulty PAR by DoPT is correct. The solution suggested based on Singapore model is also a noble thought. However many experts

feel that the suggestion fails to recognize that the success of any initiative, such as these, require 'design' interventions. The highly politicized environment, bureaucratic set-up and a deep-set culture of entitlement could come as a major roadblock to the new PAR.

Research has proven more than once that such one-of measures do not work. Copying 'best-practices' from successful organizations and imposing them on another organization, assuming that it will be solution to all the ills that plague it, is nothing more than wishful thinking. They are cosmetic reliefs that do not last long. The true face will come out sooner or later as the problems will persist.

Questions

1. Do you think performance appraisal systems in general lack objectivity? How can you make appraisals more objective?
2. Do you agree with the solution suggested by DoPT? Substantiate.

Case Study 23

S(KILL) SALES: Gaps in Sales Training

Mathew joined Pioneer Animal Pharma Ltd. recently as a Sales Executive. Mathew, along with 20 other new recruits was sent for a month long training program at the company's Delhi factory office. The sprawling campus of the Delhi factory was quite impressive. The Factory premises also resided the training facility.

Mathew and other trainees were lodged in a three star hotel in Delhi at the cost of the company. The transport and boarding was also at company's expenses. The trainees would report every day morning at the factory training facility. After finishing their breakfast, they would be taken to a nice air-conditioned training room and taken through multiple sessions, mostly on product and technical knowledge.

From the second day onwards they started to have a test on previous day's learning. The test would be objective in nature and designed purely to test the conceptual skills of the trainees. Mathew's ability to grasp the product and technical knowledge was very good and he constantly scored highest amongst the group of trainees. This was first job for Mathew after his graduation and he worked very hard in remembering the product formulations, technical aspects like amino acids, salts etc.

On the penultimate day of the training, the trainees were told about 'detailing'. Detailing is basically the way in which the sales guy makes a presentation in front of the doctor and is considered to be important in the entire pharma-sales process. The trainees were first given a demonstration by the training manager. This was followed by an in-house simulation, where one of the training manager posed as a doctor and one by one all the trainees rehearsed the act of 'detailing'. Mathew did not feel much challenge in the same. On the last day of the training Mathew received an award from the Vice-President of the firm for scoring highest aggregate marks in their month-long daily tests based on the training content. Mathew was told that his name would also be published in the quarterly pull-out of the company. Mathew was thrilled & excited and was raring to go on the field.

Mathew was posted in a small, dusty town in the northern part of the country. The otherwise sleepy town is famous for its dairy farms. The milk produced here is mainly exported to Delhi, Punjab and Rajasthan. Mathew found a place to live-in and found the first few days in his job very chaotic. The scene here was so different from the air-conditioned confines of the training room. Managing the route was a challenge in itself. Each route was of minimum 50 kilometers which meant that he had to commute an average of 100 kilometers everyday on his two-wheeler on broken rural roads. The veterinary doctors were very difficult to approach but veterinary sales being overtly a prescription market, he hardly had a choice.

Over a period of time he also learnt that in many villages instead of the veterinary doctor, it was the local self-proclaimed animal doctor who ruled the roost. Contacting them and convincing them was even more difficult. His 'detailing folders and detailing techniques hardly worked on them. Most chemists were very rugged and hardly polite. Dealing with them was not easy. At times he would have to wait for long hours at a dairy farm or a poultry farm. He did not know on such occasions whether to wait or proceed for the next call.

His clients and dealers would have strange demands at times that he never knew how to deal with. At times they even conflicted his ethical principles. The town, being a being a dairy rich place, had lot of demand of medicines for the cattle. Mathew would many times talk about all the medicines rather than specifically understand the customer needs, much to the frustration of the doctor or other clients. Mathew wondered why he was not told about all this during the training program.

Mathew story could be the story of any person working in sales. The competencies of a sales person are developed and polished by the companies through sales training programs. But many-a- times, post the training, there is gap between what sales person's performance and what is desired from the person on-the-field. We call this 'competency-gap'.

Mr. Kawaljit Singh Chadha, Director Von Remedies, Himachal Pradesh (India) feels that for a pharma sales person the basic knowledge of medicines and salts used in formulations is very important. But along with this knowledge, he should be very good in his ability to convince the doctor, who is key in pharma sales. He should have good marketing skills that should combine ethical sales. A good pharma sales person must be able to build a good team and should have leadership skills. Mr. Chadha also opined that companies must have a combination of classroom and field-based training. The classroom training would help them to gain good product and technical knowledge; on the other hand the field exposure would help them to understand the practical realties and problems on the field – like many times getting an appointment from the doctor in itself is a challenge.

Mr. Rajesh Roy, another senior pharmaceutical professional, feels that competencies in a pharma sales person can be developed only through a combination of classroom and on-the-field training. The classroom training prepares a person in terms of his product-knowledge, etiquettes & mannerisms; whereas the field training helps him to understand practical situations and how deal with them. One doctor may give 30 minutes time to a sales person while another doctor may give only 3 minutes. How does the sales person deal with both these doctors effectively can only be learnt on the field. A lot of learning is actually experiential.

According to Roland Berger Strategy Consultants, Training, coaching and development of sales reps is one of the key area to be addressed to improve the effectiveness of the sales force, that can be achieved only through upfront training for sales managers and reps.

Going back to Mathew's case the training program that he received scored well on developing product and technical knowledge but lacked from providing the trainees an experience of the field and various issues one confronts in the field. A competency-based approach to training, with a combination of classroom and field training methods, to develop such competencies would help companies to nurture more and more successful sales people in the organization, contributing to both the individual & organizational benefit.

The last time I heard Mathew had left the company and was contemplating what his future course of actions would be. As for the company, they had lost on a good potential and the cost of hiring & training Mathew, besides of course now having to incur re-hiring and re-training cost for the new candidate.

Questions

1. What do you think went wrong with training in Mathew's case?
2. What are the consequences of poorly designed training programs? Provide suggestions to design Mathew Sales Training Program better.

Case Study 24

Strike at MRF Tyre Plant

MRF is the leader in the category and holds the number 1 position since the last 21 consecutive years. The company was established by Mammen Mappillai as a toy balloon manufacturing company. Then soon MRF emerged as the leading manufacturer of tread rubber. It was the first tyre company in India to reach a turnover of INR 5000crores. The company is backed by superior R&D technology and it rolls out tyres from its 6 interdependent production facilities. It has manufacturing units in Goa, Ankenpally, Medak, Tiruvottiyur, Arakkonam, Kottayam, Puducherry and Trichy. The Arakkonam factory has a production of 45000 truck tyres and 30000 tubes every day, Puducherry plant produces 13500 truck tyres per day and Tiruvattiyur plant produces 6500 tyres a day. The output from these three factories account for around INR 4500crores per year.

All was well in the Arakkonam MRF Tyre plant, till the company decided to employ contract labours for direct production. The permanent workers started protesting such use of contractual workers by the company. The protest in the Arakkonam factory started since 3rd October 2010 that ballooned in to a full-blown strike by the workers. The workers started a sit-in strike from 10th October 2010. The local labour union, spearheading strike, backed by the United Labour Federation alleged that as a matter of policy only permanent workers were allowed in direct manufacturing of tyres. However the management had employed contract labourers on lesser wage for direct manufacturing. The Arakkonam plant employed about 5200 contract employees and 800 permanent employees. As per the company policy, the contract workers who complete 484 days were eligible for permanent employee status. However, instead of making the eligible contract workers permanent they were being merely used in direct manufacturing at a lesser wage, the union alleged. Certain permanent workers had also been dismissed by the company.

Besides the Arakkonam plant, the Puducherry and Tiruvottiyur plants workers also joined the strike and production was hit in these two plants also. The common demands of the Arakkonam and Puducherry plants employees were the reinstatement of the dismissed workers and wage revision, besides sticking to the policy on contract labours. The union also demanded the withdrawal of the CCTV cameras installed in the factory premises. They alleged that it intruded the workers privacy. The union demanded that the management should set up surveillance cameras only at the main gate and in the scrap yard, instead of in the canteen and work spaces. The Arakkonam plant union also wanted the management to recognize the "MRF United Workers Union" which claimed to have the majority of the support from the workers.

The strike went on for two days till the MRF Workers Union President asked the employees to stop the strike in all the three factories. There had been similar strike last year as well, around the same time of the year that ended without much resolution. They called off the strike taking into account the forthcoming Union elections which were to be held on 30th October. The Union leader also said that there after any struggle by the employees will be duly planned and thus the strike was paused. However the issue was far from being over.

Questions

Q. 1. Discuss the issue of contract labours in this case and analyze the same in light of the labour laws.

Q. 2. Do you think the demands of the workers are justified? Do you think frequent strikes are damaging the industrial climate of the nation?

References

Business Standard. (2010, October 12). *MRF employees call off sit-in strike*. Retrieved from Business Standard: http://www.business-standard.com/article/companies/mrf-employees-call-off-sit-in-strike-110101200232_1.html

Business Standard. (2010, October 12). *Strike halts work at 2 MRF units*. Retrieved from Business Standard: http://www.business-standard.com/article/companies/strike-halts-work-at-2-mrf-units-110101200030_1.html

ET. (2010, October 12). *Production at MRF hit after strike: Union*. Retrieved from The Economic Times: http://articles.economictimes.indiatimes.com/2010-10-12/news/27605311_1_tyres-arakkonam-mrf

Indian Express. (2010, October 12). *Staff puts the brakes on MRF Tyres*. Retrieved from Indian Express: http://archive.indianexpress.com/news/staff-puts-the-brakes-on-mrf-tyres/696519/

PTI. (2010, October 12). *Strike stalls MRF tyre unit*. Retrieved from The Hindu: http://www.thehindu.com/business/Industry/strike-stalls-mrf-tyre-unit/article826864.ece

Rediff. (2010, October 13). *MRF employees to resume work today*. Retrieved from Rediff: http://www.rediff.com/money/report/mrf-employees-to-resume-work-today/20101013.htm

Case Study 25

The New Generation Army

Violent clash between the Army soldiers and officers at Merrut cannot be ignored as an one-off incident. Neither should it be read as an impending mutiny. But definitely the times are changing and Indian army seems to be a 'generation' behind!

The Incident

The incident happened during a inter-company boxing match. One version says that a solider tried his best but lost a friendly boxing match. One of the officers confronts him after the match, publicly ridicules him and thrashes him. The soldier does not take the insult lying down and retaliates. A prolonged physical clash ensues between soldiers and officers. The ugly incident leaves army red-faced and embarrassed.

As expected a committee has been set-up to inquire into the incident. And in all possibility the erring soldiers and officers will be reprimanded and punished. But will that really put an end to what seems to be a systemic issue brewing inside the organization.

This is not the first of such incident in recent times. In the last two years this is the fourth such incident where soldiers have given back a fist for a fist. Although the top brass of the Army have come down heavily against such errants and have handed them exemplary punishments, the question is will that suffice. The repetition of such incidents, nevertheless, indicates that the problem may be lying elsewhere.

Gen Y Soldiers

Gen Y is populating the Indian Army, like many other organizations in big numbers. If reports are to be believed then the new age soldiers are not only better educated but also more aspirational. This also confirms research literature on Gen Y. A more educated, aspirational and high on self-esteem Gen Y soldier may be expecting more respect from their officers.

In fact research literature indicates that Gen Y employees do not accept authority by the virtue of organizational hierarchy. They accept authority by example and for a limited time-frame. In other words, the superior gets respect not for his position but for the exemplary performance that he/she puts forth. The respect lasts as long as the such behaviour of the superior lasts. In the coming years, as more Gen Yers will enter the Indian Army, managing this new generation soldiers will be a challenge.

Structure and Leadership

Officers and soldiers are not only differentiated by rank but also by class within the organization. A clear class system seems to be prevailing within the organization and treatment is not equal for the soldiers. A highly hierarchical structure ensures that soldiers at the bottom of the pyramid are only supposed to listen and follow. The power is highly centralized at the top.

Culture

A rigid culture of command and control is highlight of the army. The same has been followed since the British Raj and this is perhaps one of the very few institutions that has been untouched by changes in past 65 odd years of Indian independence.

Control Systems

Carrot and stick in the all practical sense, the latter being used in both letter and spirit for managing the soldiers, as is evident from the recent incidents.

Such organizational structure, culture and control systems seem totally incompatible with the new generation inducts in the Indian Army. Organizations all over the world are experiencing the phenomena of multi-generations at work. The increasing tension between Gen X bosses and Gen Y employees is not only the problem of the Army but of many organizations around the world. The organizations that are able to recognize the fact are trying to decipher Gen Y and in the process trying to find out newer and better ways to manage and engage them. The others are blissfully unaware and completely in dark.

A seminal work highlighting the need to change the organizational design of the Indian Army was recently done as a Manekshaw Paper titled 'Staff System in the Indian Army, Time for Change' by P.K. Mallick, Centre for Land Warfare Studies, New Delhi (2011), and published by Knowledge World, KW Publishers Pvt Ltd, New Delhi.

There are enough indicators to show that the Indian army's ability to attract quality officers has declined sharply following the globalization of the Indian economy. Another seminal paper titled 'The Indian Army Officers' Crisis' by Indian journalist and scholar, Dinesh Kumar, in the an issue of the academic journal, South Asia (vol. 33, no. 3, December 2010) is a must read to know the shrinking talent pool for the Indian Army.

Perhaps it's time for Army to recognize the new generation at work and re-design a new internally strong and united army.

Questions

Q. 1. Analyze the case and discuss how Generation Y soldiers might be different from their previous generation counterparts? Do you think besides the army, other organizations are also facing similar challenge? Discuss.

Q. 2. Do you think restructuring of organizations is the need of the hour to assimilate and engage the new generation workers? How can the same be done in Army?

References

Pubby, M. (2013, October 13). Officer-soldier clash again, 3 injured in boxing match brawl. Retrieved from Indian Express: http://archive.indianexpress.com/news/soldiers-and-officers-of-an-army-unit-clash-three-injured/1181260/

http://www.claws.in/administrator/uploaded_files/1316148326MP%2031%20For%20Web.pdf

Part III

COMPREHENSIVE CASES

Cases

Comprehensive Case Study 1

HRP for 2010 Winter Olympic Games

Maximizing Business, Employment, and Skills Development Opportunities throughout British Columbia

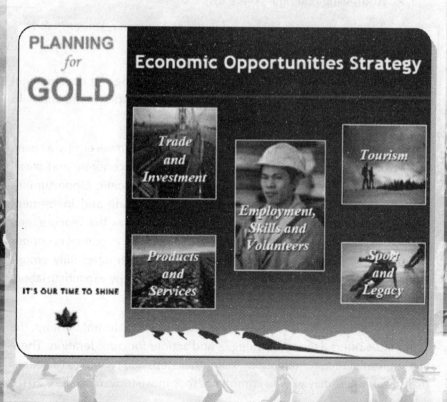

Preface

This report is the culmination of activities undertaken by the Human Resources Planning Committee over the last 12 months. It represents what the Committee learned from the research projects it sponsored and what its members heard from stakeholder groups during consultative meetings, roundtables and forums. The Committee attempted to be as comprehensive as possible in its research and consultations, however, it was not able to analyze all issues and meet with every stakeholder constituency in BC.

This report was written on behalf of the Committee, and its intended audience is all stakeholders in British Columbia who have an interest in employment and skills development opportunities resulting from the 2010 Winter Games and other major projects before, during and after the Games.

Four key, recurring themes throughout this report are:

> ➢ Maximizing economic and social opportunities
> ➢ Addressing potential skills gaps;
> ➢ Tapping the potential of under-utilized human resources; and
> ➢ Connecting labour force supply and demand

This report is very much a starting point in the planning and development of human resources required to maximize business, employment, and skills development opportunities throughout BC.

The 2010 Games were an important event in itself; however, it was even more powerful as a milestone and catalyst for BC economic and social development. A critical part of the provincial Economic Opportunities Strategy for the 2010 Games was the focus on trade and investment opportunities lasting beyond the Olympics. Measures that encouraged individuals and firms to invest in skills development were important economic tools which could also achieve social outputs through integrating groups currently under-represented in the work force and thereby expanding labour supply.

After highlighting the Committee's and stakeholders' relevant findings, the Committee offers a series of strategies and actions for consideration. These are not formal recommendations, but rather steps and examples of actions that stakeholders may wish to consider as they move forward to seize 2010-related opportunities.

Stakeholders used this report, to consider the possible strategies and actions; and to engage groups within their constituencies in planning and implementing strategies to maximize employment opportunities.

Report Highlights

Introduction

In December 2002, representatives of the federal department of Human Resources and Skills Development Canada, the provincial Olympic Secretariat, and the provincial Ministry of Skills Development and Labour formed a multi-stakeholder committee under the auspices of an Industrial Adjustment Agreement. The 2010 Human Resources Planning (HRP) Committee included representatives of Aboriginal people, Downtown Eastside Vancouver, the Vancouver Agreement, the tourism industry, the Vancouver 2010 Bid Corporation, and provincial Ministries of Advanced Education and Human Resources. An independent Committee Chair was appointed in January 2003.

The purpose of the 2010 HRP Committee was to undertake work, involving all key stakeholders, to develop potential strategies and actions for maximizing employment, skills development and volunteer opportunities associated with the 2010 Olympic and Paralympic Winter Games and broader opportunities before, during and after the Games. The Committee's formation reflected that the 2010 Winter Games can be a catalyst for achieving broader provincial employment and skills outcomes over the next several years.

The scope of inquiry included the impacts of the 2010 Winter Games, and three major projects: the Vancouver Convention and Exhibition Centre (VCEC) expansion, the Sea-to-Sky Highway (STSH) upgrade, and the Richmond-Airport-Vancouver Rapid Transit project (RAV).

2010 HR Planning Committee

The Committee terms of reference included the following components:
- ➢ Identifying the labour demand that the 2010 Games and other major projects will generate;
- ➢ Estimating the supply of skilled workers expected to be available for the Games and other projects;

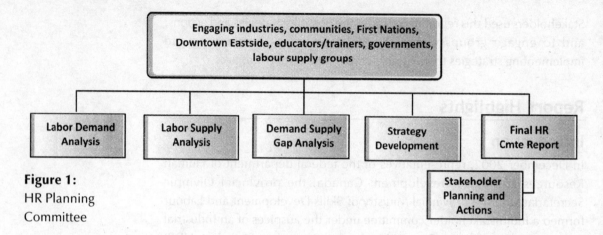

Figure 1:
HR Planning Committee

> Identifying demand-supply gaps, challenges and opportunities; and,

> Engaging stakeholders to develop strategies and action plans to address key challenges and opportunities

This Committee report is a product of research projects, a one-day stakeholder forum, and consultation with key stakeholder groups through various meetings and roundtables. The Committee's approach strongly reflected the need for linkages and integration.

The strategies and actions offered by the Committee later in this report are designed to spread the benefits of the Games throughout the province, to strengthen communities, and to honour the inclusive intent of the 2010 Olympic and Paralympic Winter Games organizers.

Research & Analysis

The two major research projects sponsored by the Committee were the 2010 Labour Demand Analysis and 2010 Labour Supply and Gap Analysis research projects completed by Roslyn Kunin & Associates, Inc. (RKA).

Labour Demand

The RKA estimates are based on the following three components of employment growth

Base Employment Growth Forecast

The first component of the model used in the labour demand analysis was to determine what employment growth would occur during the period 2003-

2015 excluding growth from the Games and the three other major projects. This is referred to as the "base growth" in employment openings. The Canadian Occupational Projection System (COPS) was used to generate this data.

Incremental Employment Growth Forecast

The second component of RKA's forecasting model for projecting labour demand was to identify the incremental growth in employment that will be created as a consequence of the Games and each of the other major projects during 2003-2015. Estimates of employment growth for the 2010 Winter Olympics draws heavily on Game impact analyses by the BC Trade Investment Office and InterVISTAS Consulting, Sea-to-Sky Highway upgrade employment estimates from the Ministry of Transportation and Highways, and Richmond-Airport-Vancouver employment estimates provided by its project office.

Table 1: Incremental Growth from 2010 Games and Three Major Capital Projects (2003-2015)

2010 Winter Olympics	76,813
Vancouver Convention and Exhibition Centre	30,660
Sea to Sky Highway	9,449
RAV Rapid Transit (low)	11,957
RAV Rapid Transit (high)	14,887
Total (low)	128,879
Total (high)	131,799

(**Source:** Prepared by Ministry of Skills Development and Labour, December, 2003)

Total Employment Growth Forecast

The final component of the RKA model was to identify the total employment growth for the period 2003–2015 if the Games and the three major capital projects proceed. This is simply calculated by adding the base growth to the incremental growth, and disaggregating by industry, occupation and region.

RKA's labour demand estimates for the period 2003-2015 include:

- Base employment growth in BC will be 913,000 job openings, consisting of almost 350,000 new jobs and almost 560,000 replacement job openings from attrition.

- The 2010 Games and three concurrent projects will generate incremental growth of almost 132,000 person years of employment in BC during 2003-2015.

- Base growth plus incremental growth will be 913,000 job openings (new and replacement) and 131,799 person years of employment, for a total of 1,045,085 opportunities.

- According to RKA, the industries with the largest amount of employment growth over the next 12 years will be Accommodation/Food/Recreation, Retail Trade, Health Services, Construction, Computer/Consulting/Business Services, and Transportation. The top growth occupations during 2003-2015 identified by RKA were Motor Vehicle and Transit Drivers, Food & Beverage Service, Managers in Retail, Managers in Food Service & Accommodation, Auditors/Accountants/Investment, Chefs & Cooks, etc.

RKA concluded that over four out of ten job openings from incremental employment growth during 2003-2015 will be in regions outside of the Lower Mainland and Southwest region of the province.

In addition to the demand for paid labour, a very major impact from the hosting of the 2010 Games was the volunteer requirements, which was considered another major component of labour demand. Volunteer work will be concentrated in the period of the Games, but is also required before the Games begin and for a time after they are concluded. In addition to its intrinsic rewards, a key benefit is that it can provide volunteers with valuable experience and networking that can benefit future employment and career development efforts.

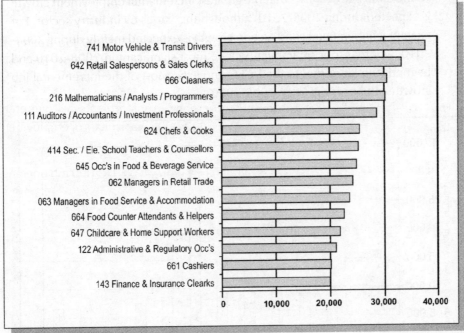

Figure 2: Occupation with Largest Number of Opening, 2003-2015

(*Source:* COPS and RKA)

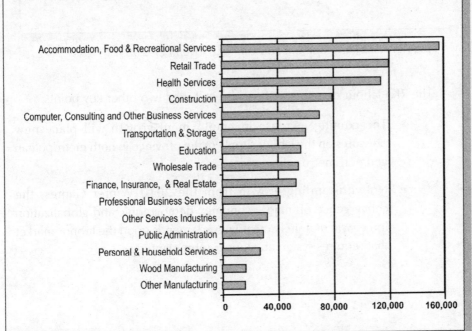

Figure 3: Industries with Largest Number of Opening, 2003-2015

(*Source:* COPS and RKA)

As the table below shows that the greatest incremental employment growth is expected during 2006-2010, although this varies by industry sector. For example, incremental construction growth is expected mainly during 2004-2010, whereas tourism impacts will be most significant in 2008-2010 and beyond (the latter due to the VCEC impacts). Most of the incremental job growth will occur between 2005-2010.

Figure 4: Incremental B.C. Job Growth Due to the 2010 Games & Related Projects, 2003-2015

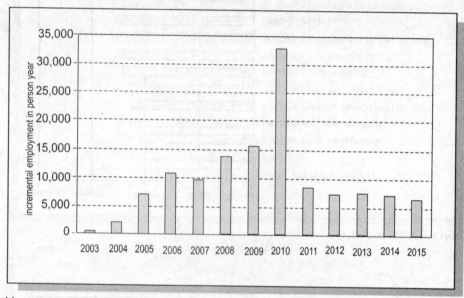

(*Source:* Prepared by Ministry of Skills Development and Labour, November, 2003)

The RKA labour demand analysis also included two other key points:

➢ The coming increase in employment growth will place new pressures on the labour supply of the province in both metropolitan and non-metropolitan areas.

➢ Notwithstanding growth from the 2010 Winter Games, the convergence of major economic, demographic and globalization forces will definitely create new demands upon the labour market that requires systematic longer-term planning.

Labour Supply and Gap Analysis

The RKA labour supply and gap analysis report complements RKA's earlier labour market demand analysis for the period 2003-2015 resulting from the 2010 Winter Games and three major projects. In combination, both reports represent one of the most comprehensive analyses of future labour market demand, supply and anticipated gaps in BC. Despite this significance, it should be noted that labour supply modeling in particular is still in its infancy in Canada, and it still remains more an "art form" than a science.

According to RKA, BC's population is projected to grow from a current level of 4.13 million to 4.9 million by 2015. The 45-64-age cohort will grow significantly to 2008 to equal the 25-44 age cohort, after which the number of older workers will continue to increase and constitute the largest cohort in the BC population. The aging of the workforce will translate into a rapid decline in labour force participation rates from 72.8% in 2001 to 67.3% in 2015 as older workers withdraw from the labour force. Nonetheless, overall the working age population (15-64) will increase from 2.8 million in 2001 to 3.4 million in 2015.

The eight major sources of incremental labour supply for BC during the 2003 – 2015 period cited by RKA are:

1. University graduates;
2. College graduates;
3. High school graduates;
4. Private training institution graduates;
5. Apprentices;
6. Inter-provincial migration;
7. International immigration; and
8. Person's leaving income assistance.

There are a number of data limitations to the amount of weight one can place on the outputs of this analysis.

The RKA labour supply analysis numbers exclude the pool of unemployed persons to avoid double-counting in estimating labour supply and because of the assumption that they are less likely to have the skills, experience and personal qualifications that match demand opportunities. The RKA supply analysis also does not take into account inter-occupational mobility.

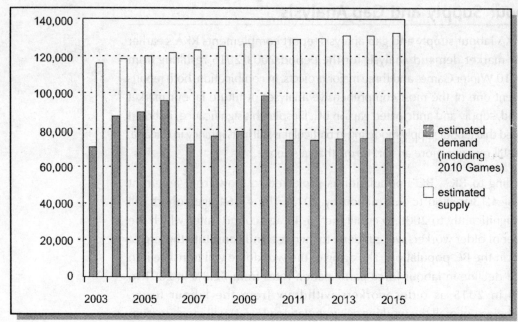

Figure 5:
RKA Labour Supply Analysis

As the above figure shows, RKA concluded that in aggregate, potential labour supply appears to be sufficient to meet incremental demand due to the 2010 Winter Games and concurrent major projects; and therefore, in broad terms there will be no wide-scale skill shortage of prospective workers.

RKA noted that the challenge is in developing the right skills and other attributes in those prospective workers to meet labour demand. For all job candidates, a good basic education is a critical first step. Strong skills in communication, client service, team work, and working with technology are essential competencies that are transferable to many occupations. For most individuals, some post-secondary training should be viewed as a "must, not a maybe" since labour analysts conclude that 70% of all new jobs now require some form of post secondary education.

However, when RKA disaggregated the supply-demand data, it found potentially significant ("severe" or "medium") gaps in the following seven of the 25 top growth occupations during 2003-2015 (extent of shortfall of workers in parentheses):

Potential "severe" gap

> Contractors & Supervisors, Trades & Related (10,857 or 70% of overall demand)

- Managers in Food Service & Accommodation (8,600 or 36% of overall demand)
- Managers in Construction & Transportation (6,731 or 59% of overall demand)

Potential "medium" gap

- Motor Vehicle & Transit Drivers (5,700 or 15% of overall demand)
- Managers in Retail Trade (3,600 or 15% of overall demand)
- Auditors, Accountants & Investment Professional (3,291 or 11% of overall demand)
- Administrative & Regulatory Occupations8 (800 or 4% of overall demand)

Occupational Category	Projected Shortfall	% of Total Demand	Level
Contractors and Supervisors, Trades and Related	10,857	70%	Severe
Managers in Food Service and Accommodation	8,600	36%	Severe
Managers in Construction and Transportation	6,371	60%	Severe
Motor Vehicle and Transit Drivers	5,700	15%	Medium
Managers in Retail Trade	3,600	15%	Medium
Auditors, Accountants and Investment Professionals	3,291	36%	Medium
Administrative and Regulatory Occupations	800	4%	Medium
Chefs and Cooks	1661	6%	Moderate
Occupation in Food and Beverage Services	826	3%	Moderate
Athletes, Coaches, Referees & Related Occ's	680	8%	Moderate
Machine Operators: Fabric, Fur or Leather	377	11%	Moderate
Creative and Performing Artists	119	1%	Moderate

Table 2: Projected Labour Supply Shortfalls (2003-2015)

In some areas of high demand, RKA's supply analysis led to projections of significant labour force surpluses during 2003-2015. This applies to four of the top 25 occupational groups

- Retail Salespersons and Sales Clerks (41,000 workers more than anticipated demands)
- Occupations in Travel and Accommodation (9,476 workers)
- Childcare and Home Support Workers (29,993 workers)
- Trades Helpers and Labourers (16,186 workers)

Top Ten Areas of Potential Surplus, 2003 2015

RKA also identified some occupations on the top 25 growth list which should be on a "watch list" for possible shortages, likely confined to only one or two years during 2003-2015:

> Creative and Performing Artists (potential shortfall of 119 workers in 2010)

> Chefs and Cooks (potential shortfall of 1661 workers over 2009-2010)

> Occupations in Food and Beverage Service (potential shortfall of 826 workers in 2010)

> Machine Operators, Fabric, Fur and Leather (potential shortfall of 377 over 2008-2010)

> Athletes, Coaches, Referees and Related Occupations (potential shortfall of 680 over 2009-2010)

Due to the limitations and assumptions on which the RKA analysis is based, more data and analyses are required before too much weight is placed on these estimates. Since some work will be concentrated in several months (i.e., one "person-year" of employment may require multiple workers), there may be dramatic increases in some Games- related demands—and then, following the Games, surpluses in these areas.

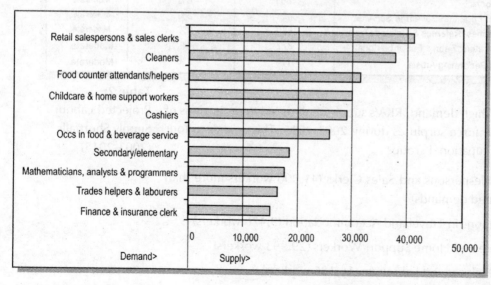

Figure 6: Top Ten Ateas of Potential Surplus, 2003-2015

The occupational groups most likely to experience the most severe pressure in 2010 are:

- Managers for Food Services and Accommodation
- Accountants and Investment Professionals
- Chefs and Cooks
- Other Occupations in Food and Beverage Services
- Motor Vehicle and Transit Drivers.

It is important to differentiate between shortages created by the 2010 Games versus by the three major projects reviewed by RKA and by base growth. Some of the potential shortages (e.g., athletes, artists and performers, etc.) are clearly created by the 2010 Games growth. Other potential shortages are clearly driven more by base growth (e.g., computer, consulting and business services); while other shortages are created by both the Games and broader growth (e.g. construction, retail and tourism occupations).

RKA offered a number of options for addressing potential labour force shortfalls including expanding apprenticeship and trades certification opportunities, expanding on-the-job training linked to career advancement into management, upgrading front-line workers, increasing the numbers of seats in training institutions, reducing unnecessary barriers to inter-provincial migration, and broadly disseminating information on future labour market demand so individuals can make better informed career choices.

In addition, it should be noted that there are a whole range of public policy and private sector options—some identified by RKA—to address potential future shortfalls of labour. The Committee cautions stakeholders not to focus exclusively on public sector and training solutions.

Labour Demand/Supply Summary

In summary, according to RKA, BC employers do not appear to face a widespread shortage in aggregate labour supply. With the exception of shortages of specialized skills in certain sectors, occupations and regions, BC employers face a shortage of "the right mix of skills and knowledge." While the research data does not project a wide-spread skills crisis in most industries, it does project a significant increase in employment opportunities that will challenge industries' capacity to recruit and train the workforce they will need.

It should be noted that this overall projection is based on the mobility of highly-skilled labour across Canada. This internal migration could be interrupted by mega-projects in other provinces and even the Pacific Northwest of the United States. Moreover, it is difficult to predict economic growth more than a year or two into the future.

For example, the final three months of 2003 saw strong job growth in BC. The labour market charged ahead, adding 36,600 jobs over the previous quarter, an increase of nearly 2%. Impressively, the gains were all in full-time jobs, while part-time employment shrunk slightly. Full-time employment is 5.1% higher than it was one year ago. The number of unemployed in the province fell sharply. 30,200 fewer people are unemployed than there were in the third quarter of 2003. In the fourth quarter of 2003, the number of unemployed fell to 164,400 – the lowest level since the quarter ending September 2001. The unemployment rate dropped to 7.4% in the fourth quarter, down a full percentage point for the same period last year. In December, the unemployment rate stood at 6.8%, falling below the cross-Canada rate for the first time since May 2001.

The point is that a sustained period of economic growth would drive the unemployment rate down even further. The labour market would then become extremely tight for those seeking to recruit skilled labour. Moreover, the labour force is rapidly changing. From 1991 to 2001, 91% of the net labour force growth was due to recent immigrants. Over the same period, fully 60 percent of the net labour force growth in BC was due to recent immigrants. However, given that a great many new Canadians do not have their skills recognized, it is difficult for them to fill the jobs for which they are qualified.

Also, in the face of "skills wastage" by not drawing on untapped labour pools, a challenge for employers is to adapt their recruitment practices and training initiatives. The hurdles in finding and preparing people for anticipated job openings can be reduced by strengthening ties among industry, community groups, educators, and other skill development and placement services. A key opportunity is for employers to recruit more from groups that have not been traditional sources of labour for them: Aboriginal persons, skilled workers re-entering the workforce after long periods of unemployment, persons with disabilities, older workers, and immigrants. This is discussed further in the next section.

Human Resource Opportunities and Challenges

Higher Growth Industry Sectors

Tourism, retail and construction are the three sectors expected to experience the greatest employment growth from the Games and related projects during 2003-2015. Together, they represent over one-third (or 400,000 job openings) of total employment growth (i.e. base and incremental) during this period; and almost 60% (or over 77,000 openings) of incremental growth.

Each sector will experience growth in a range of occupational categories because of the Games, concurrent infrastructure projects, and base growth. Managers and supervisors will be in high demand across these sectors, with other growth areas being in a combination of higher skill level (e.g. chefs & cooks, carpenters) and lower skilled jobs (e.g. food counter attendants, cashiers, trades helpers).

Top Ten Industries						
	Total Incremental Employment Growth		Total Openings in Base Model		Total Growth in Labour Demand	
	Openings	% of Total Growth	Openings	% of Total Growth	Openings	% of Total Openings
Accommodation, Food & Recreational Services	47,963	30.3	110,355	69.7	158,318	15.1
Construction	18,893	23.4	61,843	72.6	80,737	7.7
Retail Trade	10,634	8.8	109,961	91.2	120,595	11.5
Professional Business Services	8,246	19.3	34,547	80.7	42,792	4.1
Transportation & Storage	7,828	12.8	53,471	81.2	61,298	5.9
Other Manufacturing	7,330	44.1	9,302	55.9	16,632	1.2
Finance, Insurance & Real Estate	5,179	9.6	48,633	90.4	53,812	5.1
Computer, Consulting and Other Business Services	4,123	5.8	67,132	94.2	71,255	6.8
Other Services Industries	2,964	8.9	30,213	91.1	33,178	3.2
Wholesale Trade	4,895	8.7	51,233	92.3	56,128	5.4
Total	131,799	12.6	913,285	87.4	1,045,085	100

(**Source:** RKA)

Table 3: Total Labour Demand in BC from 2003 to 2015 by Industry (High Estimate)

Tourism, retail and construction sectors share challenges such as improving their image to job-seekers, recruitment and retention, competition from other sectors, capacity for training among smaller operations, and shortages of managers and supervisors. They also share opportunities to tap under-utilized labour pools, to form partnerships and alliances with educators and trainers, and to introduce innovative human resource practices. To construction in particular, and tourism to some extent, the new Industry Training Authority (ITA) may present opportunities for new, more flexible and responsive training models.

These three sectors also face unique strengths and weaknesses. Construction is more fragmented and has greater challenges in speaking with one voice and developing pan-sector strategies. Tourism, on the other hand, has completed a major sector human resources strategy and has a new cross-sector body, go2, to initiate action and solutions. Retail has a more cohesive alliance of associations, while it is in the early stages of developing a sectoral skills approach. Most additional tourism-related jobs will be generated close to and after 2010.

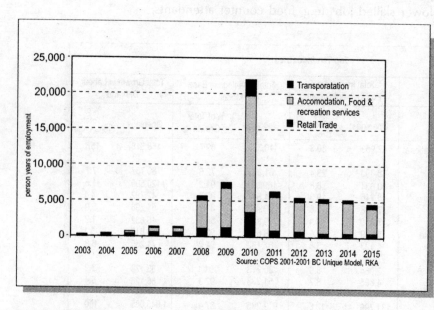

Figure 7: Incremental Employment Demand from 2010 Games & Capital Projects

(**Source:** Prepared by Ministry of Skills Development and Labour, December, 2003)

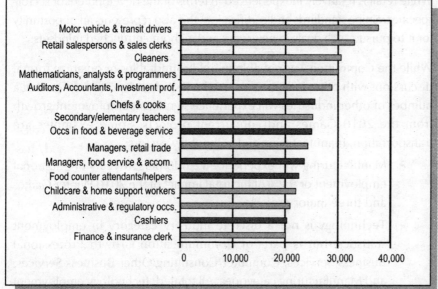

Figure 8: What Tourism-related Occupational Groups will See the Greatest Demand between 2003 and 2015?

(*Source:* Prepared by Ministry of Skills Development and Labour, December, 2003)

Construction has an advantage over other sectors with its stronger trades training culture and career opportunities which offer higher wages than sub-management/supervisory jobs in tourism and retail. However, construction experiences more "training politics" and territoriality regarding regulations and job protection than many other sectors.

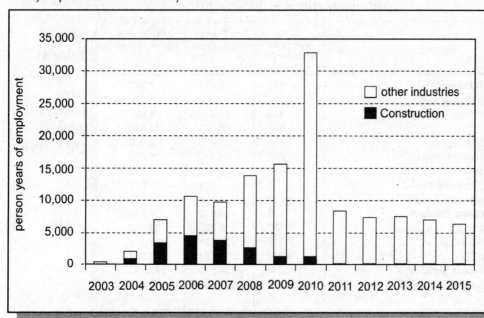

Figure 9: Incremental Employment Demand from 2010 Games & Capital Projects

(*Source:* COPS 2001-2011 BC Unique Model, RKA)

While retail is relatively inexperienced in terms of the development of sector-specific training standards and certification, this also represents an opportunity for it to pursue such goals in new ways and without entrenched mindsets.

While the Committee was not able to hold roundtables or organize formal discussions with other industry sectors, the RKA data reports predicts that a number of other industries will experience significant employment growth from the 2010 Games and concurrent projects. Some examples are transportation, manufacturing and technology sectors:

> Manufacturing will experience 12,000 person-years of additional employment or 9.2% of the total impact of the 2010 Winter Games and three major projects.

> Technology is not a discrete industry category in employment statistics, but is parts of Communication Growth Professional Business Services, Computer/Consulting/Other Business Services, and Manufacturing categories. All totaled, technology employment will experience significant incremental growth from 2010 Games and in base growth.

> Transportation is projected to experience over 61,000 job openings during 2003-2015, including anticipated demand for 37,749 motor vehicle and transit drivers—demand that RKA suggests will be particularly critical in the year 2010.

Table 4: Growth in other Industries 2003 to 2015 (High Estimate)

Sector	Total Incremental Employment Growth	Total Openings in Base Model	Total Growth in Labour Demand
Food Products & Beverages	812	6,731	7,543
Rubber, Plastics & Chemicals	304	3,162	3,466
Pulp and Paper, Paper Products	169	8,652	8,821
Wood	436	16,620	17,056
Printing and Publishing	1,190	7,719	8,909
Manufacturd Mineral Products	460	5,532	5,992
Metal Fabrication & Machinery, except electrical	880	6,042	6,922
Motor Vehicles, Trailers & Parts	0	501	501
Other Transportation Equipment	87	6,596	6,683
Electrical & Electronic Products	433	3,723	4,156
Other Manufacturing	7,330	9,302	16,632
Transportation & Storage	7,828	53,471	61,298
Communication	2,318	10,781	13,098
Professional Business Services	8,246	34,547	42,792
Computer, Consulting and other Business Services	4,123	67,132	71,255

(Source: RKA)

Communities Under-represented in the Labour Market

The research and consultation the Committee sponsored clearly showed that the skills, talents and passions of members of those British Columbians under-represented in the labour force are relatively under-utilized—particularly those of Aboriginal people, the inner city labour force, immigrants, persons with disabilities, and youth. This section of the report brings forward what the Committee heard from stakeholders about the opportunities and challenges facing these parts of the BC labour force.

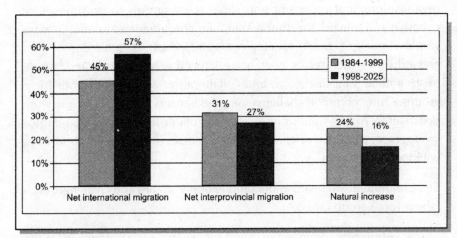

Figure 10: Past & Projected Population Growth Sources for BC 1984-1999 and 1998-2025

(**Source:** BC Stats)

Population Sector	1996	2010	% change
Persons with Disabilities			
Aged 15 Year and older	399,840		
Labour Force Size	119,952		
Labour Force Participation Rate	30%		
Aboriginal Population*			
Aged 15 years and older	96,566		
Labour Force Size	61,755		
Labour Force Participation Rate	64.0%		
BC Average**	1996		
Aged 15 years and older	3,130,300		
Labour Force Size	2,056,000		
Labour Force Participation Rate	65.7%		

Table 5: Labour Force Participation for Special Population Sector

(***Source:** The Laurier Institute)
(****Source:** BC Stats; Note that projections for 2010 were not available for BC, therefore 2008 projections are reported)

These labour force participants share a number of opportunities in common including the "inclusivity" principles and commitments in the successful 2010 Bid, the fact that they represent to employer and industries large pools of untapped labour, and the existing networks and infrastructures within each of their constituent communities.

However, such labour force groups also share significant challenges to skills development and employment. A key challenge is the need for organizations that represent and serve these groups to become more cohesive and to work together within their constituencies to offer a "one-window" point of contact for employers and industries. In turn, employers and industries, themselves, need to work together in a coordinated fashion to streamline joint discussion and collaboration with target labour force groups. Other common challenges are the barriers (e.g. lack of basic work skills, stereotypes, systemic biases, etc.) that under-represented labour force groups face; and the weak links that the agencies that represent them have with local employers.

The Committee also heard about unique opportunities and challenges each labour force group faces:

- Aboriginal communities' opportunities include a fast-growing youth population and well-developed human resources development (HRD) infrastructure of organizations and resources; major challenges include increasing high school completion and educational levels.
- The inner city labour force's opportunities are reflected in a strong network of community agencies and community economic development roots; they are challenged by chronic unemployment and the need for sustainable employment supports.
- Immigrants represent a tremendous pool of skilled and formally-trained individuals; but face language barriers and need access to more streamlined skill and credential recognition practices.
- Persons with disabilities have relatively high levels of education and can benefit from technological advances, and the Paralympic Games can be a catalyst for opportunities; however they face myths and stereotypes and need for workplace accommodations.
- Youth have opportunities to participate in the 2010 Games through

sport, volunteer and employment opportunities, but face challenges in completing high school, obtaining up-to-date information about careers and job opportunities, and significant barriers in certain populations (e.g., Aboriginal youth, youth income assistance recipients, etc.).

Workforces in Outlying Regions

In the RKA reports and other work, the Committee learned of significant potential opportunities outside of the Lower Mainland/Southwest region of the province. The 2010 Games bring both employment opportunities and challenges to outlying regions.

On one hand, RKA projects that over 40% of the new job openings, mostly in tourism, will occur in these regions, representing tens of thousands of opportunities before and during the Games. On the other hand, without community leadership and local industry and government planning and collaboration, this growth may not be fully realized. Also, local communities and industries want to ensure that they do not lose their skilled workers to the Games and major projects in the Lower Mainland, exacerbating current trends. However, outlying regions can benefit from major province-wide marketing efforts led by tourism and government agencies. The network of public post-secondary institutions throughout the province, local Chambers of Commerce, and local governments and economic development agencies will play key roles in maximizing 2010 opportunities.

Education and Training Stakeholders

Post-secondary education and training stakeholders expressed to the Committee a high level of interest in the 2010 Games. They see opportunities for partnerships with the Organizing Committee for the Olympic Games (OCOG) and with key industry groups for training volunteers and skilled workers. Since many of the new job openings will be in trades and technical occupations, industry and the new Industry Training Authority (ITA) will need help from training providers in delivering new programs and expanding successful existing ones. 2010 can be used to promote certain types of careers to young people – educators suggested that marketing directed at both K-12 and post-secondary students will be needed to get the word out about 2010-related opportunities. Young workers in the 2010 era are currently K-12 students.

Education and training stakeholders also spoke of the need for a province-wide economic strategy and the challenge of recruiting and retaining teachers and faculty members. This is a current challenge that can be exacerbated by the 2010-related growth. The Committee also heard that private training institutions need to play a substantive role in meeting future labour market needs, and that there needs to be better integration and linkages among components of the BC post-secondary education system.

Goals & Principles for Maximizing 2010-Related Opportunities

Based on the Committee's work and what it heard from stakeholders, it offers the following Vision, Goals and Principles as an organizing framework for future planning and strategy development by stakeholders. These are examples of the type of concepts stakeholders could keep in mind when undertaking 2010-related human resources planning and strategy development.

Vision

Business, employment, skills and volunteer opportunities for British Columbians are fully realized before, during and after the 2010 Olympic and Paralympic Winter Games.

Goal

- To stimulate collaborative and on-going strategic human resources planning within and among industry, government, education and training, and labour force supply stakeholders.
- To strengthen labour demand-labour supply connections through industry and labour force group leadership.
- To integrate business development, economic development and social development activities among public, private and voluntary sectors.
- To qualitatively and quantitatively increase the utilization of members of groups under-represented in employment and learning.
- To strengthen HRD and employment capacities and relationship-building within and among Aboriginal communities, the Downtown Eastside Vancouver, and outlying regional communities.
- To facilitate the consolidation and partnership-building of Aboriginal, inner cities, immigrant, and persons with disabilities communities with regards to business development, HRD and employment.

Principles

- Integration of stakeholder planning
- Comprehensiveness
- Skill transferability
- Inclusiveness
- Government facilitative role
- Demand-driven employment strategies
- Relationship-building and partnerships
- Programming flexibility
- Local community capacity-building
- Leadership and shared responsibilities of all stakeholders

Strategies and Actions for Consideration

The Committee provided a list of strategies and actions for stakeholders to consider in planning 2010-related employment and skills development initiatives. These suggestions are based on what the Committee heard during its meetings with several stakeholders and on the findings of the research projects it sponsored.

The Committee's and stakeholders' ideas were shaped by the following factors:

- The challenge of addressing potential shortages of human resources with the right knowledge, skills and attitudes;
- The economic and social imperative of addressing the under-utilization of talent among Aboriginal workers, persons with disabilities, inner city residents, and immigrants and others labour force participants;
- The need to strengthen relationships among industries, educators, other skills development and placement services, and community interest groups; and,
- The need to improve the coordination of services and reduce confusion about who provides what services in order to strengthen labour supply-demand connections.

The following Committee considerations focus on "end" statements; and each statement is followed with examples of possible actions or options for how stakeholders might achieve such ends.

Demand-side Strategies

1. **Procurement and contracting policies that meet both economic and inclusivity goals, including rewarding organizations for active recruitment and development of Aboriginal workers, inner city residents, persons with disabilities, and immigrants** - The Committee heard from industry groups who call for timely, fair and streamlined procurement practices regarding procurement and contracting for 2010-related projects. Other groups want to ensure that procurement and contracting is consistent with the inclusivity commitments and goals that were a key component in the successful bid for the 2010 Winter Games.

2. **Linked and enhanced databases to create a one-stop clearinghouse for employment and contracting opportunities and prospective suppliers** - Such a mechanism might include some of the following features:

    ➢ A regular newsletter and on-line posting of bid opportunities for suppliers of goods and services and related sub-contracts;

    ➢ A consolidated job bank (on-line) for employment openings, co-op placements, and volunteer positions arising from the 2010 Winter Games and related capital projects;

    ➢ A single point of contact for employment development services that would direct employers and industry associations to potential providers of short-term and permanent staff; and,

On-line and other resources to support local businesses and not-for-profit service agencies in responding to RFPs (i.e., increase their competitive awareness of opportunities and their capacity to respond to business development opportunities).

The clearinghouse would need to be established collaboratively with local business improvement associations, chambers of commerce, industry associations, and labour "supply side" organizations. Care should be taken to not replicate existing services but rather, link existing databases into an integrated resource with simplified on-line search capability, to minimize difficulties and duplication of effort in matching business and employment opportunities with appropriate suppliers.

3. **Increased and more effective regional and sector human resources planning throughout BC**. In order to maximize 2010-related employment opportunities and employment generated by other projects and base growth, planning and action need to occur in a bottom-up approach from within individual communities and regions and industry sectors throughout the provinces.

Supply-side Strategies

1. **Increased demand orientation within "supply side" agencies in the design and operation of their skill development and placement programs**- Increasing employers' (small business operators as well as medium-sized enterprises and large corporations) receptivity to job candidates from target populations that may otherwise be overlooked needs to be a key part of maximizing 2010-related opportunities. Employers indicated during the Committee work that success depends largely on how close a match there is between the attitudes, knowledge and skills of job candidates and the actual requirements of the jobs for which there are openings. Therefore, the Committee encourages agencies that represent and serve members of groups under-represented in the labour market to adopt new strategies or enhance existing ones to ensure a "demand" lens in their programs and services. Examples of how this could be achieved include the following:

> **Examples:** 1. Within each agency serving prospective workers, review current and proposed training programs against available labour market data on projected demands, anticipated worker supply, shortfalls and surpluses.
>
> 2. Rigorously analyze the value of program offerings and identify changes needed (in specific programs and/or resource allocations generally) to correspond to anticipated skills shortages.
>
> 3. Include demand-side representatives on advisory boards.

2. **Back-to-school alliances for Aboriginal youth throughout BC**- Approximately 48,000 Aboriginal youth are currently attending public schools (K-12) in British Columbia. They are spread throughout metro and non-metro areas of the province: three-quarters of them in off-reserve settings. These are future workers. Historically, only 40% of the Aboriginal students who enter Grade

eight go on to graduate from secondary school, yet labour market analysts report that more than 70% of new jobs now require candidates to have some post-secondary education or training.

Based on these facts and what the Committee heard from stakeholders, it encourages Aboriginal groups and education stakeholders to consider a strategic alliance between coordinators of Aboriginal back-to-school initiatives.

3. **Enhanced and integrated skills-based inventories of labour resources available through supply-side stakeholder**- The work of integrating client databases and ensuring that skills are noted could be done by five different networks of service providers, and all of this information integrated through a single portal site:

   ➢ Aboriginal workers;
   ➢ Persons with disabilities who are job-ready and actively seeking work;
   ➢ Inner City residents who are job-ready and actively seeking work
   ➢ Immigrants seeking employment; and,
   ➢ Post-secondary training programs – public and private – whose graduates are a good match for anticipated skill shortages.

Demand-supply Strategies

1. A cross-sector "Where the Opportunities Are" career information campaign directed at students, youth and unemployed persons.

2. Active recruitment practices that promote the hiring of groups under-represented in the labour force by medium and large companies.

3. Enhanced social enterprise development to expand employment and training opportunities and supports for long-term unemployed persons in the inner city.

4. Accelerated wide-scale application of prior learning assessment & recognition and foreign credential recognition systems.

5. Cross-cultural awareness-building through educational events and information for all stakeholders, including procurement coordinators for OCOG and capital projects, employers and industry associations, and "supply side" agencies.

Overall Planning and Coordination Strategies

1. On-going coordination and integration of human resources planning and development

2. Significantly more collaborative planning among the network of stakeholder organizations through inter- and intra-organizational activities.

Conclusion

While the Committee was not able to meet with all stakeholders and undertake all the work that it would have liked to, it has spent the last several months reviewing the results of some important research and engagement of several stakeholders.

The four key themes throughout this report are: maximizing economic and social opportunities; addressing potential skills gaps; increasing opportunities for under-utilized talent; and connecting labour supply and demand.

Over the course of its work, a few key factors resonate with the Committee:

- BC's future before, during and after the 2010 Games appears to bring a high volume of job opportunities in a diverse array of industry sectors and occupational categories, including a substantial amount from the Games itself and three other major projects occurring during this timeframe.

- There is a large amount of interest in and good will around the 2010 Games among all major stakeholder groups in BC, from industries to educators and trainers to Aboriginal communities to immigrant groups, persons with disabilities, and many other communities. This can be harnessed and leveraged to all British Columbians' advantage.

- This review of 2010-related opportunities, challenges and issues really demonstrates the importance of the need for real dialogue and true collaboration and partnership among stakeholders groups on both the demand and supply sides of the labour market. Leadership and vision is needed on both sides to increase relationship-building, reduce "siloism" and seize opportunities.

- Many of the 2010-related challenges and opportunities the Committee heard about revolve around the need for the strategic use of and accessibility to information. Getting the word out, sharing information, awareness and marketing will be key parts of initiatives to maximize employment opportunities.

➤ Hearing from representatives of labour force groups and the findings of the RKA, Ference Weicker and Pinay reports demonstrate the tremendous "skills wastage" or under-utilization of human resources. All added up, this represents tens of thousands or more of unemployed and/or under-employed British Columbians.

➤ The planning, coordination, strategies and actions which stakeholders undertake individually and collectively to maximize employment and skills opportunities will work most effectively if efforts are linked and integrated.

The 2010 Human Resources Planning Committee offers a few final comments. It has overseen a body of work in its sponsored research, consultations, forum and this report—it is important not to let the voices of stakeholders "sit on the shelf." The Committee urges stakeholders to take action together with others to realize their employment visions for 2010 and the labour market in general.

The Committee encourages, where appropriate, governments and the Organizing Committee for the Olympic Games to use this information in planning and implementing employment and skills development initiatives in conjunction with other stakeholder leadership bodies. This could include using an existing body or mechanism or creating a new one for continuing this body of work and to support and coordination human resources planning within and across each stakeholder constituency.

Finally, it is important that leadership bodies in each stakeholder constituency share the responsibility of acting as catalysts for their communities of interest to plan, develop and implement strategies to Maximize 2010 and Broader-Based Employment and Skills Development Opportunities throughout British Columbia.

(**This case is based on Maximizing 2010-Related Employment &Skills Opportunities in British Columbia: Connecting Labour Market Supply & Demand, Final Report of The 2010 Human Resources Planning Committee, December 15, 2003 and has been published with the permission of Kerry Jothen, Chief Executive Officer, Human Capital Strategies** {www.humancapitalstrategies.ca})

Cases

Comprehensive Case Study 2

A Metropolitan University*

> *Adapted from the book Recruitment and Selection of Vice-Chancellors for Australian Universities, Bernard O'Meara and Stanley Petzall, Victorian Universities regional Research Network Press, Ballarat, Australia, 2007.
>
> Published with permission from Bernard O'Meara.

Background

This 'Post-1985' band university is a large multi-campus dual-sector university in the CBO of a large Australian city. In 2000 the university boasted over 50,000 students, 3000 staff and an annual turnover of approximately $400 million. It has three main campuses as well as several locations in metropolitan and regional areas of the state. It has some thirty research centers that are considered extremely innovative.

The university's mission is to provide technical and professional education that develops people for leadership and employment, and to undertake research programs that address real world issues within an international and community context. Its goal is to create and sustain a distinctive world-class university at the forefront of technical and professional education and real-world research through continuous improvement with all staff committed to quality management processes

The incumbent vice-chancellor had been appointed in 1992 and had been a driving force in the development of the university.

The Incumbent VC

The vice-chancellor had originally commenced at the institution in 1970 and had been the director before being made foundation vice-chancellor in 2004, when university status had been bestowed. He therefore had a wealth of knowledge and experience, and understood the history of the university and the culture that had evolved as a consequence of the many changes the institute had undergone.

Thus, when he announced in April 2011 that he planned to retire in October 2012 when his contract expired, he gave council the opportunity to carefully consider the options available to it in seeking to appoint a new vice-chancellor. In September 2011 he confirmed his plans with the chancellor who notified council that same month.

The incumbent was fifty-four years old when he was appointed and would be sixty-two in 2012. He had, in effect, grown up with the institute and the university. He was a distinguished academic with an impressive research and publication history, and he held fellowships with institutes concerned with his areas of expertise. In conjunction with council, he had established agreed strategies for the university to follow, updated these, and it was held that the university was moving in a suitable direction.

Council subsequently adopted a policy, 'Recruitment of the Next Vice-Chancellor' (presented in Appendix 1).

The Position

In April 2011, the incumbent vice-chancellor announced he would retire from the position in October 2012. Included in the staff reporting directly to the incumbent were the deputy vice-chancellor and vice-president, and a deputy vice-chancellor (resources), together with the executive director (major projects), the chief executive officer (technology estate), and the director of planning and quality.

There were four pro vice-chancellors reporting to the deputy vice-chancellors along with seven deans and numerous directors responsible for corporate affairs, human resources management, and other branches. Many staff had worked with the incumbent vice-chancellor since he was appointed into the foundation role, and therefore there was a high degree of continuity amongst staff and activities

The primary objective of the role of vice-chancellor for the university is to provide an appropriate vision and strategic plan and ensure strong and effective leadership and clear direction within the university.

The Processes

In June 2011, the director of the university's human resource management group (HRMG) was asked to outline options available to council in the recruitment and selection of the new vice-chancellor. The director was also asked to prepare some recommendations to council, and a document, entitled 'Recruitment Strategy Guidelines' (presented in Appendix 2) was produced.

In October 2011, following submissions, a search firm was appointed to assist with the appointment. It was believed that a search firm would have the time, resources and networks to effectively complement the resources available to the university. This coincided with council considerations regarding the role of the vice-chancellor, the future direction of the university, and the characteristics sought that best suited the university in that stage of its evolution.

In addition, a timetable was produced to ensure the timelines outlined could be successfully achieved and a smooth transition from one vice-chancellor to another could occur. Apart from the draft timelines, necessary actions were outlined and responsibilities allocated accordingly. The draft timeline is presented in Appendix 3.

In accordance with the policy adopted by council, the selection panel was formed and consisted of six members. These included the chancellor, the chair of academic board, a former president of council, two external members (one from Sydney) and an incumbent vice-chancellor.

All members were specifically chosen because they had varying degrees in senior appointments either in the private sector or higher education. External members of council were senior members of the Melbourne and Sydney business communities.

Council spent a great deal of time addressing the antecedents of the university, its strategic direction, future challenges and opportunities. Thus an in-depth specification statement was produced together with a job description incorporating the results of the review of the antecedents, the role and therefore the most desirable attributes that would be sought in candidates. These comprehensive documents provided the basis for information provided to candidates and advertisements and were completed in November 2011. The specification document is presented in Appendix 4.

While advertisements were placed in newspapers locally and internationally, little was actually expected to come from them. Advertisements were placed in *The Age, The Australian, The Times: Higher Education* (UK), and *The Chronicle of Higher Education* in the US. The chancellor did not contact other chancellors or vice-chancellors to determine likely candidates.

The consultants were given all necessary information, but council did not request that the consultants contact specific potential candidates. Council was concerned that the right person with the right attributes needed to be appointed, and therefore the consultants were not limited in their search in any way.

The consultant talked to staff internally, those familiar with the university externally, and other interested parties to determine who, in their opinions, would make the most appropriate vice-chancellor Without prompting, the consultants contacted likely internal and external candidates to determine their degree of interest in the role and their objective suitability.

It is estimated that there were over thirty enquiries regarding the role and less than ten serious applications. One UK candidate underwent a preliminary interview via video conferencing in March. In April, three candidates were short-listed, one internal and two external, including one in the UK.

Each candidate was interviewed once for one to one-and-a-half-hours. The interview was roundtable, and each panel member asked questions (not set) based on areas of interest. The role of the partner was never an issue and therefore did not impact upon the processes in any way. The successful applicant reported having three interviews with the consultant and one with the selection panel.

Once the direction of the recruitment strategy was determined, the remuneration committee met twice to determine desirable candidate attributes, antecedents and strategic direction. The selection panel met once to discuss the approach to be used in the processes, questions to be asked and related issues. The review did result in the belief that the university needed a CEO, a manager and a leader who could work within the academic environment. It was considered a management role rather than solely an academic role. However, a threshold of academic credibility was still maintained.

Overall the process was relatively short and took approximately seven months, although preparation was undertaken well before this. The vice-chancellor confirmed his retirement plans in September 1999, and the final candidate was selected in April 2000. It was another six months before the appointment in October 2000, which coincided with the retirement date of the outgoing vice-chancellor.

As the incoming vice-chancellor was an internal appointment, there were some months prior to the retirement date where the two worked closely together and key issues discussed with the vice-chancellor elect.

It is this university's policy to advertise all senior appointments. Thus there was never any consideration to appoint the internal candidate without determining the suitability of other candidates, either internal or external. Succession planning was not in place with regard to the role of vice-chancellor. However, the talents of the internal candidate were so strong that the consultant suggested that the person apply.

It is reported that the consultants discovered that in their various investigations this candidate was continually put forward as a likely successor due to an established track record in academic administration. This candidate did not have a purely academic background but had held the role of deputy vice-chancellor (resources) with the university. Despite the internal candidate being appointed, the final decision was unanimous and made only on completion of all interviews.

The successful candidate was offered a five-year contract with a strong annual performance component.

The Incoming VC

The new vice-chancellor had been at the university for eleven years and had held the roles of deputy vice-chancellor (resources) and deputy vice-chancellor and vice-president. Thus, over the eleven years, the incoming vice-chancellor had worked closely with senior staff, especially the vice-chancellor, and had an especially strong grasp of the management of the university resources and strategic initiatives.

The new vice-chancellor held a PhD, was well-versed in senior academic administration, and had established a well-respected track record in this area; however, due to the positions held, this individual had worked on the periphery of core academic activities for some time and undertook to redress this quickly.

The chancellor and council were not perturbed by this situation as their review of the role led them to believe that an in-depth knowledge of all core academic activities was not essential. The incumbent had passed the threshold of academic credibility and, importantly, had demonstrated capability in the areas of administration, management, leadership and strategy. The role was deemed to require a corporate sector type CEO with these qualifications, attributes, knowledge and experience.

Council was also satisfied that major strategic change was not necessary and therefore believed the incumbent was best-placed to continue and enhance the strategic direction and initiatives of the university. There was agreement between the incumbent and the chancellor that the five-year contract should contain a performance element.

Thus it was during the research of performance-based contracts for Australian vice-chancellors that the university became acutely aware how few incumbents actually have such contracts. The performance objectives will also be published on this university's intranet so they are fully accessible to staff and the processes transparent.

(This case has been published with the written consent of Dr. Bernard O'Meara)

Appendices for the Case - A Metropolitan University

Appendix 1: Recruitment of The Next Vice-Chancellor

The Vice-Chancellor has indicated that he will be retiring from the University at the conclusion of his current contract that expires on 1st October 2012.

It is a duty of Council to appoint the Vice-Chancellor. The Act in Sections 23(1) & (2) states:
"The Council must appoint a person to be Vice-Chancellor of the University"
(and)

"for such term and on such conditions as the Council determines".

There is an appointments policy for senior appointments that was approved by Council in 1993 and although it specifies that the position of Vice-Chancellor is included within its scope, an examination of its provisions suggests that many of them are not appropriate for what is in effect an executive search.

It is therefore recommended that whilst the policy will be used where appropriate for guidance the following process will be employed for the recruitment of the next University Vice-Chancellor.

That the Chancellor be delegated authority to undertake or oversee all aspects of the recruitment process for the next Vice-Chancellor including the following:

i. using the Remuneration Committee as an advisory group: select an executive search company

ii. using the Remuneration Committee as an advisory group, approve, in concert with the executive search company, worldwide advertising, position description, and candidates' information pack;

iii. using the Remuneration Committee as an advisory group, establish a selection panel, with the following membership:

Chancellor as Chair
Two external Council Members
A staff member
A Vice-Chancellor of another University
A community member chosen for their understanding of this University
And its requirements in seeking to fill this position;

iv. Provide to Council when appropriate a recommendation on the appointment of the next Vice Chancellor.

It is proposed that the Selection Panel should confirm a short list of candidates by March 2012 with interviews taking place as soon as possible thereafter.

To note that the Remuneration Committee is delegated authority to approve on behalf of Council the contract and a remuneration package for the next Vice-Chancellor, following recommendations made to it by the Chancellor.

Appendix 2: Recruitment Strategy Guidelines
Vice-Chancellor

The Vice-Chancellor's current employment contract is due to expire on 20 October 2012.

Whilst this is still 16 months away, given the seniority of the position, the source of the pool of potential candidates and the relatively long notice periods required for senior roles particularly in this sector, the recruitment process should commence shortly.

Outlined below are the process requirements generally used as part of our Senior Appointments Policy, and options you may wish to consider in developing a recruitment strategy.

Recruitment Steps
Pre Recruitment

- Prepare position specification
- Determine recruitment strategy
- Determine selection panel.
- Select search company if one is to be used

Recruitment

- Search process begins and, if appropriate, position advertised
- Search firm regularly reports to Chair or sub-committee on search process.
- Short-listing meeting, search committee makes formal presentation to panel who then selects candidates for interview stage

Interview and offer

- Interviews
- Referee checks, and offer stage
- Approval by Council

1. Policy Requirements

The recruitment process for the position of Vice-Chancellor is covered by the University's Senior Appointment Policy.

This is a Council Appointment and requires Council approval. The initial step is to establish a selection panel. This panel will make a recommendation to Council. The Chancellor would normally be the Chair of the selection panel.

Recruitment Approach

It is usual for positions at this senior level to engage a search consultancy firm to assist in the recruitment process.

It is expected that the search would be conducted both in Australia and internationally. The position would normally also be advertised both locally and overseas. The selected search firm would manage all applications and inquiries in the first instance.

The company would be asked to provide the selection panel with a short-list of candidates from which the panel would then select for interview. The company would be expected to provide a report on the search process, make a formal presentation to the selection panel and provide documentation on the nominated candidates.

The company would liaise regularly with the Chair of the panel.

The University does not confine its recruitment search activities to one specific search company and it usually selects a company based on the requirements of the position.

One option is to invite several selected companies to provide a submission on how they would undertake such a task and then select from these.

Human Resource Management Group (HRMG) can provide names of several firms.

3. Selection Panel

The role of the selection panel is to determine the appropriate recruitment process, short-list applications, conduct interviews, assess referee reports and then make a recommendation to Council.

Whilst it is desirable to keep selection panels small, it is more important to ensure depth and range of expertise. The supervisor (in this case the Chancellor) will determine the composition of the panel. The policy states that it must include:

- The manager responsible for the position (Chancellor)
- One person elected by and from the staff of the relevant area. This person is normally selected through an election process.
- Persons with expertise in the relevant area, internal or external to the University (see Note 1)
- As this position will carry the title of Professor, at least one member of the panel should be a Professor.

Note 1: The policy provides for the panel to include representatives from Council and from within the Higher Education industry, government and private industry.

Confidentiality

The recruitment process is treated in the strictest confidence and all parties involved will be reminded of need for confidentiality.

Position Specialisation/Documentation

The University will need to produce a position specification. This will include details of the University, the position requirements and challenges and the attributes being sought.

This document will form the basis of the formal position specification and include key selection criteria.

HMRG can assist in the production of this document.

Timing

It may well be necessary to commence the process shortly in order to coincide the appointment of a new Vice-Chancellor with the expiry of the current Vice--Chancellor's contract.

Assistance

A range of support services are available to assist the recruitment process, and further information can be provided.

Director

Human Resources Management Group

15 June 1999

Appendix 3: Draft Timeline

Draft Timetable Leading to Appointment of Vice-Chancellor

Week commencing	Actions etc	Who
4 October 2011	Consultant submit draft specification, advertisement, position description and University agree fees, etc	
11 October 2011		—
18 October 2011	Finalise Specification etc and Package for interested candidates	
25 October 2011	Australian advertisement to appear	

Week commencing	Actions etc	Who
1 November 2011	International advertisement to appear	
8 November 2011	Source & Search	
15 November 2011	Source & search	
22 November 2011	Source & search	
29 November 2011	Source & search	
6 December 2011	Source & search	
13 December 2011	Deadline for applications	
20 December 2011		—
27 December 2011	Consultant office closed	
3 January 2012		—
10 January 2012		—
17 January 2012		—
24 January 2012	Preliminary review of potential candidates with Remuneration Committee	
31 January 2012	Complete interviews and reference taking	
7 February 2012		—
14 February 2012		—
21 February 2012		—
28 February 2012	Finalise Short-list of candidates	
6 March 2012		—
13 March 2012		—
20 March 2012		—
27 March 2012	Formal Council Selection committee meets	
3 April 2012		—
10 April 2012	Negotiation with preferred candidate	
17 April 2012		—
24 April 2012		—
1 May 2012	Complete assignment/announce appointment	

Appendix 4: Specification Document

Specification for Vice-Chancellor cum President of the Organisation

This University is one of Australia's largest, oldest and most successful universities. Established as the Working Men's College in 1887, the University's activities today are located on three campuses plus other sites in metropolitan Melbourne, in several areas of regional Victoria and on a number of other national and international sites. Each of the University's seven faculties offers courses ranging from certificate level vocational programs to bachelor degrees to doctoral research programs. Its thirty research centres and institutes are at the forefront of innovation. The University annual turnover approaches A$400 million and it has over 50,000 students and 3,000 staff.

The University's mission is to provide technical and professional education that develops people for leadership and employment, and to undertake research programs that address real world issues, within an international and community context. Its goal is to create and sustain a distinctive world class university at the forefront of technical and professional education and real world research through continuous improvement and with all staff committed to quality management processes. It will be characterised as an organisation and in the conduct of its staff and students by the values of client focus, practicality and relevance, global imagination, cultural diversity, fairness to all, innovation and enterprise, environmental care, learning and personal growth, ethical behaviour and responsibility and technological/professional orientation.

The present Vice-Chancellor and President retires in October 2012 having completed eleven years in the role.

The Position

The Vice-Chancellor and President is responsible for ensuring strong and effective leadership and clear direction within the University, providing the University with an appropriate vision and strategic plan. As chief executive of the organisation, the Vice-Chancellor and President reports to the University Council and is responsible for all its affairs, be they academic or of a business nature. The Vice-Chancellor and President is accountable for the achievement of key University targets which are specified in its strategic plan, oversees the preparation and management of the University budget, and directs and co-ordinates staff to ensure that the University's objectives, policy and strategic directions are achieved. The Vice-Chancellor and President is also the principal spokesperson of the University and ensures that its relationships with all stakeholders are managed effectively.

Reporting to the Vice-Chancellor and President are a number of executives responsible for the core business activities of teaching and learning, research and development, international activities and community service, and for services and support, developmental initiatives and planning and quality. In carrying out the role, the Vice-Chancellor and President will develop an outstanding senior team who are committed to the University's values and strategies and who will genuinely support their implementation and achievement.

This position offers an exciting opportunity to guide one of Australia's leading technological and vocational universities into the twenty-first century, building on its past achievements and current initiatives.

The Ideal Candidate

The ideal candidate will be an experienced manager and educator, who has developed an outstanding career in academia or in a related business or research activity, based on exceptional educational qualifications. The successful candidate will hold a Ph.D. in a discipline relevant to the University's educational activities, and demonstrate a thorough familiarity with the Australian post secondary education system.

Key Competencies

The ideal candidate will have demonstrated key competencies in a number of areas including:

Leadership competencies as shown by:

- ➢ Demonstrated success fostering a high performance
- ➢ Proven capacity to communicate an organisation's mission and vision, and to build and lead a team committed their achievement.
- ➢ A demonstrated inclusive management style which has resulted in clear definition of accountabilities, implementation of appropriate management systems and successful performance management.
- ➢ Proof of entrepreneurial flair, the ability to build support structures and evidence of shared commitment from key staff.

General management skills as shown by:

- ➢ Proven success in achieving a clearly defined set of objectives across a large organisation by delegating to key and competent staff members.
- ➢ Demonstrated ability to provide focus to an organisation ensuring the attainment of key objectives.

> Confirmed success managing an organisation in a phase of significant change or growth, ensuring its financial viability and appropriate prioritisation of key objectives.

> Demonstrated achievement in identifying and encouraging outstanding performers and in dealing appropriately with underperformers.

> Proven ability in successfully managing the sometimes conflicting ambitions of various key internal and external stakeholders.

Personal competencies as shown by:

> Illustrated adherence to the key values which the University seeks to reflect, namely client focus, practicality and relevance, global imagination. Cultural diversity, fairness to all, innovation and enterprise, environmental care, learning and personal growth, ethical behavior and responsibility, technological/professional orientation.

> Demonstrated ease the University's desire to excel in education focusing on technology and vocational relevance.

> Strong interpersonal and communication skills, both written and verbal.

> Proven ability to effectively represent an organisation to external parties.

> Established skills in successfully dealing with ambiguity.

> These Key Competencies and the Knowledge/Skill/Experience requirements

These key competencies and the knowledge/skill/Experience requirements in the Position Description should be addressed by applicants.

Location

Victoria, Australia

Remuneration

An appropriate remuneration package will be offered in order to attract, motivate and retain an outstanding Vice-Chancellor and President.

Position Description - Position: Vice-Chancellor and President

Primary Objective

Provide the University with an appropriate vision and strategic plan and ensure strong and effective leadership and clear direction within the University.

Freedom to Act/Autonomy

The Vice-Chancellor and President:

- Reports to the University Council, and provides leadership and authoritative advice on the establishment of objectives, policies, programs and the strategic plan.
- Is the principal spokesperson of the University.
  - Has the delegated authority of the University Council for the management of the University.
  - *Oversees* the preparation and management of the consolidated University budget and recommends its adoption to the University Council.
  - Is accountable for the achievement of key University targets, as specified in the Strategic Plan.
  - Ensures that the organisation is appropriately and transparently structured and staffed with superior executives and school/department heads who are committed to achieving the University's objectives.
  - Directs and co-ordinates staff to optimise the use of human, financial and physical resources of the University to achieve Council objectives, policy and strategic directions.
  - Ensures University activities comply with *relevant* Acts, legal demands and ethical standards.

University Dimensions (Approximate)

Turnover:	A$376 million (2010)
Staff Numbers:	2850
Onshore Enrolments:	35,737 EFTSU

Context

The University is a multi-level dual sector education, training and research service organisation, offering programs ranging from certificate *level* vocational programs through tailored programs for industry and community clients, to bachelor degrees to doctoral research programs. The University has *several* companies which are responsible for commercial activities relating to the University's core business activities.

The University's goal is to create and sustain a distinctive world-class university at the forefront of technical and professional education and real-world research, through continuous improvement and with all staff committed to quality management processes. As a world-class university, the University will be recognised as a leader in its teaching and learning processes, research activities and community service.

Direct Reports

- Deputy Vice-Chancellor and Vice-President
- Deputy Vice-Chancellor (Resources)

The Office of the Vice-Chancellor and President includes:

- Executive Director (Major Projects)
- Director Planning & Quality
- Chief Executive Officer University Technology Estate

Inter-relationships

A significant focus of the position is the external representation and promotion of the University to industry, the education sector, government and the community, both in Australia and internationally.

The Vice-Chancellor and President develops and communicates the Strategic Plan, with input and support from the Vice-Chancellor's Executive Group (VCEM).

The Vice-Chancellor and President reports to the University Council on the University's performance in progressing towards the objectives and targets set in the Strategic Plan.

Groups within the Office of the Vice-Chancellor and President provide support to other areas of the University in facilitating quality and planning and development initiatives.

Challenges

As Vice-Chancellor and President of the University, the position is challenged to:

- Develop the University's vision and purpose and establish stakeholder commitment.
- Lead and manage the achievement of strong growth targets for the University, with emphasis on international operations and research.
- Build on the University's past achievements and current initiatives and implement its agreed strategic direction.
- Ensure a student centred approach to teaching and learning with   an emphasis on career

development and a commitment to life-long learning.
- Ensure all University activities contribute towards a rewarding student experience that encourages a life-long association with the University.
- Maximize opportunities for access to education.
- Develop an outstanding senior team who are committed to the University's values and strategies and who will genuinely support their implementation and achievement.
- Promote the University to secure funds and resources, and build a diverse and stable revenue base in an environment where there is expected to be further deregulation, greater competition and contestability for resources.

Knowledge/Skill/Experience Requirements

The incumbent requires:

- Proven outstanding leadership ability and achievement at a senior executive management level, within an academic institution or professional environment.
- Illustrated capacity to communicate an organisation's mission and vision, and to build and lead team committed to their achievement.
- Demonstrated inclusive management style that creates and fosters a continuous Learning environment amongst University staff.
- Confirmed ability to priorities and manage accordingly.
- Strong commitment to the University's mission, goals and values.
- Demonstrated ability to think creatively and strategically to lead the University in thE achievement of its vision.
- Demonstrated understanding of local and global higher education practices.
- Demonstrated highly developed interpersonal skills appropriate for the effective externa representation of University interests to governments, relevant bodies, industry and the wider community; outstanding skills in negotiation, communication and liaison at the state, national and international levels.
- Distinguished personal academic achievement.
- A relevant Ph.D. and skills, knowledge and experience to satisfy the professional criteria of research and scholarship, educational development and practice, and institutional, professional and community leadership.

Outcomes

The following section details expected outcomes of the position.

1. Leads to Inspire

Focus is on communication and enablement of a clear, inspiring and relevant direction for the University, a commitment to quality and excellence and the realisation of outcomes.

- Ensures strategic and business planning processes and outcomes are completed, monitored and reviewed.
- Identifies and enthusiastically communicates the University's vision, mission and goals.
- Sets challenging but realistic goals, measuring performance and lor outcomes against high quality standards.
- Develops and implements strategies and initiatives that will achieve continuous improvement in systems, quality and process.
- Delegates clearly resulting in a clear definition of accountabilities.
- Responds creatively, innovatively and quickly to new challenges and opportunities.
- Make tactical and strategic choices which enhance resource flexibility and responsiveness.
- Applies marketing principles, strategies and methods which reinforce the University's competitive advantage.

2. Shapes the Future

Focus is on understanding the external environment, and identifying challenges and opportunities for the University into the future.

- Translates environmental considerations and strategic requirements into plans, objectives and actions for the University.
- Analyses and plans at a strategic and conceptual level, and balances immediate operational imperatives with long term organisational direction.
- Demonstrates a high level of tolerance for change and continues to manage effectively and efficiently in such an environment.

3. Sustains Partnerships

Focus is on establishing and maintaining positive partnerships.

- Works to build and sustain effective relationships both across the University and externally.
- Negotiates effectively to achieve outcomes of mutual benefit.

- ➢ Sustains and builds an appropriate and positive profile of the University to all stakeholders.
- ➢ Develops personal and University credibility and reputation both in Australia and internationally.

4. Develops Potential

Focus is on management style and practices for the optimum development of people.

- ➢ Develops and maintains management skills through development activities for self and team.
- ➢ Develops the potential of all staff through active performance management systems.
- ➢ Maximises the quality and contribution of others and acknowledgesand rewards their successes.

5. Models Professionalism

Focus is on modeling the highest standards of personal, professional and organisational behaviour.

- ➢ Provides a strong role model of consistent, ethical behaviour tostaff and colleagues through the demonstration of honesty, trustworthiness, commitment, loyalty, fairness and integrity.
- ➢ Espouses the highest quality of work performance.
- ➢ Is aware of personal strengths, acknowledges limitations and makes major efforts to acquire new skills and knowledge.
- ➢ Establishes and accepts personal and collective accountability.

Comprehensive Case Study

Job Characteristics of Officers and Agents: Results of a National Job Analysis*

> *Article by David R. Shetterly, Ph.D., and Anand Krishnamoorthy, Ph.D. Troy University, USA.
>
> Published with permission from David R. Shetterly.

A national Job analysis of officer and agent law enforcement positions in a large federal agency was conducted to identify the most critical job characteristics as a foundation for follow-on development of medical standards. The study employed factor analysis to identify 82 high-priority job requirements. A comparison of officer and agent job characteristics showed that any systematic difference in high-priority job requirements between the two groups was minimal. Using factor analysis in conjunction with a qualitative technique such as focus groups provides a systematic and supportable method for isolating the important job characteristics of law enforcement positions.

The law enforcement community represents a group for which the decision to hire, fire, and make many other personnel-related decisions is of critical importance. When a law enforcement officer or agent is hired, the person must be capable of meeting a wide range of job requirements. If he or she is not fully capable of performing job requirements, the officer or agent can be a danger to him or her-self, coworkers, and the general public the person was hired to protect. A particular need is for reliable and valid medical standards. Federal agencies that employ law enforcement officials must ensure that personnel are medically and psychologically fit to perform their duties at the full performance levels.

The organization studied for this article is a large federal agency that employs thousands of people across the United States. To meet its mission, the agency employs between 500 to 2,000 law enforcement officers and agents. Agents are covered by the GS-1811 occupational series and are responsible for planning and conducting investigations. Officers are uniformed personnel covered by the GS-IS02 occupational series, and they are responsible for enforcing federal laws and regulations.

In December 2003 the agency initiated data collection procedures for a job analysis of law enforcement positions focusing on identification of essential job functions for the development of medical standards. The job analysis was conducted in cooperation with the Federal Occupational Health (FOH) office, which is an element of the U.S Department of Health and Human Services. FOH has the responsibility to develop medical standards for federal law enforcement positions. A statistical analysis of the job characteristic data collected by the agency follows.

The primary objective of this analysis is to answer the question of which job requirements of the law enforcement positions are the most critical for the development of medical standards. Critical job requirements were identified by determining which job characteristics law enforcement personnel currently employed by the agency deem important to job performance and occur frequently. Job relatedness of the requirements identified by law enforcement personnel was established through the use of appropriate statistics. Discussion of related literature and an introduction of the specific design used to obtain the results of the study follow. The presentation of the data collected and the meaning of the results is also considered.

Job Analysis

According to Brannick and Levine, "Job analysis covers a host of activities, all of which are directed toward discovering, understanding, and describing what people do at work. Job analysis is important because it forms the basis for the solution of virtually every human resource problem." More directly, job analysis is a critical HR function because it establishes the extent to which characteristics of a position are job related. Weighing the job relatedness of a position's characteristic is vitally important when making personnel related decisions. For example, when selecting new employees, public employers must make hiring decisions that are consistent with important characteristics of the job. Job analysis is used for, among other things, the development and validation of selection procedures, the setting of minimum qualifications, and the validation of physical ability selection criteria for police officers.

Job-related characteristics are also important once employees are hired. In managing a public workforce, decisions related to personnel decisions such as promotions, development, discipline, reassignment, and terminations must also be based on job-related criteria. For example, job analysis has been used to develop a content-valid training report for report writing. When public employers make personnel decisions that are not related to characteristics of the job, they make themselves liable to costly legal action. In addition to litigation, personnel decisions made on criteria that are not job related leave a public employer open to loss of public confidence and degraded performance.

The conducting of job analysis can take many directions. Interviews, observations, survey questionnaires, critical incidents, and worker diaries are all means of systematically conducting job analysis that have an underlying goal of aiding decision making. A key use of job analysis is distinguishing between essential and marginal job functions. Essential job functions are those that are fundamental to a job; marginal job duties are incidental to the job. One of the goals of the research -reported here was to help isolate the essential job functions of officer and agent positions.

Only a few studies dealing with job analysis in the context of law enforcement and medical standards have been published. Three of these studies are closely related to the research on officer and agent job requirement data reported here. The three studies involved administration of a survey instrument to better understand the tasks, define job characteristics, or describe the roles and day-to-day functions of incumbents. The first study concerned the job of police chief in the state of Illinois, and it used interviews and a job analysis questionnaire to aid in development of a program for professional credentialing. The second study was a job analysis of the work of occupational and environmental health nurses in the United States. That study also involved the use of a questionnaire to collect rating data on 131 task items. As with the police chief study, the objective was to validate the contents of a professional nursing credential. The third study was similar to the job analysis of occupational and environmental health nurses in the United States, but it focused on the roles of occupational health nurses in Japan. The current study extended the use of job analysis by administering a task rating questionnaire to law enforcement personnel in a large federal agency.

Research Design

Questionnaire

The sample was 380 current law enforcement officers and agents. The survey instrument was constructed to shed light on the physical and mental job requirements of officer and agent positions. Development of the questionnaire began with a review of a standard questionnaire previously used for such purposes. The standard questionnaire contained job requirement categories and related questions developed by subject matter experts. The questions addressed topics that are commonly accepted to be relevant to federal law enforcement positions, and a standard questionnaire was adapted for use in focus groups with officers and agents.

The questionnaire used in this study was designed to explore 131 job characteristics spread among eight categories: Work Schedule, Work Environment, Mental and Cognitive Skills, Musculoskeletal/Cardiovascular, Weapons/Defensive Tactics, Senses, Vision, and Hearing. Questions in each category addressed job requirements that are thought to relate to the category. The number of questions per category ranged from seven for senses to 32 for musculoskeletal/cardiovascular.

The importance and frequency of a job characteristic was measured for each characteristic, using Likert scaling. For importance, respondents answered job requirement questions on a scale of zero (function is never related to law enforcement) to five (critically important to job performance, cannot perform the job without this job element). For frequency, respondents had to answer the job requirement questions on a scale of zero (not performed in career) to seven (performed daily).

In addition to job requirement questions, the survey asked respondents to answer eight demographic questions. Standard demographic items such as age and gender were covered in this set of questions. Job-related questions, such as type of position held (officer/agent), years of experience, job status (supervisor/nonsupervisor), and federal General Schedule grade level were also asked. A final question provided respondents the opportunity to write in information on tasks not comments by the survey and to provide comments and suggestions.

After completed surveys were submitted, they were coded into a format necessary for statistical analysis. The resulting dataset was analyzed using statistical applications in Excel and the Statistical Package for the Social Sciences (SPSS).

Statistical Analysis

There are two basic components to the data analysis reported in this article. The first component is the mean and mode for each question in the survey. The second is a factor analysis that establishes the validity of the job requirement data.

Factor analysis is especially useful when there are many variables, as in this study. A factor, which in this study can be understood as a job characteristic category, is a condensed statement of the relationship among a set of variables. In setting up the factor analysis, each of the eight categories addressed in questions one through 131 was treated as a factor. Factor analysis was used to confirm the existence of an overall job characteristic and to determine which questions were most closely associated with a given characteristic.

Associations between a job characteristic and actual practice were determined using the factor loading for a particular variable. Factor loadings are the correlation between each variable (question) and the characteristic. Factor loadings are similar to a correlation coefficient, taking on a value between zero and one and with loadings closer to one indicating higher association. Questions with a high factor loading were considered closely associated with a job characteristic, and those with a low loading were deemed to be weakly associated with the characteristic. A common practice is to use a factor loading of 0.6 or higher to indicate a high loading and 0.3 or higher to indicate a moderately high loading. A threshold factor loading of 0.6 or higher is the convention used in this study. The higher factor loading is used because of the possible detrimental impact of basing personnel decisions on a job requirement moderately related to an overall factor.

For example, the first category of job characteristics, work schedule, had nine questions. If questions three, four and seven had a factor loading above 0.6 and the rest had a factor loading less than 0.6, then the content covered by questions three, four and seven would be considered to be the most important work schedule requirements. This rule was applied to each of the job characteristic categories. Therefore, a question with a factor loading greater than 0.6, and a high importance mean value or high frequency mean value was identified as having the most support for being a job characteristic upon which to develop medical standards. A question with a low factor loading but a high importance or frequency mean value is not as reliable as a basis for medical standards, but it still merits further analysis because the characteristic is important to survey respondents.

Empirical Results

The presentation of the job analysis is divided into two parts. The first section presents the results of the statistical analyses performed with respect to the 131 job characteristics. The second section describes the differences in key job characteristics between officers and agents. The overall data set contains survey answers from 380 respondents. A large majority of the respondents are male (85 percent), officers (77 percent), and occupy nonsupervisory (79 percent) positions. The average age of respondents was 44 years, and respondents had an average of 15 years of experience in law enforcement.

Job Characteristics: Comparison among Job Requirement Categories

Summary statistics are presented in Table 1. Tables 5-12 provide details on the mean mode, and other statistical tests performed on the job requirement questions. Looking at each category, officers and agents indicate that Weapons/Defensive Tactics is of the greatest importance, although it is the lowest in terms of frequency of occurrence. Work Environment and the Mental and Cognitive Skills categories also have high importance, with respective mean values of 4.15 and 4.42. The frequency of occurrence is also high for the two categories.

Table 1:
Summary of Mean Values of Responses to Job Characteristic Questions, by Category

Category	Mean Importance	Mean Frequency	Factors/ Questions	High-Priority Questions	Low Priority Questions	Questions Needing More Research	Questions not Meeting Criteria
Work Schedule	3.85	5.03	2/9	5	1	1	2
Work Environment	4.15	4.82	3/19	11	3	4	1
Mental and Cognitive Skills performance	4.42	4.75	3/18	13	1	2	2
Musculoskeletal /Cardiovascular	4.02	2.91	4/32	14	12	2	4
Weapons/ Defensive Tactics	4.68	1.84	1/9	9	0	0	0
Senses	3.98	3.15	2/7	4	3	0	0
Vision	4.02	3.83	3/26	18	6	1	1
Hearing	4.05	4.37	1/11	8	3	0	0
Totals			19/131	82	29	10	10

Work Schedule questions had the lowest mean for importance of any of the job characteristic categories but also the highest frequency of occurrence. This reflects the ordinary things that agents and officers do on a routine basis. The Tactics/Weapons questions yielded responses that were the opposite of those for Work Schedule. Weapons/Tactics questions were identified as having the highest importance to respondents, but they were reported as being the least likely to occur. This reflects the nonroutine activity of officers and agents that, while rare in occurrence, are vitally important in terms of personal safety. The categories of Senses, Vision, Hearing, and Musculoskeletal/Cardiovascular are similar in terms of level of importance, with mean values respectively of 3.98, 4:02, 4.05, and 4.02.

Table 1 also provides summary data that is valuable for prioritizing the development of medical standards. The column titled Factors/Questions gives the number of questions asked in each category and the number of factors derived through analysis of respondents' replies. The column labeled High-Priority Questions shows the number of job requirements in each category that merit priority attention (coded as H for identification purposes in Tables 5-12). Questions in this area have a factor loading greater than 0.6 and either a mean importance value greater than four (i.e., very important to job performance), a mean frequency value greater than five (i.e., occurs monthly), or both.

In all, 82 high-priority requirements were identified. The Low-Priority column of 'lablel shows which questions regarding job requirements received a factor loading greater than 0.6 but a mean importance value of less than four and a mean frequency value of less than five (coded as L for identification purposes in Tables 5-12). There are 29 low-priority questions.

Questions with a factor loading less than 0.6 and a mean importance value greater than four or a mean frequency value greater than five were included in several categories. Ten questions merit further investigation, and these are listed in the Questions Needing More Research column of Table 1 and coded as R in Tables 5-12. The questions do not relate strongly to a category of job characteristics, but they are either very important job requirements, occur frequently, or both. Finally, 10 questions had a factor loading of less than 0.6 along with low mean importance and frequency values. The questions, in this area are shown in the Questions Not Meeting Criteria column of Table 1 and are coded as N in Tables 5-12.

Job Characteristics: Comparison within Job Requirement Categories

Since the number of high-priority job requirements is large, a subset of job requirements in each category is identified as Very High Priority. The questions about these job characteristics had a factor loading greater than 0.6 and mean values of greater than four and five on the importance and frequency scales, respectively. A total of 26 questions that fell into this Very High Priority category. Those 26 questions deserve special attention and are detailed in Table 2.

It is interesting to note the concentration of very high-priority questions within a few categories. Work Environment, Mental and Cognitive Skills, and Vision contain 22 of the very high-priority questions. Work Schedule and Hearing have a modest number (4) of very high-priority questions. The Musculoskelatal/Cardiovascular, Weapons/Defensive Tactics, and Senses categories have no high-priority questions.

The data suggests officers and agents need to be able to work long, nontraditional hours including holidays and weekends. They need to be able to drive patrol vehicles, work in extreme weather, detain individuals and conduct vehicular stops, work outside

Table 2: Very High-Priority Questions

Question	Category	Mean Importance	Mean Frequency
Work extended hours	Work Schedule	4.43	6.20
Work nontraditional hours	Work Schedule	4.19	5.98
Work over holidays and weekends	Work Schedule	4.27	5.06
Drive patrol vehicles	Work Environment	4.73	6.58
Work in > 90°F temperature	Work Environment	4.34	5.35
Work in < 30°F temperature	Work Environment	4.33	5.21
Work in high/low humidity	Work Environment	4.27	5.44
Detain individuals	Work Environment	4.7	5.98
Conduct vehicular stops	Work Environment	4.65	5.45
Work of > 50% outside office	Work Environment	4.61	6.14
Work alone while armed	Work Environment	4.85	6.52
Analyze documents	Mental and Cognitive Skills	4.74	5.77
Assess reliability of information	Mental and Cognitive Skills	4.72	5.95
Recognize inconsistencies inwords/actions	Mental and Cognitive Skills	4.67	5.87

Distinguish deception	Mental and Cognitive Skills	4.57	5.78
Respond to suddensituational changes	Mental and Cognitive Skills	4.74	6.06
Maintain calm	Mental and Cognitive Skills	4.68	5.21
Accountable for governmentfunds and records	Mental and Cognitive Skills	4.29	5.06
Identify subject by vision	Vision	4.19	5.08
Identity license plate > 20 ft	Vision	4.26	5.45
Drive in the dark	Vision	4.65	5.89
Detect! Nervousness	Vision	4.54	5.3
Read fine detail	Vision	4.17	5.82
Read gauges and dials	Vision	4.00	6.14
Estimate distance from subject	Vision	4.04	5.66
Monitor radio transmissions	Hearing	4.28	5.7

Their office, and work alone while armed. They also need to have a keen mental ability when it comes to gathering information. They need to be able to analyze documents, identify inconsistencies in spoken and written language, and identify deception. Furthermore, they need to be emotionally balanced individuals who can respond to sudden situational changes.

Vision is also an important job characteristic for agents and officers. They need to be able to read fine detail and items that are at a distance. Furthermore, they need a keen sense of night vision and must be able to detect nervousness in others. Finally, their hearing needs to be sharp enough to monitor radio transmissions through moderate background noise.

Comparison of Officers and Agents

The summary of results by position and across categories is shown in Table 3. Looking at the summary data, officers rate the questions in each category higher in terms of both importance and frequency. The sole exception is frequency for Weapons/Defensive Tactics, for which officers rank slightly, lower (1.77) than do agents (1.84).

Table 3: Mean Values for Position by Category

Category	Mean Importance Total	Mean Frequency Total	Officer Importance	Agent Importance	Officer Frequency	Agent Frequency
Work Schedule (1-9)	3.85	5.03	3.87	3.74	5.04	4.94
Work Environment (10-28)	4.15	4.82	4.22	3.89	4.98	4.17
Mental and CognitiveSkills Perfornnance (29-46)	4.42	4.75	4.43	4.36	4.76	4.73
Musculoskeletal/ Cardiovascular (47-78)	4.02	2.91	4.03	3.95	2.92	2.86
Weapons/ Defensive Tactics (79-87)	4.68	1.84	4.72	4.52	1.77	1.84
Senses (88-94)	3.98	3.15	4.03	3.86	3.26	2.68
Vision (95-120)	4.02	3.83	4.05	3.91	3.89	3.53
Hearing (121-130)	4.05	4.37	4.09	3.92	4.49	3.92

Working from these broad results, a statistical test was performed to determine any systematic differences between officers and agents in how they perceive the frequency or importance of the various job characteristics investigated in this study. Ten questions served as the basis for this test. These questions involved a switch in priority from either High Priority to Low Priority or Low Priority to High Priority when the decision criteria used in the development of Table 1 were applied to each subgroup. With the exception of the question "numerous tightly scheduled meetings," a difference on the importance scale was the determining factor in the change of classification. Table 4 provides information on the relevant questions.

On the question "numerous tightly scheduled meetings," our analysis yielded a classification of Low Priority for officers and High Priority for agents. On the remaining nine questions, application of our decision criteria yielded a classification of High priority for officers and Low Priority for agents. Our analysis yielded consistent high and low priority classifications between the two groups on the remaining High Priority and Low priority questions.

Table 4:
Test for Difference Between Officers & Agents

Question	Category	Officer Mean	Agent mean	T	P
Numerous tightly scheduled meetings	Work Schedule	4.62	5.01	-2.238	.0129
Work over holidays and weekends	Work Schedule	4.45	3.52	8.255	.0001
Work under sudden temperatu rechanges of >30°F	Work Environment	4.08	3.71	2.544	.0057
Work in snow/ice	Work Environment	4.24	3.78	3.277	.0006
Identify threat	Vision	3.10	2.66	1.683	.0466
Estimate distance from subject	Vision	4.07	3.90	1.414	.0791
Hear with moderate backgroundnoise	Hearing	4.06	3.95	0.7938	.2139
Detect soft sounds	Hearing	4.10	3.92	0.7008	.2419
Distinguish among sounds	Hearing	4.16	3.99	1.426	.0774
Localize sound source	Hearing	4.08	3.75	2.585	.0551

As can be seen from Table 4, five questions are significant at the .05 level. Three are significant at the .10 level, and two are statistically Insignificant. The small subset of five j6b characteristics that has been identified is suggestive of more stringent medical standards for officers in four instances and for agents in one instance. Taken as a whole, however, officers and agents are largely in agreement on the importance and frequency of the 131 job characteristics that are the subject of this study.

The statistical procedure discussed above has one major limitation. The number of officers who participated in the research was greater than the number of agents by a ratio of nearly 4:1. This disparity may have influenced research results. Larger sample sizes generally yield results that are more accurate. Given the disparity in sample sizes between the two groups, it is entirely possible that the results pertaining to officers are more accurate than are those pertaining to agents. For this reason, decision makers need to be more skeptical with regards to the difference between officers and agents.

Discussion

Factor analysis was used to analyze the importance and frequency of each question within the eight job characteristic categories. It was assumed that the set of questions for each of the eight categories was in fact related to the category. Each category is analogous to a factor, and factor analysis confirmed whether the questions for each category were unidimensional (i.e., reflective of one factor) or multidimensional (i.e., reflective of multiple factors). The factor analysis also identified which of the specific job characteristics are most closely related to each general category of job requirements.

The factor analysis confirmed that the set of job requirement questions addressing importance for Weapons/Defensive Tactics and Hearing categories are unidimensional. The factor analysis for the remaining categories confirmed that the questions for each category represent multiple factors. The question content for each of the factors was used to name the factors. Naming the factors is an inexact science. The approach used in this study was to provide a name that corresponded to the type of job characteristic that dominated within each set of job requirements. For example if the majority of the questions for a job requirement involved walking for extended periods of time, the requirement was named Walking.

Among the 131 questions asked, 82 were found to be high-priority questions regarding 19 factors. Further, 26 questions were identified as very high priority. The Work Environment, Mental and Cognitive Skills, and Vision categories contain all but four of the high-priority questions. An interesting finding is that law enforcement officers tend to rate importance and frequency of job characteristics higher than their agent counterparts. With the exception of importance for Work Environment and frequency for Weapons Defensive Tactics, officers have higher mean values than agents. However, only with five questions was the mean difference between officers and agents large enough to indicate a statistically significant difference between the two groups. The higher mean importance and frequency values for officers are suggestive of the possible need to consider different standards for officers and agents. Additional research is needed to gain a better understanding of what explains the difference in perception between the two groups.

The results of this analysis were used as a basis for additional qualitative analysis of essential job requirements by the federal agency. The agency did this by conducting a series of five focus groups for officers and agents. The quantitative results served as the baseline position for determination of essential job functions. To change a determination of the study required agreement of at least four out of five focus groups. The final results identified 93 essential job functions for agents and 92 essential job functions for officers.

The classification of very high-priority questions held up well under focus group scrutiny. Of the 26 questions identified as very high priority, all represented job requirements that are essential for officers. And all but two were identified as essential for agents.

The focus groups also helped reconcile a determination on the 10 questions designated as in need of additional research. Five of the questions were subsequently identified as essential job functions, two were not considered essential, and three were mixed-meaning that they are essential for one group but not the other. The result for the 10 questions that did not meet the criteria also proved interesting. Six of the questions were deemed to not be job essential, three were considered job essential, and one was essential for one group but not the other.

Job analysis ties into the HR decision making in a number of ways. This study reports on the use of job analysis data to support decisions on the development of medical standards for law enforcement agents and officers.

For example, public organizations that employ law enforcement officers and agents have an interest in physical fitness and agility standards. A standard that does not meet the rigor for a valid standard runs the risk of coming under legal attack for being an invalid predictor of successful job performance. Job analysis supports the validity of physical fitness standards by demonstrating that standards are based on concrete scientific evidence. Job analysis also applies to many other HR decision areas, such as determining training needs, developing selection procedures, and developing criteria needed for supportable performance reviews. The same essential logic that applies to the development of medical standards applies to these areas as well. HR decision making must be based on job-related criteria, and the most supportable criteria are those that have been empirically derived.

Conclusion

Taken as a whole, the questions in the survey are highly representative of the critical characteristics of the federal agency's special agent and officer positions. The size of the simple, high response rate, and scope of the questions asked demonstrate a systematic and objective approach to identifying the important characteristics of federal law enforcement positions. The contents of this article isolate the questions that are most supportable for the development of medical standards. It also isolates questions for follow-up investigation.

The approach to job analysis described here provides mangers a basis for identifying critical job requirements and for establishing priorities for developing related medical standards. When the information is supplemented by qualitative information through focus groups or other means, management is in a better position to support personnel decisions based on job-related criteria.

References

- Federal Occupational Health Law Enforcement Medical Programs (2003). General Information on Federal Occupational Health. Retrieved September 27, 2004, from http://www.foh.dhhs.gov/Public/ProductFocus!May03/LE. as p

- Brannick, M. T., & Levine, E. L. (2002). Job Analysis. Thousand Oaks, CA: Sage Publications, 2002.

- Urbanek, S. J. (1997). Job Analysis: A Local Government's Experience, *Public Personnel Management,* 26(3), 423.

- Prien, E. P. (2004). A Content-oriented approach to setting minimum qualifications, *Public Personnel Management,* 33(1), 89.

- Anderson, G. S., Plecas, D., & Segger T. (2001). Police officer physical ability testing: Re-validating a selection criterion Policing, 24(1), 8, 24.

- Truxillo, D. M., Paronto, Collins, M. E., & Sulzer). L. (2004). Effects of subject matter expert viewpoint on job analysis, *Public Personnel Management,* 33(1), 33.

- Chang, I. W., & Kleiner, B. H. (2002). How to conduct job analysis effectively. Management Research, 25(3), 73-82.

- Chow, C. M., & Kleiner B. H. (2002). How to differentiate essential job duties from marginal job? *Managerial Law,* 44(1/2), 121-128.

- Kitzman, B. C., Steven, J. (1999). Standard the job of police chief in the state of Illinois. *Public Personnel Management,* 28(3), 473-496.

- Salazar, M. K, Kemerer S., Amann M. c., & Fabrey, L. J. (2002). Defining the roles and functions of occupational and environmental health nurses: Results of a national job analysis. *AAOHN Journal,* 50(1), 16-26.

- Ishihara, I, Yoshimine, T., Horikawa,). J & Majima, J. (2004). Defining the roles and functions of occupational health nurses in Japan: Results of job analysis. *AAOHN Journal,* 52(6), 230-42.

- Kline, P. (1999). An Easy guide to factor analysis. London and New York: Routledge.

- Ibid.

Appendix 1: Tables 5-12

Table 5:
Mean, Mode, and Factor Loadings for Work Schedule Questions (1-9)

Question	Mean Importance	Mode Importance	Mean Frequency	Mode Frequency	Factor 1 Work Hours	Factor 2 Meeting Timelines	*Status
Work extended hours	4.63	5	6.20	6	.66	.28	H
Significant travel	4.16	5	5.30	6	.44	.49	R
Work nontraditional hours	4.19	5	5.98	6	.75	.01	H
Irregular meals	3.60	3	5.82	6	.68	.33	H
Sudden work detail to a different geographic area	3.67	4	3.86	4	.48	.58	N
Stringent timelines	3.86	4	5.10	5	.14	.81	H
Numerous tightly scheculeo meeting's	3.24	3	4.70	5	<.01	.85	L
Work holidays and weekends	4.27	5	5.06	6	.77	<.01	H
Work double shift	3.21	4	3.26	4	.42	.48	N

*H = High priority, L =: Low priority, R = More research needed, N = Ouestions not meeting criteria.

Table 6:
Mean, Mode, and Factor Loadings for Physical Work Environment Questions (10-28)

Question	Mean Importance	Mode importance	Mean Frequency	Mode Frequency	Factor 1 Extreme Temperatures	Factor 2 Vehicle Use	Factor 3 Airborne Hazards	*Status
Use respirator or gas mask	2.02	2	0.61	0	.16	<.01	.82	L
Withstand chemical exposwre	3.51	4	3.84	5	.19	.26	.72	L
Use body armor	4.58	5	6.32	7	.22	.51	.36	R
Drive patrol vehicles	4.73	5	6.58	7	<.01	.74	<.01	H
Pursue. suspect in government vehicle	4.17	5	2.64	1	.28	.58	.32	R

Question	Mean Importance	Mode importance	Mean Frequency	Mode Frequency	Factor 1 Extreme Temperatures	Factor 2 Vehicle Use	Factor 3 Airborne Hazards	*Status
Use government vehicle in emergencies	4.59	5	4.53	5	.26	.71	.28	H
Work in > 90°F temperatures	4.34	5	5.35	5	.78	.38	.18	H
Work in < 30°F degree temperatures	4.33	5	5.21	5	.83	.34	.10	H

18. Work under sudden temperature changes of > 30°F	4.01	5	4.24	5	.78	.23	.16	H
Work in snow/ice	4.16	5	4.76	5	.82	.26	.13	H
WHork in high/low humidity	4.27	5	5.44	5	.82	.34	.11	H
Work at high altitude	3.56	5	3.72	1	.70	.13	.17	L
Work at heights > 12 ft	3.07	3	2.8	4	.55	.14	.39	N
Walk/run on uneven terrain	4.43	5	5.75	7	.50	.55	.25	R
Detain individuals	4.7	5	5.98	7	.35	.81	<.01	H
Conduct vehicular stops	4.65	5	5.45	6	.28	.83	.14	H
Work > 50% outside office	4.61	5	6.14	7	.39	.68	<.01	H
Use multiple work sites	4.32	5	5.74	7	.50	.41	.15	R
Work alone while armed	4.85	5	6.52	7	.29	.74	<.01	H

*H = High priority, L = Low priority, R = More research needed, N = Questions not meeting criteria.

Table 7:
Mean, Mode, and Factor Loadings for Mental and Cognitive Skills Performance Questions (29-46)

Question	Mean Importance	Mode importance	Mean Frequency	Mode Frequency	Factor 1 Cognitive Skills	Factor 2 Mental Stability	Factor 3 Professional Activity	*Status
Deal with emotionally upset individuals	4.48	5	4.55	5	.69	.30	.22	H
Provide tight security	3.99	5	3.35	5	.51	.28	.31	N
Psychological tension	4.25	5	4.77	5	.39	.54	.36	R
Give deposition	4.65	5	3.99	5	.42	.71	.13	H
Analyze documents	4.74	5	5.77	6	.36	.75	.12	H
Assess reliability of information	4.72	5	5.95	7	.72	.33	.15	H
Recognize inconsistencies in words/actions	4.67	5	5.87	6	.80	.36	.13	H
Distinguish deception	4.57	5	5.78	6	.81	.24	.16	H
Learn new techniques quickly	4.26	5	4.85	5	.71	.21	.28	H
Respond to sudden situational changes	4.74	5	6.06	7	.66	.38	.22	H
Arrest subject	4.67	5	3.89	5	.69	.40	<.01	H
Make Quick decision about the use of force	4.79	5	3.58	1	.27	.77	<.01	H
Maintain calm	4.68	5	5.21	7	.32	.73	.32	H

Question									
Maintain supportive attitude	4.44	5	6.43	7	<.01	.50		.57	R
Use false identity	3.30	3	2.06	1	.58	.12		.52	N
Relationship with individuals with a criminal past	3.74	5	3.93	5	.33	.11		.69	L
Confidentiality of informants	4.51	5	4.4	5	.27	.10		.70	H
Accountable for government funds and records	4.29	5	5.06	7	<.01	.24		.71	H

*H = High priority, L = Low priority, R = More research needed,
N = Questions not meeting criteria.

Table 8:
Mean, Mode, and Factor Loadings for Musculoskeletal/Cardiovascular Questions (47-78)

Question	Mean Importance	Mode importance	Mean Frequency	Mode Frequency	Factor 1 Subdue Subject	Factor 2 Agility and Strength	Factor 3 Climbing	Factor 4 Walking	*Status
Disarm subject	4.73	5	3.66	5	.80	.15	<.01	.32	H
Subdue resisting subject alone	4.70	5	2.86	1	.82	.18	.10	.31	H
Subdue assaultive subject alone	4.68	5	1.8	1	.88	.12	.20	.18	H
Subdue resisting subject with backup	4.67	5	2.48	1	.89	.14	.18	.19	H
Subdue assaultive subject with backup	4.64	5	1.93	1	.91	.15	.18	.11	H
Subdue subject after chase	4.41	5	1.42	1	.76	.22	.36	.12	H

Control unruly crowd	4.32	5	1.84	1	.67	.26	.42	<.01	H
Stoop to assist subject	4.34	5	2.57	1	.69	.41	.33	<.01	H
Lift and carry subject	4.16	5	1.70	1	.60	.43	.43	<.01	H
Seize contraband	4.69	5	4.64	5	.83	.24	<.01	.10	H
Reach overhead	4.04	5	5.47	7	.31	.71	.18	.14	H
Bend, stoop, squat	4.36	5	4.26	5	.59	.53	.17	.21	R
Work in tight spaces	3.76	5	3.31	4	.31	.68	.31	.14	L
Rise quickly from supine position	3.82	5	3.58	4	.27	.69	.29	.31	L
Lift up to 30 pounds without assistance	3.88	5	4.54	5	.16	.76	.23	.43	L
Lift up to 50 pounds or more with assistance	3.67	3	3.79	4	.15	.73	.32	.40	L
Push/pull more than 50 pounds without assistance	3.55	5	3.41	4	.17	.71	.40	.37	L
Push/pull more than 100 pounds with assistance	3.22	3	2.57	1	.11	.56	.52	.31	N

Question	Mean Importance	Mode importance	Mean Frequency	Mode Frequency	Factor 1 Subdue Subject	Factor 2 Agility and Strength	Factor 3 Climbing	Factor 4 Walking	*Status
Use physical force to gain entrance	3.58	5	1.56	1	.27	.33	.63	.35	L
Climb over 4-foot wall	3.57	5	1.17	1	.31	.24	.75	.34	L
Climb over 6-foot wall	3.37	0	.98	0	.26	.20	.80	.30	L
Sit for extended periods	4.05	5	4.59	5	.25	.21	.35	.66	H
Stand for extended periods	3.86	5	3.92	5	.18	.29	.29	.78	L
Walk for more than 1 hours	4.09	5	4.38	5	.21	.38	.19	.79	H
Walk for more than 2 hours	3.87	5	3.55	4	.17	.33	.30	.76	L
Walk to follow subject	3.88	5	2.82	4	.30	.37	.42	.51	N
Climb ladders or stairs	3.78	5	4.49	7	.27	.52	.42	.51	N
Pursue subject on foot	3.91	5	1.69	1	.38	.30	.53	.47	N
Run up more than two flights of stairs	3.40	5	.93	0	.20	.25	.77	.26	L
Pursue subject with obstacles	4.11	5	2.01	1	.45	.35	.44	.45	R
Tread water for 10 minutes	2.82	3	.45	0	.12	.24	.61	.11	L

*H = High priority, L = Low priority, R == More research needed,
N = Questions not meeting criteria.

Table 9:
Mean, Mode, and Factor Loadings for Weapons/Defensive Tactics Questions (79-87)

Question*	Mean Importance	Mode Importance	Mean Frequency	Mode Frequency	Tactics	*Status
Handcuff compliant subject	4.63	5	3.75	4	.84	H
Handcuff noncompliant subject	4.69	5	2.54	1	.93	H
Draw baton or pepper spray	4.7	5	2.43	1	.93	H

Question*	Mean Importance	Mode Importance	Mean Frequency	Mode Frequency	Tactics	*Status
Draw handgun	4.78	5	2.5	1	.96	H
Draw handgun with weak hand	4.31	5	0.79	0	.70	H
Deploy shoulder weapons	4.64	5	2.04	1	.89	H
Make shoot/ no shoot decision	4.79	5	1.59	1	.94	H
Fire handgun	4.8	5	0.37	0	.88	H
Load weapon in an emergency	4.78	5	0,53	0	.91	H

*H = High priority, L = Low priority, R = More research needed, N = Questions not meeting criteria.

Table 10:
Mean, Mode, and Factor Loadings for Senses Questions (88-94)

Question	Mean Importance	Mode importance	Mean Frequency	Mode Frequency	Factor 1 Work Hours	Factor 2 Meeting Timelines	*Status
Use smell to detect danger	4.32	5	3.26	1	.80	.28	H
Identify alcohol/ illegal drugs	4.41	5	4.47	5	.85	.30	H
Identify object in the dark	4.35	5	2.54	1	.80	.31	H
Load weapon in the dark	4.61	5	1.48	0	.88	.14	H
Sense temperature change	3.27	3	4.25	7	.26	.84	L
Feel vibration	3.19	3	2.97	1	.18	.91	L
Maintain balance on platform	3.73	5	3.08	4	.35	.78	L

*H= High priority, L = Low priority, R = More research needed,
N = Questions not meeting criteria.

Table 11:
Mean, Mode, and Factor Loadings for Vision Questions (95-120)

Question	Mean Importance	Mode importance	Mean Frequency	Mode Frequency	Identify	Color and Stiimate	Lenses	*Status
Identity subject by vision	4.19	5	5.08	6	.66	.44	< .01	H
Identify license plate > 20 ft.	4.26	5	5.45	6	.72	.42	< .01	H
Visual surveillance of individuals	4.34	5	4.55	5	.79	.36	.10	H
Visual surveillance of vehicles or objects	4.28	5	4.49	5	.82	.27	.12	H
Surveillance from car	4.22	5	4.4	5	.78	.39	.12	H
Visually recognize individual trom photo or description	4.19	5	3.78	5	.74	.44	.12	H
Surveillance with binoculars	4.13	5	4.1	5	.75	.37	.13	H
Drive in the dark	4.65	5	5.89	6	.68	< .01	.17	H
Identify a drawn weapon	4.69	5	2.42	1	.70	< .01	.15	H
Aim weapon at a distant target	4.59	5	2.29	3	.71	< .01	.16	H
Detect nervousness	4.54	5	5.3	6	.72	.30	< .01	H
Surveillance of crowd	3.73	4	2.77	1	.57	.51	.11	N
Identify threat	3.99	5	3.01	1	.66	.36	.16	L
Use peripheral vision	4.21	5	4.07	5	.70	.25	11	H

Differentiate colors	3.95	5	6.03	7	.26	.79	.13	H
Differentiate shades of color	3.59	3	5.58	7	.18	.83	.17	H
Visually search object	4.5	5	5.44	7	.65	.40	< .01	R
Read fine detail	4.17	5	5.82	7	.39	.67	< .01	H
Read gauges and dials	4.0	5	6.14	7	.38	.71	.15	H
Estimate distance between cars	3.99	5	6.05	7	.41	.69	.13	H
Estimate distance from Subject	4.04	5	5.66	7	.54	.62	.17	H

Question	Mean Importance	Mode importance	Mean Frequency	Mode Frequency	Identify	Color and Stiimate	Lenses	*Status
Drive without corrective lenses	3.21	4	0.4	0	.13	.19	.91	L
Identify suspect without corrective lenses	3.14	4	0.41	0	.14	.17	.93	L
Disengage from situation after losing corrective lenses	3.27	5	0.15	0	.14	< .01	.94	L
Identify and handle threat without corrective lenses	3.5	5	0.12	0	.15	< .01	.94	L
Exposure to pepper spray	3.19	5	0.18	0	.15	.16	.88	L

*H = High priority, L = Low priority, R = More research needed, N = Questions not meeting criteria.

Table 12:
Mean, Mode, and Factor Loadings for Hearing Questions (121-130)

Question*	Mean Importance	Mode Importance	Mean Frequency	Mode Frequency	Tactics	*Status
Communicate effectively in private conversations with no background noise	4.05	5	4.77	7	.79	H
Understand whispering	3.9	4	4.11	5	.82	L
Hear with moderate background noise	4.04	5	49	5	.79	H
Hear verbal warnings with loud noise	4.33	5	3.4	4	.85	H
Hear on phone with moderate noise	3.98	4	5.01	5	.82	H
Monitor radio transmission with moderate noise	4.28	5	5.7	7	.85	H
Communicate in the dark	4.29	5	3.74	5	.82	H
Understand accents/ foreign dialects	3.52	3	3.42	4	.72	L
Detect soft sounds	3.99	4	4.05	5	.88	L
Distinguish among sounds	4.12	5	4.36	5	.85	H
Localize sound source	4.01	4	4.61	5	.84	H

*H = High priority, L = Low priority, R = More research needed,
N = Questions not meeting criteria.

Case Study 4

Comprehensive Case Study

Debacle of Dream Films Productions Limited (DFPL)

Ted Bieber was one of the most successful actors in the film industry. Actor, singer, and a superstar Ted Bieber was a uber-celeb. Over the years he not only grew bigger and more iconic with each passing year but he became an institution in himself. Towards the middle of his career he started his own production company.

Ted success in films did not come easy. His early failure is common knowledge and for everything that he was applauded later, was seen as a weakness when he started his journey in films. For some time it seemed that Ted's unconventional looks and great height would see him make his way back to a life of dejection. Every filmmaker that he approached thought he was too tall at 6 feet 9 inches. In desperation Ted tried to use the one other unique characteristic that he had, his deep baritone. But here too, Bieber failed. He was rejected by a production company after an audition test. So much so, that he started to be called a 'flop star'. But as destiny would have it, Ted's 15th movie became a cult film and catapulted him to superstardom.

Dream Film Production Limited (DFPL) & its Rise

Ted started Dream Film Production Limited (DFPL) that specialized in film production and event management. It was a pioneering attempt to evolve a corporatized entertainment company. DFPL was first entertainment company of its kind that had planned to notch up $2million by way of turnover in a span of 5 years. DFPL took on the mantle of branding Bieber's personality for marketing products and services covering the entire gamut of the entertainment industry—from film production and distribution, video discs, production and marketing of television software, media buying to event and celebrity management.

The star-power of Ted Bieber saw corporates and financial institutions making a beeline and picking-up equity at premium. Even leading banks participated in company's second private placement issue, shelling out good sum for every share and a premier investment banking company was roped-in as investor. Soon after, several new films starring the Ted were announced. Film distribution rights, television serials, the contract for organizing one of the most prestigious global films awards event: DFPL's rise was impressive. The first year the company did achieve its target turnover and made a decent profit. But that growth was not substantiated in the second year.

Crash - Impact

The crash came much sooner than expected. The slim profits in the beginning faded away and the company ran reportedly into a major losses in consecutive fiscals. By the end of 3 years, DFPL had piled-up accumulated losses that were well above its net worth. DFPL was on the verge of becoming a sick-industrial company.

The impact of the crash was even worse. Banks sought to attach the famous house of the Biebers'. It also sought to attach some other properties of Ted. Shortly, XYZ Production Company secured a warrant from the Court for seizure of DFPL properties. The seizure had been ordered to realise the money awarded to XYZ in arbitration proceedings. DFPL had acquired the distribution rights for a dozen films from XYZ. While DFPL wanted XYZ to take-back the flop films, XYZ wanted DFPL to pay irrespective of the film's fortunes. Another overseas firm, which had effected some of the work connected with the global awards event, had filed a winding-up petition against DFPL. The firm was claiming hefty dues plus interest. More petitions followed.

DFPL was grounded and a superstar was written-off as a huge failure.

Leadership Errors behind the Fall of DFPL

DFPL's failure can be largely attributed to Leadership errors and the subsequent wrong decisions, primarily on the part of the promoters and also of the team of managers of the company. Despite starting on a good idea, besides having the leverage of a strong star brand, DFPL crashed like a pack of cards, due to imprudent HR gaffes.

DFPL hired large number of professional managers for managing the affairs of DFPL. These were young managers who had had successful stints in the corporate world but had no experience of the entertainment industry (that was largely unorganized and informal during those times). When the debacle of DFPL happened, the promoters reportedly blamed the professionals running their company, although the reverse finger-pointing also happened. DFPL's failure is the fault of its white-collared, blue-blooded professionals. The cars, the mobile phones, the hefty salaries. They even demanded mineral water. What was the need for 150 people on the staff when even a leading director runs his show with a little over 10?

DFPL had a huge mismatch of culture internally. The professional managers could not deal with the largely informal functioning of the entertainment industry in general and the company in particular. Evidences of the informal functioning of the company could be seen in every way the company was structured or took decisions. The board of the company, comprises largely of Bieber friends who always backed the 'Bieber strategy'. Many a times this resulted in sharp differences between the promoters, board and the managers. For instance, an Audio Video, a company owned by Bieber's wife was acquired by DFPL at a mindless price. This was way too much overvalued as many say that that the actual value of the company was much lesser. Trouble started between Bieber and his professional managers when he agreed to do stage shows in overseas. The professional managers became upset that the bookings were not done through DFPL. The impasse finally resulted in the CEO putting in his papers. He was soon followed by other top leaders in the company, including, the general manager for film distribution, vice-president for television, general manager for HRD and the vice-president for marketing. The entire top team had been decimated.

Ted Bieber brought in his old friend and confidante Peter Smith to take over the operations of DFPL. Smith was responsible for the Biebers making their successful investment before. Smith adopted a different kind of a campaign for Bieber's next upcoming film by launching the first-ever interactive game package and planned to install this package at theatres. The whole idea was put forth a firm - to merchandise the film through "Touch Screen" technology. However the film crashed so badly at the box-office that one critic even went-on to say that 'The End of Bieber'.

The Biebers also reportedly took-out the entire Rs. 15 crore profit, the company earned in the first year, and extended it as loans and advances to friends and two of their privately-held companies. The star duo are also said to have placed many shares of the company with friends and relatives at par. The professional managers were at loss to understand that how could the promoters justify the sale of equity at such a low price to friends and relatives while the company has privately placed equity at seven times higher price in two rounds of private placements.

Once DFPL began its operations, it went on a overdrive. Anything and everything to do with the entertainment business was on the platter of DFPL. Many feel that the corporation spread its' resources too wide, too thin by putting its hand on too many pies. The pace of growth of the company was not in proportion keeping with the size of their pocket. Capital started becoming a major constraint, despite the fact that banks had agreed to lend money. The company began negotiating with international advertising company to sell 10 percent of the company, hoping to raise some money. It also wanted to raise some money from the public. However nothing worked. Ted Bieber had to reportedly sell-off his stake in some companies to pump more money in the company. All this seriously dented the image of the company.

The overvaluation of Audio Video Company was already weighing heavy on DFPL's shoulders. There were also enough indicators to make believe that DFPL may have also overvalued their prime assets, the personalities of Ted and his wife. The company entered into a contract with the couple, agreeing to pay a hefty annual fee for 12 years. But DFPL had only limited success in selling these two brands. Even the contract for Ted Bieber appearing in certain advertisements was not been renewed as the group decided against celebrity endorsements because it just did not get them the mileage they wanted.

Many felt that financial misadventures on the part of the Biebers also drained DFPL's revenues. Inspired by global low cost airline magnate Sam Fenandes, Ted and brother Philip floated a low-cost airline company in a Asian country. They bought some second-hand aircrafts investing hundreds of millions of dollars. But the business collapsed with the Asian meltdown. Eventually, the aircrafts were sold. In the airline business, one needs to be financially strong to sustain such losses for long periods and Biebers only had big ambition.

DFPL hit the lowest ebb while organizing the global films awards event. DFPL's attempts at event management created more problems than profits. The global films awards event, its first such attempt in that country, was riddled with controversies, beginning with protests from social acitivist groups and ending with the Spastics Society publicly denouncing the company's inability to pay up its promised charity until recently. The global films awards organization expected a fee of $2 million from the local event manager. Along with other costs, DFPL would have run up a bill of an estimated $5 million. Even a modest estimate puts DFPL's loss at about $2 million. Ted in one of his interviews admitted that the company took-up organizing global films awards event in a hurry – "We were nervous about saying yes because we had only four months to organise the event." In the same interview, Ted Bieber said - 'If we had said no to global films awards event, it would have been interpreted we didn't have the capability of doing it'. The statement is more emotional than rational and it would not be a mistake to say that it reflected more grandiose of Ted then his understanding of business and assessment of project feasibility aspects.

These serious errors in Leadership and Ted wrong counsels ensured the doom of his company. DFPL was down and out. Later in an interview when asked did he think DFPL was a unwise venture, Ted not only accepted the same but acknowledged his lack of business acumen and errors in Leadership, as well as squarely put the blame of DFPL's failure on his managers. "*I think perhaps, in many ways (what went wrong with DFPL), I myself should be the person bearing the blame. I am not a businessman. I never have been. I have problems dealing with money. My entire career has been managed by family members or managers who have looked after my affairs. I am totally ignorant as far as money matters are concerned. For me to be suddenly thrown into this huge corporate ocean without adequate managerial capacity was perhaps the unmaking of the corporation. But I was told that 'You're like the brand figure, you don't have to get into the nitty-gritty of management.' So, I very diligently kept away from it. What was required was to have an efficient executive team where you have CEOs, VPs etc. Which is what I did! I entrusted them with the job of running the corporation. I am sorry to say, but despite all this talk of professional executives and professionalism in management, this was a terrible example as far as our company was concerned. I trusted them but their feedback, their information was inadequate and false. It led to one disaster after another*".

However many experts felt that while Ted was right about his naivety, the blame that conveniently put on the heads of his managers did not represent the right picture. The fact was that he never gave his managers enough freedom to act or make decisions. The managers he recruited were not hired carefully and hence their managerial acumen did not have experience of film production. Besides Ted's grandiose image of self, made him start on a lavish scale and DFPL spread its resources too thin too soon.

DFPL was declared bankrupt. Ted was inundated by lawsuits. The superstar fell from the pedestal. Although he was able to repay all the debt, but his image took a big hit. DFPl could never recover from the losses and was closed down.

Questions

Q. 1. Analyze the case in light of leadership and HR effectiveness. Do you think poor HR effectiveness has an impact on the business strategy of the firm?

Q. 2. Imagine yourself in the place of Ted. What different would you have done in terms of leading the company and managing the human capital? Clearly outline your strategies and how that might have a favourable impact on the business.

Comprehensive Case Study

Skill-gap & Talent Shortage in India

Indian companies must take note of the fact that our economy is no longer a predominantly agrarian one. Agriculture's contribution to the rural GDP has fallen to 41.6% while the share of industry and services has risen to 58.4%. India's leap into the 21st Century service economy is both a blessing and a challenge. It's a blessing because it creates new job opportunities, especially for those at the bottom of the employment value-chain. It's a challenge because we do not seem to have enough skilled people who are equipped to do these jobs.

According to the Federation of Indian Chambers of Commerce and Industry, India churns out around 350,000 engineers and 2.5 million university graduates annually. However, at any given point in time, about 5 million graduates remain unemployable because most of them are unskilled or under-skilled.

A McKinsey Global Institute survey reveals that multinationals find only 25% of Indian engineers employable. Similarly, according to a New York Times report, only one in four engineering graduates in India is employable, based on technical skills, English fluency, teamwork and presentation skills. This kind of shortage is evident in other streams as well. If the trend continues, the National Association of Software and Service Companies (Nasscom) projects a shortage of 500,000 knowledge workers in the years to come; the BPO service sector alone will need 350,000 workers.

Essentially, this shortage represents a severe skill gap and highlights the significance of using training and development (T&D) as an intervention in a major way. Skills and knowledge are the driving forces of economic growth and social development in any country. They have become even more important given the increasing pace of globalization. Countries with higher and better levels of skills adjust more effectively to the challenges and

opportunities of globalization. As India moves progressively towards becoming a knowledge economy, it is important to focus on advancement of skills.

A Yawning Gap

According to India's demographic profile in 2002, there were 325 million (roughly 25% of the population) who were in the age group of 20-35 years, much higher than China, which had around 308 million (21% of the population) in the same age group. By the year 2020, India will have the largest population of youth in the world. This is phenomenal, as it represents a large working population.

By comparison, some developed economies, such as France, will have only 11 million people in the age group of 20-35 years by the year 2025. Despite this, there is a huge concern over the efficacy of this large pool of young people in India. This concern is fuelled by speculation over wide skill gaps both in quantitative as well as qualitative terms.

According to the National Sample Survey (61st round), only about 2% of people between the age group of 15-29 years have received formal vocational training. Those who received non-formal vocational training made up just 8%. This indicates that very few young people actually start working with some kind of formal vocational training. This proportion of trained youth is one of the lowest in the world. The corresponding figures for industrialized countries are much higher, varying between 60-96% of youth in the age group of 20-24 years.

Compared to the age group of 5-14 years, educational institution attendance rates drop by nearly half in the age group of 15-19 years and by 86% after the age of 15 years. Subsequently, labour force participation rates rise sharply after the age of 14 years, and reach close to 100% at the age group of 25–29 years. This means that a large chunk of the working population does not have proper skills.

An Ignored Imperative

It is clear that skill development has been largely ignored in our country and is one of its major needs. India's workforce will be younger than the workforces in many global economies but skill development is critical if we are to take advantage of this demographic edge.

Year 2010: Total Population 1.2 Billion		
0-18 years	18-59 years	Above 59 years
404 million	674 million	98 million

Table 1:
Demographic trend in India

Year 2022: Total Population 1.4 Billion		
0-18 years	18-59 years	Above 59 years
417 million	793 million	143 million

It is expected that the ageing-economy phenomenon will globally create a skilled manpower shortage of approximately 56.5 million by 2020. If India can get its skill development strategy right, then it could have a skilled manpower surplus of approximately 47 million. This means that in the next decade, India has the potential to become a global reservoir of skilled manpower, provided it accords high priority to skill development. By 2022 India will need to skill 240 million people if the current demographic trend continues.

Impact of Skill-gap on Corporate Sector

According to Scottish employer's skill survey 2008, the major types of skill-gaps experienced by employers are in the following areas:

1. Planning & Organizing (54%)
2. Customer-handling skills (52%)
3. Problem-solving skills (52%)
4. Team-working skills (47%)
5. Oral Communication Skills (44%)
6. Technical & practical skills (44%)
7. Written communication skills (33%)
8. Strategic management skills (29%)
9. Basic computer literacy/using IT (27%)
10. Advanced IT or software skills (24%)
11. Literacy Skills (21%)
12. Using numbers (20%)

The same survey revealed that the primary reason for the existence of skill-gaps are either people not being in jobs for not long enough or because of lack of training. People who have not been in jobs for a long-time essentially represent new employees and their incompetence. Ultimately it is the organization that faces the brunt of ill-trained employees. The various kinds of problems faced by corporate sector due to such skill-gap are:

1. Difficulties in meeting customer service objectives.
2. Difficulties in meeting quality standards.
3. Difficulties in introducing new working practices.
4. Increased operation/running costs.
5. Delays in developing new products and services.
6. Loss of business or orders to competitors.
7. Difficulties in introducing technological change.
8. At times, companies are forced to withdraw offering certain products or services to customers.

The 'Skills-Gap Survey' was conducted by the Higher Education Forum in partnership with 1SOS and Westat India Social Sciences for the Indian banking, financial services and insurance sector in March 2010. The survey revealed huge competency gaps, in terms of knowledge, skills and attitudes, between those expected by the employers and the performance of the hired MBAs.

Table 2: Employer expectation rating and performance assessment of newly hired MBAs (knowledge)

Knowledge	Expectation	Performance	
	Knowledge is very important	Knowledge is excellent or very good	Knowledge is needing improvement or lacking
Environment	75.2%	29.2%	29.2%
Organization and processes within the organization	77.9%	16.8%	46.9%
Products/solutions/services including those of competitors	77.9%	22.1%	46.9%
Consumer Behaviour	76.1%	22.1%	45.1%

Skills	Expectation	Performance	
	Skills are very important or important	Skills are excellent or very good	Skills needing improvement or lacking
Analytic Skills	90.3%	38.9%	15.9%
Computing including excel analysis	82.3%	46.0%	18.6%

Project Management	67.3%	17.7%	38.9%
Communication (Verbal and written including email communication)	92.0%	37.2%	24.8%
Presentation Skills	84.1%	37.2%	23.9%
Team work and collaboration	92.0%	28.3%	26.6%
Listening Skills	92.9%	24.8%	32.7%
Selling Skills	70.8%	26.6%	34.5%
Conflict resolution	72.6%	16.8%	49.6%

Table 3: Employer expectation rating and performance assessment of newly hired MBAs (Skill)

Attitude	Expectation	Performance	
	Attitudes is very important	Attitudes are excellent or very good	Attitudes are needing improvement or lacking
Aptitude and willingness to learn	92.9%	46.9%	9.7%
Creativity	81.4%	28.3%	21.2%
Self-discipline	92.9%	34.5%	27.4%
Self-motivated	92.0%	37.2%	31.0%
Commitment and dedication	93.8%	37.2%	27.4%
Ethical behaviour	86.7%	42.5%	17.7%

Table 4: Employer Expectation Rating and Performance Assessment of Newly Hired MBAs (Attitude)

The survey results show that newly hired MBAs lack heavily in knowledge, skills as well as attitude. The overall expectation and performance scores show a worrying gap.

Expectations	Performance	
Knowledge	4.0	2.8
Skills	4.2	3.0
Attitudes	4.4	3.2

Table 5: Overall Expectation and Performance Scores of the Hired MBAs

Bridging the Gap

But on whom does the onus of skill development rest? Some feel that the responsibility lies with the government. The government has been increasing its investments in education and training and has introduced several provisions and reforms for improvements. However, given the enormity of the skill-gap being felt in various sectors and at various levels, government interventions alone do not appear to be enough.

To effectively bridge the huge skill-gap that exists in our country, serious T&D interventions are necessary. They could take the form of: Projects involving public–private partnerships: Public-private partnerships (PPP) not only generate finances on a large scale but also provide policy, resource and infrastructure support for initiatives to impart skills training to the masses. Such projects help create a conducive environment for upscaling training.

The private sector has lent its support for the establishment of the National Skill Development Corporation (NSDC) by buying a 51% stake in it. With its capital base of Rs 10 crore, NSDC will stimulate and coordinate initiatives in the skill development sector. The corporation's mission, objectives and action plan is guided by a national policy on skill development. It will aim to improve core employability skills and competency standards, thereby creating a common platform for collaboration among private sector employers, training providers and the labour force. The government is also planning to set up a fully owned trust, the National Skill Development Fund, with a seed capital of Rs 1,000 crore. Projects involving corporate–academic partnerships: Industry and academia are the two wheels of the economic cart. If academia is the warehouse of budding talent, industry represents the talent demand and realisation. They should complement each other. On the one hand, industry is aware of critical talent-development areas while academia has large intellectual and knowledge resources at its disposal to cater to such needs.

Centum Work Skills India, a joint venture between National Skill Development Committee(NSDC) and Centum Learning, aim to skill 12 million people for the services-sector by the year 2022, targeting telecom, retail, auto, healthcare, construction, travel and hospitality sectors.

Experts feel that majority of the Indian companies do not have a development focus and lag far behind in terms of their training and development practices. The number of training and development initiatives launched by various Indian companies has increased over the last decade. However, except for companies in the IT sector, most of them still consider training as a Human

Resources (HR) support function. Many times the training department is silo-wised and lacks credibility. Business confidence on developmental interventions by their T&D departments do not seem to be high in most cases. In contrast, in the United States, training is regarded as important and treated as a skill-management function. Employees are considered as assets and are trained by their organizations as a part of their growth strategy. Such strategies have seen training departments growing into corporate universities that are capable of handling the training requirements of 30,000 to 100,000 employees. McDonald's Hamburger University, founded by Fred Turner and Ray Kroc, and Walt Disney's University of Disneyland and Disney Institute are some examples.

Leading academicians also feel that Indian academic reforms are the need of the hour. The curriculum of higher education programs should be revised in a way to make room for more skill development, rather than only imparting knowledge to the new graduates. Industry-Academia partnerships have also been encouraged for the same.

Government, Society, Academia or industry - who really holds the responsibility for skilling India? Is it fast-becoming passing-the-buck kind of story? Experts do fear such a problem. Despite the downturn, the Indian economy continues to grow, and amidst global layoffs, less than 16% of companies in India considered retrenchment. More than 60% continued hiring. India's is showing signs of turnaround in its growth rate. However, bridging the skill-gap will be critical to take our economy to the next level of growth and robustness.

Reading Exhibit 1

Accenture, the IT giant and Indira Gandhi National Open University (IGNOU) recently joined hands to develop a diploma programme for outsourcing professionals. IGNOU's extensive network will enable this programme to reach millions of students across the country, improving their understanding of a range of BPO services and upgrading their personal computing and communication skills.

Reading Exhibit 2

Nasscom is driving IT training in rural and semi-urban areas, an animation course called Anizooms being offered at subsidised rates by Nasscom Knowledge Networks (NKN) centre, has trained over 24000 youth in rural and semi-urban areas. The network plans to skill 10,000 youth in basic IT and IT related skills over the next three years. **Accenture** has partnered with Nasscom to certify their Diploma program on animations namely Anizooms. It also hires 25% Graduates from this course.

Reading Exhibit 3

The Cisco Networking Academy programme partners with over 170 institutes in India aiming to create a supply of world-class IT professionals in the country and help bridge the digital divide.

Reading Exhibit 4

Bharat Electronics, specialising in radar and naval systems, has collaborations with top institutes like the Management Development Institute in Gurgaon and the National Institute for Training in Industrial Engineering in Mumbai to train its executives.

Reading Exhibit 5

Infosys Technologies is one of the few Indian companies to take the employee training and development initiative to another level. Recently, the company's Global Education Centre (GEC) was inaugurated by Sonia Gandhi at Mysore. Built at an estimated cost of Rs 2,055 crore, the centre can train 14,000 Infosians at a time. The campus, spread over an area of 337 acres, boasts of 147 training rooms, 485 faculty rooms, 42 conference rooms and two libraries, which can house 1.4 lakh books. It also has seven food courts, a three-screen multiplex, a 1,056-seat auditorium and two helipads.

Questions

Q. 1. How acute is the skill-gap problem in India? How does it affect the industry and the graduates?

Q. 2. Who do you think has the solutions for bridging this skill gap – government, corporate sector or the academia?

Q. 3. Gather information about similar skill-gaps in other countries and elaborate the strategies that they have employed to overcome the same. Do you think any of these can be useful for India?

Index

A

About Human Capital Institute	139
Accenture	405
Acceptance by the Candidate	167
Acceptance of Offer by the Candidate	167
Accidents/Industrial Disasters	370
Adult Learning Theory for Trainers	259
Advantages of e-Recruitment Advertisements	136
Alpander	66, 67
American Accounting Association's Committee	418
American Express, India	402
Annual Appraisal	218
Anomaly of Assessment	212
Apprentices Act, 1961	408
Approaches to Audit	415
Approaches to Training Need Assessment	268
Arguments against Human Resource Accounting	422
Aspects of Preparation	428
Associated Cement Companies Ltd	420
Authourity of Incumbent	282
Automation	410
Auxillium West	412

B

Backchannel Referencing	184
Balanced Score Card(Corporate)	216
Balancing Standardization	46
Bandura's Social Learning Theory for Trainers	257
Bargaining Power of Suppliers	498
Base Pay Structure	298
Baxter Healthcare	466
Behavioural Competencies	239, 242
Benefits & Pitfalls of Automation	412
Bharat Heavy Electricals Ltd (BHEL)	419
Bibliography	62
Building Blocks of Engagement	481
Business Imperatives	36
Business Imperatives Driven-by Changed Cultural Environment	45
Business Imperatives Driven-by Changed Legal/Regul	49
Business Strategy	498

C

C.K Prahalad's n=1	465
Career Growth	483
Career Positioning	133
Categories of Return of Investment	278
Cement Corporation of India Ltd	420
Choosing the Right Rraining Method – The 3-C Mode	273
Chronology of Research in Human Resource Accountin	418
Cisco Systems	58
Cold Calling	178
Commonly Used Training Methods	271
Companies Act, 1956	422
Company Specific Factors	75
Compensable Factors	310
Compensation & Wage Administration	416
Competency & Competency Gap	265
Competency and Organizational Strategy	231
Competency and other HR Processes	232
Competency Buckets	233
Competency Dictionary	232
Competency Gap	238
Competency Mapping Process	239
Competency Mapping Exercise	250
Competition Climate	75
Competitive Business Strategy	37
Competitive Strategies	499
Competitors Strategy	128
Concurrent Validity	202
Configurational Approach	502
Contingency Approach	502
Control Systems	5
Core Responsibilities (CRs)	211
Corporate Positioning	133
Corporate Strategy	498
Corporate Talent	465
Cost Implications	68
Cost Leadership	499
Cost of Living Adjustments (COLAs)	333
Cost-minimization Approach	10
Counterfeits	125
Crash & Burn	480
Criterion Validity	202
Critical Incident Method	93
Critical Talent	465
Cultural Challenge	515
Cultural Factors	44
Customer to Employees: New Age, New Roles	28
Customisation and Personalisation	46

D

Data Collection Methods	93
Dearness Allowance	299
Decision Making/Problem Solving	116
Defining RPO	142
Deliotte	405, 470
Delphi Technique	81
Deltek Time	412
Demand & Gap Analysis HR	81

Demographic Information	159
Design Jobs	483
Diversity in Terms of Work Force	44
Divisional Score Card	216
Dock Workers (Safety, Health and Welfare) ACT, 1986	378
Doubts on Accuracy of Performance Appraisals	220
Douglas A Ready	462, 473
Dust-kickers	125

E

Ease of Trade	49
Economic Factors	34
Economic Value approach	419
Education Index	421
Edward Lifesciences	466
Elements of A Wage Structure	326
Employability	127
Employee Communications & Documents	416
Employee Engagement	7, 14, 33, 478
Employee Positioning	133
Employee Self-service Systems	411
Employee State Insurance Act 1948	404
Employee Stock Options (ESOPs)	344
Employee Training & Development	263
Employees Stock Option Programme (ESOP)	47
Employees' Provident Funds & Misc. Provisions Act, 1952	405
Employer Brand	128
Engagement Architect	61
Engagement Models	479
Engagement Trends in India	488
Engineers India Ltd	420
Entrepreneurial Environment	59
Envision	483
Equal Remuneration Act, 1974	403
Equality Concept	41
e-Recruitment Advertisements	135
Ernst & Young	401
ERP or mid-segment HCM Suite	426
Ever-seekers, Never-keepers	125
Evolution of HR	9
Evolution of Human Resource Management	8
Expectation Management	39
Explosion in Stock Markets	35
External Factors	127
External Fit	501

F

Factor Analysis of Critical Talent	161
Factories Act, 1948	376, 408
Factors Affecting Human Resource Planning	69
Factors to be Considered in Collection of Job Analysis	105
Flexible Jump Boxes	60
Food Safety and Standards Act, 2006	50
Food Safety and Standards Regulations, 2011	50
Four Parameters & Cascading Principle	213
Functional Competencies	239, 242, 243
Functional Strategies	499
Functional Talent	464

Future of Human Resource Accounting	422
Future of Industrial Relations in India	408

G

Gainsharing	356
Gain-Sharing & Profit-Sharing	343
Galagon Pat	466
GDP Growth Rate	36
Global Education Centre	466
Global Strategy Group (GSG)	494
Glocal Hiring	518
Graphic Rating Scale	219
Graphology - The Basic Analysis	175
Growing Menace	380
Growth of Income & Income Disparities	40

H

Harley Davidson Riders Club	41
High-flyers	125
Hindustan Unilever Limited (HUL)	402
Hindustan Zinc Ltd.	420
Hiring Filter	463
Hiring System	6
Hoffman, Wyatt, Gordo	67
Honeybee Preservation	41
Honeymooners and Hamsters	480
Host Country Nationals (HCNs)	508, 514
House Rent Allowance	299
Housing Allowance	521
How to Avoid Sub-conscious Bias?	181

How to Develop Brand Ambassadors?	20
Howard P. Stevens	475
HR Accounting	7
HR Analytics	7
HR Audit	7
HR Automation	6
HR Imperatives Driven by Legal Environment	51
HR Imperatives Driven by Social Context	42
HR Imperatives Driven by Technological Context	55
HR Strategies	502
HR Strategy	7
HR Systems & Processes	5
HRA at Infosys	420
HRM Effectiveness	495
Human Capital	4
Human Resource Audit	412
Human Resource Function	66
Human Resource Inventory	75
Human Resource Mobility	75
Human Resource Planning	65, 67
Human Resource Responsibilities	417

I

Identification of Functional and Role Competencies	237
Impact of Work Life Imbalance	486
Implications for Trainers	260
Implications of HR Planning on Organisation	68
Importance of Human Resource Management	11

In-basket Exercises	169	Job Evaluation	309
Increased Focus on Strategic Recruitment	38	Job Evaluations and Market Consideration	323
Indian Women's Leadership Council (IWLC)	400	Job Satisfaction	14
Individual Contribution Areas (ICAs)	211	Job Skimmers	125
Industrial Disputes Act, 1947	407	Job Specification	283
Industrial Relations	6	Judgemental Methods	81
In-house versus Outsource	425	Justlogin	412
Institute for Corporate Productivity (i4CP)	462, 468		
Instructions for Completing PAQ	102	**K**	
Interest Tests	169	Kahn	478
International Compensation	519	Key Elements of HR Planning	68
International HR Strategies	512	Kinds of Errors in Selection	192
International HRM Activities	514	Kirkpatrick's Levels	277
International Human Resource Management	508		
International Human Resource Management Roles	513	**L**	
International Labour Relations	519	Labour Acts	395
International Staffing	515	Labour Demand and Supply	127
Internationalization Strategies	512	Learning Theories	257
Interpreting Validity Coefficients	203	Leave Travel Allowance	299
Interview Method	93	Legal Approach to HR Audit	415
I-recruitment Model	455	Legal Environment	128
Is HRA Useful?	421	Legal Frameworks	50
Is Talent Management an 'Oxymoron'	462	Legal/Regulatory Factors	48
Issue of Appointment Letter	167	Letter of Intent	167
Issue of Offer Letter	167	Lev and Schwartz Model	419
		Levels of Engagement	479
J		Leverage of Legal Rights	49
		Levi-Strauss	42
Jay A Conger	462, 473	Line-of-Sight & Measurement	359
Job Analysis	89	Linking Strategic Priorities and Recruiting Practices	148
Job Analysis Interview Format	93		

List of Various Central Labour Acts	396

M

Macro Environmental Factors	69
Madras Refineries Ltd	420
Management by Objectives (MBO)	221
Management Position Description Questionnaire (MPD)	94
Manager's Role in Feedback	225
Managerial Role in Setting Objectives	216
Managing Budgets Efficiently & Meeting Biz Expecta	39
Managing Cultural Change	32
Managing Talent in a Turbulent Economy	462
Manpower Requirement (Banking, Financial Services)	79
Manpower Requirement (Building, Construction Industry)	78
Manpower Requirement Gems & Jewellery Industry)	78
Manpower Requirement (Leather & Leather Goods Industry)	79
Manpower Requirement (Organized Retail Industry)	80
Manpower Requirement (Textile & Clothing Industry)	80
Manzini, Gridley	66
Marcus Buckingham and Curt W. Coffman	463
Market Pricing/ Benchmarking	317
Markov Analysis	82
Marriott International, Inc.	404
Maruti Salesman	24
Maternity Benefit Act, 1961	406
McKinsey & Company	484
Measuring Employee Engagement	487
Medical Allowance	299
Medical Test	167
Methodology and Demographics Methodology	158
Methods of Calculating HRA	418
Michael Porter's Competitive Strategy	497
Michael Porter's Theory	497
Micro (Industry Specific) Factors	70
Mid-term Review	217
Mike Mussallem and Mckinsey & Co.	466
Minerals and Metals Trading Corporation of India	419
MINES ACT, 1952	378
Minimum Wages Act, 1948	400
Modern HR management	10
Monetary Policies	35
Money Grubbers	125
Mouly	66
Multi-channel Communication @ TCS	485

N

Narayana Murthy	417
Network Leadership	513
Networking & Communication	457
New Age HRM Model	29
New Age HRM Roles	59
New Brand Ambassadors	17
New Hire Orientation	416
Nitaqat	517

O

Objective Setting & Cascading Principle	213
Oil and Natural Gas Commission	420
Oil India Ltd	420
On-boarding and Induction	168
Open Cultures	5
Open Recruitments	494
Operational Training Need Analysis	285
Organizational Analysis of Training Needs	285
Organizational Culture	5
Organizational Design & Policies	5
Organizational Readiness	68
OSHA, 1970	379
Outsource Talent and Technology	43

P

Paper Tigers	124
Parent Country Nationals (PCNs)	508, 514
Participative Management	44
Partner Pal	60
Pay Discrimination & Glass Ceiling	398
Payment of Bonus Act, 1965	347
Payment of Gratuity Act, 1972	404
Payment of Wages Act, 1936	401
Payroll & Attendance Records	34
Payroll Automation	410
People Management	11
People Philosophy at Taj Hotels	485
PepsiCo	404
Percentage COLAs	334
Performance Appraisal Method	222
Performance Data	93
Performance Management	34
Performance Management Automation Systems	411
Performance Management Systems	6, 207
Performance Milestones	349
Performance-based Compensation	339
Performance-based Pay/ Variable Pay	341
Personnel Management	8
Political and Social Environment	128
Position Analysis Questionnaire (PAQ)	94, 95
Power Distance Index (PDI)	516
Practical Issues in ROI Computation	279
Predictive Validity	202
Preparation of People	428
Preparing Competency Buckets	237
Presence on Social Networking Websites	45
Primary Actors in Job Analysis	91
Primary Purpose	118
Process Steps in Job Analysis	92
Procter & Gamble (P&G)	457

Q

Qualitative Methods	81
Quantitative Methods	81
Quantitative Methods of Job Evaluation	314
Questionnaire Method	93
Quick Changes in Roles	47

R

Ready and Conger	474
Recognizing Women Workforce	47
Recruiting the Right One	134
Recruitment	34
Recruitment Advertisements	132
Recruitment Automation Systems	411
Recruitment Function	131
Recruitment Objectives	126
Recruitment Process Outsourcing (RPO)	156
Recruitment, Employment and Selection	416
Reference Check	167, 456
Reference Checking / Background Verification	181
Regulatory Framework	70
Relationship between Learning, Training, Education	265
Relationship Between Reliability & Validity	203
Reliability	193
Repatriation Assistance	521
Replenish Contemporary Skill Inventory?	58
Resource-based Approach	501
Robert Hayden	455
Robert L. Masternak	365
Roles of Industrial Relations	394
RPO - Challenges and Opportunities	149
RPO in Today's Economic Environment	140
Rush, Borne	68

S

Sample Exhibits of Actual Job Analysis using PAQ	105
Sample HR Audit	416
Scope of Performance Management	209
Screening Round	166
Selection Interview	179
Selection Process	166
Selection Test & Interview	166
Selection Tests	168
Seniority-based Promotions	10
Sexual Harassment & Physical Insecurity	397
Shops and Establishments Act	406
Situation Tests	169
Six Sigma Framework	475
Six Sigma Framework Applied to Talent Management	474
Social Learning Theory	257
Social Media Applications in HR	7
Social Media Applications in Managing Human Resource	453
Social Media Recruitment	139, 454
Social Networking Platforms	47
Sophisticated HRM	495
Sorting the Curriculum-Vitae (CV)	178
Sources of Recruitment	129
Southern Petrochemicals Industries Corporation	419
Species of Candidates to be Avoided	124
Sriram Ramanujam	429

Standard of Performance	282
Steel Authority of India Ltd. (SAIL)	419
Steps in Annual Appraisal Process	223
Strategic Approach to HR Audit	415
Strategic Fit	501
Strategic HRM	496
Strategic Human Resource Management	500
Strategic Management Process	500
Strategy Evaluation	500
Strategy Formulation	500
Strategy Implementation	500
Strauss, Burack	67
Structural Change in Organization	33
Success Stories	24
Supply Forecasting	82
Systems Model Approach	393

T

Taj Group of Hotels	403
Talent Acquisition and RPO - The Current State	141
Talent Catalyst	61
Talent Implications	68
Talent Management	7, 475
Talent Management in a Bust Economy	469
Talent Management: The New HRM Approach	473
Talent Managementat Edward Lifesciences	467
Tata Steel	52
Technical HRM	496
Technological Climate	54
Technological Environment	128
Technological Factors	53
Tech-savvy	61
Test-retest Reliability	194
The Appraisal Interview	224
The Industrial Employment (Standing Orders) Act, 1946	405
The Macro Environmental Factors	69
The New Age HRM	27
The Payment of Bonus Act	405
The Process of Learning	254
The Rorschach Inkblot Test	170
Thematic Apperception Test (TAT)	171
Theoretical Approaches to Industrial Relations	393
Third Country Nationals (TCNs)	508, 515
Three Cases - Divisions of Personality	176
Three Entities of Engagement	478
Trade Unions	395
Trade Unions Act, 1926	400
Traditional Appraisal Methods	218
Traditional HRM	10
Training & Development	33, 34
Training & Development System	6
Training Evaluation	275
Training for Senior/ Middle Level Management	119
Training Need Analysis	267
Training Need Analysis & Results	285
Training Process Model	266
Training versus Development	264

Training versus Education	264	Welcoming & Pre-selection Talk	166
Transfer of Learning	261	What is Human Resource Management?	4
Trend Analysis	82	What Recruiting Practices Drive RPO Today?	144
Triage Training (Virtual Training)	272	Why Engagement?	478
Turnaround/Retrenchment	499	Why Use RPO?	143
Types of Competencies	239	Woman Participation	44
Types of Performance-based Pays	341	Women Resource	399
Types of Reliability	194	Work-life Balance Myths	486
Types of Strategies	498	Work Stress	398
		Working Environment	118
		Work-life Balance & Engagement	485

U

Uncertainty Avoidance Index (UAI)	516
Unemployment Rate	128
Universalistic Approach	502
Use of Balanced Score Card (BSC) in Setting KRAs	212

Work-life Imbalance	396
Workload Analysis	82
Workmen's Compensation Act, 1923	379, 402
Workplace Health & Safety	6, 369
Workplace Positioning	133
Workplace Violence	380

V

Variable Pay Plans for Sales	299
Variable Pay Programs	299
Various Factors Affecting Recruitment	127

Y

Yoga's and Meditation	550
Yudhistra	550
YUM - Increasing Footprint through Effective Tale	585

W

Walker	66